T0181410

IFIP Advances in Information and Communication Technology 426

IFIP – The International Federation for Information Processing

IFIP was founded in 1960 under the auspices of UNESCO, following the First World Computer Congress held in Paris the previous year. An umbrella organization for societies working in information processing, IFIP's aim is two-fold: to support information processing within its member countries and to encourage technology transfer to developing nations. As its mission statement clearly states,

> *IFIP's mission is to be the leading, truly international, apolitical organization which encourages and assists in the development, exploitation and application of information technology for the bene t of all people.*

IFIP is a non-profitmaking organization, run almost solely by 2500 volunteers. It operates through a number of technical committees, which organize events and publications. IFIP's events range from an international congress to local seminars, but the most important are:

- The IFIP World Computer Congress, held every second year;
- Open conferences;
- Working conferences.

The flagship event is the IFIP World Computer Congress, at which both invited and contributed papers are presented. Contributed papers are rigorously refereed and the rejection rate is high.

As with the Congress, participation in the open conferences is open to all and papers may be invited or submitted. Again, submitted papers are stringently refereed.

The working conferences are structured differently. They are usually run by a working group and attendance is small and by invitation only. Their purpose is to create an atmosphere conducive to innovation and development. Refereeing is also rigorous and papers are subjected to extensive group discussion.

Publications arising from IFIP events vary. The papers presented at the IFIP World Computer Congress and at open conferences are published as conference proceedings, while the results of the working conferences are often published as collections of selected and edited papers.

Any national society whose primary activity is about information processing may apply to become a full member of IFIP, although full membership is restricted to one society per country. Full members are entitled to vote at the annual General Assembly, National societies preferring a less committed involvement may apply for associate or corresponding membership. Associate members enjoy the same benefits as full members, but without voting rights. Corresponding members are not represented in IFIP bodies. Affiliated membership is open to non-national societies, and individual and honorary membership schemes are also offered.

Kecheng Liu   Stephen R. Gulliver
Weizi Li   Changrui Yu (Eds.)

Service Science
and Knowledge Innovation

15th IFIP WG 8.1 International Conference
on Informatics and Semiotics in Organisations, ICISO 2014
Shanghai, China, May 23-24, 2014
Proceedings

Springer

Volume Editors

Kecheng Liu
Stephen R. Gulliver
Weizi Li
University of Reading
Henley Business School
Business Informatics Systems and Accounting
Whiteknights, Reading RG6 6UD, UK
E-mail: {k.liu, s.r.gulliver, weizi.li}@henley.ac.uk

Changrui Yu
Shanghai University of Finance and Economics
School of Information Management and Engineering
No. 777, Guoding Rd., Shanghai 200433, China
E-mail: yucr@sjtu.edu.cn

ISSN 1868-4238   e-ISSN 1868-422X
ISBN 978-3-662-52574-6   e-ISBN 978-3-642-55355-4 (eBook)
DOI 10.1007/978-3-642-55355-4
Springer Heidelberg New York Dordrecht London

Typesetting: Camera-ready by author, data conversion by Scientific Publishing Services, Chennai, India

Printed on acid-free paper

Springer is part of Springer Science+Business Media (www.springer.com)

Preface

This 2014 International Conference on Informatics and Semiotics in Organisations (ICISO 2014) was the 15th in a series of international events devoted to the latest research and application of informatics in organisations and organisational semiotics. The aim of the conference is to provide a focal forum for participants from various domains of information management and information systems, computational science, semiotics, finance and accounting, business and enterprise, service science, business and engineering. The conference enables the sharing and exchange of the latest research and practice. ICISO 2014 continued the effort of the international research community in the development of the emergent discipline of informatics and its applications. (See www.orgsem.org for earlier conferences since 1995.)

Service science is a young discipline that has attracted great attention from academia and industry because of the increasing prominence of the service economy, and the need for a scientific approach to guide the study of services. Service, as opposed to product, is regarded as an intangible commodity, which is characterised by extensive use of information and knowledge in the activities that lead to the creation and addition of social, economic, environmental or other value. Typical service industry includes financial services, hospitality, retail, health and education, as well as recent types such as data services, knowledge management and consultancy. In parallel to the service industry, other industrial sectors such as manufacturing, construction and agriculture, having realised the added value from the service associated with the product, have been incorporating service into their value network.

In the current economy, the value network of a large organisation may be connected to suppliers, customers, and many other stakeholders, often in a complex and extensive form spreading over many distributed locations and even multiple jurisdictions. In such a setting, information has two roles: one is that information itself is the valuable commodity to be delivered to the customers; and another role is that information must be effectively managed and used in communication to coordinate the human activities and the movement of materials. For small and medium-sized enterprises the value network may be simpler, information is still important in value creation through, e.g., proper use of information in coordination of production activities, marketing, customer relationship management and supply chain management.

Information is an important resource for any organisation, whether large or small; whether it is from a service or production industry. To understand the nature of information, and how it can be effectively managed and used in organisations, is highly relevant. Following the early events in the series, the key theme of this conference was on information, service and their interrelationships. Particular emphasis was placed on exploring and understanding, from both theoretical and empirical perspectives, how information enables an organisation to sustain and, furthermore, to leverage competitiveness. In both cases, the organisations will rely heavily on effective management and use of information.

Informatics is the study of information as a resource, which helps a business organisation, often through knowledge management, innovation, and service design, engineering and management. Organisational semiotics, as a discipline of studying signs, information, and human communication in organised contexts, provides an appropriate approach to examine the issues of information management and utilisation from both scholarly and practical perspectives.

ICISO 2014 received 88 paper submissions from 19 countries, which demonstrates the success and global dimension of this conference. From these, 39 were accepted for the main track (44%), and 10 were accepted for inclusion in the workshop. There numbers show the intention of preserving a high-quality forum for future editions of this conference.

The high quality of the papers received imposed difficult choices in the review process. To evaluate each submission, two rounds of paper review were performed by the Program Committee and reviewing panels, whose members are highly qualified independent researchers in the ICISO Conferences topic areas. Moreover, ICISO also featured a number of keynote lectures delivered by internationally well-known experts, namely, Daniel O'Leary (University of Southern California, Marshall School of Business, USA) and Weiguo Patrick Fan (Pamplin College of Business, USA), thus increasing the overall quality of the conferences and providing a deeper understanding of the conferences interest fields.

Two workshops were organised in association with the conference; they provided interactive fora that allowed for a more in-depth discussion of particular areas within the scope of the conference. We would like to thank the workshop chairs for their collaboration in providing this added-value event of ICISO 2014, namely: e-Health, the New Frontier of Service Science Innovation (chaired by Ping Yu, and Ying Su) and International Workshop on Information Engineering and Management (chaired by Mohammad Yamin).

Building an interesting and successful program for the conference required the dedicated effort of many people. We would like to express our thanks to all authors including those whose papers were not included in the program. We would also like to express our gratitude to all members of the Program Committee and auxiliary reviewers, who helped us with their expertise and valuable time. Furthermore, we thank the invited speakers for their invaluable contribution and for taking the time to synthesize and prepare their talks.

Moreover, we thank the workshop and session chairs whose contribution to the diversity of the program was decisive. Finally, we gratefully acknowledge the professional support of the ICISO team for all organizational processes.

March 2014

Kecheng Liu
Stephen R. Gulliver
Weizi Li
Changrui Yu

Organization

Conference Chairs

Lanjuan Liu — Shanghai University of Finance and Economics, China
Kecheng Liu — University of Reading, UK

Senior Advisory Committee

Yingluo Wang — Xian Jiaotong University, China
Renchu Gan — Beijing Institute of Technology, China
Ronald Stamper — University of Twente, The Netherlands

Program Chair

Jingti Han — Shanghai University of Finance and Economics, China

Publication Chair

Stephen Gulliver — University of Reading, UK

Organising Chair

Changrui Yu — Shanghai University of Finance and Economics, China
Weizi Li — University of Reading, UK

Conference Secretariat

Bohan Tian — University of Reading, UK
Shen Xu — University of Reading, UK
Rongfei Zhou — Shanghai University of Finance and Economics, China

Program Committee

Joseph Barjis — Delft University of Technology, The Netherlands
Adrian Benfell — Plymouth University, UK

Rodrigo Bonacin	CTI Renato Archer and Faccamp, Brazil
Auke Van Breemem	Radboud University Nijmegen, The Netherlands
M.T. Chan	Hong Kong City University, China
Pierre Charrel	IRIT, France
José Cordeiro	Technical Institute of Setubal, Portugal
Guoxi Cui	Beijing Information Science and Technology University, China
Hui Du	Beijing Jiaotong University, China
John Effah	University of Ghana Business School, Ghana
Haiqi Feng	Central University of Finance and Economics, China
Junkang Feng	University of Western Scotland, UK
Xiuzhen Feng	Beijing University of Technology, China
Florin-Gheorghe Filip	Romanian Academy, Romania
Joaquim Filip	Technical Institute of Setubal, Portugal
Hongjiao Fu	Renming University, China
Daniel Galarreta	Centre National D'Etudes Spatiales, France
Mingxing Gan	Beijing University of Science and Technology, China
Ricardo Ribeiro Gudwin	UNICAMP, Brazil
Prasad Jayaweera	University of Sri Jayewardenepura, Sri Lanka
Guorui Jiang	Beijing University of Technology, China
John Krogstie	IDI, NTNU, Norway
Angela Lacer da Nobre	Technical Institute of Setubal, Portugal
Stephen Liao	City University of Hong Kong, China
Xueshan Luo	National University of Deference Technology, China
Mark Lycett	Brunel University, UK
Keiichi Nakata	University of Reading, UK
Vania Neris	Federal University of Sao Carlos, Brazil
Andreas Oberweis	Universität Karlsruhe, Germany
Luis Quezada	University of Santiago, Chile
Wenge Rong	Beihang University, China
Janos Sarbo	University of Nijmegen, The Netherlands
Boris Shishkov	Delft University of Technology, The Netherlands
Keng Siau	Missouri University of Science and Technology, USA
Ismael Soto	University of Santiago, Chile
Ying Su	Institute of Scientific and Technical Information of China, China
Christina Tay	Chinese Culture University, Taiwan

George Tsaramirsis	King Abdulaziz University, Saudi Arabia
Hans Weigand	Tilburg University, The Netherlands
Martin Wheatman	Brightace Ltd., UK
Mohammad Yamin	King Abdulaziz University, Saudi Arabia
Zhijun Yan	Beijing Institute of Technology, China
Ping Yu	University of Wollongong, Australia
Yunchuan Zhang	Wuhan University of Science and Technology, China

Additional Reviewers

Sabah Al-Somali, Saudi Arabia
Mohammed Alsaig, Saudi Arabia
Charalampos Apostolopoulos, UK
Zainab Baker, Malaysia
Xiuxiu Chen, China
Girija Chetty, Australia
Yuri Demchenko, The Netherlands
Huiying Gao, China
Tom Gedeon, Australia
Daniel Gozman, UK
Sharif Khalid, UK
Rafiqul Khan, UK

Kamel Khoualdi, Saudi Arabia
Shixiong Liu, UK
Krikor Maroukian, UK
Omar Nasseef, Saudi Arabia
Kamran Shafi, Australia
Jeffrey Soar, Australia
Khin Win, Australia
Ling-Yun Wu, China
Sabah Al-Somali, Saudi Arabia
Wanting Wan, China
Xiaoyu Yang, China
Qing Zhang, China

Sponsors

University of Reading

Shanghai University of Finance

Incorporation with

国家人口与生殖健康
科学数据中心
National Population and Reproductive
Health Science Data Center

Supported By

Informatics Research Centre
Henley Business School
University of Reading

Keynotes

The Internet of Signs and the Semiotic Web: Signization Using Big Data and the Internet of Things and Emerging Issues

Daniel E. O'Leary

University of Southern California, USA
Oleary@usc.edu

Roughly 15 years ago the notions of the semantic web were developed (e.g., [2]). At that time it was suggested that the Semantic Web would bring structure to the content of Web pages. The Semantic Web was not seen as a separate Web but one in which information on the Web would be given well-defined meaning. The goal was to be able to better understand and process the data rather than merely display it.

In this paper I investigate "The Internet of Signs" and the "Semiotic Web" and how their development is being facilitated by notions such as "Big Data" and the "Internet of Things." For example, with the "Internet of Things" there are increasing amounts of "big data" available that can provide insights into the "Internet of Signs." Further, the increasing availability of data can facilitate increased development of the "Internet of Signs."

I will examine the relationship between so-called 'Big Data', the 'Internet of Things' (the 'Internet of People and Things,' and the 'Internet of Everything'), and the 'Internet of Signs.' In particular, I investigate how the 'things' in the 'Internet of Things' generate 'Big Data', and how both are used to generate semiotic 'signs'. In addition, I will investigate some extensions beyond those of the data generated from the Internet of Things to include signs available from the analysis of additional alternative media generally considered part of Big Data.

The Internet of Things

As noted by [1], the term the 'Internet of Things', apparently developed in 1999, initially was meant to describe the following situation: Today computers – and, therefore, the Internet – are almost wholly dependent on human beings for information.

The problem is, people have limited time, attention and accuracy – all of which means they are not very good at capturing data about things in the real world. We need to empower computers with their own means of gathering information, so they can see, hear and smell the world for themselves.

As a result, the 'Internet of Things' provides a linked set of computer programs and sensors that do not incur the same limitations of people. Those sensors are responsible for generating huge quantities of data that provide insight into the status of the things, and their relationships with other things and events in the world.

The Internet of Signs

The 'Internet of Signs' indicates that the data generated on the internet from the broad range of sources, including devices in the 'Internet of Things', information from social media (e.g. blogs) and other internet sources (often associated with 'Big Data'), provide 'signs', such as the 'sentiment' toward some issue (e.g. [3]). Those 'signs' generated from information associated with the internet provide an 'Internet of Signs'. The 'Internet of Signs' can be helpful in providing insights and other potential information about events and situations.

In particular, from the perspective of semiotics, rather than concern for an 'Internet of Things' there is concern or interest in what I would call the 'Internet of Signs'. In particular, how does the 'Internet of Things' manifest itself as 'signs' or the 'Internet of Signs' and what are the relationships between the 'things' and signs of 'things'? Ultimately, the relationships between 'things', conceptions of 'things' and symptoms of behaviors can provide a basis to better understand things, entities, events, situations, behaviors and other issues.

The Semiotic Web

Related to the Internet of Signs is the Semiotic Web. Unfortunately, the Semiotic Web, as a parallel to the Semantic Web has received limited direct attention and discussion. The Semiotic Web and the Semantic Web both draw directly on the content of the World Wide Web. The Semiotic Web is similar in concept to the Semantic Web in that it is one whereby information about signs (e.g., sentiment, things, etc.) is becoming increasingly available as greater amounts of information become available.

However, in addition to data from the Internet of Things, the Semiotic Web will need to draw increasingly on other multi-media content to draw out signs for which text is not appropriate or not sufficiently rich. This paper will examine some extensions to the Internet of Signs and the Semiotic Web and examine settings where classic text analysis is not sufficient to "see" the signs related to things, entities, locations, situations and events.

References

1. Ashton, K.: That 'Internet of Things' thing: in the real world, things matter more than ideas (June 22, 2009), http://www.rfidjournal.com/article/view/4986 (accessed January 2013)
2. Berners-Lee, T., Hendler, J., Lassila, O.: The Semantic Web. Scientific American (2001)
3. O'Leary, D.E.: Blog mining: from each according to his opinion. Decision Support Systems 51(4), 821–830 (2011)

Social Media Analytics and Its Business Applications – An Overview

Weiguo Patrick Fan

Pamplin College of Business, United States
wfan@vt.edu

Abstract. Social media analytics is concerned with developing and evaluating informatics tools and frameworks to collect, monitor, analyze, summarize, and visualize social media data to facilitate conversations and interactions to extract useful patterns and intelligence. The ubiquity of smart phones and other mobile devices, Facebook and YouTube channels devoted to companies and products, and hashtags that make it easier to instantly and broadly share experiences all combine to create a social media landscape that is rapidly growing and becoming ever more part of the fabric of businesses. As the number of users on social media sites continues to increase, so does the need for businesses to monitor and utilize these sites to their benefit. In this talk, we explore how the explosion in social media necessitates the use of social media analytics; we explain the underlying stages of the social media analytics process; we describe the most common social media analytic techniques in use; and we discuss the ways in which social media analytics create business value. In the end of the keynote speech, a case study of using social media data for product defect discovery is given to demonstrate the business value of social media.

Table of Contents

Organizational Semiotics: Theory and Concepts

Organizational Semiotics and Applications

Finance and Service Science

Enterprise Architecture

Modelling and Simulation

Decision Making and Knowledge Management

e-Health, the New Frontier of Service Science Innovation

International Workshop on Information Engineering and Management

A Semiotic Approach to Integrative Negotiation

Janos J. Sarbo

ICIS, Radboud University Nijmegen, The Netherland
janos@cs.ru.nl

Abstract. An analysis of two-party integrative negotiation reveals the potential of this type of bargaining for being interpreted as a conceptualization process. Past research on a semiotic model of human processing shows the possibility of a definition of a uniform representation of knowledge. In this paper we suggest that by combining the above results integrative negotiation can be positioned as an abductive process. We justify our hypothesis by means of experimental data.

Keywords: Negotiation, Abduction, Peircean theory, Sign aspects, Cognitive model.

1   Introduction

Arguably the most efficient strategy for negotiation is win-win or two-party integrative negotiation [1], [10]. In this paper we are concerned with the question how negotiation efficiency can be increased through goal-driven communication between the parties. We show that win-win negotiation involves a process which is isomorphic to a Peircean model of cognitive activity [8]. An analysis of the latter process reveals types of information involved by its events. A combination of the above results enables the conclusion to be drawn that, in negotiation, if the parties get stuck at some stage, this could be because of a lack of information necessary for a realization of some event in the bargaining process. Communication of the required information may enable the parties to further develop their negotiation and bring it to a successful end, eventually.

We assume that, in order to get hold of the above problem of communication, the parties need to represent, besides their own information, a possible conceptualization of the negotiation process by the other party as well. This is where the Peircean model comes handy. By virtue of its categorical foundation, this model enables a uniform representation of knowledge in any domain (or, from any perspective of interpretation) hence a merging of representations from different perspectives by the parties, into a single representation. Through analyzing the events of the arising process during negotiation, *on-line*, the parties may derive information that can be helpful for the bargaining other party. This way of communication is akin to abduction, as it may enable to establish a relation between knowledge elements, which relation could not be derived by a party on the basis of his/her actual knowledge, neither in a deductive nor an inductive fashion.

K. Liu et al. (Eds.): ICISO 2014, IFIP AICT 426, pp. 1–10, 2014.

In order to enhance the efficiency of win-win negotiation, various *off-line* methods have been developed in the past. Examples are template design and evaluation, and algorithms for developing Pareto optimal solutions [5]. A problem shared by those methods is by virtue of their distant relation with the bargaining process.

Experience with a course on negotiation at Radboud University Nijmegen, The Netherlands, shows that the use of integrative negotiation is by far not obvious. Following an analysis of exercises in bargaining, students tend to stuck at some stage in their negotiation, keep repeating their earlier arguments hence make no progress. Unless a trained mediator is involved, integrative negotiation may not arise. In order to make the parties comply with that strategy, this course applies a technique that forces the parties to co-operate.[1] This is achieved by means of setting a shared goal that both parties must agree on, and from which goal the aim of their negotiation necessarily follows. In a concrete example, a couple of students were asked to act as managers of a company. Following their instruction they had competing interests concerning the solution of a problem of the company. The shared goal was set by aiming at an increase of profit by the company. The parties were asked by a mediator (this role was played by a third student) if this goal does comply with their interest. As the answer must be positive (otherwise the managers were not able to correctly function anymore), the parties were 'primed' for acting in a co-operative fashion. Later when they were asked to develop new initiatives for a solution, they could not refuse inventing ideas that at least partly respected the interest of the negotiating other party as well.

Besides win-win bargaining, another example of integrative negotiation is problem elicitation. A distinguishing property of the latter is the existence of a spontaneous interest by the bargaining parties, for achieving a common goal. This may explain why the parties *themselves* may be able to generate helpful communication thereby enhancing their negotiation process [3]. In this paper we capitalize on the analogy between the two kinds of negotiation phenomena above and illustrate our approach with an analysis of a case study in problem elicitation. The development of a methodology enabling helpful communication is on our current agenda.

The structure of the paper is the following. We begin with an analysis of integrative negotiation from a process perspective (Sect. 2). This is followed by an introduction of a Peircean model of human information processing (Sect. 3), and how this model may enable a generation of efficient communication in win-win bargaining (Sect. 4). The proposed approach is justified by an analysis of experimental data (Sect. 5). We close the paper with a summary of results (Sect. 6).

2   Integrative Negotiation as a Conceptualization Process

Integrative negotiation, first introduced in [10], is a strategy that has the potential to achieve an agreement that gives everyone what they want and this way enables the parties to produce a more satisfactory output. This strategy is different from the one used by positional bargaining, which is based on fixed, opposing viewpoints (cf.

---

[1] Jan van den Broek (pers. comm., 2009).

positions) and tends to result in a compromise or in no agreement at all. Compromises may not satisfy the true interest of the negotiating parties.

An oft-cited example of integrative negotiation and a creation of joint value is that of the dispute between two sisters over an orange [2]. Based on their positions, their mother cuts the orange in half and gives each girl one half. This outcome represents a compromise. However, if the mother was able to find out why the girls wanted the orange – what her interests were – there could have been a different, win-win outcome. This is because one girl wanted to eat the meat of the orange, but the other just wanted the peel to use in baking some cookies. If their mother had known their interests or were able to make the girls elicit their problem, they could have both gotten all of what they wanted, rather than just half.

According to [1], [4], [9], integrative negotiation can be characterized by a process, in which, first, each side's interest is *sorted* out. Their needs and why they want that is *abstracted* into possible demands. Next, they are asked to picture how their demands may be perceived by the other side, what may be standing in the way, which *complementary* information would enable an agreement, and in that context, how the interests of the two sides could be turned into actual demands. Integrative negotiation reaches its goal when those actual demands by the parties are combined into an agreement or a *proposition* of a solution of the input problem.

From the above analysis we draw the conclusion that integrative negotiation, as a process, makes use of four types of operation on the input problem appearing as a phenomenon. These are *sorting, abstraction, complementation*, and *predication* (proposition formation). In the next section we suggest that this process can be isomorphic to a cognitively based model of human processing. By making use of the potential analogy between the two models we show that integrative negotiation can be positioned as a conceptualization process. An advantage of the application of a cognitively based model is that it may give insight in the types of events of bargaining, and how the efficiency of those events can be increased by means of communication.

3 Knowledge in Formation (KIF)

The cognitively based model of human processing, introduced by our Knowledge in Formation (KIF) research project, has been presented at various ICISO conferences in the past [6], [11]. The used representation is based on the assumption, suggested by [12], that the aim of cognitive activity is the generation of a response on the input stimulus. A process model of response generation can be given as follows.

In a single interaction, the stimulus, appearing as an effect, is affecting the observer occurring in some state. The qualities of this state (q_2) and effect (q_1), which are in focus, and complementary memory knowledge or context (C) triggered by q_2 and q_1, define the input for information processing ($[q_2\ q_1\ C]$). See Fig. 1. The goal of this process is the generation of a relation, explaining why this effect is occurring to this state. In order to achieve this goal, the observer or interpreting system has to *sort out* the two types of qualities and context ($[q_2], [q_1],[C]$); *abstract* the input qualities in focus into independent collections $((q_2), (q_1))$; *complete* them with complementary knowledge by the interpreting system $((q_2,C), (q_1,C))$; and merge the obtained representations into a single relation $((q_2,C)-(q_1,C))$ through *predication*. We assume that the above process can be executed in cyclic fashion, recursively. Note that each one of the expressions generated by this process is a representation of an interaction between already existing input expressions interpreted as a state and an effect. For instance, (q_2) is a representation of the interaction between $[q_2]$ (state) and $[q_1]$ (effect) in the sense of relative difference hence an expression of the abstract input state irrespective of the input effect. Another example is (q_2,C), which is a representation of the interaction between (q_2) (state) and $[C]$ (effect) hence an expression of the abstract input state in context.

The four types of interactions are marked by their characteristic information. In *sorting*, this is the nature of quality, focus or complementary; in *abstraction*, the difference between $[q_2]$ and $[q_1]$; in *complementation*, the possible relation(s) between q_2 and $[C]$, and between q_1 and $[C]$; in *predication*, the actual relation between (q_2,C) and (q_1,C). In our model of negotiation, in Sect. 4, we assume that efficient communication may capitalize on the above informational classification of the interpretation events.

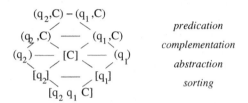

Fig. 1. The KiF process model of cognitive activity

State (q_2) and effect (q_1) stand for information in *focus*. Information, which is not in focus hence *complementary*, is represented by the context (C). Horizontal lines are used to designate interactions between input representations (cf. *positions* in the processing schema). Square brackets indicate that an entity is not yet interpreted, usual bracket symbols indicate that some interpretation is already available. The types of interpretation events are displayed on the right-hand side, in italics.

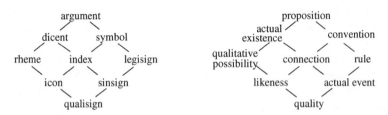

Fig. 2. The Peircean sign aspects (left) and corresponding mundane terms (right)

By virtue of the dependency between the categories, the set of sign aspects defines and induced hierarchy. Sign aspects that are higher in the hierarchy involve *all* lower category sign aspects.

In [8] we have shown that the KIF process model can be assigned a Peircean semiotic interpretation. This is illustrated by the isomorphism between the diagrams in Fig. 1 and Fig. 2. An analogy between positions in the different diagrams can be explained as follows.

The input, $[q_2 \, q_1 \, C]$, expressing a potential for information processing, corresponds to the qualisign sign aspect, or an interpretation of a phenomenon only as a quality. The representations obtained by *sorting*, $[q_2]$ (state) and $[q_1]$ (effect), expressing a potential for a relation, correspond to the icon and sinsign sign aspects, respectively. The icon sign aspect is an expression of a relation of constituency or likeness involved in the input state, the sinsign sign aspect an expression of a relation of simultaneity or an actual event involved in the input effect.[2] An explanation of a relation between other positions of the diagrams can be found in [8]. Below we can make use of the above relation between the diagrams, in Fig. 1 and Fig. 2, by referring to a stage in information processing by its Peircean sign aspect.

By virtue of its categorical foundation, KIF theory enables a definition of uniform models of information processing in any domain. As a result, different representations can be combined into a single one by means of structural coordination. This potential of the KIF process model can be used for merging individual conceptualization processes, e.g., by the bargaining parties, into a single process. The obtained structure enables pending events to be analyzed from an informational perspective in order to reveal the type of information (and communication) necessary for their realization.

According to our process model, communication can be assigned a twofold interpretation. On the one hand, it is a final relation generated by one of the parties (cf. sender), on the other hand, it is an input quality offered for processing by the other party (cf. receiver). As, in the second case, interpretation can be in need of memory information, in order to get hold of the problem of efficient communication we introduce a conceptual memory model in the next section.

4   Efficient Communication

Following [8], we assume that memory information can be represented by a graph, in which nodes stand for a collection of qualities perceived in earlier observations, edges for a relation between a pair of nodes. The above model enables our definition of qualities to be refined for interactions between memory information: q_2 can be defined by the qualities[3] shared by the nodes responding the input stimulus, q_1 by the difference between the qualities of those nodes. Formally, for a pair of nodes, n_1 and n_2, triggered by the input stimulus, $q_2 := n_1 \cap n_2$, $q_1 := n_2 \backslash n_1$ ("\" designates the operation relative difference).[4] Hence q_2 is an expression of information shared by observations of stimuli similar to the current one (cf. a state), q_1 is an expression of a change (cf. an effect). The relation between stimulus and memory response, which can be in the sense of agreement and possibility, enables memory information to be represented as focus- and complementary-type qualities, respectively.

---

[2] Note that a state may occur in itself, an effect always assumes the existence of a state.
[3] A definition of the qualities themselves is beyond the horizon of this paper.
[4] We assume that q_2 is always defined by a non-empty collection of qualities.

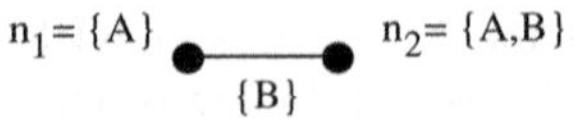

$$n_1 = \{A\} \bullet\!\!-\!\!-\!\!-\!\!-\!\!-\!\!\bullet n_2 = \{A,B\}$$
$$\{B\}$$

Fig. 3. Sample interpretation of memory information: $n_1 \cap n_2 = A$ (state), $n_2 \backslash n_1 = B$ (effect)

An algorithm for efficient communication can be defined as follows. We assume that the parties develop a representation of the negotiation process by themselves and by the bargaining other party, through merging (cf. Sect. 3). Communication (c) by one of the parties (*sender*) is offered for processing by the other party (*receiver*), who generates a hypothetical interpretation of c from the perspective of its import in the solution of the negotiation problem. As a result, a position (p) and a sign aspect is assigned to c, by *receiver*. By interpreting c, as an input quality, *receiver* may find out if, according to his representation of the negotiation process, there is an expression[5] c', in position p', which is in interaction with c. By analyzing the relation between memory response triggered by c and c', *receiver* may generate information from the perspective of the type of interaction between p and p', as follows. Qualities involved by a pair of connected nodes triggered by c and c', e.g., n_1 and n_2, respectively, can be used for the definition of a state ($n_1 \cap n_2$) and an effect ($n_1 \backslash n_2$). Information involved in the relation between this state and effect can be communicated to the other party, in the sense of difference (cf. *abstraction*), possibility (cf. *complementation*), and agreement (cf. *predication*).[6] Qualities representing the enforced perspective by *receiver* may enable *sender* to adjust his representations in p and p', and this way, enhance his interpretation process.

Through communication the parties may force one another to broaden their focus, 'see' the input from a new perspective, apply their knowledge in an abductive fashion, in order to develop a solution for their common negotiation problem.

5   A Case Study in Problem Elicitation

In a case study at the Dutch software firm Sogeti Nederland B.V., we analysed an actual elicitation process by a team of clients [13]. In this process, three clients and a professional mediator were involved in the specification of a problem with the clients' database system. The entire elicitation process, that took 4 hours, was recorded and transcribed.

A problem with the clients' application software, '*myAssignment*', is instigated in an elicitation process. The goal of *myAssignment* is to provide adequate information to employees, managers and client(s), about assignments and, most importantly, about communication between the participants of a project. The elicitation process was conducted in a separate room, in a usual setting, without intervention by the observer whose only task was to operate the fixed camera.

---

[5] Information by c' may have been generated by any one of the two parties (p and p' must be neighboring positions of the process model, depicted in Fig. 1). If it is generated by *receiver*, it can be tacit.

[6] If c does not trigger memory, or n_1 and n_2 are not connected, this may trigger a generation of a request for a re-formulation of c or a re-analysis of the input, by *sender* (cf. *sorting*).

A sample elicitation session is displayed in Fig. 4. The goal of this session is the disclosure of missing functionalities in *myAssignment*. Utterances of the sample text are interpreted from the perspective of *this* goal. The results of the analysis are given below. The representations generated are recapitulated in Fig. 5.

1. *(Pe)* *What, what I miss, ehh, in the current application ... is that ehh ... that*
   I have an overview, ehh ... of the steps that I find most logical.
   (Ca) *Hmm, hmm (with approval)*
2. *(Pe)* *What already happened.*
   (Ca) *Yes.*
   (Pe) *And ehh ... what turned out to be the result.*
3. *(Ca)* *History.*
4. *(Pe)* *Yes, history ...*
   (Ca) *Yes.*
   (Pe) *... went that, that, ehh, that description of the assignment to the ehh...*
   employee?
5. *(Pe)* *For, I think I see a check mark of that application ...*
   (Ca) *Yes.*
6. *(Pe)* *But I do not get a confirmation of anything, of ehh ...*
   (Ca) *No.*
   (Pe) *whether it, ... it has been sent.*
7. *(Pe)* *And I also do not know if it has been worked out by the employee.*
   (Ro) *Hmm, hmm.*
   (Pe) *Do you, ehh...?*
8. *(Ca)* *No, no I only know it because they tell me, like "Hi, I consulted and*
   reached agreement and ehh ... that ehh ..."
9. *(Ca)* *Yes of course, in the end you can read it off from the date of the last*
   update, but you do not get ...
   (Pe) *O.K.*
10. *(Ca)* *... an automatic mail or, or a mutation. For it is impossible to see*
    what has been changed in the brief.
    (Pe) OK.
11. *(Ca)* *So, I also miss the history, like ehh ... what was the initial assignment.*

Fig. 4. A sample conceptualization of an elicitation session by Pe (Peter) and Ca (Caroline)

(1) *logical steps*:= 'icon', *no overview*:= 'sinsign'.
   Peter admits that in the current application he is missing (cf. event) steps that he finds logical (cf. state).

(2) *what already happened*:= 'icon', *no events and result*:= 'sinsign'.
   Peter refines his judgment, by paraphrasing his earlier concepts.

(3) *no history*:= 'legisign'.
   Finally, Caroline recognizes the habitual concept of '*no history*', in the instance ('*no overview*') and corresponding form ('*logical steps*') suggested by Peter.

(4) *description of assignment*:= 'rheme'; *communication to employee*:= 'index'.
   Similarly so, Peter recognizes an abstract concept involved in the input problem: 'description of the assignment'. He also refers to 'communication' towards the '*employee*'. That concept is not further explained in this session (nor in the

encompassing text) hence it must refer to background information. From the fact that Peter is expressing his 'doubt' in a proposition about the input problem (*description of assignment to employee is lacking communication history*:= 'argument') we conclude that all less developed sign aspects[7] must be generated as well, such as the 'lack of a communication history': *lack of communication history*:= 'symbol' and, the 'description of the assignment' communicated to the employee: *description of assignment to employee*:= 'dicent'.

(5) *check mark*:= 'icon'; *presence*:= 'sinsign'.
Peter is justifying his conclusion, by referring to a possible 'presence' (cf. effect) of 'check marks' (cf. state), in *myAssignment*.

(6) *confirmation*:= 'index'.
Peter's doubt is related to his question about the existence of a conventional logging of 'confirmations' and, corresponding 'confirmed assignments': *confirmation of assignment*:= 'dicent'; *lack of confirmation history*:= 'symbol'.

(7) *working out*:= 'index'.
Peter doubts, if logging is actually 'worked out' by the employee. The appearance of this background information enables a re-evaluation of all more developed expressions: *assignment worked out by employee*:= 'dicent'; *lack of logging history*:= 'symbol', *assignment by employee is not logged*:= 'argument'.

(8) *reaching agreement*:= 'index'.
Caroline admits having the same doubts as Peter has. She points out that the employee, not the application software is providing her with information about reaching agreement with the client. According to her, a lack of logging is what is meant by 'missing communication history'. Hereby she is referring to 'reaching agreement' as a nested conceptualization process: *assignment is in agreement*:= 'argument', degenerately represented by a pointer: *reaching agreement*:= 'index', in the encompassing process of interpretation.[8] By introducing a new 'index' expression, Caroline shows her interpretation of a common term involved in the generation of Peter's conclusion (note that a generation of the 'dicent' and 'symbol' positions is coordinated by the context ('index'), in the interpretation process).

(9)-(10) Caroline is further elaborating on her conceptualization of the nested process. In (9) she pinpoints: *date of last update*:= 'icon'; *agreement*:= 'sinsign'. In (10) she introduces: *no automatic mail, no mutation information*:= 'index'; *lack of agreement information*:= 'symbol' By making use of dependencies between the sign aspects and, the assumption that 'agreement' (cf. effect) must be related to an 'assignment', enables the nested conceptualization process to be completed: *assignment*:= 'rheme'; *agreement*:= 'legisign'; *that what is changed in the assignment*:= 'dicent'.

(11) *myAssignment is missing history*:= 'argument'.
Through a proposition of the nested process, the element of a 'no mutation information' is inherited in the index position of the encompassing conceptualization process. The appearance of this information as an index expression, this time not as a sign of doubt, but as one of a hypothesis, triggers a re-evaluation of all more developed input expressions. Assuming (11) is

---

[7] The set of sign aspects defines an induced hierarchy. See Fig. 2(a).
[8] Due to a lack of space, expressions of this process are omitted in Fig. 5.

providing a conclusion of the conceptualization process so far, it follows that the subject of the process Caroline is referring to (although not explicitly mentioning) must be the application program itself: *myAssignment*:= 'rheme'; *no mutation information in myAssignment*:= 'dicent'; *lack of mutation history*:= 'symbol'. She concludes: *myAssignment is missing history*:= 'argument'.

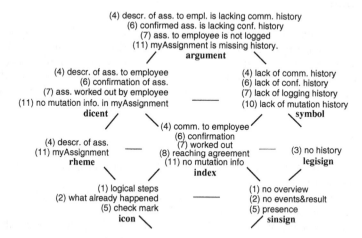

Fig. 5. A sample conceptualization session (Peircean sign aspects are recapitulated in bold face)

The above elicitation session includes two examples of efficient communication. In (1), Peter explains his first impression of a problem with *myAssignment*, which he paraphrases in (2). Although he develops different icon and sinsign expressions of the input problem, e.g., '*logical steps*' and '*no overview*', he is unable to abstract the input and represent it from the perspective of the rheme and legisign sign aspects. Caroline, noticing Peter's problem, interprets the difference between the icon (*c'*='logical steps') and sinsign positions (*c*='(no) overview'), and communicates this to Peter (*c\c'*='(no) history'). This information, which must be familiar to Peter ('*Yes, history*'), although in his conceptualization process he was not able to 'see' it, enables him to realize his pending icon-sinsign event and represent the arising relation (cf. abduction) in the legisign position ('*no history*').

The other example, in (8), is Caroline's communication, '*reaching agreement*'. In (4), Peter was able to recognize an abstract element (state) involved in the input problem (*c'*='*description of assignment*'), in the rheme position, and introduce an interpretation of this concept (*c*='*description of assignment to employee*'), in the dicent position. However, he was unable to express the context information involved. This refers to a potential asymmetry in Peter's interpretation process. Although he was able to conceptualize the input state from the perspectives of increasingly more meaningful sign aspects, he was unsuccessful in a similar development of representations of the input effect. Caroline's communication (*c\c'*) has a twofold contribution. It explains Peter's input representation, in the dicent position, and on top of this, it enables an interpretation of the legisign expression, '*no history*', in context ('*lack of logging history*'). The important element in Caroline's information about a possible relation, *'reaching agreement'* (over an *'assignment'*), is *coordination,* between the rheme-index and index-legisign interactions, which is the essential function of representations in the index position.

6   Summary

Integrative negotiation can be abstracted in a process, which is isomorphic to a Peircean model of cognitive activity. The cognitive process can be analysed from an informational perspective, in order to reveal the types of information that can be necessary for a realization of the events of this process. Those types can be used for a generation of goal-driven communication increasing the efficiency of negotiation.

References

1. Fisher, R., Ury, W.: Getting to Yes: Negotiating Agreement without Giving in. Houghton Mifflin, Boston (1981)
2. Follet, M.: Constructive conflict. In: Metcalf, H., Urwick, L. (eds.) Dynamic Administration, pp. 30–49. Harpe & Row, New York (1940)
3. Galinsky, A.D., Maddux, W.W., Gilin, D., White, J.B.: Why it pays to get inside the head of your opponent. Psychological Science 19(4), 378–394 (2008)
4. Kirk, D., Oettingen, G., Gollwitzer, M.: Mental contrasting promotes interactive bargaining. International Journal of Conflict Management 22(4), 324–341 (2011)
5. Raiffa, H.: Negotiation Analysis. Cambridge, The Belknap Press of Harvard University, Massachusetts, London (2002)
6. Sarbo, J.J.: On Well-formedness in Requirement Elicitation Processes. In: Feng, X., Liu, K., Jiang, G. (eds.) Proc. 11th Int. Conf. on Informatics and Semiotics in Organizations Beijing, China, pp. 18–25 (2009)
7. Sarbo, J.J., Farkas, J.I.: Towards meaningful information processing: A unifying representation for Peirce's signs sytems, SIGNS. Int. Journal of Semiotics 7, 1–41 (2013)
8. Sarbo, J.J., Farkas, J.I., Van Breemen, A.J.J.: Knowledge in Formation: A Computational Theory of Interpretation. Springer (2011)
9. Spanglar, B.: Integrative or Interest-based Bargaining. Beyond Intractability. In: Burgess, G., Burgess, H. (eds.) Conflict Information Consortium. University of Colorado, Boulder (2003), http://www.beyondintractability.org/essay/interest-based-bargaining
10. Walton, R.E., McKersie, R.B.: A Behavioral Theory of Labor Negotiations. McGraw-Hill, New York (1965)
11. Van Breemen, A.J.J., Sarbo, J.J.: Beyond Flatland? What does semiotics add to information sciences. In: Liu, K., Li, W., Gulliver, S.R. (eds.) Proc. of the 14th Int'l Conf. on Informatics and Semiotics in Organisations, pp. 50–55. Stockholm, Sweden (2013)
12. Harnad, S.: Categorical Perception: The groundwork of cognition. Cambridge University Press, Cambridge (1987)
13. Van Breemen, A.J.J., Farkas, J.I., Sarbo, J.J.: Knowledge representation as a tool for Intelligence Augmentation. In: Igelnik, B. (ed.) Computational Modeling and Simulation of Intellect: Current State and Future Perspectives, Hershey (PA), pp. 321–341 (2011)

A Semiotics Approach to Semantic Mismatches

Sabah Al-Fedaghi

Computer Engineering Department, Kuwait University, Kuwait
sabah.alfedaghi@ku.edu.kw

Abstract. This paper deals with modeling issues that are common to semiotics and software engineering. A major problem is that vague notions of modeling lead to difficulties in building real-world representations for use in the software development life cycle. Specifically, this paper focuses on building a consistent representation that eliminates semantic mismatches through analysis of semiotics. Semantic mismatches occur when the same term is associated with multiple concepts. Semiotics provides a good theoretical foundation for UML research, since a UML diagram can be considered a sign made up of signs. This paper introduces a new approach based on the so-called Flowthing Model (FM) to represent semiotics notions of sign, interpretant, and object, for use in studying the problem of semantic mismatches. The conclusion is that diagrammatic UML representation can lead to the appearance of such problems and that FM description provides separate streams such that no mixing can occur among terms as things that flow.

Keywords: Conceptual model, Semiotic triangle, Software engineering, Semantic mismatches, UML.

1 Introduction and Description of the Problem

A model-driven engineering approach [1] emphasizes the bridging of different technologies and the integration of various bodies of knowledge [2][3]. It is concerned with modeling standards, techniques and tools, organizational process changes, project estimation and cost [4], as well as interoperability. Modeling standards include systems (e.g., SysML), software (e.g., UML), and hardware.

A "model" of a "system", in this context, is a construct that describes and explains the modeled domain as a phase in the development of a corresponding software system. This resultant description plays a crucial role as a blueprint from which phases of development evolve. The conceptual picture describes a real-world domain while excluding technical aspects and serves as a guide for the subsequent design phase. It provides a high-level representation of relevant entities and relationships among them in a system [6].

Building such a model is a major task involving knowledge management [7] to facilitate communication among stakeholders. "Model-driven development is a technology that aims to handle software development at a higher abstraction level using models as the main development artifact" [8].

This paper targets a set of challenges related to system development, including construction of a conceptual representation to serve as the foundation for software

K. Liu et al. (Eds.): ICISO 2014, IFIP AICT 426, pp. 11–21, 2014.

development. It focuses on *analysis* of requirements in the development life cycle to specify the *what*: user requirements captured from the problem domain without technology-dependent details [9]. The design phase is concerned with specifying the *how*, when a software solution is analyzed and design artifacts are developed [10]. "'Analysis' designates some kind of understanding of a problem or situation, whilst 'design' is related to the creation of a solution for the analyzed problem" [11].

With a focus on the phase involving requirements analysis, this paper examines the specific subject of consistency through elimination of "semantic mismatches" in a system description. Without loss of generality, we describe a method that illustrates this problem and its proposed solution as used in the BRIDG (Biomedical Research Integrated Domain Group) project [12-13].

The BRIDG project is a health information system that uses UML as a modeling tool. The BRIDG project has brought together diverse standards communities "to clarify the semantics of clinical research across pharmaceutical, regulatory, and research organizations" [14]. The adopted model specifies declarative semantics through UML class diagrams that describe concepts and the relationships between them, while the business processes (the procedural semantics) are represented in UML activity and state diagrams.

Models in BRIDG were developed by teams constructing source models based on use-cases and existing standards to facilitate articulation of the semantics in UML representations. The outcome was a set of "harmonizable artifacts" for mapping relationship constructs, and use-cases that included both declarative (data) and procedural (activity and state diagram) representations of the semantics. All stakeholders then reviewed the concepts in the mapping to reach definitions of terms that satisfied all participants. "Thus, the harmonization process involved an iterative and cumulative process of knowledge assimilation and unification based on existing knowledge resources" [14].

This paper focuses on the attempt in BRIDG to build a consistent representation through the elimination of semantic mismatches by iteratively utilizing dual processes as follows:

- Analysis of "business processes" from the point in time a symptom appeared, along with an interpretation and subsequent analysis.
- Use of UML diagrams to maintain consistency between declarative and procedural semantics.

The paper proposes an alternative methodology to this oscillation of analysis of "business processes" by UML representation. It is based on the notion of streams of "flow things" (denoted by *flowthing*).

2   Semantics and the Semantic Ambiguity Problem

Consensus is a position of agreement reached by a team as a whole. It is often favored as a decision-making process by groups that support collaborative teamwork. Cooperative mechanisms in groups include sharing of information to facilitate a common "world map" view and objectives. In such a distributed information environment, it is necessary to coordinate cooperation, and that requires consensus among teams to synchronize information handling.

According to Fridsma et al. [14], consensus can be reached through *ambiguity*, *abstraction*, or *harmonization*. Consensus through ambiguity occurs when vague definitions are created that can be interpreted differently by different stakeholders, e.g., definitions purposely include vague statements on which all participants can agree. Consensus through abstraction is achieved through generalization of terms that can be interpreted or modified for the local needs of participants.

In the BRIDG project [14], harmonization was achieved as follows:

> Experts examined the *business proces*ses... to determine causal and temporal relationships between the observed change in the patient's clinical state and its association [with] the clinical trial activities. [...]
>
> Second, ... the *activity diagrams* provide an orthogonal view of the declarative semantics of the class diagrams and provide a double check of the declarative representations in the model. [14]

In the context of this project, Fridsma et al. [14] introduced an underlying notion of "semantic mismatches" in terms of semiotics signs. Semiotics theory studies the meanings carried by signs (communication). A *sign* is "something standing for something else" [15], as shown in Fig. 1. The objects that can be signified by signs can be physical (a thing), conceptual (ideas), or even other signs.

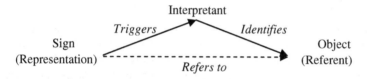

Fig. 1. Semiotic Triangle [15]

Semiotics has been used in many computer science studies. For example, according to Siau and Tian [17] "Semiotics, the study of signs, provides us good theoretical foundation for UML research as UML graphical notations are some kinds of signs." A UML diagram can be considered a sign made of signs [18-19].

Using the Semiotic triangle, Fridsma et al. [14] examined semantic mismatches in which the same term is associated with multiple concepts. They resolved this problem by creating two new concepts, with new terms applied to each of the concepts. Fig. 2 shows an example of such semantic mismatch in terms of semiotic triangles.

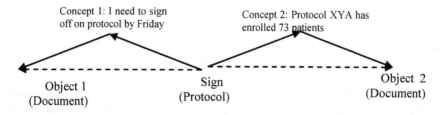

Fig. 2. Semantic mismatches: the same term associated with multiple concepts (from [14], with changes in terminology)

3   Flowthing Model

The Flowthing Model (FM) [20-22] represents some segment of reality as a web of interrelated *flows* that cross boundaries of intersecting and nested *spheres*. Ingredients in a flow include *flowthings* (things that flow), and flow systems (*flowsystems*). So-called objects, concepts, entities, and time are flowthings. A "thing" is defined as a flowthing: "what is created, released, transferred, arrived, accepted, and processed" while flowing within and among *spheres*. It has a permanent identity but impermanent form. A *flowsystem* constrains the trajectory of flow of flowthings. A particular flowsystem is the space/time for happenings and existence of flowthings. To flowthings, the flowsystem is formed from six discontinuities: being created, being released, being transferred, being arrived, being accepted, and being processed.

The ingression of a change in flowthings happens in three ways:

1. Change in *sphere* (regions in the world) through being **released**, **transferred**, and **received** from one sphere to another.
2. Change in *existence* through being created (emerging) or de-created (extinguished). An a priori snapshot of the sphere of the **creation** does not contain the flowthing, and an a posteriori snapshot contains it.
3. Change in the *form* of one or more features through being **processed**, e.g., shape, color, size.

Flows connect six *states* (also called stages) that are exclusive for flowthings; i.e., a flowthing can be in one and only one of these six states at a time: transfer, process, creation, release, arrival, and acceptance, as shown in Fig. 4. We use *Receive* as a combined stage of *Arrive* and *Accept* whenever arriving flowthings are always accepted. A *state* here is a "transmigration field" of the flowthing that is processed, created, released, arrives, is transferred, and is accepted. In Fig. 3, we assume irreversibility of flow, e.g., released flowthings flow only to transfer.

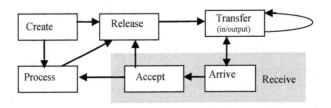

Fig. 3. Flowsystem

The exclusiveness of FM stages (i.e., a flowthing cannot be in two stages simultaneously) indicates synchronized change of the flowthing. A flowthing *cannot be changed in form and sphere simultaneously*. This is a basic systematic property of flowthings.

Initialization, stopping, and continuing of flows occur through *triggering*. Triggering is a control mechanism. It is the only linkage among elements in FM description besides flow and is indicated by dashed arrows. Synchronizations (e.g., join/fork) and logic notions (e.g., and/or) can be superimposed on the basic FM depiction.

4   Sign as a Flowthing

Sign, object, and interpretant in the semiotic triangle are viewed as flowthings in FM. Given a sign in a given sphere that includes the sign, its object, and intrepretant, each has its own flowsystem, as shown in Fig. 4. Signs can be created, released, transferred, received, and processed, but for (material) objects, an intrepretant can be only created and processed. For example, concepts cannot be transferred directly from one mind to another.

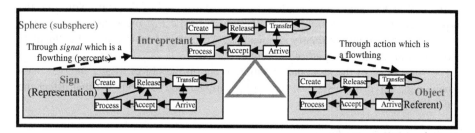

Fig. 4. The Semiotic triangle is formed from three spheres that include three different flowthings with their flowsystems

Assigning an object to a sign

Accordingly, the triangle can be supplemented with necessary flowsystems, as shown in Fig. 5. In the figure, a sign is created (appears/is generated; see circle 1). Assuming a physical sign, its appearance triggers (circle 2) physical signals, e.g., light (striking the retinas of the eyes), odor molecules, or pressure waves.

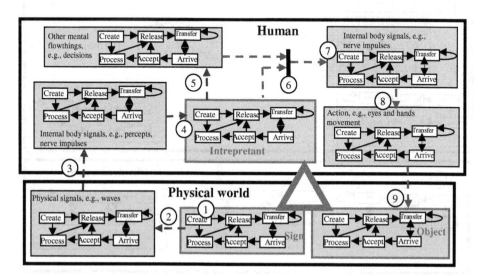

Fig. 5. The Semiotic triangle supplemented by the communication flowsystem between a human (body + mind) and the physical world.

These signals have their own flowsystems where they are created, received, etc., and they trigger (circle 3) the creation of a flowsystem of percepts/nerve impulses in the human body. These percepts/nerve impulses arrive at the brain, triggering creation of the interpretant (4), which in turn triggers other concepts (5).

With its "cluster" of associated concepts, the interpretant forms the "meaning" of the sign, thus directing attention to the thing to which the sign refers, assuming it is a physical object, through some type of action; formation of meaning triggers (6) creation of a flowsystem of percepts/nerve impulses in the human body. The vertical bar at (6) is borrowed from Petri nets notation to indicate a join of the effect of the interpretant and related concepts that form the "meaning" of the sign. Note that the purpose here is to demonstrate the methodology of the FM presentation and not to introduce a new cognitive theory of meaning. Any other description of the "mental" landscape can replace this part of the figure.

The "meaning" of the sign and intention to act on the object trigger internal body signals, e.g., nerve impulses (7), that in turn trigger body actions (8) that affect the object (9).

Assigning a sign to an object

On the other hand, assigning a sign to an object is modeled as shown in Fig. 6. Assuming physical object and sign, presence of the object (1) triggers the creation of physical signals, e.g., light (striking the retinas of the eyes), odor molecules, or pressure waves (2).

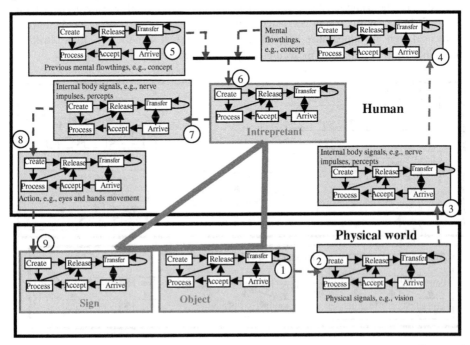

Fig. 6. The object causes creation of a sign

This, in turn, triggers the creation of a percepts/nerve impulses flowsystem in the human body (3), causing the generation of mental flowthings (4) triggered, originally, by the object, e.g., concepts of circles and lines form the concept of cylinder. Again, the purpose here is not to develop a particular cognitive process; rather, we describe assumed relationships among concepts to illustrate FM features and capability.

From the mental flowthings triggered by the signal coming from the object, and in the conjunction of mental flowthings already present in the mind from previous experiences (6), the interpretant is created. Notice that creation here does not necessarily mean no previous existence, but an emergence or appearance in the context of the current (sphere) experience caused by an encounter with the object.

The interpretant then triggers internal body signals (7) that trigger actions (8) that, in turn, trigger the creation of the physical sign, e.g., writing a word (9).

5   Consensus Re-visited

Now, in FM perspective, consider the notion advanced by Fridsma et al. [14] of semantic mismatches, in which the same term is associated with multiple concepts. Fridsma et al.'s description of the problem [14] implies that the two concepts are in two different minds (mentally separated spheres). It is difficult to imagine a person consciously using the same term for unrelated concepts. Similarly, in the context of a single organization, it is hard to imagine the same term being used for different concepts, but it might occur in disjointed or discrete suborganizational units that have indirect interaction and little personal interchange).

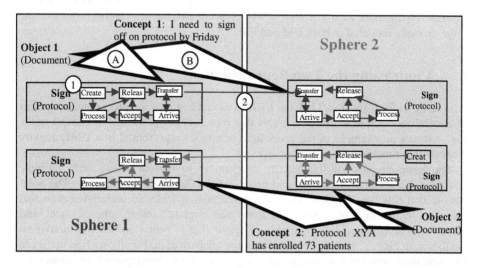

Fig. 7. The same term is associated with multiple concepts but each is recognized by its flow, under the assumption that the *same* sphere (a human) does not refer to multiple different concepts that identify multiple different objects by using one term

This means that a term corresponding to two concepts has been created in two different divisions of the organization. From the FM perspective, this means that the same term is used in two different spheres, as shown in Fig. 7, using the example given by Fridsma et al. [14] and shown previously in Fig. 2. Note that each sign is identified by its creator and its flow.

In the figure, the sign "protocol" is created by sphere 1 and flows to sphere 2. In sphere 2, this sign of "protocol" is received from sphere 1 and also another sign of "protocol" created internally in sphere 2. There is no confusion between the two signs because the FM flow description establishes the identity of each separately. Consider the sign "protocol" created in sphere 1 (circle 1). It is in the semiotic triangle labeled A. If it flows to sphere 2 (circle 2), it is in semiotic triangle B. It is just a sign in sphere 2, but its interpretant and project are still in sphere 1. Otherwise, by assumption, sphere 2 would not permit two terms to correspond to the same concept. Note that there is no *Create* stage in the upper flowsystem of sphere 2. As the sphere of a sign, sphere 2 can transfer, release, receive, and process this sign, but it is just a sign and has no corresponding concept in this sphere. If sphere 2 decides to attach a concept and object to this sign, then a mechanism is needed to import them from sphere 2. This is analogous to a postman who delivers a sealed *message* and simultaneously receives a personal message himself. Both are messages and may have the same form, but each has its own sender and receiver.

The problem in BRIDG that is discussed in this paper stems from the fragmentation of the UML representation that does not always tie each term to its stream of flow, like flows of electrical signals not bounded by wires. In FM, each kind of flowthing flows in its flowtsystem, and can be distinguished the same way electrical signals can be distinguished by following their flows from electrical sources. To illustrate such a feature of FM presentation, the next section contrasts the same example modeled in both UM and FM.

6   Contrasting the Two Representations

According to Fridsma et al. [14], the BRIDG model captures the procedural semantics of clinical research in activity diagrams that represent the processes in clinical trials. Fig. 8 shows an example of the procedural semantics represented in a UML activity diagram that functions like a storyboard.

The basic premise of the activity diagram is to present *events* with *multiple notations*, semantic *overloading*, and heterogeneous levels of descriptions. The point here is that this type of flowchart-like representation lacks an underlying web that preserves the tracking of things while they "transmigrate" among spheres, states, and existence/nonexistence. For example, a *request* that is sent vanishes into activities, databases, decisions, and processes, increasing chances of ambiguity such as occurs in the semantic mismatches discussed previously. This development of ambiguity contrasts with the FM representation with its systematic notions that all processes are categorized into stages and flowthings can be identified by flows.

Fig. 9 shows the FM representation corresponding to the activity diagram of Fig. 8 and drawn according to our understanding of the given description.

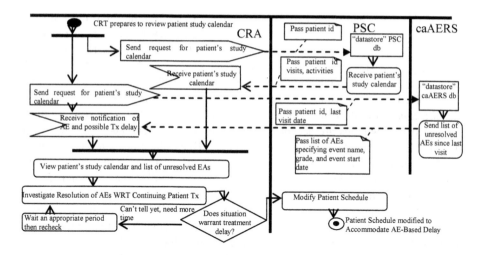

Fig. 8. Activity diagram of the example (from [14])

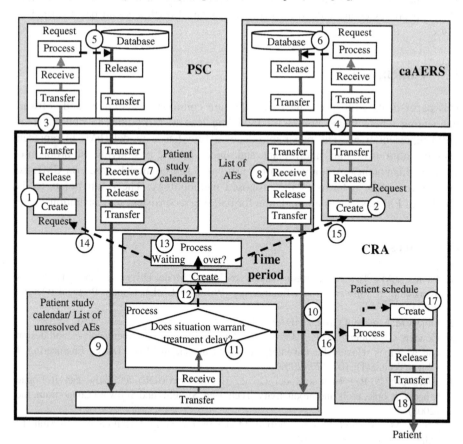

Fig. 9. FM representation that corresponds to Fig. 8

The CRT creates and sends two requests (circles 1 and 2 in the figure) to PSC and caAERS (circles 3 and 4, respectively). PSC and caAERS process these requests, triggering (5 and 6) the retrieval of "Patient study calendar" and "List of AEs", respectively. The subspheres "Patient study calendar" and "List of AEs" in CRT receive these data and send them (circles 9 and 10) to the "Patient study calendar/ List of unresolved AEs" subsphere. Note that the flowthing in this subsphere is a *generalization* of the flowthings "Patient study calendar" and "List of AEs". Both of these last two flowthings are accepted as flowthings in "Patient study calendar" and "List of AEs". When they are processed (11), "Does situation warrant treatment delay?" can lead to "Can't tell yet, need more time", triggering (12) the creation of an appropriate time period that is processed (13). "Waiting over" triggers (14 and 15) the creation of new requests. Alternatively, "Situation does not warrant treatment delay" triggers (16) the processing of "Patient schedule" (available since it is received beforehand) to create a new one (17) that is sent to the patient. Note that in the online version of the paper, each flow is drawn in a different color.

Contrasting the resultant representations side by side points to the capability of the FM methodology to construct a consistent representation with its systematic notions where all processes are categorized into stages and flowthings can be identified by flows.

7   Conclusion

This paper deals with modeling issues that are common to semiotics and software engineering where vague notions of modeling lead to difficulties in building real-world representations. The paper introduces a flow-based model (FM) to represent semiotics notions of sign, interpretant, and object, for use in studying the problem of semantic mismatches. A study case of constructing source models based on UML use cases is re-casted in terms of the proposed methodology. The result points to the viability of FM to serve as a foundation for building a consistent representation.

References

1. Favres, J.M.: Towards a Basic Theory to Model Model-Driven Engineering. In: 3rd Workshop in Software Model Engineering (WiSME@UML), Lisbon, Portugal (October 2004)
2. Object Management Group: MDA Guide Version 1.0.1, http://www.omg.org/
3. Génova, G., Valiente, M.C., Marrero, M.: On the difference between analysis and design, and why it is relevant for the interpretation of models in Model Driven Engineering. J. Object Tech. 8(1), 107–127 (2009)
4. Blackburn, M.R.: What's Model Driven Engineering(MDE) and how can it impact process, people, tools and productivity. Tech. Rep. Systems and Software Consortium, Inc. (2008)
5. Object Management Group: Unified Modeling Language Specification. Version 1.5 (March 2003), http://www.omg.org/

6. Autili, M., et al.: CHOReOS Perspective on the Future Internet and Initial Conceptual Model. Project report, version 1 (January 27, 2012),
   http://citeseerx.ist.psu.edu/viewdoc/
   download?doi=10.1.1.220.3072&rep=rep1&type=pdf
7. Brooks, F.P.: The Mythical Man-Month. Addison-Wesley (1975)
8. Silingas, D.: Model-Driven Service Choreographies for the Future Internet. In: Future Internet Symposium 2012, Vilnius, Lithuania, May 21-23 (2012)
9. Kaindl, H.: Difficulties in the Transition from OO Analysis to Design. IEEE Soft. 16(5), 94–102 (1999)
10. Høydalsvik, G.M., Sindre, G.: On the Purpose of Object-Oriented Analysis. In: VIII Conference on Object-Oriented Prog. Syst. Lang. and Appl (OOPSLA 1993), September 26–October 1, vol. 28(10), pp. 240–255. ACM SIGPLAN Notices, Washington (1993)
11. Harel, D., Rumpe, B.: Meaningful Modeling: What's the Semantics of 'Semantics'? IEEE Computer, 64–72 (October 2004)
12. BRIDG (Biomedical Research Integrated Domain Group),
    http://bridgmodel.nci.nih.gov/
13. Hastak, S.: BRIDG Update, presentation (May 15, 2012),
    http://bridgmodel.nci.nih.gov/
14. Fridsma, D.B., Evans, J., Hastak, S., Mead, C.N.: The BRIDG Project: A Technical Report, J. Am. Med. Inform. Assoc. 15(2), 130–137 (2008)
15. Eco, U.: A Theory of Semiotics. Indiana University Press (1976)
16. Marcos, E., Marcos, A.: A Philosophical Approach to the Concept of Data Model: Is a DataModel, in Fact, a Model? Inform. Syst. Frontiers 3(2), 267–274 (2001)
17. Siau, K., Tian, Y.: A Semiotics View of Modeling Method Complexity: The Case of UML. In: AMCIS 2005 Proceedings. Paper 318 (2005),
    http://aisel.aisnet.org/amcis2005/318
18. Morand, B.: Modeling: Is it Turning Informal into Formal? In: Bézivin, J., Muller, P.-A. (eds.) UML 1998. LNCS, vol. 1618, pp. 37–48. Springer, Heidelberg (1999)
19. Génova, G., Valiente, M.C., Nubiola, J.: A Semiotic Approach to UML models. In: CAiSE Workshops, vol. 2, pp. 547–557 (2005)
20. Al-Fedaghi, S.: A Conceptual Foundation for Data Loss Prevention. Int. J. Digital Content Tech. Appl. 5(3), 293–303 (2011)
21. Al-Fedaghi, S.: Interpretation of Information Processing Regulations. J. Softw. Eng. Appl. 2(2), 67–76 (2009)
22. Al-Fedaghi, S.: Conceptualizing Effects, and Uses of Information. In: The Information Seeking in Context conference (ISIC 2008), Vilnius. Lithuania, September 17-20 (2008)

Quality of Service in the Long Tail: Narratives and the Exploitation of Soft Metadata

Auke J.J. van Breemen

ICIS, Radboud University Nijmegen, The Netherlands
a.vanbreemen@science.ru.nl

Abstract. The fuzzier domains of social life come into the scope of information science. Below a method is presented that deals with exception handling or also the long tail. It is based upon the Peirce inspired KiF-model. But this time the goal is not to describe procedures or to model elicitation processes, the goal is to develop meaningful sensors that at the same time structure the analysis of the problem and facilitates the access of a database filled with stories. The domain of application is the Dutch educational system.

Keywords: Narrative method, Hard metadata, Soft metadata, Information architecture, Knowledge in Formation (KiF)-model, Education.

1 Introduction

Henry Ford felt the urge to state that any customer can have his Ford model T painted any color that he wants so long as it is black. He wanted to build a car for the great multitude: "large enough for the family, but also small enough for the individual." Within a century Anderson felt confident enough to state "Forget squeezing millions from a few megahits from the top of the charts. The future of entertainment is in the millions of niche markets at the swallow end of the bitstream."[1] Subsequently, within a decade, he extends his view from the long tail of the bit-market to the long tail of the thing-market [1, p.63] and resigns from his post as editor in chief of Wired Magazine in order to exploit the long tail in the realm of things himself.

The concept of the long tail is not only applicable to the market. Also with regard to services in the public sphere we meet the phenomenon that about 20% of the cases generates 80% of the classes. In health care the incidence of the more than 14.000[2] coded diseases diminishes rapidly if we go from the more to the less frequent. In educational and child care services,[3] were diagnostics and classification are perused in a far less serious manner, we must assume a long tail, but only some niches are well

---

[1] See http://changethis.com/manifesto/10.LongTail/
pdf/10.LongTail.pdf, C. Anderson, The long tail, 13 December 2004.

[2] For the count see the International Classification of Diseases, ICD-10, 1990.

[3] My background is the Dutch educational system, child care and health are overlapping domains . The government decided to introduce Passend Onderwijs (Fitting or Inclusive Education). If this program is taken seriously, we are in dire need to get a hold on the long tail in education.

K. Liu et al. (Eds.): ICISO 2014, IFIP AICT 426, pp. 22–31, 2014.

defined, the majority is crudely defined, if defined at all. A major contributor to the complexity is the circumstance that like personal traits, lead to different results due to the effect of circumstances and experiences on the developing personal character. This tail is besides long, very messy. Oftentimes the stakeholders disagree about the policy that ought to be effectuated. This is a result of not defined or only vaguely defined niches in combination with differences in goal orientation.

Whereas Ford could, in principle, specify every detail of the model T production process in sufficient detail, in the long tail of services a less directive approach is called for. The most we can aim at is that in the long run the classes get sorted out better and adequate policies are suggested. The solution I present below aims at just that. It consists in a narrative approach that utilizes hard (facts) and soft (perceptions) metadata for retrieval purposes. The soft metadata are part of an information architecture that helps the user to find relevant information in other stories told and, according to Kalbach an important requirement for information systems that cover niches, it makes sense by providing context [2]. Interestingly, the model together with the soft metadata proved very useful in the actual handling of long tail cases, see section 2. This offers the possibility to integrate the construction and utilization of domain specific information systems in regular workflow processes, see the conclusions section 4. For the sake of efficiency, in section 3 after the introduction of the proposed approach, I will indicate some differences with affiliated research.

2   A Case Study: Narrative Research in the Educational System

A disadvantage of strictly quantitative research in the services sector is that although one gets informed about the numbers op people that occupy the different categories distinguished, and about numerical changes through the years, one doesn't learn anything about the diverse dynamics that did lead to the membership of particular categories, nor is there any information about class hopping of particular individuals throughout their careers. As a result this kind of research is of little use for interventions in individual cases. If we want to improve on quality of service we are better off using dedicated information bases filled with Geertz' thick descriptions [3], Ginzburg's micro stories with clues [4] or Schank's scenario's and scripts [5], dealing with individual cases that are (partly) similar, than with quantitative population survey results. Although of course the combination of both is most fruitful and necessary for policy making in the system under scrutiny.

In 2012 Van Garderen of Top Innosense b.v. and I set off collecting stories with hard metadata about pupils that fell out of the educational system.[4] After some twenty five stories we organized, in cooperation with Gedragswerk,[5] a meeting with the respondents and key professionals in the problem area. Our main objective was the

---

[4] In the Dutch system this is regarded a criminal offence that instigates the officials to start prosecution regardless of the reasons to drop out, which explains why predominantly parents told their stories.

[5] Gedragswerk is an initiative of the ministry of education. If asked by parents, the organization delivers 'sparring partners' if the parents have conflicts with school regarding the teaching of their children.

development of a signifier set for soft metadata. Van Garderen working with the Cynefin model and the SenseMaking Triads in the tradition of Snowden [6], I attending with our[6] Knowledge in Formation model (KiF-model) [7] and Richmond's Trikons [8] in my mind, see section 3 for differences between both approaches.

After fifty stories it proved possible to sketch the four most relevant processes in a KiF-model and to develop a trikonic signifier set for the focal process. In 2013 I had the opportunity to follow two cases in detail. This offered the possibility to collect the scores of all stakeholders involved in one and the same model. In the first case it proved not possible to organize a meeting of all stakeholders. The negotiation process between parent and school remained a zero-sum game. Father and son recently voted with their feet in order to avoid a second criminal prosecution procedure. In the second case it proved possible to organize two such meetings and a win-win solution is realized:[7] After more than three years this son receives education again. It is worthwhile to note that the same solution would also be agreeable to the parent and child of the first case. In 2.1 I briefly describe the initial narrative environment and the hard metadata. In 2.2 I present the educational KiF-schema and the attached soft metadata.

This is not the place to delve into the content of the stories gathered in order to find some patterns. The interested reader, who mastered Dutch is referred to *De Dunne lijn; tussen naar school en thuiszitten* (The thin line between going to school and sitting at home), *De dunne lijn; perspectieven verbinden* (The thin line, connecting perspectives).[8] And, for one of the case descriptions Terug naar af Wouter! (Back to the start Wouter!).[9]

2.1   Stories and Hard Metadata

The visitor of our narrative environment first got a short introduction in the subject of interest and our goals. In the narration environment the first, and only obligatory, question we asked is: Tell your story. There are no restrictions to length in the accompanying text field. The idea is that people who go to the internet and tell their story because they experience(d) some frustrating problems are inclined to concentrate on what they deem most relevant for the state they find themselves in. Immediately after this question we asked for a title and keywords. This can be regarded as inviting user generated metadata that suffer heavily from inconsistencies, as is pointed out by Kalbach [2]. This however was not the intention. Primarily we wanted the respondent to take a somewhat distanced look at the story and at the same time prepare the respondent for a final open question: Do you have suggestions based on your experiences? Secondarily we tried to enhance the number of clues for judging the measure of credibility of the story told. The invitation to provide suggestions was put after the hard metadata questions that, besides being questions, may set off some association patterns, related to important feats of the problem area in the mind of the respondent.

---

[6] Sarbo, Farkas and Van Breemen.

[7] I don't claim that the domain specific KiF-model forces a win-win strategy. At the most it invites one by sorting out the diverse processes and arguments.

[8] Retrievable from http://www.koesch.nl/onderzoek/.

[9] Retrievable from http://www.koesch.nl/wordpress/wp-content/uploads/casuswouterd11.pdf.

Next we asked for facts (In order to give the reader at least some insight in the domain, responses are provided after a number of closed questions. N=58):

- What was the duration of the absence?
  Some days 9%, some weeks 10%, two months< 16%, 6 months< 49%, was never absent 19%.
- What was the age of the pupil?
  The main gain of this question is that by now we know we have to append the question 'duration of absence' with '1 year' and '2 years'. We got answers like from 5 to 10 years of age and 12 to 16 years of age. In general problems surface around 5 (entering primary school), around 10 (entering second part primary school), around 12 (entering secondary school) and around 15 years of age.
- Did the pupil attend a school for special education?
  Yes 52%, no 48% (special education takes about 10% of all pupils).
- What kind of school did the pupil attend?
  Kindergarten 12%, primary education 40%, secondary professional basic (vmbo) 27% professional follow up (mbo) 19%, general theoretical (havo) 8%, preparatory for university (vwo) 6%. Our evidence shows the occurrence of a downgrading of level, before a drop out.
- I am ....
  Pupil 3%, parent 79 %, grandparent 2%, friend 3%, teacher 2%, ambulant begeleider (mentors of the extra funding for pupils in regular education) 9%.
- (Open question) What were the consequences of the experiences?
- How long did those consequences last?
  Some weeks 9%, 3 months 5%, 6 months 9%, a year or longer 64%, there were no consequences 0%.
- Does the pupil attend school currently?
  Yes 53%, No 47%.
- If there has been or is a drop out, has it been reported to the officials?
  Yes 58%, no 36 %, not applicable 5%, I don't know 12%.
- Do you have suggestions based on your experiences? (lots of suggestions)
- May we know who you are, if so please provide contact details?
  7 respondents did not leave contact details.

The basic idea behind the set up thus far is that with the help of (a selection of) the hard metadata and eventual some text search (for instance autism and related terms) in the stories, a user of the database can retrieve all stories that fulfill the conditions. Thus (s)he is enabled to consult the stories or scenario's and decide which scripts may be promising and which scripts aren't for the problem (s)he is facing.

2.2   The KiF-Model

This is not the place to go into the depths of the KiF-model regarded as a model that provides a general description of interpretation processes as a procedure. In Fig. 1 the processing schema is given. The interested reader may consult [7] for details. Here it is enough to stick to the main line.

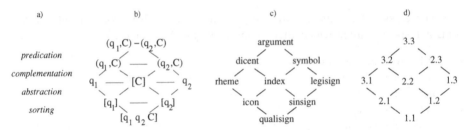

Fig. 1. a) the four stages that can be discerned in interpretation processes, b) the KiF process model of Sarbo and Farkas with the interaction of two variables q1 and q2 and the context C, c) the Peircean semiotic terms and d) the Peircean categorical values of every position on the corresponding positions.

If in analyze mode we look at an interpretation process bottom up,[10] we set off with an interpreting system in a certain *state* q1 that experiences an *effect* q2,[11] but at this point both are indiscriminately present, which is represented by the square brackets in 1.b. Since the very same effect may in different interpretation processes yield different *results* (q1,C)-(q2,C), the C represents the context and the goals, operative in the interpretive system, that determine the inclination towards the result that is going to be worked with in the stages to come.[12] From a top down perspective: at this point nothing follows, so q1 and q2 are both still regarded false, which can be regarded as an expression of doubt, see figure 2 bottom.

Fig. 2. The truth values of two variables distributed over the four compartments of the KiF-model[13]

First the state and effect are sorted out, but just that, next they must be abstracted, or 'recognized' (expressed in terms of fig. 1 b) [q1 (in the 'negation' of) q2] yields [q1] and [q2 (in the ''negation' of) q1] yields [q2]).[14] In terms of Fig. 2 the interpreting system must manage to make the state true for itself independent from but

---

[10] This does not mean we defend the bottom up stance in the old discussion about reading (bottom up vs top down). It is a mixed affair and some people are more inclined to the one or the other strategy. A person overdoing constantly in one of the directions will end up in a niche in the educational system.

[11] Notice that this is in line with Stampers actualism.

[12] What is taken as input and what as noise in the receptive field depends on C, later on we will see that also emotional predispositions bear on the outcome of interpretation processes.

[13] This is an application of Peirce's X-box which he used to derive the 16 Boolean operators.

[14] This triadic relation underlies the dependency structure of the KiF-model, cf. q1,[C]->(q1,C), This also is the relation between State, Effect->Response, that summarizes the lot. The KiF-model aims at a description of the argument in semiotic terms, cf 1c.

in light of (or in the universe co-determined by) the effect and the effect independent from but in light of the state. When 'recognized', to this end the memory [C] is addressed by q1 and q2 for complementation in the light of the goal that is operative. If as well q1 as q2 can be complemented by C - expressed by (q1,C), (q2,C) - and (q1,C) can be unified with (q2,C) (predication stage), a response can be given to the original input. Put in terms of Fig. 2: the original doubt (FF) proved to be resolvable into belief (TT). This of course does not mean that the belief is true; it only means that *this* interpreting system managed to arrive at a result on *this* input.

2.3   The KiF-Model in the Educational Domain

Learning problems experienced by pupils in class, which cannot be met in class, enter school level. Thus we have a process that has as its goal the learning activity of a pupil: Pupil(S), Class(E) ->Learning(R). If this process fails because either the S or the E cannot be made true to a satisfactory degree or both cannot be unified, a new process sets off - Pupil, School->Learning result - of which the former process is a sub-process, see Fig. 3a). If the discussion arrives at this level a serious question is regularly raised: is the class responsible for the failure or is it due to the parents? See for instance Stoutjesdijk [10], but also our stories give ample evidence for this move. So, as a parallel process we have Pupil, Parents->Interest in school, Fig. 3b)

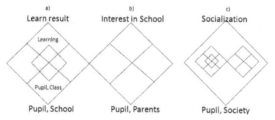

Fig. 3. After a pupil is inscribed at a school process, it enters the class sub processes. These processes are defined by their goal a). If problems arise that cannot be met in class, the discussion is transferred to the super process, but then a parallel process may be deemed relevant and questions arise about the contribution of the parent to the problem b). Both processes have society as their root. Besides that auxiliary processes may be started, indicated by the empty space c). The goal of the root process ought to pose restrictions on what can be argued about the sub processes.

Via the pupil the three processes are related and a variety of subsidiary processes may arise. Being tested by a psychologist[15] and being prosecuted by law[16] are only two of them. In Fig. 3c) Society is the agent that has its Effect on the State of the Pupil. The perspective from which this interaction must be looked at, is its goal 'Socialization'. This root process has two sub-processes of which one has a sub-process. Besides that, other parallel processes might be involved, indicated by the empty space. We must not assume the law of excluded middle holds, in our attempt to find a solution for a pupil.

---

[15] Psychologist (S), Pupil (E) -> Testreport (R) or Pupil(S), Psychologist(E)->Remediation(R).
[16] Pupil (S), Public servant (E) -> Convicted (R).

In this exposition the focus will be on the process Pupil, School->Learn result. We do not want to model this process; we want to be able to inspect it with regard to the question what the hindrances are for the achievement of a satisfactorily learning result. Since the pupil will have to do the interpretation, needed for the kernel process *learning*, we want to know whether there is a (negative) bias in the propensity to sort, abstract and complement. Next we want to know which characteristics of the child or/and of the school contribute to the problem. Finally we want to know something about propensities in the predication or unification stage. Cf. Fig.s 1a) and 5.

2.4   Soft Metadata and Trikons

Richmond [2005], following Peirce, introduces trichotomy as "the art of making threefold distinctions". "this new applied science", he continues, "rests upon Peirce's triadic categorical distinctions". Sarbo and Farkas [9] offer a way to illuminate[17] the difference between triadic and trichotomic distinctions. Interpretation processes yield signs as results. On Peircean principles a sign is something that (1) can be regarded in itself, (2) can be regarded as to its relation with its object and (3) can be regarded in the way in which it addresses its interpretant thought. If one of those relations is missing we do not have something that functions as a sign. In terms of Fig. 4 a) out of each of the bold lines a sign takes one position with the restriction that the position on a higher category cannot have a higher value than the position occupied in lower categories. As a consequence ten different sign types can be distinguished. So, in terms of Fig. 1c), a Rhematic, iconic legisign is a sign type, a symbolic, dicent legisign another. This means that for each of the triadic sign relations there is a rule restricted choice out of three, again categorically ordered, possibilities, the 1, 2 and 3 on each bold line. These are each trichotomic distinctions and not triadic relations.

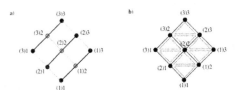

Fig. 4. Each bold line in a) presents a trichotomic distinction pertaining to signs. We get a triadic sign relation by picking a term out of each of the three trichotomies. There is a restriction: the term of a lower trichotomy may not be of lower value than the term picked in a higher trichotomy. On account of this restriction, the Trikons can be ordered in the KiF-model: Trikon (1) in the bottom square, (2) in the square left and (3) in the top square, see Fig. b). The square right is reserved for the effect processed by the interpreting system.

So, what do we want to know about the Pupil? In the first Trikon we want to know something about the sign in itself, the Pupil in this case. Especially we want to know its inclination in the sorting, abstraction and complementation phases. A shy

---

[17] A full account would demand a treatment of Peirce's extended sign system and of the differences between the static figure of semiotic terms, 1c), and the actualist, dynamical KiF-model 1b). This falls far out of the scope of this paper.

withdrawn or fearful attitude (1)1 leads to different response patterns than an angry or too assertive externally oriented inclination (1)2, which again differs in its results from a reasoned response that takes the situation into account (1)3.

In the second Trikon we want to know about the Pupils relation with its objects. Is it just the interaction with informational content that is going to make school difficult? (2)1. Is it Pupils interaction with the physical world? (2)2. Or, is it Pupils interaction with other individuals that also process information and interact with the physical world? (2)3.

Finally, we want to know how the unification process runs in the interactions between Pupil (and Pupils caretakers) and School. Are there plans without execution, but nobody makes a point of it? (3)1. Is there hostile disagreement about the action that ought to be taken? (3)2 or are all working towards a solution? (3)3. See Fig. 5.

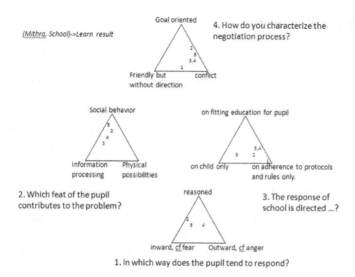

Fig. 5. The four Trikons in their KiF arrangement. The scores are from case Mithra (unpublished) in which I utilized the model to guide negotiation. 1 is the mother, 2 a teacher, 3 and 4 are pedagogical specialists. 5 is a civil servant of child care.

If we were interested in the way School interacts with Pupils in general, then we had to make a KiF-instance with school in the state position. But we are not, we only want to know how School (E) deals with this niche Pupil. This belongs on categorical level (2). School may order all kinds of tests, but leave the problem as it is in the everyday affairs (2)1, it may have protocols that are applied blindly (2)2 or it may decide its course in interaction with Pupil (and Pupils caretakers) (2)3. See Fig. 5.

Since the points in the Trikons can be calculated, it is possible to use them as pointers to stories. And, they do what Kalbach asked for. They do, together with the kiF-model, put data in a meaningful information architecture. The combination is even able to direct the negotiation process in an effective way. On top of that the educational model can be extended with embedded and parallel processes dressed with Trikons.

There is a serious objection that can be raised. It proves to be the case that even in one case different roles diverge in the scores they make. So, what is the value of a story base? Well, yes anyone taking the stories told uncritically for truth is ill advised. But, as you see in the scores in Fig. 5, the score on the top Trikon already shows that opinions strongly diverge and that it is up to the reader to sort out the promising scripts. And, even if all stories could be trusted, it would be ill advised to just do what proved to be successful. For one thing because the people concerned will not be the same, for another because the goals that are set for Pupils by their parents, will differ in terms of ambition. But also, the goal of this system is not to automate responses to problems that do arise, the goal is to empower the user by providing a model that systematically decomposes the problem into a set of questions and to deliver scripts and scenario's that other people met in dealing with similar problems.

3   Related Research

The approach proposed here is akin to cultural anthropological field work in complex societies assisted by ICT. To my knowledge, Kurz and Snowden originated this narrative approach [6]. It is quite remarkable how close the resemblance is between the Cynefin model and the KiF-model and between Triads and Trikons. There are however some significant differences. Triads are constructed in sessions with stakeholders and the terms at the corners must be in opposition with each other, Trikons are constructed in relation to goal oriented domain specific KiF-processes and the terms must adhere to categorical rules. This architectonic improves the chance that data islands, tagged with Trikons can be more easily related to each other.

Richmond's Trichotomic [8] and Keidel's Triangulation [12] are very similar. Richmond bases his Trikons on the categorical distinctions of Peirce and he applies them in grand scale philosophical musings, whereas Keidel developed his triangles in organizational science and describes them in organizational terms: autonomy (monadic, first category), hierarchy (dyadic, second category), network (triadic, third category). Anyone interested in the principles behind the Trikons is referred to Richmond, but if the interest goes to the application of Trikons, Keidel has much more to offer, cf. pp 153-167 of [12] for lots of orderly arranged triangles. In its result, the main difference between Keidel and Richmond is that Keidel uses points and lines in his Triangles[18] in order to signify situations or the direction of change in time respectively, whereas Richmond utilizes the outline of the Triads in order to indicate directionality. Technically, Trikons as I use them are ternary plots.

An important difference between Keidel and Richmond on the one hand and the proposed method on the other is that the former builds Trikonic or Triangular edifices whereas the latter integrates the Trikons with an information processing model.

4   Conclusions

The proposed narrative approach, with domain specific Kif-models that ensure a common frame of mind and deliver meaningful information architectures at the same time, and with Trikons, in order to map and retrieve perceptions, can become a sound

---

[18] Keidel is the first I know of who did.

method for dealing with quality of service in the long tail. One can imagine different ways to proceed. On categorical grounds: 1. Just throw out this conceptual net on the internet and see what the catch will be. 2. Organize for clusters of schools an environment where stories can be delivered by parents or teachers and let the schools and parents deal with it themselves. 3. Organize a specialized group of civil servants that operates on a regional or national scale and give them the task to solve problems that are brought to the fore and to follow the results in order to improve performance in the long run. In the Netherlands the local civil servants that guard the obligation to attend school and/or the national educational consultants are the most obvious candidates, but only if experienced teachers are added to the group: as it is now, the role of the servants is far too formal and their knowledge of education too scant to be able to deal with the content.

A yet unanswered, but important research question is whether it is possible to make models on the same principles in other domains, as for instance health care and child care, and in other cultures where the goals differ. The movie 一个都不能少 (Not one less), by Zang Yimou, clearly shows that in a metropolis as Shanghai it may be feasible to shift attention from the head to the tail, but that in predominantly rural areas first things still have to come first. Although, ... a lot can be learned from the devotion with which the main character handles the exception she meets.

References

1. Anderson, C.: Makers: the new industrial revolution. Crown business books. Random House Inc., New York (2012)
2. Kalbach, J.: Navigating the Long Tail. Bulletin of the American Society for Information Science and Technology 34(2), 36–38 (2008)
3. Geertz, C.: Thick description. In: The interpretation of cultures, pp. 3–33. Basic Books, Inc. (1973)
4. Ginzburg, C.: Clues: Morelli, Freud and Sherlock Holmes. In: Eco, U., Seebock, T.A. (eds.) The sign of three, pp. 81–119. Indiana university press, Bloomington (1988)
5. Schank, R.: Virtual learning; a revolutionary approach to building a highly skilled workforce. McGraw-Hill (1997)
6. Kurtz, C.F., Snowden, D.J.: The new dynamics of strategy: Sense-making in a complex and complicated World. IBM Systems Journal 42(3), 462–483 (2003)
7. Sarbo, J., Farkas, J., Breemen, A.J.J.: van: Knowledge in Formation: A computational theory of interpretation. Springer (2011)
8. Richmond, G.: Outline of *trikonic* ▷* k: Diagrammatic trichotomic. In: Dau, F., Mugnier, M.-L., Stumme, G. (eds.) ICCS 2005. LNCS (LNAI), vol. 3596, pp. 453–466. Springer, Heidelberg (2005)
9. Sarbo, J., Farkas, J.: Towards Meaningful Information Processing: A unifying representation for Peirce's sign types. Signs - International Journal of Semiotics 7, 1–44 (2013)
10. Stoutjesdijk, R.: Children with emotional and behavioral disorders in special education: Placement, progress, and family functioning. Doctoral thesis, Leiden University (2014)
11. Kurz, C.F.: Working with stories in your community or organization, 3rd edn., http://www.workingwithstories.org/
12. Keidel, R.W.: Seeing Organizational Patterns; a new theory and language of organizational design. Berret-Koehler Publishers, San Francisco (1995)

Assessing Pragmatic Interoperability of Information Systems from a Semiotic Perspective

Shixiong Liu[1], Weizi Li[1], and Kecheng Liu[1,2]

[1] Informatics Research Centre, University of Reading, UK
[2] School of Information Management and Engineering,
Shanghai University of Finance and Economics, China
Shixiong.liu@pgr.reading.ac.uk, {Weizi.li,K.liu}@henley.ac.uk

Abstract. Most of studies on interoperability of systems integration focus on technical and semantic levels, but hardly extend investigations on pragmatic level. Our past work has addressed pragmatic interoperability, which is concerned with the relationship between signs and the potential behaviour and intention of responsible agents. We also define the pragmatic interoperability as a level concerning with the aggregation and optimisation of various business processes for achieving intended purposes of different information systems. This paper, as the extension of our previous research, is to propose an assessment method for measuring pragmatic interoperability of information systems. We firstly propose interoperability analysis framework, which is based on the concept of semiosis. We then develop pragmatic interoperability assessment process from two dimensions including six aspects (informal, formal, technical, substantive, communication, and control). We finally illustrate the assessment process in an example.

Keywords: Pragmatics, Pragmatic Interoperability, Semiotic Interoperability, Systems Integration.

1   Introduction

In the study of the interoperability, most of the work focuses on discussion at a technical level. Although some of them have extended to deal with semantics, a very limited number of publications elaborate the interoperability at the pragmatic level [1]. Undoubtedly the research on technical and semantic interoperability can help establish a better understanding of data exchange and data interpretation, as well as leading to the development of supporting technologies and standards. However, the integration requires assessment of pragmatic interoperability that ensures supported process can act upon the semantic information in order to deal with the complexity. The pragmatic interoperability is concerned with the relationship between signs and the potential behaviour and intention of responsible agents. Our past work defines the pragmatic interoperability as a level concerning with the aggregation and optimisation of various business processes for achieving intended purposes of different information systems. This paper, as the extension of our previous research [1], [2], is to propose

K. Liu et al. (Eds.): ICISO 2014, IFIP AICT 426, pp. 32–41, 2014.

an assessment method for measuring pragmatic interoperability of information systems. We firstly propose interoperability analysis framework, which is based on the concept of semiosis. We then develop pragmatic interoperability assessment process from two dimensions including six aspects (informal, formal, technical, substantive, communication, and control). We finally illustrate the assessment process in an example. The next section briefs the concept of semiotic interoperability and pragmatic interoperability. Section 3 proposes the pragmatic interoperability analysis framework, and section 4 elaborates the assessment model for measuring pragmatic interoperability. The paper ends with a discussion of future work.

2   Background

Before defining pragmatic interoperability, our previous work has discussed the concept of semiotic interoperability [2], applied the concept of pragmatic interoperability in healthcare domain for analysing interoperability of systems integration at radiology department. The semiotic framework [4]–[6] that explains all aspects of how signs can be used and communicated for successful communication, determines the level of interoperability of information systems integration. Therefore we say systems are integrated at a certain interoperability level if signs among systems are successfully communicated at a certain semiotic framework level. Our previous works [1], [2] have proposed the concept of semiotic interoperability. The semiotic interoperability allows information systems to work together through communication with insight into six levels: physical, empirical, syntactical, semantic, pragmatic, and social. In addition to our definition of pragmatic interoperability, other researchers have contributed in pragmatic interoperability. Benson [7] defines it as coordination of work processes across different people to enabling work collaboration. Sadeghi et al. [8] state the pragmatic interoperability in healthcare is the ability among healthcare processes and various actors (i.e. healthcare providers and patients) that interact with information systems. We address systems interaction from the perspective of semiotic interoperability, especially at pragmatic level, which is concerned with the relationship between signs and the potential behaviour and intention of responsible agents. We define the pragmatic interoperability as a level concerning with the aggregation and optimisation of various business processes, in order to achieve intended purposes of different information systems. It is also concerned with the relationship between signs and the potential behaviour/intention of responsible agents, in a social context. Within a social community, there exist common knowledge and shared assumptions. These basic assumptions serve as a minimum basis for communication. Therefore, successful communication at this level is achieved if the hearer understands the speaker's intentions, which goes beyond the semantic interpretation of the communicative act. Interoperability is achieved at this level when processes serving different purposes under different contexts by different information systems can be composed to jointly support a common intention. The emphasis is the context awareness for processes integration. The following elements can be considered in the context: information system itself, intention, purpose, theme, time, location etc.

3   Pragmatic Interoperability Analysis Framework

Before assessing the pragmatic interoperability, our past work has developed an interoperability analysis process that pre-investigates the key factors (e.g. requirement, integration approach, interoperability measurement, knowledge foundation) of pragmatic interoperability. Based on findings of the investigation, we combine them with the semiosis concept [5] to develop an pragmatic interoperability analysis framework as shown below.

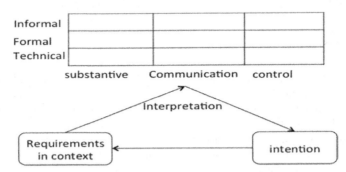

Fig. 1. Pragmatic Interoperability Analysis Framework

The development of the interoperability analysis framework is based on the concept of semiosis. Semiosis is the central concept of semiotics [5], it is a process of understanding involving transformation of signs. As a sign-mediated process, it gives meanings for understanding an object or actuality. It is also applicable to any type of sign-processing activities e.g. information systems integration. The interpretation is subjective and depending on the viewpoints of the interpretant or context. In the context of information systems integration, the context itself and its information systems are complex, artificial, and purposefully designed. They require integrated features as well as alignments between the business processes and the system functions. In order to assess and measure the pragmatic interoperability, our developed pragmatic interoperability analysis framework starts with articulating requirements in context such as interoperability environment, stakeholders, motivations, constraints, and locations. Secondly, the interpretation process assesses interoperability from two dimensions including six aspects (informal, formal, technical, substantive, communication, and control), which will be elaborated in next chapter. Thirdly, the interpretation process will help to indicate whether the requirements have been met to achieved the intentions e.g. business goals, responsibilities, and constraints.

Requirements articulation defines the problem space in which the requirements for interoperability are contextualised. Specifically it includes the identification of goals, tasks, problems, and opportunities that defines interoperation requirement in the context of organisation [9], [10]. Barriers at the informal level e.g. resources reallocation, political issue, privacy and security, people issues, culture change, and behavioural patterns are most widely highlighted in relevant researches [11]–[15].

Issues at formal level such as information flow, cross-functional integration are also discussed [11], [16]–[19]. Most interoperability requirements are articulated to overcome the interoperability barriers and realise the opportunities in organisations. Panetto and Molina [20] analyse and characterise several research challenges for Enterprise Integration and Interoperability. Their results are elaborated by a more intensive summary and contributions highlighted [21]. The challenges are classified from four dimensions (business, knowledge, applications and communications) where challenges of interoperability in enterprise are identified to include model interoperability, process interoperability and business information integration, etc. Therefore interoperability requirement can also be identified by combining conceptual, organisational and technological barriers with business, process and data concerns [22]. The integration can be also also seen as a methodological process to measuring the gap between desired interoperability goal and actual status of the system, and to adjust both the goal and interoperation actions if necessary. The step of assessment and measurement process are elaborated in next section.

4   Pragmatic Interoperability Assessment Process

The nature of information systems interoperation relies on successful signs communication [2], and each information system analysis and design must start with understanding and modelling the organisation where information system exists [5]. The organisation onion [6] stresses the distinctions as well as the interdependent links between the business process and IT systems. The organisation morphology provides a useful modelling method for understandings the norm structure of information system. Each information system can be characterised as a structure of norms that allow functions can be coordinated for certain purposes [5], and pragmatic interoperability, is to enable the purposes of each information system can be understood and perceived during interoperation, so the business processes can be aggregated accordingly. Therefore, measuring pragmatic interoperability between information systems is to measure the interoperability of norms that drive the business processes. Hence, we develop a measurement model that assesses the pragmatic interoperability from two dimensions (i.e. organisational onion, organisational morphology). The measurement model is the core of the whole assessment process. Before elaborating the model, the whole assessment process illustrates different stages and steps for measuring pragmatic interoperability as shown below:

The pragmatic interoperability assessment process starts with problem articulation. This stage defines the problem spaces of pragmatic interoperability and articulates relevant integration requirements in specific context. Various pragmatic interoperability definitions are reviewed for identifying problems. After identifying the problems, the next stage is pragmatic interoperability analysis. It identifies pragmatic interoperability requirements, and reviews various integration approaches and interoperability measurements at pragmatic level. The next stage is pragmatic interoperability measurement model, which is the core of the whole process. The model aims to measure the pragmatic interoperability from two dimensions including six aspects (formal, informal, technical, substantive, communication, and control). The last stage is to evaluate the measurement model by applying it to case study.

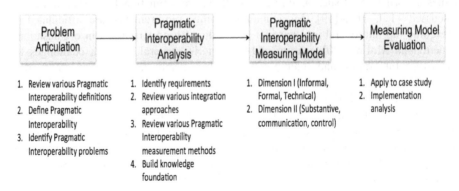

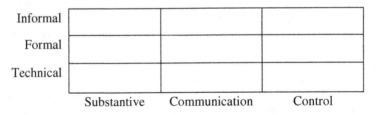

Fig. 2. Pragmatic Interoperability Assessment Process

4.1   Pragmatic Interoperability Measurement Model

The measurement model has two dimensions. Each dimension has three perspectives as displayed in the Figure below: 1) informal layer, 2) formal layer, and 3) technical layer for organisational onion; and 1) substantive area, 2) communication area, and 3) control area for organisation morphology.

	Substantive	Communication	Control
Informal			
Formal			
Technical			

Fig. 3. Pragmatic Interoperability Measurement Model

In system integration, the organisational onion illustrates on how an integrated system works, and the organisation morphology helps classify different norms that drive business processes. In pragmatic manner, the norms are regularities of perception, behaviour, belief and value that are exhibited as customs, habits, patterns of behaviour and other cultural artefacts. The developed measurement model combines both and provides coherent guideline for indicating key perspectives of measuring interoperability.

Dimension I

- Substantive

Business process and technical functions as well as cultural aspects are driven by norms in information system integration. The substantive norms are productivity-related and directly contribute to the aim and objectives. The pragmatic interoperability in this manner is to aggregate different substantive norms in order to achieve intended goal(s).

For example, in healthcare environment, the substantive norms are direct actions and orders among different information systems. Key actions such as order entry, and patient report generation, are typical substantive norms. Those could be aggregated based on the intended goals.

- Communication

The communication norms are interaction-related. They coordinate relevant people, procedures, business functions, and supported systems for undertaking substantive norms. Those communications are required to coordinate the temporal and spatial use of resources for substantive activities. Typical examples are communications by sending memoranda, announcements of meeting and events, telephones and emails. The pragmatic interoperability is to integrate different communication norms in order to eliminate the redundancy and improve communication efficiency. For example, in healthcare environment, message sending and receiving, communications between clinicians and nurses, and emergency interactions are where communication norms exist, and can be integrated for intended coordination.

- Control

The control norms are execution-related. They aim at reinforcing the whole business system running properly, particular the substantive and communication norms. Monitoring and evaluating are the main techniques of control norms. Typical examples are inter-firm agreements or contacts between organizations. The pragmatic interoperability is to ensure that the control norms function as required but consumes less, so the power of reinforcement will remain but the cost will not be increased. For example, in healthcare environment, the control norms should be regulations that reinforce the substantive and communication norms perform correctly.

Dimension II

- Informal

In informal level, culture aspect plays an important role. This aspect can be expanded as beliefs, habits and behaviour patterns of individuals. In this manner, the pragmatic interoperability is to align different culture aspects and solve conflicts of cohesiveness. An integrated information system would support perceiving of personal beliefs and organisational ground rules, whereas an un-integrated information system may be considerable conflicts between the organisational level and personal level. Issues like restriction to staff behaviour (more significant benefits from systems integration), information collaboration (information channels alignment), varieties of purchased information systems (different venders and services providers), and privacy and security concerns should be solved in this level. For example, in healthcare environment, the informal level is to concern with the understanding of the healthcare, regulatory, legislative and enterprise environment in which information systems need to be deployed to support healthcare delivery. It requires agreement on key organisational concepts such as policies, processes and roles; it also captures relevant patterns such as compliance, governance, legislative and change management.

- Formal

In formal level, business functions and procedures play dominant role that specifies on how functions should be carried out and how tasks should be performed. The pragmatic interoperability is to align procedures and rules in order to achieve higher efficiency. It defines business goals, model business processes and brings the collaboration of administrations what aim to exchange information and have different internal structures and processes. Besides, it also addresses the requirements of the user community by making services available, accessible, identifiable and user-oriented. Issues like policy (integration cuts across political boundaries), and procedure (integration causes process and operation changes) should be solved in this level. It supports seamless sharing of information, which is universal interpretation of information through data processing based on cooperating applications. For example, in healthcare environment, it is concerned with representations and interpretations of clinical, administrative and statistical information. It requires agreement on a core set of information concepts, such as information system itself and the relationships between information systems, as well as its clinical functions; it also captures relevant patterns such as quality of information and application scope.

- Technical

The technical level mostly refers to the technical computer systems and their technical functions. The systems and functions can be programmed according to norms and procedures. The pragmatic interoperability is to align technical functions and business processes in order to achieve higher system productivity. It supports seamless sharing of data, which is automated sharing of data between information systems based on a common exchange model. It also covers the technical issues of linking computer systems and services. A few key aspects are included such as interconnection services, data integration, open interface, data presentation and exchange, and accessibility will be dealt with in this level. For example, in healthcare environment, it is concerned with the understanding of technical functionality for supporting information systems. It requires agreement on a core set of technical concepts, such as technical components and devices, the interactions between components, interface and technical services; it also captures relevant patterns such as technical architecture styles and styles of component interactions.

4.2 Agent-Based Process Decomposition and Aggregation

Our developed model measuring pragmatic interoperability from 2 dimensions. Dimension 1 contains 3 aspects (substantive, communication, control), and dimension 2 contains 3 levels (informal, formal, and technical). The example of agent-based process decomposition and aggregation illustrated in figure below provides a picture of how processes are integrated in pragmatic level. The concept of Pragmatic Frame is adopted for storing pragmatic information, mainly the purpose and context of each process abstract [23]. The process can be decomposed into several sub-processes and each sub-process has its own context, purpose and semantic definition. Each process is also a set of activities, and the activity abstract contains the basic functions and pragmatic information of the process.

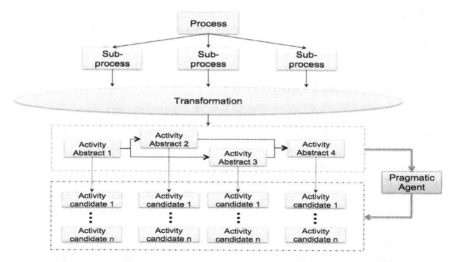

Fig. 4. Pragmatic process decomposition

After the process has been captured, it will be parsed into semantic terms that represent the meaning of the process. Each sub-process has been annotated with the semantic description and the goal to describe the detail of a list of expected activity candidates. The decomposition stage is to identify purposes for their aggregation in the next stage. The pragmatic agent uses the abstract to search the relevant activity candidates. The abstract contains semantic information, which can be searched by the agent. Finally only one candidate will succeed and be selected.

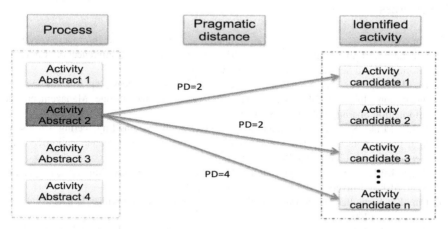

Fig. 5. Candidate selection by pragmatic distance

Each sub-process and its activities have various contexts for different purposes, and those contexts and purposes are defined based on policy designed. The activity works perfectly with its own context, but not all the activities works within their own contexts. The pragmatic ranking mechanism matches the related context (expected activity candidates) and find out the closest solution by calculating their pragmatic distance [23]. The ranking list is produced for each activity abstract and its candidates (displayed in Fig. 5).

5   Conclusion and Future Work

This paper is the extension of our previous research. It proposed an assessment method for measuring pragmatic interoperability of information systems. The developed interoperability analysis framework is based on the concept of semiosis, and contains three phrases (requirement in context, assessment model, and intentions). The developed assessment model measures pragmatic interoperability from two dimensions including six aspects (informal, formal, technical, substantive, communication, and control). The pragmatic interoperability at informal level is to align different culture aspects and solve conflicts of cohesiveness; to define business goals, model business process, and align procedures and rules in order to achieve higher efficiency at formal level; to align technical functions and business process in order to achieve higher system productivity at technical level. The substantive norms are productivity-related and directly contribute to the aim and objectives; the communication norms are interaction-related and coordinate relevant people, procedures, business functions, and supported systems for undertaking substantive norms; the control norms are execution-related and aim at reinforcing the whole business system running properly, particular the substantive and communication norms. The future work will focus on validations of the proposed assessment process.

References

1. Liu, S., Li, W., Liu, K., Han, J.: Evaluation frameworks for information systems integration: from a semiotic lens. In: The 3rd International Conference on Logistics, Informatics and Service Science, pp. 559–568 (2013)
2. Li, W., Liu, K., Liu, S.: Semiotic interoperability - a critical step towards systems integration. In: The 5th International Conference on Knowledge Management and Information Sharing, pp. 508–513 (2013)
3. Liu, K., Liao, S., Chong, S.: Semiotics for Information Systems Engineering – re-use of high level artefacts. In: The 3rd International Symposium on Communication Systems Networks and Digital Signal Processing, pp. 1–4 (2002)
4. Filipe, J.B.L.: Normative Organisational Modelling using Intelligent Multi-Agent Systems. Staffordshire University: Ph.D Thesis (2000)
5. Liu, K.: Semiotics in Information Systems Engineering. Cambridge University Press, Cambridge (2000)
6. Stamper, R.: Information in business and administrative systems. Batsford, London (1973)
7. Benson, T.: Principles of health interoperability HL7 and SNOMED. Springer (2009)
8. Sadeghi, P., Benyoucef, M., Kuziemsky, C.E.: A mashup based framework for multi level healthcare interoperability. Inf. Syst. Front. 14(1), 57–72 (2011)
9. Simon, H.: The Sciences of the Artificial, 3rd edn. MIT Press, Cambridge (1996)
10. Silver, M., Markus, M., Beath, C.: The Information Technology Interaction Model: A Foundation for the MBA Core Course. MIS Q 19(3), 361–390 (1995)

11. Allen, D.K., Karanasios, S., Norman, A.: Information sharing and interoperability: the case of major incident management. Eur. J. Inf. Syst. 22(1), 1–15 (2013)
12. Fink, L.: How do IT capabilities create strategic value? Toward greater integration of insights from reductionistic and holistic approaches. Eur. J. Inf. Syst. 20(1), 16–33 (2010)
13. Hamilton, D.: Linking strategic information systems concepts to practice: systems integration at the portfolio level. J. Inf. Technol. 14(1), 69–82 (1999)
14. Khoumbati, K., Themistocleous, M., Irani, Z.: Evaluating the Adoption of Enterprise Application Integration in Health-Care Organizations. J. Manag. Inf. Syst. 22(4), 69–108 (2006)
15. Turban, E., Watkins, P.: Integrating expert systems and decision support systems. Mis Q, 121–137 (1986)
16. Amrani, R., Rowe, F., Geffroy-Maronnat, B.: The effects of enterprise resource planning implementation strategy on cross-functionality. Inf. Syst. J. 16(1), 79–104 (2006)
17. Bidan, M., Rowe, F., Truex, D.: An empirical study of IS architectures in French SMEs: integration approaches. Eur. J. Inf. Syst. 21(3), 287–302 (2012)
18. Otjacques, B., Hitzelberger, P., Feltz, F.: Interoperability of E-Government Information Systems: Issues of Identification and Data Sharing. J. Manag. Inf. Syst. 23(4), 29–51 (2007)
19. Rai, A., Patnayakuni, R., Seth, N.: Firm Performance Impacts Of Digitally Enabled Supply Chain Integration Capabilities. Mis Q 30(2), 225–246 (2006)
20. Panetto, H., Molina, A.: Enterprise integration and interoperability in manufacturing systems: Trends and issues. Comput. Ind. 59(7), 641–646 (2008)
21. Panetto, H.: Enterprise Integration and Networking: theory and practice. Annu. Rev. Control (2012)
22. Daclin, N., Chen, D., Vallespir, B.: Methodology for enterprise interoperability. In: Proceedings of the 17th World Congress: The International Federation of Automatic Control, Seoul, Korea, pp. 128–135 (2008)
23. Liu, K.: Pragmatic Computing — A Semiotic Perspective to Web Services. Commun. Comput. Inf. Sci. 23, 3–15 (2009)

Virtual Process Modelling Informed by Organisational Semiotics: A Case of Higher Education Admission

John Effah[1] and Kecheng Liu[2]

[1] University of Ghana Business School, Ghana
[2] Informatics Research Centre, University of Reading, Reading, United Kingdom
jeffah@ug.edu.gh, k.liu@henley.ac.uk

Abstract. The purpose of this study is to explore virtual process modelling based on organisational semiotics and WebML. The Internet and the Web afford opportunities to virtualize physical processes. Research on process virtualization has so far focused on theorizing or testing which activities can or cannot be virtualized. However, studies on virtual process modelling remains limited. This study therefore uses a university's admission process as a case to explore virtual process modelling in a higher education environment.

Keywords: Process virtualization, Virtual process modelling, Web application modelling, Higher education, Organisational semiotics, WebML.

1   Introduction

Drawing from organisational semiotics and WebML, this study explores virtual process and web application modelling. Physical processes have traditionally been conducted through direct human-to-human contacts. However, the Internet and the Web afford the opportunity to virtualize such processes [1]. Process virtualization has begun to attract research attention [e.g.2, 3, 4]. However, the focus so far has been on theorizing or testing which activities can or cannot be virtualized. Research on virtual process modelling thus remains limited. This study therefore focuses on virtual process modelling to extend the existing limited research focus.

The study employs organisational semiotics [5, 6] as the theoretical foundation and WebML [7, 8] as the web interface modelling language to explore virtual admission process modelling in a higher education context. Organisational semiotics was selected for its useful information systems modelling and specification techniques [9], while WebML was chosen for its useful hypertext notations for web interface modelling [8, 10].

The rest of the paper is structured as follows. Section 2 reviews related works on organisational processes, higher education admission and WebML. Section 3 presents organisational semiotics as the theoretical foundation of the study. Section 4 illustrates the modelling of a virtualized postgraduate admission process. Section 6 concludes the paper and offers direction for future research.

K. Liu et al. (Eds.): ICISO 2014, IFIP AICT 426, pp. 42–51, 2014.

2   Related Works

2.1   Physical versus Virtualized Processes

Organisational processes comprise network of activities and their dependencies [11]. Processes can be physical or virtual. Physical processes occur through direct human-to-human contacts. Conversely, virtual processes are conducted via the Internet and the Web. Physical processes can therefore be virtualized by making them Internet and Web enabled [12].

Fig. 1 illustrates a generic process with activities and dependencies.

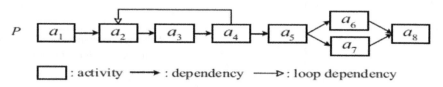

P a_1 a_2 a_3 a_4 a_5 a_6 a_7 a_8

☐ : activity ⟶ : dependency ⟶▷ : loop dependency

Fig. 1. Basic structure of a process [11]

The dependencies, which can be sequential, loop, split or joint [11], determine the directions between activities.

2.2   Higher Education Admission Process

A fundamental challenge for higher education admission is how to provide quality processes based on effective information systems [14] in order to attract highly qualified applicants. Following Harman [15] as well as McClea and Yen [16], this study views the admission process a composition of five main activities as shown in Fig. 2, namely, programmes advertisement, application, selection of qualified applicants, admission offer, and finally offer acceptance by satisfied applicants.

| Advertisement | Application | Selection | Offer | Acceptance |

Fig. 2.   Higher education admission process

The admission process is one of the major areas in need of computerization [14]. Computerizing the admission process can help to reduce printing and postage costs, improve efficiency and effectiveness, and provide real-time information access to stakeholders [16, 17]. Moreover, the Internet and the Web offer opportunities to virtualize admission processes [19]. However, such virtualization would require appropriate modelling techniques.

2.3   WebML

WebML [7, 8] is a visual web modelling language that is considered usefulness for designing data-, service-, and process-intensive web applications [20-22]. WebML supports both data and hypertext modelling. Its data model is used for designing back-end data structures, while the hypertext model is for web interface design. This study focuses on the hypertext model for the virtual admission web interface. Table 1 presents the relevant hypertext notations used in this study under their respective categories.

Table 1. Relevant WebML hypertext notations

Category	Notation	Name and description
Content units: components for entering and publishing content.		Site view: container for web pages, links, and operation units.
		Web page: container for published data, input forms and other components.
		Data units: entity instance for published data.
		Entry unit: web form for entering and accepting data.
Link units: links between web pages and other components.		Normal link: user activated hypertext link between web pages and other components
		Automatic link: system activated hypertext link between pages and other components.
Operation units: functionalities for data creation and manipulation subject to constraints.		Create operation: functionality for creating new instance of an entity in a base table.
		Modify operation: functionality for modifying or updating data in an entity instance.

In Section 4.3, the relevant hypertext notations are used to model the virtual admission web interface. The complete list of WebML notations with detailed explanations can be found in Ceri et al. [7, 8] as well as on the model's website: http://www.webml.org.

3   Organisational Semiotics

Organisational semiotics theorizes information systems as a collection of signs and symbols [23] created and consumed by actions and interactions of agents [24]. This study draws on two of its frameworks, organisational morphology and norm specification, as the theoretical foundation for the virtual admission modelling.

3.1   Organisational Morphology

Organisational morphology [25], also called organisational onion [5], views activities as norms and classifies them into three layers: informal, formal and technical, as shown in Fig. 3. Organisational norms are rules that regulate and govern how activities are performed [26].

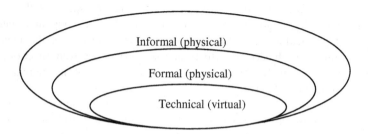

Fig. 3. The organisational onion [5]

The informal layer comprises activities that are based on implicit norms such as culture, customs and values that reflect people's beliefs, habits and practices. The formal layer consists of activities that are based explicit norms that define organisational rules and procedures. Finally, the technical layer encompasses activities that are structured and therefore are or can be computerized.

The three layers are however interrelated such that the technical layer is contained in the formal lay, which in turn is contained in the informal layer [26]. In addition, activities can be transformed from one layer to another. For example, an informal activity can be formalized, while a formal activity can computerised to become part of the technical [5].

In relation to process virtualization, the informal and formal activities constitute physical processes while the technical (computerized) form virtual processes. Virtualization therefore involves transforming physical activities (formal and informal norms) into virtual processes. According to Liu [5], transforming informal and formal activities into technical (computerised) activities require formal norm analysis and specifications. The next section discusses the formal behavioural norm specification.

3.2   Behavioural Norm Specification

Behavioural norms constitute rules that define conditions under which organisational activities should or may be performed by responsible agents [5]. Behavioural norm analysis investigates norm-based activities and specifies them in a formal structure [27]. Fig. 4 presents the generic structure for behavioural norm specification in the form of condition, state trigger, responsible agent, deontic operator and action [5].

> **WHENEVER** *<condition>*
> **IF** *<state>*
> **THEN** *<agent>*
> **IS** *<deontic operator: should, may or should not>*
> **TO** *<action>*

Fig. 4. Basic behavioural norm specification [23]

The WHENEVER <condition> and the IF <state> together define the necessary pre-conditions before an activity can start. The <agent> specifies the responsible actor for the activity. In general, an agent is an individual, a group, an organisation, a software or a physical artefact [25]. In relation to virtual processes, the agent is either physical (human or object) or virtual (internet service or web function). Deontic operator specifies whether an action is obligatory (should), optional (may) or prohibited (should not) [27].

Behavioural norms are classified into substantive, communication and control activities [25]. Substantive activities are direct operational activities; communication activities generate messages to support substantive activities; while control activities enforce rules and regulations to maintain standards for substantive and communication activities. As this study is at the exploratory stage, the current focus is on substantive norm specification.

To specify dependencies in substantive activities, the basic behavioural norm specification in Table 1 is extended to include predecessor and successor activities, as shown in Table 2. This structure is used to define the norm specifications for the virtual admission process in Section 4.2.

Table 2. Substantive behavioural norm specification for a processes

Activity ID	*<activity name>*
Specification	**WHENEVER** *<condition>* **IF** *<state>* **THEN** *<agent>* **IS** *<may>* **TO** *<online action >*
Predecessor	*<predecessor activity>*
Successor	*<successor activity>*

4   Virtual Admission Process Modelling

The study used the postgraduate admission process of University of Ghana as a case to explore virtual admission process modelling. Established in 1948, University of Ghana is one of the oldest and leading universities in Africa. In addition to undergraduate programmes, the university offers postgraduate programmes for the award of masters and doctoral degrees to both local and international students. In 2011, the first author initiated an action case research project involving himself, the university's ICT unit and the postgraduate admission office to virtualize the admission process.

Action research has a dual purpose to address an immediate practical problem in an organisation and contribute to research at the same time [28]. The study therefore aimed to improve the university's postgraduate admission by reducing processing time, data errors and data loss as well as increase online access to information for various stakeholders. It also aimed to contribute to research on virtual process modelling and organisational semiotics. Data for the study emerged from the first author's participant observation and interviews with project members and users, project and corporate documents, prototyping as well as focus group discussions with users and development team members.

4.1   Virtual Admission Process

In general, the study identified substantive, communication and control norm-based activities. However, as noted earlier, the current paper's focus is on the substantive norms. Communication norms such as advertisement, inquiries and message communication as well as control procedures are therefore not included in the current virtual process specification. This limited focus was adopted so as to first establish the substantive model before communication and control norms can be added at a later stage.

From the norm analysis involving informal and formal norms, five substantive activities were identified in the university's postgraduate admission process as shown in Fig. 5.

Fig. 5. Admission Process

The application process involves applicants completing online forms and uploading supporting documents. The web application then transfers the online data to the responsible teaching department for assessment and selection. The department reviews the application data and documents such as transcripts, certificates, research proposal, referees' reports, and selects qualified applicants. The admission office officially admits the selected applicants and those satisfied complete an online acceptance form.

4.2   Substantive Norm Specification for Virtual Admission Process

Following the norm analysis, the substantive activities were presented in a formal the extended behavioural norms specification for processes to enable their virtualization into technical norms in the university's organisational onion. As shown in Table 3, the predecessor and successor activities were added to the norm specification to account for activity dependences.

Table 3. Substantive norm specification for virtual admission process

Activity	Specification	Predecessor	Successor
Application	**WHENEVER** *<admission is open>* **IF** *<applicant likes programme>* **THEN** *<applicant>* **IS** *<may>* **TO** *<submit application>*	<open admission>	Transfer
Transfer	**WHENEVER** *<application is submitted>* **IF** *<application is complete>* **THEN** *<Website>* **IS** *<should>* **TO** *<transfer application to department>*	application	selection
Selection	**WHENEVER** *<application is received>* **IF** *<applicant is qualified and vacancy exists>* **THEN** *<Department>* **IS** *<should>* **TO** *<select applicant>*	transfer	admission
admission	**WHENEVER** *<department selects applicant>* **IF** *<applicant meets all requirements >* **THEN** *<Admission officer>* **IS** *<should>* **TO** *<offer admission through website>*	selection	acceptance
acceptance	**WHENEVER** *<admission is offered>* **IF** *<applicant likes the offer >* **THEN** *<applicant>* **IS** *<may>* **TO** *<accept offer through the website>*	admission	<enrolment>

In order to maintain dependencies, each activity has a predecessor and a successor. The emergent problem was how to get a predecessor and successor for the first and the last activity respectively. The issue was addressed by ensuring that the preceding and successive processes respectively served as the predecessor and successor for the first and last activities as shown in Table 3 with <open admission> and <enrolment>.

4.3   Hypertext Model

Following the formal substantive norm specification, WebML was used to design the hypertext architecture as the web interface to help virtualize the process activities. Fig. 6 shows a high level web interface model for the virtual admission application.

The process begins with the applicant accessing the admission website and proceeding to the application page to view information on available programmes. If the applicant identifies a programme he/she likes, the applicant completes and submits the online application form. The application is automatically transferred to the relevant department for assessment and selection. After the selection, an admission officer officially admits the applicant to the chosen programme. Finally, if the selected candidate likes the programme, he/she completes an online acceptance form for enrolment.

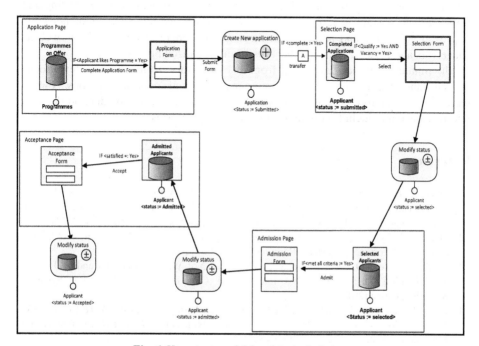

Fig. 6. Hypertext model for virtual admission

Following the implementation of the virtual admission process of the university, the post-graduate admission process has become more efficient. Reported benefits by the admission office include reduction in time, costs, human resource requirements, data errors and data losses. Other benefits include increased access to online information for all stakeholders as well as a virtual tracking facility for the applicants. Reported challenges however include frequent power failures and slow internet access during peak periods when admission is open.

5   Conclusion

This study employed organisational semiotics and WebML to explore virtual process and web application modelling with a university's postgraduate admission process as a case study. The study contributes to both organisational semiotics and process virtualization research. Based on the notion that processes consist of activities and dependencies, the study contributes to organisational semiotics research by extending the basic behavioural norm specification to include predecessor and successor activities.

The study also demonstrates the applicability of WebML to extend behavioural norm specification into Web interface modelling. By this, process modelling under organisational semiotics can be extended with WebML hypertext for web interface design. In terms of process virtualization, the study extends the existing limited research focus on theorization and testing of process to virtual process modelling and web interface design. In terms of contribution to practice, the findings demonstrate improved efficiency and reduction in time, effort, human resource, cost as well as data errors and losses as potential benefits from virtualized processes.

The limitation of the study stems from its exploratory nature and high level focus on substantive activities without communicative and control activities. Future research can therefore benefit from extending the virtual process model and the web interface design to include communication and control norms.

References

1. Overby, E.: Migrating Processes from Physical to Virtual Environments: Process Virtualization Theory. In: Dwived, Y.K., Wade, M., Schineberger, S.L. (eds.) Information Systems Theory: Explaining and Predicting Our Digital Society, pp. 107–124 (2012)
2. Overby, E., Slaughter, S.A., Konsynski, B.: The Design, Use, and Consequences of Virtual Processes. Information Systems Research 21(4), 700–710 (2010)
3. Barth, M., Veit, D.: Which Processes Do Users Not Want Online? Extending Process Virtualization Theory. In: 32nd International Conference on Information Systems, Shanghai, China (2011)
4. Balci, B., Grgecic, D.: Why People Reject or Use Virtual Processes: A Test of Process Virtualization Theory. In: Proceedings of the Nineteenth Americas Conference on Information Systems, Chicago, Illinois (2013)
5. Liu, K.: Semiotics in information systems engineering. Cambridge University Press (2000)
6. Liu, K., et al. (eds.): Proceedings of IFIP WG8.1 Working Conference Organizational Semiotics: Evolving a Science of Information Systems. Kluwer Academic Publishers, Boston (2002)
7. Ceri, S., Fraternali, P., Paraboschi, S.: Web Modeling Language (WebML): a modeling language for designing Web sites. Computer Networks 33, 137–157 (2000)
8. Ceri, S., et al.: Designing Data-Intensive Web Applications. Morgan Kaufmann, San Francisco (2002)
9. Jacobs, A., Nakata, K.: Organisational Semiotics Methods to Assess Organisational Readiness for Internal Use of Social Media. In: AMCIS 2012 Proceedings. Paper 24 (2012)
10. Brambilla, M., et al.: Designing web applications with WebML and WebRatio. In: Rossi, G., et al. (eds.) Web Engineering: Modelling and Implementing Web Applications, pp. 221–262. Springer (2007)
11. Liu, D.R., Shen, M.: Workflow modeling for virtual processes: an order-preserving process-view approach. Information Systems 28(6), 505–532 (2003)

12. Overby, E.: Process Virtualization Theory and the Impact of Information Technology. Organization Science 19(2), 277–291 (2008)
13. Overby, E., Slaughter, S.A., Konsynski, B.: Research Commentary–the Design, Use, and Consequences of Virtual Processes. Information Systems Research 21(4), 700–710 (2010)
14. Semeon, G., Negash, S., Musa, P.: The Success of Student Information Management System: The Case of Higher Education Institution in Ethiopia. In: AMCIS 2010 Proceedings. Paper 278 (2010)
15. Harman, G.: Student selection and admission to higher education: Policies and practices in the Asian region. Higher Education 27, 313–339 (1994)
16. McClea, M., Yen, D.C.: A framework for the utilization of information technology in higher education admission department. International Journal of Educational Management 19(2) (2005)
17. Hossler, D.: Using the internet in college admission: strategic choices. Journal of College Admission 162(Winter), 12–19 (1999)
18. Pollock, N.: The 'Self-service' Student: Building Enterprise-wide Systems into Universities. Prometheus: Critical Studies in Innovation 21(1), 101–119 (2003)
19. Aggarwal, A.K., Adlakha, V., Mersha, T.: Continuous Improvement Process in Web-Based Education at a Public University. E-Service Journal 4(2), 3–26 (2005)
20. Acerbis, R., Bongio, A., Brambilla, M., Butti, S., Ceri, S., Fraternali, P.: Web Applications Design and Development with WebML and WebRatio 5.0. In: Paige, R., Meyer, B. (eds.) TOOLS EUROPE 2008. LNBIP, vol. 11, pp. 392–411. Springer, Heidelberg (2008)
21. Brambilla, M., et al.: Process modeling in Web applications. ACM Transactions on Software Engineering and Methodology 15(4), 360–409 (2006)
22. Brambilla, M., Fraternali, P.: Large-scale Model-Driven Engineering of web user interaction: The WebML and WebRatio experience. Science of Computer Programming (in press)
23. Liu, K.: Requirements Reengineering from Legacy Information Systems Using Semiotic Techniques. Systems, Signs & Actions: An International Journal on Communication. Information Technology and Work 1(1), 38–61 (2005)
24. Gazendam, H.W.M.: Organizational Semiotics: a state of the art report. Semiotix 1(1), 1–5 (2004)
25. Mat Ali, N., Liu, K.: A conceptual framework for role-based knowledge profiling using semiotics approach. In: Setchi, R., Jordanov, I., Howlett, R.J., Jain, L.C. (eds.) KES 2010, Part I. LNCS, vol. 6276, pp. 554–565. Springer, Heidelberg (2010)
26. Li, W., et al.: Integrated clinical pathway management for medical quality improvement – based on a semiotically inspired systems architecture. European Journal of Information Systems, 1–18 (2013)
27. Gazendam, H.W., Liu, K.: The Evolution of Organisational Semiotics. In: Filipe, J., Liu, K. (eds.) Studies in organisational semiotics, Kluwer Academic Publishers, Dordrecht (2005)
28. Baskerville, R., Myers, A.: Special issue on action research in information systems: making IS research relevant to practice –foreword. MIS Quarterly 28(3), 329–335 (2004)

Workaround Motivation Model (WAMM): An Adaptation of Theory of Interpersonal Behaviour

Nada Nadhrah and Vaughan Michell

Business Informatics, Systems and Accounting (BISA), University of Reading,
Whitenights Reading UK, RG6 6UD
N.Nadhrah@pgr.reading.ac.uk, v.a.michell@henley.reading.ac.uk

Abstract. The study of workarounds (WA) has increased in importance due to their impact on patient safety and efficiency. However, there are no adequate theories to explain the motivation to create and use a workaround in a healthcare sitting. Although theories of technology acceptance help to understand the reasons to accept or reject technology, they fail to explain drivers for alternatives. Also workarounds involve creators and performers that have different motivations. Models such as Theory of Planned Behaviour (TPB) or Theory of Reasoned Action (TRA) can help to explain the role of workaround users, but lack explanation of workaround creators' dynamics. Our aim is to develop a theoretical foundation to explain workaround motivation behaviour models with norms that relate to sanctions to provide an integrated Workaround Motivation Model; WAMM. The development of WAMM model is explained in this paper based on workaround cases as part of further research to establish the model.

Keywords: Workaround, Behaviour, Motivation, Healthcare, Patient safety, Consequences, Norm.

1 Introduction

Healthcare professionals are continually exposed to new Information Systems (IS) that affects their daily working activities. Many healthcare workers fully use these systems; however, many choose to perform an alternative process or activity manually or via an alternative system. Some have retained old processes, and others have added additional or alternative activities to do their work. Deviations from the formal system or process, i.e. alternative activities are typically addressed in the literature as workarounds (WA) [1], [2], or sometimes deviations from dysfunctional systems [3], [4], [5]. We can define WA as "an alternative work process created by individuals or groups to achieve a benefit over the use of the existing processes" [6]. Many WA involve a single individual alternative and continuous process or action with a single actor or driver [7], Our research identified a classification of four other types. A process WA involves more than one actor working together on a sequence of different activities. A compound WA is a variant of the process WA where more than one continuous process is involved with separate performers. A consequential WA

K. Liu et al. (Eds.): ICISO 2014, IFIP AICT 426, pp. 52–62, 2014.

exists where the results of a WA drive a further and separate WA process, often used to convert the WA outputs back to a form to feed into the formal process e.g. converting manual documents to automated form. These different types of WA have different motivation impacts referred to later. Many workarounds involve a single actor. However as workarounds are in general unique alternatives to a standard formal process or system they usually have a designer or workaround creator that defines the workaround [9]. This creator is also usually the driver of the workaround. The performers in a workaround if separate from the creator can have a different behaviour in the way they are motivated to execute it. This has implications for the motivation to work around for example we may expect workaround creators motivations to execute the workaround to be higher than performers. These motivation implications will be discussed later. This paper seeks to develop a testable model of the factors affecting motivation to WA. Motivation is 'the reason or reasons one has for acting or behaving in a particular way' [8]. A number of authors have investigated the motivation reasons to perform WA. We classify these into action motives (blocks) and goal motives for WAs [9].

Many authors see positive motivations to WA as a result of a block in normal expected work activities [1]. A block is a system disruption preventing the worker from completing a task or action as desired [1]. For example in order to save time, clinicians try to avoid blocks in the system and have an action motive to work around the block. Block motivated WAs range from the complex design of processes and systems, poor system usability, inadequate user training, inflexible clinical guidelines [1], [10] and slow and time consuming processes [11]. Some users are motivated to create a WA to avoid safety features such as systems produced alarms. These are seen as inconvenient and time consuming. Overriding a system alarm that was designed intentionally to improve patient safety might be considered as a negative WA [10], or deviation and should be eliminated. However, many WAs have a positive safety benefit, For example WAs may be motivated by a physician's superior local and timely event knowledge that improves the safety of the patient [12]. A second motivating group is where there is a personal or professional benefit goal or improvement that could better be achieved by abandoning the formal process or system for a WA [9]. Pernejad cites the example of a new system reducing communication between doctors and nurses ruining their original informal communication and forcing them to WA the system to restore the communications [13]. Overworked clinicians may simply wish to reduce their workload and stress and hence choose to miss out actions or perform alternative actions to those prescribed formally [7], [6]. This often involves reversion to simpler previous habits or norms of behaviour established socially or in a team.

2   Motivation Models

Our aim is to identify which factors motivate people to the WA i.e. a general WA model i.e. most relevant factors that drive WA. There are two types – technology acceptance model and general behavioural models.

2.1   Technology Acceptance Models

Technology Acceptance Model (TAM). In TAM Davis [14] suggests the attitude of a potential user of a system has towards using it depends on the how useful they see it (perceived usefulness) and how easy it is to use the system (Perceived ease of use). This results in an attitude and behaviour to use or reject the system. However, we note that a workaround decisions is about accepting or rejecting only a very small part of a system/process and choosing an alternative ad-hoc system/process.

We have seen earlier that WA's are driven by blocks to work or goal motives resulting in improvements/changes to the activity. If an automated system provides a block, effort needs to be increased to use it. We would expect ease of use to be considered low e.g. in the case of lack or training, system complexity, slow systems etc. [9] compared with an alternative system. A system is ideally designed for ease of use e.g. by providing a record log, automatic communication and dissemination of data etc. However, if the automated system is perceived to be less useful personally to an individual they may favour an alternative WA.

TAM tells us why we might not use the automated system, but it does not tell us why we might choose to use a specific WA, manual or automated. TAM is a technology acceptance model and many WA's include both manual and other technology alternatives [7]. We also note that the professional and personal motives for perusing a WA [9] are not covered by TAM. A much deeper understanding of the behaviour is required.

Unified Theory of Acceptance and Use of Technology (UTAUT). The Unified Theory of Acceptance and Use of Technology (UTAUT) proposed by [15] extended TAM to include four new constructs. (1) Performance Expectancy is a broader version of usefulness. (2) Effort Expectancy, a broader version of ease of use identifies the extent of effort involved. (3) Social Influence measures of how much a user is influenced to use the system by people who are socially important to them[16]. Social influence relates to subjective norms of behaviour that influence individual decisions making [17]. Our research suggests social and indeed power influence is important to the workaround decisions. In previous work we identified two types of actors in the WA process, the creator and the performer [7]. Often WA are created and performed by the same person, but in process and compound WA's [9] a separate and often senior creator such as clinical consultants, senior surgeons etc. is present. Creators often allocate the WA to more junior actors to perform. The performer is the individual executes the WA process in order to achieve the task goal. They often have no decision in creating the WA and no choice to participate in it. Hence the social norms for a senior surgeon WA creator are likely to be very different from the junior doctor and different again for the nurse or porter that executes WA and need to be included in the model. (4) Facilitating conditions relates directly to whether the user behaviour is realistic and feasible [18], [19], [15], [20]. For example resources, user, experience knowledge and training. Facilitating conditions relate to many of the drivers of workarounds e.g. the availability of resources, which is known to cause technology blocks [7] or lack of training and experience [7], [21].

UTAUT assumes a user can accept or reject technology on a voluntary basis. Very often system use is mandatory and hence some WA's allow for a manual output to be converted back to system inputs, but the motivation for the WA remains. Some senior staff may mandate the WA must be done by virtue of their influence. Social influences, i.e. subjective norms for WA need to include the norms and norm relationships between WA creator and driver and those of the performer. Whilst TAM and UTAUT have limitations in their focus on technology they provide a useful basis for WA behaviour to build on. We now turn to behavioural models to help build the model.

2.2   Behavioural Models

We discuss 3 key motivational behaviour models. WA's as deviations are a decisions between the formal obligation to execute a formal process and the option to execute an informal process. We need to understand the use of a system and the extent of freedom to do something different in studying WA. Behavioural models are needed in this context to capture the formal and informal social rules for behaviour and sanctions that influence the selection of WA over the formal process and their consequences.

The Theory of Reasoned Action (TRA) and Theory of Planned Behaviour (TPB). The theory of Planned Behaviour (TPB) is driven from TRA and assumes three determinants to behaviour: : attitude, subjective norm, and perceived behavioural controls [20]. Theory of Planned Behaviour (TPB) is driven from TRA assumes independent determinants of; intention. Attitude and subjective norm, similar to TRA, TAM, UTAUT, but perceived behavioural control (PBC) is an added [22]. Perceived behavioural control relates to the level of influence a user has on the behaviour and their ability to change it– in our case the workaround.

Theory of Interpersonal Behaviour (TIB). Triandis' model considers direct variables useful for workaround behaviour: Intention (I), Habit (H), and Facilitating Conditions (FC). Intention and facilitating conditions were discussed earlier. Habit (H) is "situation-behaviour sequences that are or have become automatic, so that they occur without self-instruction" [19]. Habit is an important factor in WA motivation as many users prefer to use what is familiar to them often in place of the formal system. WA agents often revert back to old habits e.g. manual paper and pen vs automated systems as it is perceived to be easier and less effort [23]. Alternatively they may use newer habits e.g. their iPad in preference to a desktop application [24] or their iPhone as a simpler communication tool in a WA [6].
    Indirect variables (via intention) are: Affect (AF), Perceived Consequences (PC), and Social Factors (SF) [19]. Affect, relates to the individual's emotional feelings of pleasure, displeasure, toward a given behaviour [25]. Perceived behavioural consequences relate to the perception of the overall impact/benefit of the action behaviour which is the second determinant of intention [18]. The perception of workaround consequences again relates to the type of actor (creator, performer) discussed earlier. For example, a physician might avoid using a cumbersome system he dislikes by writing a   discharge summary manually as a   WA and perceive

consequential benefits of time and effort saved [7]. However, it may be a less happy and enjoyable task for the WA performer who is forced to comply with the WA and convert the text to electronic form. Perceived social norms unlike subjective norms in (TPB) or social factors adopted in UTAUT discussed. It includes two normative dimensions; normative and role beliefs [18]. Normative beliefs consist of the internalisation by an individual of referent people or groups' opinion about executing the behaviour [18], whereas role beliefs refer to the rules of the role or behaviour formally expected of the individual [18]. An additional perceived social norm added to a TIB application   is personal normative (PN) belief [26] representing the individual's personal rules of behaviour regarding whether they should perform the behaviour, i.e. do my personal rules suggest I should perform the workaround [18]. Based on the above we use TIB as the base model for WA motivation. Our previous work has identified that WA's are often discouraged and sanctions can exist. Therefore our model needs to include the impact of sanctions on motivation to the workaround. Also our research has identified the importance of the role of professional rules or norms. For example a workaround was justified if it met the professional clinical norms better than the original system [9].   The next section discusses these 2 additional factors.

2.3   Extension of Consequences and Norms Workaround Factors

Perceived Behavioural Consequences. Triandis' factor Perceived consequences (PC) refers to the probability that a given consequence or expected benefit will follow from performing the behaviour. The value of the consequence is the "impact attached to the consequence" [19]. The higher the expected value of the act, the more likely the person will intend to perform it [19]. This is an important factor for WA's as a WA is perceived as a 'deviation in medicine with potential risk and safety consequences. Hence the risk must be balanced by a superior benefit. Triandis' model does not differentiate of specify specific consideration and focuses on consequences related to the individual. For example analysis of Gagnon's paper Gagnon, et al. [18] using TIB suggests the questions related to con sequences refer to increased or reduced process time, knowledge and workload and impact on roles.

There are two separate dimensions of consequence/value related to the person, as an individual impact, and related to the process and professional medical benefit [9]. As a workaround is seen as a deviation it can have very high consequences for the individual that need to be considered separately from the benefits regarding process goal. Creating a WA may primarily save physician's time (personal goal) but it might also breach patient confidentiality policy (organisational goal) [6]. This implies a process impact in terms of patient safety and error. A clinician's professional responsibilities ensure the consequential value is not limited to individual's feelings such as satisfied, distressed, and unhappy, but related to a process/professional dimension e.g. may save time and may have a negative e.g. safety impact on the patient. The need to focus on the patient and professional/organisational goals, has been highlighted in the Stafford enquiry in the UK [26]. Unlike most behaviour models that focus on industry the health service is very person focused and safety is critical so we need to include this component.

The overall value or benefit to the clinician WA user will be determined by their feelings about both personal and professional/organisational value and benefit resulting from the WA. We divide consequences construct into two types: personal value and organisational goal or process impact value. For personal value we measure the individual's expected value in creating/ performing WA e.g. 'for me, creating/ performing WA in my practice would give me the greatest personal benefit in terms of personal WA benefits e.g. save me time, reduce stress, increase my knowledge, increased control be relaxing or satisfying and dissatisfying. So that will cover the positive and negative dimension of WA perceived personal value. The process impact value can be addressed from two benefit perspectives the impact on the process and impact on the individual client or patient. For example, a typical question to test this might be 'creating/ performing WA in my practice would provide an overall benefit to professional/organisational goals of'(1) reduce time; (2) allow to update my knowledge; for individual perspective; (3) reduce patients risk; and (4) reduce patient waiting times; (5) improve team work.

Professional Norm (PN). Our research has highlighted that an important motivator of a WA is the perceived professional rules and cultural training which influence clinicians to choose a workaround as it better meets these professional norms than the formal system. For example, there is an error in alternative drug system in pharmacy department: alternative drug is usually drop down list appears to the user when there is certain medicine not available in the stock. Although it has been updated and the alternative medicine is available, yet there is a system error message papers to physicians preventing them from completing the request. They have to call the pharmacist and indicate the problem, so the pharmacist due to their professional norm they will perform the workaround and repeat the request to order alternative drug.

Professional norms are rule based 'components of the professional behaviour 'socialized through education and training, maintained by professional colleges, and have a profound impact on professional work' [27]. We propose two aspects to test this relationship. (a) Questions relating to improvements or reduction in professional standards related to the WA users profession. (b) Questions relating to client or patient benefits.

3   WAMM an Integrated Framework of Workaround Motivation

A model of WA motivation must include the key elements of technical (section 2.1above) and behavioural (section 2.2 above) models in addition to perceived consequences and norm modification constructs. This section details the reasoning in developing the Workaround Motivational Model (WAMM). Each of the factors selected will need to be tested in relation to the intention to create or use a WA. As mentioned earlier unlike normal motivation models the WA stakeholder role e.g. as a creator of WA, user and level of use in WA must be recorded as this is expected to reflect the answers to many of the factor questions.

As mentioned, the theoretical foundation in the model is TIB which involves variables: intention, affect, social factors (normative beliefs and personal beliefs), perceived behavioural consequences, habits, and facilitating conditions. The following hypotheses will need to be tested (1) Affect is a predictor of healthcare professionals' intention to create or perform WA; (2) Perceived consequences are predictors of healthcare professionals' intention to create or perform WA; (3) Perceived social norms are predictors of healthcare professionals' intention to create or perform WA; (4) Personal normative (PN) belief is predictors of healthcare professionals' intention to create or perform WA; (5) Facilitating conditions are predictors of healthcare professionals' intention to create or perform WA; and (6) Habit are predictors of healthcare professionals' intention to create or perform WA (Fig.1).

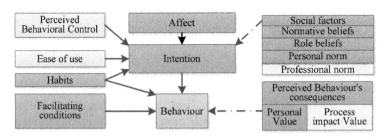

Fig. 1. Workaround Motivational Model (WAMM)

There are four constructs added: perceived behavioural controls (discussed in TPB in section 2.2). Perceived ease of use (discussed in TAM section 2.1), perceived behavioural process value consequences (discussed in section 2.2), and professional norm (discussed in section 2.3). The following hypotheses will be tested as part of the integrated model: (7) perceived behavioural controls is a predictor of healthcare professionals' intention to create or perform WA; (8) Perceived ease of use is a predictor of healthcare professionals' intention to create or perform WA; (9) perceived behavioural process value consequences is a predictor of healthcare professionals' intention to create or perform WA; and (10) Perceived professional norm is a predictor of healthcare professionals' intention to create or perform WA. Hypothesis 7 and 8 are driven from TPB and TAM respectively. Hypothesis 9 and 10 are going to be developed because they are new to the model and needed to be tested.

4   Case Examples from Practice

At this point the model questionnaires have been developed and we are in the process of gathering data from questionnaires for analysis of the factors and relationships. Timescales preclude reporting at this stage and hence we demonstrate the use of the model by showing how the variables relate to our previous case studies. The use of the WAMM model can be illustrated by a case example from our research. Many WA's are created by the same individual that performs WA and hence use of WAMM would be expected to be straightforward. However, with more complex WA's such as process and compound WA's there is a creator and separate performers. The WA motivating factors with respect to a creator of a WA are expected to be different to the actors recruited in by WA creator to perform the process. We would expect and need to test the possible positive correlations in this activity. For this reason we choose a compound WA case to show how we might expect different results for the WAMM model.

The Discharge summary (DS) report process is a compound WA case study that has been identified in one of the hospitals [6]. The DS is an electronic report that must be written and authenticated within 24 hours from the decision to be discharged by the consultant [6]. Table1 below summarises the activities performed in the DS case vs the positive or negative influence of the motivation factors and how we suggest they may vary in relation to the actor types. There are two types of actors identified: creator and performer. Creator in that case is the physician who initiated and controls the WA process by insisting on writing a discharge report manually rather than via the system. This initiated a chain of activities and involvement by other actors in the process to convert the handwritten report back to the electronic forma in the system to release DS report. From our example case the main motivational factor is likely to be the physician's habit (the case suggested a key motivator for the WA was his habit of writing, not using eth system. The facilitating condition, the factors that make WA easy are likely to be access to and control of the staff needed to convert his manual script back into the format for the system, otherwise this negates the WA benefit. The perceived behavioural controls would be expected to be high motivating factor for the physician as he is responsible and controls the patient's discharge. In terms of affect, we would expect the physician to feel very positive that he does not need to type into the system, but can simply scribble manually at high speed. We would also expect a positive correlation for the personal value impact as the physician has reduced his personal stress in using the system. These points were mentioned by different physicians in reasoning their decision to write in paper sheet rather than the system. We would expect lower or negative correlation in terms of other factors. For example professional norms generally would insist on data entry. Process impact value is likely to be negative as more resources in terms of a nurse and porter are required for the WA and reduce the process benefits.

Table 1. DS workaround case study WAMM measure of expected positive/negative influence

| Actor | Type | Activity | AF | PBC | H | FC | EU | Social norms | | PFN | PV | PIV |
								PNB	RNB			
Physician	Creator	Writing DS on a piece of Paper.	+	+	+	+	+	+	+	-	-	+
Nurse	Performer	Nurse has to photocopy three copies.	-	-	-	-	-	+	+	+	-	+
Medical secretary	Performer	MS has to type the information from paper into the computer.	-	-	-	-	-	+	+	+	-	+
Porter	Performer	Porter has to transfer one copy to MS	-	-	-	-	-	+	+	+	-	+

AF=Affect, PBC=Perceivied Behavioural Controls, H=Habit, FC=Facilitating Conditions, EU= Ease of Use, PNB= Perceived Normative Belifes, RNB= Role Normative Beleifs, PFN=Perceived Professional Norm, PV= Personal Value, PIV= Process Impact Value.

The performer actors were nurse, medical secretary, and porter. As performers of WA, we would expect different correlations as the users are lower down the power spectrum of the hospital and the nature of some of their work roles e.g. a porter, suggest different motivations from say health professional. We would expect significant motivational variables to be professional norms, and process impact value. Professional norm here was highlighted in a relation to their responsibility to get the job done and the feeling that they must do the WA as it is has become part of their job. The perceived behavioural consequences include personal and process value. We would expect a reasonable positive correlation with process value impact as many of the performers mentioned being motivated to get the job done. Also, perceived social norm were emphasized in the interviews by performers i.e. that 'doctors have asked me to do this WA'. The social norm here is highlighted because doctors must be followed according to the performers in that case. The assumption here is to what extent doctors will be followed and what is the consideration for the WA impact on the patient and the rest of the team working in the hospital whom will affected by those WA behaviours. Space precludes detailing the remaining variables.

5   Summary and Conclusion

This paper aimed to develop a theoretical foundation to explain WA motivation among healthcare professional. We explained the structure and different types of WA from the literature and our own research that had a bearing on motivational factors. We reviewed literature related to technology acceptance models and behavioural models used in healthcare context and showed how these models could be adapted to the WA motivation behaviours in healthcare. We identified additional variables to include as: perceived behavioural controls, perceived process value impact as pas part of the perceived consequences construct, and professional norm. We also identified the variation in motivational criteria that depends on the creator vs performer role in WA's. The creator role is an important factor that for obvious reasons is not included in most system and behaviour motivation applications and hence is important to identify. This study explained how these factors were integrated into the Workaround Motivational Model (WAMM). We applied WAMM factors to a compound WA example from our research to explain the type of results we might expect. These will be determined from the results of the questionnaires for creators and performers of workaround types that are currently being gathered ready for analysis. Future work is focused on completing and distributing the questionnaires, in testing heir relation to WA behaviour in healthcare context. We are particularly interested in the differences for compound WA processes and simple single actor workarounds.

References

1. Halbesleben, J.R., Wakefield, D.S., Wakefield, B.: Work-arounds in health care settings: literature review and research agenda. Health Care Management Review 33(1), 2–12 (2008)
2. Kobayashi, M., Fussell, S.R., Xiao, Y., Seagull, F.: Work coordination, workflow, and workarounds in a medical context. In: CHI 2005 Extended Abstracts on Human Factors in Computing Systems, pp. 1561–1564. ACM (2005)

3. Morath, J.M., Turnbull, J.: To do no harm. Jossey-Bass, San Francisco (2005)
4. Zhou, X., Ackerman, M., Zheng, K.: CPOE workarounds, boundary objects, and assemblages. In: Proceedings of the 2011 Annual Conference on Human Factors in Computing Systems, pp. 3353–3362. ACM (2011)
5. Reason, J.: Safety in the operating theatre – Part 2: Human error and organisational failure. Quality and Safety in Health Care 14(1), 56–60 (2005)
6. Nadhrah, N., Michell, V.: Measuring physicians WA-Implications on Work Processes and Patient Safety. In: 2013 International Conference on Logistics. Informatics and Services Sciences University of Reading (2013)
7. Nadhrah, N., Michell, V.: A Normative Method to Analyse Workarounds in a Healthcare Environment: their Motivations, Consequences, and Constraints. In: The 14th International Conference on Informatics and Semiotics in Organisations, ICISO 2013, pp. 195–204 (2013)
8. Weiner, B.: Human motivation: Metaphors, theories, and research. SAGE Publications, Incorporated (1992)
9. Nadhrah, N., Michell, V.: Workarounds: Risk or Benevolence for Patient Safety? IGI Global (2014)
10. Vogelsmeier, A.A., Halbesleben, J.R.B., Scott-Cawiezell, J.: Technology implementation and workarounds in the nursing home. Journal of the American Medical Informatics Association 15(1), 114–119 (2008)
11. Ash, J.S., Bates, D.W.: Factors and forces affecting EHR system adoption: report of a 2004 ACMI discussion. Journal of the American Medical Informatics Association 12(1), 8–12 (2005)
12. Niazkhani, Z., Pirnejad, H., van der Sijs, H., Aarts, J.: Evaluating the medication process in the context of CPOE use: the significance of working around the system. International Journal of Medical Informatics 80(7), 490–506 (2011)
13. Pirnejad, H., Niazkhani, Z., van der Sijs, H., Berg, M., Bal, R.: Impact of a computerized physician order entry system on nurse–physician collaboration in the medication process. International Journal of Medical Informatics 77(11), 735–744 (2008)
14. Davis, F.: Perceived usefulness, perceived ease of use, and user acceptance of information technology. MIS quarterly, 319–340 (1989)
15. Venkatesh, V., Morris, M.G., Davis, G.B., Davis, F.: User acceptance of information technology: Toward a unified view. MIS quarterly, 425–478 (2003)
16. Fishbein, M., Ajzen, I.: Belief, attitude, intention and behaviour: An introduction to theory and research. Addison-Wesley (1975)
17. Ajzen, I.: From intentions to actions: A theory of planned behavior. Springer (1985)
18. Gagnon, M.-P., Godin, G., Gagné, C., et al.: An adaptation of the theory of interpersonal behaviour to the study of telemedicine adoption by physicians. International Journal of Medical Informatics 71(2), 103–115 (2003)
19. Bergeron, F., Raymond, L., Rivard, S., Gara, M.-F.: Determinants of EIS use: Testing a behavioral model. Decision Support Systems 14(2), 131–146 (1995)
20. Ajzen, I.: The theory of planned behavior. Organizational behavior and human decision processes 50(2), 179–211 (1991)
21. Ferneley, E.H., Sobreperez, P.: Resist, comply or workaround? An examination of different facets of user engagement with information systems. European Journal of Information Systems 15(4), 345–356 (2006)
22. Fishbein, M., Ajzen, I.: Belief, attitude, intention and behavior: An introduction to theory and research (1975)

23. Varpio, L., Schryer, C.F., Lehoux, P., Lingard, L.: Working off the record: Physicians' and nurses' transformations of electronic patient record-based patient information. Academic Medicine 81(10), S35–S39 (2006)
24. Workflow concerns and workarounds of readers in an urban safety net teleretinal screening study. In: AMIA Annual Symposium Proceedings. American Medical Informatics Association (2011)
25. Values, attitudes, and interpersonal behavior. In: Nebraska Symposium on Motivation. University of Nebraska Press (1979)
26. Francis, R.: Report of the Mid Staffordshire NHS Foundation Trust Public Inquiry: Executive Summary: TSO Shop (2013)
27. Kirchhoff, J.W.: Norm Systems in Professional Work

Creating an iDTV Application from Inside a TV Company: A Situated and Participatory Approach

Samuel B. Buchdid, Roberto Pereira, and M. Cecília C. Baranauskas

Institute of Computing, University of Campinas (UNICAMP)
Av. Albert Einstein N1251, Campinas – SP, CEP 13083-852, Brazil
{buchdid,rpereira,cecilia}@ic.unicamp.br

Abstract. TV is a highly social and massive media that is worldwide available. The Interactive Digital TV represents a new device that is still constructing its identity. Designing applications for it is a challenging task, partially because of its intrinsic complex context and the lack of theoretical and methodological referential to support design activities. In this paper, we argue for a Socially Aware Computing approach to the design of iDTV applications, articulating artifacts and methods from Organizational Semiotics and Participatory Design. A case study on requirements for the design of an iDTV application is situated in the practical context of a Brazilian broadcasting TV Company. The results show benefits of using informed artifacts and methods in participatory and situated practices, indicating that it is possible and viable to make socially aware design in industrial settings.

Keywords: Socially Aware Computing, Organizational Semiotics, Participatory Design, Interactive Digital TV, Human-Computer Interaction.

1 Introduction

TV is recognized as a highly social technology. TV sets are displayed in living rooms, offices, restaurants and other private and public spaces. Outside their homes, people talk about football, novel/series episode, and even recommend interesting TV shows. More than high quality video and audio – including digital transmission, receiver processing capability and interactivity channel – the Interactive Digital TV (iDTV) is a medium that makes it possible the dissemination of interactive applications. With advances in Web 2.0 and Information and Communication Technologies, the iDTV is embedded and linked to other media that opens up a variety of possibilities for TV, such as its use in conjunction with mobile devices to complement the TV content, or even as a gateway to information via the Internet [6].

Considering the complex social context in which people live and the TV is inserted, Buchdid and Baranauskas [4] highlight the need for studies that consider the TV within a digital and social ecosystem, recognizing and addressing technical and social issues in order to design solutions that make sense to people. In the same way, Cesar et al. [6] highlight that research on social iDTV, which incorporates features of viewers and contextual information, has been scarce. In fact, several research works have

K. Liu et al. (Eds.): ICISO 2014, IFIP AICT 426, pp. 63–73, 2014.
© IFIP International Federation for Information Processing 2014

suggested the importance of comprehensive and contextual studies to propose devices, services and applications that make sense for the diversified population reached by iDTV (e.g.; [5], [6], [15]).

For TV broadcaster companies, while there is a demand for producing interactive content, the development of an application is a new element for their supply chain. Developing applications for iDTV is different from developing traditional software systems (e.g., Web); thus it can hardly be supported by an existing software development methodology [19]. Furthermore, as it is common for an emerging technology, the iDTV suffers with lack of references (e.g., sample applications, processes, mechanisms for evaluation, good practices guides) to assist any development processes [8].

In this sense, there is a demand for a design process suitable to the needs of the complex and dynamic context of a TV Company, while meets the needs of diverse audience reached by TV. Therefore, this study investigates the possibility of conducting design practices inside the context of an organization in order to understand the organizational culture and deal with the different forces that exist in its complex context. For this, in this paper, we draw on the Socially Aware Computing [2] to clarify requirements for an iDTV application, with Participatory Practices supported by Organizational Semiotics artefacts in situated contexts. A case study in the context of EPTV [7], a Brazilian broadcasting company, presents the design of an application for the "Terra da Gente" (TdG) ("Our Land", in English) TV show [18], and shows the results of our practices in an industrial setting.

The paper is organized as follows: Section 2 introduces the background of our work; Section 3 presents the case study in which the practices were conducted and Section 4 presents and discusses the main findings from the case study analysis. Finally, Section 5 presents our final considerations and directions for future research.

2   Theoretical and Methodological Foundation

The Socially Aware Computing (SAC) [2] is an approach to the design of information systems that extends and articulates ideas from Organizational Semiotics (SO) [9, 17] and Participatory Design (PD) [12] to make design socially responsible, participatory and universal as a process and a product. The SAC supports the understanding of the organization, the solution to be designed, and the context in which the solution will be inserted, so that it can potentially meet the sociotechnical needs of a particular group or organization.

The SAC has been used to support design in scenarios of high diversity of users (regarding skills, age, gender, special needs, literacy, intentions) [13]. Specifically for the iDTV context, SAC has been used to support the consideration of stakeholders' values and culture during the design process [14], for proposing recommendations to iDTV applications [15] as well for designing physical interaction devices for TV [11].

The SAC draws on the Semiotic Onion [17] to represent the idea that a design process needs to be conducted through its three nested levels: informal, formal and technical. The informal level refers to social norms that regulate behavior, beliefs, values, habits, culture, etc., that drive people's behavior. The formal level involves rules and procedures are created to explain mechanistic and repetitive tasks. The technical system is only part of the formal level of an organization, which can be automated.

Therefore, a design process should be understood as a wave that begins from outside to inside the Semiotic Onion, crossing the informal and formal layers to result in a technical system – see "SAC" detail in Fig. 1. This wave brings to the technical system relevant aspects of the informal and formal layers. Therefore, returning back to the social world, the technical system will impact on formal and informal layers alike, including the target-users, the environment in which it is/will be inserted, potentially promoting acceptance/adoption [2].

In SAC, design activities are conducted in Semio-participatory Workshops (SpW) [3] with individuals in their different roles (e.g., designer, developer, user, other stakeholders) – the ones who may direct or indirectly influence or be influenced by the problem being discussed and the solution to be designed. The idea is to bring up the viewpoint of different stakeholders situated in different layers of the organization to understand its situational context and the system inside it.

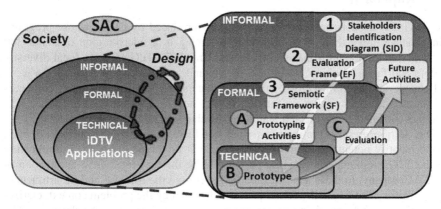

Fig. 1. Proposed design process from SAC's meta-model for design

Inspired by Baranauskas' SAC approach [2], we draw on artifacts from OS and design practices from PD in order to propose practices for supporting design activities in a situated context. Fig. 1 presents details indicating three semiotics artifacts chosen for supporting the problem clarification and solution proposal in a participatory and situated context: (1) Stakeholders Identification Diagram (SID); (2) Evaluation Frame (EF); and (3) Semiotic Framework (SF).

The SID [10] is an artifact from OS that facilitates the identification of the parties involved in a particular design situation; going beyond obvious classes of stakeholders (e.g., user, client, manager), it pays attention to different levels of involvement, interests, and expectation. The EF, proposed by Baranauskas [1], extends the SID to support reasoning about problems and solutions related to each stakeholder; it favors the clarification and identification of requirements as well as the anticipation of issues that may impact/influence the solution to be designed. Finally, the SF [16] is an artifact from OS that, in the context of our work, favors the identification and organization of requirements according to six different communication levels. The first three levels are related to technological issues (the physical, empirics, and syntactics), and the other three levels are related to aspects of human information functions (semantics, pragmatics and social world) [9].

The artifacts articulate information from each other, not linearly: e.g., if during the practice with the SF or the EF a new stakeholder is identified, the SID must be updated, eventually resulting in an update of SF and/or EF. The information produced through the artifacts and the practices support further design activities, such as drawing, constructing and evaluating a prototype for the solution (see details "A", "B" and "C" in Fig. 1). Therefore, the SID, EF and SF are articulated in participatory practices with key stakeholders: while the SID and EF lead participants to think about aspects related to the stakeholders, their needs, expectations, problems, challenges and ideas, the SF supports the organization and specification of these aspects as requirements for design decisions regarding the prospective application.

3   Case Study: The Situated Context and Methodological Approach

The TdG TV show is one of several programs produced by EPTV whose programming reaches more than 10 million citizens living in a micro-region of about 300 cities, in São Paulo and Minas Gerais States, Brazil [7]. TdG explores local diversity in flora and fauna, cooking, traditional music, and sport fishing; it runs once a week and counts on a team of editors, writers, producers, designers, technicians, engineers and journalists, among other staff members. Besides the TV show, the TdG team also produces a printed magazine and maintains a web portal related to the subject [18].

This section presents the main activities conducted to clarify the problem domain and to identify potential requirements for the first prototype of an iDTV application for the TdG program, named iTG. This would be the first interactive application in the TV Company. In these activities, participants used the SID, EF and SF artifacts in 2 participatory and situated workshops for understanding the problem context, clarifying, analyzing and organizing requirements for the application to be designed. The activities were conducted from January to July, 2013, and involved 8 participants playing different roles at EPTV: *TdG Chief Editor:* coordinates the production team (e.g., editors) of the TV show and the web portal. *Designer:* is responsible for the graphic art of the TV show, web portal, and iDTV application. *Operational and Technological Development Manager:* coordinates the department of new technologies. *Supervisor of Development and Projects:* coordinates the staff in the identification and implementation of new technologies. *Engineer on Technological and Operational Development:* works on infrastructure, and content production and distribution. *Technician on Technological and Operational Development:* is responsible for the implementation, support and maintenance of production department. *Intern:* an engineering student who is in training at EPTV. Three researchers in Human-Computer Interaction were responsible for preparing and conducting the workshops: two are experts in the SAC approach and the third is an expert in iDTV technologies.

The activities started with the identification of the interested parties. As an **input**, a poster with the SID was previously filled in with post its containing stakeholders related to iDTV applications coming from literature [5] and adapted to the TdG scenario. The participants were invited to propose new stakeholders, remove irrelevant ones, and exchange the position of stakeholders inside the diagram. Every change should be discussed among the group members (see "A" detail in Fig. 2). The **output** was a diagram that reflects the stakeholders involved in the problem domain according to the participants point of view. This activity was key for identifying the main forces as well as constraints that the team would face during the project.

Fig. 2. Participatory activities in a situated context

Having identified the stakeholders, the participants were invited to fill in the **EF** artifact in order to think about possible important issues related to the different stakeholders, and the way they could affect the project ("B" detail in Fig. 2). As **input**, the participants used the SID previously filled in, and their practical knowledge about the domain. The **output** was a collaboratively filled frame that presents requirements and constraints, observations and ideas, problems and suggestions related to different stakeholders' issues. This practice was important to identify the forces (interests) among the participants in the situated context, generating discussion and ideas for the iDTV application to be designed.

Finally, a workshop with the **SF** was conducted to organize the material produced from the previous practices in order to make explicit the requirements for the prospective iDTV application. As **input** for the activity, the SF was filled in with post its containing requirements identified through the EF, and with requirements for iDTV applications coming from literature [5]. Therefore, participants were asked to discuss and validate the diagram previously filled in, keeping, removing, and proposing new requirements for the application to be designed. All the decisions came from the group discussion ("C" detail in Fig. 2). The **output** of this activity was an organized list of requirements for the application to be designed.

Before each activity, the results obtained from the previous activities were presented and discussed in a summarized way, and the techniques to be used, as well as their methodologies and purposes were introduced to the participants. Posters with printed artifacts, pens and post its were prepared and provided to participants in each activity. During all the practices, the participants worked in a single group. Table 1 presents, for each activity presented in this paper, the time spent by researchers for introducing the artifacts and explaining how the participatory practices should be performed ("Introduction Time" column), the time spent by participants to perform each activity ("Practice Time" column), and the total time spent in each practice ("Total" column).

The results from these activities (e.g., artefacts filled in) were used to generate design ideas for the first iTG prototype. These ideas were materialized through an

Table 1. Time spent for conducting the activities presented in this paper

Practices	Introduction Time	Practice Time	Total
Stakeholders Identification Diagram (SID)	15 min	30 min	**45 min**
Evaluation Frame (EF)	10 min	35 min	**45 min**
Semiotic Framework (SF)	15 min	50 min	**65 min**
Total	**40 min**	**1h 55 min**	**2h 35 min**

adapted version of the Brain Draw participatory technique ("A" detail in Fig. 1) guided by Design Patterns for iDTV [8], supporting the construction of interfaces as well as an interactive prototype for the application. The final prototype was evaluated both interactively in a participatory practice and with representatives of end users ("C" detail in Fig. 1); the materials and results produced in these activities were used to inform requirements for the design of the iTG application.

4   Results and Discussion

The SID resulting from the participatory practices at EPTV (Fig.3) shows that there are many stakeholders potentially involved in the iTG application. The interested parties directly connected with the Broadcaster Company and iTG application are in *italics*, while the audience, which will be directly affected by the iTG application is underlined. The other stakeholders were brought from the literature [5] and were validated by the participants in the workshop.

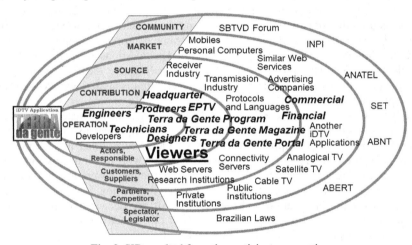

Fig. 3. SID resulted from the participatory practice

For example, in the operation layer there are Engineers and Technicians. Between the operation and contribution layers are the Producers and Designers. The EPTV as well as the TdG program are in the contribution layer because they are directly responsible for the development of the iDTV application. The "Terra da Gente" printed Magazine and Web Portal are crossing layers because they may advertise the iDTV application. The Commercial and Financial departments are between the source and market layer because they can define the economic viability of iDTV applications. Most stakeholders removed during the workshop were in the community layer. Some stakeholders were removed because participants understood that these stakeholders were already incorporated into the ABNT (acronym for Brazilian Association of Technical Norms) standard, or entities such as ANATEL (National Telecommunications Agency) and other regulators. The headquarter, which was initially proposed in the community layer, was moved to the contribution layer due to the great influence of its premises and rules on the iDTV applications. Software companies were also removed since they intended to hire developers as staff of the EPTV to do the job.

Other stakeholders were validated by participants due to their importance in the context of the application being developed (e.g., mobiles and personal computers can directly compete with iDTV applications).

Table 2 shows the EF resulted from the practice. It indicates that most issues were found in the contribution layer. The main problem emphasized during the activity was the "*Competition of the iDTV application with the TV content*": the main concern of the participants is that the interactive application should not disrupt the viewers from the main content of the TV show. The solution proposal for this issue was to "*Develop an application with the lower possible impact on the TV content*". The market layer was not worked out by the participants because the application would not have advertisements competing with the TV show sponsors.

Table 2. EF resulted from the participatory practice

Stakeholders	Problems and Issues	Ideas and Solutions
Operation	1. Labor (Human resources). 2. Application maintenance.	1. Hire professionals. 2. Simplify operations.
Contribution	1. Headquarter approval. 2. How to attract the viewer? 3. Competition of iDTV application with the TV content. 4. Policies of call the iDTV application. 5. Return channel constraints. 6. Graphic patterns.	1. Respect pre-established premises. 2. Advertise in the TdG website and magazine. 3. Develop an application with the lower possible impact on the TV content. 4. Broadcast the application in a transparent way for the user. 5. Identify the existence of return channel before trying to use it. 6. Experience different design elements.
Source	1. Existence and adequacy of receivers in accordance with standards.	1. Develop applications according to the standard, regardless of the receiver brand and model.
Market	--------	--------
Community	1. How to identify iTG acceptance?	1. Use the web portal to support measurement.

Table 3 presents the requirements proposed for the iTG application, organized according to the SF artifact. The requirements in *italics* were identified during practice with the EF, while the underlined requirements were identified during the practice with the SF artifact. The other requirements were brought from literature [5] and were adapted to the TdG context. All requirements were validated by the participants.

Table 3. SF instanced from the participatory practice

Level	Requirements
Social World	*1. Provide the least possible impact on TV content;* 2. Consider the diversity of the target audience; 3. The remote control should be the main interaction device (due to costs).
Pragmatics	*1. Integration with other communication channels (content, website and magazine);* 2. Application with short interaction paths (few steps to reach the goal); 3. The application must challenge and encourage users to interact (motivation should be associated with the application content); 4. The application should be easy to understand and use.
Semantics	*1. Respect headquarter premises; 2. Identify when it is possible to use the return channel and adapt the application for it; 3. Use the TdG portal to prospect the application acceptance;* 4. Ensure accessibility, usability and universal design; 5. clearly show the application features and relate them to the remote control's buttons.
Syntactics	*1. It should be easy to maintain; 2. Respect graphic patterns (characteristic of the TV);* 3. Must be asynchronous to the TV content; 4. Indicate to users when the application and updates are available (conditional); 5. Observe the constraints of the programming language used.
Empirics	1. Develop mechanisms to reduce the low speed transmission; 2. Consider the quality of the connectivity service available; 3. Use a web server suitable to a large number of connections.
Physical World	*1. Follow the ABNT standard;* 2. Consider the receiver limitations (memory and processing); 3. Consider different kinds of receiver brands and models.

Some initially proposed requirements were excluded from the artifact by the participants. For example: i) "*the need to transmit the application for mobile devices*" was removed because the participants decided that the iDTV application should transmit just to TV devices; and ii) "*alert users when using the return channel*" (associated with costs of using it) was removed because there will be no additional costs for those who already have internet connection.

As results of these practices, participants stated that the iTG application should be informational, so that users could have extra information that do not fit in the TV show content, not disturbing the audience´s attention to the program content. The application should reach the same audience of the TV show: people from all ages, mainly adults and elderly people that enjoy fauna and flora, fishing, ecotourism and regional cuisine.

The results from the practices supported the construction and evaluation of an interactive prototype for iTG (Fig. 4). For example: "A" detail shows the simple layout that covers only the screen edges, following the headquarter premises to "*provide least possible impact on TV content*"; the "B" detail shows a menu with few options and few hierarchical levels, which is directly linked to the requirements: "*the application should be easy to understand and use*" and "*application with short interaction path (with a few steps to reach the goal)*". The "C" detail represents treatment for the requirements: "*clearly show the application features and relate them to the remote control's buttons*" and "*the remote control should be the main interaction device (due to costs)*". Finally, "D" detail shows a game to motivate the viewers to interact with the program content; this feature represents the requirement: "*the application must challenge and encourage users to interact (motivation should be associated with the application content)*".

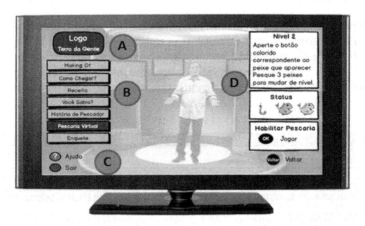

Fig. 4. First Prototype for the iTG application

The situated and participatory practices supported by the informed artifacts were essential to provide an understanding about the problem domain, the solution to be designed and the different forces and interests that should be taken into account. The practices led to the construction of a collective knowledge about the problems that we would face during the process of designing an iDTV application, revealing interests of the participants, favoring discussions and the comparison of different viewpoints, levels of abstraction (informal, formal and technical), and so on. For example, envisaged Poll and/or Quiz features generated discussions among participants throughout the design process. From a technical viewpoint, the return channel required for these features is only possible if the TV is connected to the Internet, which does not occur with most Brazilian TVs (see "Contribution" layer in Table 2). From a practical perspective, a Poll could captivate viewers, becoming a direct communication channel between them and the TV show. However, according to some influential stakeholders, it could disperse the viewers' attention. After discussion, the participants agreed to use the return channel and its services, specifying the following requirement: "*Identify when it is possible to use the return channel and adapt the application for it*".

The practices allowed participants to see the problem from different perspectives, generating ideas for the application; e.g., the participants became aware that, besides maintenance issues that may spend human and financial resources, the application must be primarily concerned with the end user, respecting accessibility and usability issues, as well as normative questions, such as the headquarter premises and the TV show content. Moreover, issues that go toward the informal layer gained notoriety during the process: when faced with the amount of stakeholders in SID, one participant said: "*We had never thought of that range of stakeholders; only about the ones closer to the problem and those related to technical issues*". Concerns, such as "*How to evaluate the application acceptance?*" and "*Consider the diversity of the target audience*" also represent issues that would hardly be thought without the artifacts and practices conducted.

The SID allowed us to observe that only those who are immersed in the situated context can measure the importance of some stakeholders: e.g., several stakeholders at the community layer were grouped into stakeholders that really made sense to the participants. The same was perceived with the EF and SF, in which some requirements would not be easily identified whether no participatory practice was conducted in a situated scenario. For example, the requirement: "*It should be easy to maintain*" is directly linked to the problem "*Labor (Human resources department)*" and the lack of developers in the broadcasting company.

Filling in the SID and EF beforehand was important to give participants a starting point as well as to reduce the workshop time. The initial stakeholders and requirements promoted discussion between the participants, leading them beyond their initial viewpoint/opinion. For example, ethical issues associated to the use of the return channel were remembered and discussed during the activities. These issues are of utmost importance in technologies for human use, even more in applications that reach a wide audience, not only because of the user, but also because of the reputation of both the broadcasting company and the TV show.

Using SO artifacts and conducting participatory design in the company settings was not considered expensive, as it could be supposed to be: only two workshops, lasting less than 2 hours each, were sufficient to the phase of clarifying the problem reported in this case study. Considering the whole design process, from the problem clarification to the prototype evaluation, less than 12 hours were required from the group. These results suggest that the Social Aware Computing in a situated context is a possible and viable approach to the design of iDTV applications.

Finally, as lessons learned from our practices, we point out the importance of having a person from the organization that acts as a mediator between the organization's members and external participants (e.g., researchers). This person must understand the differences in language and culture, as well as the interests of different participants and stakeholders in the activities to be conducted in order to deal with different tradeoffs. Also, during the practices it was possible to perceive among the insiders the existence of two groups with competitive views: those who were betting on interactivity as a mechanism to attract the audience, and those who were not, arguing that interactivity could disturb the viewers from the TV Show content. In this case, the researchers, supported by OS artifacts, acted as the mediators in the negotiation for reaching final decisions.

5   Conclusion

The design of iDTV applications presupposes a comprehensive and contextual analysis for the application to make sense for the diversity of possible audience. In a broadcasting company, the design of iDTV application is a new activity that is not yet in its supply chain. In this sense, practices that understand the company's needs, that is suitable to their production chain, and that favor the design of applications that make sense to viewers are welcome. In this paper, we presented three participatory practices with artifacts adapted from the Organizational Semiotics to understand a situated context at different levels of abstraction and from different viewpoints in order to clarify requirements for an iDTV application.

The practices were important to generate discussions among participants, promoting the understanding of the main interests and conflicts inside the company's context, the constraints and possibilities of the application being designed, the role of the application within the TV show, what it should provide to the viewers, and so on. Understanding the situated context was also important to the proposition of participatory practices suitable to the broadcasting company reality, allowing the participants to effectively clarify the problem and propose design solutions for an iDTV application in a collaborative way. The findings suggest that the practices are viable to be conducted in practical contexts, requiring reasonable time and few resources of the broadcasting company.

Other OS methods and artefacts may still be used for further studies. For example: the semantic analysis and the norm analysis could be previously elaborated and worked in a participatory workshop as well. The application designed from the activities presented in this paper is being implemented and tested to be broadcasted with the TV show.

Acknowledgments. This research is partially funded by CNPq (#165430/2013-3) and FAPESP (#2013/02821-1). The authors specially thank the EPTV team, and the participants who collaborated and authorized the use of the documentation of the project in this paper.

References

1. Baranauskas, M.C.C., Schimiguel, J., Simoni, C.A.C., Medeiros, C.M.B.: Guiding the Process of Requirements Elicitation with a Semiotic Approach. In: 11th International Conference on Human-Computer Interaction, pp. 100–111 (2005)
2. Baranauskas, M.C.C.: Socially Aware Computing. In: VI International Conference on Engineering and Computer Education (ICECE 2009), pp. 1–5 (2009)
3. Baranauskas, M.C.C.: Modelo Semio-participativo de Design. Codesign De Redes Digitais - Tecnologia e Educacao a Servico da Inclusao, Penso 1, 38–66 (2013)
4. Buchdid, S.B., Baranauskas, M.C.C.: Interactive Digital TV as revealed through Words: Focuses and Research Sources. In: 19th Brazilian Symposium on Multimedia and the Web (WebMedia 2013), pp. 289–296. ACM Press, New York (2013)
5. Buchdid, S.B., Baranauskas, M.C.C.: Situating iDTV in Brazil: A Study on Requirements Informed by Cultural Valuation. In: 14th International Conference on Informatics and Semiotics in Organisations (ICISO 2013), pp. 228–237 (2013)
6. Cesar, P., Chorianopoulos, K., Jensen, J.F.: Social Television and User Interaction. Computers in Entertainment 6(1), 1–10 (2008)
7. EPTV news portal (January 10, 2014), http://www.viaeptv.com
8. Kunert, T.: User-Centered Interaction Design Patterns for Interactive Digital Television Applications. Springer (2009)
9. Liu, K.: Semiotics in Information Systems Engineering. Cambridge University Press (2000)
10. Liu, X.: Employing MEASUR Methods for Business Process Reengineering in China, PhD Thesis University of Twente, Ensgede, the Netherlands (2001)
11. Miranda, L.C., Hornung, H., Baranauskas, M.C.C.: Adjustable interactive rings for iDTV. IEEE Transactions on Consumer Electronics 56, 1988–1996 (2010)
12. Müller, M.J., Haslwanter, J.H., Dayton, T.: Participatory Practices in the Software Lifecycle. In: Handbook of Human-Computer Interaction, 2nd edn., pp. 255–297. Elsevier (1997)
13. Pereira, R.: Key Pedagogic Thinkers: Maria Cecília Calani Baranauskas. Journal of Pedagogic Development, 18–19 (2013)
14. Pereira, R., Buchdid, S.B., Baranauskas, M.C.C.: Keeping Values in Mind: Artifacts for a Value-Oriented and Culturally Informed Design. In: 14th International Conference on Enterprise Information Systems (ICEIS 2012), pp. 25–34 (2012)
15. Piccolo, L.S.G., Melo, A.M., Baranauskas, M.C.C.: Accessibility and interactive TV: Design recommendations for the brazilian scenario. In: Baranauskas, C., Abascal, J., Barbosa, S.D.J. (eds.) INTERACT 2007. LNCS, vol. 4662, pp. 361–374. Springer, Heidelberg (2007)
16. Stamper, R.K.: Information in Business and Administrative Systems. John Wiley and Sons, New York (1973)
17. Stamper, R.K., Liu, K., Hafkamp, M., Ades, A.: Understanding the Roles of Signs and Norms in Organisations: a semiotic approach to information system design. Journal of Behaviour & Information Technology 19(1), 15–27 (2000)
18. Terra da Gente Portal (January 13, 2014), http://www.terradagente.com.br
19. Veiga, E.G.: Modelo de Processo de Desenvolvimento de Programas para TV Digital e Interativa. 141 f. Masters' dissertation - Computer Networks, University of Salvador (2006)

A Semiotic Approach for Guiding the Visualizing of Time and Space in Enterprise Models

John Krogstie[1] and Alexander Nossum[2]

[1] Norwegian University of Science and Technology (NTNU)
[2] Norkart A/S
krogstie@idi.ntnu.no

Abstract. Even if geographical aspects such as *location* are included already in the Zachman framework (as the *where*-perspective), it is not common to have detailed geographical aspects included in enterprise models. Cartography is the science of visualizing geographical information in maps. Traditionally the field has not included conceptual relationships that you find in enterprise models. Both cartography and enterprise modelling have developed guidelines for obtaining high quality visualizations. SEQUAL is a quality framework developed for understanding quality of models and modelling languages based on semiotic theory. In cartography such frameworks are not common. An adaptation of SEQUAL in the context of cartographic maps called MAPQUAL has been presented earlier. Differences between quality of maps and quality of conceptual models, pointing to guidelines for combined representations have been performed, and we try in this paper to investigate the utility of these guidelines in a simple trial. The result of the trial is presented, indicating that it is possible to represent conceptual, temporal, and spatial aspects in the same models in many ways, but that the choice of main perspective should depend on participant appropriateness.

Keywords: Quality of models, Spatial enterprise models, Maps, Semiotics.

1   Introduction

A *conceptual model* is traditionally defined as a description of the phenomena in a domain at some level of abstraction, which is expressed in a semi-formal or formal visual language. An enterprise model can be regarded as a kind of conceptual model. The field has spawn from information systems development and computer science with methodologies like Data Flow Diagram (DFD), Entity Relationship diagrams (ER) and more recently Unified Modeling Language (UML), Business Process Model and Notation (BPMN) and Archimate. The languages used for conceptual modelling largely contain nodes and links between nodes, and containment relationships. In enterprise modelling a number of perspectives to modelling are distinguished. For instance the Zachman Framework [22] describes 6 perspectives; *What* (material) it is made of, *How* (process) it works and *Where* (location) the components are, relative to

K. Liu et al. (Eds.): ICISO 2014, IFIP AICT 426, pp. 74–86, 2014.

one another, *Who* is involved, *When* are tasks done relative to each other and *Why*. In conceptual and enterprise modelling, we traditionally deal with *what* (data modelling), *how* (process modelling), *who* (organizational and actor modelling), *when* (behavioural and temporal modelling), and *why* (goal-oriented modelling). On the other hand the location aspect (*where*) is seldom dealt with in detail, although as we see e.g. in the development of BIM [21] of buildings that topological aspects get more and more important to represent.

Cartography on the other hand, focuses on aspects of location through maps. Maps at first sight appear to be very different from conceptual models. However, many similarities among these representations can be found.

The ultimate goal of the work is to develop an understanding of quality of enterprise models when also including geographical/topological constructs. To get to this we have earlier developed a framework for understanding and assessing quality of maps (MAPQUAL [18]), based on the SEQUAL-framework [10] for quality of models and modelling languages. Differences between SEQUAL and MAPQUAL are used to assess how combined geographical and conceptual models should be developed to achieve high quality models, and the aim of this paper is to report in experiences with modelling notations that takes into account both conceptual, topological and temporal issues.

In section 2, we present background on quality of maps and conceptual models. Section 3 describes the case and section 4 present a simple trial with two alternative visualizations of situations in the case-domain. In section 5 we sum up the experience and describe further work on an integrated approach.

2 Background and Related Work

A map is a kind of model. An underlying assumption has been that cartographic maps represent, primarily, geographic concepts. Some research has been put into applying cartographic visualization techniques as described by [4] on general non-geographic information [1, 15, 20] and the opposite, applying general information visualization techniques on geographic information. However, little work has looked on combining conceptual models with cartographic maps.

Earlier work on quality of models and quality of maps described in MAPQUAL [18] has illustrated that the main semiotic levels related to quality of models as described in SEQUAL applies also to maps. There are also distinct differences, which is a challenge when you want to visualize both geographical and conceptual aspects.

The differentiation between language and model (map) are usually not discussed in cartography. There exists no tradition of defining the syntax for languages for making maps, although standardizations towards both symbol sets and rules for applying them exist. MAPQUAL recognize this and aims at investigating how existing cartographic research can be structured following the SEQUAL structure inspired by semiotics.

Generally the visualization in maps can be said to comprise three graphic primitives; point, line and area and relations between these (Points being within an area, line crossing an area or being the border of an area etc). This is inherently different from meta-meta models in conceptual modelling which usually comprise of only nodes and links between nodes, in addition to visual containment.

The main aspects of the basic MAPQUAL [18], extended to take into account additional aspects of indoor maps [16] is described here.

2.1   Comparing Quality of Maps and Quality of Models

We here discuss the different levels of quality according to the semiotic ladder first described in the work of Stamper [6].

- Physical quality: The basic quality goal is that the model exists physically and is available to the relevant actors. Cartography is traditionally more geared towards making tangible representation of maps (i.e. printed maps) -although this is shifting towards more intangible representations for instance in a software environment (i.e. web mapping tools). SEQUAL focus much on guidelines for a modelling environment and different functionalities that it should provide. It should be noted that these guidelines are adapted to an information systems context, however, the guidelines should hold true for a cartographic environment as well. Also aspects of security (privacy) and currency as discussed in [16] is relevant for both types of representations.

- Empirical quality deals with comprehension when a visual model M is read by different social actors. MAPQUAL is significantly different from SEQUAL in this area. This is mainly due to the differences in meta-meta model discussed above. Colours are heavily used in cartography to separate different concepts from each other. In conceptual modelling the use of colours has been avoided to a large degree. Gopalakrishnan et al. [8] suggest using colours more in conceptual models. The inherent topological attributes of cartographic concepts often restricts the freedom of layout modifications, such as choosing where a concept should be placed on a map. Guidelines for increasing empirical quality of conceptual models base themselves, mostly, on the freedom of layout, supported by guidelines for graph aesthetics. These guidelines are thus not directly applicable to a map. In cartography one could see the aesthetics and geographical attributes as orthogonal dimensions. Conceptual modelling and cartography share the background for the guidelines for empirical quality.

- Syntactical quality: Is the model according to the syntax of the language. In cartography there is a lack of definition of formal languages in designing maps.

- Semantic and perceived semantic quality is the relation between the domain, map/model and social actor knowledge and interpretation. Thus, this facet is assumed to be generally applicable for cartography as well as for conceptual modelling. In cartography the quality of the data, in terms of measure errors, is quite common to use as a semantic quality measure.

- Pragmatic quality relates to that human interpreters understand the model. MAPQUAL does not include an extensive investigation in the research of human interpretation of maps in cartography, but recognise that there are many similarities between this and SEQUAL' focus on human interpretation of models. MAPQUAL and SEQUAL are thus more or less equal with respect to pragmatic quality, although with increasing focus on interactivity of digital maps [16].

- Social quality: Do different stakeholders agree on their interpretation of the model. MAPQUAL base the discussion of social quality of cartographic maps solely on the discussion of social quality in SEQUAL.
- Deontic quality: Do the model help to achieve the overall goal of modelling? Emphasise is put on how maps can support the achievement of goals of the map.

Looking on language quality we have found the following:

- Domain appropriateness: Due to the lack of discussion and formal separation of domain and language in cartography, MAPQUAL is similar to SEQUAL with respect to domain appropriateness (is it possible to represent the domain using the language).
- Participant appropriateness: Cartography has a tradition of exploiting the "natural" or cognitive knowledge of participants to a large extent. E.g. the use of colour for type of areas in a map reflects the colour in the real world. In conceptual modelling the tradition of creating a new language and thus disseminate this knowledge in a tailored way is more common.
- Modeller (cartographer) appropriateness: Similar to participant appropriateness, MAPQUAL and SEQUAL are similar with respect to modeller appropriateness.
- Comprehensibility appropriateness: Comprehensibility is divided into two areas; conceptual basis and external representation. Conceptual basis comprise the discussion on which concepts that are included in the language. SEQUAL provides several concrete guidelines for the conceptual basis. These guidelines have validity in cartography as well as for conceptual modelling. External representation focus on how the notation of the language is formed, i.e. the graphical aspects of the language. In this area there are significant differences between MAPQUAL and SEQUAL. Cartography has a strong tradition of investigating graphic design principles based on so-called visual variables [4]. Traditionally maps have a larger focus on the use of colours and the use of texture as a visual technique. SEQUAL encourage being able to support a free approach to composition of symbols. Such free composition of symbols cannot be a general guideline in cartography since the geographical reality often is constraining this freedom.
- Tool appropriateness: Tool appropriateness is traditionally not considered in cartography. Thus MAPQUAL adopts SEQUAL on the discussion of tool appropriateness, although with less focus on executional semantics.
- Organisational appropriateness: Here MAPQUAL focus more on a cartographic context and the current standardisation efforts in this area.

Thus, two interrelated facets have large differences: comprehensibility appropriateness for language quality and empirical quality for map/model quality. When investigating and comparing MAPQUAL and SEQUAL, we devise some important guidelines when using both conceptual and geographical aspects:

1. Clearly discriminate between geographical oriented lines and conceptual lines.
2. Clearly differentiate between nodes (concept) which are often depicted by a geometric shape, and geographic areas (by texture or colour for instance)
3. Indicate topological information by positioning of conceptual nodes according to the topology when possible.
4. Position concepts according to their temporal nearness.
5. Use visual variables where appropriate, especially the use of colour and shading for differentiation is necessary for integrated models.
6. Design the visualization based on the participants' cognitive metaphor of the most important information attribute. For instance, temporal attributes tend to be lean towards a sequential metaphor. Spatial attributes, like nearness, tend to lean towards a distance metaphor (i.e. closer is nearer).

3 Quality of Integrated Conceptual and Topological Models

In the investigation of developing quality guidelines for integrated visualizations that exhibit both conceptual and geographic information, a case study has been performed. The case study is in the health-care domain, which is an area where space support is found to be very important [9] and which lends itself well to these kinds of visualizations. Research suggests that providing awareness of the hospital environment is one mean to lower the complexity of the decision-making. Both a focus towards the spatial dimension (i.e. location), but also the conceptual dimension (i.e. state, relationship etc.) is needed [2, 3].

The spatial dimension in indoor environments is commonly visualized either directly in a floor-plan (i.e. an indoor map) [13] or as an attribute in a diagram-like fashion [3]. Both approaches aim at visualizing the spatial dimension as well as the conceptual dimension including relationships, states and similar. However, both approaches focus the visualization towards their respective field (i.e. floor map on the spatial dimension, diagrams on the conceptual dimension) without successfully obtaining a good communication of both dimensions at the same time. This section will describe the background for the case and the perspective chosen for the trial, as well as a concrete situation that instantiates the information space under investigation.

3.1 Self-coordination of Hospital Staff

The primary focus for the case is the self-coordination of hospital-staff. A typical work situation for hospital staff includes various tasks that can either be scheduled or occur spontaneously. The tasks may require different equipment, several other staff members may be involved in a task, either throughout the whole duration of the task or only briefly, and often involving patients. Additionally, the staff member may have special interests in specific patients. This can be modelled by concepts in the information space, with relationships among them. Moreover, all the concepts have a spatial relationship of some sort. Concepts also have several non-physical properties, such as state, importance, staff type and so on.

The spatial dimension of the information is regarded as highly important and relevant for collaboration and coordination. The absolute location of concepts is not necessarily what best satisfies the actors' information needs. Deduced information, based on the absolute location of concepts may prove to be more suitable, especially towards the topology of concepts. Topology aspects may be spatial or temporal. Spatial topology is commonly exhibited in cartography for instance in subway maps, where less emphasis is put on distance than in topographical maps. Temporal aspects can be deduced by, for instance, the travelling distance divided by the travelling speed. In an indoor environment, this is very useful as the distances may be large, but conceptual entities can travel fast, for instance by elevators across floors. Additional obstacles that slow actors down are also present, such as wardrobes, bathrooms, disinfection areas, etc, where actors are held up temporarily.

3.2   Concrete Case Relative to Trial

Since the conceptual information model can attain fairly high complexity, it is important to constrain the case-study to a moderately complex sub-domain. The case-study revolves around one specific actor as the intended main user. The user has certain interests, or relevant information associated with him/her, this information is a subset of the total information available. The goal for the trial was to provide a visual communication method which satisfies this users specific information needs. However, the method developed and investigated should also be able to be adapted to satisfy similar scenarios with other user types.

The scenario focuses on a typical working day for an anaesthetist. An anaesthetist's tasks are typically distributed throughout the hospital and each task has a small time span. Often the anaesthetist is working in parallel on two or more tasks, providing a need to self-coordinate in an effective matter, often requiring the knowledge of spatial attributes.

Development of the visual representations could be performed in several different ways, each with different benefits. For the initial investigation, a paper-prototype inspired approach was taken. Paper-prototypes supports for fairly rapid development, allowing for several ideas to be manifested and iteratively developed. The development of paper-prototypes ended with primarily two different kinds of visual representation methods, spatial Gantt charts (see example in Fig. 2) and Spatial Circles (see example in Figure 1). Both take into account the guidelines in the end of section 2, but Spatial Gantt chart have a higher emphasis on the temporal dimension. Due to the previous experiences of the subject (with Gantt-charts), we expected that the Spatial Gantt chart would perform best. A full description of the notation and snapshots used in the trial is found in [17].

4   Trial

The design of the trial was inspired by experiments conducted by [19] on differences between two conceptual modelling techniques. It should, however, be noted that the trial in this project was never intended to be as comprehensive as Opdahl and Sindre [18], especially with respect to the number of participants. Since it was not meaningful to use proxies (e.g. students) in the case, the number of available subjects was also too small to use statistical methods.

The trial is designed with strong inspiration from both the Latin-Square experimental design method, work by [7] and the Technology Acceptance Model (TAM) [5]. The main intention of the trial is to investigate the properties of comprehension of the different types of visual representations and their acceptance.

In the trial the participants were given an introduction to the area, and then presented with a tutorial of the visualization to be presented. Then the visualization representing the scenario snapshot was presented. Instructions were given to answer a questionnaire -the time frame of this was 5 minutes. This process was performed iteratively for each of the snapshots in the scenario, but by changing the order of visualization types presented i.e. changing the order in which the different visualizations were presented, and having different visualizations representing similar information for the two different trials to leverage the potential learning factor for the visualization types. Additionally it is desirable to be able to compare the two different visualization types against the same information without repeating the presentation of the same scenario snapshots to the same participant. One potential shortcoming of this design is the differences in the participants -if the number of participants is small the impact of this will increase and can lead to wrong conclusions if not taken into account.

The questionnaires are essentially of two different types, one which is to be answered during the presentations of the different visualizations and one to be answered after finishing the presentations. One questionnaire for each of the scenario snapshots was created. The users' comprehension and potential knowledge gain from the visualization are evaluated by investigating the questionnaires. Comprehensibility deals with whether the user understands what the visualization depicts. Knowledge gain deals with whether the user is able to use the information in the visualization and potentially create new knowledge, or take decisions based on the information gained. Typical questions included for these two topics are:

- Comprehensibility "Is task 1 far away?, When is task 2 starting?
- Knowledge gains "What do you decide to do next?

The post-presentation questionnaire was more comprehensive and aims primarily at investigating the user *acceptance* of the two different visualization types. Categorization and questions were inspired by the Technology Acceptance Model and [19] with the following categories:

- Perceived usefulness
- Perceived ease-of-use
- Intention to use

The post-presentation questionnaire used a 5-point Likert scale with the "opposing statements" format of the questions. The answer options indicated to which degree the subject agreed with the statements. In order to avoid repetition and monotony, the questions ordering was randomized.

4.1 Results from the Trial

Two participants were recruited to the trial, both staff at the local hospital. One participant was an anaesthetist and the other a general practitioner. Neither one received any compensation for their participation. Both trials were set up identically with respect to both equipment and introduction of the participants to the trial. Each trial took approximately 30 minutes.

This section will present and discuss the results from the trial categorized according to comprehensibility, knowledge gain and technology acceptance briefly (due to the strict page limitations of the conference).

Comprehensibility: The results of the comprehensibility investigation were calculated as an average over all questions related to comprehensibility, regardless of the information depicted. The questions were not designed to necessarily have a yes/no answer. Coding of the answers given was performed by mapping each answer to correct, semi-correct or wrong. This could potentially introduce bias or errors in the results since it was done by one person only, however due to the limited scope of the trial this was regarded as tolerable. The results indicate a slightly higher proportion of correct answers for the Spatial Circle layout than the Spatial Gantt layout. However the difference is marginal.

Knowledge Gain: The results were calculated by first coding the answers in three different categories; correct, semi-correct and wrong. It is noted, as for results under comprehensibility, that this can introduce biased results. A standard arithmetical average was then calculated for each of the category over the answers related to knowledge gain. A differentiation between the two visualization types was kept, in order to compare their performance. The results indicate that Spatial Circle layout performs slightly better than the Spatial Gantt layout. However, the difference between the two is marginal.

Technology Acceptance: The final and most comprehensive questionnaire revolved around investigating the participants' acceptance of the visualizations. Results from the technology acceptance investigation were produced by calculating an average of the degree of acceptance in the different categories of acceptance for each of the visualizations. Additionally, an average over the three categories was calculated to provide a summary of the acceptance. The degree of acceptance used the 5-point Likert scale which was coded as a range from -2 to +2. The result was that the Spatial Gantt layout appears to be superior to Spatial Circle layout in all categories of acceptance. Spatial Circle layout received negative degree of acceptance in all categories. It is not justifiable to draw a solid conclusion based on these results -however the results is regarded as indicative with respect to the comparison between the two visualization types.

The superior acceptance of Spatial Gantt is attributed to the participants' familiarity with the Gantt, or Gantt-like, metaphor. This familiarity was recognized in the design of the visualization types and was thus not unexpected. On the other hand, it is interesting that even if the performance (as for comprehension and knowledge gain) seems relatively equal, the difference in acceptance of the approach appear this clear. Similar results are found in other studies of modelling notations [8].

5   Conclusion and Future Work

This work is aimed at investigating properties of visual representation of geographical, temporal and conceptual representations. Integrating spatial and non-spatial information is needed in meeting the increased amount of spatial and conceptual information. Information is increasingly including a spatial attribute [11] which indicates a need to understand how integrated visual representations works. One way of eliciting this is to merge current understanding of quality in cartography and conceptual modelling and thus create an integrated understanding of quality. In earlier work, the development of MAPQUAL has contributed to a broader understanding of integrated visual representations.

In order to investigate properties of different visual representation techniques a case study was performed. The health-care domain was chosen, with the specific scenario of an anaesthetist work day. Two distinctly different visual representation methods were developed for the scenario following the guidelines for mixed representations. In order to investigate their appropriateness a simple trial was designed and conducted. Due to limited resources the trial was intended to be illustrative rather than provide statistically valid conclusions, largely due to the limited number of participants involved. Further efforts relating to integrated visual representations can benefit by revising and extending the experiment design based on the experience presented in this article.

Through the investigations of visual representations, several issues were discovered. The information was perceived by the participants as through a sequential metaphor, favouring a sequential alignment of the temporal attributes. Thus, the non-sequential layout (i.e. Spatial Circles) was not favoured for the scenario. More generally this is formulated as a guideline which relates to sequentiality of the visual representation relative to the participants cognitive metaphor of the information.

Introducing spatial attributes to a traditionally non-spatial information space, such as schedule information, is new and unfamiliar to the participants. This can introduce issues with the acceptance of the visual representation developed. Moody [15] identifies a similar issue with development of modelling languages.

The investigations did not look on tool support for any of the visual representations. This is intentionally left up to further work. It is strongly encouraged that further efforts delve into the investigation of relevant techniques for tool support. Filtering techniques from conceptual modelling combined with generalization and zooming techniques from cartography and GISc are reckoned to be highly successful and a necessity for the success of integrated visual representations. Additional tool support could introduce the notion of interactive models/maps.

Experience from this work has illustrated that integrating visual representation techniques from cartography and conceptual modelling is feasible and potentially useful. The work reported here has only briefly investigated some of this potential. The close collaboration with domain experts from the application domain proved highly beneficial and led to development which otherwise could not have been possible. Further investigations similar to this one, is encouraged to look into the perceived usefulness for the participants and the effects on collaboration between relevant participants. Additionally, more complex scenarios should be developed and investigated, preferably spatial-intensive scenarios, i.e. where spatial attributes are recognized in advance as important by the participants.

References

1. van der Aalst, W.M.P.: TomTom for business process management (TomTom4BPM). In: van Eck, P., Gordijn, J., Wieringa, R. (eds.) CAiSE 2009. LNCS, vol. 5565, pp. 2–5. Springer, Heidelberg (2009)
2. Bardram, J., Bossen, C.: Mobility Work: The Spatial Dimension of Collaboration at a Hospital. Computer Supported Cooperative Work 14, 131–160 (2005)
3. Bardram, J., Hansen, T.R., Soegaard, M.: AwareMedia – A Shared Interactive Display Supporting Social, Temporal, and Spatial Awareness in Surgery. In: Proceedings of CSCW 2006, Banff, Alberta, Canada, November 4-8 (2006)
4. Bertin, J.: Semiology of Graphics: Diagrams, Networks, Maps. University of Wisconsin Press, Madison (1983)
5. Davis, F.: Perceived usefulness, perceived ease of use, and user acceptance of information technology. MIS quarterly, 319–340 (1989)
6. Falkenberg, E.D., Hesse, W., Lindgreen, P., Nilsson, B.E., Oei, J.L.H., Rolland, C., Stamper, R.K., Assche, F.J.M.V., Verrijn-Stuart, A.A., Voss, K.: A Framework of information system concepts - The FRISCO Report, IFIP WG 8.1 Task Group FRISCO (1996)
7. Gemino, A., Wand, Y.: Evaluating modeling techniques based on models of learning. Communications of the ACM 46(10), 79–84 (2003)
8. Gopalakrishnan, S., Krogstie, J., Sindre, G.: Capturing Location in Process Models: Comparing Small Adaptations of Mainstream Notation. International Journal of Information System Modeling and Design (IJISMD) 3(3), 424–459 (2012)
9. Gulliver, S.R., Grzybek, H., Radosavljevic, M., Wiafe, I.: Changing Building User Attitude and Organisational Policy towards Sustainable Resource use in healthcare. Health Policy and Technology 2(2), 75–84 (2013)
10. Krogstie, J.: Model-based Development and Evolution of Information Systems. Springer (2012)
11. MacEachren, A., Kraak, M.: Research challenges in geovisualization. Cartography and Geographic Information Science 28(1), 3–12 (2001)
12. Marjamaa, R., Torkki, P., Torkki, M., Kirvela, O.: Time Accuracy of a Radio Frequency Identification Patient Tracking System for Recording Operating Room Timestamps. Anesthesia & Analgesia 102(4), 1183–1186 (2006)

13. McCarthy, J.F., Meidel, E.S.: ACTIVEMAP: A visualization tool for location awareness to support informal interactions. In: Gellersen, H.-W. (ed.) HUC 1999. LNCS, vol. 1707, p. 158. Springer, Heidelberg (1999)
14. Moody, D.: Theoretical and Practical Issues in Evaluating the Quality of Conceptual Models. Data & Knowledge Engineering 55(3), 243–276 (2005)
15. Moody, D., van Hillegersberg, J.: Evaluating the Visual Syntax of UML: An Analysis of the Cognitive Effectiveness of the UML Family of Diagrams. In: Gašević, D., Lämmel, R., Van Wyk, E. (eds.) SLE 2008. LNCS, vol. 5452, pp. 16–34. Springer, Heidelberg (2009)
16. Nossum, A.: Developing a Framework for Describing and Comparing Indoor Maps. The Cartographic Journal 50(3), 218–224 (2013)
17. Nossum, A.: Visual Representation of Integrated Information, Master Thesis, Norwegian Technical University of Science and Technology (2009)
18. Nossum, A., Krogstie, J.: Integrated Quality of Models and Quality of Maps. In: Halpin, T., Krogstie, J., Nurcan, S., Proper, E., Schmidt, R., Soffer, P., Ukor, R. (eds.) BPMDS 2009 and EMMSAD 2009. LNBIP, vol. 29, pp. 264–276. Springer, Heidelberg (2009)
19. Opdahl, A., Sindre, G.: Experimental comparison of attack trees and misuse cases for security threat identification. Information and Software Technology 51(5), 916–932 (2009)
20. Skupin, A., Fabrikant, S.: Spatialisation Methods: A Cartographic Research Agenda for Non-geographic Information Visualization. Cartography and Geographic Information Science 30(2), 99–119 (2003)
21. Succar, B.: Building information modelling framework: a research and delivery foundation for industry stakeholders. Automation in Construction 18(3), 357–375 (2009)
22. Zachman, J.A.: A framework for information systems architecture. IBM Systems Journal 26(3), 276–291 (1987)

Appendix A: Examples of Visualizations

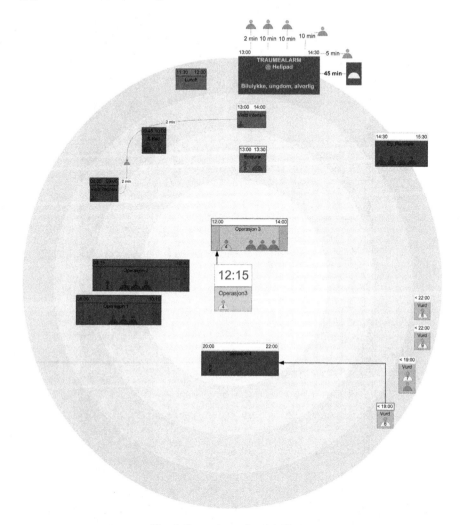

Fig. 1. Example on Spatial Circles

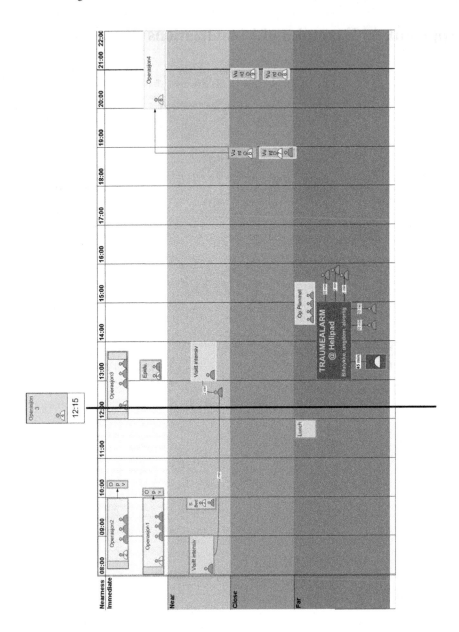

Fig. 2. Example on Spatial Gantt

Exploring Interface Sign Ontologies for Web User Interface Design and Evaluation: A User Study

Muhammad Nazrul Islam

Turku Centre for Computer Science (TUCS),
Department of Information Technologies,
Åbo Akademi University,
Turku - 20520, Finland
nislam@abo.fi, nazrulturku@gmail.com

Abstract. The aim of this paper is twofold: firstly, to find the set of ontologies (i.e., the set of concepts and skills) presupposed by users when interpreting the meaning of web interface signs (i.e., the smallest elements of web user interfaces), and secondly, to investigate users' difficulties in interpreting the meanings of interface signs belonging to different kinds of ontologies. In order to achieve these aims an empirical user study was conducted with 26 test participants. The study data was gathered by semi-structured interviews and questionnaires. Following an empirical research approach, descriptive statistics and qualitative data analysis were used to analyze the data. The study results provide a total of twelve ontologies and reveal the users' difficulties in interpreting the meanings of interface signs belonging to different kinds of ontologies.

Keywords: Web user interface, Ontology, Semiotics, Interface sign, Web usability, User interface design.

1 Introduction

1.1 Web Interface Sign and Ontology

The web user interface (UI) is the 'window to the world' through which interactions between end users and web applications are mediated, organizations communicate with customers, and the like [1]. A web UI encompasses a number of navigational links, symbols, command buttons, thumbnails, icons, small images, etc. These smallest elements are defined in this paper as interface signs (see Fig. 1, example interface signs are marked by ovals). Interface signs are treated as one of the most crucial elements of web UIs. The main reasons are [2-4]: (a) the content and functions of web applications are essentially directed by interface signs, (b) users interact with web applications by means of interface signs, (c) an interface sign is designed by designer(s) as an encoded form and users should properly decode or interpret the sign to get the meaning of this sign, and (d) inaccurate interpretation of interface signs leads users to usability problems and to low task performance. Designing user

K. Liu et al. (Eds.): ICISO 2014, IFIP AICT 426, pp. 87–96, 2014.

intuitive interface signs is essential to ensure effective and efficient system use, to maintain the user satisfied, to achieve system's learnability, to provide users the means to communicate, etc. i.e., to improve the usability of web applications [3], [5], [6-7]. Interface sign design principles are semiotics by nature as semiotics is considered as the doctrine or science of signs [8-10]. Semiotics can be defined as "the study of signs, signification, and signifying systems" [11].

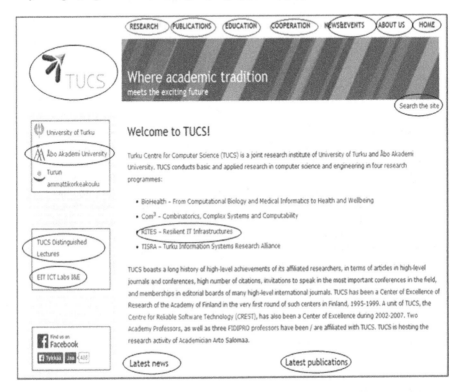

Fig. 1. Example interface signs marked by ovals; snapshot of Turku Centre for Computer Science retrieved from www.tucs.fi on January 2014

The term 'ontology' is defined as the set of concepts and skills that a user should have for understanding the referential meaning of an interface sign [2] [12]. From the user's perspective, ontology refers to the knowledge or concepts that are needed to understand and properly interpret the meaning of an interface sign. From the designers' perspective, ontology refers to the knowledge or concepts presupposed and referred to by an interface sign. For example, an interface sign 'Inbox' in an email application may be well designed in terms of color, layout, position, etc. but will not make any sense to the users who do not know what the concept of 'Inbox' refers to. Here, this 'concept' is defined as 'ontology'. The concept and definition of ontology provided by Speroni [12] and Bolchini et al. [2] are considered as background theory of this paper. According to Speroni [12], the most common ontologies used in information intensive websites are: Internet Ontology (knowledge related to the internet use), InterLocutor/Institution Ontology (knowledge related to the owner of the website), Commonsense Ontology (knowledge belonging to the user's background, and referring to common and everyday terms), Website Ontology (knowledge related to a particular website), Web Domain Ontology (knowledge related to a specific web domain), Context Ontology (knowledge related to a specific context of interface sign), and Topic Ontology (knowledge related to a specific topic or subject of a website).

1.2   Motivation and Study Questions

Ontologies are important for interface sign design and evaluation for the following reasons [2] [12] [13-15]:

i)   Users hold a set of ontologies to interpret the meaning of interface signs. In other words, users interpret the meaning of interface signs based on their presupposed knowledge.

ii)   A proper matching between the ontology or ontologies referred to by an interface sign and the ones known by a user helps the user to properly interpret the meaning of this sign.

iii)   UI practitioners should know the users of a system in order to design or evaluate it (i.e., 'knowing the users'). In other words, practitioners need to know what kind of presupposed knowledge (i.e., ontologies) is used by the end-users when interpreting the meaning of interface signs.

iv)   Practitioners can model the profiles of end-users based on their familiarity with different kinds of ontologies. This model assists practitioners to create a design or evaluation paradigm for web user interface design and evaluation.

However, the set of ontologies provided by Speroni [12] and Bolchini et al. [2] was an example list of most common ontologies used in information intensive web UI. In their work, they have also stated that the set of ontologies can be different depending on different websites. A few studies were conducted to observe users difficulties in interpreting the meaning of interface signs belonging to different kinds of ontologies [13-15]. These studies were conducted mainly using an expert inspection as a method, considered the ontologies proposed by Speroni [12], and focused only on information intensive websites.

Therefore, the objectives of this paper were to find the set of ontologies presupposed by users when interpreting the meaning of web interface signs, and to investigate users' difficulties in interpreting the meanings of interface signs belonging to different kinds of ontologies. The fundamental question was: *what ontologies are used to interpret the meaning of web interface signs?* In order to achieve these objectives, an empirical study was conducted with a total of 26 test participants. The study results provide a set of twelve ontologies, a few features related to ontology mapping in interpreting the meaning of the interface signs, and reveal the participants' difficulties in interpreting the meaning of interface sign belonging to different kinds of ontologies. It is important to mention here that an earlier version of this paper is published in [16].

The paper proceeds as follows. Section 2 presents the study method. The study results are discussed in section 3. The discussion and ideas for future work are presented in the final section.

2   Study Method

The study followed an empirical research approach. The study data was collected by semi-structured interviews and questionnaires. The empirical study was designed and conducted primarily to find the determinants (themes) and the attributes (sub-themes) of user-intuitive interface signs. However, the scope of this paper was limited to a specific objective, which was a part of the primary objective of the aforementioned study, - i.e., to explore the web interface sign ontologies for interface sign design and evaluation. Thus this paper focused only on users' presupposed knowledge or ontologies (a determinant of user-intuitive interface signs), and considered data related to web sign ontologies. The study data was analysed by descriptive analysis and qualitative data analysis. The profiles of test participants and study procedure are discussed briefly here. The methodology is discussed more comprehensively in [17].

Participants: A total of 6 female and 20 male participants (i.e., a total of 26 participants) were recruited to conduct this study. Participants were aged 22-41 [M (SD) = 25.85(4.86)]. 5 participants were company employees, 1 research personal, and remaining 20 were graduate students at Åbo Akademi University (AAU), Finland. Company employees were also studying as graduate students at ÅAU. Each participant had good experience in accessing university websites and using email applications. 5 participants had experience in accessing museum websites, and 17 participants had prior experience with use of online calendars. Each participant had experience with (real-world) calendars and visited a few (real-world) museums.

Study procedure: The study was conducted in a usability test laboratory in Finland. A total of 72 interface signs were selected from user interfaces of two web application domains (online calendar and email) and two web domains (university and museum websites). Three types of questions: open ended, probing, and closed questions were developed following the interview guidelines suggested by Stanton & Young [18].

Each test was conducted one by one. The following activities were followed in each test session with each participant. Firstly test subjects filled up pre-test questionnaires and signed a test-consent form; secondly a short lecture was given to inform the test subjects about the test in general: test procedure, test participants' roles, etc.; and finally test subjects were asked to answer a set of questions for each interface sign presented to them. Selected interface signs were presented to test subjects in two arrangements: *sign without context* and *sign with context*. Test subjects were not allowed to click on the signs; they were only supposed to respond to a number of questions for each interface sign such as: What could be the referential meaning of this sign? Why do you think this (user's response for the first question) is the meaning of this sign? How certain or confident are you that you are correct in your interpretation (score: 1(very low) – 7(very high))? What complications or difficulty do you feel to interpret this sign (score: 1(very easy) – 7(extremely difficult))? Each test-session generally took about 100-120 minutes for each participant. Each test session was audio-video recorded. Both qualitative and quantitative data were collected and analyzed.

3   Study Results

The study provides the following results:

- A set of twelve interface sign ontologies.
- A few features of ontology mapping in interpreting the meaning of the interface signs.
- Reveal the participants' difficulties in interpreting the meaning of interface signs belonging to different kinds of ontologies.

Next we will discuss each study results more comprehensively.

3.1   Set of Ontologies

The study found a total set of twelve ontologies to interpret the meaning of the interface signs. A few of them (i.e., number *i, vi-viii, x,* and *xii*), as discussed in section 1.1, are also proposed by Speroni and Bolchini et al. in (Bolchini et al. 2009; Speroni 2006). The set of ontologies, their definition and examples are briefly presented in table 1.

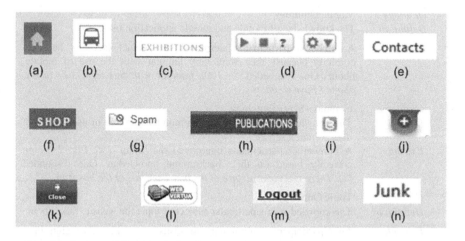

Fig. 2. A set of interface signs

Table 1. Set of interface sign ontologies

#		Ontologies
i	*Ontology*	Internet Ontology
	Definition	The knowledge of world of web, web browsing and its concepts and conventions.
	Example	A number of participants interpreted the <Home > (see Fig. 2.a) sign correctly because they were familiar with the world of web and internet browsing. One responded *"....It is for home page...my experience of browsing on internet; it is a home icon for web entrance...."*
ii	*Ontology*	Real World Ontology
	Definition	The knowledge of the real world experiences and concepts.
	Example	One participant interpreted the <Bus> (see Fig. 2.b) sign correctly because he was familiar with it. He responded *"....There is a clear picture of the bus. I see this at the bus stop....."*
iii	*Ontology*	System Ontology
	Definition	The knowledge of the (studied) system, its functionalities & concepts.
	Example	One participant interpreted the 'Exhibition' (see Fig. 2.c) sign correctly because he had experience with museum though he never visited museum website. He responded *"....The term is known to me. It is a general term. I have heard this term in the museum....."*
iv	*Ontology*	Computer Ontology
	Definition	The knowledge of computers and computer uses.
	Example	One participant interpreted the <media player> (see Fig. 2.d) sign correctly because he had used the Windows Media Player in his computer. He responded *"....I am familiar with these sign from the Windows Media Player ...."*
v	*Ontology*	Mobile Ontology
	Definition	The knowledge of mobile and mobile application uses.
	Example	A number of participants interpreted the 'Contact' (see Fig. 2.e) sign correctly because they were very familiar with the use of mobile phone. One responded *"....I am familiar with this sign...like in my phone I have contacts....."*
vi	*Ontology*	Common-Sense Ontology
	Definition	The knowledge belonging to a common background of users and that uses common sense.
	Example	A number of participants interpreted the 'Shop' (see Fig. 2.f) sign correctly based on their background knowledge. One responded *"....There is a clear picture of the bus. I see this at the bus stop....."*
vii	*Ontology*	Topic Ontology
	Definition	The knowledge of a particular subject or topic the website talks about.
	Example	Two participants interpreted the <Bus> (see Fig. 2.b) sign in a museum website inaccurately because they thought that the icon stands for a specific exhibition related to vehicles. One responded *"....It is kind of bus exhibition....."* The sign actually stands for providing information on how to reach the museum.

Table 1. (*continued*)

#		Ontologies
viii	*Ontology*	Current Web Domain Ontology
	Definition	The knowledge of web interface signs which are specific enough to the current web domain (e.g., email application domain).
	Example	A number of participants interpreted the <Spam> (see Fig. 2.g) sign in an email application correctly because of their familiarity with the email application. One responded "....*I know this meaning because of my previous knowledge of using email applications....*"
ix	*Ontology*	Other Web Domain Ontology
	Definition	The knowledge of web interface signs which are specific enough to a particular web domain other than the web domain where the sign is currently available.
	Example	One participant interpreted the 'Publications' (see Fig. 2.h) sign in a museum website correctly because of his familiarity with university websites (i.e., educational web domain). He responded "....*From university domain, I know what is a publication. I never had seen 'Publications' in a museum website...*"
x	*Ontology*	Organization Ontology
	Definition	The knowledge of web interface signs that refer to the institution or organization that owns a website or an application.
	Example	A number of participants interpreted the <Twitter> (see Fig. 2.i) sign correctly because they were familiar with Twitter. One responded "...*I never use Twitter. But I know what Twitter is .....*"
xi	*Ontology*	Cultural Ontology
	Definition	The knowledge of web interface signs which are specific to a particular cultural context.
	Example	One participant interpreted the <red color plus> (see Fig. 2.j) sign in a museum website as 'the museum's hospital or medical help center information', because this kind of sign (i.e., red color plus sign) represents hospital or medical help in her country of origin.
xii	*Ontology*	Website Ontology
	Definition	The knowledge of web interface signs which are specific to a particular website.
	Example	A number of participants were unable to interpret the <Close> sign (see Fig. 2.k) sign in an email application because they never visited this website and also were not familiar with the sign. One responded "....*I think it is something different because if it is for close then it should be X, but it has an arrow. So, may be it is for proceed. I never use this sign with arrow icon. However, it may mean closing a tab or email...*" This sign was actually designed for logging-out.

3.2   Ontology Mapping

The following features, related to ontology mapping in interpreting the meaning of interface signs, were also found in the study.

(i)   The set of ontologies found in this study includes both the designers' perspectives in interface signs design and the users' perspectives in interface signs interpretation. In other words, ontology derived from the users' perspective implies that it is referred to by the interface signs. For example, when a participant interpreted the 'Junk' sign (see Fig. 2.n) in an email application because of his familiarity with *Current Web Domain Ontology*, it shows that *Current Web Domain Ontology* is referred to by the 'Junk' sign from the designers' perspective.

(ii)   Participants used single or multiple ontologies to interpret the meaning of the interface sign. Similarly, an interface sign may belong to a single ontology or to multiple ontologies. However, a proper matching between ontology/ontologies referred to by an interface sign and the one(s) owned by the participants led them to interpret the meaning of interface signs correctly. For example, the <Spam> (see Fig. 2.g) sign in an email application pointed to the *Current Web Domain Ontology*. Participants familiar with the email application domain interpreted the meaning of this sign accurately. Again, the 'Contact' (see Fig. 2.e) sign in an email application built on multiple ontologies such as *Mobile Ontology, Current Web Domain Ontology, Internet Ontology, Other Web Domain Ontology,* and *Common-Sense Ontology*. A number of participants interpreted the meaning of this sign accurately because of their familiarity with these ontologies.

(iii) When multiple ontologies are referred to by an interface sign, then participants interpreted the sign meaning only for ontology/ontologies with which they were familiar (i.e., a familiar ontology supports an unfamiliar ontology to get the sign meaning). For example, the <Web Virtua> sign (see Fig. 2.l) in a university website assumed the *Current Web Domain Ontology, Cultural Ontology, Internet Ontology,* and *Website Ontology*. A few participants interpreted the meaning of this sign properly because of their familiarity with *Current Web Domain Ontology* (the appended images refer to the university library in a university website) and *Internet Ontology* (the term 'web' is familiar from internet access).

(iv)   An ontology conflict [12] occurred when participants were confused with which ontology/ontologies to consider in interpreting the meaning of an interface sign. Ontology conflict increased perceived interpretation difficulty as well as decreased meaning interpretations' accuracy. For example, the 'Close' (see Fig. 2.k) sign in an email application built on the *Website Ontology*, because the 'Close' sign was specific to this application for signing-out. A number of participants' treated this sign as built on *Computer Ontology, Common-Sense Ontology, Internet Ontology, or Mobile Ontology* to close an open or pop-up window. Thus, an ontology conflict occurred.

3.3   Difficulties Related to Different Kinds of Ontologies

This study also investigated the participants' difficulties in interpreting the meanings of interface signs belonging to different kinds of ontologies. The study found that difficulty experienced to interpret an interface sign by an individual depends on his or her familiarity with the ontology / ontologies assumed for the interface sign. For example, a participant familiar with *Current Web Domain Ontology* led him/her to interpret the meaning of interface signs that belong to the *Current Web Domain Ontology* with comparatively low perceived difficulty. However, because participants had heterogeneous profiles (i.e., they had different levels of familiarity with each kind of ontology), the study also found that participants experienced (a) lower level of perceived meaning interpretation difficulty with interface signs that belong to *Internet Ontology, Computer Ontology, Mobile Ontology, Current Web Domain Ontology, and Common-Sense Ontology;* (b) average level of perceived meaning interpretation difficulty with interface signs that belong to *Other Web Domain Ontology, System Ontology, Real World Ontology, Cultural Ontology, Organizational Ontology,* and *Topic Ontology;* and (c) higher level of perceived meaning interpretation difficulty with interface signs that belong to *Website Ontology*. For example, both 'logout' (see Fig. 2.m) and 'Close' (see Fig. 2.k) signs stand for logging-out from email applications. Participants experienced less perceived difficulty to interpret the meaning of 'Logout' sign and high perceived difficulty to interpret the meaning of the 'Close' sign because these signs belong to *Internet Ontology* and *Website Ontology* respectively and participants' familiarity level with these ontologies was high and less respectively.

4   Discussion and Conclusions

This paper explores ontologies of web interface signs for designing and evaluating web interfaces. The study results provide a set of ontologies to interpret the meaning of interface signs and a set of features of ontology mapping in interpreting the meaning of interface signs; and reveal the users' difficulty in interpreting the meaning of interface sign.

The results will help practitioners at least in the following two ways: Firstly, the results will assist practitioners to model the users' profiles based on their familiarity with ontologies, which in turn assist them to design and evaluate interface signs. Secondly, the results will provide the following set of ontological guidelines for interface sign design and evaluation:

(i)   design interface signs based on users' familiarity level with ontologies;

(ii)   design interface signs that belong to multiple ontologies;

(iii)   avoid ontology conflict when creating interface signs;

(iv)   (re)design interface signs which belong to ontologies, with which user experienced lower level of perceived difficulty (e.g., Internet Ontology); and

(v)   avoid to create interface signs that belong only to the 'Website Ontology'.

For researchers, a number of ways of fruitful research still remain such as conducting similar studies on mobile interfaces, conducting action research to validate the study outcomes, and the like. However, the author intends to conduct future work to validate the study results and alleviate the subjectivity of ontologies in web UI design and evaluation process to improve system usability.

Acknowledgements. The author would like to thank all the participants of this study. Finnish Economic Education Foundation and Nokia Foundation provided the grant that has made this research possible. For this, they are gratefully acknowledged.

References

1. Benbasat, I.: Human-Computer Interaction for Electronic Commerce: A Program of Studies to Improve the Communication between Customers and Online Stores. In: Galletta, D., Zing, P. (eds.) Human-Computer Interaction and Management Information Systems: Application, Armonk, NY, pp. 17–28 (2006)
2. Bolchini, D., Chatterji, R., Speroni, M.: Developing heuristics for the semiotics inspection of websites. In: Proceedings of the 27th ACM International Conference on Design of Communication, pp. 67–71. ACM Press, USA (2009)
3. De Souze, C.S.: The Semiotic Engineering of Human-Computer Interaction. MIT Press, Cambridge (2005)
4. Islam, M.N., Tétard, F.: Exploring the Impact of Interface Signs' Interpretation Accuracy, Design, and Evaluation on Web Usability: A Semiotics Perspective. Journal of Systems and Information Technology (2014)
5. de Souza, C.S., Leitão, C.F., Prates, R.O., da Silva, E.J.: The Semiotic Inspection Method. In: Proceedings of the VII Brazilian Symposium on Human Factors in Computing Systems, pp. 148–157. ACM Press, New York (2006)
6. Islam, M.N.: A Systematic Literature Review of Semiotics Perception in User Interfaces. Journal of Systems and Information Technology, 45–77 (2013)
7. Islam, M.N., Tétard, F.: Integrating Semiotics Perception in Usability Testing to Improve Usability Evaluation. In: Ruiz, M.A.G. (ed.) Cases on Usability Engineering: Design and Development of Digital Products, pp. 144–168. IGI Global, USA (2013)
8. Peirce, C.S.: Collected Writings. In. Hartshorne, C., Weiss&, P., Burks, A. (eds.), 8 vols. Harvard University Press, Cambridge (1931-1958)
9. Andersen, P.: Computer Semiotics. Scandinavian J. of Information Systems, 3–30 (1992)
10. Saussure, F.D.: Course in General Linguistics (trans. Harris, R.). Duckworth, London (1983)
11. Stam, R., Burgoyne, R., Lewis, S.F.: New Vocabularies in Film Semiotics: Structuralism, Post-Structuralism and Beyond. Taylor & Francis, London (1992)
12. Speroni, M.: Mastering the Semiotics of Information-Intensive Web Interfaces, Unpublished doctoral dissertation. University of Lugano, Switzerland (2006)
13. Islam, M.N.: Semiotics Perception towards Designing Users' Intuitive Web User Interface: A Study on Interface Signs. In: Rahman, H., Mesquita, A., Ramos, I., Pernici, B. (eds.) MCIS 2012. LNBIP, vol. 129, pp. 139–155. Springer, Heidelberg (2012)
14. Islam, M.N., Ali, M., Al-Mamun, A., Islam, M.: Semiotics Explorations on Designing the Information Intensive Web Interfaces. International Arab Journal of Information Technology, 45–54 (2010)
15. Islam, M.N.: Towards Designing Users' Intuitive Web Interface. In: Proceedings of the 6th International Conference on Complex, Intelligent, and Software Intensive Systems, pp. 513–518. IEEE CS, Sicilia (2012)
16. Islam, M.N.: Towards Exploring Web Interface Sign Ontology: A User Study. In: Stephanidis, C. (ed.) HCII 2013, Part I. Communications in Computer and Information Science, vol. 373, pp. 41–45. Springer, Heidelberg (2013)
17. Islam, M.N.: Towards Determinants of User-Intuitive Web Interface Signs. In: Marcus, A. (ed.) DUXU 2013, Part I. LNCS, vol. 8012, pp. 84–93. Springer, Heidelberg (2013)
18. Stanton, N.S., Young, M.S.: Guide to Methodology in Ergonomics: Designing for Human Use. Taylor and Francis, UK (1999)

Incorporating Semiotics into Fuzzy Logic to Enhance Clinical Decision Support Systems

Xiuxiu Chen[1,2], Huiying Gao[1], Kecheng Liu[2], and Ying Zhang[1,3]

[1] School of Management and Economics, Beijing Institute of Technology, Beijing, China
[2] Informatics Research Centre, Henley Business School, University of Reading, Reading, UK
[3] School of Management, University of Jinan, Shandong, China
Xiuxiu.Chen@pgr.reading.ac.uk, huiying@bit.edu.cn,
k.liu@reading.ac.uk, 172210826@qq.com

Abstract. In order to enhance the quality of care, healthcare organisations are increasingly resorting to clinical decision support systems (CDSSs), which provide physicians with appropriate health care decisions or recommendations. However, how to explicitly represent the diverse vague medical knowledge and effectively reason in the decision-making process are still problems we are confronted. In this paper, we incorporate semiotics into fuzzy logic to enhance CDSSs with the aim of providing both the abilities of describing medical domain concepts contextually and reasoning with vague knowledge. A semiotically inspired fuzzy CDSSs framework is presented, based on which the vague knowledge representation and reasoning process are demonstrated.

Keywords: Semiotics, Fuzzy logic theory, CDSSs, Knowledge representation, Knowledge reasoning.

1 Introduction

Clinical decision support systems (CDSSs) – known as the provision of patient-specific assessments or recommendations to support the clinical decision making [1], have been increasingly applied in various healthcare institutions. Previous studies have shown that CDSSs can improve the clinical practices [2], reduce serious medication errors and enhance the delivery of healthcare services. However, multiple challenges continue to impede the effective implementation of CDSSs. As vague information exists almost everywhere in the whole clinical decision making process, the interactions between organisational and technical factors should be considered when we design the CDSSs, especially during the representation and interpretation processes of the domain knowledge. Sources of vagueness or imprecision may be qualitative and quantitative. Qualitative vagueness is generated by lacking of precise measurements. For example, some symptoms (patients' facial expressions, feelings and behaviours) are usually described in some subjective terms. Quantitative vagueness is generated by lacking of precision in a measurement even when corresponding precise measurement exists. For example, the value of Body Mass Index (BMI) can be accurately calculated with height and weight. However, not

K. Liu et al. (Eds.): ICISO 2014, IFIP AICT 426, pp. 97–106, 2014.

everyone with a high BMI is obese, especially the one who exercises regularly. Besides, knowledge is usually characterized by a high level of context-dependency [3] and evolvement [4]; therefore, it cannot be defined independently without their pragmatic meanings. Thus, without appropriately handling with these challenges, the CDSSs might not support the clinical practice effectively. In order to address the aforementioned issues, we draw a refined underpinning and methodology to offer an adaptive framework of CDSSs integrating with more accurate knowledge representation and interpretation mechanism. By integrating the organisational semiotics and fuzzy theory, the proposed framework of CDSSs allows describing medical domain concepts contextually and reasoning with vague knowledge.

The reminder of the paper is organized as follows. Section 2 outlines the related theoretical background and main previous researches. The subsequent section provides a detailed illustration of the semiotically inspired fuzzy CDSSs framework; especially the knowledge representation is designed and reasoning process is discussed. Finally, section 4 draws our discussion and conclusions.

2   Theoretical Background

The proposed hybrid framework integrates two techniques, namely organisational semiotics and fuzzy logic theory, which are shortly outlined in the following sub-sections.

2.1   Organisational Semiotics

Organisational semiotics (OS) is a particularly branch of semiotics related to organisations, business and the IT system. From the OS perspective, IT systems or computer-based systems can be seen as the inside layer of the formal system in the organisational onion as shown in Fig.1, that means only a small part of the entire organisation. Therefore, in the IT system analysis and design, the related informal and formal aspects of the business should be firstly understood. Based on this view, the effective implementation of CDSSs requires a clear understanding and modelling of the interactions among these three aspects.

Moreover, the performance of CDSSs largely depends on its underlying knowledge base [7]. Stamper shares the view that knowledge is those signs interpreted at the

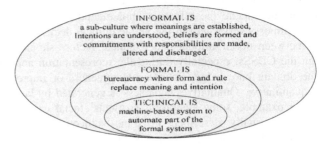

Fig. 1. The organisational onion [5-6]

social level of semiotic ladder (composed of physical word, empirics, syntax, semantics, pragmatics and social world), and it is equated with norms and attitudes [8]. Therefore, the explicit representation of knowledge should realize the mapping from the informal layer to the formal layer.

2.2 Fuzzy Logic Methodology

Fuzzy logic resembles human reasoning in its use of vague information to generate decisions [9]. Unlike classical set theory, fuzzy logic provides an alternative way of thinking about the complex system modelling, characterized with the membership of an element instead of the crisp value. The difference between the classical set and fuzzy set is shown in Fig. 2.

Definition 1. Fuzzy set A is described by some predefined range X (known as the universe of discourse) and the membership function μ_A, then

$$A = \left\{ \, (x_i, \mu_A(x_i)) \mid \forall x_i \in X, \mu_A(x_i) \in [0, 1] \, \right\} \qquad (1)$$

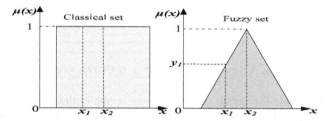

Fig. 2. Difference between classical set (*left*) and fuzzy set (e.g. triangular membership function) (*right*)

Because of the inherent vagueness of the medical knowledge, fuzzy logic has been utilized in many medical applications, such as the fuzzy expert support system for coronary artery disease screening using clinical parameters [10], determining the caloric intake requirement [11], and monitoring the multiple sclerosis [12]. However, fuzzy logic theory has limited ability to elicit the variables/elements and reflect their contextual interpretation. Therefore, incorporating the semiotic approach into fuzzy logic is a candidate solution for conceptual and computational modelling, which allows for the explicit representation of the contextual interpretation [3] and ensures the effective implementation of CDSSs.

3   Semiotically Inspired Fuzzy CDSSs Framework

In this paper, we propose the semiotically inspired fuzzy CDSSs framework, which is shown in the Fig. 3. It is based on the organisational onion, which integrates the informal and formal factors during the IT system design process. Moreover, the use of fuzzy logic enables the quantitative representation with the aim of reducing the ambiguity of knowledge, so that the reasoning as well as the utilization of the vague knowledge can be more effective to support the decision-making.

As shown in the Fig. 3, the proposed CDSSs framework can be described in three levels: informal, formal and technical level.

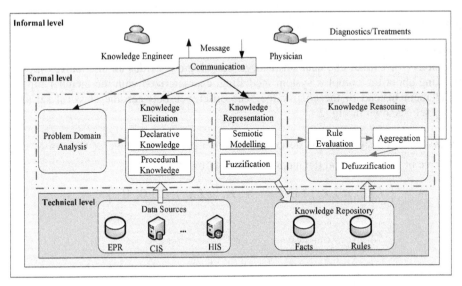

Fig. 3. Semiotically-inspired fuzzy CDDSs model

(1) Informal level: We define system users as agents in this paper, e.g. physicians, nurses, any other healthcare professionals and knowledge engineers. In this paper, we just take two main perspectives (knowledge engineer and physician) to illustrate the mechanism of this model in Fig. 3. The shared beliefs and values on the medical quality improvement and accuracy decision support strategy through the treatment process will be established. In real scenarios, all kinds of agents have to acquire various related data and deliver them to the computer-based system. But the substantial common understanding and explicit representation of these inputs are definitely based on the communications/interactions between the informal level and the formal level. For the physicians, the communication also provides the preparatory work for the following knowledge reasoning and treatment/diagnostics recommendations.

(2) Formal level: including the problem domain analysis, knowledge elicitation, knowledge representation and knowledge reasoning. We analysis these modules following the activity lines for knowledge engineer and physician, respectively.

As what we have discussed above, a good and effective decision support system cannot be independent on its underlying knowledge base. Therefore, for the knowledge engineers, they will firstly conduct the problem domain analysis, which focuses on the understanding of the organisation from both the informal and formal perspectives and investigating of the potential problem to be dealt with. Subsequently, they will elicit clinical knowledge from multiple sources and represent them with formalized specifications. During this elicitation and representation process, knowledge engineers have to coordinate the formal aspects with many informal aspects in the organisation with the communication module. For example, different physicians may have different preferences on the diagnostic criteria or subjective assessments on the non-verbal expressions; they may also have different beliefs such as low healthcare cost, high quality healthcare services and low healthcare risks; therefore, all of the vagueness should be considered when constructing the knowledge repository. All the elicited knowledge can be classified along two axes: declarative knowledge and procedural knowledge [13]. In particular, declarative knowledge describes all kinds of medical domain concepts, their attributes as well as the interrelationships between the concepts and attributes. On the other hand, procedural knowledge specifies a set of prescriptions for actions in relation to certain types of conditions or conclusions to be drawn from the declarative knowledge. In this paper, we introduce the context analysis based on the semiotic triangle model to represent and interpret imprecise knowledge. Specially, declarative knowledge will be interpreted with the semiotic triangle model (section 3.1) and stored in the knowledge facts repository, while procedural knowledge will be demonstrated with fuzzy set theory (section 3.2) and saved in fuzzy rules repository.

For the physicians, their activity line includes the knowledge representation and knowledge reasoning. Knowledge representation mainly addresses the definition of membership according to own understanding and context. In this paper, we adopt the Mamdani-style fuzzy inference procedures [14] to implement the fuzzy system, mainly composed of fuzzification of input variables, rule evaluation, aggregation of the rule outputs, and defuzzification.

(3) Technical level: automate the well-defined work procedures of the fuzzy clinical decision support system. It is developed to read signs, re-arrange signs, process and finally display them. Multiple sources of knowledge in this research are also defined in this level: (i) clinical data derived from other current healthcare IT applications including electronic patient record (EPR), clinical information system (CIS), laboratory information system (LIS), picture archiving and communications system (PACS), etc.; (ii) existing clinical pathways and other business processes/ procedures in use in hospitals; (iii) social knowledge or shared clinical experiences (recorded and observed) from community members; (iv) existing medical entities (basic statements about the medical concepts) and public medical classification terminologies such as SNOMED CT (Systematized Nomenclature of Medicine Clinical Terms); (v) medical educational resources for practitioners and (vi) academic resources like medical literatures and case studies. Besides, the implementation of knowledge repository including the facts and rules are built according to the informal and formal factors.

Obviously, the computer-based system presupposes a formal system, just as the formal system relies on an informal system. Information flow and interactions among these three levels should be considered in the design of the CDSSs, especially facing the inherent vagueness of the medical knowledge.

3.1   Knowledge Fact Representation

In this sub-section, we will further discuss the conceptual modelling in a broader context of knowledge fact representation, mainly focus on the understanding and interpreting of medical knowledge.

An explicit representation of the medical knowledge is critical for the proper functions of CDSSs. However, the elements of medical knowledge must be defined within a context of their usage for a specific patient, at a specific time, for a specific purpose, by a specific healthcare professional. Although many existing clinical diagnostic criteria and domain terminology (e.g. SNOMED CT, ICD-10) indicate the diagnosis and treatment for diseases, the definition of domain concepts is not context-aware and still requires the communication in the creation of their meanings, especially for the inherent characteristics of medical knowledge such as the vagueness and context-dependency. Therefore, in this paper, the knowledge representation approach based on the peircean semiotic triangle (object, representamen and interpretant) is introduced, as shown in Fig. 4. We define the object as multi-dimensional variables /concepts including the quantitatively measurable variables and qualitative (subjective) ones, meanwhile, the sign stands for several specific measurements such as multi-parameters on various types of instruments/sensors, laboratory report, CT, observations, questionnaires and psychological scales. Interpretant is the most complex notion in this model and it provides not only semantic meaning but also pragmatic significance. The intepretant is identified by the context in several dimensions: agents (e.g. healthcare professionals, nurses, patients), intentions (e.g. treatment, assessment), preferences (e.g. subjective assessment for the measurements), and temporal information. Therefore, the meanings of any medical elements will be quite different according to their possible interpretations.

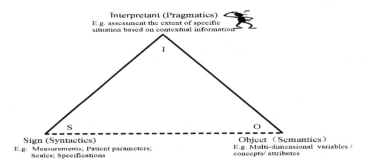

Fig. 4. Semiotic triangle for knowledge fact representation process (adapted from Peirce's theory)

For the qualitative measurable variables mentioned above, for example, physical activeness, dietary habits, sedentary behaviour and quality of life, they are quite difficult to define, measure, or quantify. Even for some quantitatively measurable variables, e.g. age, the group they belong to might be more meaningful than the actual values for the healthcare professionals. Besides, several cut-off values for existing diagnosis criteria are often arbitrarily established. For example, the value of Body Mass Index (BMI) greater than or equal to 30 indicates obesity; however, somebody whose BMI equals to 29 and be with small muscle mass may means higher fat than a muscular person with BMI = 32. Therefore, fuzzy logic theory is adopted in the interpretation process.

Based on the analysis above, a piece of knowledge fact can be represented by a quintuple:

$$KF = \langle C, T(C), U, I(P, H, M, T) \rangle \tag{2}$$

Where C is a set of related concepts/variables; $T(C)$ is the set of terms for C, U is the universe of discourse; I, the function of P, H, M and T, means the interpretation process; P stands for a specific patient; H stands for a specific health professional; M represents the possible measurements; T means a specific time. Set of the terms will be identified for each concept, such as 'very mild', 'mild', 'moderate', 'severe', and 'extremely severe' for the concept of *stress*. It is also worth mentioning that attributes of the concepts can also be defined when required, e.g. *frequency* and *intensity* for the concept of *stress*. The measurements are mapped into these defined terms according to the interpretation process. With the function I, crisp assessment value for various measurements (especially for the qualitative measurable variables) will be produced as the input data of the fuzzy CDSSs.

3.2 Fuzzy Reasoning Process

The medical domain knowledge must be translated into a computational model in order to be identified by the computer-based system. This sub-section will describe the fuzzy reasoning process in four steps, namely fuzzification, rule evaluation, aggregation, defuzzification, as shown in Fig. 5.

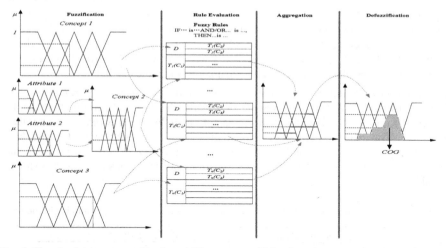

Fig. 5. Sketch of the computational modelling process (Take three-input process as an example. D means the output concept for final decision, which is also described as a fuzzy set).

Step 1: Fuzzification. With the interpretation process, not only the quantitative variables but also the qualitative ones will be assigned an appropriate crisp value belongs to the universe of discourse. In this step, crisp input values will be converted into corresponding fuzzy terms with appropriate membership degree values. Fig. 6 shows the membership functions for five defined terms of concept "*physical activeness*". The membership functions will be constructed with the communication

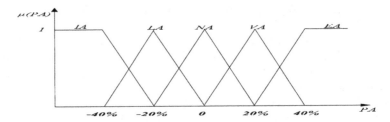

Fig. 6. Example for the membership functions of physical activeness

between knowledge engineers and healthcare professionals, with the consideration of the context information.

In Fig. 6, the *PA* axis refers to the universe of the discourse for the physical activeness, whereas the $\mu(PA)$ axis represents the degrees of membership in the [0, 1] interval. The terms of the subset *PA* are $\{IA, LA, NA, VA, EA\}$ where *IA* = inactive; *LA* = lightly active; *NA* = neutral active, *VA* = very active; *EA* = extremely active. Trapezoids and triangles are chosen to represent the membership functions, e.g., the membership function of *LA* is triangular (-40%,-20%, 0).

***Step 2:** Rule evaluation.* In this step, multiple fuzzy inputs generated last step can be seen as the antecedents of the fuzzy rules. All the possible values for these antecedents will be calculated according to the defined fuzzy rules. These fuzzy rules are developed by integrating the experiences of healthcare professionals and those of knowledge engineers with the consideration of the problem characteristics. The formal format of fuzzy rule is "If antecedent is…, then consequent is …". Take the type-2 diabetes mellitus (T2DM) prediction as an example. If we adopt *BMI, Physical activeness and Stress* as three variables, therefore, one typical knowledge rule can be:

If *BMI* is *very high* and *Physical activeness* is *inactive* and *Stress* is *extremely severe,* then *the risk for the T2DM* is *very high*. Especially, the "*Stress*" variable here can be qualified with two attributes of this concept, namely the *has-intensity* and *has-frequency*. The reasoning process also applies the fuzzy logic, e.g. If stress *has-intensity* is *extremely high* and stress *has-frequency* is *almost-all-the-time*, then the *stress* is *extremely severe*. Part of the classifications of fuzzy rules repository is shown in Table 1.

Table 1. Classifications of fuzzy rules (based on our previous work [15-16] and background)

Rule repository classification	Potential application scenario
Clinical diagnosis	Evaluation of a patient's condition;
	Evaluation of clinician's suggestions.
Preventive reminders	Health maintenance;
	Clinical prevention for certain diseases.
Nutrition	Caloric intake requirement;
	Form healthy dietary habits.
Behaviour recommendation	Physical activity and calorie consumption.
Examination	Recommended examinations for certain diseases
Consultation	Assessment for the mental disorders.

Suppose we have predefined n variables, according to membership functions for a group of defined terms, 2^n fuzzy rules in one form can be activated at the same time. The values of consequents for these activated rules can be calculated with Mamdani Operator [11], shown in Eq. 3.

$$\mu(V_1, V_2, \ldots, V_n) = \phi \left[\mu_{V_1}(v_1), \mu_{V_2}(v_2), \ldots, \mu_{V_n}(v_n) \right]$$

$$= \mu_{V_1}(v_1) \wedge \mu_{V_2}(v_2) \wedge \ldots \wedge \mu_{V_n}(v_n)$$

(3)

Step 3: *Aggregation.* In this step, all the results of consequents in step 2 will be integrated into a final fuzzy set with the aggregation operator, union ($\vee$). The process can be seen clearly in the Fig. 5 with the comparison of aggregation step and defuzzification step. The shade area in the defuzzifation diagram indicates the final aggregation result.

Step 4: *Defuzzification.* It is the final step for the computer-based system. In this step, linguistic or crisp value (if required) can be obtained. The most popular technique to convert fuzzy set into a single number is calculating the centre of gravity (COG) of the fuzzy set (shaded area in Fig.5), using Eq. 4.

$$COG(A) = \frac{\int_a^b \mu_A(x) \, x \, dx}{\int_a^b \mu_A(x) \, dx}$$

(4)

Where A represents the final aggregation fuzzy set, its universe of course is $[a, b]$.

4   Discussion and Conclusions

CDSS is increasingly important in supporting the clinical practices including prevention, diagnosis, treatment, evaluation and long-term care. Its performance can be affected by the communication between the business and technical factors in the healthcare organisations, especially because of these characteristics of medical knowledge such as vagueness and context-dependency. In this paper, a semiotically-inspired fuzzy CDSS framework is proposed, while two key points, namely vague knowledge representation and reasoning, are illustrated. The innovation of this study is twofold. Firstly, we emphasize the role of informal factors with the organisational onion in the design phase and operation of CDSS, as the vagueness and imprecision are the intrinsic characteristics of medical knowledge. The contextual information and communication are considered in their definition and interpretation processes. Specifically, we explain the knowledge presentation process with semiosis and construct the knowledge representation model. Secondly, we modify the reasoning process with the semiotic thinking to support CDSS, which is also the formal part of the proposed framework. Although the application of fuzzy logic in healthcare is definitely not new, integrating the fuzzy logic and semiotics in an organisational perspective is necessary for the decision-making process, especially in the definition of membership functions of various linguistic variables and their attributes. Besides, we have applied this approach in a CDSS for the purpose of supporting the diagnosis and treatment of T2DM in a clinical setting in China.

On the other hand, this research faces some potential challenges. The most obvious one would be the computational efficiency. The active knowledge rules will be much more complicated with the increasing of the input variables and the complexity of membership functions. Therefore, future work could involve how to elicit the most significant variables and how to further refine the knowledge rule. Moreover, some potential application area could be integrating the multiple sensors with the proposed framework with the aim of providing a wider range of support, such as the homecare and mobile hospital for the chronic patients.

Acknowledgments. The research is supported by the Beijing Municipal Natural Science Foundation under Grant 9133020 and scholarship program sponsored by China Scholarship Council (CSC). Special thanks to Hongqiao Yang, the Director of the Information Centre of Hospital 309 of People's Liberation Army, China, for providing the research background and valuable guidance.

References

1. Hunt, D.L., Haynes, R.B., Hanna, S.E., Smith, K.: Effects of computer-based clinical decision support systems on physician's performance and patient outcomes: a systematic review. The Journal of American Medical Association 280, 1339–1946 (1998)
2. Kawamoto, K., Houlihan, C.A., Balas, E.A., Lobach, D.F.: Improving clinical practice using clinical decision support systems: a systematic review of trials to identify features critical to success. British Medical Journal 330, 765–768 (2005)
3. Kwiatkowska, M., Kielan, K.: Fuzzy logic and semiotic methods in modelling of medical concepts. Fuzzy Sets and Systems 214, 35–50 (2013)
4. Taborsky, E.: Semiosis, information and knowledge. Organisational Semiotics - Evolving a science of information systems, 189–210 (2002)
5. Stamper, R.K.: Language and computer in organized behaviour. Linguistic Instruments in Knowledge Engineering, 143–163 (1992)
6. Liu, K.: Semiotics in information systems engineering. Cambridge University Press, Cambridge (2000)
7. Purcell, G.P.: What makes a good clinical decision support system? British Medical Journal 330, 740–741 (2005)
8. Stamper, R.K.: Organisational semiotics: informatics without the computer? In: Information, Organisation and Technology: Studies in Organisational Semiotics, pp. 115–171. Kluwer Academic Publishers, Boston (2001)
9. Zadeh, L.A.: Fuzzy sets. Information and Control 8, 338–353 (1965)
10. Pal, D., Mandana, K.M., Pal, S., Sarkar, D., Chakraborty, C.: Fuzzy expert system approach for coronary artery disease screening using clinical parameters. Knowledge-Based Systems 36, 162–174 (2012)
11. Nakandala, D., Lau, H.C.W.: A novel approach to determining change of caloric intake requirement based on fuzzy logic methodology. Knowledge-Based Systems 36, 51–58 (2012)
12. Cox, E.: Fuzzy modelling and genetic algorithms for data mining and exploration. Morgan Kaufmann (2005)
13. Ryle, G.: The concept of mind. Hutchinson of London (1949)
14. Esposito, M., Pietro, G.D.: An ontology-based fuzzy decision support system for multiple sclerosis. Engineering Applications of Artificial Intelligence 24, 1340–1354 (2011)
15. Li, W., Liu, K., Yang, H., Yu, C.: Integrated clinical pathway management for medical quality improvement-based on a semiotically inspired systems architecture. European Journal of Information Systems, 1–18 (2013)
16. Yang, H., Li, W., Liu, K., Zhang, J.: Knowledge-based clinical pathway for medical quality improvement. Information Systems Frontiers 14, 105–117 (2012)

Multifractal Analysis on the Return Series of Stock Markets Using MF-DFA Method

Wanting Wang[1,2], Kecheng Liu[1,2], and Zheng Qin[2,3]

[1] Henley Business School, University of Reading,
RG6 6UD, Reading, UK
wwt159753@gmail.com
[2] School of Information Management and Engineering,
Shanghai University of Finance and Economics, 777 Guoding Rd,
200433 Shanghai, China
k.liu@henley.ac.uk
[3] South University of Science and Technology of China, 1028 Xueyuan Ave,
518055 Shenzhen, China
qinzheng@mail.shufe.edu.cn

Abstract. Analyzing the daily returns of NASDAQ Composite Index by using MF-DFA method has led to findings that the return series does not fit the normal distribution and its leptokurtic indicates that a single-scale index is insufficient to describe the stock price fluctuation. Furthermore, it is found that the long-term memory characteristics are a main source of multifractality in time series. Based on the main reason causing multifractality, a contrast of the original return series and the reordered return series is made to demonstrate the stock price index fluctuation, suggesting that the both return series have multifractality. In addition, the empirical results verify the validity of the measures which illustrates that the stock market fails to reach the weak form efficiency.

Keywords: Stock market fluctuations, Generalized Hurst Exponent, Multifractal, MF-DFA, Time series.

1 Introduction

Since the stock market was established, there are numerous bull and bear markets. It is hard to find a proper way to understand the unusual patterns, but the efficient market theory provides a widely applicable opinion. The efficient market theory is the cornerstone of modern finance, which is first proposed by Bachelier [1]. Fama establishes EMH (Efficient Market Hypothesis) theory [2]. However, the efficient theory cannot explain many actual phenomena that appear in stock markets, such as Black Monday or the breakdown of U.S. stock market in October 1987. Also, the statistical characteristics of financial data appear the fat tail, long-term memory characteristics, volatility clustering, self-similarity, and so on. For these visions, it is necessary to develop a new method to capture the characteristics of stock price fluctuations in order to perform better risk estimation, prevention and control.

K. Liu et al. (Eds.): ICISO 2014, IFIP AICT 426, pp. 107–115, 2014.

2   Literature Review

Mandelbrot first proposes fractal theory in the 1970s [3]. In 1997, Mandelbrot proposes a multifractal model of asset returns to describe the variation of financial asset prices and he points out that the multifractal analysis can be reproduced volatile financial transactions and provide information on the predicted value of market trends, thus showing some regularity of various financial markets [4]. It has been verified that multifractality widely exists in financial markets such as stock markets, future markets, spot markets, foreign exchange markets, derivative markets, interest rate markets and so on [5-9].

MF-DFA, short for multifractal detrended fluctuation analysis, is first proposed by Kantelhardt [10], which can describe different statistical characteristics of time series on different time scales, also is an efficient way to test whether non-stationary time series is multifractal. It considers the average volatility of time series of each interval as a statistical point to calculate volatility functions, and then determines the generalized Hurst exponents based on the power law of volatility functions. Its advantages are the ability to discover the long-term correlation in non-stationary time series and to avoid the misjudgment of correlation. Norouzzadeh et al. studies the Iranian Rial-US dollar exchange rate logarithmic variations through MF-DFA [11]. They find that the time series exhibits multifractality, which is mostly due to different long-range correlations for small and large fluctuations. Ying et al. measures multifractality in Shanghai stock market using MF-DFA [12] and finds that the generalized Hurst exponent can capture multifractality better. Panigrahi et al. characterizes price index behavior through fluctuation dynamics, involving companies listed on New York Stock Exchange [13]. They use wavelet based multifractal detrended fluctuation analysis to analyze companies' self-similar and non-statistical properties.

However, most recent studies are focused on the original price series or its deformation; thus they have not detected the contribution of long-term memory characteristics on multifractality. This paper uses both the original return series and the reordered return series in order to study stock price fluctuations and discuss their connection; therefore, providing a better way to understand the stock price fluctuations.

3   Methodology

For series $\{x(i)\}$, where $i = (1, 2, \cdots, N)$ and N is the length of $\{x(i)\}$, the MF-DFA method is as following.

Through the sum process, the original series $\{x(i)\}$ merges into a new series $\{y(j)\}$, with $\bar{x}$ indicating the mean value of series $\{x(i)\}$.

$$y(j) = \sum_{i=1}^{j} [x(i) - \bar{x}], \ i = (1, 2, \cdots, N) \tag{1}$$

Next, divide the new series $\{y(j)\}$ into $N_s = int\left(\frac{N}{s}\right)$ non-overlapping segments of equal length s. Usually time scale s is not an integer multiple of length N, so repeating the same procedure from the opposite end to get the whole part of series $\{y(j)\}$ other than disregard extra parts. Therefore, total $2N_s$ segments are obtained.

$$y_v(j) = y(l + j), j = (1, 2, \cdots, s), \; v = (1, 2, \cdots, 2N_s), \; l = (v - 1)s \tag{2}$$

Fit local trend function $\tilde{y}_v(j)$ on $2N_s$ sub segments v by the least squares method in order to eliminate the local trends in each sub segments v and get the residuals series $\varepsilon_v(j)$.

$$\varepsilon_v(j) = y_v(j) - \tilde{y}_v(j), \; j = (1, 2, \cdots, s) \tag{3}$$

Then calculate the mean squared value of $2N_s$ sub segments without local trends.

$$F^2(s, v) = \frac{1}{s}\sum_{j=1}^{s}\varepsilon_v^2(j) = \frac{1}{s}\sum_{j=1}^{s}\{y[(v - 1)s + j] - \tilde{y}_v(j)\}^2, \tag{4}$$

$$v = (1, 2, \cdots, N_s)$$

$$F^2(s, v) = \frac{1}{s}\sum_{j=1}^{s}\{y[N - (v - N_s)s + j] - \tilde{y}_v(j)\}^2, \tag{5}$$

$$v = (N_s + 1, N_s + 2, \cdots, 2N_s)$$

Also average all segments to get the q-th order fluctuation function.

$$\begin{cases} F_q(s) = \left\{\dfrac{1}{2N_s}\sum_{v=1}^{2N_s}[F^2(s, v)]^{\frac{q}{2}}\right\}^{\frac{1}{q}}, \; q \neq 0 \\[3mm] F_0(s) = \exp\left\{\dfrac{1}{4N_s}\sum_{v=1}^{2N_s}\ln[F^2(v, s)]\right\}, \; q = 0 \end{cases} \tag{6}$$

To any fixed q, determine the scaling exponent of fluctuation function, and the relationship between $F_q(s)$ and s is obtained.

$$F_q(s) \propto s^{h(q)} \tag{7}$$

For every time scale s, we can get a correspondent value $F_q(s)$. The q-th order generalized Hurst exponent is the slope of $Ln(F_q(s)) \sim Ln(s)$. Here, if $h(q)$ is a constant and independent from q, the series $\{x(i)\}$ is monofractal; and if $h(q)$ is a function of q, the series $\{x(i)\}$ is multifractal.

The multifractal spectrum $f(\alpha)$ is another efficient way to describe the multifractal time series. The $h(q)$ generated by MF-DFA is related to Renyi exponent $\tau(q)$.

$$\tau(q) = qh(q) - 1 \tag{8}$$

Thus the multifractal spectrum $f(\alpha)$ can be generated by formula (9) and (10).

$$\alpha = h(q) + qh'(q) \qquad (9)$$

$$f(\alpha) = q[\alpha - h(q)] + 1 \qquad (10)$$

Furthermore, we define the range Δh of generalized Hurst exponents $h(q)$ to measure the degree of multifractality. The greater the Δh is, the stronger the degree of multifractality is and the more severe the fluctuation is.

$$\Delta h = h_{\max}(q) - h_{min}(q) \qquad (11)$$

4   Empirical Research

4.1   Data Description

The daily closing prices of NASDAQ Composite Index (IXIC) from 31 December 2008 to 31 December 2013 are selected as the sample data. Total 1259 data are derived from Yahoo! Finance and calculated in MATLAB R2012b. Based on the original prices, we assume I_t represents the closing price in time t; thus the logarithmic rate of return R_t in time t is as formula (12).

$$R_t = \ln(I_t) - \ln(I_{t-1}) \qquad (12)$$

Therefore, total 1258 daily logarithmic rates of return R_t ($t = 1, 2, \cdots, 1258$) are obtained, shown as Fig. 1.

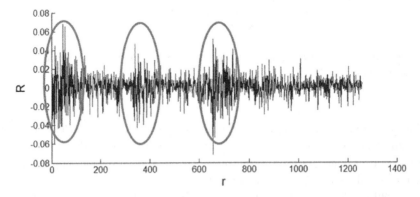

Fig. 1. Daily logarithmic rates of return R of NASDAQ Composite Index (IXIC) from 01 January 2009 to 31 December 2013 have three obvious aggregated fluctuations, illustrating the long-term memory characteristics of NASDAQ

Table 1. The fundamental statistics of R

Series	Mean	Median	Variance	Kurtosis	Skewness
R	0.000744	0.0011	0.0132	6.3116	-0.2028

The table 1 illustrates the skewness of return series is not equal to 0 and the kurtosis is much larger than it of normal distribution, which is approximately equal to 3. The fundamental statistics show that the return series is not normally distributed and has leptokartic characteristics, indicating that traditional EMH is not a proper way to describe the return series.

However, the long-term memory characteristics of low or high volatility in time series also cause multifractal behaviors. In this paper, random reordering process is used to eliminate the data correlation and keep the volatility, demonstrating the volatility of reordered series is the same as the original one, without long-term memory characteristics. Figure 2 is generated by the following random reordering procedures.

First, to generate a random pair of natural numbers (a, b), in which a and b are less than or equal to the length N of time series.

Second, to change the a-th and the b-th number in time series.

Third, to repeat the above two procedures $20*N$ times, in order to make sure the order fully disrupted.

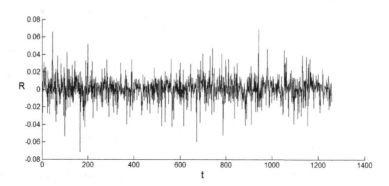

Fig. 2. Reordered return series $R_{reordered}$ of NASDAQ Composite Index (IXIC) from 01 January 2009 to 31 December 2013 has the same fluctuation distribution as the original one. Also, there are no obvious aggregated fluctuations, indicating the reordering process is effective.

4.2   Empirical Research Results

The MF-DFA method is applied to the daily logarithmic rates of return R and its reordered series $R_{reordered}$. Here we define parameter q is [-10, -8, -6, -4, -2, 0, 2, 4, 6, 8, 10] and s is an integer array, ranging from 3 to $\frac{N}{5}$, where N is the length of R and $R_{reordered}$. Fig. 3 shows the fluctuation function $F_q(s)$ of both R and $R_{reordered}$

series in NASDAQ. Fig. 4 shows the generalized Hurst exponents H_q of two series, which depends on q, by $3 \leq s \leq \frac{N}{5}$. The different values of $h(q)$, the results of MF-DFA, are illustrated in table 2, when q changes from -10 to 10.

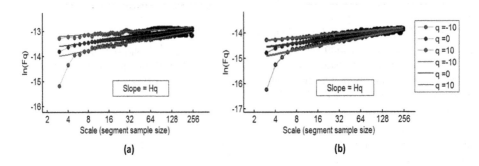

Fig. 3. The multifractal fluctuation function $F_q(s)$ of the return series R for NASDAQ is figure (a); and $F_q(s)$ of $R_{reordered}$ is figure (b). The upper, the middle and the lower curves are the curves of $q=10$, $q=0$, and $q=-10$. This figure also shows the generalized Hurst exponents H_q of $R_{reordered}$ is slightly greater than those of R; and the goodness of fit is better. E.g. When $q=-10$, $H_q(R) = 0.757591165$ and $H_q(R_{reordered}) = 0.809184708$.

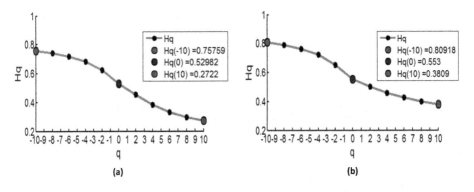

Fig. 4. The generalized Hurst exponents H_q of R and $R_{reordered}$ are not constants but the function with respect to q, indicating multifractality in R and $R_{reordered}$. Figure (a) is for R and figure (b) is for $R_{reordered}$.

As can be seen in table 2, when q changes from -10 to10, the $h(q)$ of original return series descends from 0.757591 to 0.272200 and the $h(q)$ of reordered return series descends from 0.809185 to 0.380904. Both $h(q)$ are not constant, indicating that there is obvious multfractality. So using monofractal model to describe is not appropriate.

Comparing both return series, the $h(q)$ of reordered one is closer to 0.5 than it of original one, because $Var(h(R)) = 0.035$ and $Var(h(R_{reordered})) = 0.027$. Therefore, the relevance of $R_{reordered}$ is higher than it of R.

Table 2. The generalized Hurst exponents $h(q)$ of R and $R_{reordered}$, when q is from -10 to 10

Order q	$h(q)$ of R	$h(q)$ of $R_{reordered}$
-10	0.757591	0.809185
-8	0.741504	0.789698
-6	0.718603	0.761953
-4	0.684111	0.720634
-2	0.623898	0.651603
0	0.529818	0.552996
2	0.452512	0.500296
4	0.382411	0.458481
6	0.330822	0.424952
8	0.295986	0.399629
10	0.272200	0.380904
Δh	0.485391	0.428281

When q is a negative or relatively small positive number, $h(q) > 0.5$. The small fluctuations of the rates of return are amplified, expressing the persistent feature. Correspondingly, when q is a relatively large positive number, $h(q) < 0.5$, indicating that the large fluctuations are dominant; therefore, anti-persistent feature is clear.

For a given q, each $h(q)$ of original return series is less than it of reordered one, indicating that the persistent characteristic of $R_{reordered}$ is stronger and the anti-persistent characteristic is more weaken. Meanwhile, after reordering, Δh reduces and the multifractality weakens. Because $h(q)$ changes slightly with q, which is not significant, it is a proof that the long-term memory characteristics of returns can lead to multifractality. $\Delta h(R) > \Delta h(R_{reordered})$, so the multifractality of R is more obvious.

Furthermore, the characteristics of multifractality are analyzed by combining MF-DFA and multifractal spectrum. According to formula (8), the relationship between $\tau(q)$ and q can be obtained, shown as Fig. 5. For monofractal, $\tau(q)$ is linear; for multifractal, $\tau(q)$ is nonlinear. And the stronger the nonlinearity is, the stronger the multifractality is. As can be seen from Fig. 5, the nonlinearity in $\tau(q)$ of reordered return series is obviously more weaken than it of original one. It also illustrates our interpretation of Fig. 4 and table 2.

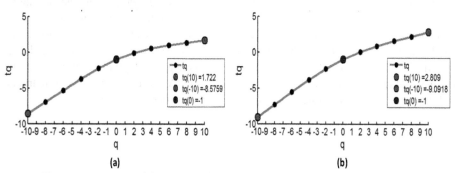

Fig. 5. Multifractal $\tau(q) \sim q$: Figure (a) is for R and figure (b) is for $R_{reordered}$

Finally, according to formula (9) and (10), the multifractal spectrums of both series can be captured, shown as Fig. 6. The multifractal spectrum width of reordered return series is less than it of original one, illustrating the interpretation of Fig. 5. The variety of reordered return series confirms that persistent relevance is an important factor to the multi-scaling changes in price volatility.

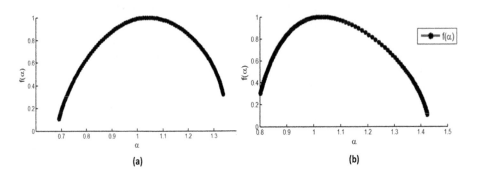

(a)   (b)

Fig. 6. Multifractal Spectrum $f(\alpha) \sim \alpha$: Figure (a) is for R and figure (b) is for $R_{reordered}$.

5   Conclusions

The multifractal model is more appropriate to describe the price variance. MF-DFA, which is executed in this paper, captures the multifractality in both the original return series and the reordered one.

Through the statistical research on NASDAQ Composite Index using MF-DFA, it is discovered that the long-term memory characteristics of the return volatility are a main reason of multifractality in the stock market. The empirical results also suggest that the entire stock market is not a random process, but a process affected by large and small fluctuations in some periods. The correlation of return volatility, especially the persistent relevance, contributes to the multi-scaling changes in price volatility.

In fact, the long-term memory enables us to recall noise, opaque prices in stock markets and other complex information. In addition, investors also respond to the market in a non-linear way. They begin to act only when the information accumulated to a certain extent and to trade at an accepted price other than a fair price. Their behaviours lead to the stock price walking in a biased random way; therefore, the stock market is hard to reach the weak form efficiency. How to understand the multifratcality in financial markets and how to characterize the multifractal indicators of financial risks are the two key issues in the future. A fresh look at financial markets will help make more accurate risk estimation and control.

References

1. Barchelier, L.: The theory of speculation. Annales Scientifiques de l'École Normale Supérieure 3(17), 21–86 (1990)
2. Fama, F.E.: Efficient Capital Markets: A Review of Theory and Empirical Work. The Journal of Finance 25(2), 385–417 (1970)
3. Mandelbrot, B.B.: Fractals: Form, Chance and Dimension. W.H. Freeman, San Francisco (1977)
4. Mandelbrot, B.B., Fisher, J.A., Calvet, E.L.: A Multifractal Model of Asset Return. Working paper in Yale University (1997)
5. Karuppiah, J., Los, C.A.: Wavelet Multiresolution Analysis of High-frequency Asian FX Rates. International Review of Financial Analysis 14, 211–246 (2005)
6. Norouzzadeh, P., Jafari, G.R.: Application of Multifractal Measures to Tehran Price Index. Physica A. 356, 609–627 (2005)
7. Cajueiro, D.O., Tabak, B.M.: Long-range Dependence and Multifractality in the Term Structure of LIBOR Interest Rates. Physica A. 373, 603–614 (2007)
8. Lee, K.E., Lee, L.W.: Probability Distribution Function and Multiscaling Properties in the Korean Stock Market. Physica A. 383(1), 65–70 (2007)
9. Lim, G., Kim, S.Y., Lee, H., Kim, K., Lee, D.I.: Multifractal Detrended Fluctuation Analysis of Derivative and Spot Markets. Physica A. 386, 259–266 (2007)
10. Kantelhardt, J.W., Zschiegner, S.A., Koscielny-Bunde, E., et al.: Multifractal Detrended Fluctuation Analysis of Non-stationary Time Series. Physica A. 361, 87–114 (2002)
11. Norouzzadeh, P., Rahmani, B.: A Multifractal Detrended Fluctuation Description of Iranian Rial-US Dollar Exchange Rate. Physica A. 367, 328–336 (2006)
12. Ying, Y., Zhuang, X.T., Jin, X.: Measuring Multifractality of Stock Price Fluctuation Using multifractal Detrended Fluctuation Analysis. Physica A. 388, 2189–2197 (2009)
13. Panigrahi, K.P., Ghosh, S., Banerjee, A., Bahadur, J., Manimaran, P.: Econophysics of Systemic Risk and Network Dynamics, pp. 287–295. Springer (2013)

Exploiting Linked Data in Financial Engineering

Vivian Lee[*], Masatomo Goto, Bo Hu, Aisha Naseer, Pierre-Yves Vandenbussche,
Gofran Shakair, and Eduarda Mendes Rodrigues

Fujitsu
vivian.lee@uk.fujitsu.com

Abstract. In this paper, we report on a recent initiative that exploiting Linked
Data for financial data integration. Financial data present high heterogeneity.
Linked Data helps to reveal the true data semantics and "hidden" connection,
upon which meaningful mappings can be constructed. The work reported in this
paper has been well-accepted at several public events and conferences, including
the 26th XBRL conference, involving the realisation of the XBRL (eXtensible
Business Reporting Language) prototype called HIKAKU, which means
"comparison" in Japanese. It demonstrates our approach to exploit the power of
Linked Data in enhancing flexibility for data integration in the financial domain.

Keywords: Financial Engineering, Financial Reporting, XBRL (eXtensible
Business Reporting Language), Governmental Data, Linked Data, Data driven
platform.

1 Introduction

The Ki2NA platform is a data-centric platform whose applications are driven by
interactions with Linked Data in a unified way. It is developed with shorten the
development cycles and thus the time to the market as the main design principle. To
achieve this goal, adopts a universal approach to treat data is the key. The Linked Data
basis of the platform is designed to ensure the universal data treatment is applied. This
is evident from the following design decisions: 1) the underlying data storage is
heterogeneous and can be assembled for optimisation according to the specific needs of
each application? 2) metadata services from LOD4all provide data discovery services?
3) modelling constructs such as the data-cube observation model are transferable across
multiple application domains? 4) APIs and query language provide consistent access to
data and associated services that drive applications.

The purpose of the HIKAKU application is twofold: i) the business value of the
LOD4all service (a Linked Open Data Repository being developed in the scope of
Ki2NA) through the development of a financial prototype featuring XBRL data and ii)
the benefit of using Linked Data technologies to combine XBRL data with open data to
enhance financial analysts' experience.

In order to motivate our research and development, we firstly outline current issues
in the financial domain and how this impacts on corporate financial reporting. This is

---

[*] Corresponding author.

K. Liu et al. (Eds.): ICISO 2014, IFIP AICT 426, pp. 116–125, 2014.

then followed by a review of related work and an exploration of the potential of Linked Data to address these issues. The current HIKAKU application is also discussed in detail, together with the key user benefits. In conclusion, we provide the future roadmap and proposed extensions to this prototype.

1.1   Financial Reporting

Financial reporting is the communication of financial information about an enterprise to the external world/public. Thus far, the corporate financial reporting practice has been questioned on two counts. On the one hand, the current financial reporting framework was largely shaped during and immediately after the first industrial revolution in response to the emergence of corporate form, stock market, and the regulation of accounting and auditing practices. Due to the intricate nature of financial instruments, the complexity of financial reporting is inevitable. Obscure legal terms designed to avoid stating responsibility in a black-white fashion have aggravated the magnitude of complexity. As a result, it becomes increasingly challenging for investors, who are not professionally educated/trained, to distil the messages conveyed in such reports [5]. Financial report tooling should, therefore, not only assist authoring, but also facilitate comprehension.

On the other hand, since the latest technological revolution, the corporate structure has undergone fundamental changes that start to render the conventional reporting approach less desirable for modern companies. Some of such fundamental changes include the difference between the market value and book value of company assets, the establishment of off-shore financial centres and off-shore financing channels, far-reaching globalisation, etc. Evidence of rigid constraints and a general lack of flexibility translate into financial reporting that is based on conventional auditing and accounting methodology, which starts to struggle in faithfully reflecting the performance of companies. This is particularly true for social media and e-commerce businesses, whose true value can only be revealed using data other than balance sheets, profit/loss statements, and cash flow statements.

However, there have been some efforts to address such problems. The recent advances in ICT, especially in the automation of data integration, has already been embraced by the business world and paved the way of for financial reporting mechanism that is well aligned with the emerging business practice.

1.2   Related Work

One important benefit of applying Linked Data principles to the financial domain is the increased data inter-operability across multiple financial systems and financial instruments [7]. The financial industry has long acknowledged the necessity of aligning different data providers[2]. This is evident in the Financial Reporting arena, where international collaboration is already firmly established. For instance, the US Securities and Exchange Commission (SEC) has mandated that by 2014 all financial entities should adopt the eXtensible Business Reporting Language (XBRL). XBRL is a family of XML-based global standards, enabling the automated exchange of business information through machine-interpretable tags. XBRL taxonomies are constantly revised to reflect the regulations/rules. Apart from the US SEC, major players of XBRL include US FFIEC, Japan Financial Supervisory Agency , Bank of Japan, Tokyo Stock Exchange, UK HMRC and many other European and Asian financial regulators.

Despite the benefits of adopting established standards, these can also become barriers, hindering the adoption of new technologies that are not fully compatible with existing ones. In recent years, the value of semantically enriched XBRL has been recognised [6]. The semantics of XBRL constructs are to benefit significantly from the ongoing Financial Industry Business Ontology (FIBO) initiative, aiming to provide an industry-wide generic ontology [1]. To the best of our knowledge, however, there are not yet any deployed XBRL tools that take advantage of Linked Data offerings and release the full power of XBRL. Leaving non-technical issues aside, the lack of large scale adoption can be attributed to several reasons. Firstly, full-scale conversion from XML-based XBRL instance and taxonomy documents to genuine Linked Data format (i.e., a graph data model coded in the Resource Description Framework, RDF) is not straightforward. Naive conversion can lead to badly distorted RDF graphs, missing relations, and knowledge loss [4]. Secondly, without properly populated RDF models, the advantage of semantic inferences cannot be fully appreciated. Thirdly, XBRL leverages a large number of operational knowledge, defining how financial figures are computed. However, RDF, a knowledge representation paradigm that is rooted in Description Logic and specialises in non-numeric-conceptual modelling, may find difficulties in reasoning and reconstructing such knowledge. Finally, XBRL presents well-defined semantics for a well-defined purpose. Portraying complete pictures of companies requires data that are not annotated with XBRL. Using a single model for such a diverse mission may result in modifying or extending the XBRL models and thus raise operating costs and incur doubts among the established XBRL community.

2   HIKAKU-A Company Comparison Application

Better financial data integration allows both professional analysts and amateur individual investors to understand the performance of a particular company more efficiently. HIKAKU provides capabilities for seamlessly linking heterogeneous financial data and trace their provenance, thus enriching current financial reporting practice with the Linked Data computing paradigm [3]. It addresses the shortcomings of the current state of the art tools, in terms of data timeliness, data completeness, and data consumption. A key differentiator is that we compile data across multiple companies to offer performance comparison instead of isolated figures from individual ones. In the mean time, we hide the unnecessary financial reporting complexity and just present the data to ordinary investors/analysts in an easy-to-understand fashion. In addition, we expand the scope of where data is solicited from, linking not only conventional financial reporting information sources, but also Linked Open Data in order to construct performance summaries that go well beyond balance sheets.

Currently, the HIKAKU application utilises three main sources XBRL as a freely available and global mechanism for exchanging business information? Linked Open Data such as DBPedia and Crunchbase, which offer general information about companies? and finally, company sentiment extracted from news media (e.g. NY Times), which provides up-to-date information of a particular company that is attracting lots of media attention due to their performance or internal affair. The application aims to address the following inefficiencies in the current offering:

1. Semantic and syntactical discrepancies abound in individual reports, even with authoring support.
2. Lack of tooling for analysis across multi-sources reports.
3. Analysis is largely single faceted whereas financial requirements become increasingly multiple faceted.
4. Financial reports with release and audit latency fail to give timely results.
5. Failure to provide contextual information, helping a user to understand a company's performance.

2.1   Linked Data Driven Platform

The HIKAKU application is powered by the Ki2NA platform, which is a flexible, large-scale data processing platform that builds applications capable of delivering value to the user through knowledge-enabled networks (interconnected data systems supported and driven by Linked Data). The Linked Data model is used both at the data layer to deliver the end-user application, and also on the process-layer to model data flows between processes and define the interaction between all platform components.

The architecture and interaction of different processes are driven by the flow of information/data. Linked Data allows data, which is stored in the platform, to easily be further enriched and new knowledge to be produced by integrating and connecting existing information. Fig. 1 shows the Ki2NA architecture, consisting of three tiers and eight layers.

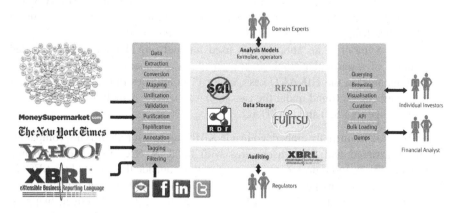

Fig. 1. Ki2NA Platform Architecture

The architecture can be divided into three tiers: a typical presentation tier, a (business) logic tier and a data tier. Whereas the presentation tier provides the communication interface between applications and clients on the one hand and the underlying system on the other hand, the logic tier executes system and application specific (business) logic. The data tier provides all necessary data management functionalities.

In the data tier, the platform deals with data heterogeneity and aims to handle a wide variety of data formats and storage solutions through a uniformed access mechanism to the above logic tier. This flexibility is a prerequisite of the HIKAKU financial use case. HIKAKU mashes up data from a variety of sources, integrating them into financial reports and therefore greatly assisting the decision-making process.

2.2   Financial Regulation and Governmental Data

As already mentioned in section 1.2, XBRL is a standard that enables the communication and exchange of business information especially in the financial sector. Reporting information such as financial figures is usually provided in the form of an XBRL instance, and each semantic definition is defined in a taxonomy. XBRL includes a family of XML-based standards e.g. NewsML and MathML. Since each XBRL taxonomy definition gives additional semantics, it is considered as a specialised data type. In addition to XBRL documents, there are also three other types of identifiers that are considered crucial when reconciling financial information from different sources to a single individual or company entity.

These identifiers are:

- Legal Entity Identifier (LEI) is a global system of identifiers designated by the Financial Stability Board (FSB) in an effort to overcome the current fragmented systems of firm identifiers and to create a common identifier for financial institutions. The LEI code can be retrieved from https://www.ciciutility.org.
- Central Index Key (CIK) is a number given to an individual or a company by the United States Securities and Exchange Commission. The CIK code can be searched from http://www.sec.gov/edgar/searchedgar/cik.htm.
- Ticker Symbol is an abbreviation used uniquely to identify publicly traded shares of a particular stock on a particular stock market. Depending on the companies (in the HIKAKU case, major IT companies in the U.S.), the ticker symbol can be found under the two stock exchanges, namely New York Stock Exchange (NYSE) and NASDAQ.

The CIK code is normally embedded inside XBRL reports for identifying companies that have registered and filed disclosures with the U.S. Securities and Exchange Commission (SEC), and it does not cover corporations outside the scope of the SEC. In order to broaden company performance comparisons into a global view, it is important to use LEI as the ultimate global identifier for company entities. Moreover, mapping ticker symbols to LEI is also essential in order to extract accurate stock price data from stock markets for particular companies, enabling companies' stock prices to be brought into financial reports. The architecture of mash-up, extraction, and integration governmental public data can be shown in Fig. 2:

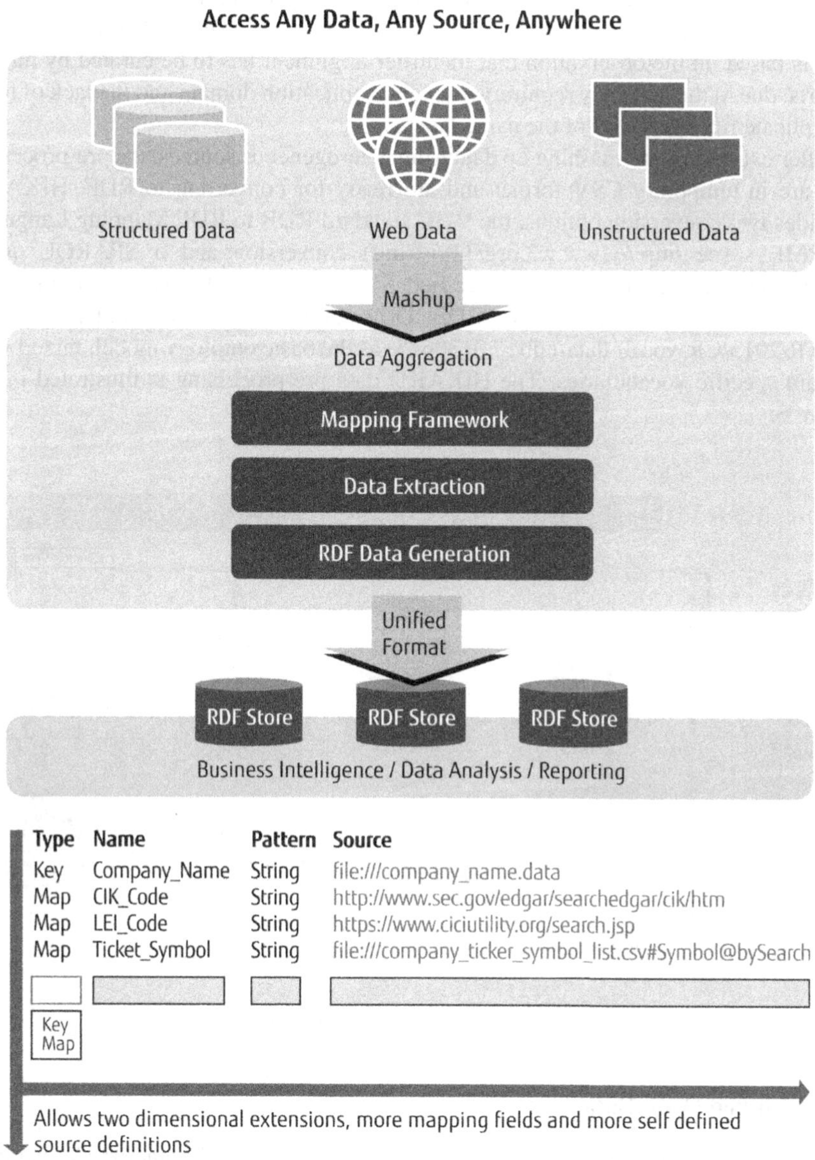

Access Any Data, Any Source, Anywhere

Fig. 2. Data Aggregation Architecture

Within HIKAKU, we elected to use company names as the key for searching and indexing other identifiers from the respective websites, enabling these different identifiers to be reconciled. This approach did raise some challenges. For example, MICROSOFT CORP can also be written as Microsoft Corporation while Yahoo can also be called YAHOO INC or Yahoo! Inc. etc., which ruled out exact string matching.

In the initial prototype, the solution involves manually fixing the problematic names into a consumable format for each website on top of string similarity based algorithms. This is based on the observation that identifier alignment has to be curated by human experts, due to the accuracy requirement of the application domain and the lack of tools to explicate full semantics of the name labels.

After extracting and mashing up data from heterogeneous sources, the pre-processed data are in temporary CSV format and are ready for converting to RDF. HIKAKU provides two conversion options, the W3C standard RDB to RDF Mapping Language (R2RML - see http://www.w3.org/TR/r2rml/) conversion and a SPARQL query construction that leverages a use-specified SV column to RDF type mapping. The second method treats the W3C RDF Data Cube Vocabulary (http://www.w3.org/TR/2013/CR-vocab-data-cube-20130625) as the basic ontology model, mixed with domain specific vocabularies. The HIKAKU data pre-processing is illustrated in the Figure 3:

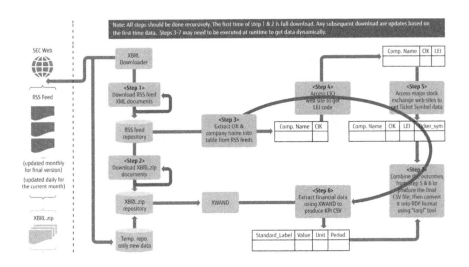

Fig. 3. Data Processing Flow

2.3   Linked Open Data

Numeric figures in financial reports can be unintentionally and/or deliberately manipulated to present a false and misleading image of a company (c.f. the recent scandalous acquisition of Autonomy by Hewlett-Packard [3]). Even though such incidents cannot be entirely avoided, incorporating other sources of data can promote informed decision making and minimise potential risks and mistakes due to a lack of transparency. Typical public data that can complement financial reports include stock price data, digitised mass media contents, mailing list/online bulletin board systems (BBS) and the emerging social media. The use of public data is based on the following observations: 1) Official financial reports are normally published quarterly (aka 10Q) and yearly (aka 10K). They normally lag behind media coverage of major events concerning the subject company; 2) Official financial reports tend to be summarising over a long period of time and may not reflect the stock price fluctuation at given time points in that period; and 3) More and more users or customers are starting to share their opinions about a product, a service or a company in channels other than customer services. We witnessed customers' sentiments (boycott/promotional activities) campaigned through news articles that have strongly affected a company's performance in the real world.

Choosing the most appropriate data sets not only can impinge the scope and accuracy but also system performance in terms of query execution time and memory consumption. The data sets being considered by HIKAKU can be grouped into several categories.

LOD Data Sets. When comparing financial performance, one needs to cover a wide spectrum of aspects of corporate entities. Even though data sets published on LOD cloud may not explicitly bear a "finance" label in their titles, they can be of great assistance in discovering relevant information, which is otherwise hard to access. The following LOD data sets have been chosen at this stage.

- DBPedia is used for general company data such as logo and location, as well as KPIs such as the number of employees, revenue assets, equity, net income, etc. We also compose a company's subsidiaries out of DBPedia data. The quality of data varies. Hence, data collected from DBPedia are cross-validated and complimented with those from other sources.
- Linked CrunchBase is a free database of technology companies, people, and investors. From CrunchBase, we retrieve such data as funding, competitors, company acquisitions, main people in charge, and products. It allows us to identify similar and comparable company profiles. For instance, companies with similar size, products and competitors can be grouped together and recommended for performance comparison.
- Linked NewYork-Times, as of 13 January 2010, has published approximately 10,000 subject headings as linked open data8. It complements company profiles compiled from the above two sources.

Mass Media. Mass media coverage provides more up-to-date information of a company and, on many occasions, actually leads/misleads the market on a wide and profound basis, e.g. causing stock briefly to plunge or rise. HIKAKU reflects this through the sentiment analysis of new articles. As an example, the NY Times is used to gather news articles and commentaries about a specific company, with Yahoo! Finance APIs used to get the stock price. Sentiment scores are then computed with off-the-shelf tools/services and accumulated to reflect a company's mass media image.

3   Implementation of the HIKAKU Prototype

The Ki2NA platform uses a triple store for data storage to meet the requirements of the HIKAKU application. This triple store contains all the heterogeneous data-sets represented according to the Linked Data guidelines (using HTTP URIs, RDF, and linking related resources together), making it easy to query for data from different sources using a single interface.

For end-users, the comparative results of the selected companies are centred on the web interface where users can decide whether to drill down into individual KPIs or roll-up to acquire an overview. The KPIs are extracted from the previously described heterogeneous data sources. The user interface uses a colour code to demonstrate the integration of such heterogeneous data to compose more complete information about companies, while at the same time serves as a legend for provenance information. For example, a company's description comes from DBPedia LOD data-source, whereas the CIK code is sourced from the U.S. Security Exchange Commission. These two KPIs will show up in the UI with distinct colours (DBpedia KPI in yellow and US SEC in blue).

There are three distinct types of visual analytics: bar chart view, time-line view and table view. Users can navigate between the bar and the time-line chart using the upper tabs while the table view is always visible. Users' interactions with the table view are reflected and synchronised on the bar chart and time-line views.

The current prototype also provide a feature for specifying new KPIs (i.e. new financial concepts) by arbitrarily combining pre-defined KPIs in mathematical formulae. The system will then calculate the formula on-the-fly and display the result as a normal concept. Such feature also demonstrates the strong data integration capability by enabling combine KPIs from different data sources.

4   Benefits

During HIKAKU research and development, we have acquired a better understanding of the socio-technical considerations, and our findings will be potentially valuable to researchers and practitioners planning similar initiatives. In particular, we highlight the following two aspects:

Early-adopter: In many application domains, the existing technologies create resistant old "habits". Finding the cutting point and early adopters becomes crucial. We decided to centre our Linked Financial Data application on financial reporting, and more specifically XBRL. The Financial Reporting community has already established a consensus on a common language for computer enabled data exchange? and has reached out to major technology vendors for help. Building our solution around established XBRL expertise therefore ensures a vast population of potential adopters. Moreover, as the beneficiaries of XBRL range from authorities/regulators, to financial institutes, and even to individual investors, the selected target group presents a wide diversity to allow us to implement different roll-out strategies.

Positioning: HIKAKU is designed as a value-added service on top of XBRL, consuming and unlocking the value of the latter. On the other hand, HIKAKU offers functionalities that are not available should XBRL be used in an isolated fashion. We acknowledge that XBRL and many other semantic-less XML-based languages will still serve as data exchange technologies in specialist domains. Linked Data technology is to assist rather than replace such technologies, offering better functionality and a better user experience. Meanwhile, Linked Data technology is not the answer to all the data integration challenges faced by the XBRL community (for instance, unambiguous alignment with universal identifier). It is always desirable to communicate any disadvantages fully at an early stage. During the conceptual design and development of the HIKAKU application, this strategy has helped us focus on true add-on values.

5   Conclusions and Future Plans

The public data enhancements, including Linked Open Data, social media, XBRL, LEI, and ticker symbol, allow us to extend conventional financial reports with: i) better comparison through semantic alignment, ii) support of unconventional, on-the-fly KPI definitions, and iii) timely access to external data other than the official financial reports.

The crux of our future work lies in improving the current prototype to reflect feedback from various public events and extended quantitative studies of employed technologies in the financial domain. More evaluations have already been scheduled. With the XBRL community already becoming the initial adopter, reach-out to other financial communities can be facilitated through the XBRL "channel".

Future plans also include an improved HIKAKU financial dashboard with features such as 1) time series analysis (e.g. "Fujitsu's performance since the latest tsunami disaster.", "is Fujitsu performing better this year comparing with other Japanese companies? "), 2) a data set explorer and quality-checker (e.g. "FT.com with a quality score of 0.8 and a trust score of 0.75"), and 3) user-defined KPI validation (e.g. "combining sentiment score and total number of employees does not make sense.").

References

1. Bennett, M.: Fibo: Best practice in big data. Journal of Banking Regulation (3-4), 255–268 (2013)
2. Burdick, D., Hernández, M.A., Ho, H., Koutrika, G., Krishnamurthy, R., Popa, L., Stanoi, I., Vaithyanathan, S., Das, S.R.: Extracting, linking and integrating data from public sources: A financial case study. IEEE Data Eng. Bull. 34(3), 60–67 (2011)
3. Florian, B., Martin, K.: Linked Open Data: The Essentials - A Quick Start Guide for Decision Makers. edition mono/monochrom, Vienna, Austria (2012)
4. García, R., Gil, R.: Triplificating and linking xbrl financial data. In: Proceedings of the 6th International Conference on Semantic Systems, pp. 3:1–3:8. ACM (2010)
5. Omberg, T., Sakr, S., Sethi, S., Murrell, B., Popken, A.: Key factors shaping financial reporting: The decade ahead. Deloitte (2011)
6. O'Riain, S., Curry, E., Harth, A.: Xbrl and open data for global financial ecosystems: A linked data approach. International Journal of Accounting Information Systems 13(2), 141–162 (2012)
7. O'Riain, S., Harth, A., Curry, E.: Linked Data Driven Information Systems as an Enabler for Integrating Financial Data. In: Yap, A. (ed.) Information Systems for Global Financial Markets: Emerging Developments and Effects, ch. 10, pp. 239–270. IGI Global (2012)

An Interdisciplinary Perspective on Education Service Systems

Christina Tay

Chinese Culture University, Taipei, Taiwan
Christina@sce.pccu.edu.tw

Abstract. The increased complexity in education systems has given rise to a number of intersecting trends and calling for a discipline to integrate across academic silos. As the concept of service innovation advances more rapidly into education services; industry, government, and academy are awakened to the concept of embedding services innovation. This theoretical paper offers an integrated framework for education systems (IFES) covering two intersecting dimensions where service innovation and service science can take place. As an effort to contribute in the area of service innovation and service sciences, an interdisciplinary approach is applied, interconnecting an array of competences across the different stakeholders. It is hypothesized that to increase productivity in education industries, interconnecting knowledge and resources from diverse areas and across different stakeholders through the co-lineation of four dimensions: (1) information, communications and technology; (2) skills and tools; (3) people and attitudes; (4) systems, processes and management; are essential to creating service innovation. This paper contributes a perspective of interconnectivity balanced with harmony that are crucial for effective productivity and service innovation by adopting a service science approach.

Keywords: service science, productivity, service innovation, service quality, education.

1   Introduction

As societies become more diverse, individualistic and more educated, the various stakeholders in the education system also become more demanding. The importance of diverse local contexts can only be expected to increase in order to cope with such externalities. Education services in institutions are increasingly expected to ensure high quality, efficient, equitable and innovative education. At the same time, the education service sector has also become a place of burgeoning economic activities and one of the fastest rising stars contributing to Gross Domestic Product (GDP). First, in developed economies, and now in many developing economies as well, the education sector injects into the GDP of many developed economies. For Singapore, New Zealand, Australia, the U.K., the U.S. and Canada, the education sector contributes 1.9%, 1.13%, 1.06%, 0.4%, 0.5%, 0.25% to their GDPs [2], [5], [6], [13]. Due to such ascendance, industry, government, and institutions have awakened to the

K. Liu et al. (Eds.): ICISO 2014, IFIP AICT 426, pp. 126–134, 2014.
© IFIP International Federation for Information Processing 2014

realization that embedding the concept of service innovation in the education sector is crucial to enhancing productivity as it contributes generously to the economic growth of education institutions as well as the national economies.

Productivity and service innovation levels in the education industry are relatively slow to develop owing to the complexity of its system resulting in its stakeholders to be less satisfied with the current assessment and distribution of value that they feel should be attainable. For example, the number of intangible units such as total number of credit hours of education produced, the number of degrees conferred and the number of courses offered by a service provider are normally referred to as outputs in service productivity. The downside of such an assessment often results in service providers being overly-focused on 'producing' credit hours, degrees, and courses rather than bundling offerings that precludes elements that matter to its stakeholders like instruction, credentialing, accreditation, student support and services during the period of their academic studies, student career services and placement prior to graduation, alumni socialization and connectivity after graduation to produce better end results rather than lead to an improvement in calculable outputs such as credit hours, degrees conferred or courses offered.

The emergence of the service science discipline creates new opportunities to study and explore transformations in education services, because it is such an important actor in knowledge economies. The providence of education services is now seen through the lens of multidisciplinary studies that converges and interconnects to create greater productivity. Service science offers a fresh perspective on the challenges faced by service providers when productivity issues are being challenged. Thus, service science emerges as a discipline that coagulates a loosely coupled of networked entities by attempting to interconnect and hold together trust propositions by applying knowledge and resources aimed at creating mutual benefits and more sustainable service-for-service interaction patterns amongst the stakeholders in an entity. Service science is motivated by a lack of integrated, foundational knowledge to inform its normative goal of assisting organizations in the process and provision of service innovation in order to realize more predictable outcomes [15]. Diversity is seen as enabling the different actors to learn from each other that enables greater productivity in the entity.

Service science seeks the elements such as those aforementioned and examines them scientifically, investigating them through the lenses of existing academic disciplines to raise productivity. It also aims to create win-win value propositions that interconnect all the stakeholders including parents, faculty, deans, heads of departments, administrators, owners, regulatory bodies(e.g. Ministry of Education, Accreditation Boards), community leaders, in conjunction with skills, technology, rules and policies improving productivity, quality, sustainability, learning by molding them to become strong backbones of a service provider through the mathematical modeling of business processes. [9] suggest that the key to understanding the exchange of resources within service systems is found in the distribution of competences, such as knowledge and skills, among service systems and understanding the value propositions that connect such systems[17]. Education is viewed as a service system that has been re-imagined as a continuous improvement process by service scientists [16].

Nevertheless, an integrated framework on education systems (IFES) binding several disciplines is lacking in existing literature in service sciences. In addition, literature examining service science in the education service industry is seriously lacking In this paper, the service science discipline is utilized to integrate across academic silos and advance service innovation more rapidly into the area of the education industry by presenting an IFES framework of service science web that interconnects knowledge and resources from diverse areas and the different stakeholders, embedding the core notion of continuous improvement with the final aim of optimizing productivity, enhancing quality, creating sustainability, stimulating learning with the final aims of creating service innovation in an entity. Then, in the third section, issues and opportunities for new managerial knowledge for services-oriented systems are explored through the (a) information, communication and technology, (b) skills and tools, (c) people and attitudes, and (d) systems, processes and management perspectives. The fourth section explains the interconnections and relationships between the input and output factors as prescribed in the third section. The last section then concludes with some recommendations.

2   IFES Framework of Service Science Web Interconnectivity

In contrast to applying manufacturing and service orientations to service organizations, little scholarly attention has been given to the applying service orientations to education services, a sector of burgeoning growth in many developed countries [3-4], [14]. In this section, a framework that captures the complex relationships amongst stakeholders to produce knowledge and resources that advance service innovation is presented. An integrated framework on education systems(IFES) is modeled to present the complex service science web of interconnectivity that holds together knowledge and resources essential to creating mutual benefits amongst the various stakeholders in the education service industry.

The IFES framework is aimed at interconnecting the diverse competences of the various stakeholders with the final aims of developing a more sustainable service-for-service interaction patterns amongst them. The y-axis of the IFES framework takes on a multidisciplinary approach that coagulates the interests of industry, academia and government at aims enhancing and/or producing service innovation in the education industry. If the interests of such actors are not considered, the likelihood of success in service innovation is going to be low. Actors gather information and knowledge in a multi-disciplinary manner, from business administration, engineering, information science, socio-informatics, and computer-adaptive systems. The stages of service innovation is presented on the x-axis where ideas for service innovation develops from an abstract stage to a more concrete stage as the actors in the IFES framework interact with each other. As we traverse through the inner levels of the IFES framework, an aggregate effect occurs across the two inner circular dimensions where the effects present at the previous level(s) will also be present at the subsequent level(s) of analysis in order to optimize productivity, enhance quality, create sustainability and stimulate learning with the final aim to create service innovation.

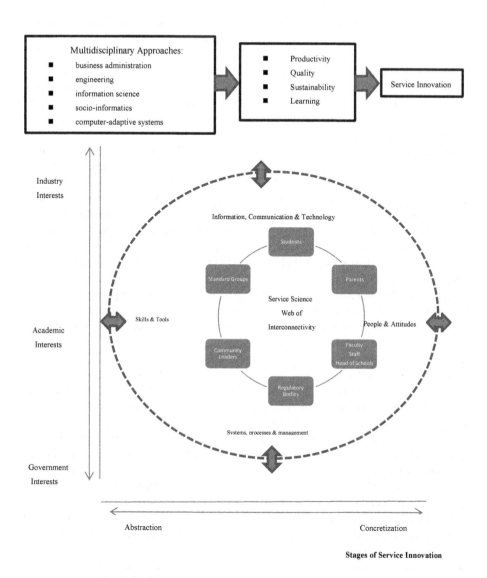

Fig. 1. An integrated framework on education systems (IFES)

The inner framework works along two dimensions. The first inner dimension involves stakeholders who interact with one another directly or indirectly. The stakeholders may be from different parts of the same organization, or across a couple of different organizations. The second dimension is how these stakeholders utilize their different competences. The inner circle of Fig. 1 shows first dimension: the stakeholders. Typical stakeholders have private profit incentive–driven and social welfare–driven considerations related to the economic, organizational, human, and technological issues that may arise [1]. In this paper, the term stakeholder refers to an agent who has interest in a service entity and who may be able to affect change through his/her own actions, or is affected by other change agents due to the actions of another stakeholder. The resulting changes vary in their impact dimensions on service productivity and service innovation.

The ripples of our inner circle portray the effects of the different stakeholders upon each other due to their individual actions. [8] have characterized these contrasting stakeholder roles as value makers and value takers, as they are at opposite ends of the spectrum of production and consumption. One example of contrasting stakeholder roles are student & parent stakeholders(value takers) as opposed to faculty, staff and head of schools(value makers) may hold conflicting goals; for example, lower school fees versus maximizing payback on services provided to stakeholders. The same holds true for regulatory bodies(value takers) versus head of schools(value makers) where the former may be interested to regulating or standardizing processes to optimize social welfare, whilst the latter may be more interested in possessing greater flexibility in their operational processes in order to achieve meet the agile needs of stakeholders, faculty and staff. From the student & parent stakeholders (value takers) perspective of the latter, regulatory bodies (e.g. the Department of Education, Accreditation Bodies) are the value makers for them.

Another class of stakeholders may not play a direct role in consumption of education services, but may represent the views of other stakeholders. These are the community leaders (value takers/makers) who may interact with faculty, staff and head of schools (value makers/takers). Their value derives from carrying out or preserving the interests of other stakeholders related to the education entity so that services offered possess continuous improvement qualities and that the rights of other stakeholders are heard and protected. The concept embedded in the IFES framework is that no stakeholder group is considered more important than the other but one of opposing interests and shared concerns.

The final outputs in service productivity and service innovation emphasize on harmony between the different stakeholders whilst interconnecting their different competences: information, communications and technology; skills and tools; people and attitudes; systems, processes and management. The interconnectivity process of attempting to hold together knowledge and resources could mean some sacrifices will have to be made, career paths may be changed and skills enhanced. There are renewed endeavor for an integrated discipline in modern education entities of today. Thus, this paper contributes a perspective of interconnectivity balanced with harmony in productivity elements that are crucial for effective productivity and service innovation.

The outer circle of Fig. 1 shows the second dimension: the competences of the different stakeholders. In the IFES framework, the cascading effects of both dimensions are required to drive the creation and diffusion of de facto outputs. Without them, the forces that are needed to evolve greater productivity cease to exist.

The IFES captures the countervailing forces and effects of these processes. The concept of synergizing the countervailing forces and effects of these processes is represented with a circular design. Each arrow represents a unique force that influences service productivity which could, in return promote service innovation, and vise-versa. The inner circle reflects the reality and complexity as the various stakeholders interact with each other. Complexity increases with the addition of new stakeholders and as more stakeholders interact with each other. The ripples on the circles illustrate the cascading effects of the stakeholders and competences as these forces interconnect and interact with each other. Since it is possible that these outcomes may not occur during all interactions, ripples are used instead of solid lines to provide an accurate depiction.

To produce the desired output consisting productivity, quality, sustainability, learning and service innovation, the co-lineation of the various dimensions in the inner and outer circles must occur in a harmonious pattern. The noise produced during this dynamic interaction must be separated from signals in order to differentiate what makes up the desired outputs.

3   The Interconnectivity between Inputs and Outputs

By developing a service mindset, education institutions are more easily able to recognize the interactive nature of services output. Each stakeholder in the system (whether student or institution) must be aware that the outcomes produced is co-produced through a shared vision that is of mutual benefit to all actors. The economic definition of productivity is, fundamentally, the relation between the physical quantities of outputs and the physical quantities of inputs[10].Service quality is where both input and output quantities are adjusted to yield the intended results.

The old adage of productivity represents some measure of the ratio of a producer's output to input. For example, completion-to-enrollment ratio, time to degree, cost per credit/degree, student-faculty ratio and cost or "profit" per faculty member. But, such conventional perspectives do not address the perspectives of the different stakeholders. Taking an example of student-faculty ratio, the problem with such a conventional approach to boosting productivity is its failure to consider the inputs of stakeholders on student perception of teacher quality into the process as well as the outputs experienced by the stakeholders such as student learning satisfaction. Instead, its approach would be to try to maximize student-faculty ratio by depleting student numbers or increasing faculty number and/or by setting stringent performance standards for faculty, which could result in the suffering of one stakeholder (teacher subject to more stringent performance standards) at the expense of innovation in teaching, which can be depicted as a form of service innovation.

Thus, such a conventional approach to productivity takes into account, the customer's perspective – defined as the ratio of the service output experienced by a customer to the output experienced by a customer as a participant in service production – suffers when managers in service-producing businesses blindly mimic the productivity improvement methods of their peers in product- producing businesses[11]. A customer(student's) perspective on productivity, when considered separately, often ends up with one stakeholder at odds with the other; increasing productivity for one at the stake of the other.

A totally different approach to productivity has to be taken to obtain a global measure of how well a service provider uses resources to create outputs in the form of acceptable perceived quality and customer value. In services, it is not only the inputs that are difficult to calculate, it is also difficult to get a useful measurement of the outputs. Hence, productivity cannot be understood without taking into account the *interrelationship* between the use of inputs or production resources and the perceived quality of the output produced with these resources[7].

The service science perspective presented in the IFES framework offers an *interconnectivity perspective* that examines productivity from the different stakeholder, where stakeholders benefit from the synergies of their respective competencies. The outer circle of Fig. 1 presents a conceptual IFES framework that captures this very essence of synergizing the competences of the various stakeholders and portrays the central role of service quality in linking the two. The arrows from the core of the IFES framework that lead to the outer circle implies how the inputs from the stakeholders along with their competences influence service quality. Service quality, in return, influences the outputs of the different stakeholders.

In services, productivity and service innovation cannot be separated. Through inputs such as (a) information, communication and technology, (b) skills and tools, (c) people and attitudes, and (d) systems, processes and management perspectives; stakeholders participate in the derivation of productivity and service innovation. They may also have an impact on how fellow stakeholders participate in the process and perceive the quality of the service produced. Such an interaction-induced stakeholder system integrated with their respective competencies contributes to productivity and service innovation.

The interrelationship depicted here reflects a constant interactive relationship amongst the stakeholders. Service productivity and service innovation is rather dependent on the progress of relationships amongst these actors, at the same time involves co-learning experiences of both or all parties. In the process, the various stakeholders will learn how to interact with one other so that service inefficacies, service quality deficiencies and information asymmetries can be minimized and so as not to create unnecessary costs for both or all parties. As this interconnectivity pattern continues, the stakeholders attain greater experience and learn to be able to more effectively participate in outputting greater productivity and enhancing service innovation values. During this process, the stakeholders also learn more about each other's competences that allows increased productivity and service innovation.

It is important for service productivity that one realizes that customer relationships are learning relationships, where both parties learn about each other, and that they last over a long period of time [7], [12]. The development of service productivity is one of a mutual learning experience consisting constant interactions amongst its stakeholders, whilst understanding their individual competences along the way.

4   Conclusion

The service industry evolves in a dynamic environment where different stakeholders may have conflicting expectations of what makes up productivity and service innovation, thus, making it harder than ever to separate noise from signals. This paper presented a framework from a service science perspective which utilizes an interdisciplinary approach to integrate across academic silos and advance service innovation more rapidly into the area of the education industry. The IFES framework interconnects knowledge and resources from diverse areas and across the different stakeholders, embedding the core notion of continuous improvement with the final aim of optimizing productivity, enhancing quality, creating sustainability and stimulating learning with the final aims of creating service innovation.

The IFES framework emphasizes the multiple roles of different stakeholders in an education entity including stakeholders, parents, faculty, staff, regulatory bodies (e.g. Ministry of Education, Accreditation Boards), community leaders and standard groups. No stakeholder group is considered more important than the other. Instead, the perspective under-planted in this IFES framework is one of opposing interests and shared concerns. The IFES framework presented points out how the co-lineation of information, communications and technology; skills and tools; people and attitudes; systems, processes and management; can find an important place in the founding of emerging discipline of service science.

In the process of creating greater productivity and enhanced service innovation, stakeholders will learn how to interact with one another as well as about others' individual competences. Such interrelationship is one that emphasizes on harmony amongst the various stakeholders, whilst interconnecting their different competences. During the interconnectivity process of attempting to hold together knowledge and resources for the mutual benefits for the various stakeholders could mean some sacrifices will have to be made, career paths may be changed and skills enhanced. There are renewed endeavor for an integrated discipline in modern education entities of today. Thus, this paper contributes a perspective of interconnectivity balanced with harmony that are crucial for effective productivity and service innovation in an increasingly complex service system by undertaking a service science approach.

References

1. Bardhan, I.R., Dermirkan, H., Kanna, P.K., Kauffman, R., Soufstad, R.: An Interdisciplinary Perspective on IT Services Management and Service Science. Journal of Management Information Systems 26(4), 13–64 (2010)
2. Boag, S.: New Zealand punching above its weight in Export Education. Media Release, Education New Zealand (November 26, 2010),
http://www.educationnz.org.nz/comm/Mediarealeases/
Punching%20Above%20Weight-26-11-08.pdf (retrieved on November 10, 2013)
3. Bowen, D.E., Siehl, C., Schneider, B.: A Framework for Analyzing Customer Service Orientations in Manufacturing. Academy of Management Review 14(1), 75–95 (1989)

4. Castelacci, F.: Technological paradigms, regimes and trajectories: Manufacturing and service industries in a new taxonomy of sectoral patterns of innovation. Research Policy 37, 978–994 (2008)
5. Crawford, R.: Universities Key to Building Export Education Industry, Te Pokai Tara (February 20, 2009), http://www.universitiesnz.ac.nz/node/364
6. Douglass, J.A., Edelstein, R., Hoaraeu, C.: US Higher Education as an Export: It is about the money, but also much more, Center of Studies in Higher Education (April 28, 2011) (retrieved on November 10, 2013)
   http://cshe.berkeley.edu/news/index.php?id=89
7. Grönroos, C., Ojasalo, K.: Service productivity: Towards a conceptualization of the transformation of inputs into economic results in services. Journal of Business Research 54(4), 414–423 (2004)
8. Kauffman, R.J., Walden, E.: Economics and electronic commerce: Survey and directions for research. International Journal of Electronic Commerce 5(4), 5–116 (2001)
9. Maglio, P.P., Spohrer, J.: Fundamentals of Service Science. Journal of the Academy of Marketing Science 36(1), 18–20 (2008)
10. Massy, W.F., Sullivan, T.A., Mackie, C.: Data Needed for Improving Productivity Measurement in Higher Education. Research and Practice in Assessment 7, 5–15 (2012)
11. Parasuraman, A.: Service quality and productivity: a synergistic perspective. Managing Service Quality 12(1), 6–9 (2002)
12. Peppers, D., Rogers, M., Dorf, B.: Is your company ready for one-to-one marketing? Harvard Business Review 77, 151–160 (1999)
13. Singapore Ministry of Trade, Developing Singapore's education industry (2013), http://www.mti.gov.sg/../ERC_SVS_EDU_MainReport.pdf (Retrieved on November 14, 2013)
14. Saara, B.: A manufacturer becoming service provider – challenges and a paradox. Managing Service Quality 15(2), 142–155 (2005)
15. Spohrer, J., Maglio, P.P., Bailey, J., Gruhl, D.: Steps Toward a Science of Service Systems. Computer 40, 71–77 (2007)
16. Sphorer, J., Fodell, D., Murphy, W.: Ten Reasons Service Science Matters to Universities, Educause Review Online (2012), http://www.educause.edu/ero/article/ten-reasons-service-science-matters-universities (retrieved on November 9, 2013)
17. Vargo, S.L., Akaka, M.A.: Service-Dominant Logic as a Foundation for Service Science: Clarifications. Service Science 1(1), 32–41 (2009)

Goal Oriented Value Object Classification
for Healthcare Service Development

Gilmini Dantanarayana[1], Chathurika Wickramage[1], and Prasad Jayaweera[2]

[1] Department of Computer Science, Faculty of Science, University of Ruhuna, Sri Lanka
[2] Department of Computer Science, Faculty of Applied Sciences,
University of Sri Jayewardenepura, Sri Lanka
{gilmini,chathurika}@dcs.ruh.ac.lk, pja@sjp.ac.lk

Abstract. In present day, performance of inter and intra cooperative enterprise systems can be guaranteed by provisioning e-Services. Modeling values for e-Service is challenging due to inherited complexity of service constellations. In this research, we present a classification to guide identification of different types of value objects that could be considered as mostly relevant and appropriate in healthcare trading scenarios. Further we propose a set of guidelines that direct construction of e^3-Value model along with the instructions to figure out the value objects. The classification and the guidelines are capable enough to provide clear and precise understanding of goal aligned e-Services to be developed and deployed by e-Service designers. Thus the proposed approach also facilitates business/IT alignment by realizing business motivations and top level goals in e^3-Value model which directly assist in defining business system requirements.

Keywords: Healthcare Services, Standards, Motivations & Value Modeling.

1 Introduction

Nowadays most enterprise solution developments are based on service orientation and related modeling concepts in order to cope with demanding flexibility, portability and agility for successful and sustainable business service deployments. Especially requirements of healthcare domain can be modeled as services offering wide spectrum of services to its customer, the patient. A notable global standardization effort in this direction is SAIF [7]. However, these efforts still lacks complete and systematic guidelines or approaches that could facilitate healthcare service designing and deployment. This paper attempts to propose a service oriented Value Objects (VO) identification based on BMM and e^3-Value constructs as part of an ongoing research for a complete framework for health solution development in line with global standardizations efforts introduced briefly in the next section of the paper.

The composition of concepts used, actions performed and relationships among users in an enterprise should be represented and visualized to facilitate the development effort of e-Service solutions. Development of a value model is one type of enterprise modeling at very early stages that focus on actors, resources and resource exchanges.

K. Liu et al. (Eds.): ICISO 2014, IFIP AICT 426, pp. 135–144, 2014.
© IFIP International Federation for Information Processing 2014

In this research, we propose a classification schema related to value objects mostly relevant to healthcare industry. Initially BMM [12] is used in analyzing healthcare motivational requirements that leads to classify the value objects. Each value object is represented as a pattern with a description, the motivation for identification and a concrete example illustrating the value object. Further, a set of guidelines is defined in figuring the value objects in an e^3-Value model that helps to develop and deploy e-Services effectively.

The value object categorization is described based on a case study from healthcare industry where a patient who needs to admit for a surgery who has already been investigated for a health problem is considered in this paper. Additionally, the proposed classification supports health solution development with the identification of value objects with recurrent use, co-created values and authentication requirements.

The rest of the paper is structured as follows. Section 2 explains research background with relevant standards and related work on how service identification leads to business-IT alignments. Section 3, clearly outlines the proposed Value Object Classification and the set of guidelines to capture the value modeling aspects. Next, Section 4 illustrates how the Value Object Classification and the guidelines are applied to identify services of an enterprise. Finally, Section 5 concludes with discussions.

2   Related Work and Research Background

Two main sub-sections are to be introduced here. Firstly the standardizations adopted as the foundations for motivation/goal modeling and healthcare value modeling in our proposed framework. In this context main focus is given on to BMM and e^3-Value briefly introduce below. Secondly some of the research contributions related to our work in this paper.

2.1   Service Aware Interoperability Framework (SAIF)

SAIF is the leading framework that primarily combine recommendations from two global standardization organizations; OMG (Object Management Group–Non-profit organization that introduces standards related to Object Orientated and related IT solution development standards) and HL7 (the internationally recognized organization that introduces messaging standards for Healthcare domain). SAIF focuses to ensure interoperability among healthcare applications [7]. However, SAIF is not completely established with its recommendations and adoptable approach in healthcare solution development. Therefore some research work could be found arguing and proposing different extensions [10]. In this context, our work proposed here could also be considered as possible extensions to SAIF sub-frameworks; Enterprise Conformance and Compliance Framework (ECCF) and Governance Framework (GF).

2.2   Goal Modeling

The main composition of a Business Motivation Model (BMM) [12] are ends (such as goals and objectives) and means (such as strategies, tactics, policies, rules) for a business environment. BMM shows how goals can be captured and represented using such higher level modeling concepts. Each component of the BMM provides a way to understand the overall business plan and then to facilitate lower level technical realization. Building up components of the BMM consequently may help to identify value objects and the business service processes needed for their exchanges.

Part of such a motivation model developed for the running case introduced here has been illustrated in Fig. 1.

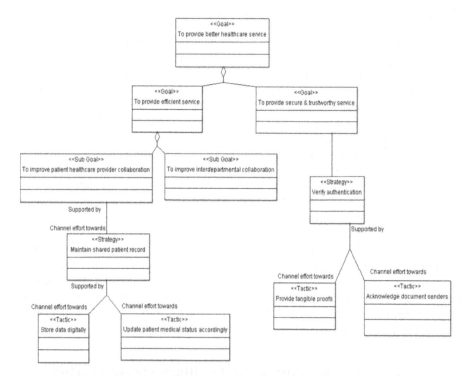

Fig. 1. Motivation model for surgery case

2.3   e³-Value Constructs

e³-Value modeling approach is based on an ontology, which has a set of concepts and related notations covering all these major value modeling concepts [3]. It also has methodology to model networked businesses in terms of values and analyzing profitability. Its notation provides graphical representation of businesses by means of value actor, market segment, value object, value port, value interface, value activity, value exchange, etc [4]. A value actor is an economically independent entity who is responsible for profit and loss in business. Market segment represents a set of actors having common economic interests in particular business setup. A commodity that has some economic value for a value actor and involved in exchanges between actors is a value object. A value object can be service, good, money or experience. Value ports at value interface of actor's are used to send or receive value objects from/to other actors. Value activities carried out by actors to create/add value to value objects.

2.4   Motivations/Value Oriented Service Designing

When representing business environment in value modeling, several methodologies have been proposed by the researchers in order to simplify and to facilitate the process of business solutions development [8], [1], [9], [13].

Recent research works [2], [11] on designing e-Business systems are trying to ensure business-IT alignment by proposing systematic approaches to capture higher level motivational requirements and realizing them on subsequent modeling level of development workflows. Often business models describe what aspects of the organization by focusing on what value is exchanged among actors [11]. It is quite evident the importance of initiating ICT solution development with designing of business models preceded with motivation/goal modeling in order also to guarantee successful business-IT integrations [11], [6].

Mainly values that are exchanging among actors in health industry is considered and analyzed further in our work. Additionally, we focus on identification of e-Services in healthcare industry, that facilitate creating values to intended users by analyzing the common characteristics. Our recommendation of healthcare motivation modeling is founded on Business Motivation Model while e^3-Value modeling is used as basis for healthcare value modeling in this context. Recent research suggests that how different modeling aspects for identification and development of e-Service of an enterprise. They also suggest a systematic approach that make use of two goal modeling steps and one business modeling step based on i* and e^3-Value modeling methods [1]. Considering goal oriented business modeling researches, we have proposed an alternative approach for identification of Value Objects and thereby initial development of related e-Service for their exchanges among actors.

3   Value Object Identification in Healthcare Service Sector

Identification and categorization of different value objects that are being exchanged among different actors in business collaborations are fundamental in designing and development of services. This is the main challenge that e-Service designers are facing and need guidelines and support for business contexts that they engaged in. When considering against typical business collaborations where economic commodities are exchanges, in healthcare industry this situation is very much challenging due to the factors such as involvement of ever increasing numbers of different healthcare service providers and complexity of value objects exchanged among them mostly in the forms of intangible healthcare services.

As a remedy to the situation briefed above, in this work we propose Value Objects Classification for healthcare service industry. Occurrence of following value object patterns have been subjected to this study provoked with the standardization efforts and research work summarized in the above section.

3.1   VO Classification

Intrinsic Value Objects (IVO)
These are the value objects used in value transfers but the receiving party has no immediate interest other than personal consumption or personal usage with respect to the concerned collaboration context.

Example: The patient fee, a payment is transferred to the admission office from the patient. The received payment will not be transferred in another value transfer in the healthcare collaborations for the case under consideration.

Motivation: IVO have specific usage meant for a single value actor in a particular collaboration.

Recurrent Value Objects (RVO)
Value objects that are repeatedly used in many different value transfers of a value model. In circumstances receiving party may have some usage or value with RVO and could then again be transferred with or without any value addition to yet another party.

Example: In this case study, same set of medical reports of a patient is transferred among the several actors; from medical laboratory to ward and ward to operation theater, etc. As it is more important to ensure the health state of the patient prior to any medical/surgical treatment related activities, the medical reports are being transferred repeatedly in order to provide necessary patient health state information.

Motivation: RVO are exchanged between many different actors with the same or different value object usages and with or without possible value additions to the received value object.

Co-created Value Objects (CVO)
These are the value objects that could also be transferred via value transfers but they could also be accesses or/and add value separately or simultaneously by different value actors.

Example: In the case, patient's health records are transferred as patient referral from the admission office to the ward and being updated continuously, same records are accessed and updated by operation theater as well.

Motivation: CVO models the situation where value objects needed to be accessed, continuously updated with possible value additions by many different value actors in a collaboration context.

Affirmative Value Objects (AVO)
These are kind of auxiliary value objects that in occasions composed with other regular value objects mainly for the authorization and for the verification purposes. These AVO are to be transferred together with other regular value objects.

Example: In the case study for instance certification of issuer in medical reports, certified surgery results and authorized referral statements should be signed by an authorized healthcare service provider. Unless verified with the signature the necessary actions may not be carried out due to policy/regulatory concerns in a particular governing setup.

Motivation: Authorization, approval and certification of some healthcare value objects are critical. In order to accommodate these requirements we proposed composing regular value objects with AVO through with confirmatory value actor information could be released.

3.2   e³-Value Modeling Guidelines for the VO Classification

Set of guidelines can be derived for the afore mentioned Value Object categories as follows and further a relevant framework is provided for the categories to build up the e³-Value model. We have proposed a systematic approach, first to identify Value Objects from these different categories.

Guideline 1
Identify IVO by looking at goals of value actors' participation in (healthcare/business) collaborations.
 Example: Physician's intension of getting fee, patient's intension of getting health service, etc.

Guideline 2
Identify RVO that is needed from another party in order to create IVO by a value actor.
 Example: Physician in need of a medical report (patient history or pervious treatments, etc)

Guideline 3
Identify CVO that is created in a single or several steps by two or more value actors. This is where multi-party involvement is needed in creation/adding value of objects.
 Example: In the operation theater surgeon, antitheists, nursing staff, etc are involved.

Guideline 4
Identify AVO that is with or without other type of VO where authority and authorization factors are to be considered as necessary requirement.
 Example: Medicine (treatment) of a prescription, its dosage & usage to be signed and approved by a physician, etc.

| Ward | Medicine (Treatment) + Physician's Approval/ Certification | Patient |

4   Application of Proposed Classification

One of the primary requirements in initiating motivation/goal modeling is deciding on a stakeholder's perspective of the concerned business situation. When considering healthcare scenarios it is notable that the ultimate customer is patient and we refer patient's perspective as Primary Perspective in motivation modeling effort. In addition to the Primary Perspective all the other service providers could be considered compassioning healthcare service industry. This could be collectively referred as Healthcare Enterprise Perspective in motivation modeling.

When carefully analyzing healthcare service collaborations, it is evident that there are Governing Collaborations (between Physicians and Patients) that enact and control all the other Auxiliary Collaborations between other supportive healthcare service providers such as Medical Laboratory Technicians, Pharmacists, etc. Therefore, we recommend also to consider these two sub perspectives; Governing Perspective and Auxiliary Perspective also during motivation modeling efforts.

Phase 1: Two perspectives on goal modeling
>   a.Primary Perspective → HC service concerned goals
>   b. Enterprise Perspective
>   - Governing Perspective → Overseeing and controlling goals
>   - Auxiliary Perspective → Healthcare Service supportive goals

Phase 2: Goal driven VO identification
>   a.VOs connected with primary perspective goals
>   - Primitive VOs
>   Basically these transfers are IVOs in order to obtain the service.
>   Ex: Patient to Enterprise → Fee (a monitory value)
>   b. VOs connected with enterprise perspective goals
>   - Composite VOs
>   Ex: Enterprise to Patient → Healthcare Service (a composite service)

Phase 3: Decomposition of composite value offerings
>   a.VOs used repeatedly within enterprise with or without value addition
>   - These transfers are RVOs.
>   Ex: MLT to Physician → Medical Reports
>   b. VOs involved multi parties who perform co-creations
>   - These transfers are CVOs.
>   Ex: Ward to Patient →Electronic Health Record (EHR)
>   c.VOs required authenticity
>   - These transfers are AVOs.
>   Ex: Medical Lab to Patient →Medical Reports (with MLT's endorsement)

Completed examples have been summarized in Table 1.

Phase 4: Identification of Actors (supported/intended in the motivation model) who create/consume VOs

Phase 5: Develop e³-Value model by annotating with above VO categories.

According to the proposed guidelines now it is possible to complete the e³-Value model components for the VOs and actors identified in above phases thus verify the completeness of the final e³-Value model.

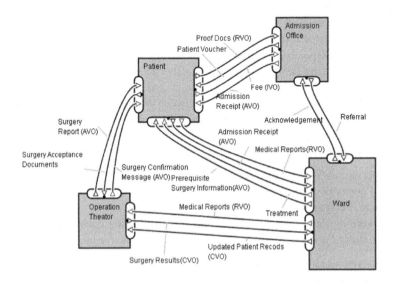

Fig. 2. e3-Value model for surgery case

To illustrate the usage of VO categorization and the guidelines proposed, we developed a simplified value model for the running case according to the above mentioned guidelines and phases. Fig. 2 depicts the extended e³-Value model for the surgery case in health care industry that was verified against the proposed service oriented value object classification.

This work leads easy recognition of VOs transferred among actors in a particular scenario. Then they can be mapped with the proposed VO classification that guides to design e³-Value models by realizing the value actors and the related service activities easily. Table 1 depicts the composition of the value actors, objects and service activities of e³-Value model based on proposed VO categories, for healthcare domain.

In the implementation phase, when developing the IT service solution, several system requirements can be easily realized from the proposed value object classification in line with [1]. Every RVO object is reusable. CVO objects are always shared data that can be accessed concurrently which may demands maintaining information consistencies. Policy, Privacy and Security requirements of value exchanges can also be captured. For instance authenticity of AVO objects can be shown.

Table 1. VO category for surgery case

Value Object Category	Value Object	Service	Service Provider	Service Recipient
IVO	Fee	Payment	Health Care Institute	Patient
RVO	Medical Report*	Medical Report Provision	Medical Lab	Patient
		Medical Report Provision	Patient	Ward
CVO	Patient Records→Personal Information	Patient Records Provision	Admission Office	Patient
	Patient Records →Personal Information + Symptoms	Patient Records Provision	Ward	Patient
	Patient Records →Personal Information + Symptoms + Diagnosis Reports	Patient Records Provision	Ward	Operation Theater
	Patient Records →Personal Information + Symptoms + Diagnosis Reports + Surgery Results	Patient Records Provision	Operation Theater	Ward
AVO	Medical Report**	Medical Report Provision	Medical Lab	Patient
	Patient Records***	Patient Records Provision	Ward	Patient

* To be produced to the physician, no immediate consumption by patient.

** Medical report together with Medical Laboratory Technician's authorization

*** Patient Records together with Consultant's certification

The 05 phases discussed above clearly and precisely shows the applicability of the proposed service oriented value object classification in healthcare domain.

5   Conclusions

This work proposes a classification that facilitates identification of different categories of value objects that could exist in healthcare service sector. Since this classification based on goal standardization efforts, our initial experiences show that such taxonomy is capable enough to provide better understanding of services to be developed and deployed by e-Service designers in healthcare industry. The adoption and utilization of the classification could be completed in parallel with business value modeling. Further, it could provide early identification of e-Services of the concerned enterprise application as we have briefly illustrated under the application of the classification. A set of guidelines associated with the value object categories confirms the applicability of proposed classification. This could also help in analyzing the collaborative states and dynamic behavior of different value objects in a service oriented enterprise. This comprehensive set of guidelines assists to build precise e^3-Value model based on goals.

Further this can be improved and applied in different specializations and various application areas even within the health industry as well as in other possible domains. We wish to propose a complete framework that combines this classification and set of guidelines along with service rules to different domains that addresses major requirements directly influence service process modeling of an organization where it helps to develop and deploy e-Services effectively.

References

1. Andersson, B., Johannesson, P., Zdravkovic, J.: Aligning goals and services through goal and business modelling. In: Information Systems and e-Business Management, vol. 7(2), pp. 143–169 (March 2009)
2. Baida, Z., Gordijn, J., Sæle, H., Akkermans, H., Morch, A.: An Ontological Approach for Eliciting and Understanding Needs in e-Services. In: Pastor, Ó., Falcão e Cunha, J. (eds.) CAiSE 2005. LNCS, vol. 3520, pp. 400–414. Springer, Heidelberg (2005)
3. Gordijn, J., et al.: The e3-Value methodology (December 17, 2012), http://e3value.few.vu.nl/
4. Gordijn, J., Akkermans, H.: e3-Value: Design and Evaluation of e-Business Models. IEEE Intelligent Systems 16(4) (2001)
5. Gordijn, J., Kartseva, V., Schildwacht, J., Wieringa, R.J., Akkermans, J.M.: Developing a Domain-Specific Cross-Organizational RE Method. In: Proceedings of The 12th International Conference on Requirements Engineering, RE 2004 (2004)
6. Gordijn, J., Petit, M.: Understanding Business Strategies of Networked Value Constallations Using Value and Goal Modeling. In: Proceedings of 14th IEEE International Conference on Requirements Engineering (2006)
7. HL7 Architecture Board (ed.): HL7 Service Aware Interoperability Framework: Canonical Version, Release 1 (Unique Ballot ID: SAIF CANON R1 I1 2011MAY). HL7 (2011), http://www.hl7.org/ctl.cfm?action=ballots.home
8. Jayaweera, P., Petit, M.: Classifying Business Rules to Guide the Systematic Alignment of a Business Value Model to Business Motivation. In: Proceedings of the Fourth International Workshop on Business/IT Alignment and Interoperability (BUSITAL 2009), Collection CEUR Workshop Proceedings, vol. 456 (2009)
9. Jayaweera, P., Rathnayaka, N.: Rule Framework for Motivation/Service Process Alignment (October 10, 2013), http://ict1.tbm.tudelft.nl/vmbo2013/lib/exe/fetch.php?media=vmbo2013_submission_23.pdf
10. Landgrebe, L., Smith, B.: The HL7 Approach to Semantic Interoperability. In: ICBO: International Conference on Biomedical Ontology, July 28-30 (2011)
11. Martin, H., Paul, J., Erik, P., Jelena, Z.: Value and Goal Driven Design of E-Services. In: IEEE International Conference on E-Business Engineering (ICEBE 2007), pp. 295–303 (2007)
12. Object Management Group, Inc. Business Motivation Model, BMM (December17, 2012), http://www.omg.org/spec/BMM/
13. Raadt van der, B., Gordijn, J., Yu, E.: Exploring web services ideas from a business value perspective. In: Atlee, J., Roland, C. (eds.) Proceedings of the 2005 13th IEEE International Conference on Requirements Engineering (RE 2005), pp. 53–62. IEEE Computer Society, Los Alamitos (2005)
14. Semantics Of Business Vocabulary And Business Rules (SBVR), Version 1.0. (January 03, 2014), http://www.omg.org/spec/SBVR/1.0/

A Design Science Oriented Framework for Experimental Research in Information Quality

Mouzhi Ge[1] and Markus Helfert[2]

[1] Free University of Bozen-Bolzano,
I-39100, Bolzano, Italy
[2] Dublin City University, Glasnevin
Dublin 9, Ireland
mouzhi.ge@unibz.it,
markus.helfert@computing.dcu.ie

Abstract. Design science has been used as a new research paradigm in information quality research. Within design science, experimental validation has been recognized as one of the most important research methodologies. However, as there is a lack of a coherent framework for conducting experimental research, different information quality studies may produce different results, which can be even conflicting. In order to reduce this ambiguity, we have proposed a framework that is used to (1) refine the experimental methodology in information quality research, (2) advance the rigorous information quality research in design science, and (3) demonstrate an exemplary experimental validation in design science.

Keywords: Design science, experimental design, information quality, experimental research methodology, information system framework.

1 Introduction

Design science research (DSR) focuses on creations of artificial systems. It addresses research through the *building* and *evaluation* of artifacts designed to meet stated objectives [10]. *Building* refers to the process of constructing an artifact for a specific purpose and *evaluation* assesses how well the artifact meets objectives. Evaluation is considered as the centre of DSR focusing on the output of design science research. Although evaluation strategies and guidelines have been proposed, practical evaluation of design artifacts is still challenging, as many approaches are subjective and designed for a small number of application scenarios or specific projects. Limited contributions have addressed the practicalities of evaluating research outputs that are designed within a complex research environment.

Recent methodological research has confirmed that experimental research is an effective way to evaluate artifacts, however, when incorporating experimental research into practical research scenario, we are yet facing the problem of how to conduct the experiment in design science. Therefore in this paper, we have proposed a framework to refine the experimental research in design science in an application level. We demonstrate the framework in information quality research.

K. Liu et al. (Eds.): ICISO 2014, IFIP AICT 426, pp. 145–154, 2014.
© IFIP International Federation for Information Processing 2014

Information quality research has been well developed during the last two decades. DeLone and McLean [3] proposed a comprehensive IS success model that considers information quality and system quality are the influencing factors to IS use and user satisfaction. In turn they will cause individual and organizational impact. This work not only lead to a large number of validation research on this model but also bring further attention of information quality into the IS community. Afterwards, different information quality research such as information quality dimensions [21, 30], information quality assessment [5, 9, 31] and information quality management [12, 32] has been conducted.

With the emerging research paradigm of design science, more and more researchers are using design science to conduct information quality research [13, 33, 34]. Given the nature that information quality research can be conducted with experimental research methodology in design science, we therefore donate our demonstration in this research area.

2   Design Science

In information system research, researchers distinguished two paradigms: behavioral science research and design science research [10]. The former is understood as a "problem understanding paradigm", the latter as a "problem solving paradigm". A key characteristic of DSR is that it resolves an important, previously unsolved problem, for a class of businesses or environments, while making a contribution to the knowledge base [29].

Design researchers investigate the current knowledge and solutions to insure they do not just replicate past work of others. The value of a new solution may come from various activities such as solving a known or expected problem, satisfying needs, or innovating something new. However, the new knowledge comes from "the number of unknowns in the proposed design which when successfully surmounted provides the new information that makes the effort research and assures its value" [26]. The research may involve searching the existing knowledge base, or collecting primary data through empirical work such as case studies, interviews, experiments or surveys. Research should stop if the problem has already been solved, or if it is found to be unimportant for the targeted objectives. Through this research process, the design science researcher satisfies the relevance condition for DSR in IS [11], while also addressing generalizability [1]. Characteristic for DSR is that rich phenomena that emerge from the interaction of people, organizations, and technology may need to be qualitatively assessed to yield an understanding of the phenomena adequate for theory development or problem solving [15]. The process of constructing and exercising innovative IT artifact enable design-science researchers to understand the problem addressed by the artifact and the feasibility of their approach to its solution [19].

It is generally agreed, that design science research develops knowledge that can be used by professionals in the field in question to design innovative solutions to their field problems [25]. To obtain knowledge for innovative solutions, Van de Ven [27] proposed engaged scholarship as a participative form of design science research.

It accommodates points of views of key stakeholders to understand complex problems. By exploiting differences between stakeholders, engaged scholarship develops knowledge that is more penetrating and insightful than when researchers work alone. Sein et al. [22] propose action design research method to interlink the buil-ding and evaluation phases and thereby emphasising the organisational context. Illust-rating the complexity of developing innovative outputs, Leonard [18] outlines that working across boundaries between disciplines, specializations, or expertise is a key ingredient for most innovative solutions.

Since design is inherently an iterative and incremental activity, the evaluation phase provides essential feedback to the build phase concerning the quality and utility of the design output under development and its design process. Evaluation delivers evidence that an artifact developed achieves the purpose for which it was designed and consequently provides indications for the design process. Experimental research has been recoganized as one the most important methods to evaluate and confirm the artifact.

3   Experimental Research in Design Science

Researchers identified a number of methods that can be used for evaluation of design science artifact. Hevner, et al. [10] proposed five classes of evaluation methods: (1) Observational methods include case study and field study. (2) Analytical methods include static analysis, architecture analysis, optimization, and dynamic analysis. (3) Experimental methods include controlled experiment and simulation. (4) Testing methods include functional testing and structural testing. (5) Descriptive methods include informed argument and scenarios.

As a further study, Venable [28] divides evaluation into artificial and naturalistic. Artificial evaluation includes laboratory experiments, field experiments, simulations, criteria-based analysis, theoretical arguments, and mathematical proofs. It evaluates a solution in a contrived and non-realistic way. Naturalistic evaluation explores the performance of a solution in its real environment. By performing evaluation in a real environment (real people, real systems, and real settings [23], naturalistic evaluation embraces all of the complexities of human practice in real organizations. This approach is always empirical, and includes methods such as case studies, field studies, surveys, and action research [29]. While the dominance of the naturalistic paradigm brings to naturalistic DSR evaluation the benefits of stronger internal validity [8], limited research has been done on the artificial evaluation such as laboratory and field experiments.

Experimental research involves directly manipulating a small number of variables and identifying the relationship between these variables. Using quantitative analysis, we can use the analysis results to test hypotheses or validate the artifact. An ideal experiment is designed to control all other possible factors affecting the experimental outcome and show how independent variables affect dependent variables [17]. It has been found that laboratory experiments are an effective methodology in addressing the cause and effect relationship [2, 6, 14], especially in investigating the cause and effect relationship between attributes of the decision environment, characteristics of information system and decision performance [4].

One critical concern in experimental research is the validity. Experiment validity can be divided into internal validity and external validity. The lack of internal validity means the experimental result is affected by uncontrolled factors. To improve internal validity, Field and Hole [6] proposed eight factors potentially threatening internal validity: group threats, regression to mean, time thread, history, maturation, instrument change, different mortality, reactivity, and experimenter effects. The above threats can be resolved or minimized by experimental controls, such as providing monetary incentive to subjects and selecting appropriate subjects at random. External validity tests how well the research findings generalize to other populations and circumstances. Two threats are associated with external validity: over-use of the special participants and restricted numbers of participants [6]. Considering the two threats, external validity can be increased by carrying out empirical tests across different participants and situations.

4   Experimental Research Framework in Design Science

In order to develop the experimental research framework, we have firstly reviewed the methodological issues that may occur in experimental research. Jarvenpaa et al. [14] proposed four open methodological issues in experimental information system research: research strategy, measuring instruments, research design, and experimental task. Research strategy emphasizes that the research program should be performed under a theory, a model or a framework. Two issues are related to the research strategy: a lack of theories for guiding the research [24], and studies which fail to build upon the work of others [14]. Measuring instruments focus on the reliability and validity of the measurements. Research designs concentrate on two issues: the importance of the research and the absence of experimental control [14]. Experimental task refers to a work that is taken by subjects in the experiment. The task is considered inappropriate when it is ambiguous or excessively complex. An ambiguous task might consist of inconsistent, incomplete and incorrect problems. An overly complex task may foster in the subjective influences such as preference, experience and even gambling.

Table 1. Methodological issues in experimental research

Methodological issues in experimental research [14]		
Research Strategy	•	Lack of theories for guiding the research
	•	Studies without building upon other's work
Measuring Instrument	•	Reliability
	•	Validity
Research design	•	The importance of the research
	•	The lacking of the experimental control
Experimental task	•	Ambiguous
	•	Overly complex

Considering the methodological issues mentioned in Jarvenpaa et al. [14], we have proposed a framework as shown in Figure 1. This framework consists of three components, which are artifact, experiment and data analysis. Along with each component, we provided a set of guidelines to deal with the methodological issues in experimental research.

Given the nature of design science, this paradigm is used to solve the practical problems, thus artifact should intend to solve a real-world problem. In order to build the artifact with theoretical basis, certain theory should be used to support for building this artifact. To highlight the novelty and importance of the artifact, an extensive literature review needs to be conducted. The artifact building will provide basis for the experimental design. In the experimental design, a validation of measuring instrument is needed, this is to intensify the experiment validity. The external factors that may influence the experiment should be kept under control. From the participant's perspective, the experiment should be easy to understand and easy to operate. After collecting the experimental data, we need to firstly understand which type of data is collected such as nominal data, ordinal data, interval data or ratio data, based on the data type, the according data analysis can be carried out. In turn, the data analysis can used to validate, evaluate and improve the artifact.

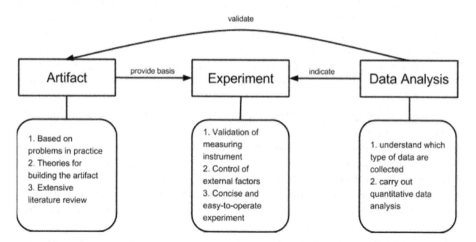

Fig. 1. Experimental Research Framework in Design Science

5   Validation with Information Quality Research

In order to demonstrate the usage of our framework, we have conducted an empirical information quality research design. In today's organizations, one important factor concerning information quality is that it directly influences decision-making. Owing to this, recent information quality research shows an increasing tendency to study the relationship between information quality and decision-making. Although their research findings confirmed that making correct decisions is dependent upon high quality information, exactly how information quality affects decision-making is still not entirely understood [7].

Case studies concerning poor information quality in decision support system are frequently documented in recent years and relate to a broad range of domains. Information quality issues may not only cause errors in business operations but also potentially impact society and wider aspects. For example, in 1986 NASA lost the space shuttle Challenger with seven astronauts onboard. The Presidential Commission investigated the Challenger accident and found that NASA's decision-making process was based on incomplete and misleading data. Just 2 years later the US Navy Cruiser USS Vincennes shot accidentally an Iranian commercial aircraft with 290 passengers onboard. Officials who investigated the Vincennes accident ad mitted that poor-quality information was a major factor. Yet not only in the space and military industries but also in our daily decision, certain information quality problems can lead to severe results; for instance, Pirani [20] reported that one piece of wrong biopsy information caused a patient's death in an Australian hospital. Real-world examples such as these illustrate cases in which poor information quality has significant impact on decision-making and may lead to irreversible damages.

From different case studies, we can conclude a real-world problem: *"How to build a decision support system with high quality information?"* To investigate this research question, one key question is to find out how information quality affects decision-making. As we have mentioned in Section 3, experimental research is an effective way to address the cause and effect relationship. We therefore use experiment to conduct this research. As we mainly focus on the experimental research in design science, we in the following only detail the research design related to the experiment part.

To start the design science procedure, first we need to define our artifact. As derived from the practical case study, our artifact is a *decision support system with high quality information*. To build this artifact, we use DeLone and McLean IS success theory to guild the design. It can be seen that high quality information can affect the decision-making (*Use*) and user satisfaction, and it will in turn generate individual impact and organizational impact. Literature across the domain information system, information management and information quality is related to this research work.

The experimental design is based on a well-known management game, the BeerGame. This game is a role-playing simulation, which involves managing supply and demand in a beer supply chain. The concept for this game was first developed at the Massachusetts Institute of Technology in the 1960s. Since then, several extensions and modifications have been suggested. Kaminsky and Simchi-Levi [16] identified several weaknesses in this traditional game and consequently developed the computerized Beer Game.

Based on the computerized Beer Game, we provide various quality levels of marketing and selling information to subjects. Using the given information, subjects are asked to make inventory control decisions. In the experiment, we have adopted a set of validated information quality measurements from [30]. Also we have also considered 10 external factors that may influence the experiment such as task complexity, decision time, expertise, decision strategy, interaction, information overload, information presentation, decision aids, decision model and environment. All the external factors are kept under control. That means keeping the same status of all the external factors for every experimental treatment. By conducting a pilot study, we can find out if the experiment task is clear and easy to operate to the participants.

For this experiment we use a four-component beer supply chain: manufacturer, distributor, retailer and customer. One episode of the experiment includes 10 weeks. In each week, the order of events is as follows: (1) Manufacturer fills the distributor's demands of last week. (2) Distributor fills the retailer's demands of last week and places an order with manufacturer for next week. (3) Retailer fills the customer's demands of this week and places an order with distributor for next week. If the demands are not catered for, the unsatisfied demands are recorded as back orders. The manufacturer is guaranteed to provide enough products for the distributor. Therefore there is no back order with the manufacturer. At the beginning of the game, there is no back order in each component and the demands of last week are perfectly satisfied.

A software-based system is developed to deliver the experimental scenario (figure 2). Subjects play the role of distributors who place orders to manufacturers and meet demands of retailers. The other three roles are taken over by the computer. To simplify the design of JIT inventory control, no lead time is set between distributors and manufacturers. This is to encourage subjects not to stock any product, accordingly, to achieve zero inventories. In each week, we provide the marketing information and selling history to subjects. According to the given information, subjects are able to make more reliable and reasonable inventory decisions. In one episode, subjects are asked to place 10 orders to manufacturers. Orders which conform to the best decision are recorded as the correct inventory decision. Since the goal of this experiment is to minimize the inventory to zero, the best decision is determined by the order which equals the retailer's need plus existing back orders.

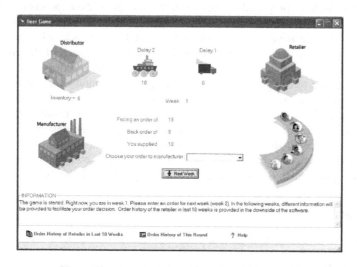

Fig. 2. Experiment of Beer Game inventory control

From the experiment, we can then collect the ratio date from the beer game. Therefore, parametric statistical analysis such as ANOVA is used to analyze the data. Afterwards, the data analysis can validate and evaluate our proposed artifact. A list of detailed design is shown in Table 2.

Table 2. Demonstration in information quality research

Artifact	Experiment	Data Analysis
Decision support system with high quality information	Beer Game experiment from MIT	Parametric statistical analysis
Practical problem: Different case studies have demonstrated that decision support system has information quality problem.	**Validation of measuring instrument:** Adopted validated measuring instrument from [30]	**Data collection:** Ratio Data
Theory: DeLone and McLean IS success theory	**Control of external factors:** A total of 10 external factors such as Task Complexity And decision time are controlled	**Data analysis:** AVONA and descriptive analysis
Literature review: Papers in information quality, information management and information system.	**Concise and easy-to-operate experiment:** We adopted a computerized beer game and carried out pilot study	

6   Conclusion

In this paper, we have proposed a framework that can guild the experimental research in design science. Based on the methodological issues in experimental research pointed by [14], we have proposed an experimental framework, which consists of three components: artifact, experiment, and data analysis. In each of the component, we have taken the methodological issues into consideration and proposed a set of detailed guidelines to design the experiment. In order to demonstrate and validate our proposed framework, we have conducted an empirical study in information quality research by using the framework. Under this framework, we can primitively avoid the possible methodological issues for experimental research in design science. The validation has not only shown that it is feasible to apply our framework in empirical information quality research, but also indicated that the framework can enhance more rigorous and quantitative design science oriented experimental research.

References

1. Benbasat, I., Zmud, R.: Empirical Research in Information Systems- The Practice of Relevance. MIS Quarterly 23(1), 3–36 (1999)
2. Campbell, D.T., Stanley, J.: Experimental and quasi-experimental designs for research. Houghton-Mifflin, Boston (1963)

3. DeLone, W.H., McLean, E.R.: Information system success: the quest for dependent variables. Information System Research 3(1), 60–96 (1992)
4. Dickson, G., Senn, J., Chervany, N.: Research in management information systems: the Minnesota experiments. Management Science 23(9), 913–923 (1977)
5. English, L.P.: Improving data warehouse and business information quality: methods for reducing costs and increasing profits. Wiley, New York (1999)
6. Field, A., Hole, G.: How to design and report experiments. Sage publication, London (2003)
7. Fisher, C.W., Chengalur-Smith, I., Ballou, D.P.: The impact of experience and time on the use of data quality information in decision making. Information Systems Research 14(2), 170–188 (2003)
8. Gummesson, E.: Qualitative Methods in Management Research. Chart-well-Bratt, Lund (1988)
9. Ge, M., Helfert, M.: A Review of Information Quality Research - Develop a Research Agenda. In: International Conference on Information Quality, MIT, Cambridge (2007)
10. Hevner, A.R., March, S.T., Park, J., Ram, S.: Design Science in Information Systems Research. MIS Quarterly 28(1), 75–105 (2004)
11. Hevner, A.R.: A Three Cycle View of Design Science. Scandinavian Journal of Information Systems 19(2), 87–92 (2007)
12. Huang, K.T., Lee, Y., Wang, R.Y.: Quality information and knowledge management. Prentice Hall, New Jersey (1999)
13. Helfert, M., O'Brien, T.: Sustaining data quality – creating and sustaining data quality within diverse enterprise resource planning and information systems. In: Nüttgens, M., Blinn, N. (eds.) Governance and Sustainability in IS. IFIP AICT, vol. 366, pp. 317–324. Springer, Heidelberg (2011)
14. Jarvenpaa, S.L., Dickson, G.W., DeSanctis, G.: Methodological issues in experimental IS research: experiences and recommendations. MIS Quarterly 9(2), 141–156 (1985)
15. Klein, H.K., Myers, M.D.: A Set of Principles for Conducting and Evaluating Interpretive Field Studies in Information Systems. MIS Quarterly 23(1), 67–93 (1999)
16. Kaminsky, P., Simchi-Levi, D.: A new computerized beer game: a tool for teaching the value of integrated supply chain management. In: Lee, H., Ng, S.M. (eds.) Supply Chain and Technology Management, The Production and Operations Management Society, Miami (1998)
17. Kerlinger, F.N., Lee, H.B.: Foundation of Behavioral Research. Harcourt College Publisher, Fort Worth (2000)
18. Leonard-Barton, D.: Well Springs of Knowledge: Building and Sustaining the Sources of Innovation. Harvard Business School Press, Boston (1995)
19. Nunamaker, J.F., Dennis, A.R., Valacich, J.S., Vogel, D., George, J.F.: Electronic Meeting Systems to Support Group Work. Communications of the ACM 34(7), 40–61 (1991)
20. Pirani, C.: How safe are you hospital? The Weekend, Australia (2004)
21. Pipino, L., Lee, Y., Wang, R.Y.: Data quality assessment. Communications of the ACM 45(4), 211–218 (2002)
22. Sein, M., Henfridsson, O., Purao, S., Rossi, M., Lindgren, R.: Action Design Research. MIS Quarterly 35(1), 37–56 (2011)
23. Sun, Y., Kantor, P.B.: Cross-Evaluation: A New Model for Information System Evaluation. Journal of the American Society for Information Science and Technology 57(5), 614–662 (2006)

24. Taylor, R.N., Benbasat, I.: Cognitive styles research and managerial information use: problems and prospects. In: Joint National Meeting of the Operations Research Society of America and The Institute of Management Sciences, Colorado Springs, Colorado (1980)
25. Van Aken, J.E.: Management Research as a Design Science: Articulating the Research Products of Mode 2 Knowledge Production in Management. British Journal of Management 16(1), 19–36 (2005)
26. Vaishnavi, V.K., Kuechler, W.: Design Science Research in Information Systems (January 20, 2004), http://www.desrist.org/desrist (last updated September 30, 2011)
27. Van de Ven, A.H.: Engaged Scholarship: A Guide for Organizational and Social Research. Oxford Univ. Press, Oxford (2007)
28. Venable, J.R.: A Framework for Design Science Research Activities. In: Proceedings of the Information Resource Management Association Conference, Washington, DC, USA, May 21-24 (2006)
29. Venable, J., Pries-Heje, J., Baskerville, R.: A Comprehensive Framework for Evaluation in Design Science Research. In: Peffers, K., Rothenberger, M., Kuechler, B. (eds.) DESRIST 2012. LNCS, vol. 7286, pp. 423–438. Springer, Heidelberg (2012)
30. Wang, R.Y., Strong, D.M.: Beyond accuracy: what data quality means to data consumers. Journal of Management Information Systems 12(4), 5–34 (1996)
31. Wand, Y., Wang, R.Y.: Anchoring data quality dimensions in ontological foundations. Communications of the ACM 39(11), 86–95 (1996)
32. Wang, R.Y.: A product perspective on total data quality management. Communications of the ACM 41(2), 58–65 (1998)
33. Xie, S., Helfert, M.: An assessment technique for information quality support in emergency response. Int. J. Business Continuity and Risk Management 3(4), 373–393 (2012)
34. Xie, S., Helfert, M., Ostrowski, L.: Human involvement in designing an information quality assessment technique – demonstrated in a healthcare setting –. In: Huang, R., Ghorbani, A.A., Pasi, G., Yamaguchi, T., Yen, N.Y., Jin, B. (eds.) AMT 2012. LNCS, vol. 7669, pp. 630–645. Springer, Heidelberg (2012)

Rationality of Service Composition of Workflow Net in a Service Oriented Architecture

Guangqi Huang[1], Li Huang[1], Xiuxiu Chen[2], and Lily Sun[3]

[1] Science and Technology on Information Systems Engineering Laboratory,
National University of Defense Technology, Changsha, Hunan, China
[2] School of Management and Economics, Beijing Institute of Technology, Beijing, China
[3] School of Systems Engineering, University of Reading, UK
{guangqi.huang,l.huang,Xiuxiu.Chen,lily.sun}@reading.ac.uk

Abstract. Users' requirements change drives an information system evolution. Consequently, such evolution affects those atomic services which provide functional operations from one state of their composition to another state of composition. A challenging issue associated with such evolution of the state of service composition is to ensure a resultant service composition remaining rational. This paper presents a method of Service Composition Atomic-Operation Set (SCAOS). SCAOS defines 2 classes of atomic operations and 13 kinds of basic service compositions to aid a state change process by using Workflow Net. The workflow net has algorithmic capabilities to compose the required services with rationality and maintain any changes to the services in a different composition also rational. This method can improve the adaptability to the ever changing business requirements of information systems in the dynamic environment.

Keywords: Service Composition, Service Composition Atomic-Operation Set, Rationality, Workflow Net, SOA.

1 Introduction

With the extensive utilization of service oriented architecture (SOA) [1][2] in the field of information systems, the concept of service is employed in design and implementation of information systems. A software component can be described as technical service. A technical service consists of a composition of functional workflow which can be represented by an atomic-operation set. Technical services can be integrated to construct an information system. As [3] pointed out, technical services can be mapped on to business processes for meeting users' complicated requirements in various business domains [4].

In an information system application, its behavior and process of services composition evolve which is driven by orchestrating business services. Consequently, it affects the executable functional workflow to change from one stage of service composition to another state of composition. Therefore, the service composition process should have abilities to facilitate evolutions supported by the internal strategy

K. Liu et al. (Eds.): ICISO 2014, IFIP AICT 426, pp. 155–165, 2014.

and external environment [5-7]. The evolution of service composition refers to services set or flow structure will add, update and adjust dynamically according to the changing requirements of business application during the implementation process. Generally, it includes two major forms, namely, services set change and service workflow structure adjustment [5][8]. In this paper, we focus on the methods to ensure the rationality of the process of service composition evolution behavior in SOA system.

Some achievements on the evolution of service composition have been made. Ref. [6] summarizes several common types of service composition evolution, including shallow and deep service evolution, and puts forward a service life cycle method. Ref. [9] proposes the solutions for dynamic composite service evolution problems from the research field of the trustworthy software, and discusses the existing work of dynamic service composition [10-11], including evolution time, evolution operation classification and evolution influence, etc. In ref.[12], the instance dynamic migration (IDM) of the Web service composition evolution is studied, the processing framework is built, and the optional rules and arithmetic to execute the IDM from the service choreography perspective are addressed. Regarding to the business process analysis and modelling, existing researches have illustrated series of WS-BPEL analysis methods and technologies based on Petri network [13-15], which provide the research method for this paper.

Therefore, this paper argues that how to correctly judge the rationality of business logic of the service composition behavior evolution is a basic problem in the SOA information systems. Based on the workflow-net theory, this paper studies the basic service composition operations according to the requirement in the SOA information system, puts forward the service composition atomic-operation set (SCAOS), and defines a kind of service composition atomic operations, which ensure the rationality of service composition process evolution. The following paper will be organized as follows. Section 2 illustrates the problems of the service composition. Section 3 describes the theory for analysis of the rationality of service composition. Section 4 proposes SCAOS while a sample is given to illustrate this process in section 5. Section 6 gives our conclusion and outlook.

2   Description of the Service Composition

Service composition problem is essentially a procedure that a set of services orchestrate according to the business process. It can be described as: $C = < S : R >, C \in Service, S \subset Service$. C means the composite service, S means the set of atomic services, R means the relationship between the services in S. If the number of atomic services in S is 0 or 1, R will lose significance, service composition cannot be built. Therefore, in this paper, we define:

$$C \in CService \Leftrightarrow C = < \{se_0, se_1, ..., se_n\} : R >, se_i \in EService, 0 \leq i \leq n, n > 0$$

It means that the service C is a composite service, if and only if it is composed of two or more atomic services.

Generally, service composition behavior evolution of the SOA system is mainly caused by two factors: their services set and business process. Service composition behavior evolution caused by changes of services set can also be called S evolution of service composition, denoted as E_S. In this process, the atomic services set S changes, which results in a change of C. The evolution caused by changes of business process is also called as R evolution of service composition, denoted as E_R. In this process, the atomic services set S is not changed, while the relationship R changes, which results in a change of C.

3   Theory for Analysis on the Rationality of Service Composition Operation

The use of workflow net (WF-net) to describe the service composition and analysis the rationality of service composition behavior evolution can be defined as follows:

Definition 1. *A Petri net* $WFN = (P,T,F)$ *is called as WF-net [9][16], if and only if:*

- Exists an initial place $i \in P$, its precursor is empty, $^\bullet i = \varnothing$.
- Exists an end place $o \in P$, its successor is empty, $o^\bullet = \varnothing$.
- For any node $x \in P \cup T$, all belongs to a path from i to o .

WF-net can be used to describe the internal logic of service composition dynamically.
For $WFN = (P,T,F)$,

- The set of place p is used to describe the conditions of service calling.
- The set of transition T is used to describe the collection of service units of composite service, it is actually an operation.
- The set of flow relationship F is used to describe the logical relationships between service units of composite service.

The distribution of the Tokens in all places is identified as network state, initial state (final state) of WF-net denoted as $M_0(M_{end})$. In $M_0(M_{end})$, only the initial place (the end place) is marked.

Definition 2. *Rational WF-net [9]. A WF-net* $WFN = (P,T,F,i,o,M_0)$ *is rational, if and only if:*

(1) For any state M can be reached from the initial state M_0 . There is a transition sequence that drives the state M to the end state M_{end} , the formalization description is:

$$\forall M\ (M_0 \xrightarrow{\ *\ } M\ ) \Rightarrow (M \xrightarrow{\ *\ } M_{end})$$

(2) The end state M_{end} is the only final state which can be reached from the initial state M_0 , and M_{end} will have at least one mark, the formalization description is:

$$\forall M \ (M_0 \overset{\centerdot}{\longrightarrow} M \wedge M \geq M_{end}) \Rightarrow (M = M_{end})$$

(3) Dead transition does not exist in the WF-net, the formalization description is:

$$\forall t \in T, \exists M, M' \ s.t. \ M_0 \overset{\centerdot}{\longrightarrow} M \overset{t}{\longrightarrow} M'$$

The rationality of a WF-net, can be used to judge whether a service composition behavior evolution is rational:

- The rationality of a WF-net can ensure that the evolved process of service composition can be smoothly completed.
- Internal constitution service should all stop until the end of service composition.
- All internal constitution service of service composition could be called.

Theorem 1. For WF-net $WFN_1 = (P_1, T_1, F_1)$ and $WFN_2 = (P_2, T_2, F_2)$, $T_1 \cap T_2 = \varnothing$, $P_1 \cap P_2 = \{i, o\}$ and $t^* \in F_1$. The WF-net $WFN_3 = (P_3, T_3, F_3)$ which replaces the transition t^* of WFN_1 with WFN_2 can be built with $F_3 = \{(x, y) \in F_1 | x \neq t^* \wedge y \neq t^*\} \cup \{(x, y) \in F_2 | (x, y) \cap \{i, o\} = \varnothing\} \cup \{(x, y) \in P_1 \times T_2 | (x, t^*) \in F_1 \wedge (i, y) \in F_2\} \cup \{(x, y) \in T_2 \times P_1 | (t^*, y) \in F_1 \wedge (x, o) \in F_2\}$, $P_3 = P_1 \cup P_2$, $T_3 = (T_1 \setminus \{t^*\}) \cup T_2$.
Therefore, WFN_1 and WFN_2 are rational if and only if WFN_3 is rational. Proof of this theorem is proved by [7].

4   Service Composition Atomic-Operation Set

Based on the WF-net theory of service composition description, this paper puts forward the service composition atomic-operation set (SCAOS). Faced with business logic evolution requirements in the information system, this paper defines 2 classes and 13 kinds of basic service composition of atomic operations. It can be used to specify the service composition behavior in SOA system, in order to guarantee the rationality of evolution process of service composition behavior. The service composition that can be described by rational WF-net is also called as rational service composition.

4.1   Internal Relationships in the Service Composition

Without considering the cycle of calls, the relationships between service units of composite service include the following three types: sequence, switch and flow. Here, we define that $\forall a, b \in S$ are represented by the transition t_a and transition t_b, respectively. Therefore,

(1) Sequence: Two service units are sequentially called, that is $\exists p_s \in P \ s.t. \ p_s \in t_a^* \wedge p_s \in {}^*t_b$, as shown in Fig. 1:

Fig. 1. Sequence relationship

(2) Switch: Two service units are selected to call according to the specific condition, that is $\exists p_{in}, p_{out} \in P$ s.t. $p_{in} \in {}^{\bullet}t_a \wedge p_{in} \in {}^{\bullet}t_b \wedge p_{out} \in t_a^{\bullet} \wedge p_{out} \in t_b^{\bullet}$ (shown in Fig. 2)

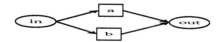

Fig. 2. Switch relationship

(3) Flow: Two service units are called at the same time (shown in Fig. 3), that is $\exists p_{in}, p_{in'}, p_{out'}, p_{out} \in P \wedge t_{split}, t_{join} \in T$, s.t.

$$\{p_{in}, p_{in'}\} \subset t_{split}^{\bullet} \wedge p_{in} \in {}^{\bullet}t_a \wedge p_{in'} \in {}^{\bullet}t_b \wedge p_{out'} \in t_a^{\bullet} \wedge p_{out} \in t_b^{\bullet} \wedge \{p_{out}, p_{out'}\} \subset {}^{\bullet}t_{join}.$$

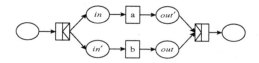

Fig. 3. Flow relationship

4.2   Evolution of Service Composition Behavior Caused by the Change of Services Set

For composite service $C = <S:R>$, service composition behavior evolution caused by the change of services set can be defined as follows:

Definition 3. *S Evolution* E_S : *Refers to the composite services set* $S = dom(C)$ *changes, which also led to a change in the relationship. It includes two aspects, namely, increase and decrease. Considering the above three kinds of basic internal relationships of service composition, it is divided into the following 6 kinds of evolution:*

(1) Sequence Increase Evolution b_{sq^+} (Shown in Fig. 4):

$$T^N = T^O \cup \{t_b\} \wedge P^N = P^O \cup \{p_s\} \wedge F^N = F^O \cup \{(t_a, p_s), (p_s, t_b), (t_b, p_{out})\} \setminus \{(t_a, p_{out})\}$$

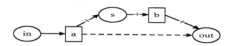

Fig. 4. Sequence Increase Evolution

(2) Switch Increase Evolution b_{sw^+} (Shown in Fig. 5):

$$T^N = T^O \cup \{t_b\} \wedge P^N = P^O \wedge F^N = F^O \cup \{(t_b, p_{out}), (p_{in}, t_b)\}$$

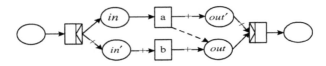

Fig. 5. Switch Increase Evolution

(3) Flow Increase Evolution b_{fl^+} (Shown in Fig. 6):

$$T^N = T^O \cup \{t_b\} \wedge P^N = P^O \cup \{p_{in'}, p_{out'}\} \wedge F^N$$

$$= F^O \cup \{(t_{split}, p_{in'}), (p_{in'}, t_b), (t_b, p_{out}), (t_a, p_{out'}), (p_{out'}, t_{join})\} \setminus \{(t_a, p_{out})\}$$

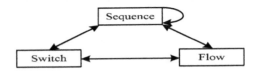

Fig. 6. Flow increase Evolution

The inverse evolution behavior of the above evolutions can be defined as: Sequence Decrease Evolution b_{sq^-} , Switch Decrease b_{sw^-} , and Flow Decrease Evolution b_{fl^-} . They are similar with the above evolutions, so here we do not describe them in detail.

4.3   Service Composition Behavior Evolution Caused by the Business Process Change

For composite service $C = <S : R>$, service composition behavior evolution caused by changes of business process can be defined as follows:

Definition 4. *R Evolution (E_R): Refers to the relationship R changes but the composite services set* $S = dom(C)$ *remains. In other words, the service business process is changed.*

According to the actual requirement of service composition behavior evolution, considering the above three kinds of basic internal relationships of service composition, 7 kinds of evolutions can be got as follows, as shown in Fig. 7:

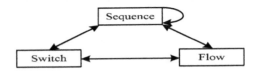

Fig. 7. 7 kinds of R evolution behaviors (indicated by the directions of arrows)

Define the relative start and end WF-net of evolution as $WFN^O = (P^O, T^O, F^O, i^O, o^O, M_0^O)$ and $WFN^N = (P^N, T^N, F^N, i^N, o^N, M_0^N)$, WFN^O is a rational WF-net, $A \setminus B$ means set out the elements like set B from set A, then the following 7 kind of evolution behaviors maybe occur in $WFN^O \rightarrow WFN^N$:

(1) Reverse Evolution b_{sq2sq}: the sequence execution of service a and service b is reversed, described as:

$$T^N = T^O \wedge P^N = P^O \wedge F^N = F^O \cup \{(t_b, p_s), (p_s, t_a)\} \setminus \{(t_a, p_s), (p_s, t_b)\}$$

(2) Sequence to Switch Evolution b_{sq2sw}: the sequence execution of service a and service b is changed to switch execution, described as:

$$T^N = T \wedge P^N = P^O \setminus \{p_s\} \wedge F^N = F^O \cup \{(p_{in}, t_b), (t_a, p_{out})\} \setminus \{(t_a, p_s), (p_s, t_b)\}$$

(3) Sequence to Flow Evolution b_{sq2fl}: the sequence execution of service a and service b is changed to flow execution, described as:

$$T^N = T^O \wedge P^N = P^O \cup \{p_{in'}, p_{out'}\} \setminus \{p_s\} \wedge F^N$$
$$= F^O \cup \{(t_{split}, p_{in'}), (t_a, p_{out'}), (p_{in'}, t_b), (p_{out'}, t_{join})\} \setminus \{(t_a, p_s), (p_s, t_b)\}$$

(4) Switch to Flow Evolution b_{sw2fl} : the switch execution of service a and service b is changed to flow execution, here $\{t_{split}, t_{join}\} \subset T^O$, described as:

$$T^N = T^O \wedge P^N = P^O \cup \{p_{in'}, p_{out'}\} \wedge F^N$$
$$= F^O \cup \{(t_{split}, p_{in'}), (p_{in'}, t_b), (t_a, p_{out'}), (p_{out'}, t_{join})\} \setminus \{(p_{in}, t_b), (t_a, p_{out})\}$$

The inverse evolution behavior of the last three evolutions mentioned above can be defined as: Switch to Sequence Evolution b_{sw2sq} , Flow to Sequence Evolution b_{fl2sq} , and Flow to Switch Evolution b_{fl2sw} . They are similar with the above evolutions, so we do not describe them here in detail.

4.4   Rationality Analysis of Service Composition Behavior Evolution

The verification of the rationality of operations of service composition behavior evolution can be transferred to the verification of rationality of relative WF-net. It is proved that the service composition atomic-operation set can keep the rationality of evolved composite service. The following propositions are true:

Proposition   1.   *Atomic-operation   set   of   S   Evolution,* $E_S = \{b_{sq^+}, b_{sq^-}, b_{sw^+}, b_{sw^-}, b_{fl^+}, b_{fl^-}\}$ *can keep the rationality of evolved composite service.*

Proposition   2.   Atomic-operation   set   of   R   Evolution,
$E_R = \{b_{sq2sq}, b_{sq2sw}, b_{sw2sq}, b_{sq2fl}, b_{fl2sq}, b_{sw2fl}, b_{fl2sw}\}$ *can   keep   the   rationality   of evolved composite service.*

In this paper, we take the switch to flow evolution b_{sw2fl} as an example to prove the above propositions.

Proof: According   to   the   switch   relationship,   a   WF-net WFN_{sw}^O is   built,

$$P_{sw}^O = \{i, o, p_{in}, p_{out}\}, T_{sw}^O = \{t_{split}, t_{join}, t_a, t_b\}, F_{sw}^O = \{(i, t_{split}), (t_{split}, p_{in}), ..., (t_{join}, o)\}$$

as shown in Fig. 8a. Similarly, according to the flow relationship, the other one WFN_{fl}^N is built, as shown in Fig. 8b.

According   to   Theorem   1,   the   WF-net   before   evolution $WFN^O = WFN_{sw}^O + WFN_{other}$ can be got. WFN_{other} is the residual network of the WF-net before evolution, is similar with the WFN_1 in [Theorem 1]. WFN^O is rational, so WFN_{other} is rational. Obviously that the WF-net WFN_{fl}^N is rational, then the evolved WF-net $WFN^N = WFN_{fl}^N + WFN_{other}$ is rational too.

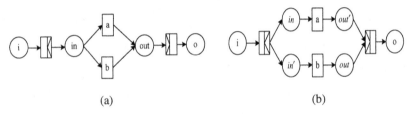

(a)   (b)

Fig. 8. Proof of the rationality of evolution behavior

4.5   Rationality Analysis of Mixed Service Composition Behavior Evolution Operations

In the application of actual SOA system, a whole service composition behavior can be decomposed into multiple mixed service composition atomic operations, so a service composition behavior is essentially an operation sequence of atomic operations. Based on [Proposition 1] and [Proposition 2], it is guaranteed that the rationality of the whole service composition behavior remains unchanged. In addition, for the nested service composition behavior, according to [Theorem 1], if we transfer the transitions t_a and t_b of S evolution and R evolution behavior and replaced it with a rational WF-net, then the evolved WF-net is still rational. It is consistent with the inclusion of service, so a rational WF-net corresponds to a rational composite service. This rational composite service can be used as a basic service unit to participate higher level service composition, and this evolution behavior is rational too.

In summary, for the defined service composition atomic-operation set in the SOA system $SCAOS = E_S \cup E_R$, every operation $\forall b \in SCAOS$, the evolved service composition process is rational.

5 Sample of Service Composition Behavior Evolution

Suppose in the information service center of a bank system, the user information query process is implemented as a composite service. Its logic process is designed as follows: firstly, input the user account code, and call user identification service **Service0**; then, according to the category of user account, call the VIP user account financial information query service **Service1** or common user account financial information query service **Service2**; subsequently, call user basic information query service **Service3**;   and finally, call user information comprehensive analysis and processing service **Service4**, return the results of user account information analysis.

We found that if the bank system query the account financial information using **Service1** or **Service2** and query the basic information using **Services3** at the same time, the reaction rate of user account information analysis will maybe increase. Thus the original business logic is changed and the service composition process evolution happens. The relationships among **Service3** and selective **Service1** and **Service2** are the order of sequence execution before evolution, while their relationships are changed to the order of concurrent execution after evolution, as shown in Fig. 9:

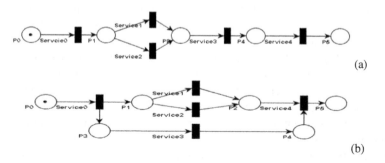

(a)

(b)

Fig. 9. Relative WF-net before evolution (a) and after evolution (b)

Thus, the above service composition evolution is essentially a kind of R evolution - Sequence to Flow Evolution b_{sq2fl} . It is rational. Then, we build the state reachability graph of the relative WF-net before evolution and after evolution, as shown in Fig. 10:

Comparing the state reachability graph before evolution and after evolution, obviously the evolution behavior is rational and the results of the business processes are consistent.

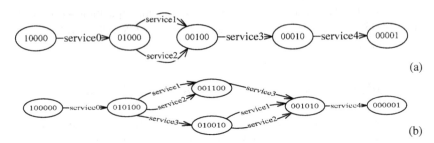

Fig. 10. State reachability graph before evolution (a) and after evolution (b)

6   Conclusions

A challenging issue associated with service composition is to remain the rationality of service composition. In order to ensure the rationality of the service composition behavior, this paper studies the service composition operations according to the requirement in the SOA information system, puts forward the SCAOS, defines 2 classes and 13 kinds of basic service composition atomic operations, including service composition operations caused by the changes of services set and business process. Specifically, S evolution operations includes Sequence Increase Evolution, Switch Increase Evolution, Flow Increase Evolution, Sequence Decrease Evolution, Switch Decrease and Flow Decrease Evolution; R evolution operations includes Reverse Evolution, Sequence to Switch Evolution, Sequence to Flow Evolution, Switch to Flow Evolution, Switch to Sequence Evolution, Flow to Sequence Evolution and Flow to Switch Evolution.

Using the WF-net theory, this paper proves that SCAOS can maintain the rationality of service composition operations of SOA system when the service composition behavior occurs. The workflow net has algorithmic capabilities to compose the required services with rationality and maintain that any changes to the services in different compositions are also rational. SCAOS remains the rationality of the internal process logic in the SOA information system. This method can enhance the adaptability of SOA information systems to respond to the ever changing business requirements in the dynamic environment.

References

1. Newcomer, E., Lomow, G.: Understanding SOA with Web Services. Addison Wesley Professional (2004)
2. Xiaolu, C., Yuqi, L.: Web Services technology, architecture and Application. Electronics Industry Press, Beijing (2002)
3. Jian, Y., Yanbo, H.: Service oriented computing-principle and application. Tsinghua university press, Beijing (2006)
4. Zhongyu, Z., Guangqi, H.: Transparency of Information System Service Evolution. Computer Engineering and Design 32 (2011)

5. Ryu, S.H., Casati, F., Skogsrud, H., Benatallah, B., Saint-Paul, R.: Supporting the dynamic evolution of Web service protocols in service-oriented architectures. ACM Transactions on the Web 2, 1–45 (2008)

6. Papazoglou, M.P.: The challenges of service evolution. In: Bellahsène, Z., Léonard, M. (eds.) CAiSE 2008. LNCS, vol. 5074, pp. 1–15. Springer, Heidelberg (2008)

7. Zhongyu, Z., Guangqi, H., Tao, C., Pei, Z.: Approach of QoS-Oriented Services Run-Time Binding. Computer Engineering and Design 32, 2700–2703 (2011)

8. Guangqi, H., Chuanqing, C., Chenping, S., Zhongyu, Z.: Study on Evolution Behavior of Service Combination under Unchanged Set. Compute Science 39 (2012)

9. Jin, Z., Hailong, S., Xudong, L., Ting, D., Jinpeng, H.: Dynamic evolution mechanism for trustworthy software based on service composition. Institute of Software 21, 261–276 (2010)

10. Von de Aalst, W.M.P., Jablonski, S.: Dealing with workflow change: Identification of issues and solutions. Int'l Journal of Computer System Science & Engineering 15, 267–276 (2000)

11. Andrikopoulos, V., Benbernou, S., Papazoglou, M.P.: Managing the evolution of service specifications. In: Bellahsène, Z., Léonard, M. (eds.) CAiSE 2008. LNCS, vol. 5074, pp. 359–374. Springer, Heidelberg (2008)

12. Wei, S., Xiaoxing, M., Jian, L.: Instance migration in dynamic evolution of web service compositions. Chinese Journals of Computers 32, 1816–1831 (2009)

13. Lohmann, N.: A feature-complete petri net semantics for WS-BPEL 2.0. In: Dumas, M., Heckel, R. (eds.) WS-FM 2007. LNCS, vol. 4937, pp. 77–91. Springer, Heidelberg (2008)

14. Lohmann, N., Wolf, K.: How to implement a theory of correctness in the area of business processes and services. In: Hull, R., Mendling, J., Tai, S. (eds.) BPM 2010. LNCS, vol. 6336, pp. 61–77. Springer, Heidelberg (2010)

15. Liske, N., Lohmann, N., Stahl, C., Wolf, K.: Another Approach to Service Instance, Service-Oriented Computing. In: 7th International Joint Conference, pp. 24–27 (2009)

16. Van der Aalst, W.: Workflow Management Models, Methods, and Systems. The MIT Press Cambridge, Massachusetts (2002)

Process Oriented Dependency Modelling for Service Identification

Wenge Rong[1,2], Ting Li[3], Yuanxin Ouyang[1,2], Chao Li[1,2], and Zhang Xiong[1,2]

[1] School of Computer Science and Engineering, Beihang University, Beijing, China
[2] Research Institute of Beihang University in Shenzhen, Shenzhen, China
[3] Sino-French Engineering School, Beihang University, Beijing, China
{w.rong@,liting@ecpk.,oyyx@,licc@,xiongz@}buaa.edu.cn

Abstract. Service-Oriented Architecture (SOA) is important for organisations to achieve dynamic business process and build business agility. One of the first step for service oriented applications implementation is to properly identify a set of fine-grained services. A right service granularity is necessary to satisfy lower coupling and higher cohesion principles for reusable software services. To meet this challenge, a lot of efforts have been attached to support service identification. In this paper, by considering the dependency combined with the idea of graph partition, a service identification method is proposed from the business process's perspective. The illustration example has shown its promising and it is expected that the proposed service identification method can offer researchers further insight into service granularity analysis.

Keywords: Service Identification, Semiotics, Semantic Analysis, Granularity.

1 Introduction

In recent years, the evolving businesses environment has put unpredictable pressure than ever on the way the business is conducted. The success of a business heavily relies on its ability of implementing dynamic business processes in terms of the business model and operations to adjust the changing market, which is one of the major options for effect creation. During the process of building business agility, the concept of Service Oriented Architecture (SOA) has been proposed and widely lauded as an innovative business oriented solution [2].

The implementation of SOA based systems lines in the provision of a set of loosely coupled services. A service can be generally considered as a piece of applications that encapsulate and implement certain business logic for invocation by internal or external partners through well defined interfaces. In reality it is normally scalable in terms of its scope. It can be as simple as a single file compression action or as complicated as a whole software package abstracted for a specific business solution. Though its principle is primary and simple, its analysis, design, realization and implementation are of much importance and difficulty [2,9]. To solve these problems, a preliminary challenge called service

K. Liu et al. (Eds.): ICISO 2014, IFIP AICT 426, pp. 166–175, 2014.
© IFIP International Federation for Information Processing 2014

identification must be solved and has attracted much attention from scholars in this domain.

Service identification is an essential process for successful SOA based system implementation since errors made during the procedure of identification will be carried on in next procedures and leads to a chain reaction [8] and thereby influencing the effectiveness of the SOA architecture [3]. In fact, service identification has impact on the goals like the composability of loosely-coupled services and the reusability of individual services in different contexts [11].

The granularity in service identification process generally varies over time and can be classified in term of data, functions, and business value [7]. One of the widely used methods relies on business process decomposition by analysing related tasks and activities [6]. Though process oriented service identification has shown its potential, its potential has not been fully realized [4] and how to analyse in-depth the business process and fulfil the requirements that they represent is still difficult [1].

To deal with demands of examining and articulating possible services with operations of service candidate, in this paper a semantic analysis method inspired by semiotics theory [13] has been proposed to clarifying the meaning and dependency within a business process, thereby supporting the possible service candidate selection.

The remainder of the paper is organized as follows. Section 2 describes the most related works in the domains of service identification. The proposed model of the service identification will be elaborated in section 3. Section 4 will describe the details of proposed approach with an illustration example. Section 5 concludes the paper with some suggestions and recommendations for the future work.

2   Related Work

Since SOA is involved in the whole business process, different stakeholders will probably have their own viewpoints on its scope and capacity from different perspectives. As a result, the service identification methods are also diversified. Some of them consider services from lower level implementation, such as data, features and etc. [10], while others consider service granularity from higher level like application domain and business process [12].

In the literature, most approaches of service identification are based on business process due to its intention to realize the reusability to create business value [6]. Wang et al. investigated the service scope analysis by conducting review on inter-/intra-enterprise business processes to identify the qualities which a good service should have [15]. They consider a service as the composition of a set of legacy software components with larger granularity. Based on this, they proposed a service normal form and a normalized method to solve the problem that service are difficult to integrate closely with information systems.

Inaganti and Behara thoroughly studied the handshake between SOA and business process management [8]. Their work conducts value-chain analysis by in-depth analysing process coupled with use case study. Afterwards they identify services with the combination of top-down and bottom-up approaches. Similarly Dwivedi and Kulkarni also proposed a method for service identification by utilizing process map [4].

Another interesting work is the one by Kim et al., who tried to build a formal approach with the right granularity from the business process model [11]. With the concept of graph partitioning, they distinguish the distance of activities within a role and those belong to different roles so that they can minimise the network round-up costs incurred during the service execution.

Mani et al. proposed a novel method by focusing on the performance of users on the interfaces and use the interface design as an input to identify service [14]. They captured the appropriate references to data and process models, and analysis the requirements from data displayed in the user interface, identify business service requirements from the UI navigation flow and links between the UI and the business process model.

3   Methodology

In this research, the semantic analysis method proposed in organisational semiotics theory is employed [13] to get service candidates for an organization by analysing the business process. The proposed methodology is organized into four main phases: 1) map the process onto a semantic chart according to the rules of constructing ontology chart, 2) calculate the similarity between every two affordances in the ontology chart, 3) cluster the affordances based on their similarities, 4) choose an appropriate criterion to partition the ontology chart to cut the service into sub-services with right-granularities. Publishing the services with right-granularities can lower the cost and can be convenient for the consumers.

3.1   Semantic Chart Annotation

The first step is to map the business process onto a semantic chart, which provides a graphic representation describing the ontological dependencies between the concepts [13]. An semantic chart is comprised of a set of semantics units. According to the ontological relationships, these units are set in the ontology chart at different places. The ontology chart presents the essential elements and the atomic-level functions during the business process, that is why a ontology chart can explain the participants in a process and what they do exactly. Fig. 2 is an example of semantic chart which consists of agent, affordance, role and determiner [13].

- *Agent*: an agent is represented by rounded rectangle in the ontology chart. It means the the stakeholder(autonomous individuals) who is in charge of some operations in a certain field, and it can be an a group, an organization, an individual and etc.

- *Affordance*: an affordance is represented by rectangle in the chart. It describes action possibilities of which an actor is aware, and it can exhibit the connections between entities and some behaviour patterns in a field. [5].
- *Role*: a role is represented by ellipse in the chart. While the agent describes the class of individuals, the role defines the instance of an agent, and some of the behaviours that an agent has, which means, the role allows explicate the meaning of the concepts in the ontology by designating the agent to whom this authority is released.
- *Determiner*: an determiner is prefixed with # in the chart. It is used to describe the properties of semantic units. The determiners of each affordance are very important in our approach of service identification.

3.2   Service Similarity Calculation

To calculate the similarity, two hypotheses are employed, i.e., h_1: the interaction between two affordances provided by different places will cause a lot of long-distance communication cost. h_2: two affordances who have tighter ontological dependency are more relative to each other, which means, the similarity between them is higher. Based on these two hypotheses, it is then possible to empirically define the similarity between affordance a_i and a_j as:

$$S_{i,j} = w_1 * S^1 + w_2 * S^2$$

where S^1 and S^2 denote two indexes who measure the similarity associated to the former two hypotheses and w_1 and w_2 refer to the weight assigned to each similarity factor.

According to h_1, S^1 depends on whether these two affordances have the same provided physical place. As presented before, the first determiner of every affordance is noted as $\#p$. As such in this paper it is determined that if two affordances have the same $\#p$, their similarity is set to 1, otherwise their similarity is 0, as shown below:

$$S^1 = \begin{cases} 1 & if \ \ a_i.\#p = a_j.\#p \\ 0 & if \ \ a_i.\#p \neq a_j.\#p \end{cases}$$

According to h_2, the ontological dependencies in the ontology chart have a very important influence. Accordingly the similarity S^2 is associated to hypothesis h_2. The ontological dependencies are denoted by lines in the ontology chart. If two affordances are connected by one single line, they have a first-order ontological dependency; if they are connected by two lines, they have a second-order ontological dependency; and if they are connected by three or more than three lines, they have a multi-order ontological dependency. It is obvious that the smaller the order of ontological dependency is, the more similar the two affordances are. Formally, the similarity S^2 is assigned as below:

$$S^2 = \begin{cases} 1 & if\ a_i\ and\ a_j\ are\ the\ same \\ 0.75 & if\ a_i\ and\ a_j\ have\ a\ first-order\ ontological\ dependency \\ 0.5 & if\ a_i\ and\ a_j\ have\ a\ second-order\ ontological\ dependency \\ 0 & if\ a_i\ and\ a_j\ have\ a\ multi-order\ ontological\ dependency \end{cases}$$

3.3 Affordances Clustering and Service Refinement

A service is essentially a combination of affordances who satisfy some given conditions, as shown below:

$$Service = \{\ \sum affordance | constraints\ \}$$

According to this definition, this service identification approach is substantially about how to determine the constraints who differentiate services. That is why we choose to identify the service with the idea of cluster analysis.

4 Case Study

In this research an illustration example is given in form of a basic library service process, which is presented by flowcharts in the Fig. 1, where some basic library functions are presented.

4.1 Semantic Chart Generation

With the business process chart, it is able to obtain the service semantic chart. The mapping rules are listed below and part of the semantic chart of this process is shown in Fig. 2.

1. The functions in the process chart are mapped as affordances.
2. The role (provider or consumer) relative to the function is placed in a certain place in the semantic chart based on the link between them, and each role must have an antecedent agent.

The determiners of affordances is listed in the table I and each of affordance is numbered to simplify the expression in the rest of this paper. In the column of 'deternimers' in this table, it is found that the first determiner is always the physical place where the affordance is provided. In this library service process, the physical places are online, book management department division, reading room management division, card management division and logistics. The rest determiners describe the dependencies among all these affordances.

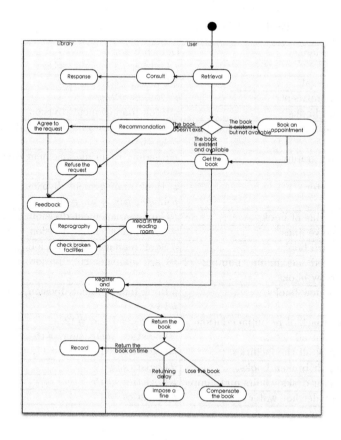

Fig. 1. The basic library process

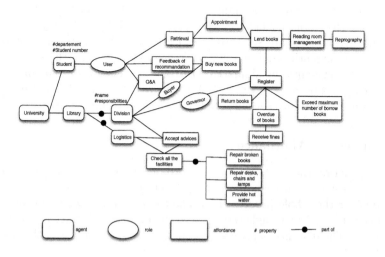

Fig. 2. The library service ontology chart

Table 1. Determiners of all the affordances

Number	Affordance	Determiners
1	Q&A	#Online, #Division, #User
2	Retrieval	#Online, #user, #3, #4
3	Appointment	#Online, #2, #4
4	Lend books	#Book management division, #2, #5
5	Reading room management	#Reading room management division, #4, #6
6	Reprography	#Reading room management division, #5
7	Register	# Book management division, #Division, #4, #8, #9, #10, #11
8	Overdue of books	#Card management division, #7, #9
9	Receive fines	#Card management division, #8
10	Return books	#Book management division, #7
11	Exceed maximum number of borrow books	#Card management division, #7
12	Buy new books	#Book management division, #Division, #13
13	Feedback of recommendation	#Online, #User, #12
14	Accept advices	#Logistics, #Division, #15
15	Check all the facilities	#Logistics, #14, #16, #17, #18
16	Repair broken books	#Logistics, #15
17	Repair desks, chairs and lamps	#Logistics, #15
18	Provider hot water	#Logistics, #15

4.2 Similarity Calculation

In this case study, we use the similarity equation presented in previous section to determine the similarity between each service candidate. To simplify the case study, the two weights are set to 0.5 respectively. With these rules, it is able to derive a eighteenth-order matrix where the element in i-th row and j-th column $M_{i,j}$ represents the similarity of a_i and a_j. Obviously, this matrix is a symmetric matrix because $S_{i,j} = S_{j,i}$. With the results of calculating similarities, the affordance can be further clustered to identify possible services.

4.3 Cluster the Affordance

After constructing the ontology chart, affordance need to be clustered together to generate proper service candidates and the clustering process contains 4 steps:

1) Consider the whole process as an one-to-one service, which means, every affordance is treated as a single service, and calculate the distance between every two services. The distance is inversely proportional to the similarity because the

closer two services are, the more similar they are, and the higher the similarity is. As such the distance between two services can be defined as:

$$D_{i,j} = \frac{1}{S_{i,j}}$$

There is problem that the distance between a service with itself is 1, which is not correspond with the reality. In this paper we set the distance of this case to 0. Also, we admit that if $S_{i,j} = 0$, $D_{i,j}$ is defined as 10 to allow the calculate.

2) Find out the closed two services, put these two services into one service. In this way, the number of services is one less than before.

3) Re-calculate the similarities between the new services derived from step 2.

4) Repeat step 2 and step 3 until an all-to-one service is finally realized, which means all the affordances are regarded as one single service.

These results can be presented in a tree in Fig. 3, with which it is able to obtain the services with the right granularities.

4.4   Service Refinement

The graph of the tree which presents the results of clustering is shown in Fig. 3. In this figure, we can see clearly that this bottom-up approach transfer these one-to-one services into a all-to-one service step by step. In this process, we can choose some many-to-many results.

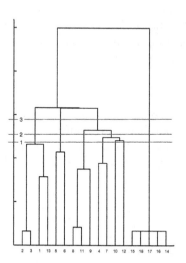

Fig. 3. Results of clustering

The three red lines gives three possible service recommendations. For example, the line 2 gives a result of five services. All the affordances connected by lines below line 2 are placed together like {2, 3, 1, 13}, {5, 6}, {8, 11, 9}, etc. These three kinds of results have their own advantages and disadvantages. The first result is more flexible for consumers to use, while it needs more cost of library to manage and maintain. The third result costs less, but it is less flexible and it loses some reusability at the same time. With these provided results, people should choose their preferable result according to their real needs.

As illustrated before, different disciplines will result in different service candidates generation. Here the second result as mentioned above is chosen to make some further illustrations. According to the second result, this library process service can be separated into five services which can be named as: $Service_1$: online service, $Service_2$: facility service, $Service_3$: library card service, $Service_4$: library service, $Service_5$: logistics service. These five right-granularity services can achieve the objective of high-cohesion and low coupling.

5   Conclusion

The concept of SOA has been debated in recent years, the service granularity is a crucial issue in designing the SOA in order to satisfy low coupling, high cohesion and low reuse cost principles. Although the coarse-grained services have their own significance, its important to deal with other possible granularity levels. In this paper, we have attempted to come up with a new service identification approach which takes advantage of features of semantic analysis. This approach takes the business process as handling object to construct an ontology chart and partition the chart to get the identified services to reduce the coupling of remote functions and to increase the local function cohesion. This proposed framework is being instantiated in the library process to be evaluated but it still needs some improvements. The application of this method challenges us to concentrate our work on designing a special service identification tool, and to validate it in other domains in the future.

Acknowledgements. This work was partially supported by the State Key Laboratory of Software Development Environment of China (No. SKLSDE-2013ZX-25), the National Natural Science Foundation of China (No. 61103095), and the National High Technology Research and Development Program of China (No. 2013AA01A601).

References

1. Amsden, J.: Modeling soa: Part 1. service identification (2007),
   http://www.ibm.com/developerworks/rational/library/07/
2. Bianchini, D., Cappiello, C., De Antonellis, V., Pernici, B.: P2S: A methodology to enable inter-organizational process design through web services. In: van Eck, P., Gordijn, J., Wieringa, R. (eds.) CAiSE 2009. LNCS, vol. 5565, pp. 334–348. Springer, Heidelberg (2009)
3. Bianchini, D., Pernici, B., Cappiello, C., Antonellis, V.D.: Service identification in inter-organizational process design. IEEE Transactions on Services Computing (2013) (in press)

4. Dwivedi, V., Kulkarni, N.: A model driven service identification approach for process centric systems. In: Proceedings of 2008 IEEE Congress on Services, Part II, pp. 65–72 (2008)
5. Gibson, J.J.: The ecological approach to visual perception. Routledge (1986)
6. Gu, Q., Lago, P.: Service identification methods: A systematic literature review. In: Di Nitto, E., Yahyapour, R. (eds.) ServiceWave 2010. LNCS, vol. 6481, pp. 37–50. Springer, Heidelberg (2010)
7. Haesen, R., Snoeck, M., Lemahieu, W., Poelmans, S.: On the definition of service granularity and its architectural impact. In: Bellahsène, Z., Léonard, M. (eds.) CAiSE 2008. LNCS, vol. 5074, pp. 375–389. Springer, Heidelberg (2008)
8. Inaganti, S., Behara, G.K.: Service identification: BPM and SOA handshake. BPTrends 3, 1–12 (2007)
9. Jamshidi, P., Sharifi, M., Mansour, S.: To establish enterprise service model from enterprise business model. In: Proceedings of 2008 IEEE International Conference on Services Computing, pp. 93–100 (2008)
10. Kang, D., Song, C.-y., Baik, D.-K.: A method of service identification for product line. In: Proceedings of 3rd International Conference on Convergence and Hybrid Information Technology, vol. 2, pp. 1040–1045 (2008)
11. Kim, Y., Doh, K.-G.: Pragmatic granularity decision for right-grained services in service-oriented modelling. International Journal of Web and Grid Services 8(2), 111–133 (2012)
12. Kohlborn, T., Korthaus, A., Chan, T., Rosemann, M.: Identification and analysis of business and software services - a consolidated approach. IEEE Transaction on Services Computing 2(1), 50–64 (2009)
13. Liu, K.: Semiotics in Information Systems Engineering. Cambridge University Press (2000)
14. Mani, S., Sinha, V., Sukaviriya, N., Ramachandra, T.: Using user interface design to enhance service identification. In: Proceedings of 2008 IEEE International Conference on Web Services, pp. 78–87 (2008)
15. Wang, Z., Xu, X., Zhan, D.: Normal forms and normalized design method for business service. In: Proceedings of 2005 IEEE International Conference on E-Business Engineering, pp. 79–86 (2005)

A Research on Interaction and Merging between Modern Manufacturing and Producer Services

Jiemei Zhang

Business Management Institute of Henan University,
Kaifeng, China
jiemei1226@163.com

Abstract. The paper defines modern manufacturing and producer services and analyzes the interaction mechanism between these two industries from the perspectives of professional labor division, outsourcing, the production value chain and the ecological community respectively. It reaches the conclusion that a merging mode of interaction is the future development for modern manufacturing and producer services, and that it is imperative to boost such a merging mode in the industrialization of China.

Keywords: modern manufacturing, producer services, outsourcing, interaction and merging.

1 Overview of Modern Manufacturing and Producer Services

1.1 The Definition of Modern Manufacturing

Modern manufacturing is a new concept raised during the economic restructuring of China. *Proposals on Revitalizing Modern Manufcturing in Beijing*, a document issued by Beijing municipal government in Feb., 2003, specified the tasks, objectives and measures of accelerating the development of modern manufacturing in Beijing in the years to come. Statistics Bureau of Beijing city, in accordance with the requirements of sustainable development, put forward the definition of and criteria for modern manufacturing, which was approved by the Statistics Bureau of the State.

Modern manufacturing refers to manufacturing armed with modern science and technology, or a combination of the two. In essence, it means to optimize and upgrade the structure of manufacturing sectors, and it include all the firms and enterprises involved in processing and reprocessing raw materials with high and latest technology. Modern manufacturing is featured by high technology and high added value. It attaches great importance to input of knowledge and technology and therefore into processing, equipment and materials, therefore the products are high in technical content and added value. Modern manufacturing is so closely associated with other sectors that it could largely propel the national economy and serve as an important backbone of the whole industry. It complies with the sustainable development in that it is energy efficient and environment friendly.

K. Liu et al. (Eds.): ICISO 2014, IFIP AICT 426, pp. 176–186, 2014.

Compared with traditional manufacturing, modern manufacturing puts more stress on the input of knowledge and technology and on the application of modern technology, manufacturing organization systems and management concepts in the whole industry organization system with high technical content, more added value and long industry chain, which boasts modern integration production, intensive knowledge and high efficiency.

1.2   The Definition of Producer Services

Some scholars and institutes defined producer services from the angle of service activities involved. The concept of producer service was firstly proposed by American economist H.Greenfield in 1966 when he was studying services sectors and their classification. In 1975, Browning and Singelman also used "producer services" and stated that the services include knowledge-intensive and client-oriented services in finance, insurance, law, taxes and brokerage. Hubbard and Nutter (1982), Daniels (1985) classified services into producer services and consumer services, with the former involving the areas beyond the latter, also including goods storage and distribution, office cleaning and security services. Howells and Green (1986) held that producer services include insurance, banking, finance and other business-related services such as advertising and market research, profession and science services such as accounting and law, research and development services for other companies. Hong Kong Trade Development Council (HKTDC) believes that producer services involve professional services, information and intermediary services, finance and insurance services and other trade-related services.

Some scholars and institutes define producer services from the angle of service functions. Gruble and Walker (1989), Coffer (2000) proposed that producer services neither aim for consumption nor yield products directly, instead, they are the input within the process, playing a role of intermediary for the production of other final products or services. They further pointed out that the producers mainly employ labor and knowledge capital as input sources, with output involving enormous services for labor and knowledge capital, and that producer services can contribute to the professionalization of production, expand capital-intensive and knowledge-intensive production and finally enhance the productivity of labor force and other production elements. Hansen (1990, 1994) indicated that producer services act as an intermediary, present both in upstream activities like research and development, and in downstream ones like market. United States Department of Commerce further divided these functions into two types, one being "allied producer services", responsible for the transactions between the headquarters with branches of foreign-funded producer services corporations (taking up 10% of the total services), the other being "independent producer services" directly collaborating with foreign firms, private enterprises and foreign governments (taking up 90% of the total services). According to Chinese scholars Zhong Yun and Yan Xiaopei (2005), producer services offer services to manufacturing, business activities and governmental management rather than individual consumers, and they do not directly engage in producing process or transformation, though they are the indispensable activity in any industry.

Theoretically, producer services refer to the input services from the market into the producing process, which are employed for further production of the commodities and services. Producer services are the services bought by the producers from the given market and offered for production and business activities instead of individual consumers. They also means the externalization and marketization of services, a trend that internal sectors for producer services are separated from and independent of original enterprises with purposes of reducing costs, improving productivity and enhancing the professional levels of corporate management.

2   The Mode of Interaction between Modern Manufacturing and Producer Services

As a division of labor, producer services are originated from manufacturing, and have a kind of innate kinship with the latter. Producer services are intermediate knowledge input, with manufacturing sectors as their major consumers. They rely on the demands of the manufacturing and contribute to the industry upgrade of the manufacturing. In a nutshell, the two are mutually reliant and stimulative. Their interactive mode can be further divided into an alternative mode and a merging mode.

2.1   The Alternative Mode of Interaction between Modern Manufacturing and Producer Services

This mode is based on the outsourcing of services realized by the market mechanism. The outsource of services refers to the practices that original internal service sectors of the corporation operate independently, free from the control of the corporation or that the corporation seek services or resources from other professional enterprises instead of from its own internal sectors. The practices mainly include outsourcing of services. There is a tendency of resorting to market means during the development of services. Producer services were once conducted through non-market means by the producing sectors, while manufacturers could buy various producer services on the market with the emergence of numerous enterprises specializing in finance, marketing and consultancy.

Outsourcing of services is the main way manufacturers interact with service industries. Manufacturers outsource to professional services enterprises the services that are not directly related to production activities or corporate strategies, such as human resources management, accounting and logistics. Producer services enterprises will in turn expand and diversify their services in order to meet ever-increasing intermediate needs from manufacturers, and hence became more professionalized and larger in size.

Newly-independent services enterprises. These enterprises are originally the internal sectors of large-scale and powerful manufacturers, which grow with much more services capacities than needed by their own enterprises. Hence, the independent professional services enterprises provide services not only for their parent enterprises but for other enterprises. Examples can be found in the independent logistics company and mould designing company of Hair Groups.

These newly-independent services enterprises intensify the competition in the services industry, which boost the internal development of the industry and also contribute to the higher productivity of the manufacturers.

2.2 The Merging Mode of Interaction between Modern Manufacturing and Producer Services

In this mode of deep-level interaction between manufacturers and services enterprises appears a merging tendency characteristic of ambiguity in features of products, organization and products confines. The definite trends are services going industrialized and manufacturing services-oriented. See Figure 1.

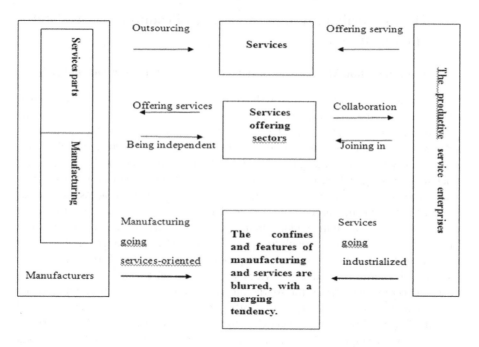

Fig. 1. The Merging Mode of Interaction Between Modern Manufacturing and Producer Services

Services enterprises became the dominant forces of economy with increased productivity and enlarged sizes fulfilled through industrialization of services. Against such a background, a number of large-sized aggressive producer services enterprises spring up and take up the top level of the industry chain, offering services to manufacturers and other services enterprises as well. They expand into other parts of the chain, turning into integrative services enterprises and providing comprehensive services to manufacturers. In the meantime, large-sized manufacturers gradually change from the pure manufacturing mode into a combination of manufacturing and producer services provision. Hence the growing ambiguity of the confines between manufacturers and services enterprises and a merging trend.

In general, the modes of interaction between manufacturers and services enterprises are not classified strictly according to their development phases, rather, they coexist. For instance, market-based practices like outsourcing of services and independent services sectors abound within the merging mode. The differences lie in the conditions under which the modes are applied. A case in point can be found in the newly-independent services enterprises that are operated mainly by large manufacturers instead of small or medium-sized ones. It is certain that only large-sized manufactures capable of developing and offering services stand the chance to become services providers and join the mass producer services industry.

3   The Interaction Mechanism between Producer Services and Manufacturers

3.1   The Interaction Mechanism Based on Labor Division and Outsourcing

According to labor division theory held by the school of Classic Economics, outsourcing of producer services embodies the deep level of labor division and professionalization. Scholars from the school of New System Economics approach the matter with the theory of transaction costs. Coffey & Drolet (1996) thinks that each enterprise is faced with a strategic choice of "DIY of Buy it" which will affect its costs structure, producing and organizing modes, its place in the region or even the structure of the economy. The fact is that enterprises always hope to have access to various recourses and capacities needed to yield products or services at the lowest possible costs so as to stay competitive. Outsourcing of producer services refers to the practice that enterprises get services though transactions with services providers on the market including manufacturers and services enterprises as well. Manufacturers once were the producers of a series of producer services such as internal R & D sectors, wholesale and retail sectors and internal transportation facilities, which were all be provided by the headquarters of the enterprises (Coffey & Polese, 1987). Through "vertical delegating", they now outsource services otherwise provided from inside. In services sectors, externalization is achieved through the so-called soft process of "horizontal delegating" (Michalak & Fairbairn, 1993).

3.2   The Interaction Mechanism Based on the Industry Chain

The concept of "Industry Chain" was first proposed by American scholar, Michael Porter in 1985. He described how customers' value could be formed through a series of practices aimed for final products or services. He split the practices in half, namely, fundamental ones and supporting ones. Later he redefined the industry chain as a series of value-creating practices from fundamental raw materials and providers, through producers to the final products being consumed or transported. Porter (1998) verified that producer services enterprises permeate into every link of the industry chin of manufacturers and provide 5 interrelated input elements during the production process: (1) What products to be made; (2) How to make the products; (3) Process cooperation; (4) Other beneficial services; (5) Distribution. In his opinion, the process for an enterprise to create value can be broken up into different yet correlated value-added activities such as design, production and sale which constitute the industry chain of the enterprise. Not every link can create value which actually comes from some certain activities known as strategic links. The competitive edge of an enterprise in one of these links determines its competitive power in the market. The economic competition of the world indicates that the competitive power of an enterprise relies less on processing and manufacturing than on producer services activities as the market competition intensifies.

From the perspective of the industry value chain, the functions of producer services are as follows: (1) producer services act as a channel through which labor, knowledge and technology capital enter the production process. The application of technology and knowledge in the manufacturing sectors are mainly fulfilled by means of the input of producer services like science and technology development, management consultancy and etc.; (2) producer services are the major sources of added value of products. It is said that in modern manufacturing, the profits of enterprises come mainly from the services links of design and marketing of products rather than processing; (3) producer services are the important approaches for enterprises to form product diversity and to compete with others in aspects other than prices.

3.3   The Interaction Mechanism Based on Ecological Community

The community is originally short for a biotic community, a collection of living species confined in a certain space during a specific period of time. There are three features about the biotic community. Firstly, living creatures in a given community are not scattered by accident, rather, there are complex relations between them in the forms of recycling of matters and transfer of energy. Therefore, there are some structures of constitution and nutrition in a given community. Secondly, biotic communities frequently change their appearances in a certain order as time goes by, with dynamic characteristics of constant development and evolution. Thirdly, the features of a community are not simply the sum of features of all the creatures within it.

In view of the theory of ecology, an economic community refers to a certain organization in the ecological system of economy, one being inherently related to another. The economic community consists of agricultural community, industrial community and modern services community, together with the indispensable manufacturing sub-community and producer services sub-community. See Figure 2.

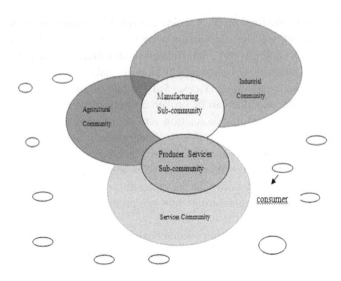

Fig. 2. Composition of the Ecological Community

The fundamental agricultural, industrial and services communities are interacted with each other, the services community being more involved with other communalities. Shelp (1984) pointed out, "Agriculture, excavating and manufacturing are the bricks of the building of economic development with services enterprises being the plaster." Riddle also believes that the services industry contributes to the expansion of other sectors, that they are the adhesive of the economy, providing convenience to the business transaction and impetus to the commodity production and that services are not marginalized or luxurious economic activities but the core of economy. Producer services, as the major part of services, the "adhesive", make it possible for services community to interact and coexist with the other two, forming a organic economic community.

In ecological community of national economy, the labor distribution of manufacturing, outsourcing of services and derivation of industry chain bring about the producer services industry. The upgrade of manufacturing itself requires large quantities of knowledge input, accelerating the development of producer services which, in turn, enhances the competitive power of manufacturing. To summarize, the two industries coexist and develop simultaneously.

Manufacturing sub-community and producer services sub-community can be blended with each other. On the one hand, manufacturing provides a living environment for services in that (1) producer services are derived from manufacturing and (2) manufacturing community are the principal consumers of services. On the other hand, producer services sub-community offer nutrition and knowledge essential to the upgrade of manufacturing.

4   Roads for the Merging Development of Modern Manufacturing and Producer Services Industry

There is an inherent evolution mechanism between producer services and manufacturing that is featured by two-way interaction, close correlation and positive feedback. The services play an important role in the upgrading of manufacturing, with their level of development determining that of manufacturing. On the other hand, manufacturing provides momentum and support as in infrastructure for the upgrading of producer services. The paper proposes the following suggestions from the perspective of the interactive development of the two industries.

4.1   The Hierarchical Level of Manufacturing Should Be Improved So As to Achieve a Positive Interaction with Producer Services

Many manufacturers in China are invested by foreign capital though China is tuning into the world factory. The manufacturing industry of China mainly follows the mode of international subcontracting, which takes advantage of cheap labor pool in China but cannot cultivate strong competitive power.

As the criteria of international labor division convert from industry levels to value chain levels, the power of a nation lies not in certain industries or products but in the chains or processing stages it holds in the whole industry chain. It is imperative for Chinese manufacturers to improve their hierarchical levels in the industry chain. As for those low-level processing stages, the manufacturers can reinforce their control over logistic purchasing, systematic production and quality control and the like by means of modern information technology. They should also master core technology, enhance their core competitive power and build their own brands. With the deepening of labor division, sectors of producer services have already been merged into every link of manufacturing. Services for the higher hierarchical level of manufacturing involve industry research and feasibility research of investment, product development and design, marketing research and venture capital and etc. Services for the middle level involve quality control, accounting, human resources, law consultancy, information and insurance and etc. Services for the low level include the areas in sales, advertising, logistics, maintenance and clients training, etc. These activities are gradually turning into strategic parts for manufacturers to enhance their power. The integration of manufacturing and producer services can optimize resources and affect the product costs at the lower level. It also merges the shared knowledge and other resources of enterprises to the best, providing powerful momentum for the corporate creation, and contributing to the technology innovation, industry transformation and upgrading of manufacturing (Lin Lei, 2008).

4.2   The Soft Environment for Producer Services Should Be Optimized, and the Obstacles in System Abolished

A perfect environment is the important basis on which modern services industry develop. Beside the hardware environment such as modern communications facilities and convenient networks, a soft environment including laws and governmental regulations and policies, systems and mechanisms is also indispensable to modern manufacturing. For instance, the government can establish and consummate policies concerning intermediary services agencies of science and technology, support them in finance, subsidies and taxes and aid innovative practices of higher hierarchical level (Sun, 2009). The notion of "Big Market, Small Government" held by Hong Kong government has set us a good example that the government reduces social transaction costs of public services and social integrity, cultivate an open business environment with moderate supervision, and offer enough space for civilian capital in fields of intermediary agencies, shipping and finance, etc.

In addition, the government should regard developing services industry as an important means to promote manufacturing and the living standard of people while drafting macro policies. Regulations that discriminate or restrict the further development of services industries should be abolished in order for services industry to enjoy the same treatment with manufacturing in aspects of investment, market entrance qualifications, governmental financial support, water and electricity supplies. Strict rules regulation over monopoly sectors as telecom and banking, railroad transportation and broadcasting should give way to a competition mechanism and less control over price and investment for enterprises to enter the market freely so as to enhance service quality and efficiency.

4.3   The Financial Industry as the Core of Cervices Industry Should Be Accelerated and the Industry Code Reinforced

The services industry with the financial services as the core is the important back-up of the upgrading and development of Chinese manufacturing. Therefore, it is vital to complete the development mechanism of financial services industry, set up and improve regional financial service center and reasonably integrate regional financial resources. One top priority now is to reform regional financial agencies and abrogate obstacles inherent in the system. Favorable conditions should be offered to small and medium-sized manufacturers in applying for loans. Professional corporations offering financial guarantee for small and medium-sized manufacturers could be cultivated step by step to fund these enterprises for their turning into high-tech and capital-intensive ones. For another, various financial innovation mechanisms could be adopted to lower the risks for financial services industry and to improve their efficiency, which will greatly benefit the competitive power of manufacturing in China. What's more, the infrastructure for the financial services industry should be strengthened, so is the financial system of multi-layer and great variety. The initial advance of manufacturing relies to great extent on fund, while enterprises in China have to raise money on their own, deriving only a small sum of capital from financial agencies. Since lack of fund will retard the development of manufacturing on the higher part of industry chain, it is important to broaden the financial channel for manufacturing and create a positive environment for the upgrading of manufacturing.

The intermediary services of science and technology, as a type of technology capital, provide powerful technology support for the upgrading of manufacturing in

China. As China's economy develops and social labor division deepens, creation initiatives will gradually involve with the upgrading process of manufacturing and exert increasingly great influence. The service quality of intermediary agencies of science and technology should be improved with more coverage of services and a set of qualification evaluation criteria, against the background in which such agencies abound recently. Meanwhile, great efforts should be made to raise practitioners' awareness of service and their professional capacity and morality, preventing the immoral behaviors from happening. Furthermore, compound talents of high level should be admitted into intermediary agencies of services to optimize the personnel structure, which will enable intermediary agencies of science and technology to contribute to the creation system and the whole industry value chain, bringing added value to the industry.

4.4 More Efforts Should Be Made to Cultivate Talents, Building a Talents Pool for the Further Development of Manufacturing and Services Industry

The government should give top priority to producer services, lowering the market entrance qualifications, building a sound market for competition and offering favorable treatment in policies. Talents are the most crucial element for the new type, knowledge-intensive producer services industry. So the government is expected to do well in cultivation of needed talents to virtually enhance the efficiency, quality and development level of producer services industry in China, which can be realized through close cooperation of enterprises, universities and research institutes.

The development of services industry and the upgrading of manufacturing require highly professionalized talents. In order to meet such need, more capital should be invested into human resources and cooperation between enterprises and universities should be intensified to cultivate professionals of high level. Besides, measures should be taken to attract overseas professionals, turning China into a real power rich in human capital other than human resources. This calls for complete systems in talents cultivation and movement and creative systems to prevent brain drain. Last, due attention should be paid to the training of competent ordinary laborers and technicians who are also indispensable to the sustainable development and competitive power of manufacturing of China.

References

1. Baldonado, M., Chang, C.-C.K., Gravano, L., Paepcke, A.: The Stanford Digital Library Metadata Architecture. Int. J. Digit. Libr. 1, 108–121 (1997)
2. Bruce, K.B., Cardelli, L., Pierce, B.C.: Comparing Object Encodings. In: Ito, T., Abadi, M. (eds.) TACS 1997. LNCS, vol. 1281, pp. 415–438. Springer, Heidelberg (1997)
3. van Leeuwen, J. (ed.): Computer Science Today. LNCS, vol. 1000. Springer, Heidelberg (1995)
4. Michalewicz, Z.: Genetic Algorithms + Data Structures = Evolution Programs, 3rd edn. Springer, Heidelberg (1996)

5. Cohen, S., Zyman, J.: Manufacturing Matters: the Myth of the Post Industrial Economy Basic Books. New York (1987)
6. Rowthorn, P., Ramaswamy, R.: Growth, Trade and Deindustrialization I Mf Staff Papers, pp. 18–41 (1999)
7. Klodt, H.: Structural Change Towards Services: the German Experience University of Birmingham. IGS Discussion Paper (2000)
8. Gurrierp, M.: International Competitiveness in Produces. Paper Presented at the SETI Meeting Room (2003)
9. Pappas, N., Sheehan, P.: The New Manufacturing; Linkage Between Production and Service Activities. In: Sheehan, P., Tegart, G. (eds.) Working for the Future Melbourne, pp. 127–155. Victoria University Press (1998)
10. Karaomerlioglu, D., Carlsson, B.: Manufacturing in Decline? A Matter of Definition Economy, Innovation, NewTechnology, 175–196 (1999)
11. Linyan, S.: Theory and Practice of Service-oriented Manufacturing. Tsinghua University Press, Beijing (2009)
12. Lei, L., Guisheng, W.: The Development of Manufacturing and Services Innovation. Science Press, Beijing (2008)

An Architecture for Improving Hajj Management

Mohammad Yamin[1] and Moteb Ayesh Albugami[2]

[1] Department of MIS, King Abdulaziz University, Saudi Arabia,
[2] Faculty of Business Adminstration, Tabuk University, Saudi Arabia
myamin@kau.edu.sa, malbugami@ut.edu.sa

Abstract. The effective management of crowded events such as the Muslim Hajj in Saudi Arabia and the Hindu Kumbh in India continues to remain a challenge mainly due to uncontrollable buildup of crowds or mismanagement. Despite regular occurrence of catastrophes such as stampedes and fires, resulting in significant loss of lives, there are no international binding standards for controlling and managing large crowds. Indeed, the use of advanced technology, including tracking and monitoring tools, and sensor and biometric identification methods, can assist towards better crowd management but technology alone cannot be a solution to overcrowding. Because of the congestion, resulting from overcrowding, timely cleaning and sanitation becomes unmanageable, which causes spread of diseases. This article discusses some factors which are critically important and provide an architecture for better management of Hajj.

Keywords: Management, Crowd, Hajj, Kumbh, Stampedes, RFID, Sensor Networks, Biometric, pilgrims, tawaf.

1   Introduction

In the last decade alone, thousands of people have perished in stampedes, fires and other incidents resulting from overcrowding or mismanagement of large gatherings of people. Ironically most of the crowded events happen to be religious in nature. On 13th October 2013, more than one hundred people died due to overcrowding on a bridge in India [1]. On 10th February 2013, dozens of people were crushed to death in Kumbh [17]. On the eve of 2013, more than sixty people were killed and hundreds injured in Ivory Coast [2]. Excessive death toll (over eleven hundred) and injuries (over two and a half thousands) in a building collapse in Bangladesh on 24th April, 2013 was also partly due to overcrowding [18]. In Hajj alone, during the last twenty years, several stampedes and fires have resulted in thousands of deaths, the most recent [3] being in October 2012. To analyze and describe the problems of overcrowding, we have chosen the case of Hajj, which is an annual event involving a gathering of more than three million with very intense activities.

The Hajj is a pilgrimage to Makkah in Saudi Arabia that takes place every year during 8th-12th Dhulhijja, a month in the Islamic (lunar) calendar. Every year millions of pilgrims from more than one hundred and fifty countries perform Hajj. Although

K. Liu et al. (Eds.): ICISO 2014, IFIP AICT 426, pp. 187–196, 2014.

the Hajj rituals span only four fixed days, but partly due to limited air and sea transportation, many of the pilgrims spend four to six weeks in and around Makkah (Mecca) and Madinah (Medina), the two holiest cities for Muslims. The Hajj is a unique, very complex, challenging and costly exercise to manage as it involves frequent mass movement of more than three million pilgrims. Some of the problems and aspects of Hajj can be found in [10], [11], [12], [13], [14] and [15]

The most critical factors in crowd management are the extent of the crowd and its management. To minimize the chances of stampedes and other catastrophes, event organisers need to limit the crowds to acceptable levels. However, there is no binding international standard for setting a limit on the number of people which could be allowed to gather in a specified space or area. Event organization would become significantly easier to manage if such standards were agreed upon and implemented. Crowd management can also be improved significantly with the help of sensor and biometric technology, tools and gadgets. Some of the intensely crowded events like the Hajj often involve simultaneous movement of the entire congregation, which creates problems of transportation and uncontrollable buildup of crowd. In such situations, tracking, accessibility and identification of pilgrims becomes very difficult. Many of the sensor and wireless devices available today, including Radio Frequency Identification (RFID) [5] can be used for controlling and monitoring the movement of crowds. These technologies are now being widely used for improving management and administration of many business functions. However, these technologies are still going through a transitional phase [9] and one would hope to see significant refinement of them to become usable and effective for managing very large and dense crowds. Nevertheless, these technologies in their present form could have been used in saving thousands of precious lives in many of the past incidents of stampedes and fires. A description of ubiquitous technologies including RFID, sensor networks, biometric and scanning devices can be found in [5].

There are serious health issues for crowded events with a span of three or more days, if cleaning and disposal of rubbish cannot be carried out regularly. Lack of cleaning gives rise to the growth of dangerous bacteria, which has been witnessed in some cases [6]. Another serious health risk is from the mismanagement of the pilgrims carrying communicable and contagious viruses, bacteria and diseases. Due to inability to control entry, many pilgrims may carry deadly bacteria such as HIV Aids and Hepatitis. Many of these infected pilgrims may not be known to the management and hence cannot be isolated. Indeed the infected pilgrims must be isolated from the rest of the pilgrims. For managing the health and wellbeing of the pilgrims, including those infected with contagious bacteria, the RFID technology can play a very significant role [21].

In this paper we present and analyze a number of problems of hajj management, and offer some solutions including architecture for improving the management. These solutions can indeed be applied in many other and similar crowded events such as Kumbh.

2   The Hajj Management Issues

Hajj is a set of highly complex and intense activities which makes it a very challenging event to manage. Overseas pilgrims start arriving in Saudi Arabia five weeks before the actual hajj period. Late arrivals stay back for up to five weeks after the event. The hajj rituals however only span over four days, from 8-12 of the Arabic (lunar) month of Dhulhijja. The problems and challenges of Hajj are generally not known to many researchers mainly because of the entry restrictions and poor press and media coverage.

2.1   Pilgrims Numbers

Due to an overwhelming number of requests, which cannot be accommodated, people (including the Saudi citizens) are restricted to perform Hajj once in five years. However, this moratorium has so far not been successfully implemented. Current facilities for hajj are adequate only for two million people. One of the main problems for the Hajj mangers is to deal with a large number of illegal pilgrims. Makkah region, which has a population of about two million, largely contributes to the illegal pilgrims. According to the governor of Makkah [16], in 2012, up to 3.65 million pilgrims performed hajj, which nearly doubled the maximum accommodation capacity. Some other sources, including eye witness accounts of congestions put these figures even much higher which demonstrates that the number of the hajj pilgrims is often uncontrollable. Most of the expatriates, living in the kingdom of Saudi Arabia, are always very eager to perform hajj every year and many of them happen to be illegal migrants. Presence of the unauthorized pilgrims, especially the illegal immigrants, is a cause of great concern, particularly in relation to law and order agencies. The hajj managers do not have any personal and health data for these pilgrims. Hence they also pose serious health risks, severely strain the pilgrim movement, sometimes causing stampedes. During the 2012 Hajj, due to overcrowding, walking on roads became very strenuous and sometimes resulted in minor stampedes. In the case of an emergency, due to the lack of data, illegal pilgrims are very vulnerable

2.2   Visa and Immigration

Anyone outside Saudi Arabia, intending to perform Hajj, applies for a visa through a travel agent in their country of residence by furnishing information and undergoing some medical examination and immunisation. The hajj visa is granted by the Saudi government if the visa conditions are met. Once a Hajj visa is granted, each pilgrim is assigned to a Hajj Management group, known as Munazzim, who are responsible for organising travel and accommodation before, during and after the hajj. The Munazzim groups are the official representatives of the Ministry of Hajj.

For an overseas pilgrim, there are very strict visa requirements for entering in the kingdom of Saudi Arabia. The foreign pilgrims are mainly processed at Jeddah and

Madinah airports, which are about ninety and four hundred kilometers away from Makkah, respectively. Jeddah is not only the designated airport of Makkah but also has the main sea port where hundreds of thousands of pilgrims, mainly from Africa, are processed. So far there is only one 4x4 lane road link between Jeddah and Makkah but currently a rail link is also under construction. Most of the pilgrims also visit Madinah, which houses the grand mosque of the prophet Muhammad and is also his final resting place. After the immigration processing, the pilgrims are required to hand over their passports to their Munazzim and travel to their hotels in Makkah or Madinah in the care of the Munazzim group.

2.3   Assemblies in Mina, Arafat and Muzdalifah

As part of the core activities of Hajj, all pilgrims are required to spend some time in Mina, Arafat and Muzdalifah. The tent city of Mina [7], separated from Makkah by about seven kilometers of very thick hills, has historically predefined perimeters. It covers an area of about twenty square kilometers and has thousands of nonflammable tents that can accommodate about one and half million pilgrims . All pilgrims are required to spend three days in Mina. By a very simple arithmetic calculation, it is easy to determine that Mina cannot accommodate more than two million pilgrims.

The Valley of Arafat [19] hills are about twenty kilometers away from Mina. All pilgrims must spend the best part of the day of 9th Dhulhijja there. This area has a capacity to accommodate about two million pilgrims. Muzdalifah is a small village between Mina and Arafat. All pilgrims are required to spend the night of 9th Dhulhijja in Muzdalifah, which nowadays can accommodate up to a maximum of one million people as a large portion of its area has been consumed by the multiple roads running between Mina and Arafat. On their way back from Arafat valley, all pilgrims are required to spend the night of the 9th Dhulhijja in the open space, previously a hill, near the town of Muzdalifah. The space in Muzdalifah is much smaller than that of Arafat or Mina. There is not enough space for even one million people. As a result, roads get jammed for many hours and many pilgrims cannot make it to Muzdalifah until the morning of the next day.

The journey from Mina to Arafat on the morning of the 9th of Dhulhijja and then from Arafat to Muzdalifah in the evening is a very complex exercise. The hajj management ought to be congratulated for transporting more than three million people from Mina to Arafat and back on the same day. Since 2010, there is a train service linking Mina, Muzdalifah and Arafat; however this service can transport only a fraction of the three million passengers. Sometimes, the number of pilgrims' swells to four millions as it did in 2012. In desperate situations, many pilgrims would find alternative accommodation in adjoining townships, roadsides, hills, pathways, and rooftops, endangering their lives and those of others.

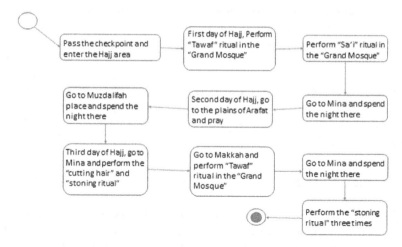

Fig. 1. Diagram of core activities of hajj

2.4   Core Rituals of Hajj

Fig 1 shows a diagram of the core activities of Hajj. On the 8th day of Dhulhijja, the first day of hajj, all pilgrims travel to, and spend the night in the tent city of Mina. On the 9th day of Dhulhijja, all pilgrims travel to the Valley of Arafat Mountains, located about twenty kilometers from Mina. Assembly in the Arafat valley on the afternoon of the 9th day of Dhulhijja is mandatory for all pilgrims. After the sunset, all pilgrims must travel to Muzdalifah, a hill town between the valley of Arafat and Mina. At Muzdalifah pilgrims are normally required to offer prayers and to spend the night in the open space. In the morning of the 10th day of Dhulhijja, all pilgrims arrive back in Mina where they perform a set of rituals. These rituals include symbolic stoning, known as 'Rami' at sites of devils, popularly known as Jamarat, and a journey to grand mosque in Makkah where they perform tawaf (circumvolution) of Kaaba and offer prayers in the holy mosque. On the 11th day of Dhulhijja, pilgrims remain in Mina and perform a set of rituals including another act of stoning at Jamarat. On the 12th day of Dhulhijja, after another set of stoning rituals, the hajj is completed and the pilgrims return back to their hotels or homes. After a few days, foreign pilgrims gradually start returning back to their home countries. Some pilgrims have to wait for up to five weeks to return to their home countries.

2.5   Health Risks and Lost Pilgrims

Currently hajj permissions may be granted for people suffering from serious medical conditions. However, the management of pilgrims suffering from contagious and communicable diseases is highly desirable. It is extremely dangerous to allow pilgrims carrying HIV, hepatitis, swine flu, bird flu, and tuberculosis to live with other pilgrims. Such pilgrims must be identified and isolated. On the other hand, lack of cleaning and sanitation due to intense crowding, especially during the four days of hajj, causes many pilgrims to develop a cough and fever.

As the hajj involves frequent mass movement and activities, many pilgrims disperse from their groups and lose their way. Due to communication problems, lack of education, congestion, poor network reception and many other reasons these pilgrims go on missing for days and sometimes weeks. Some of these pilgrims are injured and require urgent medical attention. Currently, pilgrims carry a non-electronic wristband, which only identifies a pilgrim belonging to group of thousands of pilgrims under a Munazzim.

3   Some Solutions

Although the Saudi Arabian government has provided extensive and superior infrastructure to facilitate Hajj but still, some problems of congestion, resulting in disasters like stampedes, fires and spread of diseases persist. In the case of road congestion, extra infrastructure just increases the usage and doesn't reduce congestion [4]. Thus a good infrastructure is not necessarily a viable substitute for effective management. Here we present some solutions to the problems, including an architecture, to improve the management of hajj.

3.1   Controlling the Pilgrim Numbers

In order to be able to effectively manage hajj, it is absolutely necessary to limit the number of pilgrims to an acceptable level. Some extraordinary measures are required to be implemented for stopping illegal pilgrims. The lack of these measures has witnessed a swelling crowd in 2012. Learning from the problems encountered earlier, during the hajj of 2013, the management ran a very successful campaign of effective advertisements at all levels of media vowing to very severe punitive measure for unauthorized pilgrims. These measures did succeed in limiting the number of pilgrims to about two million, but still there were no significant reduction in the number of illegal pilgrims from Makkah region. To minimize the chances of locals contributing to the catastrophes, it is highly desirable to organize crowd management training programs and encourage the people, especially the ones from Makkah region, to participate.

3.2   Pilgrim Tracking and Identification

Currently many organizations and businesses are using RFID chips with a sensor or a WiFi network to track and monitor people and products. For example, passports of many countries are now RFID enabled, which leads to immigration processing without human intervention. Some RFID tags [8] such as shown in Fig 2 can be used to replace traditional wristbands. The RFID tags can carry vital data and can be supported with a sensor, GPS or a 3G network to relay data to the data center. An account of the description, usage and usefulness of RFID can be found in [5].

Fig. 2. RFIDs for human use and tracking

3.3 Prevention of Spread of Diseases

There are two prerequisites for preventing the spread of diseases during hajj namely, controlling the number of illegal pilgrims and availability of data of every pilgrim's health including diseases that can affect others. By preventing illegal pilgrims, the management can effectively get the hajj precinct regularly cleaned and hence prevent the outbreaks of bacteria that normally develop within seventy-two hours of non-disposal of garbage. Instead of preventing pilgrims with diseases like HIV Aids, tuberculosis and Hepatitis, hajj management should create a secluded isolation area for the infected pilgrims. Socially and religiously, it would be very hard to deny pilgrimage to people on their deathbeds. So if they cannot be stopped, they should be properly managed.

The problems of crowding in Mina, Arafat and Muzdalifah are dependent on pilgrim numbers, religious interpretations and infrastructure. It is simply impossible to accommodate two million people in Muzdalifah, prompting religious decree to ease the overcrowding. Some traffic congestion problems may ease in coming years once the rail links (under construction) between Jeddah, Makkah, Mina, and Madinah become operational. Currently, there are hundreds of towers and many other large buildings under construction to meet the increasing demand of accommodation.

3.4 Operations Overview

While there are a lot of issues associated with the Hajj, the most important is the need to managing the crowd and facilities during the Hajj period. The component diagram in Fig 3 shows an overview of the proposed operations architecture.

As shown in Fig 3, the crowd controller will be responsible for monitoring and managing, transportation, health care services, security services and ritual sites. The transportation is managed by scheduling, based on the number of people in a ritual site at given time. In case of emergency, the controller will inform and request help from health care and security services. The controller will liaise with the security services in a two ways communication, where they can report and receive reports about security issues. The controller receives information about the situation and status in the various ritual sites. Accommodation will be available for all pilgrims upon arrival in the ritual sites, of Mina, Arafat and Muzdalifah, which would be equipped with the required facilities. Buses and trains would transport pilgrims

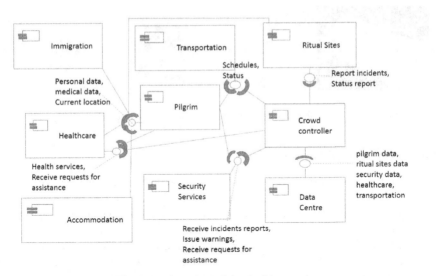

Fig. 3. An Overview of the Architecture

between sites. The rituals sites would be monitored and receive instructions or request help from the controller. Additionally, the controller would monitor the movements of individuals and crowd for security, health and traffic reason.

The architecture and other solutions proposed in this paper can be useful in managing many other crowded events such as Kumbh and Badrinath Yatra [20].

4   Conclusions

People continue to die due to mismanagement of crowded events. The culture of blame game needs to change by squarely making the local management and government responsible for all overcrowding and preventable catastrophes in their jurisdiction. Surely, better and improved infrastructure may help in checking overcrowding but infrastructure alone is not sufficient to prevent hazardous incidents. There is a need for well-coordinated management of crowds with modern tools and technology. The technology, if used as part of a whole solution, can be very effective in controlling crowds but may not bring desired results if used in a standalone mode as is the case of hajj or Kumbh management. The hajj rituals are based on Abrahamic traditions mentioned in the holy Quran which were enacted by Mohammed, the prophet of Islam. Thus being deeply enshrined in religious teachings and faith, some changes cannot be implemented unless approved by the clerics.

Technological solutions, irrespective of their sophistication, become ineffective because of the ignorance, which prevails in almost all religious gatherings. Incidentally, most of the large gatherings are religious in nature and sadly most of the stampedes are associated with religious gatherings. These religious assemblies gather people from diverse ethnicities, beliefs and cultures, which make it very difficult to make simple changes against sectarian religious perceptions. However, through persistent cross-cultural consultation, and discussions at national and international levels, managers of such events can bring many desirable changes.

Acknowledgment. The inspiration for this article has come from personal experiences of the authors who have performed hajj several times, and who have also participated in many other crowded events including the Kumbh. The authors acknowledge support from the faculty of Economics and Administration of the King Abdulaziz University. The authors also acknowledge the help provided by various individuals and organisations involved in the hajj management including the Hajj Research Centre in Makkah and the Ministry of Interior of Saudi Arabia.

References

1. ABC Online News, Scores dead after bridge stampede near Hindu temple in India, http://www.abc.net.au/news/2013-10-13/scores-killed-in-indian-bridge-collapse-during-hindu-gathering/5019484 (retrieved January 10, 2014)
2. CNN, Ivory Coast mourns 60 killed in New Year's stampede (January 2, 2013), http://edition.cnn.com/2013/01/01/world/africa/ivory-coast-deaths (retrieved January 10, 2014)
3. Daily Mail, 50 pilgrims' dead in Hajj stampede, http://www.dailymail.co.uk/news/article-07141/50-pilgrims-dead-Hajj-stampede.html (retrieved February 15, 2013)
4. Duranton, G., Turner, M.A.: The fundamental law of road congestion: Evidence from US cities. The American Economic Review 101(6), 2616–2652 (2011)
5. Finkenzeller, K.: RFID Handbook: Fundamentals and Applications in Contactless Smart Cards, Radio Frequency Identification and Near-Field Communication, 3rd edn. Wiley (2010)
6. McConnell, J.: The Lancet Infectious Diseases. Mass gatherings health Series, vol. 12(1), pp. 8–9 (January 2012)
7. Mina, Saudi Arabia, http://en.wikipedia.org/wiki/Mina,_Saudi_Arabia (retrieved January 10, 2014)
8. Rfid stock photos and images, http://www.fotosearch.com/photos-images/rfid.html (retrieved February 23, 2014)
9. Talevski, A., Wu, C., Chang, E.: Wireless Sensors, SOA and Web Based Approaches for Remote Operation and Control. In: 7th IEEE International Conference on Industrial Informatics, INDIN (2009)
10. Yamin, M., Ades, Y.: Crowd Management with RFID & Wireless Technologies. In: Proceedings of First International Conference on Networks & Communications. IEEE Computer Society Washington, DC (2009)
11. Yamin, M., Huang, X., Dharmendra, S.: Wireless & Sensor Technology and Crowd Management. Journal of Cooperation among University, Research and Industrial Enterprises 2(1) (April 2009)
12. Yamin, M., Masoud, M., Huang, X., Sharma, D.: RFID Technology and Crowded Event Management. In: Proceedings of International Conference on Intelligent Agents, Web Technologies and Internet Commerce, Vienna, December 10-12 (2008)

13. Yamin, M.: A Framework For Improved Hajj Management And Future Research. ENTIC Bull. 2(08) (2008)
14. Yamin, M.: A Framework For Improved Hajj Management And Future Research. In: Proceedings of International Engineering Convention Jeddah, Saudi Arabia, March 10-14 (2007)
15. Yamin, M.: Wireless Systems to Manage Large Congregations, Proceedings of Keynote Addresses and Invited Lectures. In: 2nd International Conference on Wireless Communications and Sensor Networks, Allahabad India, pp. 17–19 (2006)
16. Saudi Gazette (November 10, 2012), http://www.pressdisplay.com/pressdisplay/viewer.aspx (retrieved January 10, 2014)
17. The Guardian, Kumbh Mela stampede leaves dozens of Hindu pilgrims dead – video (retrieved February 15, 2013), http://www.guardian.co.uk/world/video/2013/feb/11/kumbh-mela-stampede-hindu-video (retrieved January 10, 2014)
18. Wikipedia, Savar Building Collapse (2013), http://en.wikipedia.org/wiki/2013_Savar_buil-ding_collapse (retrieved February 15, 2013)
19. Wikipedia, Mount Arafat, http://en.wikipedia.org/wiki/Mount_Arafat (retrieved January 10, 2014)
20. Wikipedia, Badrinath, http://en.wikipedia.org/wiki/Badrinath (retrieved February 15, 2013)
21. Yao, W.: The use of RFID in healthcare: Benefits and barriers. In: Proceedings of IEEE International Conference on RFID-Technology and Applications, RFID-TA (2010)

How Enterprise Architecture Formative Critical Success Facets Might Affect Enterprise Architecture Success: A Literature Analysis

Haining Wan, Aimin Luo, and Xueshan Luo

Science and Technology on Information Systems Engineering Laboratory,
National University of Defence Technology, 410072 Changsha, P.R. China
{hnwan,amluo,xsluo}@nudt.edu.cn

Abstract. Though Enterprise Architecture (EA) is getting increasing attentions from both academics and practitioners, EA research around EA success factors remains modest and immature. This study explores how EA formative critical success facets/factors would affect the achievement of EA success. This research highlights the importance of four mediators, i.e., (I) Real and mature business needs; (II) Real and continuous commitment; (III) Actionable EA programs; and (IV) Well-controlled execution of EA programs. This study deepens our understanding of EA success and would be of explanatory contribution to EA value development and action-guiding contribution to EA adoption and implementation.

Keywords: Enterprise architecture success, Success facets, Formative factors, Casual relationship, Literature analysis.

1   Introduction

Enterprise architecture now is emerging as an enterprise problem-oriented discipline [1], and actually problem-finding is more concerned than problem-solving [2]. Though Enterprise architecture gains increasing attentions from both academics and practitioners, "we are far from establishing a solid empirical base for enterprise architecture" [3]. EA is multi-dimensional [4, 5]. As a result, EA success sounds somewhat multi-dimensional. Similarly, formative EA success factors sounds multi-faceted. Partly due to this reason, still there is no single commonly agreed-upon definition for Enterprise Architecture[6, 7], as a result, "defining EA is highly debated in both academia and industry" [8].

Several studies around EA success factors (cf. [3, 9]) are dedicated to demystifying the potential formative success factors of enterprise architecture. Still, understanding of EA success remains modest. In practice, measure, trace and control of EA success look quite immature [8, 10-13] with inadequate success measurement [14]. The casual relationships between EA success factors and EA success are not well conceptualized and keep constantly unclear.

This research is dedicated to demystify these casual relationships. The rest of this paper is organized as follows. Section 2 details the research design. After that,

K. Liu et al. (Eds.): ICISO 2014, IFIP AICT 426, pp. 197–209, 2014.

Section 3 briefly presents the many EA success factors/facets. Then Section 4 as the core of this study proposes a synthesizing model. Finally, Section 5 concludes the paper.

2   Research Design

The research model is illustrated in Fig. 1. With EA success in the center, matters as to EA success factors in two directions are present in Fig. 1, i.e., (I) formative-affective EA success factors, and (II) reflective-indicative EA success factors. The inherent distinction between formative and reflective factors could be found in [15, 16]. It is noteworthy that *lag effects* and *EA reflective factors* are **excluded** in our focus; instead, as highlighted in **bold** in Fig. 1, we concentrate on EA formative factors and their relations to EA success.

Fundamentally, (time) *lag effect* between EA investment and its payoff objectively exists. Therein it is quite a challenge to make a balance between long-term interest and short-term payoff [17]. And it is somewhat necessary to "focus architectural decisions where the payoff is highest and maximize your likelihood of success"[18]. From the organization learning theory [19], lag effect is quite important in measuring EA success, but at the same time makes it quite problematic to measure EA success.

Fig. 1. Research model

Concerning EA reflective factors, EA quality as used in [9] includes process quality and outcome quality [5, 20, 21]. Therein, outcome quality includes design quality and implementation quality. Correspondingly, in EA implementation, project/program effectiveness and the achievement of objectives might be used to determine the extent of achieved success. Regarding process quality, EA maturity and EA capability could be employed as indicators.

Two research steps are applied, i.e.,

(I) Literature review to extract EA success factors/facets. In this step, we focus on identifying EA success factors. Further, by individual reflection and collective communication, the many identified EA success factors are categorized into four facets.

(II) Literature analysis and synthesis to reveal the connections. This step is the core of this research. Around the four facets, we analyze and synthesize the literature with our understandings. A conceptual model is presented to theorize the casual relationships between the four categorized EA success facets and EA success.

Further, the main research structure is summarized in Table 1.

Table 1. Research structure

Constructs	Notes
Research question	How does EA formative success factors/facets contribute to EA success?
Research objective	This study aims to demystify the casual relationships between the many potential EA formative success factors/facets and EA success.
Research assumption	• As to different organizational EA adoption and implementation, we assume that there are some common EA success factors and those success factors could be organized to form some particular facets. • We also assume that their (the success factors/facets) casual relationship to EA success is observable, somewhat objective, constructible and understandable.
Research methodology	• Prescriptive literature analysis within which research critiques, analyzes and extends existing literature and attempts to build new groundwork [22]. • Abductive reasoning
Research contribution	Theoretically, this study conceptualizes EA by connecting EA success factors/facets and EA success within four mediators. The four mediators are also of practical value as guiding checkpoints in EA adoption and implementation.
Potential pitfall	• At present, no well-defined understanding of EA success with reflective indicators is openly-accessibly present. • At present, no well-accepted collection of EA success factors/facets is openly-accessibly present.

3   EA Formative Success Facets

A pilot title search with keywords "enterprise architecture" from 1990 through 2012 was conducted in a website[1], where we can set our target database as the eight senior basket journals [23]. That test search got merely four relevant articles. Further detailed check showed that those four articles were actually irrelevant to our present research. Thus we changed our search strategy. With keywords of "enterprise architecture" and "success factors OR failure factors", a computerized content search based on Google Scholar was applied to gather related materials. A three-step checking-verifying process was applied in order to identify pertinent literature and to exclude the irrelevant ones.

We **firstly** checked the *title* and *abstract*. If the material was relevant, then we went to the second step, otherwise, the material was left abandoned. The relevance of material was dependent on the answer to questions whether the material was about EA and whether it was possible for success factors to be addressed in the material. If 'yes' for both questions, then the material was labeled as relevant, otherwise, the

---

[1] cf. URL: http://www.vvenkatesh.com/ISranking/AdvSearch.asp

Table 2. EA formative success factors and facets

Facet	Factors terminology [3, 9, 24-43]
EA readiness and preparation	Terms, definitions, and understandings of EA
	Understanding of high-level business formal structure (e.g., strategy, vision, mission, objective, etc.)
	Purpose and EA scenarios
	Definition and refinement of the scope of architecture
	Business linkage (the extent for business to be linked in EA practice)
	Business cases (e.g., best practice)
	Organization culture
	Business model
	Sensibility and awareness of the need of change
	EA team skills
	Domain knowledge
	Training and education
Top commitment and leadership	Support & commitment from/of top executives
	Active involvement of top executives
	Identification of stakeholders
	Participation and coordination of stakeholders
	Communication between stakeholders
	Achieving consensuses
EA domain techniques	EA deliverables & artifacts
	Innovation and creativity in EA design
	EA resources and architecture repository management
	Architecture analyzing, satisfying, optimizing, assessing and evaluating
	Architectural principles
	Modeling techniques, languages & Software tools
	Architectural frameworks and methodologies, process
EA governance and program management	Governance model & structure and monitoring
	Sourcing and outsourcing (Involvement of external consultant service)
	Roles, accountability, responsibility
	Project and program management
	Transition management (The planning, arrangement of transitions in EA implementation)
	Risk control
	Cost control
	Investment policy (strategy)

material would be labeled as irrelevant. **Secondly**, we continued to check the content of the material. In this step, we questioned whether there were any insightful findings or summaries about factors in relation to EA success. If so, we went to the third step. Otherwise, the material would still be left abandoned. **Thirdly**, we would check the *socio-technical context* in which success factors were presented and discussed. We would label the success factors if the specific context was compatible with lifecycle-long EA success.

From final 24 searched materials, we gathered 33 success factors. The labeled success factors are then categorized into four facets, as shown in Table 2. Avoiding the situation of EA as an end in itself [14] and regarding the objective existence of lag effect, Here the lens of lifecycle-long EA success, is employed in facet categorization. Consequently, four EA success facets overarch the many potential EA critical success factors, i.e.,

- *EA readiness and preparation.* This facet deals with organizational fundamental understanding towards EA, the introduction of EA to a specific, and organizational preparation for introducing EA. In principle, this facet affects not only EA introduction but also change execution in EA implementation.
- *Top Commitment and leadership.* This facet relates to the commitment from top executives and other stakeholders and provides sufficient power to perform organizational changes.
- *EA domain techniques.* This facet refers to the professional EA techniques, affairs or the skills what enterprise architecture should acquire.
- *EA governance and program management.* Factors in this category concern mainly management-control issues in relation to incremental EA implementation and lifecycle-long EA maintain.

Detailed meanings and potential contextual application of these success factors could be found in the literature. Due the limit of pages and that it is not the focus of this paper, hereby related information are not attached.

4   The Synthesizing Research Model

With the research model in Section 2 at hand, based on literature analysis and synthesis, we develop a new conceptual model to illustrate how these extracted EA success factors could contribute to achieving EA success, as shown in Fig. 2. In the following subsections, we will explain the model step-by-step.

The many success factors together contribute to EA success through four mediators, including: (I) ensuring that there are real and mature business needs; (II) ensuring that real and continuous commitment is available; (III) facilitating actionable EA programs; and (IV) ensuring that there would be well controlled (in the sense of time, budget, and other resources) execution of EA programs in organizations.

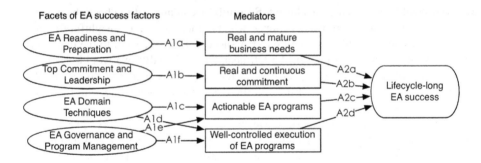

Fig. 2. Synthesizing model: revised research model

4.1   Discussion

Obviously, in the synthesizing model, factors in the first two facets (i.e., *EA readiness and preparation* and *Top commitment and leadership*) bridges '**what - why**'-related issues. These two facets help to answer fundamental questions like 'what is EA' and 'why to adopt EA in an organization'. The 'what - why'-related issues help to ensure that EA is adopted necessarily, timely, readily and promisingly.

In contrast, factors in the latter two facets (i.e., EA techniques and EA governance and program management) address '**how**'-related issues of EA practice. The 'how'-related issues connect the consequential affairs, including *creation, implementation, maintenance* and *upgrade* of EA design in accordance to the four steps (i.e., as illustrated in [44], *plan, do, check, action*).

In the synthesizing model, the arrows (A2a, A2b, A2c, and A2d) from mediators to EA success represent that there are full of pitfalls, risks, difficulties, resistances, problems, etc., in relation to the four mediators in achieving EA success. Any failure in relation to every single success factor, through the transfer of mediators, might finally lead to an EA failure.

It is important to differentiate every single factor from others. At the same time, we need to acknowledge that the many factors are actually interrelated to one another. The interrelationships will be left as a part of our future research. There seems to be a virtual success chain, in which the many factors are the connecting points. In such a success chain, the many factors could also be called *failure points*. Given that any point in the chain fails, the whole net might lead to a final failure.

4.2   Real and Mature Business Needs

Business needs might explain the urgency and importance of EA adoption and implementation in a concrete organization. A mature, smooth application seems quite important for EA justification and legitimacy. The reason could be backed with the ambition to gain relative competitive advantage [45] and with the desire to improve the overall enterprise performance.

EA could not be cost-justified [46]. Potential EA benefits could just be realized ex post but should not promised ex ante in that a divergence between realizability and desirability of EA benefits really exists and matters [47]. Additionally, "the architecture effort's effectiveness is only measurable by the degree to which it contributes to the business' success"[11].

EA adoption and implementation could also be motivated by the existing enterprise-wide problems like misalignment of business and IT, etc. As well, the target (to-be) architecture in EA implementation might evolve with evolving business needs [48].

As to various EA application scenarios [49, 50] in different organizations, a common but serious problem is that business needs are **not** always **real** or **mature enough** for EA introduction and implementation. This implies that from the internal aspects, (an) enterprise might not have sufficient motivation to introduce EA as a tool to solve their enterprise-wide problems. Alternatively, if business needs (for EA adoption and implementation in an organization) turn weak or immature anytime during EA adoption and implementation, EA adoption and implementation might become not so necessary anymore. More precisely, in this situation, the enterprise is then actually not in urgent need for EA adoption and implementation.

Therefore, real and mature business needs help shape, justify, and legitimize the foundation for enterprise to introduce changes.

Proposition A2a: Real and mature business needs are crucial for EA success.

EA readiness and preparation could positively affect the achievement of real and mature business needs [33]. A systematic understanding towards EA and a contextual understanding of an enterprise could help reshape and facilitate the fit between EA benefits and the real motivations in an enterprise. Business needs could also be assessed with such a fit. The understanding of this sort of fit could help (an) enterprise better comprehend where the enterprise is in the 'EA journey' and how to be better prepared towards its vision in the future,

Proposition A1a: Factors in the facet of *EA readiness and preparation* could promote EA success *by* facilitating the achievement of *real and mature business needs*.

4.3   Real and Continuous Commitment

People-Business-IT socio-technical changes in lifecycle-long EA management are quite common [39, 51, 52]. Change sometimes might confront organizational-political-cultural obstacles[53]. Essentially, socio-technical changes call for sufficient understanding, coordination, communication and support of stakeholders. In People-Business-IT socio-technical changes, enterprise architects are thought to just play a role of coordinator to understand the strategy, to create architecture models, and to gain power in order to execute changes [2, 4, 54, 55]. In this sense, commitment implies power providing. Only with sufficient power, could EA be implemented and could the obstacles brought about by involved changes be overcome.

Similar to business needs, a common but serious problem concerning commitment is that commitment in EA practice is **not** always **real, continuous** and thus not **adequate** [48, 56, 57]. If commitment turns disappeared or exhausted sometime during EA implementation, EA implementation would be doomed to fail in that no adequate resources would be available to do EA implementation.

Many matters might lead to an absence of adequate commitment, for example, problems relating to communication, trust, and some other socio-cultural-political issues, like change of leadership, cultural resistances, etc.

Therefore, sufficient power sounds crucial. Without sufficient power, it will be quite problematic to implement changes and to overcome obstacles,

> **Proposition A2b:** Real and continuous commitment are crucial for EA success.

Unreal or discontinuous commitment will probably result in dangerous delays or final cancellations of EA implementation. Being aware of this reality, in accordance with the factors in the facet of top commitment and leadership, EA team in enterprises could keep more cautious and more realistic, which further would facilitate that the commitment is real and continuous,

> **Proposition A1b:** Factors in the facet of *top commitment and leadership* could promote EA success *by* facilitating the achievement of *real and continuous commitment*.

4.4   Actionable EA Programs

As addressed in [39], with given mature business needs and real, continuous commitment in EA adoption and implementation, another question arises: How and when will project/program plans be reviewed, assessed for EA compliance? Here good project/program plans would facilitate EA compliance, where, in principle, those plans are often made within given/reasonable time, budget and some other constraints. With these plans, gradually, EA implementation, which enable business IT convergence [58], becomes methodologically actionable [48, 59].

EA compliance is the core of EA management (cf. [7, 13]). In reality, the ground of EA practice relies much on the connections between enterprise portfolio management and tactic EA programs and then operational EA projects. To a large extent, compliance between the three levels of managements ensures correct executions of strategy.

Obviously, actionable EA programs would ultimately contribute to EA compliance. Particularly, actionable EA programs bridging enterprise top-level strategy, vision with EA operational detailed projects appear crucial for implementing EA smoothly, progressively and successfully.

From the contrary perspective, if real EA implementation proves that EA program/project plans are not actionable anymore, certain adjustments of organizational constraints need to be considered as to concrete business needs and commitments. In general, such kind of adjustments might happen at any time in EA implementation. From this point, validation of enterprise architecture design (and plans as well) before implementation is quite necessary and helpful [60].

In summary, we could come to the following propositions.

Proposition A2c: Actionable EA programs are crucial for EA success.

EA techniques provide philosophical supports for the forming and planning of EA programs. Methodological frameworks, method supports, and together with professional guidelines could help enterprises move towards doable EA planning. Systematic modeling and analyzing facilitate the improvement of EA design.

Proposition A1c: Factors in the facet of EA techniques could promote EA success by facilitating the achievement of actionable EA programs.

Contextual adjustment of EA programs could make EA programs more actionable. Systematic planning and aligning could make EA programs more orthogonally compatible to overarch the enterprise vision.

Proposition A1e: Factors in the facet of *EA governance and program management could* promote EA success by facilitating the achievement of actionable EA programs.

4.5   Well-Controlled Execution of EA Programs

Execution of EA programs means that EA programs would be divided into concrete EA projects with concrete budget and time limits. Critical problems remain being there in controls of the execution. Often in EA practice, enterprise suffers from excesses of money or time to accomplish planned changes. Sometimes, the risk may go out of control. Another common problem is that the execution of EA programs might not be traceable in terms of accountability. These crucial issues relating to control and controllability of execution of EA programs are critical for EA success,

Proposition A2d: Well-controlled execution of EA programs is crucial for EA success.

Though there is no detailed auditing and accounting supports (like that in ITIL, Information Technology Infrastructure Library [61]) in present mainstream EA frameworks, still, methodological steps as provided in many EA frameworks could indeed more or less help to gain better control of execution of EA programs. The systematic guidelines with 'steps after steps' are quite prescriptively helpful in executing EA programs, i.e.,

Proposition A1d: Factors in the facet of EA techniques could promote EA success by facilitating the achievement of well-controlled execution of EA programs.

Well-controlled execution means that challenges [29, 62], pitfalls [11, 12, 63] are controlled according to the investment strategy. As well, the accountability as to risks, costs is also considered. An overall alignment between stage-crossing EA governance and concrete EA programs could facilitate better control in execution of EA programs.

Proposition A1f: Factors in the facet of *EA governance and program management* could promote EA success by facilitating the achievement of well-controlled execution of EA programs.

5   Concluding Remark

As a part of our continuous studies around EA success, the progress made here is an elaboration of connections between EA success facets and EA success. The emerged idea is that actually the four mediators in the synthesizing research model are crucial but at the same time quite problematic in real EA implementations. This might help explain why EA failure rate keeps high for years [64]. With regard to our theoretical synthetic analysis herein and our previous observation on EA practice in industry, this emerged idea seems to be of high generalizability.

This paper as an explanatory and exploratory study primarily provides a theoretical groundwork for further research in EA success and EA success factors. In addition, this elaboration deepens our understanding towards EA as a problem-finding and problem-solving tool by leveraging various complimentary boundary objects [2]. Besides this theoretical contribution, we believe that the four mediators as concrete checkpoints may potentially help increase the probability of EA success in practice.

The future research includes factors analysis with empirical data for better understanding the interrelationships between EA success factors. Another direction is to bridge EA formative success factors with EA reflective success factors.

Acknowledgments. This research has been funded by China National Natural Science Foundation (No. 71171197).

References

1. Robertson-Dunn, B.: Beyond the Zachman framework: Problem-oriented system architecture. IBM Journal of Research and Development 56, 10:11-10:19 (2012)
2. Gotze, J.: The Changing Role of the Enterprise Architect. In: 2013 17th IEEE International Enterprise Distributed Object Computing Conference Workshops (EDOCW), pp. 319–326. IEEE (2013)
3. Bricknall, R., Darrell, G., Nilsson, H., Pessi, K.: Enterprise architecture: critical factors affecting modelling and management. In: Proceedings of European Conference on Information Systems (2006)
4. Strano, C., Rehmani, Q.: The role of the enterprise architect. Information Systems and E-Business Management 5, 379–396 (2007)
5. Khayami, R.: Qualitative characteristics of enterprise architecture. Procedia Computer Science 3, 1277–1282 (2011)
6. Rood, M.A.: Enterprise architecture: definition, content, and utility. In: Proceedings of Third Workshop on Enabling Technologies: Infrastructure for Collaborative Enterprises, pp. 106–111. IEEE (1994)

7. Sebis(Software Engineering for Business Information Systems), The definition of enterprise architecture management, http://wwwmatthes.in.tum.de/pages/b3ucy89rqu5d/Definitions-of-Enterprise-Architecture-Management

8. Cameron, B.H., McMillan, E.: Enterprise Architecture Valuation and Metrics: A Survey-Based Research Study. Journal of Enterprise Architecture 9, number 9(1) (2013)

9. Ylimäki, T.: Potential Critical Success Factors for Enterprise Architecture. Journal of Enterprise Architecture 2, 29–40 (2006)

10. Wan, H., Johansson, B., Luo, X., Carlsson, S.: Realization of enterprise architecture (EA) benefits. In: Harmsen, F., Proper, H.A. (eds.) PRET 2013. Lecture Notes in Business Information Processing, vol. 151, pp. 92–105. Springer, Heidelberg (2013)

11. Rehkopf, T.W., Wybolt, N.: Top 10 architecture land mines. IT Professional 5, 36–43 (2003)

12. Weiss, D.: Why enterprise architecture measurement programs fail: The common pitfalls. Gartner (2006)

13. Lange, M., Mendling, J., Recker, J.C.: Measuring the realization of benefits from enterprise architecture management. Journal of Enterprise Architecture 8, 30–44 (2012)

14. Labusch, N., Koebele, F., Aier, S., Winter, R.: The architects' perspective on enterprise transformation: An explorative study. In: Harmsen, F., Proper, H.A. (eds.) PRET 2013. Lecture Notes in Business Information Processing, vol. 151, pp. 106–124. Springer, Heidelberg (2013)

15. Diamantopoulos, A., Siguaw, J.A.: Formative versus reflective indicators in organizational measure development: a comparison and empirical illustration. British Journal of Management 17, 263–282 (2006)

16. Coltman, T., Devinney, T.M., Midgley, D.F., Venaik, S.: Formative versus reflective measurement models: Two applications of formative measurement. Journal of Business Research 61, 1250–1262 (2008)

17. Cumps, B., Viaene, S., Dussart, P., Vanden Brande, J.: Towards enterprise architecture infused organizations. Journal of Enterprise Architecture 9, 8–18 (2013)

18. Malan, R., Bredemeyer, D.: Less is more with minimalist architecture. IT Professional 4 4(48), 46–47 (2002)

19. Argyris, C.: On Organizational Learning. Wiley (1999)

20. Jacobson, C.P.: Quality in Architecture-Centric Engineering.Dissertation/Thesis (2011)

21. Razavi, M., Aliee, F.S., Badie, K.: An AHP-based approach toward enterprise architecture analysis based on enterprise architecture quality attributes. Knowl. Inf. Syst. 28, 449–472 (2011)

22. Palvia, P., Mao, E., Salam, A., Soliman, K.S.: Management information systems research: what's there in a methodology? Communications of the Association for Information Systems (CAIS) 11, 289–309 (2003)

23. Asscoation for Information Systems. Senior Scholars' Basket of Journals, http://start.aisnet.org/?SeniorScholarBasket (December 27, 2013)

24. Aier, S., Schelp, J.: A reassessment of enterprise architecture implementation. In: Dan, A., Gittler, F., Toumani, F. (eds.) ICSOC/ServiceWave 2009. LNCS, vol. 6275, pp. 35–47. Springer, Heidelberg (2010)

25. Gabier, B., Seymour, L.F., Van Belle, J.P.: Benefits and Factors Driving Enterprise Architecture Development in a Large South African Utility Company. In: Proceedings of the IV IFIP International Conference on Research and Practical Issues of Enterprise Information Systems. (2010)

26. Iyamu, T.: The Factors Affecting Institutionalisation of Enterprise Architecture in the Organisation. In: IEEE Conference on Commerce and Enterprise Computing, CEC 2009, pp. 221–225. IEEE (2009)
27. Lange, M., Mendling, J., Recker, J.: A Comprehensive EA Benefit Realization Model–An Exploratory Study. In: Proceedings of the 2012 45th Hawaii International Conference on System Sciences, pp. 4230–4239. IEEE Computer Society Press (2012)
28. Mezzanotte, D., Dehlinger, J., Chakraborty, S.: On Applying the Theory of Structuration in Enterprise Architecture Design. In: 2010 IEEE/ACIS 9th International Conference on Computer and Information Science (ICIS), pp. 859–863. IEEE (2010)
29. Nakakawa, A., Bommel, P., Proper, H.: Challenges of involving stakeholders when creating enterprise architecture. In: 5th SIKS/BENAIS Conference on Enterprise Information Systems, pp. 43–55 (2010)
30. Ojo, A., Janowski, T., Estevez, E.: Improving Government Enterprise Architecture Practice–Maturity Factor Analysis. In: 2012 45th Hawaii International Conference on System Science (HICSS), pp. 4260–4269 (2012)
31. Steenbergen, M., Berg, M., Brinkkemper, S.: A Balanced Approach to Developing the Enterprise Architecture Practice. In: Filipe, J., Cordeiro, J., Cardoso, J. (eds.) ICEIS 2007. LNBIP, vol. 12, pp. 240–253. Springer, Heidelberg (2008)
32. van der Raadt, B., Soetendal, J., Perdeck, M., van Vliet, H.: Polyphony in architecture. In: Proceedings of the 26th International Conference on Software Engineering, ICSE 2004, pp. 533–542 (2004)
33. Jahani, B., Javadein, S.R.S., Jafari, H.A.: Measurement of enterprise architecture readiness within organizations. Business Strategy Series 11, 177–191 (2010)
34. Matthee, M.C., Tobin, P.K.J., Van der Merwe, P.: The status quo of enterprise architecture implementation in South African financial services companies. South African Journal of Business Management 38, 11–23 (2007)
35. Schmidt, C., Buxmann, P.: Outcomes and success factors of enterprise IT architecture management: empirical insight from the international financial services industry. European Journal of Information Systems 20, 168–185 (2011)
36. Handley, J.: Enterprise Architecture Best Practice Handbook: Building. In: Running and Managing Effective Enterprise Architecture Programs - Ready to use supporting documents bringing Enterprise Architecture Theory into Practice, Emereo Pty Ltd, London (2008)
37. Niemann, K.D.: From Enterprise Architecture to IT Governance: Elements of Effective IT Management, Friedr. Vieweg & Sohn Verlag | GWV Fachverlage GmbH, Wiesbaden (2006)
38. Ross, J.W., Weill, P., Robertson, D.C.: Enterprise architecture as strategy: creating a foundation for business execution. Harvard Business School, Boston (2006)
39. Schekkerman, J.: How to survive in the jungle of enterprise architecture frameworks: Creating or choosing an enterprise architecture framework. Trafford Publishing (2003)
40. Ambler, S.W.: Agile Strategies for Enterprise Architects (January 15, 2014), http://74.208.162.151/Atlanta/PDF/Ambler.pdf
41. Daneva, M., van Eck, P.A.T.: What Enterprise Architecture and Enterprise Systems Usage Can and Can not Tell about Each Other. In: Rolland, C., Pastor, O., Cavarejo, J.L. (eds.) Proceedings of the First International Conference on Research Challenges in Information Science, RCIS 2007, pp. 133–142. Ecole Marocaine des Sciences de l'Ingénieur - University Press, Ouarzazate (2007)
42. DoD Architecture Framework Working Group: DoD Architecture Framework Version 2.0 (2009)
43. OpenGroup: TOGAF version 9.0 - A Pocket Guide (2009)

44. Platje, A., Wadman, S.: From Plan-Do-Check-Action to PIDCAM: the further evolution of the deming-wheel. International Journal of Project Management 16, 201–208 (1998)
45. Porter, M.E.: Competitive Advantage: Creating and Sustaining Superior Performance. Free Press (1998)
46. Zachman, J.A.: You Can't 'Cost-Justify' Architecture. DataToKnowledge Newsletter (Business Rule Solutions LLC) 29, 1–10 (2001)
47. Wan, H., Luo, X., Johansson, B., Chen, H.: Enterprise architecture benefits: the divergence between its desirability and realizability. In: 14th International Conference on Informatics and Semiotics in Organizations(ICISO2013, IFIP WG 8,1 Working Conference). SciTePress (2013)
48. Armour, F.J., Kaisler, S.H., Liu, S.Y.: Building an enterprise architecture step by step. IT Professional 1, 31–39 (1999)
49. Aier, S., Riege, C., Winter, R.: Classification of Enterprise Architecture Scenarios–An Exploratory Analysis. Enterprise Modelling and Information Systems Architectures 3, 14–23 (2008)
50. Bucher, T., Fischer, R., Kurpjuweit, S., Winter, R.: Analysis and Application Scenarios of Enterprise Architecture: An Exploratory Study. In: Proceeding of 10th IEEE International Enterprise Distributed Object Computing Conference Workshops, IEEE Computer Society, Hong Kong (2006)
51. Hoogervorst, J.: Enterprise architecture: Enabling integration, agility and change. International Journal of Cooperative Information Systems 13, 213–233 (2004)
52. Zachman, J.A.: Enterprise architecture: The issue of the century. Database Programming and Design 10, 44–53 (1997)
53. Lines, R.: Influence of participation in strategic change: resistance, organizational commitment and change goal achievement. Journal of Change Management 4, 193–215 (2004)
54. Bradley, R., Pratt, R., Byrd, T.A., Simmons, L.: The role of enterprise architecture in the quest for it value. Mis Quarterly Executive 10, 19–27 (2011)
55. Op't Land, M., Waage, M., Cloo, J., Steghuis, C.: Positioning Enterprise Architecture, pp. 25–47. Springer, Heidelberg (2009)
56. Kaisler, S.H., Armour, F., Valivullah, M.: In: Proceedings of the 38th Annual Hawaii International Conference on System Sciences, HICSS 2005, p. 224b. IEEE (2005)
57. Seppanen, V., Heikkila, J., Liimatainen, K.: Key issues in EA-implementation: case study of two Finnish government agencies. In: IEEE Conference on Commerce and Enterprise Computing, CEC 2009, pp. 114–120. IEEE (2009)
58. Harishankar, R., Daley, S.K.: Actionable Business Architecture. In: 2011 IEEE 13th Conference on Commerce and Enterprise Computing (CEC), pp. 318–324. IEEE (2011)
59. Armour, F.J., Kaisler, S.H.: Enterprise architecture: Agile transition and implementation. IT Professional 3, 30–37 (2001)
60. Schekkerman, J.: Enterprise architecture validation (2005)
61. Information Technology Infrastructure Library (January 15, 2014), http://en.wikipedia.org/wiki/ Information_Technology_Infrastructure_Library
62. Chuang, C.-H., van Loggerenberg, J.: Challenges Facing Enterprise Architects: A South African Perspective. In: 43rd Hawaii International Conference on System Sciences (HICSS), pp. 1–10. IEEE (2010)
63. Gartner, Gartner Identifies Ten Enterprise Architecture Pitfalls (May 09, 2013), http://www.gartner.com/newsroom/id/1159617
64. Shaw, B.: Enterprise Architecture – Will Yours Fail (December 08, 2013), http://www.itprojecttemplates.com/WP_EA_Will_Yours_Fail.htm

An UML-Based Meta-modeling Method
of Building Architecture Product

Jiong Fu, Aimin Luo, and Xueshan Luo

Science and Technology on Information Systems Engineering Laboratory
of National University of Defense Technology, Changsha, P.R. China
fu9jiong2@163.com, {amluo,xsluo}@nudt.edu.cn

Abstract. Architecture product modeling is an important means to collect enterprise-wide decision-making data. DoDAF2.0 proposes meta-model theory to facilitate organizing and collecting data, but still no clear concrete modeling methods for collecting data are available. This paper presents an UML-based meta-modeling method of building architecture product. This method contributes by solving the existing problem within product modeling, and by using the method we can get the modeling tool easily.

Keywords: Architecture, Meta-model, Meta-modeling, UML.

1 Introduction

Information system architecture is defined as the structure of components consisting of its system, relationships, and the disciplines and guidelines governing their design and evolution over time [1]. At present, much research on information system architecture is generally conducted based on the research of DoDAF, and thus research around modeling of architecture product is an important part. Though DoDAF2.0 [2] provides the criterion and method for data organizing and collecting, the method and process for product modeling is left absent. As a result, there is a lack of maneuverable guidance for product modeling, and this lack will affect data collecting and moreover affect decision-making. Presently, Object Management Group(OMG) recommended MOF as the standard of meta-meta-model, but still not accepted widely [3]. Lan [4] introduced the basic building process of executable meta-model in MDA domain. However, the research on architecture product modeling has little progress.

In order to settle the problem, refer to the meta-modeling method and technologies in MDA domain, this paper proposes a meta-modeling method framework and elaborates the basic process of information system architecture product modeling. Further, this paper studies three key technologies of the meta-modeling of architecture product, i.e., (I) meta-meta-model, (II) meta-model and (III) meta-modeling tool. By using the method of meta-modeling of architecture product, we can solve the problem of product modeling, and it can provide the modeling tool easily.

This paper is organized as follows. In section 2, we present the architecture of the product element modeling framework. Section 3 discusses the method and basic

K. Liu et al. (Eds.): ICISO 2014, IFIP AICT 426, pp. 210–220, 2014.

process of modeling meta-meta-model. In section 4, we propose a construction method based on UML for architecture product meta-modeling. In Section 5 we take Operational Resource Flow Description (OV-2) as an example to illustrate our method and the meta-model tool. Section 6 concludes the paper by noting the future works.

2   The Meta-modeling Method Framework of Architecture Product

No unified and standardized definition of architecture meta-model is available now. Based on its application, the architecture meta-model can be categorized into two categories, i.e., data meta-model and product meta-model. Data meta-model focuses on the criterions of architecture data, it can better support us to collect and store data. This part (Data meta-model) is the core of DoDAF2.0; while product meta-model focuses on the direct guidance for various architecture products modeling. It (product meta-model) is very important in process of architecture development and design. This paper mainly focuses on latter one, i.e., product meta-model.

The meta-modeling of architecture product is defined as the process of characterizing the meta-model of the modeling language of architecture product, customizing the modeling language of view product and configuring the modeling tool which supports the modeling language. The process of meta-modeling involves several important elements, including meta-meta-model, meta-model, model, meta-modeling tool and modeling tool. Different from the methods used to build DoDAF Meta Model(DM2), the product meta-modeling approach is mainly to solve the problem as to how to build meta-meta-model, product meta-model and to customize modeling tool.

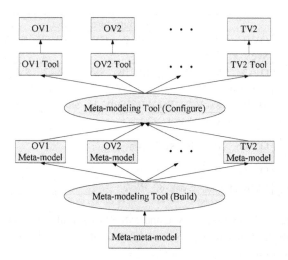

Fig. 1. The meta-modeling method framework of architecture product

For the problem of the lack of guidance and progress of the architecture product meta-modeling, refer to the meta-modeling method and technologies in MDA domain, this section presented a meta-modeling method framework of architecture product and analyzed basic processes and main technologies of meta-modeling. Through the research, we improve the modeling framework of architecture product under the meta-model theory, and provide a method for architecture product modeling.

The meta-modeling method framework of architecture product is presented here, as shown in Figure 1. The meta-modeling method framework includes two main processes. One is the process of product meta-model built by meta-meta-model, and the other is the process of configuring modeling tool by product meta-model. Two processes are all based on the architecture meta-modeling tool.

3   Architecture Meta-meta-model

Architecture meta-meta-model is the basis for building architecture product meta-model, the contents of meta-meta-model directly impact on the contents of the product meta-model. In this section, we build a set of meta-meta-model that can be used to construct and describe architecture product meta-model.

The basic method of establishing architecture meta-meta-model is to extract all the essential attributes that describe the architecture, under the deep analysis of the 52 View product models in DoDAF2.0. And then extend specific attributes in architecture domain, refer to Ecore model [5] in MDA. Specific steps can be divided into the followings:

Step 1: Classify the 52 products of DoDAF2.0 by different visual styles, shown in Table 1.

Table 1. Classification of Architecture Products by Visualization Style

Visualization Style	Architecture Products
Digraph/Graph	OV-1、OV-2、SV-1、SV-2、CV-1、CV-2、SvcV-1、SvcV-2、SvcV-4、DIV-1
Table/Matrix	OV-3、SV-3、SV-5a、SV-5b、SV-6、SV-7、SV-9、AV-1、AV-2、CV-4、CV-5、CV-6、CV-7、SvcV-3a、SvcV-3b、SvcV-5、SvcV-6、SvcV-7、SvcV-9、StdV-1、StdV-2、PV-1、PV-3
Hierarchy Diagram	OV-4、OV-5、SV-4、CV-2
State Transition Diagram	OV-6b、SV-10b、SvcV-10b
Timing Diagram	OV-6c、SV-10c、SvcV-10c
Timeline Diagram	SV-8、CV-3、SvcV-8、PV-2

Step 2: For each visual style, analyze and extract essential elements.

The visualization styles in step 1 can be roughly divided into two categories: "Node + Connection" type , including digraph/graph, hierarchy diagram, state transition diagram, timing diagram; and "Table" type, including table and matrix , timeline diagram.

For the "Node + Connection" type, entity and relationship are the core data elements. There are some other data elements, e.g. property and type. Entity can be in place of icon, vertex and node in products, also refers to specific activities or functions. Relationship can be in place of connection, arc, input connection or output connection. Entity and relationship can have a number of categories and attributes, relationship can be subdivided into binary relationship, inheritance relationship, association, aggregation relationship, etc.

For the "Table" type, the row, column, or cell of the table can be seen as an entity, while other data elements include property, type and comment.

Therefore, summarizing the above analyses, the essential elements of different visualization style are shown in Table 2. The essential data elements of architecture products include: Entity Relationship (binary relations, inheritance, association and aggregation), property, type and comment.

Table 2. Essential Elements of Different Visual Style

Type	Visual Style	Core Data Elements	Other Data Elements
"Node + Connection" Type	Digraph/Graph	Entity 、 Relationship	Property、 Type
	Hierarchy Diagram		
	State Transition Diagram		
	Timing Diagram		
"Table" Type	Table/Matrix	Entity	Property 、 Type 、 Comment
	Timeline Diagram		

Step 3: Refer to Ecore model, extend specific attributes in architecture domain, and we get architecture meta-meta-model, as shown in Fig. 2.

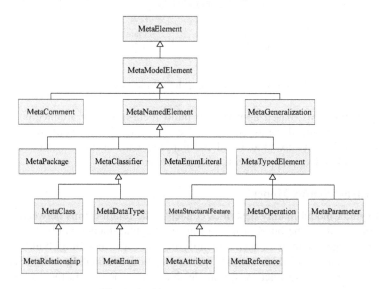

Fig. 2. Architecture meta-meta-model

The elements used for meta-modeling in architecture meta-meta-model shown in Fig. 2 include: MetaClass, MetaRelationship, MetaEnum, MetaPackage, MetaComment, MetaReference, MetaGeneralization and MetaAttribute.

MetaClass is used to define building blocks of the modeling language, for example, when building meta-model of Operational Resource Flow Description (OV-2), the MetaClass is used to describe operational nodes and operational activities. MetaRelationship is used to define binary relationship in modeling language, such as association, generalization, realization, etc. MetaEnum is used to define enumeration types of modeling language. MetaPackage is used to manage and organize the blocks defined. MetaComment is used to define the annotation to aid in understanding the modeling language. MetaReference is used to define association and aggregation relationship between blocks. MetaGeneralization defines inheritance relationship between blocks. MetaAttribute defines the properties of elements defined.

4   The Architecture Meta-model

The meta-model of architecture product includes abstract syntax model, surface syntax model, semantic model. This section uses UML-based approach to build meta-model of architecture product. The idea is shown in Fig. 3.

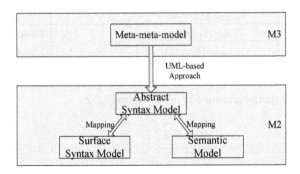

Fig. 3. UML-based Approach to Build Meta-model

In Fig. 3, the UML-based approach to build meta-model of architecture product contains the following three aspects: the abstract syntax model built by meta-meta-model, the surface syntax model and its mapping with abstract syntax model, the semantic model and its mapping with abstract syntax model.

4.1   Abstract Syntax Model

Abstract syntax model mainly describes concepts, the relationships between concepts and constraint rules. The build process of abstract syntax model can be broken down into several stages, namely concepts identifying, concepts modeling, building formal rules between concepts, add necessary operations, model validating and model testing [6]. Fig. 4 shows the abstract syntax model building process and the corresponding relevant contents.

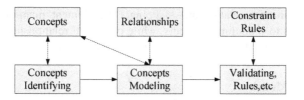

Fig. 4. The Abstract Syntax Model Building Process

Concepts modeling is the core stage of building the abstract syntax, it can be divided into the following two steps:

Step1: Classify the identified concepts.

Here to sort out which concepts are MetaClass, which concepts are MetaRelationship, which concepts are MetaAttribute. Typically, the concept which means entity can use MetaClass to describe, the relationship between entities can use MetaRelationship to describe, and the attributes of entity or relationship can use MetaAttribute to describe.

Step2: Use UML-based approach for modeling.

After classifying the identified concepts, we can use UML-based approach to model the concepts and relationships of abstract syntax model.

4.2   Surface Syntax Model

Surface syntax model describes the details of the abstract syntax model. Surface syntax model divides into two parts: text surface syntax and graphical surface syntax, this paper only discusses its graphical surface syntax, specifically including four aspects, namely, graphical elements, combination layout, location and mapping between the abstract syntax model and graphical surface syntax model [7].

Graphical elements are the basic structural elements of graphic symbols, such as line, rectangle, ellipse, and so on. In follow of the principles of usability, completeness, conciseness, we get the basic graphical elements, including rectangle, round rectangle, diamond, triangle, polygon, ellipse, circle, line, polygonal line, arc, text object, image object and angular rectangle.

Combination layout is a combination of several elements combined in a certain way to become a complex graphical symbol. Combination layout reflects the internal structure of the surface syntax model. Combination layout divides into two types: one is nested combination between block graphical elements, while the other is the combination of linear graphical elements combined with other graphical elements.

Unlike combination layout, location reflects possible positional relationship of graphic symbols. There are many kinds of positional relationships between graphic symbols, and we summarize as five types: nested type, connected type, block-block attached type, block-line attached type and line-line attached type.

After defining combination layout and basic positional relationships between graphical symbols, the mapping between the abstract syntax model and graphical surface syntax model is also very important. The mapping can be divided into element mapping and positional relationship mapping. The element mapping is to attach graphical symbols to modeling elements, while positional relationship mapping is to attach location to the relationships between modeling elements.

4.3   Semantic Model

Abstract syntax model describes the structure of modeling language, and surface syntax model describes the manifestation of modeling language. In contrast, semantic model describes the meaning of the concept of modeling language.

Abstract syntax model describes the structure of modeling language, and surface syntax model describes the manifestation of modeling language. In contrast, semantic model describes the meaning of the concept of modeling language.

In this paper, we use UML-based extensional semantics [8] approach to describe the semantic model. The so-called UML-based extensional semantics approach is to extend the existing UML semantics specification to adapt the semantic description of architecture model language. The way of extension is by the way of object-oriented inheriting with precise semantics of the UML model elements, thus reusing existing language semantics.

The core elements of UML models with precise semantics include Class, Package, Association and Property, while the sorts of the core elements of the abstract syntax model of the architecture modeling language include MetaClass, MetaPackage, MetaRelationship and MetaAttribute. Let them inherit from Class, Package, Association and Property of the UML language, as shown in Fig. 5, so that they have semantics when building abstract syntax model.

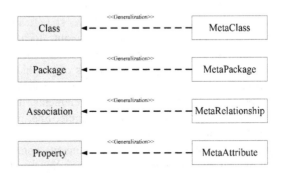

Fig. 5. UML-based Extensional Semantics

5   The Architecture Meta-modeling Tool and Case Study

Architecture meta-modeling tool is the carrier of meta-modeling process, as well as the manifestation of the meta-modeling method of architecture product. Architecture meta-modeling tool should be able to construct product meta-model, and also can customize the corresponding modeling tool. So compared with the traditional architecture modeling tool, meta-modeling tool has better expansibility, and meta-modeling can greatly reduce workload of tool development.

By developing our architecture meta-modeling tool prototype, we use Java language which is platform-independent to code, and use integrated development platform Eclipse to develop the tool. Besides we use Graphical Editing Framework (GEF) to achieve the graphical representation of modeling elements. The visual interface of the tool includes six parts, followed by toolbar, palette, editing area, navigation area, property area and outline area, as shown in Fig. 6.

We take Operational Resource Flow Description (OV-2) as an instance to illustrate the meta-modeling method and the tool introduced above.

Operational Resource Flow Description (OV-2) describes the resource information exchanged between operational activities. Now assume a simple scenario: we assume that a combat unit has a simple process including intelligence gathering, information processing, combat command ordering and combat performing. Table 3 lists all the scenarios including operational activity, operational information and operational node.

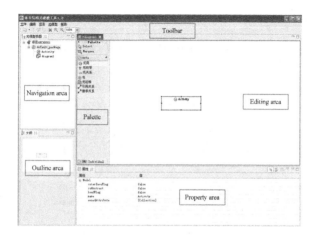

Fig. 6. The Visual Interface of The Tool

Table 3. Activities, Information and Node

Operational Activity	Operational Information	Operational Node
Intelligence gathering	Intelligence information	Accused node
Information processing	Processed information	Processing node
Combat command ordering	Combat command	Firepower node
Combat performing		

(1) Build meta-model of OV-2

Firstly, we need to build OV-2 abstract syntax model. The concepts meaning entity include Activity, OperationalNode, Information, Organization, Condition, and they can be created by MetaClass. NeedLine is a kind of relationship and can be created by MetaRelationship, while ActivityConsumesResource, ActivityProducesResource, ActivityPerformedUnderCondition and ActivityPerformedByPerformer are detailed description of relationships, and they can be created by MetaReference. So OV-2 abstract syntax model is shown in Fig. 7.

Fig. 7 shows that OperationalNode contains Activity, while Activity contains Condition and Organization. NeedLine contains Information, and both source end and target end of NeedLine are Activity.

Then, build OV-2 surface syntax model. Since Organization and Condition can be regard as attributes of Activity, they don't need graphical symbols, the same to Information. Only OperationalNode, Activity and NeedLine need to define graphical symbols. The OV-2 surface syntax model is shown in Fig. 8.

Fig. 8(a) shows that rectangle represents OperationalNode, and round rectangle represents Activity, while the combined symbol of a solid line with an arrow represents NeedLine. The location of OperationalNode and Activity is belong to block-block attached type, while the location of Activity and NeedLine is belong to connected type. Fig. 8(b) shows the modeling interface of surface syntax model.

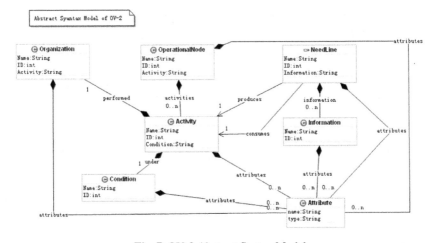

Fig. 7. OV-2 Abstract Syntax Model

Concepts/Relationships	Graphical Symbol/Location	Type
OperationalNode		
Activity		Element Mapping
NeedLine		
OperationalNode & Activity		Positional Relationship Mapping
NeedLine & Activity		

(a)

(b)

Fig. 8. OV-2 Surface Syntax Model

Besides, by analyzing OV-2 abstract syntax model, we can find that Activity, OperationalNode, Information, Organization, Condition are instances of MetaClass, so they inherit semantics from Class. NeedLine is an instance of MetaRelationship, and it inherits semantics from Association. Attribute is an instance of MetaAttribute, and therefore it inherits semantics from property.

(2) Configure to generate OV-2 modeling tool

Architecture meta-modeling tool is able to analyze the product meta-model we build, and customize the modeling tool which supports the product. Fig. 9 shows the modeling interface of OV-2 modeling tool, which is created by the meta-modeling tool after analyzing OV-2 meta-model.

Fig. 9 shows that yellow round rectangle represents Activity, and rectangle represents OperationalNode, and the straight line with arrow represents Needline. When modeling, Activity can only attach to the boundary of OperationalNode, while Needline can only be created between activities.

From the content and visual style of the OV-2 product we built, we can find they correctly reflect the meaning of OV-2. Thus, the architecture meta-modeling tool has validated our meta-modeling method of architecture product.

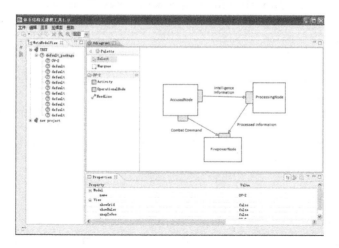

Fig. 9. The Modeling Interface of OV-2 Modeling Tool

6   Conclusions

This paper presents a meta-modeling method of architecture product. We analyze the main technical issues of meta-modeling, including meta-meta-model, product meta-model and meta-modeling tool. Based on the tool, we analyze and validate the meta-modeling method of architecture product via a case. This research provides a new method for architecture product modeling with the theory of meta-modeling. This new method enables enterprise modeling with meta-models. Future work will be conducted with a focus on integrating other modeling methods into the as is tool.

References

1. IEEE Architecture Working Group, IEEE Recommended Practice for Architecture Description, IEEE Std 1471, Draft Version 3.0, USA (1998)
2. DoD Architecture Framework Working Group. DoD Architecture Framework Version 2.0: Architect's Guide-Architecural Data and Models.U.S. Department of Defense (2009)
3. Hui, L., Zhi-Yi, M., Wei-Zhong, S.: Progress of Research on Metamodeling. Journal of Software 19(6), 1317–1327 (2008)
4. Qingguo, L.: Research on the Key Technology of Executable Metamodel. Jilin University (2006)
5. Ecore. The Core of EMF, Package org.eclipse.emf.core
6. Zhi-ping, J., Ming, H., Zhi-xue, W., Hang-ping, Q.: The Research on the Data-centered C4ISR System Architecture Development Method. Fire Control & Command Control 34(1) (January 2009)
7. Xiao, H., Zhi-Yi, M., Wei-Zhong, S.: A Metamodel for the Notation of Graphical Modeling Languages. Journal of Software 19(8) (August 2008)
8. Clark, T., Evans, A., Sammut, P., Willans, J.: Applied Metamodeling A Foundation for Language Driven Development Version 0.1, http://albini.xactium.com/content/index.php?option=com_remository&Itemid=28

A Component Data-Focused Method to Build the Executable Model for a DoDAF Compliant Architecture

Li Huang[1,2], Guangqi Huang[1,2], Yaohong Zhang[1], Weizi Li[2], and Xueshan Luo[1]

[1] Science and Technology on Information Systems Engineering Laboratory,
National University of Defense Technology,
410073 Changsha, China
[2] Informatics Research Centre, University of Reading, Whiteknights,
RG6 6UD Reading, UK
{nudthli,luoxueshan}@gmail.com,
cscsyz@163.com, zhang_yaohong@263.net,
weizi.li@henley.ac.uk

Abstract. An executable model plays an important role on verifying the behavior and performance of an architecture. This paper summarizes the state of the art on the synthesis methods of the executable model for an architecture that is compliant with the Department of Defense Architecture Framework (DoDAF). To overcome the deficiencies of current executable modeling studies, a component data-focused method is proposed. Following the introduction of an executable modeling language named OPDL, the data elements of DoDAF Meta-model (DM2) required for building executable model is analyzed. The mapping relations between partial DM2 and OPDL elements are built. Finally, a process to create executable model is explained in detail.

Keywords: Architecture, Architecture Verification, Executable Model, DoDAF, DM2.

1   Introduction

The Department of Defense (DoD) Architecture Framework (DoDAF) [1] is the overarching, comprehensive framework and conceptual model enabling the development of architectures in the DoD. A DoDAF compliant architecture is presented by dividing all kinds of architecture descriptive data into manageable pieces, according to the stakeholder's viewpoint. Furthermore, data pertained to each viewpoint are described by a few predefined models respectively.

In order to verify the behavior and performance of the architecture and address the concerns of the customer, Levis and Wagenhals [2] proposed that an executable model which is synthesized from architecture models is needed. An executable model of architecture enables the architect to analyze the dynamic behaviors of the architecture, identify logical and behavioral errors that are not easily seen in the static descriptions of its models, and demonstrate the capabilities of the architecture to the users.

K. Liu et al. (Eds.): ICISO 2014, IFIP AICT 426, pp. 221–230, 2014.
© IFIP International Federation for Information Processing 2014

Wagenhals et al. [3-5] use Colored Petri Nets (CPN) language for creating the executable model of the architecture. The approaches have also been developed that allow the derivation of CPN model of an architecture designed by either structured analysis or object-oriented methodology. Wang et al. [6] proposes the method of transforming System Modeling Language (SysML) based architecture models to CPN. Baumgarten and Silverman [7] converted several architecture models to ExtendSim model which enables workload, timing, and process analysis that can help identify gaps, bottlenecks and overloads to queues. Mittal, Zeigler, et al. [8-9] presented extensions to the DoDAF to support specification of DoDAF architectures within a development environment based on Discrete Event System Specification (DEVS) model, and demonstrated how DoDAF-DEVS model mapping can actually take place from the existing DoDAF UML specifications. As part of the Architecture-based Technology Evaluation and Capability Tradeoff (ARCHITECT) methodology developed by Griendling and Mavris [10], an approach adopting a standard set of DoDAF models and the associated data to create four types of executables models is detailed.

Overall, the aforementioned executable modeling studies have the following characteristics: 1) every method has its specific executable modeling languages, most of which are some extensions to original Petri net. 2) every method contains algorithms to transform static architectural models described by different methodologies into executable models. These algorithms are generally different in various architecture methodologies due to the emphasis on architectural model instead of the underlying architecture data, which is one of the deficiencies of previous version of DoDAF. 3) most methods focus on validating the correctness of the logic and behavior of architecture, hence they usually extract much information from activity or state related models in the architecture to build executable models, but little information from component related models.

Methodology-specific executable model conversion algorithms need architect to be familiar with both original architectural modeling languages and target executable formalisms, and it is also difficult to be commonly understood and compared across multiple instances [11]. Hence, it is almost impossible to popularize these methods widely. As the latest DoDAF version 2.0 [12] has shifted to a "data-centric" approach by building the DoDAF Meta-model (DM2), it places greater emphasis on architecture data as the necessary ingredient for architecture development. DM2 defines architectural data elements, their associations and attributes, thus providing a high-level view of the data normally collected, organized, and maintained in an architectural description effort. It is feasible to make research on new executable model synthetic methods which are architectural modeling methodology-independent, such as those done by [11] and [13].

But the executable models built by these new studies still lack system component information. System component information plays an important role on the verification of architectural behavior and performance, which are affected by architectural components and structure. The lack of system component information in the generated executable models will constrain their ability in evaluating more user concerns such as system structural fitness, measures of performance and measures of effectiveness of system, and etc.

In order to solve the issues mentioned above, we propose a component data-focused method to build the executable model for a DoDAF based architecture. It will build the executable model upon DM2, which is architectural modeling methodology-independent. At the same time, component information will be extracted from the underlying data of architecture models and embodied in the generated executable model as a main part. As to the selection of executable modeling language, we select the Object Petri Nets based Description Language (OPDL) [14], which was developed by our laboratory. OPDL is an extension of original Petri net. It offers an advantage of combining a well-defined mathematical foundation, the graphical representation and interactive simulation capabilities to check both the logical and functional correctness of a system and to make performance analysis. Many architectural elements, e.g. information, materiel, and data can be defined by different types of tokens in OPDL. These features make OPDL flexible and capable of modeling complex systems. Furthermore, OPDL is simple to use, whereas CPN is relatively more complicated.

The remainder of this paper is organized as follows. Section 2 gives a brief introduction of OPDL. Section 3 examines DM2 data elements which are related to component information for building executable model. In the meantime the mapping relations between DM2 and OPDL elements are established. Section 4 presents the steps for building OPDL based executable model.

2   OPDL

To implement object model in the original Petri net, an Object Petri Nets based Description Language (OPDL) is designed [14]. OPDL extents Petri nets on two aspects. First, it introduces object-oriented methodology into Petri nets to form Object Petri Nets (OPN), where the object is the basic modeling unit and reusable module. Second, OPDL adds new model elements to original Petri net, such as switch, and attributions to all of the model elements.

Below is a simple explanation for the basic model elements of OPDL.

Class. An OPN class includes four parts, which are property table, OPN description, initialization function and post-instancing function. 1) Property table is a data space used by the object. Each item in the table is composed of a property name and a property value. A property value can be accessed via its name. 2) OPN description is an OPN graph. Different graphs connect together through their input ports and output ports. 3) Initialization function is used to initialize the object instance when it is created, such as setting the initial value of a property. 4) Post-instancing function will be executed after the object instance has been created. All the classes are stored in a class library. Modeler builds and organizes model based on the class library. Class quotation mechanism supports the reuse of model. Hence, modeling is the process of designing and using classes.

Object. An OPN object is an instance of some class. The attributions of an object can be modified by its instance function. There are two sorts of relations between two different objects, i.e. interactive relation and nesting relation. By interactive relation, two objects connect together via their input ports and output ports. By nesting relation, two objects form hierarchy model.

Place. A place is a kind of data structure, which has a queue to buffer tokens. Each place corresponds to a color. Only those tokens which have the same color can enter into the place. The attributions of a place include rule of queue, token capacity and the event processing function. When a token enters or gets out the place, its event processing function will be invoked. OPDL also defines a special kind of place named port. A port has the same attributions as a place. Ports are divided into input ports and output ports. The successor of an output port should be an input port, and the predecessor of an input port should be an output port.

Transition. The attributions of a transition include priority, delay function, predicate function, action function, and event processing function. Priority is used to handle conflicts. Delay function is used to determine the process time of a transition. Predicate function is a condition which needs to be satisfied for a transition to be enabled. Action function is a sequence of operations that a transition will carry out after it fires. When a transition begins to fire, the event processing function will be executed.

Switch. A switch can be regarded as a special kind of transition. Unlike a common transition, it does not distribute any tokens automatically at the end of its firing, and it is up to the modeler to determine how to distribute the tokens to its successive places.

Arc. An Arc is used to connect the place and the transition just as the original Petri nets. Moreover, it is used to connect an input port and an output port.

Token. A token is defined as a structural data and corresponds to a color. A token has a property table. In the functions of a transition, the items of property table can be inserted and accessed.

To implement OPDL, we developed a software tool named OPMSE [14], which is a kind of integrated modeling and simulation environment.

3   DM2 Data Elements Required for Building Executable Model

As mentioned above, the aim of our method is to create an executable model that can be used to verify system structural fitness, measures of performance and measures of effectiveness of system, and so on. Thereby, component information of the whole architecture which describes a system is required for building the executable model. The data elements in DM2 related to component information need to be examined. Then, the mapping relations between DM2 and OPDL elements need to be established to create OPDL based executable model.

3.1   DM2 Data Elements Related to System Component

The essence of DM2 is to answer the set of standard interrogatives, which are the set of questions, Who, What, When, Where, Why, and How [1]. Accordingly, data elements in DM2 is divided into 12 categories of data groups, which are Performers,

Resource Flows, Information and Data, Activities, Training/Skill/Education, Capability, Services, Projects, Goals, Rules, Measures, and Locations.

We begin by finding the data element that is used to represent system component information. It is easy to determine that the Performers data group answers the Who question, and its *System* data element represents system component information. Then, the data element that represents system function information is *Activity*, which is in the Activities data group. A *System* may have several *Activities*. And also, a system function transforms input information into output information, which is represented by *Information* data element in the Information and Data group. A system may have several performance parameters, which are represented by *Measure* data element in the Measures data group. Thus, *System*, *Activity*, *Information* and *Measure* form the basic DM2 data elements related to system component, as shown in Fig. 1.

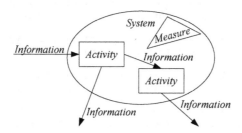

Fig. 1. DM2 data elements related to system component

Besides data elements, the associations between them need to be considered. We can find these associations which are *activityPerformedByPerformer*, *activityResourceOverlap*, *wholePartType*, and *measureOfTypeResource*. The *activityPerformedByPerformer* association represents that an *Activity* is performed by a *System*. The *activityResourceOverlap* association represents that a piece of *Information* is produced by an *Activity* and consumed by another *Activity*. The *wholePartType* association represents that a *System* is a part of another *System*. The *measureOfTypeResource* association represents that a *Measure* belongs to a *System*.

According to DM2, architecture data can be saved in XML format. The figures from Fig. 2 to Fig. 6 illustrate some architecture data segments related to system component information of a notional system.

```
- <System ideas:FoundationCategory="IndividualType" id="s2">
    <ideas:Name exemplarText="System A" namingScheme="ns1" id="n89" />
  </System>
- <System ideas:FoundationCategory="IndividualType" id="s3">
    <ideas:Name exemplarText="System B" namingScheme="ns1" id="n90" />
  </System>
- <System ideas:FoundationCategory="IndividualType" id="s4">
    <ideas:Name exemplarText="System C" namingScheme="ns1" id="n91" />
  </System>
- <System ideas:FoundationCategory="IndividualType" id="s5">
    <ideas:Name exemplarText="System D" namingScheme="ns1" id="n92" />
  </System>
```

Fig. 2. System segment of architecture data

```
-  <Activity ideas:FoundationCategory="IndividualType" id="a18">
    <ideas:Name exemplarText="Act A" namingScheme="ns1" id="n74" />
   </Activity>
-  <Activity ideas:FoundationCategory="IndividualType" id="a19">
    <ideas:Name exemplarText="Act B" namingScheme="ns1" id="n75" />
   </Activity>
-  <Activity ideas:FoundationCategory="IndividualType" id="a20">
    <ideas:Name exemplarText="Act C" namingScheme="ns1" id="n76" />
   </Activity>
-  <Activity ideas:FoundationCategory="IndividualType" id="a21">
    <ideas:Name exemplarText="Act D" namingScheme="ns1" id="n77" />
   </Activity>
```

Fig. 3. Activity segment of architecture data

```
-  <Information ideas:FoundationCategory="IndividualType" id="di14">
    <ideas:Name exemplarText="Info A" namingScheme="ns1" id="n84" />
   </Information>
-  <Information ideas:FoundationCategory="IndividualType" id="di15">
    <ideas:Name exemplarText="Info B" namingScheme="ns1" id="n85" />
   </Information>
-  <Information ideas:FoundationCategory="IndividualType" id="di16">
    <ideas:Name exemplarText="Info C" namingScheme="ns1" id="n86" />
   </Information>
-  <Information ideas:FoundationCategory="IndividualType" id="di17">
    <ideas:Name exemplarText="Info D" namingScheme="ns1" id="n87" />
   </Information>
```

Fig. 4. Information segment of architecture data

```
<activityPerformedByPerformer ideas:FoundationCategory="TripleType"
id="app19" place1Type="s2" place2Type="a18" place3Type="apuc17" />
<activityPerformedByPerformer ideas:FoundationCategory="TripleType"
id="app20" place1Type="s2" place2Type="a19" place3Type="apuc18" />
<activityPerformedByPerformer ideas:FoundationCategory="TripleType"
id="app21" place1Type="s3" place2Type="a20" place3Type="apuc19" />
<activityPerformedByPerformer ideas:FoundationCategory="TripleType"
id="app22" place1Type="s3" place2Type="a21" place3Type="apuc20" />
```

Fig. 5. activityPerformedByPerformer segment of architecture data

```
<activityResourceOverlap ideas:FoundationCategory="TripleType"
id="aro14" place1Type="a18" place3Type="a20" place2Type="di14" />
<activityResourceOverlap ideas:FoundationCategory="TripleType"
id="aro15" place1Type="a18" place3Type="a21" place2Type="di15" />
<activityResourceOverlap ideas:FoundationCategory="TripleType"
id="aro16" place1Type="a19" place3Type="a22" place2Type="di16" />
<activityResourceOverlap ideas:FoundationCategory="TripleType"
id="aro17" place1Type="a18" place3Type="a19" place2Type="di17" />
```

Fig. 6. activityResourceOverlap segment of architecture data

3.2   Mapping Relations between DM2 and OPDL Elements

After the analysis of DM2 data elements related to system component information, the mapping relations between DM2 and OPDL elements is established according to their features, which is shown in Table 1.

Table 1. Elements mapping between partial DM2 and OPDL

DM2 data elements		OPDL model elements
data elements	*System*	class, object
	Activity	transition
	Information	place (input port, output port) , property of class
	Measure	property of class
associations between data elements	*activityPerformedByPerformer*	transition of class's OPN graph
	activityResourceOverlap	arcs
	wholePartType	constituent relation between two objects
	measureOfTypeResource	property of certain class

Each *System* can be mapped to an object in OPDL. For those objects have the same properties and OPN graphs, a class can be defined. If a *wholePartType* association exists between two *Systems*, then a parent-child relation exists between their corresponding objects.

Each *Activity* can be mapped to a transition in OPDL. If an *activityPerformedByPerformer* association exists between an *Activity* and a *System*, it means that the corresponding transition is part of the corresponding class's OPN graph.

Each piece of *Information* can be mapped to a place, an input port, an output port, or a property of class in OPDL. If an *activityResourceOverlap* association exists between two *Activities* and a piece of *Information*, then two arcs are needed to connect between each corresponding transition and the corresponding place or port.

Each *Measure* can be mapped to a property of class. If a *measureOfTypeResource* association exists between a *Measure* and a *System*, it means that the corresponding property belongs to the corresponding class.

4   Process of Building Executable Model

A process to build executable model is shown in Fig. 7. Firstly, we extract part information from architecture data that is saved following DM2, including *System*, *Activity*, *Information*, *Measure* and their associations. Then convert into their OPDL counterparts according to above established mapping relations. Some OPN classes will be created at this step, which we call initial OPN classes. Secondly, depending on the simulation purposes of executable model, some edits on these initial OPN classes need to be done, such as adding new places and transitions in their OPN graphs, initializing properties of classes in their initialization functions and post-instancing functions, and defining the process time and operations of transitions in their delay functions and action functions respectively. All the OPN classes will be ready and organized in an OPN class library at this step. Lastly, we instantiate the top level OPN class in the library, which will also instantiate its descendent objects, and an executable model will be produced.

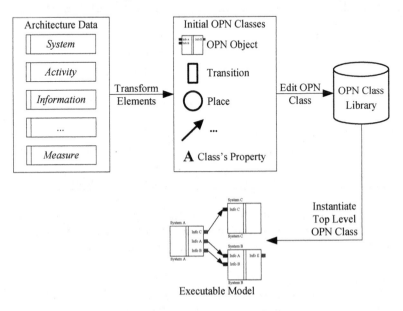

Fig. 7. A process to build executable model

The first step in above process can be subdivided into several sub steps as follows.

(1) Determination of OPN objects. For each *System* in architecture data, we define an object with the same name.

(2) Creation of OPN classes. For each object with particular features, a class is created. For those objects have similar features, we only create one class for them. Additionally, a top level class is always created in view of the modeling mechanism of OPDL. For composite classes determined by *wholePartType* association, their child objects are built into their OPN graphs.

(3) Creation of graph elements for OPN classes. Each *activityResourceOverlap* association involves three elements, i.e. an *Activity* which produces information, a piece of *Information*, and an *Activity* which consumes information. The *System* which performs activity to produce or consume information can be determined by *activityPerformedByPerformer* association. For each *Activity* that produces or consumes information, we create a transition in the class which is the counterpart of *System* that produce or consume information. For an *activityResourceOverlap*

association, if it is the same *System* that produce and consume information, we create one place in the class; otherwise, we create an output port in one class and an input port in another class. Two arcs are built to connect two pairs of transitions and places respectively. Arcs connecting the ports of child objects of a composite class need to be created based on *activityResourceOverlap* association too.

(4) Creation of properties for OPN classes. *Measures* in *measureOfTypeResource* association and *Information* in *activityResourceOverlap* association can be used to define candidate properties for class.

According to above process, we can build an OPN class library based on the part architecture data shown in Fig. 2 to Fig. 6. The OPN graph of top level class in the library is shown in Fig. 8. Fig. 9 illustrates the OPN graph of class "System A". We can get an executable model by instantiating the top level OPN class in OPMSE.

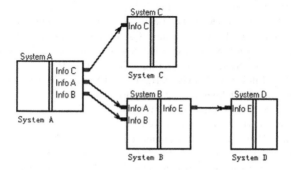

Fig. 8. The OPN graph of top level class

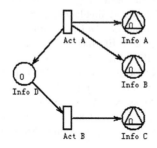

Fig. 9. The OPN graph of class "System A"

5   Conclusion

This paper presents a component data-focused method to synthesize the executable model for an architecture that is described compliant with the DoDAF. It is architectural modeling methodology-independent and is fit for the verification of architectural behavior and performance. Future research will involve adding additional data elements which are related to service, rule, and communication. This helps the transformation from architecture data into the executable model to enable more widely evaluation on user concerns. At the same time, a method to enable automatic executable model generation will also be studied.

Acknowledgments. This research was supported in part by the State Scholarship Fund (No. 201206115006) from China Scholarship Council.

References

1. DoD Architecture Framework Working Group.: DoD Architecture Framework version 2.0, Introduction, Overview, and Concepts, vol. 1. Department of Defense, Washington (2009)
2. Levis, A.H., Wagenhals, L.W.: C4ISR Architectures I: Developing a Process for C4ISR Architecture Design. Systems Engineering 3, 225–247 (2000)
3. Wagenhals, L.W., Shin, I., Kim, D., Levis, A.H.: C4ISR Architectures II: Structured Analysis Approach for Architecture Design. Systems Engineering 3, 248–287 (2000)
4. Wagenhals, L.W., Haider, S., Levis, A.H.: Synthesizing Executable Models of Object Oriented Architectures. Systems Engineering 6, 266–300 (2003)
5. Wagenhals, L.W., Liles, S.W., Levis, A.H.: Toward Executable Architectures to Support Evaluation. In: The 2009 International Symposium on Collaborative Technologies and Systems, pp. 502–511. IEEE Press, New York (2009)
6. Wang, R.Z., Dagli, C.H.: An Executable System Architecture Approach to Discrete Events System Modeling Using SysML in Conjunction with Colored Petri Net. In: 2nd Annual IEEE Systems Conference, pp. 1–8. IEEE Press, New York (2008)
7. Baumgarten, E., Silverman, S.J.: Dynamic DoDAF and Executable Architectures. In: 2007 Military Communications Conference, pp. 1–5. IEEE Press, New York (2007)
8. Mittal, S.: Extending DoDAF to Allow Integrated DEVS-based Modeling and Simulation. The Journal of Defense Modeling and Simulation 3, 95–123 (2006)
9. Zeigler, B.P., Mittal, S.: Enhancing DoDAF with a DEVS-based System Lifecycle Development Process. In: 2005 IEEE International Conference on Systems, Man and Cybernetics, pp. 3244–3251. IEEE Press, New York (2005)
10. Griendling, K., Mavris, D.N.: Development of a DoDAF-Based Executable Architecting Approach to Analyze System-of-Systems Alternatives. In: 2011 IEEE Aerospace Conference, pp. 1–15. IEEE Press, New York (2011)
11. Ge, B.F., Hipel, K.W., Yang, K.W., Chen, Y.W.: A Data-Centric Capability-Focused Approach for System-of-Systems Architecture Modeling and Analysis. Systems Engineering 16, 363–377 (2013)
12. DoD Architecture Framework Working Group.: DoD Architecture Framework version 2.0, Architectural Data and Models, vol. 2. Department of Defense, Washington (2009)
13. Zhang, X.X., Luo, X.S., Luo, A.M.: Method of Architecture Executable Evaluation Based on DM2. In: 3rd International Conference on System Science, Engineering Design and Manufacturing Informatization, pp. 213–217. IEEE Press, New York (2012)
14. Luo, X.S., Qiu, D.S., Rao, X.H., Bao, W.D.: OPMSE: An Object Petri Nets based Modeling and Simulation Environment. In: Mortensen, K.H. (ed.) Tool Demonstrations of 21st International Conference on Application and Theory of Petri Nets, Denmark, pp. 65–69 (2000)

What Do Partners Share in Strategic Alliances?

Lee Li

York University, 4700 Keele St. Toronto, Canada
Leeli@yorku.ca

Abstract. This study categorizes resources into firm-specific and general resource; costs into accounting and non-accounting cost; and risks into visible and invisible risks. Using data from 167 Canadian firms in technology industries, we find that sharing firm-specific resources and non-accounting costs are negatively correlated with environmental dynamism but sharing general resources, accounting costs and visible risks are positively correlated with environmental dynamism. Findings suggest that sharing certain resources, costs and risks do not necessarily incur high transaction costs.

Keywords: Strategic alliances, Environmental dynamism.

1   Introduction

What do partners share in their strategic alliances? The mainstream management literature suggests that they share resources, costs and risks [1]. However, the literature also acknowledges that such sharing increases transaction costs which are positively correlated with environmental dynamism [2]. The costs include partner opportunism, coordination costs, equity hostage and dependence, etc. Empirical studies show that these costs, under certain conditions, can surpass benefits provided by strategic alliances and may even make partners' R&D and production activities unproductive. As such, an important question emerges as to why partners share resources, costs and risks even at such high transaction costs. A logical answer to the question would be the possibility that partners share different resources, costs and risks in diverse environments to minimize the transaction costs and maximize the sharing benefits. However, the existing studies do not differentiate between these resources, costs and risks and associate them with sharing costs and sharing environments.

This paper aims to make such contributions. It develops and tests the hypotheses that both the costs and the benefits of sharing depend, to a great extent, on categories of resources, costs and risks that partners share and the environments within which such sharing occurs. In a highly dynamic market, for example, the costs of sharing knowledge resources between technology-based partners may be much higher than the costs of sharing financial resources between the same partners. The partners can specify how they share the risks and costs when they share financial resources in the contract but they can hardly determine accurately the partner's opportunistic behavior

K. Liu et al. (Eds.): ICISO 2014, IFIP AICT 426, pp. 231–237, 2014.

in sharing the knowledge resources and the impacts of environmental dynamism on such sharing. This study will differentiate between these resources, costs and risks and clarify the relationships between the benefits and the cost of sharing against the background of environmental dynamism.

In this study, we define resources as assets that are tied semipermanently to a firm; costs as the sacrifice a firm makes to achieve a particular purpose; and risks as negative variance in performance beyond the control of decision makers. Accordingly, we classify resources, costs and risks, each into two categories: resources into firm-specific and general resources; costs into accounting costs and non-accounting costs; and risks into visible and invisible risks. Firm-specific resources are those unique to a particular firm while general resources are those available in the market. Accounting costs include operation costs, such as fixed and variable costs, which are specified in firms' income statements. Non-accounting costs are those costs unidentified in firms' income statements, including transaction costs and opportunity costs. Visible risks are the possibilities predicted and specified in the partnership contracts while invisible risks are those unspecified in the contracts.

Evidence collected in this study shows that partners share firm-specific resources and non-accounting costs in a relatively stable environment. In contrast, they share general resources, accounting costs and visible risks when environments grow highly dynamic. The findings of this study make significant contributions to the existing literature on two fronts. First, it clarifies the fact that the benefits and the costs of sharing resources, costs and risks between partners depend on the types of resources, costs and risks they share and the environments within which the sharing occurs. Second, it explains why firms use strategic alliances even when sharing resources, costs and risks may lead to high transaction costs.

2   Hypotheses Development

2.1   Firm-Specific and General Resources

Research-based view (RBV) suggests that firms' ability to sustain their competitive advantage is based on their firm-specific resources which are not easily tradable or redeployable outside the firm and thus are difficult for competitors to imitate [3]. Firm-specific resources include property based resources and knowledge-based resources. Property-based resources are protected by property rights while knowledge-based are protected by knowledge barriers which are subtle, hard-to-understand, or built on accumulation of experiences and knowledge, and continuous financial and human investments [4].

Partners may share property-based and knowledge-based resources through licensing/franchising, joint ventures or R&D consortia. In other words, partners give up, to varying degrees, the property rights or knowledge barriers in partnership cooperation. Therefore, the firms who own the property-based and knowledge-based resources have to use partnership contracts to safeguard the value of these resources in order to maximize its economic rents from alliances and sustain the value of these resources. Environmental dynamism makes such safeguards difficult because, with the ambiguity associated with the environmental dynamism, partners can hardly specify each partner's responsibilities and obligations in the contracts [5]. Monitoring partners' behavior is difficult in a highly dynamic environment. Moreover, sharing property-based and knowledge-based resources is a firm-specific investment and such investments have, by definition, limited economic value in alternative settings. If the alliance agreements are terminated unexpectedly due to the environmental changes, firms can hardly recoup their initial investments.

General resources are different from firm-specific ones in that general resources are subject to ready imitation by other firms. Capital, land and unskilled labor are examples of general resources. Environmental dynamism provides a flow of opportunities that typically is fast, complex, ambiguous, and unpredictable [6]. Firms may not have sufficient general resources under their direct control to exploit these opportunities. Direct control over abundant general resources results in inflexibility which makes firms inefficient to manage the complexities and ambiguity. Strategic alliances enable these firms to get access to external general resources. Through joint venture in foreign countries, for example, partners can have access to local production infrastructure and low-cost labor. Sharing general resources rather than owning general resources provides important strategic benefits, such as loose coupling, ambidexterity and improvisation, which increase firms' learning speed and responsiveness to manage environmental dynamism More importantly, sharing general resources reduces investment risks. As such, firms tend to get access to these resources through strategic alliances when they experience high environmental dynamism. Accordingly, we predict that:

Hypothesis 1a: The higher the environmental dynamism, the more general resources partners will share.

Hypothesis 1b: The higher the environmental dynamism, the fewer firm-specific resources partners will share.

2.2   Accounting Costs and Non-accounting Costs

Environmental dynamism raises firms' accounting costs because the dynamism leads to both opportunities and threats, and managing increased opportunities and threats incurs accounting costs. Partners may not have sufficient financial resources to cover the costs on their own. More importantly, unexpected accounting costs may increase substantially in dynamic environments due to the high unpredictability and velocity and sourcing from partners is an effective way to manage such sharp cost fluctuations. Sourcing cash from partners, for example, is a frequently used option for firms in high-tech industries. Because accounting costs are specified in numbers, both parties' responsibilities and obligations in sharing these costs can be relatively precisely defined in partnership contracts. In other words, transaction costs for such sharing is minimal.

Non-accounting costs include transaction costs and opportunity costs. Non-accounting costs are mutual between partners. Both partners share such costs when they form strategic alliances. Existing studies have shown that both parties may earn private benefits unilaterally from the alliance [7]. Such private benefits vary from cheating to learning by observation without other party's permission. Consequently, both partners have to monitor each other's behavior to reduce the possibilities of opportunism because both partners invest in the alliances and they have to protect such partner-specific investments.

High levels of environmental dynamism not only increase non-accounting costs but also make the non-accounting cost forecasting inaccurate. Dynamism creates the causal ambiguity which blurs the links between non-accounting costs and the effectiveness to reduce transaction costs and opportunity costs, and many contingencies will distort cost estimates [8]. Because accurate cost forecasting is difficult to achieve, partners have to identify and correct their forecasting problems by frequently re-estimating and reallocating costs between them. Such frequent re-estimation and reallocation not only make existing partnership agreements non-binding, but also create enormous uncertainties for the future of these agreements. Accordingly, we predict that:

Hypothesis 2a: The higher the environmental dynamism, the more accounting costs partners will share.

Hypothesis 2b: The higher the environmental dynamism, the less non-accounting costs partners will share.

2.3   Visible and Invisible Risks

Visible risks are the possibilities that a hazard may occur in a decision-maker's perception. In other words, they can be defined and specified in partnership contracts [9]. When partners jointly develop a new product, for example, they may predict the possible failure of the new product. Invisible risks are unforeseeable risks. For example, the sudden death or resignation of a firm's CEO may cause sharp fluctuations in the firm's stock value. Because of such unforeseeablity and unexpectedness, invisible risks can hardly be specified and each party's responsibility and obligations in sharing these invisible risks can hardly be clearly determined in the partnership contracts.

Environmental dynamism increases both visible and invisible risks. However, its impacts on these risks are different. Environmental dynamism enhances partners' desire to share the visible risks because the dynamism increases the risks and the costs to cover the risks [10]. Firms may not have sufficient resources, such as cash, to manage these risks on their own [11]. More importantly, the responsibilities and obligations to share risks between partners can be specified in partnership contracts so the possibilities of partner opportunism are minimal [12].

Because the invisible risks are unforeseeable, the responsibilities and obligations in sharing invisible risks are mainly based on partners' mutual trusts [13]. However, existing studies have shown that such trusts are negatively correlated with environmental dynamism. Generally, firms share invisible risks only when they are confident that the risk-adjusted returns of a joint project will be positive [14]. High levels of environmental dynamism may reduce or even damage the confidence because risk forecasting and measurements become highly inaccurate, if not impossible, in such environments. Accordingly, we predict that:

Hypothesis 3a: The higher the environmental dynamism, the more visible risks partners will share.

Hypothesis 3b: The higher the environmental dynamism, the less invisible risks partners will share.

3   Method

3.1   Setting, Sample, and Data

This study used data of Canadian technology firms to test the hypotheses. Two waves of questionnaires were mailed to the CEOs or the highest-ranking officers of the target firms. All questions in the questionnaires were presented as a seven-point Likert-type scale (ranging from 1 = strongly disagree to 7 = strongly agree).

3.2   Main Variables

Firm-specific resources consist of five measurement items: (1) patents; (2) expertise in making a product; (3) possession of a unique technology; (4) skilled labor; and (5) brand equity. *General resources* are composed of four measurement items: (1) cash; (2) production and storage infrastructure; (3) unskilled labor; and (4) communication/transportation/distribution facilities. *Accounting costs* include: (1) prime costs; (2) conversion costs; and (3) non-manufacturing costs. *Non-accounting costs* are composed of both transaction costs and opportunity costs. Measurement items of transaction costs include (1) monitoring/controlling costs; (2) coordination costs; (3) information collecting/processing costs; (4) partner maximizing unilateral interests; and (5) partner cheating. Measurement items of opportunity costs include (1) the loss of other market opportunities; (2) failure to address other threats; and (3) loss of possible profits in other business. Measurement items of *visible risks* consist of (1) magnitude of possible loss; (2) chances of possible loss; and (3) exposure to possible loss. Measurement items of *invisible risks* include (1) feelings that unfavorable hazards would occur; (2) the perceived possibilities that unknown unfavorable hazards would occur; and (3) past experiences that unfavorable hazards which were undefined in partnership contracts occurred when contracts were executed.

We used a composite index of four items to measure *sharing* of each above-mentioned category between partners. These four items include necessity, magnitude, duration, and possible impacts of sharing. Measurement of *environmental dynamism* (EV) was based on the items developed by Boyd and associates (1993) and Zahra and associates (1997), and there were seven such items that compose the construct (see Appendix 1). Both linear and squared terms of the variable (EV and EV^2) were used to denote low and high levels of environmental changes. All data will be provided upon request.

4   Discussion and Conclusions

The evidence collected in this study indicates that sharing firm-specific resources and non-accounting costs is feasible at low level of environmental dynamism. In other words, a low level of environmental dynamism does not impede such sharing. When environmental dynamism grows high, however, sharing firm-specific resources and non-accounting costs becomes unlikely. In contrast, partners share general resources, accounting costs and visible risks in a highly dynamic environment. It should be noted that sharing invisible risks between partners may not be affected by the levels of environmental dynamism. Two possible interpretations emerge from this study. Frist, invisible risks increase substantially when environments grow dynamic. As such, partners have to share more invisible risks if they want to keep their partnerships. Second, it is difficult for managers to define invisible risks regardless of the level of environmental dynamism and they cannot negotiate and specify such risks in the partnership contracts. Consequently, they do not have a clear idea of how to deal with such risks. Perhaps both causes co-exist and they work in combination.

The findings of this study have important theoretical implications. First, partners share more general resources, accounting costs and visible risks when environments grow dynamic. As such, sharing general resources, accounting costs and visible risks may not necessarily increase transaction costs and increased environmental dynamism enhances the needs for partners to share general resources, accounting costs and visible risks. The evidence explains why firms use strategic alliances in highly dynamic environments. Transaction costs are associated not only with environmental dynamism but also with the nature of the resources, costs and risks that partners share. Second, sharing firm-specific resources and non-accounting costs between partners decreases with environmental dynamism. The evidence confirms the traditional belief that sharing firm-specific resources incurs transaction costs in dynamic environments. Moreover, such sharing may also increase opportunity costs which have been ignored in the mainstream literature. Both transaction costs and opportunity costs vary positively with environmental dynamism and both of them are sacrifice partners make in their partnerships. Transaction costs have been widely discussed in the existing literature but opportunity costs do not receive a similar attention. Finally, in contrast to the existing literature, partners are willing to share more visible risks when environments are dynamic. Even their sharing of invisible risks may not necessarily decrease in highly dynamic environments. In other words, the traditional belief that environmental dynamism is negatively correlated with partners' wishes to share risks may not be true.

References

1. Borch, O.J., Huse, M., Senneseth, K.: Resource configuration, competitive strategies, and corporate entrepreneurship: An empirical examination of small firms. Entrepreneurship Theory and Practice 24(1), 49–70 (1999)
2. Das, T., Teng, B.: Strategic alliance constellations: A social exchange perspective. Academy of Management Review 27, 445–456 (2002)

3. Glover, S.I., Wasserman, C.M.: International strategic alliances, joint Ventures & strategic alliances. Law Journal Press, The US (2003)
4. Goerzen, A.: Alliance networks and firm performance: The impact of repeated international strategic alliances. Strategic Management Journal 28, 487–509 (2007)
5. Gulati, R., Khanna, T., Nohria, N.: Unilateral commitments and the importance of process in alliances. Sloan Management Review 35(3), 61–69 (1994)
6. Lecocq, X., Demil, B.: Strategizing industry structure: The case of open systems in a low-tech industry. Strategic Management Journal 27, 891–898 (2006)
7. Ireland, R.D., Hoskisson, R.E., Hitt, M.A.: The management of strategy: Concepts and cases. South-Western, Mason (2009)
8. Dess, G.G., Beard, D.W.: Dimensions of organizational task environments. Administrative Science Quarterly 29(1), 52–73 (1984)
9. Qian, G., Li, L.: Profitability of small- and medium-sized enterprises in high-tech industries: The case of the biotechnology industry. Strategic Management Journal 24(9), 881–887 (2003)
10. Lu, J.W., Beamish, P.: The internationalization and performance of SMEs. Strategic Management Journal 22, 565–586 (2001)
11. Amburgey, T.L., Kelly, D., Barnett, W.: Resetting the clock: The dynamics of organizational change and failure. Administrative Science Quarterly 38, 51–73 (1993)
12. Hannan, M.T., Freeman, J.: Structural inertia and organizational change. American Sociological Review 49, 149–164 (1984)
13. Baum, J., Calabrese, T., Silverman, B.: Don't go it alone: alliance network composition and startup's performance in Canadian biotechnology. Strategic Management Journal 21, 267–294 (2000)
14. Luo, Y.: Are joint venture international strategic alliances more opportunistic in more volatile environment? Strategic Management Journal 28, 39–60 (2007)

More Sensors or Better Algorithm?

Zoltan Horvath[1,*] and Hanna Horvath[2]

[1] University of Pecs, Ifjusag st. 6., Pecs, 7623, Hungary
hz@gamma.ttk.pte.hu
[2] Leowey Klara Secondary School, 8-10. Szent Istvan Sqr., Pecs, 7624, Hungary
hhzs1995@yahoo.com

Abstract. For the development of a successful indoor navigation system it is essential to know the nature of signals broadcasted by different access points and other signal broadcasting/transmitting equipments, since we can't rely on the help of navigation satellites inside buildings. However we need to use the original signal in each case for accurate positioning, so we have to be able to filter out the interfering signals with the help of different algorithms.

Keywords: GPS, L1 regression analysis, Kalman Filter, GLONASS.

1 Introduction

We examined the precision and inaccuracy of GPS sensors built in different smartphones in a previous research of ours [12]. From the experiment it turned out, that the data provided by the devices are quite inaccurate. The primary cause of this is attributable to the scattered signal, which stems from the device not always seeing the original "clear" signal broadcasted by the navigation satellites. This is why the spread of GLONASS system is of great importance, as smartphones using GLONASS provide more precise data for the users. On the one hand the device uses two independent navigation system here, also GLONASS has ground reference stations where the device gets further clarification. Nevertheless it does not always mean a solution. This is why the usage of different "signal-cleaner" algorithms is necessary, because these algorithms are able to filter out scattered, disturbing signals from the originals. Thereby the measurement becomes much more accurate. Filtering out the scattered signals and those which come from the interference is also essential, because when using indoor navigation, the ratio of scattered signals increases significantly compared to the original.

---

* Corresponding author.

K. Liu et al. (Eds.): ICISO 2014, IFIP AICT 426, pp. 238–245, 2014.
© IFIP International Federation for Information Processing 2014

2   Material and Method

2.1   Devices

In our research we used the next smart phones and a tablet. These were the following: HTC HD (Windows mobile 6), HTC 8x (Windows mobile 8), Sonny Xperia J (Google Android OS v4,0), iPhone 4 (iOs 4), iPad2 (iOs 6), Nokia Lumia 1520.

By choosing these devices, we can try out most of the used operation systems of our times'. In addition, the HTC 8X device applies GLONASS support in order to allocate our location. This support is available up from the series of iPhone 4S.

2.2   GLONASS

Before the research, we required the HTC 8X to be the most precise since this device has GLONASS support besides GPS [7]. This means that the traditional GPS system is expanded with the data of the satellites developed by Russians, therefore it makes it more precise to the users. Presently there are 51 reference stations in Hungary. Pecs is a good location in this network because there are three stations near at hand. These are Siklos (20km from Pecs), Barcs (50km from Pecs) and Kaposvar (50km from Pecs). Structure of GPS signal.

All signal components are derived from the output of a highly stable atomic clock. In the operational (Block II/IIA) GPS system each satellite is equipped with two caesium and two rubidium atomic clocks. The clocks generate a pure sine wave at a frequency $f0 = 10.23MHz$, with a stability of the order of 1 part in 1013 over one day. This is referred to as the fundamental frequency.

Multiplying the fundamental frequency f0 by integer factors yields the two microwave L-band carrier waves L1 and L2 respectively (above two figures). The frequency of the two waves is obtained as follows:

$$fL1 = f0 \times 154 = 1575.42MHz \tag{1}$$

equivalent wavelength: $\lambda L1 = c / fL1 \approx 19cm$

$$fL2 = f0 \times 120 = 1227.60MHz \tag{2}$$

equivalent wavelength: $\lambda L2 = c / fL2 \approx 24cm$

These are right-hand circularly polarised radio frequency waves capable of transmission through the atmosphere over great distances, but they contain no information. All satellites broadcast the same frequencies (though the received frequencies are slightly different because of the Doppler shift).

2.3   Clear GPS Signal

We performed measurements on planes during flight, when the aircrafts reached the altitude. During the measurements we experienced that certain mobiles were unable to detect GPS signal. The mensuration was necessary, because we couldn't get closer to the satellites broadcasting navigation signals than the aforementioned altitude, furthermore no artificial object could interfere with the signals. This way we can work with relatively clean signals, free of scattered signals. Since at flight altitude we can't designate a fixed length area, every measurement lasted for exactly 10 minutes. The results can be seen in the following figure.

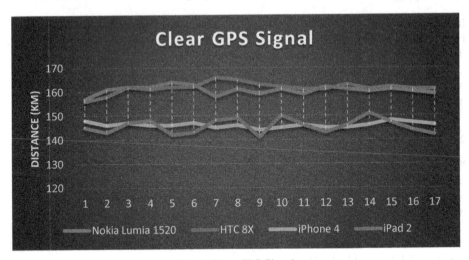

Fig. 1. Clear GPS Signal

2.4   L1 Regression Analysis

We investigate our results first time with L1 regression. Consider the linear regression model (1):

$$Y_i = \beta_0 + \beta_1 x_{li} + \cdots + \beta_p x_{pi} + \varepsilon_i \tag{3}$$

Where $\beta_0, \beta_1, \ldots, \beta_p$ are unknown parameters and $\{\varepsilon_i\}$ are unobservable independent, identically distributed random variables each with median 0. For simplicity, we will assume that the x_{ki}'s are non-random although the results will typically hold for random x_{ki}'s. We will consider the asymptotic behavior of L1-estimators of $\beta = (\beta_0, \ldots, \beta_p)$; that is $\widetilde{\beta_0} \widetilde{\beta_1}, \ldots \ldots, \widetilde{\beta_p}$ minimize the objective function (2)

$$g_n(\Phi) = \sum_{i=1}^{n} |Y_i - \phi_0 - \phi_1 x_{li} - \cdots - \phi_p x_{pi}| \tag{4}$$

over all $\phi = (\phi_0, \ldots, \phi_p)$.

In Petros Hadjicostas (2012) optimization program he seeks to minimize [8] (over all $k \in \{2,\ldots, n\text{-}2\}$) (3)

$$z_k = \sum_{i=1}^{k} |\theta_i - \gamma_0 - \beta \phi_i| + \sum_{i=k+1}^{n} |\theta_i - \delta_0 - \beta \phi_i| \tag{5}$$

Subject to at least one of the following conditions:

1A: $\beta \geq 0$ and $\beta(\phi_{k+1} - \phi_k) \geq \gamma_0 - \delta_0$
1B: $\beta \geq 0$ and $\beta(\phi_n - \phi_1) \leq \gamma_0 - \delta_0$
2A: $\beta \leq 0$ and $\beta(\phi_{k+1} - \phi_k) \leq \gamma_0 - \delta_0$
2B: $\beta \leq 0$ and $\beta(\phi_n - \phi_1) \geq \gamma_0 - \delta_0$

This minimization problem can be solved using standard Linear Programming techniques. L1 Linear regression assumes that an intercept term is to be included and takes two parameters: the independent variables (a matrix whose columns represent the independent variables) and the dependent variable (in a column vector). L-1 regression is less affected by large errors than least squares regression [4]. Reflectanced GPS signal filtering with Kalman filter.

2.5   Kalman Filter

We can filter the reflectanced GPS signal with Kalman filter because we can monitor the GPS. If we know which particular signal our smartphone is using then we know what this satellite frequency is. After this, we can use the Kalman filter where we give the original frequency (this will the right data) and we say that the other results are the errors [9].

It is instructive first to review the analysis step in the standard Kalman filter where the analyzed estimate is determined by a linear combination of the vector of measurements d and the forecasted model state vector ψ^f[10]. The linear combination is chosen to minimize the variance in the analyzed estimate ψ^a, which is then given by the equation

$$\psi^a = \psi^f + K(d - H\psi^f) \tag{6}$$

The Kalman gain matrix K is given by

$$K = P^f H^T (HP^f H^T + W)^{-1} \tag{7}$$

The error covariance of the analyzed model state vector is reduced with respect to the error covariance of the forecasted state as

$$P^a = \overline{(\psi^a - \psi^t)(\psi^a - \psi^t)^\mathsf{T}}$$

$$
\begin{aligned}
&= \overline{[\psi^f - \psi^t + K(d - d^t - H\psi^f + H\psi^f][\psi^f - \psi^t + K(d - d^t - H\psi^f + H\psi^f)]} \\
&= (I - KH)\overline{(\psi^f - \psi^t)(\psi^f - \psi^t)}^\mathsf{T}(I - KH)\mathsf{T}\, K\overline{(d - d^t)(d - d^t)}^\mathsf{T}K^T \\
&= (I - KH)P^f(I - H^t K^t) + KWK^t \\
&= P^f - KPH^f - P^f H^T K^T + K(HP^f H^t + W)K^T \\
&= (I - KH)P^f \tag{8}
\end{aligned}
$$

The analyzed model state is the best linear unbiased estimate [1]. This means that ψa is the linear combination of ψf and d that minimizes $TrP = \overline{(\psi - \psi^t)(\psi - \psi^t)}$, if model errors and observations errors are unibased and are not correlated [2].

3   Results

During our research we examined how much some algorithm can refine the results of the measurements compared to the raw data. In fig. 2 we can see how the result changes if we clean the data measured at high altitude with the help of the algorithms.

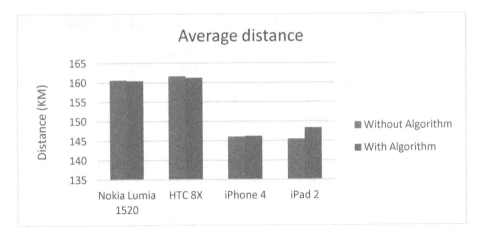

Fig. 2. Average distance (Transition altitude) with and without algorithm

Before the purification of the original signals we expected not to have significant difference, for at flight altitude the devices detects the original signal. It is not distorted so much by atmospheric phenomena, natural and artificial objects. The analyzed values confirms this, as we can see it. Perhaps the data measured by iPad 2 is the only exception. As we can see in the graph (fig. 3), the data collected by these the devices has only a digression of a couple of centimetres. To sum up, we can say that if we measure one point in an open area, where the zenith is 92% visible; there is no significant difference between the two operation systems.

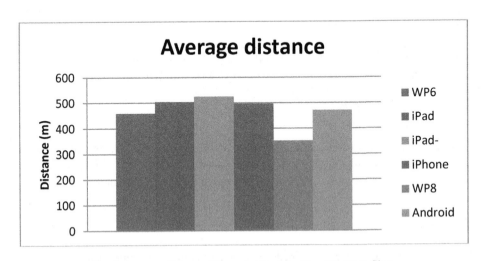

Fig. 3. Average distance (Ground altitude) without Kalman filter

When we started our research we were in an opinion that the most homogeneous data will be collected by the device which applies GLONASS support as well. As it can be seen in Fig. 3, the WP8 device was the one which made this result. From the second place, we did not experience big difference. That is to say, there is no significant difference between the results achieved by the devices which only use GPS. On the other hand, the HTC 8X (WP8) is the absolute number one with big difference. As we can see, there are two results for the iPad: results from Sports Tracker as well as Outdoor Navigation. The difference is evident and interesting as a single device produced two different results during the same time interval. It is extremely important to point out that the measurement circumstances were exactly the same! Will similar devices using different applications bring similar results or will the same problem not be there in such a case. And most importantly: can this problem be solved using different algorithms? We will examine this in the frame of another project.

What is then if we can filter the satellite signal at the measurement? Because the smart phones can use small mobile apps where this application can recording all signal. After we can analysed this results and we can separate the signal and the reflectance signal, we can see the results between the original data and the filtered data on the next figures (fig. 4).

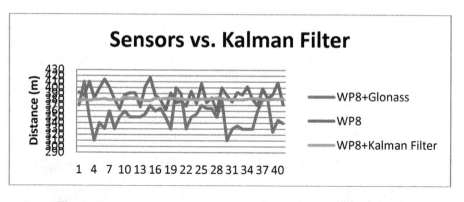

Fig. 4. Modify distance with Kalman Filter, Glonass and without Glonass

We can see in these figures that the different is huge. In the first situation, where we used the GPS+Glonass than was the deviation 22.36 and the average distance 352.19m until then when we used the filter the deviation was 1.47 and the average distance was 371.65 meter. If our smartphone use just the basic GPS system then the deviation is 14.35 and the average distance was 378 meter. As shown in fig. 5, we can see how the values of average distance change if we clean the original raw data with the algorithms. In this case we can provide comparatively accurate (few meters difference) data also with smartphones with not so good sensors.

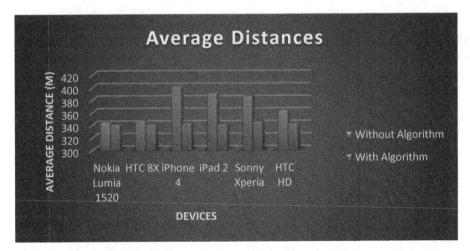

Fig. 5. Average distances with and without algorithm

4   Conclusion

In our measurements, we have proved that the sensor itself does not provide enough accurate information in terms of navigation. To access the precise information we need different algorithms. Thus, a full-whipped cheaper smart can be achieved in a more accurate geolokalizációt. The indoor navigation also it will be the most important thing is that the original signal can be filtered out of the scattered signals. Since most of the signals (according to preliminary measurements) seem close to 74% of the scattered or reflected signal. This greatly reduces the accurate position determination. At indoor navigation is not enough to precision some thirty feet. After filtration of the signal device with GPS with the smooth result of the device and result in GLONASS + GPS, the average was 8.68% of the difference. We can see in fig 6.

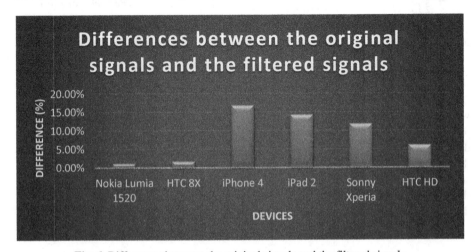

Fig. 6. Differences between the original signals and the filtered signals

The measurements are all available today, operating systems performed. As a reference, and the higher layers of the airspace (flight altitude) measurements were performed in order to eliminate inaccuracies caused by stray signals.

Acknowledgement. Supported by the SROP-4.2.2.C-11/1/KONV-2012-0005 grant.

References

1. Gerrit, B., van. Leeuwen, P.J., Evensen, G.: Analysis Scheme in the Ensemble Kalman Filter. Mon. Wea. Rev. 126, 1719–1724 (1998)
2. Cheng, D., Hadjicostas, P.: Right-invariant metrics applied to rank correlation coefficients (2012) (submitted for publication)
3. Brachmann, F.: About performance requirements set against consumer-grade geolocation technologies (2013) (submitted for publication)
4. Fisher, N.I.: Statistical analysis of circular data, vol. 23. Cambridge University Press, New York (1995)
5. Gartner, https://www.gartner.com/newsroom/id/2573415
6. GLONASS masked area, http://www.gnssnet.hu/ASfigures.php?station=SIKL&button=%E1br%E1k
7. GLONASS, http://www.novatel.com/assets/Documents/Papers/GLONASSOverview.pdf
8. Hadjicostas, P.: Using L1-Regression to Estimate a Monotone Two-Piece Linear Relationship Between Two Angular Variables. In: 46th Annual Conference on the operations research society of New Zealand, December 10-11, pp. 139–147 (2012)
9. Yang, S.-C., Kalnay, E., Hunt, B.: Handling Nonlinearity in an Ensemble Kalman Filter: Experiments with the Three-Variable Lorenz Model. Monthly Weather Review 140(8), 2628–2646 (2012)
10. Jung, Y., Xue, M., Tong, M.: Ensemble Kalman Filter Analyses of the 29–30 May 2004 Oklahoma Tornadic Thunderstorm Using One- and Two-Moment Bulk Microphysics Schemes, with Verification against Polarimetric Radar Data. Monthly Weather Review 140(5), 1457–1475 (2012)
11. Horvath, Z., Brachmann, F.: smartphones and tablets integrated GPS accuracy, SZAMOKT 2013 (2013) (submitted publication)
12. Horvath, Z., Horvath, H.: The Measurement Preciseness of the GPS Built in Smartphones and Tablets. International Journal of Electronics & Communication Technology (IJECT) 5(SPL-I), 2230–7109 (2014)

A Combining Forecasting Modeling and Its Application

Dengmei Qiu and WenJie Wang[*]

Glorious Sun School of Business and Management, Donghua University
Shanghai, 200051, China
{dmqiu,wenjiew}@dhu.edu.cn

Abstract. The supply chain coordination has abstracted more and more attention from industries and academics. This paper studies a Bayesian combination forecasting model to integrate multiple forecasting resources and coordinate forecasting process among partners in retail supply chain. The simulation results based on the retail sales data show the effectiveness of this Bayesian combination forecasting model to coordinate the collaborative forecasting process. This Bayesian combination forecasting model can improve demand forecasting accuracy of supply chain.

Keywords: Combination forecasting, Bayesian model, Supply chain.

1   Introduction

With the development of information and network technology, various innovative supply chain solutions are created. Collaborative planning, forecasting and replenishment (CPFR), which is an retailing supply chain coordination innovation based on the network technology, has been adopted and implemented by many world-renowned retailers and manufacturers, such as Wal-Mart, Proctor & Gamble, etc.. CPFR concerns the collaboration where two or more parties in the supply chain jointly plan a number of promotional activities and work out synchronized forecasts, on the basis of which the production and replenishment processes are determined [1]. The first CPFR project was piloted by Wal-Mart with its suppliers in 1995. The results of two-year project showed that CPFR could simultaneously reduce inventory levels and increase sales for both retailers and suppliers. Since its original application was initiated, CPFR has had many successful applications in North America, Europe and China [2].

The collaborative forecasting plays an important part in CPFR implementation procedure. We will briefly review the CPFR concept and its implementation process at the beginning of this paper. And then, the collaborative forecasting process which is the core part of CPFR will be mainly discussed. As the basics phase of the implementation of CPFR, the collaborative forecasting process is the cornerstone to the success of

---

[*] Corresponding author.

K. Liu et al. (Eds.): ICISO 2014, IFIP AICT 426, pp. 246–252, 2014.

CPFR projects. The collaborative forecasting process of CPFR requires a solid forecasting approach to synthesis information and knowledge from multiply parties in the supply chain. The combination forecasting method can combines forecasting models from different parties to smooth coordination in the supply chain and reduce forecasting discrepancies. Thus, considering the multiple forms of forecasting resources in the retail supply chain, the Bayesian combination forecasting method is applied for CPFR collaborative forecasting modeling with improved forecasting accuracy and supply chain collaboration performance in this paper.

Combining forecasts is a well-established procedure for improving forecasting accuracy which takes advantage of the availability of both multiple information and computing resources for data intensive forecasting [3]. Since Bates-Granger first proposed the combination forecasting method in 1969 [4], many kinds of combining methods have been developed [3]. Zeng et al [5] studied the combination forecasting model with error correction and changing weight coefficient. Hoogerheide et al [6] compared several Bayesian combination schemes in terms of forecast accuracy and economic gains. Bayesian combination methods use the distributional properties of the individual forecasts to construct the combination. The demand forecasting in retail supply chain is impacted by many factors such as product promotion or social development trend. And, subjective forecasting based on the expert experiments is often used in retail market forecasting. So, the Bayesian combination forecasting model is considered as the collaborative forecasting approach in retail supply chain coordination.

In the first part of this paper, the CPFR retail supply chain coordination and collaborative forecasting process are discussed briefly. In the second part of the paper, a Bayesian combination forecasting method is modeled to coordinate forecasting process in retail supply chain. Finally, the simulation for this model is completed based on the Carrefour sales data. The simulation results showed the effective of this Bayesian combination forecasting model in retail supply chain collaboration process.

2   Bayesian Combination Forecasting Modeling for Collaborative Forecasting Process

The combination method proposed by Bates and Branger in 1969 is normally called as optimal linear combination model or B-G method. The forecasting results $f_{c1}, f_{c2} \cdots f_{cn}$ are supposed as random variables with the covariance matrix $\sum$ in this model. Based on the minimizing the variance criteria (MV), the optimal forecasting results can be calculated as the following formula (1)

$$f_c = \sum_{k=1}^{n} W_k f_k = W^T \bullet f \tag{1}$$

Here, weighting vector $W^T = (1_n^T \sum {}^{-1} 1_n)^{-1} 1_n^T \sum {}^{-1} = (W_1, W_2 ..., W_n)$, $1_n^T = (1,1,...,1)$.

The Bayesian combination forecasting model is developed based on the B-G method and uses the distributional properties of the individual forecasts to construct the combination. Supposed the Y is presenting the samples of actual demand. The forecasting results obtained from the different parties in the supply chain which are forecasted with m kinds of individual forecasting methods are presented by $f_1, f_2, \cdots f_m$ $(j=1,2,\ldots,m)$. $i = 1,2,\cdots,n$ present different forecasting time periods. The Bayesian combination forecasting method makes use of the Bayesian rule to decide the optimal combination ways and weights of individual forecasting methods in combination model and get the combined forecasting results in different time periods $\hat{f}_{ic}$ $(i = 1,2,\cdots,n)$, which can be fully approximated to actual demand values.

Set $z_i^T = (f_1, f_2, \cdots f_m)$, $i = 1,2,\cdots,n$, and then the joint probability density function of m individual forecasting samples on independent time $z_1, z_2, \cdots, z_n$ can be calculated as follows.

$$f(z_1, z_2, \cdots, z_n | Y; \varphi) = \prod_{i=1}^{n} f(z_i | Y_i; \varphi) \tag{2}$$

Here φ is parameter vector, and $Y^T = (y_1, y_2, \cdots, y_n)$ is the vector of the actual demand samples on the different forecasting time periods.

According to the Bayesian rule, the probability density function that Y is specified as a vector value y is as follows:

$$f(y | z_1, z_2, \cdots, z_n) = \frac{\prod\limits_{i=1}^{n} f(z_i | y_i) f(y_i)}{\prod\limits_{i=1}^{n} \int_{A_i} f(z_i | y_i) f(y_i) dy_i} = \prod_{i=1}^{n} \frac{f(f_{i1}, f_{i2}, \cdots f_{im} | y_i) f(y_i)}{\int_{A_i} f(f_{i1}, f_{i2}, \cdots f_{im} | y_i) f(y_i) dy_i} \tag{3}$$

Here $f(y_i)(i = 1,2,\cdots,n)$ is the prior probability distribution of y_i, which presents the prior estimation or preference of decision maker to y_i. A_i is the definition set of y_i.

If only one forecasting time period is considered as the general case and prior distribution $f(y)$ is uniform distribution form, that is $f(y) \propto 1$, the formula (2) can be simplified as the following.

$$f(y | f_1, f_2, \cdots, f_m) = \frac{f(f_1, f_2, \cdots f_m | y)}{\int_A f(f_1, f_2, \cdots f_m | y) dy} \tag{4}$$

The forecasting error distribution of individual forecasting results $(f_1, f_2, \cdots f_m)$ is chosen as normal distribution or logarithm normal distribution in most case. In this paper, more general distribution of forecasting error is introduced through $Box-Cox$ conversion.

$$Z^{(\lambda)} = \begin{cases} \dfrac{Z^{\lambda} - 1}{\lambda} & \lambda \neq 0 \\ \ln Z & \lambda = 0 \end{cases} \tag{5}$$

Here, λ is conversion parameter

Supposed $\sum$ is the covariance matrix of $(f_1, f_2, \cdots f_m)$ and Wi presents the weights of individual forecasting fi. Then, weights can be calculated as following formula based on the minimum error variance criteria:

$$W^T = \left(1_m^T \sum{}^{-1} 1_m\right)^{-1} 1_m^T \sum{}^{-1} = \left(W_1, W_2 ..., W_m\right) \tag{6}$$

And, nonlinear combination forecasting formula can be obtained through Bayesian analysis as follows, which will be used to calculate the optimal combination forecasting results approximated to the actual values Y.

$$\hat{f}_c = \begin{cases} \displaystyle\prod_{i=1}^{m} f_i^{w_i} \times e^{\frac{s^2}{2}} & \lambda = 0 \\ \left[1 + \displaystyle\sum_{i=1}^{m} \lambda W_i f_i^{(\lambda)}\right]^{\frac{1}{\lambda}} = \left[\displaystyle\sum_{i=1}^{m} W_i f_i^{\lambda}\right]^{\frac{1}{\lambda}} & \lambda \neq 0 \end{cases} \tag{7}$$

Here, $\dfrac{1}{S^2} = 1_m^T \sum{}^{-1} 1_m = \dfrac{1}{|\sum|} 1_m^T \sum{}^{*} 1_m$, and $\displaystyle\sum_{i=1}^{n} W_{it} = 1$

And, the optimal conversion parameter λ^* can be calculated as the following formula.

$$\lambda^* = \arg\min_{\lambda} \sum_{j=1}^{t} \left[Y_j - \left(\sum_{i=1}^{n} W_i f_{ij}^{\lambda}\right)^{\frac{1}{\lambda}}\right]^2 \tag{8}$$

Here, f_{ij} present the forecasting result on j time period by i individual forecasting methods. The weights W_i can be calculated by formula (4). The covariance matrix $\sum$ can be determined by prior value or estimated by past proximate samples values.

3 Simulation

The simulation of the Bayesian combination forecasting model will be based on the sales data of one kind of biscuit product in Carrefour China in this paper. The detailed sales data of this biscuit product in 39 weeks in Carrefour China is showed in table 1. During the simulation process, the sales data from week 1 to week 28 are used to estimate parameters in Bayesian combination forecasting model creation. The sales data from week 29 to week 39 are used to compare with the forecasting results obtained from combination forecasting methods.

Table 1. The Sales Data of Biscuit in Carrefour Supermarket

Week	1	2	3	4	5	6	7	8	9	10	11	12	13
Demand	64	78	62	38	59	13	99	82	105	56	56	88	93
Week	14	15	16	17	18	19	20	21	22	23	24	25	26
Demand	100	110	135	124	105	86	117	172	185	169	192	195	156
Week	27	28	29	30	31	32	33	34	35	36	37	38	39
Demand	136	132	183	84	92	119	137	107	80	218	167	156	170

Based on the Carrefour biscuit sale data and statics analysis, the Bayesian forecasting model can be created following three main steps, which includes proper individual forecasting methods selection, combination ways determination and optimal parameter estimation. The characteristics of the individual forecasts combining in the model has substantial implications on the overall forecasting performance of model, and thus it is very important to make a rigorous analysis on the individual forecast errors. The first step of combination modeling is to compare and select proper individual forecasting methods for combination.

Table 2. Forecasting Results of Five Individual Forecasting Methods

Week	Actual Demand	F1	F2	F3	F4	F5
29	183	141.3333	138.9865	179.2469	136.3747	125.3344
30	84	150.3333	165.3946	184.8024	173.2965	159.2878
31	92	133	116.5578	190.4484	112.6916	68.3652
32	119	119.6667	101.8231	196.185	93.30308	111.0044
33	137	98.3333	112.1293	202.0121	115.4397	106.5959
34	107	116	127.0517	207.9297	135.7434	117.6981
35	80	121	115.0207	213.9379	118.0299	93.1682
36	218	108	94.0083	220.0367	90.26195	82.5842
37	167	135	168.4033	226.2259	186.0273	177.1399
38	156	155	167.5613	232.5058	183.4052	115.0543
39	170	180.3333	160.6245	238.8761	162.1665	150.9677

In general, different parties in the retail supply chain may use the different patterns of individual forecasting. So, the different patterns of individual forecasting methods, which include the simple moving average, the exponential smoothing, the trend extrapolation method, ARIMA (autoregressive integrated moving average) method and artificial neural network method, are applied to combine model to forecast Carrefour biscuit demand from week 29 to week 39. Through comparison study of forecasting results of each individual forecasting method, the best parameters of each individual forecasting method are estimated. The forecasting results of five different individual forecasting methods are indicated in Table 2. The F1 row data indicated the best result forecasted by the simple moving average method when moving period N equal to 3. The F2 row data indicated the best result forecasted by the exponential smoothing method when smoothing coefficient *a* equal to 0.6. The F3 row data indicated the best result forecasted by the two polynomial regression method (n=2). The F4 row data indicated the best result forecasted by the ARIMA method when parameter d equal to 1. The F5 row data indicated the best result forecasted by the artificial neural network method when there are three neurons and two hidden layers in the neural network.

After the five individual forecasting methods selected, the second step of combination modeling is to determine proper combination ways of these individual methods. With the Matlab simulation tool, the forecasting results are calculated using different combination ways of these individual forecasting methods. As it is widely accepted that only ``good" forecasts should be included in a combination, strong differences in forecast error variances between the individual forecasts are not to be expected [7]. Four individual methods (F1、F2、F4、F5) which have good forecasting performance is decided to be combined into Bayesian combination model.

The optimal conversion parameter λ^* can be calculated according to the formula (8). The sum of square of forecasting error is minimized when $\lambda^* = 6.9419$. The optimal conversion parameter λ^* could be simplified as $\lambda^*=7$ in the Bayesian combination modeling. The forecasting error between forecasting result and actual demand are used as the evaluation standards of forecasting methods performance. There are many kinds of measure indexes of forecasting errors [8]. In this paper, four main measure indexes of forecasting error, which are the squares sum error (SSE), the mean square error (MSE), the mean absolute percentage error (MAPE) and the mean square percentage error (MSPE), are applied to comprehensively evaluate the forecasting accuracy of Bayesian combination forecasting model.

Table 3. The Comparison of Bayesian Combination Models Forecasting Accuracy

Combination Forecasting	SSE	MSE	MAPE	MSPE
Simple Average Method	2.64E+04	2.40E+03	0.3589	0.3725
Optimal Linear Method	2.52E+04	2.29E+03	0.2734	0.3416
Bayesian Combination $\lambda^*=7$	1.92E+03	1.74E+02	0.0803	0.0561

The Bayesian combination models with different parameters λ are compared with the simple average method and optimal linear methods in the simulation based on Carrefour biscuit sale data. The forecasting errors of different combination forecasting methods are showed in the table 3. It can be found that the four measure indexes of forecasting error of optimal Bayesian combination method when $\lambda^* =7$ are lower than those of simple combination methods. So, the optimal Bayesian combination forecasting model performs better than other combination models in retail collaborative forecasting process. This simulation research proved that the optimal Bayesian combination forecasting method is an effective approach to integrate and coordinate the forecasting process among partners in retail supply chain. Bayesian combination forecasting method can highly improve the demand forecasting accuracy of collaborative forecasting activity in the retail supply chain.

4   Conclusion

The collaborative planning, forecasting and replenishment framework provides the practical roadmap for retail supply chain coordination. The collaborative forecasting is taken as the core part in CPFR solution implementation. A Bayesian combination forecasting method, which can combine individual forecasting methods from different parties in the retail supply chain, is modeled for CPFR collaborative forecasting process. The simulation results showed that forecasting discrepancies are reduced and collaborative forecasting accuracy is improved after integrating forecasting process with the optimal Bayesian combination forecasting model. It is turned out that the Bayesian combination forecasting method is an effective means for collaborative forecasting process in retail supply chain. The further research on collaborative forecasting methodology for supply chain coordination will be extended into different statistic features of product demand situation in the future.

Acknowledgments. This research was supported by a grant from the Shanghai Science Foundation Council (12ZR1400900) and the Chinese National Science Foundation Council (71172174).

References

1. Liu, X., Sun, Y.: Information Integration of CPFR in Inbound Logistics of Automotive Manufactures Based on Internet of Things. Journal of Computers 7(2), 349–355 (2012)
2. Danese, P.: Designing CPFR collaborations: insights from seven case studies. International Journal of Operations & Production Management 27(2), 181–204 (2007)
3. Bunn, D.W.: Forecasting with more than one model. Journal of Forecasting 8(3), 161–166 (1989)
4. Bates, J.M., Greanger, C.W.J.: Combination of Forecasts. Operational Research Quarterly 20(4), 451–468 (1969)
5. Zeng, Y., Tang, X., Zheng, W.: Combination forecasting based on Stein-rule estimation and error correction. Journal of Management Sciences in China 4(6), 39–47 (2001)
6. Hoogerheide, L., Kleijn, R., Ravazzolo, F., Van Dijk, H.K., Verbeek, M.: Forecast Accuracy and Economic Gains from Bayesian Model Averaging Using Time-Varying Weights. Journal of Forecasting 29(1-2), 251–269 (2010)
7. Menezes, L.M., de, B.D.W., Taylor, J.W.: Review of guidelines for the use of combined forecasts. European Journal of Operational Research 120(1), 190–204 (2000)
8. Zhang, C., Huang, L., Zhao, Z.: Research on combination forecast of port cargo throughput based on time series and causality analysis. Journal of Industrial Engineering and Management 6(1), 124–134 (2013)

System Structure Risk Metric Method
Based on Information Flow

Mengmeng Zhang, Junxian Liu, Aimin Luo, and Xueshan Luo

Information Systems Engineering Laboratory,
National University of Defense Technology, China
377019128@qq.com, 18674864900@163.com,
amluo@nudt.edu.cn, luoxueshan@gmail.com

Abstract. The measurement of structure risk aims to analysis and evaluate the not occurred, potential, and the objectively exist risk in system structure. It is an essential way to validate system function and system quality. This paper proposes the risk metric model and algorithm based on information flow and analysis risk trend between traditional tree structure and network-centric structure.

Keywords: System Structure, Risk, Information Flow, GIG.

1   Introduction

With the development of information and network technology, the environment's uncertainty, the mission's complexity and the system functions' diversity have made the traditional platform-centric, tree structure information systems become network-centric information systems. System structure is the sum of the various relationships between the various components in information system. System functions are the characteristics and capabilities represented by system unit and relationship. System structure reflects the functions of the system through connection and topology. The optimalization of system structure can improve the ability of information system.

Structure risk is an important limiting factor in structure optimalization. The basic meaning of risk is uncertainty of loss. However, there isn't common concept applied to all areas . This paper argues that the risk of system structure refers to the risk probability and consequences of the risk event due to system specifications immaturity. System structure risk metric utilizes a certain method to calculate risk value by quantifying and integrated process .

The generating of information superiority in information systems rely on the producing, processing and utilizing of all kinds of information. When optimizing system structure, it should analysis the information flow in-depth. The system function can be abstracted as an orderly flow of intelligence, command and control and state information, including structure risk.

K. Liu et al. (Eds.): ICISO 2014, IFIP AICT 426, pp. 253–262, 2014.
© IFIP International Federation for Information Processing 2014

2   Background

Generally speaking, risk is the possibility of loss, injury, disadvantage or destruction, which is usually calculated through matrix or multiplication. While system structure risk consists of two levels of meaning: the first is the system performance risk; the second is the risk in the process of system structure migration.

Performance risk is the possibility that missions couldn't be completed because the stoppage of system units or relationships. System structure migration risk is mainly used to measure the influence of system migration failure or cost and schedule impacted than expected because of technological immaturity and uncertainty when system structure program development or system migration. The system structure migration risk includes technical risk, schedule risk and cost risk. Because this paper mainly considers the design phase of system structure, the system structure migration risk is not the main content of the study.

Complex network [1] is a complex structure consisting of huge number of nodes and relationships, which is a new and important method to represent system structure. However, complex network mainly considers the structure ability represented by topology while ignoring role of nodes. OPDAR model is an extended model of complex network through the classification of nodes which express the system structure better.

3   Risk Metric Method Based on Information Flow

System structure risk metric utilizes a certain method to calculate risk value that form quantified and integrated process of system structure risk. Usually the system structure risk can be used as one of the necessary constraints to optimize a system structure, of course, also used as a separate target to evaluate system structure.

3.1   System Structure Information Flow Model

This paper adopts OPDAR information flow model in references [2] to describe the information system structure, in which exists four basic units, namely Observer, Processor, Decision and Actor, also the relationships between the system units.

There are three kinds of information flow through the combination of system units and relationships: Intelligence information flow, Command and Control information flow, Cooperation information flow. Each kind of information flow refers to a functional link that information generating, and utilizing.

Analyzing the information flow of Intelligence support and share reflect the system's ability to safeguard intelligence, analyzing the information flow of command and control reflect the system's ability of decision making, analyzing the information flow of feedback and cooperation reflect the system's ability of synchronization . And then the overall performance of the system structure can be obtained through information flow.

3.2   Information Flow Risk Model

In OPDAR model, the information flow is a link combined by relationships end to end in structure. From a risk perspective, the relationships and units in system structure in the information flow are all risk factors. Each node or arc in information flow corresponds a risk event, contains a certain probability of occurrence and consequence.

Supposing information flow $f = v_0 e_1 v_1 e_2 v_2 \cdots e_n v_n$ is a simple path from system unit v_0 to system unit v_n. The occurrence probability of risk event A_i of unit v_i is p_i, and risk consequence is $c_i, 0 \le i \le n$; the occurrence probability of risk event B_i of arc e_i is q_i, and risk consequence is $d_i, 0 \le i \le n$. Thus the risk of $f = v_0 e_1 v_1 e_2 v_2 \cdots e_n v_n$ can be represented as follows.

$$
\begin{aligned}
R(f) = {} & P(A_0)c_0 \\
& + P(\overline{A}_0)\big(P(B_1)d_1 + P(\overline{B}_1, A_1)c_1\big) \\
& + \cdots \\
& + P(\overline{A}_0 \cdots \overline{A}_{i-1}, \overline{B}_1 \cdots \overline{B}_{i-1})\big(P(B_i)d_i + P(\overline{B}_i, A_i)c_i\big) \\
& + \cdots \\
& + P(\overline{A}_0 \cdots \overline{A}_{n-1}, \overline{B}_1 \cdots \overline{B}_{n-1})\big(P(B_n)d_n + P(\overline{B}_n, A_n)c_n\big)
\end{aligned}
$$

Assuming the risk events corresponded to nodes and arcs in information flow occur or not are independent to each other, so

$$
R(f) = p_0 c_0 + \sum_{i=1}^{n}(q_i d_i + (1-q_i)p_i c_i)\prod_{j=0}^{i-1}(1-p_j)\prod_{j=1}^{i-1}(1-q_j) \tag{3.1}
$$

Obviously, the key factor of the   system structure risk is how to calculate the risk of each information flow, which have to rely on the system unit as well as the relationship in information flow.

In system design phase, it is difficult to calculate the failure rate of the system unit because the actual system units have not been finished. Therefore, when calculating the probability of system structure performance risk, we can assume system units themselves run without a fault and only consider fault caused by the accessing and supporting the structure.

Under the above assumption, regardless of the kind of system unit, the failure rate is identical, denoted p, $0 \le p \le 1$; system relationship is denoted as $q, 0 \le q \le 1$. That in (3.1), $p_0 = p_1 = \cdots = p_n = p, q_1 = q_2 = \cdots = q_n = q$, so

$$
R(f) = pc_0 + \sum_{i=1}^{n}(qd_i + (1-q)pc_i)\prod_{j=0}^{i-1}(1-p)\prod_{j=1}^{i-1}(1-q) \tag{3.2}
$$

Which is

$$R(f) = pc_0 + \sum_{i=1}^{n}(qd_i + (1-q)pc_i)(1-p)^i(1-q)^{i-1} \qquad (3.3)$$

(3.3) illustrates the key of information flow risk calculation is to determine the consequences of risk events occur, such as system units or relationships failure or interruption. In this paper, we use the "contribution" of unit(relationship) to repress the consequence of the unit's(relationship's) risk event occur, which consists the ratio between the number of information flows contained the unit(relationship) and all the information flows in structure and the rank in each information flow.

System Unit Risk Model

Assuming the set of intelligence information flow in system structure is $S_f^{IS} = \{f_i^{IS} \mid i = 1,2,\cdots,N_f^{IS}\}$, the set of command and control information flow is $S_f^{CC} = \{f_i^{CC} \mid i = 1,2,\cdots,N_f^{CC}\}$, the set of cooperation information flow is $S_f^{CO} = \{f_i^{CO} \mid i = 1,2,\cdots,N_f^{CO}\}$. The weight of each kind of information flow is β^{IS}, β^{CC} and β^{CO}.

For each system unit $node_i$ $(1 \le i \le N_n)$, denoting the number of information flow which contain this unit is v_i^{CC}, v_i^{IS} and v_i^{CO}, denoting the system unit weight of each kind of information flow is α^{CC}, α^{IS} and α^{CO}. Assuming $node_i$ as v_i, according to (3.3), the "contribution" the system unit to the risk of the information flow is

$$p\left(\frac{\alpha^{CC}v_i^{CC}}{N_f^{CC}} + \frac{\alpha^{IS}v_i^{IS}}{N_f^{IS}} + \frac{\alpha^{CO}v_i^{CO}}{N_f^{CO}}\right)(1-p)^i(1-q)^i \qquad (3.4)$$

Supposing v_i^{CC}, v_i^{IS}, v_i^{CO} is denoted as v_i, given that $0 \le 1 - p \le 1$ and $0 \le 1 - q \le 1$, so the more forward position v_i in the flow $f = v_0 e_1 v_1 e_2 v_2 \cdots e_n v_n$ (i smaller), the more contribution to flow risk; the more rearward position in the flow(i bigger), the little contribution to flow risk.

If the rank of $node_i$ in intelligence information flow is $\sigma^{IS}(i,j), 1 \le j \le v_i^{IS}$, the system unit's "contribution" for the system structure intelligence risk is

$$Risk^{IS}(node_i) = \frac{p\beta^{IS}}{N_f^{IS}}\left(\frac{\alpha^{CC}v_i^{CC}}{N_f^{CC}} + \frac{\alpha^{IS}v_i^{IS}}{N_f^{IS}} + \frac{\alpha^{CO}v_i^{CO}}{N_f^{CO}}\right)\sum_{j=1}^{v_i^{IS}}((1-p)(1-q))^{\sigma^{IS}(i,j)} \qquad (3.5)$$

If the rank of $node_i$ in command and control information flow is $\sigma^{CC}(i,j), 1 \le j \le v_i^{CC}$, the system unit's "contribution" for the system structure command and control risk is

$$Risk^{CC}(node_i) = \frac{p\beta^{CC}}{N_f^{CC}}\left(\frac{\alpha^{CC}v_i^{CC}}{N_f^{CC}} + \frac{\alpha^{IS}v_i^{IS}}{N_f^{IS}} + \frac{\alpha^{CO}v_i^{CO}}{N_f^{CO}}\right)\sum_{j=1}^{v_i^{CC}}((1-p)(1-q))^{\sigma^{CC}(i,j)} \quad (3.6)$$

If the rank of $node_i$ in cooperation information flow is $\sigma^{CO}(i,j), 1 \le j \le v_i^{CO}$, the system unit's "contribution" for the system structure cooperation risk is

$$Risk^{CO}(node_i) = \frac{p\beta^{CO}}{N_f^{CO}}\left(\frac{\alpha^{CC}v_i^{CC}}{N_f^{CC}} + \frac{\alpha^{IS}v_i^{IS}}{N_f^{IS}} + \frac{\alpha^{CO}v_i^{CO}}{N_f^{CO}}\right)\sum_{j=1}^{v_i^{CO}}((1-p)(1-q))^{\sigma^{CO}(i,j)} \quad (3.7)$$

Therefore, the system unit's total risk for system structure is

$$Risk(node_i) = Risk^{IS}(node_i) + Risk^{CC}(node_i) + Risk^{CO}(node_i)$$

$$= \frac{p\beta^{IS}}{N_f^{IS}}\left(\frac{\alpha^{CC}v_i^{CC}}{N_f^{CC}} + \frac{\alpha^{IS}v_i^{IS}}{N_f^{IS}} + \frac{\alpha^{CO}v_i^{CO}}{N_f^{CO}}\right)\sum_{j=1}^{v_i^{IS}}((1-p)(1-q))^{\sigma^{IS}(i,j)}$$

$$+ \frac{p\beta^{CC}}{N_f^{CC}}\left(\frac{\alpha^{CC}v_i^{CC}}{N_f^{CC}} + \frac{\alpha^{IS}v_i^{IS}}{N_f^{IS}} + \frac{\alpha^{CO}v_i^{CO}}{N_f^{CO}}\right)\sum_{j=1}^{v_i^{CC}}((1-p)(1-q))^{\sigma^{CC}(i,j)} \quad (3.8)$$

$$+ \frac{p\beta^{CO}}{N_f^{CO}}\left(\frac{\alpha^{CC}v_i^{CC}}{N_f^{CC}} + \frac{\alpha^{IS}v_i^{IS}}{N_f^{IS}} + \frac{\alpha^{CO}v_i^{CO}}{N_f^{CO}}\right)\sum_{j=1}^{v_i^{CO}}((1-p)(1-q))^{\sigma^{CO}(i,j)}$$

System Relationship Risk Model

For each system relationship e_i, denoting the number of information flow which contain this relationship is ε_i^{CC}, ε_i^{IS} and ε_i^{CO}, denoting the system relationship weight of each kind of information flow is $\lambda^{CC}, \lambda^{IS}$ and λ^{CO}. According to (3.3), the "contribution" the system relationship for the risk of the information flow is

$$q\left(\frac{\lambda^{CC}\varepsilon_i^{CC}}{N_f^{CC}} + \frac{\lambda^{IS}\varepsilon_i^{IS}}{N_f^{IS}} + \frac{\lambda^{CO}\varepsilon_i^{CO}}{N_f^{CO}}\right)(1-p)^i(1-q)^{i-1} \quad (3.9)$$

Similar to system unit, the more forward position e_i in the flow $f = v_0e_1v_1e_2v_2\cdots e_nv_n$, the more contribution to flow risk, conversely smaller.

Denoting the set of system relationship in system structure is $S_r = \{r_i = (node_i^s, node_i^e) \mid node_i^s, node_i^e \in S_{node}, i = 1,2,\cdots, N_r\}$.

For each system relationship r_i $(1 \leq i \leq N_r)$, if the rank of r_i in intelligence information flow is $\delta^{IS}(i, j), 1 \leq j \leq \varepsilon_i^{IS}$, the system relationship's "contribution" for the system structure intelligence risk is

$$Risk^{IS}(r_i) = \frac{q\beta^{IS}}{N_f^{IS}}\left(\frac{\lambda^{CC}\varepsilon_i^{CC}}{N_f^{CC}} + \frac{\lambda^{IS}\varepsilon_i^{IS}}{N_f^{IS}} + \frac{\lambda^{CO}\varepsilon_i^{CO}}{N_f^{CO}}\right)\sum_{j=1}^{\varepsilon_i^{IS}}((1-p)(1-q))^{\delta^{IS}(i,j)} \quad (3.10)$$

If the rank of r_i in command and control information flow is $\delta^{CC}(i, j), 1 \leq j \leq \varepsilon_i^{CC}$, the system relationship's "contribution" for the system structure command and control risk is

$$Risk^{CC}(r_i) = \frac{q\beta^{CC}}{N_f^{CC}}\left(\frac{\lambda^{CC}\varepsilon_i^{CC}}{N_f^{CC}} + \frac{\lambda^{IS}\varepsilon_i^{IS}}{N_f^{IS}} + \frac{\lambda^{CO}\varepsilon_i^{CO}}{N_f^{CO}}\right)\sum_{j=1}^{\varepsilon_i^{CC}}((1-p)(1-q))^{\delta^{CC}(i,j)} \quad (3.11)$$

If the rank of r_i in cooperation information flow is $\delta^{CO}(i, j), 1 \leq j \leq \varepsilon_i^{CO}$, the system relationship's "contribution" for the system structure cooperation risk is

$$Risk^{CO}(r_i) = \frac{q\beta^{CO}}{N_f^{CO}}\left(\frac{\lambda^{CC}\varepsilon_i^{CC}}{N_f^{CC}} + \frac{\lambda^{IS}\varepsilon_i^{IS}}{N_f^{IS}} + \frac{\lambda^{CO}\varepsilon_i^{CO}}{N_f^{CO}}\right)\sum_{j=1}^{\varepsilon_i^{CO}}((1-p)(1-q))^{\delta^{CO}(i,j)} \quad (3.12)$$

Therefore, the system relationship's total risk (r_i) for system structure is

$$\begin{aligned}
Risk(r_i) &= Risk^{IS}(r_i) + Risk^{CC}(r_i) + Risk^{CO}(r_i) \\
&= \frac{q\beta^{IS}}{N_f^{IS}}\left(\frac{\lambda^{CC}\varepsilon_i^{CC}}{N_f^{CC}} + \frac{\lambda^{IS}\varepsilon_i^{IS}}{N_f^{IS}} + \frac{\lambda^{CO}\varepsilon_i^{CO}}{N_f^{CO}}\right)\sum_{j=1}^{\varepsilon_i^{IS}}((1-p)(1-q))^{\delta^{IS}(i,j)} \\
&+ \frac{q\beta^{CC}}{N_f^{CC}}\left(\frac{\lambda^{CC}\varepsilon_i^{CC}}{N_f^{CC}} + \frac{\lambda^{IS}\varepsilon_i^{IS}}{N_f^{IS}} + \frac{\lambda^{CO}\varepsilon_i^{CO}}{N_f^{CO}}\right)\sum_{j=1}^{\varepsilon_i^{CC}}((1-p)(1-q))^{\delta^{CC}(i,j)} \\
&+ \frac{q\beta^{CO}}{N_f^{CO}}\left(\frac{\lambda^{CC}\varepsilon_i^{CC}}{N_f^{CC}} + \frac{\lambda^{IS}\varepsilon_i^{IS}}{N_f^{IS}} + \frac{\lambda^{CO}\varepsilon_i^{CO}}{N_f^{CO}}\right)\sum_{j=1}^{\varepsilon_i^{CO}}((1-p)(1-q))^{\delta^{CO}(i,j)}
\end{aligned} \quad (3.13)$$

Therefore, the calculating process of system structure risk consists four steps: first, traversing all information flows in system structure; second, determining every system unit's rank in each information flow and computing the total contribution; third, determining every system relationship's rank in each information flow and computing the total contribution; forth, summing all system units' risk and system relationships' risk to obtain the system structure's risk.

4   Case Study

This paper compares traditional tree network structure with network-centric structure, which is good for comparative analyzing risk trend in network-centric structure and providing guidance for network development.

Network-centric structure dynamic organize and optimize the distribution of the loosely coupled system component in network, which can maximize system's function and capability and then realize the goal of dynamically adaptation to environmental changes. Reflected in the physical structure is that none of the system component is a must exist one, named "equality." Its manifestation includes circle, center or connection of tertiary-level in structure and so on.

The selected structure is Fig.1 and 2. Respectively, circle, triangle, square and diamond represent observer unit, process unit, decision unit and actor unit. Fig. 1 shows a traditional three-tree network which according to the triangular organization. Each decision unit has three child decision units and bottom decision unit controls two actor units. Each processor unit guarantees six decision units and has three father observer units. Fig. 2 adds some "horizontal" factor. (1) forms a p-circle by adding some cooperation relations among processor units. (2) forms a p-center by adding some intelligence relations among processor units and decision units. (3) joins some command and control relationships of tertiary-level. (4) joins intelligence relationships between processor units and actor units which forming safeguarding of tertiary-level.

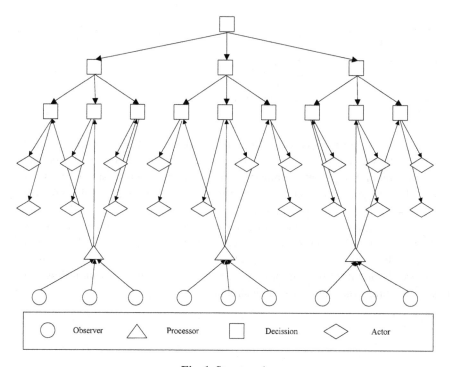

Fig. 1. Structure 1

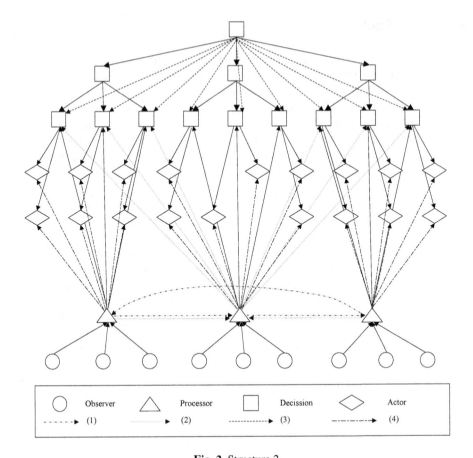

Fig. 2. Structure 2

Assuming the probability of system unit's risk event occurrence is 0.1, the probability of system relationship's risk event occurrence is 0.1.Because the command and control relationship is more important in information transmission in information system, flow weight of command and control information flow is 0.5, the other two is 0.25. The same is with unit weight and relationship weight . To analysis the change of risk in-depth, extract the common law, we analysis the risk change process with the combination. The risk value of different combinations((1)(2)(3)(4)) is in Fig. 3 and Fig. 4. The intelflow represents intelligence information flow, c2flow represents command and control information flow, coflow represents cooperation information flow. Fig. 4 shows the average risk value of system structure.

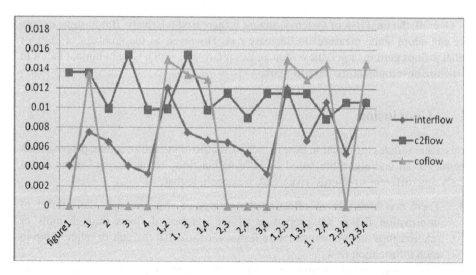

Fig. 3. Risk value of each flow kind

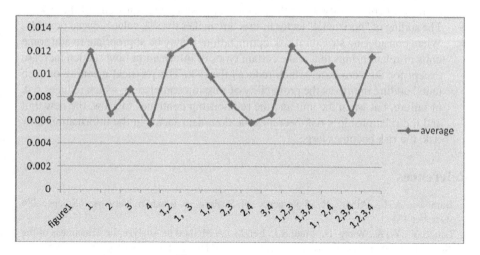

Fig. 4. Average risk value

Fig. 4 shows the risk value in system structure in about 0.01, to the more realistic.

After analyzing the result, when adopting (1), the risk of cooperation flow appears. Because the number of cooperation flows is few, the risk value is relatively large. If we want to decrease the influence of cooperation flows, we can add the number of cooperation flows or decrease the ratio that flow through cooperation units. When adopting (2) and (4), the number of intelligence flows is increased, therefore risk of intelligence flow increases. However, the ratio that through decision units decreases, the risk of command and control information flows decreases. When adopting (3), the number of command and control flows is increased, therefore risk of command and control flow increases.

Overall, the total risk of system structure is increased relatively. But to some extent, we can adopt some measures to decrease risk. However, as the numbers of units or relationships getting larger, the cost increases relatively, which is an important factor in structure development we have to think.

5   Conclusion

This paper utilizes information flow in the risk metric of system structure, proposes risk metric model and algorithm based on information flow. In the basis of comparative analyzing different structures' risk trend, we conclude that:

- There are three reasons affecting the change of structure risk: the number of information flows; the proportion of the number of flows through units or relationships and system structure flows; the rank that the unit or relationship in each information flow;
- The general trend of structure risk is increased. Risk can used as a main consideration indicator of structural optimization, considering how to improve the system structure utility under the premise of meeting the constraint of the risk;
- The adding of "horizontal" factor in structure makes the risk value reduced possibly;
- When considering structural risk optimization, it may be appropriate to add some units or relationships that make certain types of information flow sudden increase except for the zero case, which reduces the risk. The physical meaning of such units' adding improves the probability of mission completing, which reduces risk of failure, but when the unit and the relationship continues to grow, the new unit and the relationship's risk becomes the dominant factor in the information flow risk, the risk becomes large.

References

1. Barabási, A.-L., Albert, R.: Emergence of Scaling in Random Networks. Science 286 (October 15)
2. Lan, S.Y., Yi, K., Wang, H., Mao, S.J., Lei, M.: A Method to Analyze the Timeliness of the Networked C4ISR System. System Engineering and Digital Technology 蓝羽石，易侃，王珩，毛少杰，雷鸣。网络化C4ISR系统结构时效性分析方法。系统工程与电子技术。9, 1908–1914 (2013)
3. Levchuk, G.M., Merina, C., Levchuk, Y.N., et al.: Design and Analysis of Robust and Adaptive Organizations. In: Proceedings of Command and Control Research and Technology Symposium(A2C2 session), Annapolis, MD (2001)
4. Levchuk, G.M., Levchuk, Y.N., Merina, C., et al.: Normative Design of Organizations-Part 3: Modeling Congruent, Robust, and Adaptive Organizations. IEEE Transactions on SMC 34(3), 337–350 (2004)
5. Yang, D.S., Zhang, W.M., Liu, Z.: Task Allocating among Group of Agents. In: Proceedings of International Conference on Web Intelligence, pp. 574–578. IEEE Press, Beijing (2004)
6. Yu, F., Tu, F., Pattipati, K.R.: A Novel Congruent Organizational Design Methodology Using Group Technology and a Nested Genetics Algorithm. IEEE Transactions on Systems, Man, and Cybernetics-Part A: Systems and Humans 36(1), 5–18 (2006)

An Empirical Study about the Marketization Degree of Labor Market from the Perspective of Wage Determination Mechanism

Qiushuo He

Shenzhen Institute of Information Technology, Shenzhen 518029, China
heqs@sziit.com.cn

Abstract. Ten years ago, economists had raised the issue of whether economic freedom can be measured, and there are a large number of domestic and foreign institutions and individuals had researched the measure of marketization degree, but it is few to measure the market degree of the labor market from the perspective of wage determination mechanism. This article attempts to investigate by using the stochastic frontier method of wage determination mechanisms from the micro-perspective, and measure the marketization degree of labor market, but also examine China's labor market and wage reform process, understand and grasp the labor market. At the same time, the research result will feedback the effect of labor market reform and promote the reform of labor market.

Keywords: Labor market, Wage determination mechanism, Marketization degree.

1   Background and Objective

Ten years ago, economists had raised the issue of whether economic freedom can be measured, and there are a large number of domestic and foreign institutions and individuals who had researched the measure of marketization degree, but it is few to measure the market degree of the labor market from the perspective of wage determination mechanism ([2] degree of market about wage). Most researches focus on the part of measure of labor market, which is the part of the measure of overall market. This article attempts to use stochastic frontier method to measure the trend about the degree of marketization of wage determination of Chinese labor market from the perspective of individual human capital promoting the potential income (i.e. market value), thereby measuring the marketization degree of the labor market.

2   The Research Methods

This article attempts to use stochastic frontier method from the perspective of wage determination mechanism to measure marketization degree of labor market, it will refer

K. Liu et al. (Eds.): ICISO 2014, IFIP AICT 426, pp. 263–271, 2014.

to Contreras' method of robustness test and add to more related omitted variables such as work experience squared, marital status, sex, occupation nature except level of education, work experience.

3   The Empirical Analysis

3.1   Stochastic Frontier Approach

The basic idea of the stochastic frontier method is as follows. Considering a group of individuals, each individual has the same level of human capital. It is obvious that each individual won't own the same income level, because even assuming the same level of human capital, different individual is in different environments such as the department environment, family environment, working industry etc. and this will effect the income level of individual. And so different individual will get different income level, and degree of marketization of the wage determination mechanism will be different. Therefore, if the individuals can get their potential income, then it indicates that the labor market in their wage determination mechanism is completely market-oriented.

Stochastic frontier model is as follows[1]:

$$\ln E_{it} = \alpha + \beta X_{it} + v_{it} - \mu_{it}$$

Potential wage (wage border)

Random wages border

Observations wage (real wage)

That $\varepsilon_{it} = v_{it} - \mu_{it}$, $\mu_{it} \sim N(m_{it}, \sigma_{it}^2)$, $v_{it} \sim N(0, \sigma_v^2)$

Where i represents the number of samples, $i=1$, ...n ; t is the time series, $t=1$, ...T, Since this article attempts to get the marketization degree of wage determination mechanism on the labor market each year, so this article will adopt sectional data, and T=1。 Thus, the equation becomes:

$$\ln E_i = \alpha_0 + \alpha_i X_i + v_i - \mu_i \qquad i=1, 2, ...N \qquad (1)$$

Here E_i is the observable income of individual i, Xi is a vector of explanatory variables, v_i is the white noise, representative of the random error term, subject to the normal distribution of the expected value of 0, and variance σ_v^2, and is independent to μ_i . μ_i is non-negative random variables and can measure the degree of non-marketization, subject to the normal distribution of the expected value m_i, variance σ_μ^2 and discontinuous at 0. Here μ_i reflects the degree of

---

[1] The prototype of the model equation derived from the income equation belonging to Jacob, but here we use stochastic frontier approach to estimate.

non-marketization of individual i obtaining the potential wage, random items μ_i is limited to non-negative, because some individuals may get random wages border which is $\alpha + \beta X_i + v_i$. The parameters in the Equation 1 are estimated to use the least squares method and the method of maximum likelihood estimation method.

$$\lambda = \frac{\sigma_\mu^2}{\sigma_\mu^2 + \sigma_v^2} \quad (0 \le \lambda \le 1 \text{ can make } \sigma^2 = \sigma_v^2 + \sigma_\mu^2) \tag{2}$$

Which λ represents the proportion of non-marketization in the random disturbance term, σ_μ^2 is the variance of the difference of marketization degree, σ^2 is the summation between σ_μ^2 and the variance of the random noise ($\sigma^2 = \sigma_v^2 + \sigma_\mu^2$).

We won't use OLS estimation unless $\gamma = \alpha_0 = \alpha_1 = \dots = \delta_i = 0$. When λ is close to 1, it indicates that the deviation of the stochastic frontier income function comes mainly from random variables μ_i, and also indicates that the gap between the real income and the boundary income (ie, potential revenue) primarily dues to the non-market of wage determination mechanism. When γ is close to 0, it indicates that the gap between the real income and the maximum possible income mainly dues to the statistical error.

3.2   Data Description and Variable Description

In this paper, we use the Chinese Nutrition and Health Survey (CHNS) data. CHNS is operated by international research team, and funded by the American University of North Carolina Carolina Population Research Center (since 1989). The survey included 3800 towns and villages; 14,000 people in total. This paper uses 1989, 1991, 1993, 1997, 2000 and 2004. Since this paper attempts to find the trend of the different marketization degree of wage determination mechanism, so each year is as a cross-section data to analyze in this paper. It will remove the rural areas sample and only leave the working-age population in urban areas sample (survey for the resident

Table 1. Definition of the variables

Variable name	
lnWage	logarithm of hourly wage
Education	years of education (years)
Age	Age
exp	Age - years of education -6
Exp^2	work experience squared
Gender	1: Men 0: Female
Marriage	1: Unmarried 0: Married
The nature of a work unit	1 : SOE 0: Non-state-owned enterprises
Regional dummies	1: Elsewhere 0: Guizhou

population, except to the floating population) because this paper will focus mainly on of the urban labor market, and remove the observed samples, which miss basic personal information and employment, income information. The remaining samples number is 2013 in 1989, 2530 in 1993, 1725 in 1991,1451 in 1997,741 in 2004,1659 in 2000.

3.3   Empirical Results and Discussion

This paper uses stochastic frontier method to estimate the existence of non-market in the model. The results are shown in Table 2. Here we use stata statistical software.

3.4   Analysis

First we examine the result in Table 3 (a). The empirical result of using the maximum likelihood method shows that the degree of wage determination mechanism of the market is not simply random error distribution. Empirical results suggest that it can reject the null hypothesis at the 5% significance level. The difference of marketization degree is existed in the individual of the sample.

T-statistics of λ shows that λ is statistically non-zero from the Table 3 (a). Table 3 (a) indicates that the parameter at the 5% significance level is significant. λ is close to 1. It indicates that there are factors from the non-market in the random disturbance term, other factors come from other exogenous variables such as the statistical error. In addition, based on the results in 2004, we can estimate degree of marketization of each individual and calculate the average marketization degree of all individuals in the sample is 63%, which indicates that the degree of non-marketization is about 37 percent comparing to the individual of the highest marketization level of wage determination on the random border (the highest marketization level of wage determination is 1)[^2].

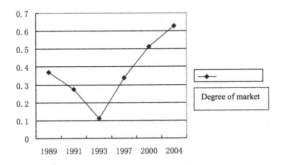

Fig. 1. Degree of wage determination market trend

---

[^2]: Mentioned before, the results of marketization degree of wage determination in [2] were 5.44%, 28.98%, 32.63% and 78.80% in 1979, 1985, 1990 and 1995, although this measure is about different year, but from the overlap of the Year 1990 and the 1995, the result is less than Chen's results, which may be due to the different methods and the different measurement range, so the contrast is not very strong.

Table 2. Sample statistics description

Years	State sector						Non-state sector					
	1989	1991	1993	1997	2000	2004	1989	1991	1993	1997	2000	2004
Hourly wage(Yuan/hour)	0.667	0.594	0.952	3.524	4.017	5.953	0.705	1.047	2.235	3.429	4.784	6.649
	(1.498)	(0.436)	(1.713)	(24.37)	(5.507)	(5.109)	(0.875)	(1.221)	(4.620)	(4.416)	(8.889)	(5.435)
Weekly working hours(H)	49.00	48.206	47.45	41.6549	48.873	42.203	46.340	45.930	44.977	49.457	40.942	51.757
	(7.596)	(7.230)	(8.594)	(9.333)	(15.138)	(10.366)	(20.238)	(16.095)	(19.540)	(17.257)	(10.587)	(16.777)
Age (years)	34.085	34.767	35.576	36.322	39.096	40.571	33.134	34.583	35.972	33.506	38.021	37.756
	(10.875)	(10.595)	(10.584)	(10.109)	(11.711)	(9.818)	(12.056)	(11.282)	(10.221)	(11.911)	(10.315)	(10.864)
Work experience (years)	18.211	18.800	19.501	18.951	2106	22.372	16.615	17.097	18.727	17.843	20.47	21.893
	(11.501)	(11.222)	(11.084)	(10.831)	(12.569)	(10.510)	(12.839)	(12.164)	(10.621)	(12.779)	(10.891)	(11.761)
College and above%	0.073	0.081	0.087	0.175	0.074	0.264	0.002	0.027	0.00	0.048	0.089	0.166
	(0.260)	(0.273)	(0.282)	(0.380)	(0.263)	(0.441)	(0.054)	(0.165)	(0.00)	(0.215)	(0.485)	(0.249)
High school%	0.315	0.317	0.314	0.455	0.201	0.486	0.173	0.083	0.150	0.301	0.273	0.303
	(0.464)	(0.465)	(0.464)	(0.498)	(0.401)	(0.500)	(0.378)	(0.278)	(0.367)	(0.461)	(0.446)	(0.460)
Junior%	0.417	0.415	0.437	0.296	0.526	0.210	0.483	0.569	0.431	0.457	0.288	0.358
	(0.493)	(0.492)	(0.496)	(0.457)	(0.499)	(0.407)	(0.500)	(0.498)	(0.491)	(0.501)	(0.453)	(0.498)
Primary and below%	0.195	0.187	0.162	0.249	0.199	0.058	0.342	0.321	0.419	0.194	0.349	0.173
	(0.204)	(0.196)	(0.184)	(0.221)	(0.310)	(0.066)	(0.427)	(0.503)	(0.505)	(0.218)	(0.442)	(0.183)
Sex% (Man = 1)	0.590	0.597	0.590	0.579	0.606	0.607	03753	0.383	0.438	0.518	0.609	0.579
	(0.491)	(0.490)	(0.491)	(0.493)	(0.488)	(0.488)	(0.431)	(0.496)	(0.441)	(0.502)	(0.488)	(0.493)
Marital status%(Married = 1)	0.202	0.210	0.202	0.155	0.361	0.095	0.258	0.263	0.170	0.253	0.186	0.151
	(0.402)	(0.407)	(0.402)	(0.362)	(0.480)	(0.293)	(0.438)	(0.443)	(0.378)	(0.437)	(0.389)	(0.358)

Note: Figures in brackets the standard error of the corresponding variable; Source: Chinese Nutrition and Health Survey (CHNS)

From Fig. 1, we are sure that marketization degree of wage determination mechanism first decreased and then increased gradually in the entire time series, in 1993 it is obvious turning point. Marketization degree of wage determination has been low before this point. The average degree of the whole marketization degree is approximately 20%, the average marketization degree gradually increases to above 50% after 1997, which partly shows that Chinese labor market reform is successful. But in absolute terms, compared to developed countries it is substantially lower, because in United States it is 86% in the same period [7].

From the perspective of human capital investment, Table 3 (a) shows that the impact of education on wages border is very significant, and its coefficient indicates that wage boundary will rise as the year of education is added one (it was 0.7% in 1989, and has been increased to 3% in 2004). And this suggests that the impact year of education on wage border is increased year by year, and the impact of experience on wage border is very significant, but little change.

Overall, the marketization degree of wage determination mechanisms is low, and its evolution path has been relatively consistent with China's development. For example in Fig. 1, the marketization is lower in the early 1990s, which may be mainly two reasons. On the one hand, although the government had began to reform wage before 1993, such as proposing the wage relevant to economic efficiency of enterprises in 1984 and also practiced various forms of wage system. But the reforms didn't change the wage determination of enterprise. The difference of wage determination is huge between the two types of market. In result, the income gap between the two markets is not only reduced, but expanded.

On the other hand, the affection of wage system reform is not obvious. There are two reasons: One is that the concept of return on human capital in the early 1990s might not be very clear. At that time, China adopted a unified wage policy and the gap is not obvious between the wages of various positions, so the status of competitive price system about the marginal productivity compensation paid to workers is not yet stable, especially in the Chinese state-owned sector, competitive wage payment mechanism is far from established. Second is the price information has been vacant in the state-owned economy, because the information is inefficient and the fact was that workers were short of the information about the work accumulation with workers' human capital. More seriously, the country's income level is very consistent, especially in state-owned enterprises. Although the wage was higher in non- state-owned enterprises but the staff mobility was not high due to social security and labor ideology. Because labors were lazy to learn about wage information of other companies, so the wage of workers cannot reach its borders largely.

Also from Fig. 1, marketization degree of wage determination mechanism began to shoot up after 1993, which indicates that the labor market situation had improved significantly. In 1993, the government officially announced the goal as the socialist market economic system reform, and selects the 100 state-owned enterprises to implement the corporate system. State-owned enterprises speed up to change from the planning system to market economy system. At the same time, the government began efforts to build a comprehensive social security system. Labor law formally was enacted in 1995. The government began to build macro-guidance system of enterprise wage income and establish wage guidelines system. Thus series of market-oriented reform made the individual human capital returns to rise naturally. The marketization degree of wage determination mechanism had been continuously improved.

3.5   Stability Test

This paper discusses whether the result is significantly changed after adding more relevant omitted variables using Contreras method. This paper used the same method to estimate [Equation 1]. In addition to the above estimates used by the relevant variables (level of education, work experience and work experience squared), we now add new variables which include the level of education (education), work experience (exp) and work experience squared (exp^2), marital status (mar), gender, occupation nature, where corporate ownership dummy variable (SOE) - to estimate the equation [Equation 1].

Estimation results are in Table 3 (b). it is worth noting that the change of marketization degree is small in all time, and basically all the newly added variables were significant. Thus confirms our results stability.

We see that adding gender variable is significant, suggesting that the impact of gender on wages boundary is significant, and wages border of men is average higher around 7% than women. But we examine that men coefficient is 0.0693 in 1989 and rises to 0.0743 in 1993, but began to decline after 1993. This suggests that the impact of gender on wages border is waning after 1993. Marital status variables are most significant, and results also indicate that unmarried can raise wages border around 6% relative to married persons, the most important fact is the coefficient of sector is significant at the 1% level of significance. Before 2000 coefficient is negative which showed that wage boundary in state-owned enterprises was lower than in non-state-owned enterprise. It is consistent with our expectation.

Due to lack of competitive in SOE labor market early, wages and employment determination were more planned (which has been demonstrated in previous chapters), so the wages of workers were lower. Rather than non-state-owned enterprises had been in a competitive labor market, so its wages were relatively higher. However this situation has changed from 2004 (2004's coefficient symbol is changed and a very significant), which also indirectly shows that a series policies about wage and employment of state-owned enterprises play a role and reforms began to show results, particularly human capital returns gradually increased significantly which suggests that the marketization degree of wage determination mechanism gradually increased and also shows that the marketization degree of the labor market is also improving.

Table 3. Estimated wage equation

	1989		1991		1993		1997		2000		2004	
	(a)	(b)	(a)	(b)	(a)	(b)	(a)	(b)	(a)	(b)	(a)	(b)
Constant term	-0.6109***	-0.5558***	-.5349***	-.3925***	-.272	-.1688**	.1894	.2454**	.2152***	.2083**	.0832	.1683**
Years of education	0.0076***	.0077***	.0111***	.0103***	.0001	.003	.039***	.0037	.0489***	.048***	.0668***	.0701***
Experience	0.0133***	.0129***	.0106***	.0104***	.0124***	.0126***	.009***	.0096***	.0077***	.008***	.009***	.005**
Experience squared	-0.0001***	-.0001***	-.0001***	-.0001***	-.0001***	-.0001***	-.0001***	-.0001***	-.0001***	-.0001**	-.0001**	-.00006
Gender	—	.0578***	—	.0499***	—	.0647***	—	.0616***	—	.0577***	—	.0687***
Marital status	—	-.0063**	—	-.00004	—	.0055	—	-.0214	—	.0053***	—	-.05002**
State-owned enterprises	—	-.5558***	—	-.1715***	—	-.1639***	—	-.1015***	—	-.0116	—	.0647***
σ^2*	.0892***	.0869***	.0372***	.0355***	.0625***	.0601***	.0671***	.0652***	.0812***	.079***	.066***	.074***
λ*	0.85**	0.84**	0.85**	0.88**	0.83**	0.83**	0.74**	0.73**	0.78**	0.86**	0.68**	0.67**
The average value of the log-likelihood	-533.0257	-500.71	455.25	501.86	-575	-43.29	-50.97	-39.96	-237.37	-224.94	-110.44	-70.66
Number of samples	2530	2530	2013	2013	1725	1725	741	741	1451	1451	1659	1659
Years	1989	1989	1991	1991	1993	1993	1997	1997	2000	2000	2004	2004
The average degree of market	0.37158	0.37158	0.27245	0.27245	0.111	0.111	0.339	0.339	0.5123	0.5123	0.63	0.63

Note: *, **, and *** represent 10%, 5% and 1% significance level, λ is the variance estimation parameters

4   Conclusions

This paper estimates the marketization degree of the wage determination mechanism. We found that the marketization degree of wage determination mechanism is very low before the 1990s.1993 was a turning point. The marketization degree of the wage determination mechanism had been low before this point. The average degree of the whole marketization degree is approximately 20%, the average marketization degree gradually increases to above 50% after 1997, which partly shows that Chinese labor market reform is successful. But in absolute terms, compared to developed countries it is substantially lower, because in United States it is 86% in the same period [7].

Overall, the result is consistent with the path of China's labor market reform.

These empirical studies show that there are some factors that affect non-market-oriented. There is not a bargaining system between labor and State-owned enterprise, and the government still plays a key role in wages of workers' determination. Enterprises have not the autonomy of wage determination. The marketization degree of wage determination in the market is low. While workers' bargaining power has increased in the non-state-owned enterprises, but it is thin in an oversupply of labor market, which also shows that China's labor market need to deepen reform, improve the marketization of wage determination mechanism.

References

1. SDPC Market and Price Research Group: Judgment of China's economic marketization degree. Macroeconomic management (2) (1996)
2. Zongsheng, C.: Marketization process research of China's economic system. Shanghai People's Publishing House, Shanghai (1999)
3. Zhenhua, Z.: Institutional change and economic growth. Shanghai Joint Publishing, Shanghai People's Publishing House, Shanghai (1999)
4. Chunbing, X.: The wage determination mechanism research of different ownership enterprises. Economic Research (6), 16–26 (2005)
5. Contreras, D., Bravo, D., Medrano, P.: Measurement error, unobservable and skill bias in estimating the return to education in Chile. Working Paper. Universidad de Chile, 1–45 (1999)
6. Dickens, W., Kevin, L.: The Reemergence of Segmented Labor Market Theory. The American Economic Review (5), 129–134 (1988)
7. Greene, W.: Maximum likelihood estimation of econometric frontier functions. Journal of Econometrics 13, 27–56 (1980)
8. Kumbhakar, S.C., Lovell, C.A.K.: Stochastic Frontier Analysis. Cambridge University Press (2000)

Pipeline and Data Parallel Hybrid Indexing Algorithm for Multi-core Platform

Suqing Zhang and Jirui Li

Information Engineer Department,Henan Vocational and Technical Institute,
Zhengzhou, China
280946342@qq.com, ljrokyes@163.com

Abstract. The scale and growth rate of today's text collection bring new challenges for index construction. To tackle this problem, Pipeline and Data Parallel Hybrid Algorithm (PDPH), is proposed to improve the indexing performance for multi-core platform. Compared to existing sequential indexing algorithms, Pipeline and data parallelism are introduced by the PDPH to improve the algorithm flexibility and scale the performance with more cores. Evaluations showed this algorithm can improve index construction speed for multi-core platform.

Keywords: Multi-core platform, Indexing Algorithms, Data Parallel, PHPD.

1 Introduction

The world's data is increasing at an astonishing rate. The scale and growth rate of text collection bring new challenges for index construction. Building an index for a large text collection may involve parsing billions of documents, handling millions of distinct words, and processing billions of occurrences of words in the text. Text collections have become so large and are growing so rapidly that traditional indexing schemes become unmanageable, requiring huge resources and taking days to complete. More powerful computing resources and more efficient algorithms are needed to tackle this problem. T

With the growth of data, the computing power also increases according to Moore's law. Computing power is increasing because of the multi-core technology. Multi-core technology packs two or more execution cores into a single processor so a single chip can provide multiple execution resources. Multi-core architecture is in essence a divide-and-conquer strategy. By divvying up computational work and then spreading it over multiple execution cores, a multi-core processor can perform more work in a given clock cycle than a traditional single core processor. Multi-core processors provide thread-level parallelism. However, to make full use of thread-level parallelism, an application should be threaded so that it can spread its workload across multiple execution cores.

In a multi-core system, there are usually several execution cores, shared memory and disks. However, those existing sequential indexing algorithms, which are mostly

K. Liu et al. (Eds.): ICISO 2014, IFIP AICT 426, pp. 272–280, 2014.

single-threaded, treat the multi-core system the same as the traditional single-core system and cannot make use of the multiple execution cores. Also, semiconductor manufacturers of multi-core processors choose to scale back the clock speed so that the chips run cooler, so the performance of single-threaded sequential indexing algorithms in a multi-core system will decrease a little compared with the traditional single-core environment.

We present an efficient indexing algorithm that can be deployed on multi-core systems. It is the Pipeline and Data Parallel Hybrid (PDPH) algorithm. In addition to employing a pipeline, the PDPH algorithm also introduces data parallelism into the indexing process. This algorithm has good performance. It is also more scalable than the existing sequential algorithms.

2   Sequential Indexing Algorithms

There are several proposed algorithms to construct index files(inverted files). The Simple In-Memory algorithm keeps all index data in the main memory. It is only suitable for small text collections. The Disk-Based algorithm makes use of temporal files in order to reduce the need for the main memory. However, because there are many random disk accesses, the Disk-Based approach is too slow for large collections. The Two-Pass In-Memory approach introduces compression to limit temporal disk space usage, but it uses two passes over the collections that means it needs to traverse the text collection twice. For large text collections, for example a terabyte scale collection, just traversing the whole collection will take a long time. Both of the Sort-Based algorithm and the Single-Pass algorithm are scalable methods. They can be used for text collections with any size and can work with limited main memory. However, because the Single-Pass algorithm stores compressed index data in memory, it makes better use of memory than the Sort-Based algorithm. Because of this, the Single-Pass algorithm is the most efficient sequential indexing algorithm.

The Single-Pass algorithm travels only one pass over the collection. The Single-Pass algorithm maintains a lexicon for distinct terms of the collection in memory first. Each term in the lexicon is assigned a dynamic in-memory bit-vector for its inverted list. The bit-vector is used to accumulate a term's corresponding postings in a compressed format. Each document is read into the main memory and then parsed into postings. For each posting delivered from the parsing stream, a lookup for its corresponding term in the lexicon is made. If the term does not exist in the lexicon, the term is inserted into the lexicon and the corresponding bit-vector is allocated and initialized. The posting is inserted into the bit-vector and compressed on the fly. The process is repeated as long as the main memory is available. When the main memory is used up, the terms and their inverted lists in the lexicon are written to a temporary disk index in lexicographical term order. The allocated space for terms is freed and the process repeats until all the documents in the collection are processed. When all the documents are processed, there could be several temporary disk indices. These indices should be merged into a single inverted index for fast query. Suppose the number of indices is N; then an N-way merge requires only one merging pass over the

N indices. To avoid excessive disk costs, an in-memory input buffer is assigned to each of the N indices. During merging, inverted lists are processed in lexicographical order. Inverted lists are decompressed, re-compressed, and merged into the final inverted list.

The merged lists can be written to a new file directly. In this case, the Single-Pass algorithm requires temporary disk space more than twice the size of the final inverted file. To save disk space, the Single-Pass algorithm can also write merged lists back in place into the temporary disk index. However, the temporary disk space is saved at the cost of indexing time. The Single-Pass algorithm is shown in Fig. 1.

Fig. 1. Structure of the Single-Pass algorithm

3   Pipeline and Data Parallel Hybrid algorithm

3.1   Algorithm Design

The PDPH algorithm is a pipeline algorithm. The indexing process is divided into four stages: the loading stage, the processing stage ,the flushing stage and the merging stage. Loading, processing and flushing are executed in order so they form a pipeline. The loading stage loads documents into the document buffer from the disk or network. In the processing stage, we launch multiple threads for processing. The works of these processing threads are the same: The segmentation stage is designed especially for Chinese, Japanese and Korean text collections. During this stage, sentences are segmented into words. This stage is useful only when the text collection contains Chinese, Japanese or Korean text because only sentences in these three languages do not have any delimiters between words. The parsing stage parses documents and tokenizes documents into terms. During the parsing stage, postings are extracted and fed into the following stage - the compression stage. The compressing stage processes the posting stream, accumulating lists in the main memory in a compressed format. Each thread accumulates the compressed inverted lists in the memory individually. We refer to the compressed inverted lists maintained by a thread as a memory index. When the memory is exhausted, the memory indices of all processing threads are written onto the disk as a temporal disk index during the flushing stage. During merging stage, those temporal disk indices are merged into a single memory index and then written onto the disk. The PDPH algorithm is shown in Fig. 2.

Among these stages, the loading and the flushing stages are I/O-intensive. the disk conflict between these two stages is not serious. The segmentation stage, the parsing stage and the compression stage are all CPU-intensive.

All processing threads do the same work. If they are fed with the same amount of data, their run times should be approximate to each other. In a multi-core system with n execution cores, we can launch n processing threads and assign each processing thread to a core. When the core number increases, the PDPH algorithm still can make use of the multiple computing resources by increasing the processing thread number. It is also suitable for optimization. Optimized parsing or compression can improve the performance of the algorithm.

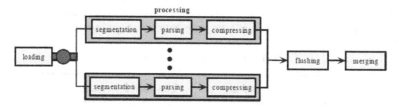

Fig. 2. Structure of the PDPH algorithm

For a threaded program, communication between threads is a critical issue for the performance of the program. Main memory buffer is used for thread communication. Generally speaking, the size of the memory buffer is important to the communication efficiency. If the buffer size is too small, it will decrease the communication efficiency. If the buffer size is too big, the buffer will take up too many memory resources. So the goal of the buffer design is to maximum the performance with a minimum buffer size. In the evaluation section we will show that we can get good performance in the cost of a moderate size buffer.

Synchronization is another critical issue for a threaded program. Since the pipeline stages are in sequence, we only have to handle synchronization for adjacent stages. Lock is a common mechanism for thread synchronization. Lock mechanism should be carefully designed because it not only affects the performance of the program, but more important, it affects the correction of the program.

Careless lock design may cause a very common problem in multi thread program - dead lock. Since adjacent stages communicate by the memory buffer, we can handle thread synchronization in the memory buffer, for example, making the buffer operation thread-safe. When a thread is operating in a buffer, other threads which want to access the buffer at the same time will be blocked.The granularity of the lock is important to performance. If the granularity is too big, other threads will wait a long time to grab a lock. If the granularity is too small, threads will grab and release lock more frequently and introduce much overhead. For simplicity, in our implementation, the granularity is a document. That means to put a document in the buffer or get a document from the buffer, a thread has to grab and release the lock one time. Of course some other sophisticated lock mechanisms will provide better lock performance, but we can see that even with this simple lock design, the PDPH algorithm will outperform the Single-Pass algorithm a lot.

3.2   Experimental Evaluations

We used three text collections to test our algorithm. The statistics of these collections were shown in Table 1. These three collections are drawn from the Terabyte track in the TREC 2011. The Terabyte track consists of a collection of Web data crawled from Web sites in the .gov domain during early 2011. This collection ("GOV2") contains a large proportion of the crawlable pages in .gov, including HTML and text, plus the extracted text of PDF, Word, and Postscript files. The GOV2 collection is 426GB in size and contains about 25 million documents. Collection 1, Collection 2 and Collection 3 were disjointed subsets of the GOV2 collection. Since the test collections are English text collection, so we omit the segmentation stage in our indexing process.

Table 1. Collection description

	Collection 1	Collection 2	Collection 3
Size	5.5GB	22GB	40GB
Documents	349900	13,43,092	2,214,327
Distinct terms	3,448,052	10,016,184	13,686,308
Term occurrences	261,373,711	1,086,543,215	2,112,867,468
Average file size	17KB	17KB	19KB

The test machine had two Intel Woodcrest 2.66GHz CPUs. Each CPU had four cores, so there were eight cores in the system. However, one of the eight cores had a defect, so we only use the other seven cores in the system. There was 2GB memory in the system and we used 1.5GB memory for constructing the inverted files. The disk was an Ultra320 SCSI disk. And the text collection and the inverted files were placed on the same disk. The operating system running on the test machine is a Linux operating system with kernel 2.4.22.

We measured the indexing performance when different numbers of processing threads were launched for a certain number of cores. Each processing thread maintained a memory index. When the main memory was used up, all of the memory indices were merged together and then flushed to the disk as a temporal disk index. For comparison purposes, we also measured the performance of the Single-Pass algorithm. The result of test is shown in Table 2.

The Single-Pass program is a modification of indri 2.8, which is an efficient indexing and searching engine. The Single-Pass program is composed of three threads. The first thread each time loads a document into the memory, parsing it into postings and compressing the postings. The first thread keeps running until there is no free memory space. Then the first thread is paused and the flushing thread is activated. The flushing thread writes compressed inverted lists in memory onto the disk as a temporal disk index and then it frees the memory. When there is available memory space, the first thread is awakened up and continues to run. When all documents in the text collection are processed, the merging thread merges all temporal disk indices into a final inverted index. The indexing process in the Single-Pass program has a slight difference from the standard Single-Pass algorithm. In the standard Single-Pass algorithm, Golomb codes and Elias codes are used to compress

Table 2. Elapsed time in seconds to construct inverted files with the PDPH algorithm

Case	Cores / Algorithm	1	2	3	4	5	6	7
Collection 1	Single-Pass	400						
	PDPH1	296	259	260				
	PDPH2	397	261	210	224			
	PDPH4	408	266	242	236	224	220	
	PDPH6	401	264	239	229	233	228	221
	PDPH8	418	264	237	236	233	233	236
Collection 2	Single-Pass	1680						
	PDPH1	1285	1090	1060				
	PDPH2	1743	1130	951	913			
	PDPH4	1720	1136	1035	969	944	937	
	PDPH6	1706	1125	1027	968	947	943	933
	PDPH8	1723	1146	1026	989	971	963	952
Collection 3	Single-Pass	3112						
	PDPH1	2299	1981	1979				
	PDPH2	3186	2048	1736	1692			
	PDPH4	3163	2044	1895	1806	1707	1670	
	PDPH6	3171	2108	1896	1797	1783	1748	1725
	PDPH8	3150	2073	1854	1773	1732	1749	1740

postings. However, use of byte-aligned codes or word-aligned codes can reduce the query evaluation time compared to the Golomb or Elias codes. The overhead of byte-aligned codes is only a modest amount of temporal disk space. Since the word-aligned codes are more complex but have similar performance with byte-aligned codes, for the simplicity, the byte-aligned code is adopted to compress postings instead of the Golomb and Elias codes in the Single-Pass program.

The PDPH algorithm needs two buffers in the memory: the original document buffer and the the parsed document buffer. The loading thread loads documents into the original document buffer. The parsing thread fetches documents from the original document buffer, parsing these documents and filling the parsed documents into the parsed document buffer.Since the average file size of these three collections is less than 20KB, we test buffer size 512KB, 1MB and 10MB and find that they all have similar performances. Besides, we also generate some bigger documents by aggregating some small documents. The average file size of these bigger documents is 17MB. Then we test buffer size 20M, 50M, 100M and 200M and find that they also have similar performances. So we can achieve good performance in the cost of a little memory for buffering.

In Table 2, PDPHn (n = 1...8) means n processing threads were launched for the processing stage. For example, PDPH1 means there was only one processing thread. When only one core was available, PDPH1 outperformed the Single-Pass algorithm by 24%. For PDPHn (n>1), their indexing times were close to the Single-Pass algorithm. The reason is that the benefit of the pipeline was offset by the overhead introduced by the context switching and thread synchronization.

When there were two cores available, the indexing times for PDPH1 and PDPHn were very close. The performance improvement was about 32%. When three cores were used, the PDPH1 had no further performance improvement. For PDPH2, the performance improvement compared to the Single-Pass algorithm was about 44%. Fig.3 shows the running time of each stage in PDPH2 when three cores were used to construct the inverted files for collection 3. Processing1 and processing2 were the two processing threads. The running times of these two threads were almost the same. The loading stage was the stage with the longest running time, so the pipelining time was approximate to the loading time.

For PDPHn (n>2), when the number of cores was increased from two to three, their performances was also improved, but the improvement was not as significant as the improvement of PDPH2. This was because the number of threads in PDPH2, which require large amount of processor resources, matched the number of cores in the system. In PDPH2, in addition to the two processing threads, the loading thread also required many processor cycles, so there were three threads that had a large amount of computing work. There were exactly three cores in the system, so each thread could be served by an individual core. In PDPHn (n>2), there were at least four threads which represented heavy computing work. Context switching brought some overhead, so PDPH2 outperformed PDPHn (n>2) when only three cores were available. More generally, we also can conclude that if there are n cores in the system, PDPH (n-1) will outperform PDPHk (k > n).

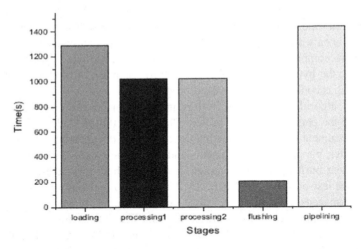

Fig. 3. Running time of each stage in PDPH2 when three cores are used

When the number of cores is increased from 4 to 7, the performance of PDPHn (n=1...8) did not change much. This was also the result of the pipeline. Fig.3 shows that the loading stage is the most time-consuming stage. When the number of cores was increased, the processing times decreased, but the loading time was left unchanged. The loading time hid the processing times and the pipelining time was approximate to the loading time, so even if the processing times were totally eliminated, the pipelining time would not change much. In order to improve the scalability of the PDPH algorithm, I/O optimization is a critical issue.

We compared the Single-Pass algorithm, and PDPH algorithm in Fig.4. As can be seen, the FDPH algorithm can greatly save time than the serial algorithm in multi-core environment.

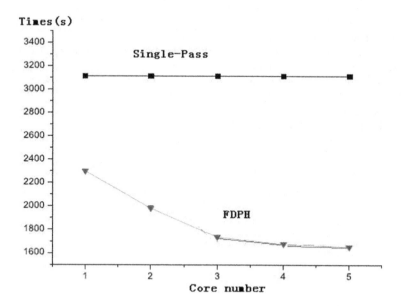

Fig. 4. Performance and scalability of the four algorithms

4   Conclusions

In multi-core environments, traditional sequential indexing algorithms cannot make use of all the cores in a system. They are also not scalable when the number of cores increases. In this paper, we present an efficient indexing algorithm for multi-core systems: the PDPH algorithm. The PDPH algorithm divides the indexing process into pipeline stages. However, it does not divide the computing work into several stages. Instead, the computing work is kept in one single stage but data parallel is introduced so this computing stage will run in parallel on several execution cores. The I/O operation is kept in one stage and it also can overlap with the computing stage. The PDPH algorithm can achieve good performance. When one, two, three or four cores are used, the performance improvement is 26%, 36%, 44% or 46%.

References

1. Anh, V.N., Moffat, A.: Inverted Index Compression Using Word-Aligned Binary Codes. Information Retrieval, 151–166 (2005)
2. Anh, V.N., Moffat, A.: Improved Word-Aligned Binary Compression for Text Indexing. IEEE Transactions on Knowledge and Data Engineering 18, 857–861 (2006)

3. Trotman, A.: Compressing Inverted Files. Information Retrieval, 5–19 (2003)
4. Heinz, S., Zobel, J.: Efficient single-pass index construction for text databases. Journal of the American Society for Information Science and Technology, 713–729 (2003)
5. Yue, M., Li, W.: Dynamic indexing for large-scale collections. Journal of Beijing Normal University (Natural Science), 134–137 (2009)
6. Ling, S., Xue-jun, Y., Lan, M.: Research on Data Organization and Index of EMMDB. Journal of Frontiers of Computer Science & Technology, 742–748 (2010)
7. Dejiao, N., Tao, C., Yong-zhao, Z., Shiguang, J.: Hierarchical metadata indexing algorithm of mass storage system. Application Research of Computers, 510–513 (2010)
8. Feng, W.: Study of XML Search Engines Based on Document Type Definition. Journal of Anhui Science and Technology University, 35–39 (2010)
9. Yue, Z., Hao-min, Y., Qi, Z., Xuan-jing, H.: Distributed Index for Near Duplicate Detection. Journal of Chinese Information Processing, 91–97 (2011)

Hierarchical Clustering Based Web Service Discovery

Huiying Gao[1], Susu Wang[1], Lily Sun[2], and Fuxing Nian[1]

[1] School of Management and Economics, Beijing Institute of Technology, Beijing, China
huiying@bit.edu.cn, susu_cheer@sina.com, nfx1228@163.com
[2] School of Systems Engineering, University of Reading, Whiteknights, UK
lily.sun@reading.ac.uk

Abstract. This paper presents a hierarchical clustering method for semantic Web service discovery. This method aims to improve the accuracy and efficiency of the traditional service discovery using vector space model. The Web service is converted into a standard vector format through the Web service description document. With the help of WordNet, a semantic analysis is conducted to reduce the dimension of the term vector and to make semantic expansion to meet the user's service request. The process and algorithm of hierarchical clustering based semantic Web service discovery is discussed. Validation is carried out on the dataset.

Keywords: Web service discovery, semantic analysis, hierarchical clustering, service matching, vector space model, Web service description.

1   Introduction

Web services describe a standardized way of integrating Web-based applications using open standards, such as Extensible Markup Language (XML), Simple Object Access Protocol (SOAP), Web service description language (WSDL) and the Universal Description, Discovery, and Integration (UDDI) over an Internet protocol backbone[1]. Popova et al. [2] believe that Web service can enable the applications built on different servers to be accessed more easily, independent of platforms and programming languages. In recent years, especially with the development of cloud computing, different types of Web services are emerging [3]. As the rapid increase in the number of Web services, however, looking for the Web service in the online registry is like looking for a needle in the haystack. A better way for Web services discovery is to classify the Web services into different categories based on semantic analysis when they are published so that the matching algorithm can be done only in the related category with high efficiency and accuracy.

There are many approaches to build automatic taxonomies, such as rule based approach, semantic analysis, cluster analysis and learning algorithms. The trend by more and more taxonomy systems is to combine multiple methods based on various algorithms using statistical method, semantic analysis and clustering technique. This paper aims at a hybrid solution for Web service discovery by combining semantic analysis with the techniques of hierarchical clustering.

K. Liu et al. (Eds.): ICISO 2014, IFIP AICT 426, pp. 281–291, 2014.

The remainder of the paper is organised as follows: Section 2 discusses the state of art in relation to the methods of Web service matching. Clustering analysis is also argued. In Section 3 the semantic expansion of Web service is described and a hierarchical clustering based Web service discovery algorithm is put forwarded to classify and discover the Web services automatically. By using a Web service testing set, Section 4 illustrates the discovery process and validates the feasibility of the proposed method. Finally Section 5 draws the conclusion and flowed by the outlook.

2   Literature Review

2.1   Web Service Matching

A lot of research work has been conducted to solve the problem of Web service discovery. Two important ones are 1) Web service matching algorithm with high recall, precision and efficiency, and 2) the effective services selection and ranking methods in the found preliminary services set. The Web service matching is mainly through three stages [4]: a grammatical matching method based on keyword or vector space model such as UDDI systems of IBM, Microsoft, and SUN; a semantic matching method based on ontology such as OWL-S, METEOR-S and WSMO; a service matching method based on information search technology, for example, Niu et al. [5] have devised a semantic Web service discovery method based on context and action inference.

2.2   Clustering Algorithm

Clustering is a process of dividing data objects into several classes or clusters to make the similarity between different clusters maximal and the similarity between objects within one cluster minimal [6]. Clustering algorithm can generally be divided into five categories [7][8]: hierarchy-based approach, division-based approach, density-based approach, grid-based approach and model-based approach. Each method has its own advantages and disadvantages. As the hierarchy clustering method can show all the whole process of clustering, so we can confirm the number of categories by analyzing the process. It may reduce the time spending on determining the number of categories.

The basic hierarchical clustering algorithm can be divided into agglomerate hierarchy clustering algorithm (AGNES) and divisive hierarchy clustering algorithm (DIANA). The idea of agglomerate algorithm is that treat every object as a separate class, then merge the two closest clusters and update the original distance between clusters and the new cluster, repeat this step until all objects are in one cluster; while the idea of divisive algorithm is contrary [9].

As a technique widely used in the field of information search, clustering method improve the efficiency of information discovery to some extent. There are also some studies on the utilization of service clustering to improve efficiency of Web service discovery. For example, Rajagopal et al. [10] propose a service discovery method which is based on ontology clustering for grid service. Sudha et al. [11] complete the service clustering based on the WSDL to improve the efficiency of service discovery. Sun et al. [12] cluster the services with high function and process similarities based on Petri Net. Wang et al. [13] propose a service discovery method by combining the ideas of P2P and clustering. Xu et al. [14] propose a discovery method based on graph theory. Yahyaoui et al. [15] introduce a novel matching approach which allows reducing the matching space through fuzzy classification rules. Facing the explosive increase of Web service, combine semantic analysis together with clustering technique to improve the accuracy and efficiency of Web service discovery is a trend.

3   The Method of Hierarchical Clustering Based Web Service Discovery

In our approach, we aim to realize the semantic Web service discovery process based on a hierarchical clustering. The advantage of this approach is that it can generate a hierarchically nested clustering and has high accuracy.

3.1   Web Service Description

In order to conduct similarity calculation on Web services, Web service description documents should be abstracted mathematically based on WSDL [16]. According to the structure of the WSDL document, Web service can be defined as follows.

Definition 1 [4]. Service description is an abstract of functional attributes and process model of Web service which can be expressed as a four-tuples:

$$WS =< sName, sDescription, sInput, sOutput >$$

among which,

$sName$ is the service name

$sDescription$ is the service description

$sInput = \{I_1, I_2, ..., I_m\}$ shows the input set of service

$sOutput = \{O_1, O_2, ... O_m\}$ shows the output set of service

Corresponding to the description of Web service, we can define the functional similarity of two services as follows.

Definition 2 [17]. Define the similarity of service ws_1 and ws_2 in Equation (1).

$$Sim(ws_1, ws_2) = \alpha_1 Sim(Sn_1, Sn_2) + \alpha_2 Sim(Sd_1, Sd_2) + \alpha_3 Sim(Si_1, Si_2) + \alpha_4 Sim(So_1 + So_2) \quad (1)$$

Among which, α_1, α_2, α_3, α_4 are respectively the weight of name similarity, description similarity, input similarity, output similarity of Web service in the whole similarity, and $\alpha_1 + \alpha_2 + \alpha_3 + \alpha_4 = 1, 0 \leq \alpha_1 \leq 1, \ 0 \leq \alpha_2 \leq 1, 0 \leq \alpha_3 \leq 1, 0 \leq \alpha_4 \leq 1$.

Service name similarity can be calculated by using:

$$Sim(Sn_1, Sn_2) = \frac{1}{p+q} \sum_{j=1}^{q} \sum_{i=1}^{p} Sim_{concept}(n_i^{(1)}, n_j^{(2)})$$

Service description similarity can be calculated by using:

$$Sim(Sd_1, Sd_2) = \frac{1}{p+q} \sum_{j=1}^{q} \sum_{i=1}^{p} Sim_{concept}(d_i^{(1)}, d_j^{(2)})$$

Service input similarity can be calculated by using:

$$Sim(Si_1, Si_2) = \frac{1}{p+q} \sum_{j=1}^{q} \sum_{i=1}^{p} Sim_{concept}(i_i^{(1)}, i_j^{(2)})$$

Service output similarity can be calculated by using:

$$Sim(So_1, So_2) = \frac{1}{p+q} \sum_{j=1}^{q} \sum_{i=1}^{p} Sim_{concept}(o_i^{(1)}, o_j^{(2)})$$

among which, p, q are respectively the number of concepts in S_n, S_d, S_i, S_o of the two services. If we ignore the difference between the name, description, input and output of service, then $\alpha_1 = \alpha_2 = \alpha_3 = \alpha_4$.

Similar to the description of Web service, a service request can be defined as follows.

Definition 3 The description information of service request of a Web service requestor can be defined as the four-tuples:

$$RS = < rName, rDescription, rInput, rOutput >$$

in which,

rName represents the service name that the requestor is looking for

rDescription represents the service functional description that requestor needs

$rInput = \{rI_1, rI_2, ..., rI_m\}$ is the input set that service requestor provides

$rOutput = \{rO_1, rO_2, ..., rO_m\}$ is the output set that service requestor provides

Semantics is introduced through the calculation of concept similarity and in generally, the similarity between two concepts can be defined as follows.

Definition 4[18]. In a ontology category, the similarity of two concepts can be defined by Equation (2). The value of Sim is between [0,1].

$$sim(c_1, c_2) = \frac{2 * depth(LCS(c_1, c_2))}{dis(c_1, LCS(c_1, c_2)) + dis(c_2, LCS(c_1, c_2)) + 2 * depth(LCS(c_1, c_2))} \tag{2}$$

in which,

LCS refers to the smallest common ancestor node of two concepts,
depth represents the hierarchy depth of the repository,
dis represents the shortest path length between two concepts.

3.2   Web Service Discovery Processes Based on Clustering

Web service discovery consists mainly of two basic processes: the clustering and matching of Web services. The introduction of semantic technology and clustering method may affect both the two processes and ultimately impact the efficiency and accuracy of Web service discovery.

3.2.1   Process of Web Service Clustering

Web service can be seen as a kind of a short text. It can be described by using the service name, service description, service input and service output at the same time. So the process of text clustering can be equally applicable to Web service clustering as shown in Fig.1[19].

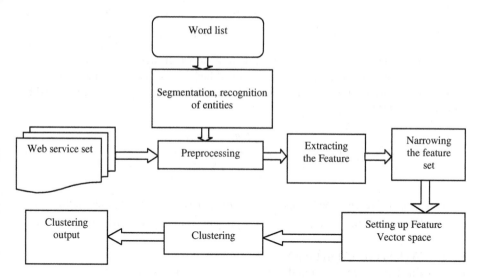

Fig. 1. The clustering process of Web service based on service description documents

The main process of hierarchical clustering are described as follows.

Step 1. Preprocessing of Web services: To preprocess the Web service description text to complete the Web service description segmentation and stemming process.

Step 2. The establishment of Web service feature space: There is a variety of feature representations of Web service information. We adopt the vector space model[20] (VSM) which is one of the methods that have been widely used and got better results in recent years and Term Frequency-Inverse Document Frequency (TF-IDF) which is a weighting technique commonly used for information retrieval and text mining.

Step 3. Reduction of Web service information feature set: Filter the words extracted from the Web service description text, remove prepositions, pronouns etc that have no actual meaning, and then stemming. For the feature vector space of Web service got from Step 2, calculate the similarity of feature words and reduce the dimension of the semantic vector space. According to definition 4, similarities can be calculated.

Step 4. The description of Web services collection: After reducing the feature set, the establishment of feature vector space of Web services is completed. Assuming that $WS = \{ws_1, ws_2, ..., ws_n\}$ represents a Web services set containing n Web services, in which ws_i represents the number i service, then the service set can be represented abstractly by Equation (3).

$$WS = \begin{pmatrix} tfidf_{1,1} & tfidf_{1,2} & \cdots & tfidf_{1,s} \\ tfidf_{2,1} & tfidf_{2,2} & \cdots & tfidf_{2,s} \\ \cdots & \cdots & tfidf_{i,j} & \cdots \\ tfidf_{n,1} & tfidf_{n,2} & \cdots & tfidf_{n,s} \end{pmatrix} \tag{3}$$

in which each row of the matrix represents a service, element $tfidf_{i,j}$ represents the weight of service i on feature word j, s is the dimension of feature word vector.

Step 5. Web services clustering: The prerequisite of clustering is determining the similarity between Web services. As mentioned before, TF-IDF is normally applying together with cosine similarity. Therefore, the cosine coefficients can be calculated by Equation (4) [21].

$$Sim(d_i, d_j) = Cos(d_i, d_j) = \frac{\sum_{k=1}^{|T|} tfidf_{i,k} \times tfidf_{j,k}}{\sqrt{\sum_{k=1}^{|T|} tfidf_{i,k}^2 \times \sum_{k=1}^{|T|} tfidf_{j,k}^2}} \tag{4}$$

in which $tfidf$ represents the TF-IDF weight of two Web service in the feature vector space, d represents the documents and T represents the feature word set.

3.2.2   Web Service Matching Process

Three main steps are involved in the Web service matching process.

Step 1. Service request description: according to definition 3, we can describe the service request as $R_{ws} = (Rt_1, Rt_2, ...Rt_i, ...Rt_m)$, in which Rt_i represents the number i feature word of request entered by users, m is the number of valid service request feature words.

Step 2. The semantic matching of service requests: according to definition 1 and 2, supposing that the feature vector of Web service set is $T = \{t_1, t_2, ..., t_s\}$, then the matching process of traditional method will be: for all feature word in T, judge whether there is R_{ws}. If there is, note the frequency of the word as 1; otherwise as 0; then treat it as a Web service to calculate the TF-IDF value in the space of T, represented as $R_{tfidf} = (R_{tfidf,1}, R_{tfidf,2}, ..., R_{tfidf,m})$. Therefore, the matching process is namely the process of calculating the similarity between R_{tfidf} and all services in ws. Among them, the conversion from service request vector space to Web service feature word vector space can be achieved by Hungarian algorithm and the concept similarity is calculated based on WordNet.

Step 3. Service request matching based on clustering: After clustering based on Equation (4) the Web services storing in the database, the storage of Web service become different. Each cluster has a representative. If the new service has a higher similarity with a representative, it might mean that the similarity between the new service and all services in the cluster which the representative is in is higher than others. Before calculating the similarity between service request and all services, the similarity between Web service request and each representative should be compared. Select the clusters whose representatives have the top n similarity with the service request, calculate the similarity between the service request and all services in these clusters and finally return them to users by the similarity.

4   Results and Discussion

In our research work we choose OWL-TC 4.0 as the data set. It is the fourth version of OWL-S service test set which provides 1083 semantic Web services from nine different areas. The method mentioned in the paper and the traditional method of Web service matching is realized on the same data set. Comparative analysis is conducted on the recall, precision and time efficiency.

According to the advice of Lehmann that the number of categories should be between $n/30$ and $n/60$[9] (in which n represents the number of samples), we can implement clustering using SPSS19.0 based on the above results. The cosine similarity can be the measurement of similarity between Web services according to the process of Web service clustering mentioned in Section 3.2.1. Comparing the clustering distribution with 19-36 clusters, some of the results are shown in Fig.2.

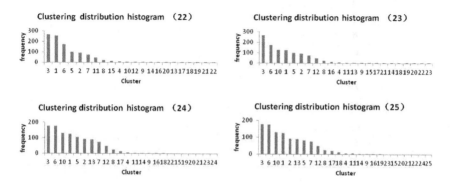

Fig. 2. The clustering distribution histogram with 22-25 clusters

The distribution with 24 clusters is relatively the most average and thereafter every time a cluster is added, the distribution only adds a cluster with the frequency less than 5 while the impaction on the clusters with higher frequency is weak. So considering both average and simplicity of computation, we choose 24 as the number of clusters of experimental data.

According to the Web service matching process of Section 3.2.2, we take "movie price" as a service request and complement the experiment while "movie" does not appear in the feature vector and "price" exists in the feature vector. The gravity of every cluster is taken as representative and cosine similarity between all representatives and service request is calculated by software Matlab to compare the results of matching. Table 1 shows the results of similarity between representatives and service request.

Table 1. The calculating results of similarity between representatives and service request

Cluster NO	Cluster size	Similarity (high to low)
13	88	0.483482
1	126	0.101886
10	129	0.081205
3	177	0.058091
11	5	0.053409
16	3	0.035541
20	1	0.020473
4	7	0.014712
9	3	0.014255
17	13	0.01176
18	3	0.009699
12	48	0.009568
5	103	0.00072
6	176	0.000445
2	92	0
7	74	0
8	24	0
14	4	0
15	1	0
19	1	0
21	1	0
22	2	0
23	1	0
24	1	0

After clustering, the top ten clusters are chosen which have the greatest similarity between representatives and service request and are returned to users in the descending order.

Taking the reality into consideration, users' browse focuses on the results in the top pages, we select the top 100 Web services to calculate the evaluation indicators after the matching results are returned. Let average of ten times calculating results be the indicator value of two methods on time efficiency and let

Recall rate = (number of related service discovered/total number of related)*100%

Precision rate = (number of related service discovered/total number of service discovered)*100%.

The results are shown in Table 2, from which we can see that the recall rate and precision rate in the experiment of the method proposed in this paper are 0,4167 and 0,2 respectively, both are higher than that of the traditional method without hierarchical clustering and semantic analysis. Yet the time consuming of our method is 0.1086 seconds which is less than that of the traditional method of 0.4441seconds.

Table 2. The comparison between Web service discovery method based on traditional keywords and hierarchical clustering (based on the top 100 return results)

	Recall	Precision	Time-consuming(s)
Traditional method	0	0	0.4441
This method	0.4167	0.2000	0.1086

The verification results show the advantages of hierarchical clustering based Web discovery on recall rate, precision rate and time efficiency which indicates the effectiveness of the method.

5   Conclusions

The method of hierarchical clustering based Web services discovery is devised to improve the efficiency and accuracy of Web service discovery. The hybrid solution for building and populating a taxonomy structure of web services are studied by combining semantic analysis with clustering techniques. The verification is carried out by using the dataset of OWL-TC4.0 to demonstrate the acceptance of the hierarchical clustering method in Web service discovery.

The work to convert the Web services into term vectors as well as the semantic expansion of the query of the user is done on WordNet, based on which a service provider and consumer would derive a meaning of the text or key word of the query or the Web service description document in a semantic level. However, a full understanding of web service potentiality can only be reached when the effects of the sign, made by contextual interpretation, is made by the service provider and consumer through consensus (pragmatics) [22]. In order to overcome limitations of this work, the future work will consider introducing domain ontologies in a semiotics way to make the Web service discovery context aware so as to improve the accuracy of service discovery in further step. Additionally, more properties like the preconditions and results of Web services in the Web service description document should be taken into account when the semantic vector space are set up.

Acknowledgments. This work was supported in part by the Beijing Natural Science Foundation (Grant No. 9133020) and by the National Natural Science Foundation of China under Grant 71102111.

References

1. Thomas, E.: Service-oriented Architecture Concepts, Technology, and Design, pp. 56–80. China Machine Press (2007) (in Chinese)
2. Popova, G., Nedeva, V.: Web Services-an Instrument to Resolve the Problems of Information Systems Integration. Rakia Journal of Sciences, 61–64 (2006)
3. Yue, K., Wang, X., Zhou, A.: The Core Support Technology of Web Service: Review. Journal of Software 15(3), 428–440 (2004) (in Chinese)
4. Liao, Z., Liu, J., Liu, Y., Liu, H.: Review of Web Service Discovery Technology. Journal of The China Society for Scientific and Technical Information 27(2), 186–192 (2008) (in Chinese)
5. Niu, W., Chang, L., Wang, X., Han, X., Shi, Z.: Semantic Web Service Discovery Based on Context and Action Reasoning. Pattern Recognition and Artificial Intelligence 23(1), 65–71 (2010) (in Chinese)
6. Ertel, W.: Introduction to artificial intelligence. Springer (2011)
7. He, L., Wu, L., Cai, Y.: Summary of Clustering Algorithm in Data Mining. Computer Application Research, 10–13 (2007) (in Chinese)
8. Hu, Q., Ye, N., Zhu, M.: Summary of Clustering Algorithm in Data Mining. Computer and Digital Engineering (2007) (in Chinese)
9. Liang, B.: Detection of Top-n Global Outliers in Datasets Based on Hierarchical Clustering. Computer Engineering and Applications 48(9), 101–103 (2012)
10. Rajagopal, S., Selvi, T.: Semantic grad service discovery approach using clustering of service ontologies. In: Proceedings of IEEE TENCON 2006, pp. 1–4 (2006)
11. Sudha, R., Yousub, H., Zhao, H.: A Clustering Based Approach for Facilitating Semantic Web Service Discovery. In: Proceedings of the 15th Annual Workshop on Information Technologies & Systems, Las Vegas, USA (2006)
12. Sun, P., Jiang, C.: Process Model-oriented Semantic Web Service Discovery Using Service Clustering Optimization. Journal of Computers 31(8), 1340–1353 (2008) (in Chinese)
13. Wang, L., Hu, X.: Web Clustering and Composition based on P2P. Computer Engineering 35(17), 7–10 (2009) (in Chinese)
14. Xu, X., Chen, J., Wu, Y.: Web Service Discovery Method based on Clustering Optimization. Computer Engineering 37(9), 68–70 (2011)
15. Yahyaoui, H., Almulla, M., Own, H.: A Novel Non-functional Matchmaking Approach between Fuzzy User Queries and Real World Web Services Based on Rough Sets. Future Generation Computer Systems (2014)
16. Gao, H., Stucky, W., Liu, L.: Web Services Classification Based on Intelligent Clustering Techniques. In: Proceedings of 2009 International Forum on Information Technology and Applications, pp. 242–245 (2009)
17. Ma, Y., Jin, B., Feng, Y.: Semantic Web service Dynamic Discovery based on Evolution Distributed Ontology. Journal of Computers 28(4), 603–614 (2005) (in Chinese)

18. Wu, Z., Palmer, M.: Verb semantics and lexical selection. In: Proceedings of the 32nd Annual Meeting of the Associations for Computational Linguistics, pp. 133–138 (1994)
19. Qing, Y., Gong, L., Xiang, L.: Text Clustering Algorithm based on Vector Space Model. Computer Engineering 34(18), 39–44 (2008)
20. Hamadi, R., Benatallah, B.: A Petri Net based Model for Web Service Composition. In: Proc. of the 14th Australasian Database Conference on Research and Practice in Information Technology, pp. 19–200 (2003)
21. Jing, P., Dong, Y.: A Text Clustering Algorithm Based on Semantic Inner Product Space Model. Journal of Computer 30(8), 1354–1362 (2007)
22. Liu, K., Benfell, A.: Software and Data Technologies Communications in Computer and Information Science. 50, 18–32 (2011)

A Comprehensive Evaluation Approach that Highlights the 'Equilibrium' and Its Application in Evaluation on Regional Innovation Capability

Yanru Qi, Yun Liu, and Jing An

School of Management and Economic, Beijing Institute of Technology, Beijing, China
yrqits@163.com, liuyun@bit.edu.cn, anjing@tobacco.gov.cn

Abstract. In this paper we proposed a novel method that aggregates the "Functionality" and the "Equilibrium" to calculate the weight of comprehensive evaluation problem, The method calculate the weight coefficient according to the principle of "variance drive" firstly, then considering the development of the system balance with relative equilibrium coefficient to arrive at the comprehensive evaluation results of various systems. The method reflects the scientificity, impartiality and rationality. So it can avoid the phenomenon "one swallow make a summer", which can promote the healthy development of the whole system. Finally, a numerical example was given to illustrate the effectiveness of the proposed method.

Keywords: Comprehensive Evaluation, Multiple Attribute Decision Making, Relatively Balanced Coefficient.

1 Introduction

Many comprehensive evaluation problems can be met frequently in realistic society, such as evaluation of the region innovation capability or urban competitiveness of a country or area. The method use now for this problems are classified into 9 classes, such as Comprehensive Evaluation methods [1-4], Operational Research methods [5-7], Statistical methods [8-9], Systematic Engineering methods [10-12], Fuzzy Mathematics methods [13-16].

Multi-index comprehensive evaluation is a kind of method to get a comprehensive index to make an overall evaluation and a vertical or horizontal comparison on evaluation object, by integrating the multiple index information which describes the different aspects of the evaluation object. This method is widely used in many areas since it could make accurate description for evaluation objects and process the dynamic objects which have many decision makers and indexes.

In the evaluation process, the comprehensive evaluation result is directly influenced by the determination of weight coefficient and evaluation index. There are several methods of determining the weight, which can be grossly divided into subjective and objective weighting method [17]. Subjective weighting method such as Delphi and AHP often depends on subjective experience, the result of which instability with the

K. Liu et al. (Eds.): ICISO 2014, IFIP AICT 426, pp. 292–301, 2014.

influence of the expert experience or preference. Objective methods such as Maximizing Deviation Method[18] and Mean Square Difference Method[19] depends on practical data of every index, the result of these methods based on principle that "the difference is driven" may led to lopsided development of the evaluation system. To avoid the defects of subjective and objective weighting methods, a new weighting method is proposed[20], and the new mathematical programming model synthesized both subjective and objective characters is established. This research will set up a comprehensive evaluation model that introduce "relative equilibrium coefficient" into the objective weighting method to encouraging the advanced and urging on the backward in evaluation. With all these efforts, we can expect to realize the health development of system.

In the real evaluation process, fewer scholars consider whether the indexes of evaluation objects are in balanced development. In this paper we proposed a novel method that aggregates the "Functionality" and the "Equilibrium" to calculate the weight of comprehensive evaluation problem, the method utilize the deviations between each indicator and the average value to calculate the in the multi-index comprehensive evaluation, then considering the development of the system balance with relative equilibrium coefficient to arrive at the comprehensive evaluation results of various systems. The case analysis result is given to prove the effectiveness of this method in the end of this paper. This method gives consideration to both functionality and equilibrium of evaluation objects and realize the function of encourage advanced spur lagging behind.

2   Determination of Index Weight Coefficients

2.1   Based on the Weight Determination Method of "Variance Drive"

Setting the evaluation object set

$$O = \{o_1, o_2, \cdots, o_n\} \tag{1}$$

Index set

$$P = \{p_1, p_2, \cdots, p_m\}$$
$$x_{ij} = x_j(o_i)(i = 1, 2, \cdots, n; j = 1, 2, \cdots m) \tag{2}$$

which is short-cut process of scheme o_i about the indicator p_j. Then the index matrix about scheme set O and index set P can expressed as

$$A = \left[x_{ij} \right]_{n \times m} = \begin{bmatrix} x_{11} & x_{12} & \cdots & x_{1m} \\ x_{21} & x_{22} & \cdots & x_{2m} \\ \vdots & \vdots & & \vdots \\ x_{n1} & x_{n2} & \cdots & x_{nm} \end{bmatrix} \tag{3}$$

Without loss of generality, assume the index of index set P are all extra-large, carry out the dimensionless treatment with the data in A as below:

$$x_{ij}^* = \frac{x_{ij}}{\min_i \{x_{ij}\}}, \left(i=1,2,\cdots,n; j=1,2,\cdots,m\right) \tag{4}$$

We mark x_{ij}^* as x_{ij} below for convenience

Gather the multi-target information with linear weighted model; assume that y_i is the evaluating value of scheme o_i, then,

$$y_i = \omega_1 x_{i1} + \omega_2 x_{i2} + \cdots + \omega_m x_{im}$$
$$= \sum_{j=1}^m \omega_j x_{ij} = \omega^T x_i \tag{5}$$
$$(i=1,2,3,\cdots,n)$$

In the formula $x_i = (x_{i1}, x_{i2}, \cdots, x_{im})^T$, $\omega = (\omega_1, \omega_2, \cdots, \omega_m)^T$ is m-dimensional vector, name x_i as the index vector of o_i, ω as index weight vector.

If $y = \begin{bmatrix} y_1 & y_2 & \cdots & y_n \end{bmatrix}^T$, then the formula (5) can be written as :

$$y = A\omega \tag{6}$$

We can regard n evaluation objects as n dots or vectors of m-dimensional space that consist of m- evaluation indexes. Then what we should do is select index weight coefficient to enlarge the difference of each evaluation objects and highlight the overall differences of each evaluation objects, based on that improved the method of maximizing deviations which was mentioned in literature [18], and build the function

$$H = MAX \sum_{j=1}^m \omega_j \cdot (\sum_{i=1}^n |x_{ij} - x_j|) \tag{7}$$

If define

$$\sum_{j=1}^m \omega^2_j = 1 \tag{8}$$

in advance, then we can transform the issue into the maximum problem of type(7) under this Limited-Term, that is select ω to make

$$H = MAX \sum_{j=1}^{m} \omega_j \cdot (\sum_{i=1}^{n} |x_{ij} - x_j|)$$

$$s.t. \sum_{j=1}^{m} \omega^2_j = 1$$

$$\omega > 0$$

(9)

Apply Lagrange conditional extreme to type (9), we can get

$$\sum_{i=1}^{n} |x_{ij} - x_j| = 2\lambda \omega_j$$

$$\sum_{j=1}^{m} \omega^2_j = 1$$

(10)

And we can obtain the weight coefficient after normalization processing as follows,

$$\omega^*_j = \frac{\sum\limits_{i=1}^{n} |x_{ij} - x_j|}{\sum\limits_{j=1}^{m} \sum\limits_{i=1}^{n} |x_{ij} - x_j|}$$

(21)

Utilize the weight coefficient obtained from formula (11) with formula (5), we can get the comprehensive index y based on 'differences drive'.

The analysis result of the system which is obtained from the evaluating value is independent on people's subjective judgment and strong objectivity. However, this evaluating value has the character of highlight indicators intrinsic difference, which can cause the system appear the "deformed" development phenomenon that focus on strengthening an index because of optimizing. In order to avoid the occurrence of this phenomenon, we introduce the system relative equilibrium coefficient concept. Meanwhile, we encourage these balanced development systems and punish these deformed development systems through the above coefficient to get the more close to the actual situation and acceptable evaluation result.

2.2   The Introduction of Relative Equilibrium Coefficient

In this paper, we will utilize the reciprocal of the coefficient of variation of decentralized characterization data to describe the balance of the system [21]. We define system o_i (while the index value of o_i is data after dimensionless process)

$$JH_i = \begin{cases} \dfrac{\frac{1}{m}\sum\limits_{j=1}^{m} x_{ij}}{s_i} \quad (s_i = \sqrt{\dfrac{\sum\limits_{j=1}^{m}(x_{ij} - x_i)^2}{m-1}} \neq 0; i = 1, 2, \cdots, n) \\ \max\{JH_d\} + c, (s_i = 0; s_d \neq 0) \end{cases}$$

(32)

It is observed that the larger JH_i, the smaller volatility of numerical value between the indicators in the system is. Otherwise, the bigger volatility of the system indicators, the less balanced development of the system is. We use formula (14) to define the relative equilibrium coefficient of system.

$$JH^*_i = n \cdot \frac{JH_i}{\sum\limits_{i=1}^{n} JH_i}$$

$$\sum\limits_{i=1}^{n} JH^*_i = n$$

(43)

There from we can deduce that, for these n systems, if JH^*_i is less than 1, then there is a gap between the indicators of this system; if JH^*_i is bigger than 1, then indicators in the system is relatively balanced; if JH^*_i is equal to 1, then the development of indicators in the system is in a middle position among all the systems. For these systems that JH^*_i is bigger than 1, we should increase its value to some extent as motivation. Meanwhile, for these "deformed" developed systems, we should decrease its value as punishment so as to realize the disciplinary role of evaluation model.

2.3   A Build-Up Model That Introduce the Relative Equilibrium Coefficient

On the base of relative equilibrium coefficient, we concentrate the system over again and obtain that

$$y_i^* = y_i + \frac{(JH_i^* - 1) * \sum\limits_{i=1}^{n} y_i}{n * \sum\limits_{i=1}^{n} \left| JH_i^* - 1 \right|}$$

(54)

Via the objective evaluation of the difference process of formula (14), we can realize the function of promoting the smooth development and punish imbalanced development.

3   Example

Utilize the functionality and balanced aggregate model to calculate the region innovation capacity data of 31 provinces as tab 1 in *literature [22]*,

Table 1. The region innovation capacity index of each province of 2011

Regions	The Utility Value of Knowledge Creation	The Utility Value of Knowledge Acquisition	The Utility Value of Enterprise Innovation	The Utility Value of Innovation Environment	The Utility Value of Innovation Performance
Jiangsu	40.94	50.59	62.85	50.85	50.58
Guangdong	48.92	44.54	50.81	55.10	56.95
Beijing	79.96	40.65	46.26	36.70	45.44
Shanghai	47.60	63.82	44.93	37.37	44.68
Zhejiang	31.89	30.91	56.53	41.22	36.87
Shandong	31.42	25.12	44.09	39.72	39.54
Tianjin	28.36	37.49	41.04	32.85	37.69
Hubei	24.89	21.33	36.79	30.27	34.57
Sichuang	26.00	26.18	29.17	34.41	31.12
Chongqing	20.6	25.43	35.66	32.01	30.12
Hunan	29.27	25.51	28.27	29.30	35.91
Liaoning	23.59	38.66	26.20	30.36	27.26
Anhui	19.65	15.88	33.29	30.54	36.35
Shaanxi	30.25	18.62	26.74	33.41	27.10
Henan	22.39	20.83	23.69	29.58	30.81
Fujian	17.38	21.50	21.88	26.71	30.91
Shanxi	20.61	15.69	30.85	21.80	26.12
Hebei	18.92	22.64	20.12	24.75	29.07
Heilongjiang	22.87	17.54	20.66	23.06	29.24
Guangxi	14.81	16.08	25.40	23.65	28.33
Jilin	17.58	13.37	19.04	24.43	33.47
Jiangxi	13.43	17.02	16.31	28.51	31.49
Hainan	18.74	26.06	12.35	23.27	31.65
Ningxia	13.06	16.82	24.44	23.87	19.41
Yunnan	18.03	17.09	21.86	20.22	24.75
Inner Mongolia	12.29	20.64	14.67	24.70	28.41
Xinjiang	12.95	17.49	16.83	23.05	29.22
Gansu	19.29	17.64	21.99	18.18	21.24
Guizhou	16.33	13.39	18.6	20.34	24.02
Xizang	5.79	5.82	14.6	24.95	34.00
Qinghai	7.30	17.43	14.16	20.67	19.41

from formula (11) that the weight of each index as table 2:

Table 2. The weight of each index

	The Utility Value of Knowledge Creation	The Utility Value of Knowledge Acquisition	The Utility Value of Enterprise Innovation	The Utility Value of Innovation Environment	The Utility Value of Innovation Performance
weight	0.196032	0.181183	0.211934	0.130354	0.125122

x_{ij} Was separately substituted into formula (5), we can get the comprehensive evaluation value of innovation capacity of provinces, autonomous regions and municipalities. We sort the value and compared with *literature [22]* and the results as shown table 3.

Table 3. The relative equilibrium coefficient, evaluating value of assembled and sorting result of provinces, autonomous regions and municipalities

| Regions | Relative Equilibrium Coefficient | Calculations | | Sorting Result of Literature[22] | Sorting Result of This Paper |
		Evaluation Value of Literature[22]	Evaluation Value of This Paper		
Jiangsu	1.336999	52.27	51.76501	1	1
Guangdong	2.105035	51.89	51.58099	2	2
Beijing	0.585137	47.92	50.9122	3	3
Shanghai	0.989686	46.23	48.38886	4	4
Zhejiang	0.772414	41.23	39.83768	5	5
Shandong	0.961705	37.34	35.98531	6	7
Tianjin	1.460951	35.89	35.69753	7	6
Hubei	0.928789	30.61	29.71281	8	10
Sichuang	1.687775	29.95	29.50226	9	9
Chongqing	0.996219	29.85	29.31325	10	12
Hunan	1.57561	29.79	29.08532	11	8
Liaoning	1.021588	28.93	28.58283	12	11
Anhui	0.619462	28.56	26.89815	13	14
Shaanxi	1.00293	27.79	26.07996	14	13
Henan	1.159824	25.96	24.88072	15	15
Fujian	0.921067	24.16	22.95871	16	17
Shanxi	0.814262	23.83	22.76698	17	16
Hebei	1.165102	23.26	22.56933	18	18
Heilongjiang	1.073299	22.84	22.21028	19	19
Guangxi	0.742462	22.56	20.98269	20	21
Jilin	0.566841	22.2	20.87774	21	24
Jiangxi	0.537177	22.07	20.71971	22	25
Hainan	0.622538	21.95	20.43453	23	20
Ningxia	0.826361	20.89	20.06905	24	26
Yunnan	1.350361	20.74	19.51379	25	23
Inner Mongolia	0.608492	20.46	19.17662	26	27
Xinjiang	0.639	20.38	18.63339	27	28
Gansu	2.111367	19.83	18.54533	28	22
Guizhou	0.936691	19	17.97067	29	29
Xizang	0.280583	18.43	14.69616	30	30
Qinghai	0.600275	16.3	14.50313	31	31

The weight of each index provided by the *literature* [22] was $\omega = \{0.15, 0.15, 0.25, 0.25, 0.20\}$, compared with the weight indexes provided by the *literature* [22], this paper pays more attention on the role of enterprise innovation while studying the regional innovation capability. And accordingly, the weights of innovation environment and innovation performance are relatively reduced. After calculating the comprehensive evaluation value of each region's innovation capability by using the aggregation model which focuses more on equilibrium, we get an evaluation result which is close to the one from *literature [22]*.

During the calculation process, we find that, the innovation capabilities of Jiangsu province, Beijing city, Guangdong province, Shanghai city and Zhejiang province are ranked from 1 to 5 based on the 2 calculation results. That is, in the development process, all of these 5 regions have got leading advantage in innovation even they have different equilibrium in knowledge creation, knowledge acquisition, enterprise innovation, innovation environment and innovation performance.

At the same time it shows that, all the index developments from Guangdong province are in a more balanced pace than the other 4 regions. There is still room for Zhejiang province to improve its capabilities on knowledge creation and knowledge acquisition. And we also find Shanghai city has obvious shortcomings on innovation environment.

The regions ranked from 6-9 have no obvious differences from these 2 calculations. Most of these 14 provinces, cities and autonomous regions are located in eastern China. Considering the development equilibrium of each index, the innovation capability of Hunan province climbs up 3 places to the 8th comparing with the first time. While Hubei and Chongqing slips down 2 places.

The result shows that the utility value rankings of each index for Hunan province are the 8th, the 10th, the 13th, the 15th and the 9th, which means it has better equilibrium. By contrast of that, Hubei province should improve its capability of knowledge acquisition. And Chongqing should pay more attention on the development of knowledge creation capability.

The countries rank low in west of china, the innovation capabilities of most regions in western China are ranked backward. In the backward ranked regions, the regional innovation capability of Gansu province moves up 6 positions to the 22nd. Hainan and Yunnan move up 3 and 2 positions respectively to the 20th and 23th. While both of Jilin and Jiangxi declines 3 positions to the 24th and 25th respectively.

The analysis shows that the enterprise innovation capability of Gansu province is ranked at the 2nd in the last 12 regions. In addition, the developments of its knowledge creation, knowledge acquisition, innovation environment and innovation performance are in balance and without obvious differences. Among the last 12 regions, Jilin and Jiangxi have more advantages in the innovation performance than the other regions. But the former should improve its capabilities of knowledge acquisition and enterprise innovation. And the latter should pay more attention on its capabilities of knowledge creation and enterprise innovation.

4   Conclusions

For the issue of less consideration on whether the system is in balanced development when evaluating the regional economic development and industry innovation capability, this paper proposes a comprehensive evaluation model which could highlight the 'Equilibrium' of each evaluation index development from the evaluation object. And also, this model is applied to the comprehensive evaluation on our country's regional innovation capabilities. This model not only considers the influence on the evaluation result from each index value, and also, it considers the equilibrium of system development. During the evaluation process, it 'promotes' the system which has balanced development in each index. While it 'punishes' the system which only focuses on the development of some index and ignores the others' development. Finally that will aggregate the 'difference' and 'equilibrium' to get a more reasonable and reliable evaluation result. And it will really work on 'encourage the developed ones, and motivate the developing ones'.

References

1. Zongjun, W.: On the methods, problems and research trends of comprehensive evaluation. Journal of Management Sciences in China 1, 75–79 (1998) (in Chinese)
2. Hwang, C.L., Md Aasud, A.S.: Multiple Objective Decision Making Methods and Applications, vol. 2, pp. 325–355. Spring (1979)
3. Lichtenberg, F.R.: Issues in measuring industrial R&D. Research Policy, 157–163 (1990)
4. Charnes, A., Cooper, W.W., Rhodes, E.: Measuring the efficiency of decision making units. European Journal of Operational Research, 429–444 (February 1978)
5. Coooper, W.W., Tone, K.: Measures of inefficiency in data envelopment analysis and stochastic frontier estimation. European Journal of Operational Research, 72–78 (February 1997)
6. Junxia, W., Jiancheng, G.: The application of composition DEA method in measuring the performance of knowledge management of enterprise. Studies in Science of Science, 84–88 (2002) (in Chinese)
7. Xiaoqun, H.: The Methods of Modern Statistics Analysis. Press of Renming University of China, Beijing (1998) (in Chinese)
8. Savoy, J.: Statistical inference in retrieval effectiveness evaluation. Information Processing and Management 33, 495–512 (1997)
9. Torkel, W.J.: Quality of research measured by citation method and by peer review-a comparison. IEEE Trans on Engineering Management 4, 218–222 (1986)
10. Saaty, T.L.: Fundamentals of Decision Making and Priority Theory with the Analytic Hierarchy Process, pp. 35–127. RWS Publications, Princeton (1994)
11. Schen, K.S.: Avoiding rank reversal in AHP decision-support models. European Journal of Operational, 36–38 (March 1998)
12. Carrettoni, F., Castano, S., et al.: RETISS: A real time security system for threat detection using fuzzy logic. In: Proceedings of 25th IEEE International Carnahan Conference on Security Technology, pp. 247–269. Taipei (1991)
13. Chen, S.J., Hwang, C.L.: Fuzzy Multiple Attribute Decision Making, pp. 163–287. Springer Press (1992)

14. Guohong, C.: Fuzzy mode identification in R&D project termination. Studies in Science of Science 16, 68–74 (1998) (in Chinese)
15. Dimitras, A.I., Slowinski, R., Susmaga, R., et al.: Business failure prediction using rough sets. European Journal of Operational Research 95, 24–37 (1999)
16. Grabowski, M.R., Wallace, W.A.: An expert system for maritime pilots: Its design and assessment using gaming. Management Science 3, 1506–1520 (1993)
17. Fan, Z., Zhang, Q., Ma, J.: An integration weight determine method of multiple attribute decision making. Journal of Management 1, 50–53 (1998) (in Chinese)
18. Wang, Y.: Multiple attribute decision making and sorting with maximizing deviations method. China Soft Science, 36–38 (1998) (in Chinese)
19. Wang, M.: Weight coefficient to determine the deviation and mean square deviation decision method in multi-index evaluation. China Soft Science, 100–103 (1999) (in Chinese)
20. Fan, Z., Zhao, X.: The subjective and objective method in multiple attribute decision making. Decision Making and Decision Support System 7, 87–91 (1997) (in Chinese)
21. Mei, C., Fan, J.: Data Analysis Method. Higher Education Press, Beijing (2006) (in Chinese)
22. Guo, Y., Zhong, T.: The report of Chinese regional innovation capacity of 2011- Study of regional innovation system in the Pearl River Delta. Science Press, Beijing (2011)

Comparative Studies between the Regional Economic Growth Levels Based on the Three-Stage Weight Dynamic Comprehensive Evaluation

Jing An, Yanru Qi, and Yun Liu

Beijing Institute of Technology
anjing@tobacco.gov.cn, yrqits@163.com

Abstract. This paper proposes a dynamic comprehensive evaluation method based on three times weight. Firstly, this paper determines the index weight based on the twice stage difference driving features. Then it introduces the relative balance coefficient to calculate the comprehensive evaluation value. This method has the following characteristics: 1) The comprehensive evaluation result is totally based on the information provided by the evaluating indicator system, without the influence from subjective factors; 2) The results have direct comparability among different evaluation systems at each time; 3) Motivation or punishment are the characteristics of this method. This approach has been applied to an empirical study of the regional economic growth level during the years of 2001 and 2011. Finally this paper makes related suggestions to the economic development of eight domestic economic regions.

Keywords: Twice stage difference features, Relative balance coefficient, Three times weight, Dynamic comprehensive evaluation, Regional economic growth.

1 Introduction

The economic development level of every region in China is in disequilibrium because there are variously economic and social differences in the growth rate and configuration mode of the production factors. For the issues above, the government has significantly improved the economic development levels of western and northeastern China, by refining and adjusting the regional development strategies like western development, Revitalizing old industrial base of northeastern China. But comparing with the other regions, there is still a great advantage in the developed regions of eastern and middle China because of their strong economic base. And the differences are still very obvious if we talk about the specific provinces, cities and autonomous regions. Comprehensive evaluation, analysis and comparison on the economic development levels of each region in China are of great significance to enhance the Macro-control and promote the coordinated development of national economy.

The domestic research about regional economic development is primarily in the 20th century, 90 years later. Most of the scholars adopt various statistics techniques to analysis the difference change law of regional economic [1-3]; DEA was used for evaluating the difference of regional economic development of 12 cities in Liaoning by

K. Liu et al. (Eds.): ICISO 2014, IFIP AICT 426, pp. 302–311, 2014.

liangjian and mojianfang [4-6]; Yangzhuxin put forward those who be based on the collect bisect analyze to be able to evaluate the economic development of Bohai sea [6]. Yuebing proposed a uniform approximation comprehensive evaluation method to estimate the level of economic development of 12 provinces and cities of china [7]. Existing research focus on difference analysis on regional economic development, there is little research that is directed to the change of regional economic development level for a period of time, For this reason the paper establish a set of complete scientific and comprehensive system of evaluation indicators, and proposes a dynamic comprehensive evaluation method based on three times weight, and then compared the economic development of 31 provinces, autonomous regions and municipalities during the years of 2001 and 2011, finally, the paper ranked the cities according to their economic development level.

2   Index Selection

In according with the principle of systematic and comprehensive, reliability and easy to operate, an evaluation index system, which contains seven indexes, was established as shown in table 1:

Table 1. Evaluation index system

Index code	Index	Unit
x1	Regional GDP	Million Yuan
x2	Regional Add Value of the Tertiary Industry	Billion Yuan
x3	Per-capita Disposable Income of Urban Residents	Yuan/person
x4	Per-capita Disposable Income of Rural Residents	Yuan/person
x5	Region Tax Revenue	Billion Yuan
x6	Foreign Trade	Billion Yuan
x7	Social Productivity (region GDP/region employed person)	Billion Yuan/ Million Person

We choose 2387 data series during the year of 2001 and 2011, all the data from "china statistical yearbook".

3   A Dynamic Comprehensive Evaluation Method based on Three Times Weight

In the real world, data series which own large amount of data according to the order of time like a data cartridge, we call it multi-dimensional time series [8-9], Dynamic comprehensive evaluation is a problem base on multi-dimensional time series, it generally denoted as:

$$y_i(t_k) = f(\omega_1(t_k), \omega_2(t_k), \cdots, \omega_m(t_k); x_{i1}(t_k), x_{i2}(t_k), \cdots, x_{im}(t_k)), (k = 1, 2, \cdots, N) \tag{1}$$

$y_i(t_k)$ is the comprehensive evaluation value of system s_i at the time of t_k.

The paper proposed a dynamic comprehensive evaluation method based on three times weight, the method follow the principle of greatest extends reflects the difference between the object as described in the following procedure:

3.1   The Weight Determination Process Based on the Twice Variance Drive

a) Handling dimensionless. Without loss of generality, assume the index of index set $x_1, x_2, \cdots, x_m$ are all extra-large, in order to combat the effects of different dimension and different type, need carry out the dimensionless treatment with the data as below:

$$x'_{ij}(t_k) = \frac{x_{ij}(t_k) - x_{ij}^{min}(t_k)}{x_{ij}^{max}(t_k) - x_{ij}^{min}(t_k)} (i=1,2,\cdots,n; j=1,2,\cdots,m; k=1,2,\cdots,r) \tag{2}$$

b) Determine the weight coefficients ω_{jk} of each year by using mean square error. The basic principle of this method is the weight coefficient depend on the relative dispersion degree of the evaluation object, the greater the dispersion degree of index values, the greater the weight coefficient [10]. Therefore, the method reflects the importance of index by using mean square error, operation step as fellows:

$$\omega_{jk} = \frac{R(X_j(t_k))}{\sum\limits_{j=1}^{m} R(X_j(t_k))} \tag{3}$$

c) Determine the weight coefficient w_j: If there were obvious difference between the index value of the x_j at moment t_k and the index value of the other moment, the weight at same time should play a biggish role in the process of evaluation in order to expose this difference. The fluctuant circumstance of index x_j at moment $t_k(k=1,2,L,N)$ can be boiled down to a formula:

$$\theta_{jk} = \frac{\sum\limits_{s \neq k} \cos\langle x_j(t_k), x_j(t_s)\rangle}{N-1} \tag{4}$$

The bigger the θ_{jk}, the index value at moment $t_k(k=1,2,L,N)$ closer to the index at other time, and the moment play a small role in the whole evaluation process, so the overall weight of the index x_j can be expressed as:

$$\omega_j = \frac{\sum\limits_{k=1}^{N} \frac{1}{\theta_{jk}} \cdot \omega_{jk}}{\sum\limits_{j=1}^{m}\sum\limits_{k=1}^{N} \frac{1}{\theta_{jk}} \cdot \omega_{jk}} \tag{5}$$

The ω_j as a final weight value of index, the bigger the ω_j, the greater index influence, but rather the contrary.

3.2   Result Based on the Three Stage Weight Dynamic Comprehensive Evaluation

When analyze the overall situation of s_i, we expect the comprehensive evaluation value in the period of $[t_1, t_N]$ of the bigger the better [11], but the fluctuation of s_i in this period as small as possible.

a) Determine the synthetic evaluation indexes by using method based on twice-weighted. To determined the weight by using the method shows above, and built a synthesizing evaluation function at some point such as $t_k(k = 1, 2, \cdots, N)$:

$$y_i(t_k) = \sum_{j=1}^{m} \omega_j \cdot x_{ij}(t_k), k = 1, 2, \cdots, N; i = 1, 2, \cdots n \tag{6}$$

The comprehensive evaluation value, is calculated from the above formula has direct comparability. s_i has different 'performance' in different moment. During the study process on the execution status of the entire system, in order to embody the thinking about thick thin now thou and emphasize the differences between different moments, the comprehensive evaluation index is defined as [8]

$$h_i = \sum_{k=1}^{N} \exp\{\lambda t_k\} \cdot y_i(t_k), i = 1, 2, \cdots, n \tag{7}$$

λ is the time discount factor. In order to avoid the randomness of λ value, it is defined that $\lambda = (2N)^{-1}$

b) Introduce the 'relatively balanced coefficient' to implement triple weighting. In the calculation process of comprehensive evaluation index, the situation like $h_i = h_j (i \neq j)$ may happened because of the appearance of complementary. At this stage, the paper using the reciprocal of the coefficient of variation to describe the balance of the system:

$$JH^*_i = n \cdot \frac{JH_i}{\sum_{i=1}^{n} JH_i} \tag{8}$$

$$JH_i = \begin{cases} \dfrac{h_i}{s_i}, (s_i \neq 0) \\ \max\{JH_d\} + c, (s_i = 0; s_d \neq 0) \end{cases} , (i = 1, 2, \cdots, n)$$

$$h_i = \frac{1}{N} \sum_{k=1}^{N} h_{ik}$$

$$s_i = \sqrt{\frac{\sum_{k=1}^{N} (h_{ik} - h_i)^2}{N-1}} \tag{9}$$

Formula 8/9 shows that the bigger JH_i, the smaller fluctuation of the system value, which means the system development is more balanced. Otherwise, the bigger fluctuation means the development is more imbalanced. We should increase the comprehensive evaluation value in some extent to encourage the system, which developed balanced. While for the system of lopsided development, we need to reduce their comprehensive evaluation value for punishment.

c) An evaluation model based on relatively balanced coefficient. On the basis of getting relatively balanced coefficient, we make the aggregation once more:

$$h_i^* = (\lambda_1 + \lambda_2 \cdot JH_i^*) \cdot h_i \tag{10}$$

$$\lambda_1 + \lambda_2 = 1$$

$$\lambda_2 = \frac{\sum_{i=1}^{n} \left| JH_i^* - 1 \right| \cdot h_i}{\sum_{i=1}^{n} h_i} \tag{11}$$

The s_i is sorted from big to small according to the value of h_i^*. The sorting result reflects both the comprehensive evaluation result in each year. And meanwhile, the comprehensive evaluation result given from this method is completely based on the information provided by evaluation indexes.

4   Instance

4.1   The Weight Determination Process Based on the Twice Variance Drive

To determine the weight for each economic index from the 31 provinces, cities and autonomous regions from 2001-2011, we further discuss the change degree of the development trends from each economic index between different years (see table 2).

Table 2a. The calculations of index weights and change degree

| | The Economic Index Weight of 2001-2011 | | | | | | |
	X1	X2	X3	X4	X5	X6	X7
2001	0.167	0.130	0.134	0.137	0.139	0.164	0.129
2002	0.173	0.124	0.113	0.144	0.142	0.169	0.136
2003	0.164	0.127	0.136	0.140	0.135	0.169	0.129
2004	0.164	0.130	0.128	0.148	0.134	0.170	0.128
2005	0.169	0.125	0.126	0.156	0.134	0.162	0.128
2006	0.149	0.128	0.145	0.157	0.136	0.149	0.136
2007	0.150	0.131	0.141	0.154	0.137	0.151	0.136
2008	0.149	0.134	0.134	0.156	0.137	0.157	0.133
2009	0.153	0.136	0.124	0.155	0.140	0.158	0.133
2010	0.149	0.135	0.130	0.153	0.139	0.157	0.138
2011	0.148	0.143	0.129	0.149	0.141	0.153	0.136

Table 2b. The calculateions of index weights and change degree - The Average Cosine Value

	X1	X2	X3	X4	X5	X6	X7
2001	0.995	0.970	0.963	0.983	0.996	0.967	0.983
2002	0.996	0.978	0.963	0.990	0.997	0.968	0.985
2003	0.997	0.983	0.933	0.993	0.998	0.973	0.989
2004	0.997	0.984	0.962	0.995	0.998	0.976	0.991
2005	0.997	0.983	0.965	0.994	0.998	0.980	0.991
2006	0.997	0.985	0.953	0.994	0.998	0.982	0.991
2007	0.997	0.985	0.961	0.995	0.998	0.983	0.992
2008	0.997	0.983	0.968	0.995	0.998	0.981	0.992
2009	0.997	0.981	0.954	0.994	0.998	0.974	0.990
2010	0.996	0.981	0.968	0.993	0.997	0.965	0.985
2011	0.996	0.975	0.968	0.990	0.995	0.959	0.983

Based on the basic principle of twice variance drive, this paper reduces the economic indicator weights with the same development trends and increases the indicator weights of those with big changes. These paper determines the comprehensive weights for each kind of economic indicators like that shown in next table:

Table 3. Comprehensive weight values of every kind of economic indicators

	X1	X2	X3	X4	X5	X6	X7
Weight	0.1558	0.1314	0.1342	0.1487	0.1358	0.1616	0.1324

The comprehensive evaluation values of each region from 2000 to 2010 are calculated by using linear weighted comprehensive method. The value is shown in table 4.

4.2   Introduce the Relatively Balanced Coefficient to Make Triple Weighting

Considering the fluctuation status of each province, city and autonomous region from 2001 to 2011, we calculate the relatively balanced coefficient and the overall evaluation. The ranking of overall evaluation values are shown in table 5:

5   Research Findings and Policy recommendations

As the overall evaluation result, the economic developments among the eastern, central and western China are very imbalanced. The developed areas mainly concentrate in eastern area while the undeveloped areas mainly concentrate in the western area. All of the provinces, cities and autonomous regions with top 10 economic development level are from the eastern area. On the contrary, 8 of the 12 regions from western area are in

Table 4. Comprehensive evaluation of economic development in each region (2001-2011)

Regions	2001	2002	2003	2004	2005	2006	2007	2008	2009	2010	2011
Beijing	0.44	0.46	0.47	0.47	0.47	0.53	0.52	0.53	0.51	0.51	0.53
Tianjin	0.29	0.31	0.3	0.31	0.31	0.3	0.31	0.31	0.33	0.35	0.37
Hebei	0.32	0.32	0.31	0.3	0.31	0.28	0.29	0.3	0.32	0.31	0.32
Shanxi	0.12	0.11	0.12	0.13	0.14	0.15	0.15	0.16	0.18	0.17	0.18
Inner Mongolia	0.11	0.11	0.13	0.15	0.16	0.17	0.2	0.22	0.25	0.27	0.28
Liaoning	0.36	0.36	0.35	0.32	0.32	0.32	0.32	0.34	0.38	0.37	0.41
Jilin	0.16	0.17	0.16	0.16	0.16	0.14	0.16	0.18	0.2	0.2	0.2
Heilongjiang	0.23	0.24	0.23	0.22	0.21	0.17	0.16	0.17	0.19	0.18	0.19
Shanghai	0.73	0.72	0.73	0.73	0.74	0.72	0.7	0.7	0.69	0.68	0.66
Jiangsu	0.56	0.56	0.58	0.6	0.62	0.6	0.62	0.65	0.67	0.68	0.71
Zhejiang	0.51	0.54	0.57	0.6	0.58	0.57	0.57	0.56	0.54	0.53	0.56
Anhui	0.2	0.2	0.19	0.18	0.18	0.16	0.17	0.19	0.21	0.21	0.23
Fujian	0.35	0.34	0.32	0.31	0.31	0.26	0.27	0.29	0.31	0.29	0.31
Jiangxi	0.14	0.14	0.14	0.14	0.15	0.14	0.14	0.14	0.16	0.16	0.18
Shandong	0.53	0.52	0.53	0.55	0.57	0.55	0.57	0.56	0.59	0.58	0.59
Henan	0.27	0.27	0.27	0.27	0.28	0.27	0.29	0.3	0.33	0.32	0.33
Hubei	0.28	0.28	0.28	0.26	0.24	0.2	0.21	0.23	0.25	0.24	0.26
Hunan	0.24	0.23	0.23	0.21	0.22	0.21	0.21	0.22	0.24	0.24	0.25
Guangdong	0.78	0.76	0.76	0.73	0.72	0.73	0.72	0.72	0.72	0.71	0.71
Guangxi	0.14	0.14	0.14	0.13	0.13	0.12	0.13	0.13	0.16	0.15	0.16
Hainan	0.09	0.09	0.08	0.08	0.07	0.06	0.06	0.06	0.08	0.06	0.07
Chongqing	0.17	0.14	0.15	0.15	0.15	0.13	0.13	0.14	0.19	0.16	0.17
Sichuan	0.24	0.26	0.26	0.25	0.24	0.22	0.22	0.24	0.26	0.27	0.29
Guizhou	0.07	0.07	0.06	0.06	0.06	0.06	0.06	0.07	0.08	0.07	0.08
Yunnan	0.17	0.14	0.14	0.13	0.14	0.12	0.12	0.12	0.13	0.13	0.14
Tibet	0.03	0.03	0.1	0.06	0.06	0.04	0.02	0.02	0.02	0.01	0.01
Shaanxi	0.13	0.13	0.13	0.13	0.13	0.13	0.14	0.15	0.18	0.18	0.2
Gansu	0.08	0.08	0.07	0.06	0.06	0.06	0.06	0.07	0.08	0.07	0.07
Qinghai	0.04	0.05	0.05	0.05	0.05	0.03	0.04	0.04	0.06	0.05	0.06
Ningxia	0.04	0.05	0.04	0.04	0.05	0.05	0.06	0.06	0.09	0.08	0.09
Xinjiang	0.14	0.14	0.14	0.13	0.12	0.11	0.11	0.11	0.13	0.11	0.13

the last 10 places. The other 4 regions are Inner Mongolia, Sichuan, Yunnan and Xinjiang, whose ranks are also in the backward places 18th, 13th, 19th and 20th respectively. For the 11 years development, the economic development level of Jiangsu province is always ranked at the 3rd place. The economic development level of Beijing city is always ranked at the 6th place. The economic development level of Liaoning province is always ranked at the 7th. The sequences of Tianjin, Inner Mongolia, Henan and Sichuan are stably rising up. In addition to Inner Mongolia, the rising rates of the other regions are very small. Besides, the changes of the regional economic status in China have the character like 'rigid body translation'. So it is very difficult to break the existed economic pattern because of the forming from a lot of years.

Table 5. The sorting result of the dynamic comprehensive evaluation result for each region's

Regions	Relatively Balanced Coefficient	Evaluation Value	Rank Results
Beijing	0.950678	0.647108	6
Tianjin	0.863093	0.401213	10
Hebei	1.226271	0.431684	9
Shanxi	0.615723	0.170316	25
Inner Mongolia	0.407585	0.206644	18
Liaoning	0.919504	0.448882	8
Jilin	0.759644	0.208418	17
Heilongjiang	1.737191	0.310575	14
Shanghai	1.645028	1.109446	2
Jiangsu	0.847437	0.791767	4
Zhejiang	1.278549	0.792838	3
Anhui	0.819529	0.236511	16
Fujian	1.496676	0.456686	7
Jiangxi	0.764263	0.177665	22
Shandong	1.014575	0.743778	5
Henan	0.844111	0.366211	11
Hubei	1.302635	0.351772	12
Hunan	1.017027	0.297138	15
Guangdong	1.56975	1.125752	1
Guangxi	0.851985	0.173828	23
Hainan	1.314329	0.098503	26
Chongqing	0.82172	0.185603	21
Sichuan	0.93464	0.321178	13
Guizhou	0.776897	0.078473	28
Yunnan	1.537235	0.198961	19
Tibet	0.251214	0.031996	31
Shaanxi	0.580093	0.170543	24
Gansu	1.107278	0.088641	27
Qinghai	0.64729	0.052347	30
Ningxia	0.422798	0.061456	29
Xinjiang	1.675251	0.19069	20

The southeast coastal area of China consists of Guangdong, Fujian and Hainan provinces. Unlike the development of eastern coastal area, the economic development of this area is very imbalanced. The comprehensive ranking of Guangdong province is No.1 while the ranking of Hainan province is only 26. So for these 2 backward provinces, especially for Hainan province, the major issue is how to utilize the overseas social resources and high-level openness from its neighbors Hongkong, Macao and Taiwan to accelerate the economic development.

The northern coastal area of China consists of 2 provinces (Hebei and Shandong) and 2 cities (Beijing and Tianjin). These 4 cities and provinces are always in steady development status (maximum ranking difference) during the 11 years. And finally, their comprehensive evaluation values are respectively ranked at the 6th, the 10th, the 9th and the 5th. This area should continue to utilize their superior geographical location, convenient transportation and developed technology, education and cultural undertakings, in order that, it can enlarge its opening to the outside world and seek progress in stability.

The middle reaches of the Yellow River in China consists of 3 provinces and 1 autonomous region, which are Shanxi, Shanxi, Henan and Inner Mongolia. It shows that the economic development levels of these 4 areas are improved year by year in this 11 years. Especially, the economic development level of Inner Mongolia has risen to the 13th in 2010 comparing with its 25th position in 2000. In these 4 regions, the economic development mainly relies on their rich natural resources. So, accelerating the steps to open to the outside world and adjust the economic structure become the major problem without any delay. And meanwhile, Shanxi, Shanxi and Henan provinces could take the development model of Inner Mongolia as reference to promote their big progress in economic development.

The middle reaches of the Yangtze River in China consist of Hubei, Hunan, Jiangxi and Anhui provinces, whose comprehensive ranking are in lower locations. This region should vigorously develop its agricultural production, increase the degree of opening to the outside world and accelerate industry transformation. Besides, because of the large population of this region, the effective improvement of per capita economic level is also the major task in its development.

The northeastern China consists of 3 provinces, which are Liaoning, Jilin and Heilongjiang. The major issues this region faces are resources depletion and the urgent requirement of industrial structure upgrading. So this region should increase the proportion of gross product from the non-public economics and the small and medium-sized business, speed up the technological progress and improve its capacity for independent innovation, consolidate the foundation position of agriculture, improve the resource utilization, promote the foreign economic cooperation and improve the usage quality of foreign investment. During the development progress, Jilin and Heilongjiang provinces could take the development process of Liaoning province as reference. They should deepen the collaboration between provinces and promote the integration development of regional economy.

Besides, the southwestern and northwestern China consists of 5 provinces and 1 city. Because of the historical existence and excessive enlargement of the development gap with eastern region, 90% of the regional economic development in this area belongs to underdeveloped region. The problems of this region such as remote location, poor soils, bad natural conditions and large number of poor people make the western region construction as a long and difficult task. The western development provides a series of policy guarantees and funding for the economic development of western China. So we must insist carrying out the western development strategy, accelerate the infrastructure construction, strengthen the ecological protection, positively adjust the industrial structure, develop the technology and education and accelerate the talent development. Under the premise of our country's stable increase in financial resources, our country should gradually increase the support on western region and fully encourage western region's initiatives, to push on the economic development of western region with specific target and phases.

References

1. Chen, L.: Analysis the Levels of Development of the East. Science & Technology Information 21, 645–646 (2008)
2. Feng, L., Jianhua, X.: Exploratory Spatial Data Analysis of the Regional Economc Disparities in China. Journal of East China Normal University (Natural Science) 2, 44–51 (2007)

3. Shidai, W., Qiang, W.: Regional Economic Disparities and Coordination of Economic Development in Coastal Areas of Southeastern China. ACTA Geographic Sinica 63(2), 123–134 (2008)
4. Jie, L., Yan, L., Yapeng, J.: The analysis of Regional Disparities Economic Development Based on DEA. Communication of Finance and Accounting (5), 119–122 (2010)
5. Jianfang, M., Shiqi, Y.: The Application of DEA Method for Evaluating the Development of Region Economics. Systems Engineering 19(2), 18–21 (2001)
6. Zhuxin, Y.: Research on the Comprehensive Evaluation of Development of Economic Zone Ability Based on Set Pair Analysis-Around The Bohai Sea. Mathematics in Practice and Theory 39(2), 10–17 (2009)
7. Bing, Y., Hongjuan, F., Xuemei, W.: Study on the Comprehensive Evaluation Method of the Economic Development Level in China Areas. Journal of Tianjin University Science and Technology 36(6), 725–729 (2000)
8. Yajun, G.: Comprehensive Evaluation: Theory, Methods and Applications. Science Press, Beijin (2007)
9. Xuesen, Q.: A New Discipline of Scienci—The Study of Open Complex Giant System and Its Methodology. Urban Studies (1), 3–10 (1990)
10. Yajun, G.: Method of Dynamic Comprehensive Evaluation Based on Twice Driving. Journal of Northeastern University 15(5), 547–550 (1995)
11. Wang, Y.: Multiple attribute decision making and sorting with maximizing deviations method. China Soft Science (3), 36–38 (1998) (in Chinese)
12. Wang, M.: Weight coefficient to determine the deviation and mean square deviation decision method in multi-index evaluation. China Soft Science (8), 100–103 (1999) (in Chinese)

Competitive and Cooperative Degree in Supply Chain: Supplier Selection between Competitors and Third-Party Suppliers

Bo Xie[1], Xianjia Wang[1], and Chuan Zhou[2]

[1] Wuhan University, Economics and Management School, 430072 Wuhan, China
xie040304@gmail.com
[2] Chian Unicom, 471001 Luoyang, China
bo6193@163.com

Abstract. This work explores the firm's supplier selection question that the competitor firm and the third-party supplier can supply the substitutable component. We consider a supply chain with two competing original equipment manufacturers (OEMs) and two third-party suppliers. The two OEMs produce the competing products which are comprised by two main components. Each OEM only can produce one component in-house and each third-party supplier only supplies one component. The OEMs must decide whether to outsource the other component to the competing OEM or to a third-party supplier. We discuss the different supplier selection strategies and compare the OEMs profits in different decision. We find that there are conditions where, while one of the OEMs should outsource to the competing firm, outsourcing to a third-party supplier is the optimal strategy for the other OEM even when the cost of the third-party supplier is more expensive and the competition is intense.

Keywords: Outsourcing selection, Co-opetition, Price competition.

1   Introduction

Competitors Nissan and Daimler's Mercedes are both outsourcees and outsourcers of one another. In particular, Nissan uses Daimler's Mercedes front-wheel-drive architecture platform for its Infiniti luxury vehicle and supplies Daimler with diesel and gas engines [1]. Moreover, Samsung and Google, Leica and Panasonic also compete with the end product in the market and supply the component to each other in the component wholesale market [2] [3]. We call this relationship is co-opetition. The previous research literature (e.g., [4] [5] [6]) has researched the co-opetition problem about the competing firms and points out that the competitor can earn revenue from both competing products with two firms cooperation. Consequently, the competitor will not price its own product aggressively, thus leading to a lower degree of competition.

In this paper, we consider the supplier-selection problem of two competing OEMs. The OEMs can produce one component in-house and must outsource the other component to a third-party supplier or to the competing OEM. We consider the case

K. Liu et al. (Eds.): ICISO 2014, IFIP AICT 426, pp. 312–319, 2014.
© IFIP International Federation for Information Processing 2014

where competing OEMs will cooperate as supply-chain partners only if their total profit is higher than that they can get if they do not cooperate.

2   Literature Review

Our work in this paper relates to the stream of research on the topic of forming a supply-chain relationship with competitors. Bengtsson and Kock [7] define the co-opetition as a strategy embodying simultaneous cooperation and competition between firms. Gnyawali and Park [8] investigate why and how co-opetition between large firms and impact the participating firms and the industry. Venkatesh et al. [4] find that the manufacturers of proprietary component brands often have the ability to effect for the end-products and face to choose its role from sole entrant, co-optor and component supplier in the market. Lim and Tan [9] focus on the outsourcing of the supplier as a direct competitor of the buyer firm in the downstream marketplace. Wang et al. [6] investigate the advantage of being the first mover when a contract manufacturer acts as both supplier and competitor. Moreover, Pun [10] considers the supplier selection of a manufacturer can either outsource to an independent supplier or to its competitor when the firm wants to do R&D for the end-product.

Our paper differs from these papers in the following ways: First, we assume that there are two OEMs competing in the market and each of them can supply the component with its brand. Second, in our paper, we assume that there is price competition for the OEMs in the market. The OEM's decision about the outsourcing will have impact for total profit. To the best of our knowledge, the case that the competing OEMs supply the component to each other is a new type in supply chain.

3   Model Framework

We consider a supply chain with two OEMs (firms G and S) and two third-party suppliers and each OEM sales a competing product. And each product consists of two main components, A and B. Firm G (firm S) produces component A (component B) in-house and must outsource component B (component A) either to a third-party supplier firm B (firm A) or to the competing OEM firm S (firm G). The basic frame work of the model is similar to that in Pun and Bo [11]. The OEM and the third-party supplier each produce the component with different costs. Specifically, the production cost of the OEMs is normalized to zero, and the production cost of the third-party suppliers is Δc, so that the third-party suppliers have higher production cost when $\Delta c > 0$ and the OEMs have higher production cost when $\Delta c < 0$. We use the demand model presented by McGuire and Staelin [12] and Staelin [13]. Specifically, the demand of the end-product of firm $i \in \{G, S\}$ is as follows:

$$D_i = 1 - \frac{1}{1-\theta} p_i + \frac{\theta}{1-\theta} p_{\bar{i}} \tag{1}$$

$\bar{i}$ is the competitor of firm i and pi is the price of product i. $0 \le \theta < 1$ is the degree of competition between the two products, so that the two products are not competing when θ is zero and competition increases in θ.

In this game, the two OEMs first choose the outsourcing strategy. Then, as commonly assumed in the literature (e.g. [14] [15] [16]), the suppliers set the wholesale price w simultaneously. Lastly, the two competing OEMs choose the retail price p. The OEM can choose to outsource to the competing OEM or to the third-party supplier. We use the abbreviations T and C (Third-party supplier and Competing OEM) to denote the different suppliers and the first letter to denote the component supplier for firm G and the second letter for firm S. As a result, we will get four strategies as {TT, TC, CT, CC}, where TT denotes that firm G outsources to the third-party supplier and firm S outsources to the third-party supplier. Since strategy TC and strategy CT are symmetrical, without loss of generality, we omit the results of strategy CT to avoid redundancy.

Table 1. The profits of firms in different strategies

Firm	Strategy TT	Strategy TC	Strategy CC
G (OEM)	$(p_G - w_B)D_G$	$(p_G - w_B)D_G + w_G D_S$	$(p_G - w_S)D_G + w_G D_S$
S (OEM)	$(p_S - w_A)D_S$	$(p_S - w_G)D_S$	$(p_S - w_G)D_S + w_S D_G$
A (3rd-party)	$(w_A - \Delta c)D_S$	0	0
B (3rd-party)	$(w_B - \Delta c)D_G$	$(w_B - \Delta c)D_G$	0

In the next analysis, we will use π_G and π_S to represent the profits of the two OEMs. And we use superscripts to denote the outsourcing strategy. For example, π_S^{TC} represents the profit of firm S under strategy TC. Specifically, firm G and firm S will cooperate (strategy TC or CC) only if they can earn higher total profits than they do under strategy TT. For notational convenience, let the total profit of the two firms be $\pi_{GS} = \pi_G + \pi_S$. Then the two competing OEMs will choose the strategy that gives them the largest total profit.

4   Analysis

In this section, we will compare total profit and present the optimal outsourcing strategy. Throughout the analysis, we will focus on the region where demands of both products are positive. We consider another strategy that two OEMs both produce the two main components in-house and use π_{GS}^{II} as the total profit under this strategy. We will compare the total profit in the following and discuss the competition and cooperation.

Proposition 1. The comparisons of the total profit of the two OEMs are as follows.

 a. $\pi_{GS}^{II} > \pi_{GS}^{TT} \Leftrightarrow \Delta c > \Gamma_0(\theta)$,

 b. $\pi_{GS}^{II} > \pi_{GS}^{CC} \Leftrightarrow \theta < \sqrt{13} - 3$,

 c. $\pi_{GS}^{TT} < \pi_{GS}^{CC} \Leftrightarrow \Delta c > \Gamma_1(\theta)$,

 d. $\pi_{GS}^{TT} < \pi_{GS}^{TC} \Leftrightarrow \Delta c > \Gamma_2(\theta)$,

 e. $\pi_{GS}^{TC} < \pi_{GS}^{CC} \Leftrightarrow \Gamma_{3a}(\theta) < \Delta c < \Gamma_{3b}(\theta)$.

It has been shown that selling through third-party retailers can mitigate competition between competing manufacturers (e.g. [12]). Proposition 2a states that competition between OEMs can also be mitigated with outsourcing to the third-party suppliers. In particular, when the two products are independent ($\theta = 0$), the OEMs should produce both components in-house (strategy II) in order to eliminate the inefficiency of double marginalization unless the third-party supplier has a very low cost ($\Delta c < \Gamma_0(0) = -1$). It can be shown that $\Gamma_0(\theta)$ increases in θ. Consequently, when compared to strategy II, strategy TT becomes more valuable as competition intensifies since outsourcing to a third-party supplier can mitigate competition.

Since the third-party suppliers are not responsible for producing any of the components under strategies II and CC, the comparison of the total profit between these two strategies remains independent of Δc (cf. Proposition 2b). Two drivers in particular have an impact on the comparison between strategies II and CC. First, outsourcing to a competitor can minimize competition; second, producing all components in-house can eliminate the inefficiency of double marginalization. When all firms have the same production costs ($\Delta c = 0$), Proposition 2a shows that the advantage of mitigating competition by outsourcing to a third-party supplier is smaller than the inefficiency of double marginalization introduced by deploying strategy TT. Consequently, the total profit is larger under strategy II than it would be under strategy TT, regardless of the degree of competition. Proposition 2b extends the result of Proposition 2a by illustrating that, compared with outsourcing to a third-party supplier, outsourcing to a competitor is more effective in mitigating competition. In particular, when competition is sufficiently strong ($\theta > \sqrt{13} - 3$) and all firms have the same production costs ($\Delta c = 0$), the two OEMs are better off mitigating competition by deploying strategy CC than by deploying strategy II despite incurring the inefficiency of double marginalization.

Proposition 2c further illustrates that outsourcing to a competitor does a better job of mitigating competition compared to a strategy of outsourcing to a third-party supplier. Specifically, when the level of competition between the two products is intermediate (e.g., $\theta = 1/2$), then mitigating competition is marginally valuable, and the total profit under strategy CC is higher as long as the costs of the third-party suppliers are sufficiently high ($\Delta c > \Gamma_1(1/2) \approx -0.62$). When the level of competition is intense ($\theta \to 1$), mitigating competition becomes very important and, hence, strategy CC is always superior to strategy TT, even when the third-party suppliers costs are extremely low ($\Delta c > \lim_{\theta \to 1} \Gamma_1(\theta) = -\infty$). It can be shown that $\Gamma_2(0) = \Gamma_{3b}(0)$ (cf. Propositions 2d-e). Therefore, depending on the relative cost efficiency between the OEMs and the third-party suppliers, when there is no competition, the OEMs would choose between two options: both would outsource to one another or both would outsource to third-party suppliers. When there is no competition, the firms are never better off in deploying the asymmetric strategy (strategy TC). In the presence of competition, however, the comparisons of the total profit under strategies TT, TC and CC are not monotonic in the degree of cooperation between the two competing OEMs. Specifically, Proposition 2d shows that some degree of cooperation between competitors (strategy TC) is better than no cooperation (strategy TT) as long as the third-party suppliers' costs are larger than $\Gamma_2(\theta)$. As θ increases, $\Gamma_2(\theta)$ decreases, hence, a certain degree of cooperation (strategy TC) becomes relatively more valuable when compared to strategy TT because the third-party suppliers must be relatively more cost effective ($\Gamma_2(\theta)$ more negative) for strategy TT to be optimal. However, Proposition 2e demonstrates that maximum cooperation (strategy CC) is not always better than some cooperation (strategy TC). When the degree of competition is small, it can be shown that the total profit under maximum cooperation (strategy CC) is larger than what it would be under some degree of cooperation (strategy TC) as long as the third-party suppliers' costs are not too low ($\Delta c > \Gamma_{3a}(\theta)$ where $\Gamma_{3a}(\theta) < 0$). However when competition is strong, we find that π_{GS}^{TC} is larger than π_{GS}^{CC} when the OEMs' costs are similar to those of the third-party suppliers. Therefore, cases do exist where the total profit under strategy TC is larger than it would be under strategy CC in spite of the cost disadvantage of the third-party supplier ($\Delta c > 0$). We present the optimal strategy in Proposition 3. The outside region represents the cases in which no demand of both products is positive.

Proposition 2. The optimal outsourcing strategy is presented in Fig. 1.

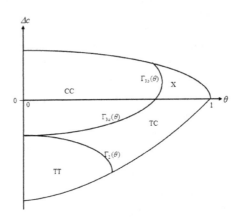

Fig. 1. Optimal outsourcing strategy

When being the outsourcee of the competitor (firm S), the OEM (firm G) can have two revenue sources: one from the wholesale market and the other from the end product market. Therefore, when there is no competition between the two competing products ($\theta = 0$), the two OEMs will outsource to one another (strategy CC). However, if the third-party supplier is significantly more cost effective ($\Delta c \ll 0$), they will outsource to the third-party supplier (strategy TT).

Previous research has shown that competitors cooperating as supply-chain partners can minimize competition. Therefore, one might expect that when competition intensifies (θ increases), the region where strategy CC is optimal will also increase because there is more cooperation under strategy CC than that of strategy TC. We find, however, that this insight might not hold. The total profit of both OEMs consists of two drivers. The first is the relative cost efficiency between the OEMs and the third-party suppliers Δc, and, numerically, we observe that this relative production cost has more impact to the total profit under strategy CC (π_{GS}^{CC}) than to the total profit under strategy TC (π_{GS}^{TC}). The other factor that affects the total profit is the degree of competition between the two products (θ). We find that the total profit under strategy TC is more likely to be larger than it would be under strategies TT and CC when θ is large (cf. Proposition 2). As a result, one of the firms can be better off outsourcing to the third-party supplier (strategy TC), even when the third-party supplier's production costs are higher than those of the competitor and when the competition is strong (cf. Point X in Fig. 1).

Next, we extend our results by altering some assumptions in the model. We assume the difference between third-party supplier and competing OEM is the quality of the components rather than the cost. Under this discussion, the basic framework of the model and the game sequence are similar to that in the previous discussion but the demand function is different. All firms have the same production costs ($\Delta c = 0$).

$$D_i = Q_i(N) - \frac{1}{1-\theta} p_i + \frac{\theta}{1-\theta} p_{\bar{i}}, \quad Q_i(N) = \begin{cases} \alpha & N = C \\ 1 & N = T \end{cases} \qquad (2)$$

The solution process in this section can be proved in the same way as in the previous solution, respectively, and thus the proofs are omitted for brevity. We just summarize the main findings here.

Proposition 3. The optimal outsourcing strategy is presented in Fig. 2 and is expressed mathematically as follows (where Λ, Γ and γ are threshold value).

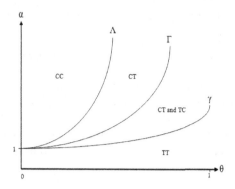

Fig. 2. Optimal Outsourcing Strategy for Different Quality

When $\alpha < \gamma$, the equilibrium strategy is that firm G and firm S both choose to outsource to the third-party suppliers so that they are just pure competitors in the market. It is because when α is small, outsource to the third-party supplier is better. When $1 < \alpha < \gamma$, outsourcing to the third-party supplier, OEM will also get the larger profit than outsourcing to the competitor. When $\Lambda < \alpha$, the best choice for both OEMs is outsourcing the ingredient to each other, even in this case OEMs could not price its product aggressively. When compared to the profit of OEMs under others strategies, it shows that both OEMs get the largest profit for outsourcing to each other (strategy CC).

And we consider the case where outsourcing to competitor, the OEM will get high quality end-product (i.e., $\alpha > 1$). In strategy CT, firm G will get the high quality end-product with outsourcing to firm S and firm S just outsources to the third-party supplier. The demands and the prices of firm G and firm S are better off with the increases of α simultaneously in strategy CT. We know when firm G outsources to the competitor firm S; it will manufacture the different quality end-product. With $\alpha > 1$, the quality of firm G's end-product is high. The high quality end-product brings the larger total market demand for firm G and therefore allows firm G to charge a higher price. Since firm G charges a higher price which has the positive impact on firm S's end-product demand even firm S's total market demand is unchanged. So the demand of firm S is also increasing and allows firm S to charge a higher price even its end-product's quality is lower than that of firm G. We also get that the increasing speed of price for firm G is faster than it for firm S (i.e., $\dfrac{\partial P_G^{CT}}{\partial \alpha} > \dfrac{\partial P_S^{CT}}{\partial \alpha}$). As a result, the demands and the prices for both OEMs are better off with α increasing in strategy CT (strategy TC).

Next, consider the case where outsourcing to competitor, the OEM will get low quality end-product (i.e., $\alpha < 1$). In strategy CT, firm G will get the low quality end-product with outsourcing to firm S. We know that the demands and the prices of firm G and firm S are better off with the increases of α simultaneously in strategy CT. With α increasing, the total market demand of firm G is increasing even which is less than that of firm S. The increasing total market demand allows firm G to charge a higher price. When firm G charges the higher price, firm S will get larger end-product demand since the price of firm G has the positive impact on firm S's demand and allowing firm S to charge a higher price. And we can know $\dfrac{\partial P_G^{CT}}{\partial \alpha} > \dfrac{\partial P_S^{CT}}{\partial \alpha}$. So we get the result that the demands and the prices for both OEMs are better off with α increasing in strategy CT even $\alpha < 1$. Similarly, in strategy TC, the demands and the prices of firm G and firm S are better off with the increasing of α simultaneously in strategy TC.

So we know that under strategy CT and strategy TC, the demand and the price of the both OEMs will increase consistently whether $\alpha > 1$ or $\alpha < 1$.

5   Conclusion

In this paper we talk about the outsourcing strategy of two OEMs. Because the cooperation between the competitors could reduce the competition, people think more cooperation is the better. But in the research, we find that since two OEMs have the price competition in the market, one OEM had better outsource to the third-party supplier even if the competitor OEM's production cost is lower. So the cooperation degree is important.

We research the supplier selection question with some limitations. First we assume that the information about the production cost is complete information. When the cost is private, we must think about the information sharing or information leakage question. Second, we study the market where the demand of the market is certain. If the demand is uncertain, the firm must think about the inventory problem and leftover problem. These will make the supply chain inefficient.

References

1. Nissan, C.L.: Daimler planners confer weekly on more deals. Automotive News 86(6512) (2012)
2. Marketing Weekly News. Panasonic introduces ultra-slim LUMIX digital cameras with 10x optical zoom and wide-angle Leica lens. Marketing Weekly News (January 2012)
3. Digital Life. Leica goes digital. Digital Life (February 2007)
4. Venkatesh, R., Chintagunta, P., Mahajan, V.: Research note-sole entrant, co-optor, or component supplier: optimal end-product strategies for manufactures of proprietary component brands. Management Science 52(4), 613–622 (2006)
5. Xu, Y., Gurnani, H., Desiraju, R.: Strategic supply chain structure design for proprietary component manufacturer. Production and Operations Management 19(4), 371–389 (2010)
6. Wang, Y., Niu, B., Guo, P.: On the advantage of quantity leadership when outsourcing production to a competitive contract manufacturer. Production and Operations Management 22(1), 104–119 (2013)
7. Bengtsson, M., Kock, S.: "Coopetition" in business networks-to cooperate and compete. Industrial Marketing Management (29), 411–426 (2000)
8. Gnyawali, D.R., Park, B.J.: Co-opetition between giants: Collaboration with competitors for technological innovation. Research Policy 40(2011), 650–663 (2011)
9. Lim, W.S., Tan, S.J.: Outsourcing suppliers as downstream competitors: biting the hand that feeds. European Journal of Operational Research 203(2), 360–369 (2010)
10. Pun, H.: Supplier selection when the production process can be improved. Working Paper
11. Pun, H., Bo, X.: The more the better? Optimal degree of supply-chain cooperation between competitors. Working Paper (2013)
12. McGuire, T., Staelin, R.: An industry equilibrium analysis of downstream vertical integration. Marketing Science 2(2), 161–191 (1983)
13. Staelin, R.: Commentary - an industry equilibrium analysis of downstream vertical integration: Twenty-five years later. Marketing Science 27(1), 111–114 (2008)
14. Gerchak, Y., Wang, Y.Z.: Revenue-sharing vs. wholesale-price contracts in assembly systems with random demand. Production and Operations Management 13(1), 23–33 (2004)
15. Granot, D., Yin, S.Y.: Competition and cooperation in decentralized push and pull assembly systems. Management Science 54(4), 733–747 (2008)
16. Nagarajan, M., Sosic, G.: Coalition stability in assembly models. Operations Research 57(1), 131–145 (2009)

A Multi-attribute Collaborative Filtering Recommendation Algorithm Based on Improved Group Decision-Making

Changrui Yu[1], Yan Luo[2], and Kecheng Liu[1,3]

[1] School of Information Management and Engineering, Shanghai University of Finance and Economics, Shanghai 200433, China
yucr@sjtu.edu.cn
[2] The Sydney Institute of Language and Commerce,Shanghai University, 20 Chengzhong RD, Shanghai 201800, China
luoyan@shu.edu.cn
[3] Informatics Research Centre, Henley BusinessSchool, University of Reading, Reading, RG6 3XA, U.K.
k.liu@reading.ac.uk

Abstract. The paper builds an evaluation model of user interest based on resource multi-attributes, proposes a modified Pearson-Compatibility multi-attribute group decision-making algorithm, and introduces the algorithm to solve the recommendation problem of k-neighbor similar users. Considering the characteristics of collaborative filtering recommendation, the paper addresses the issues on the preference differences of similar users, incomplete values, and advanced converge of the algorithm. Thus the paper realizes multi-attribute collaborative filtering. Finally, the effectiveness of the algorithm is proved by an experiment of collaborative recommendation among multi-users based on virtual environment.

Keywords: Personalized recommendation, Pearson-Compatibility, Group decision-making, Multi-attribute, Collaborative filtering.

1 Introduction

The goal of a recommender system is to generate meaningful recommendations to users for items or products that might interest them [1]. In many markets, consumers are faced with a wealth of products and information from which they can choose. To alleviate this problem, many web sites attempt to help users by incorporating a recommender system that provides users with a list of items and/or web pages that are likely to interest them. There are real-world operations of industry strength recommender systems, for example the recommendations for books on Amazon, or movies on Netflix, and so forth.

As one of the most successful approaches to building recommender systems, collaborative filtering (CF) uses the known preferences of a group of users to make

K. Liu et al. (Eds.): ICISO 2014, IFIP AICT 426, pp. 320–330, 2014.
© IFIP International Federation for Information Processing 2014

recommendations or predictions of the unknown preferences for other users[2]. The developers of one of the first recommender systems, Tapestry [1] (other earlier recommendation systems include rule-based recommenders and user-customization), coined the phrase "collaborative filtering (CF)," which has been widely adopted regardless of the facts that recommenders may not explicitly collaborate with recipients and recommendations may suggest particularly interesting items, in addition to indicating those that should be filtered out. The fundamental assumption of CF is that if users X and Y rate n items similarly, or have similar behaviors (e.g., buying, watching, listening), and hence will rate or act on other items similarly.

Literature [3] studies have shown that users' interest to a product or service are affected by user topic preferences, content preferences, user habits, public evaluation and other factors, and these factors is decided by the different attributes of items. For example, the reasons of users liking a new movie may be caused by one or more attributes of the movie, such as the director, star, theme, content, style, public comment and other factors. Thus, in the application of collaborative filtering algorithm, it is necessary to use multi-attribute analysis model, that the user rating to an item should be from a different perspective (attributes) to describe their interests preferences.

However, the current research work of multi-attribute collaborative filtering focus on clustering users and resources based on the attribute information, and the recommended method is still more traditional. Such methods can only obtain a set of potential interest items of target users, but the reasons of such a recommendation is not given to the target user. In addition, the present study do not consider the characteristics differences of similar users interested in the item attributes. It can lead to recommendations deviation. For example, in the traditional way, User B is the most similar to the target user A, because A and B on the same film have the same degree of interest. But if they prefer the film properties are completely different, it will lead to recommendations deviation when we give greater weight given to B used to predict interest preferences of A.

We think that the multi-attribute collaborative filtering can be regarded as a group decision-making process. By building the rating matrix of target items for the similar users, we can remove the user who has a large attribute preference difference with target user from the nearest user set, and save the problem of recommendations deviation. And we can analyze the user's interest performance from the view of item's attributes, give the reasons descriptions for the recommendation. In order to achieve this goal, the paper has proposes a modified Pearson-Compatibility multi-attribute group decision-making algorithm, and introduces the algorithm to solve the recommendation problem of k-neighbor similar users. The organization of the paper is as follows. We review recommender systems and multi-attribute utility theory in Section 2.In section 3, with applied ontology method to describe user profile, we introduce detailed how to build a user interest model. In section 4, we expound the algorithm in each steps specifically. In section 5, an experiment is reported and the findings also be discussed.

2   Descriptions of Basic Model

A user's comment on a certain item is usually an integration of multi-attribute comments made from different angles. Suppose an item is shown as follows:

$$P = \{ a_1, a_2, a_3, ... a_n \}$$

Based on the revised rating model, the paper establishes the user rating matrix. Suppose the user set is denoted as $U = \{ U_1, U_2, ... U_p \}$ and the user U_j rating for item P_i is denoted as $A(U_j, P_i)$:

$$
A(U_j, P_i) = \begin{array}{cccccc}
 & a_1 & a_2 & a_3 & a_{n-1} & a_n \\
\begin{bmatrix}
\omega_{11} & \omega_{12} & \omega_{13} & \cdots & \omega_{1n-1} & \omega_{1n} \\
\omega_{21} & \omega_{22} & \omega_{23} & \cdots & \omega_{2n-1} & \omega_{2n} \\
\omega_{31} & \omega_{32} & \omega_{33} & \cdots & \omega_{3n-1} & \omega_{3n} \\
\cdots & \cdots & \cdots & \cdots & \cdots & \cdots \\
\omega_{(n-1)1} & \omega_{(n-1)2} & \omega_{(n-1)3} & \cdots & \omega_{(n-1)(n-1)} & \omega_{(n-1)n} \\
\omega_{n1} & \omega_{n2} & \omega_{n3} & \cdots & \omega_{n(n-1)} & \omega_{nn}
\end{bmatrix}
\begin{array}{c}
a_1 \\ a_2 \\ a_3 \\ \cdots \\ a_{n-1} \\ a_n
\end{array}
\end{array}
$$

Where ω_{xy} is the importance of attribute a_x of product P_i in comparison with attribute a_y for user U_j. Here we use the 1-9 scale Paired comparison method to analyze the compared importance level of each attribute of the product that a user evaluates [19]. The rating matrix of an item is mainly acquired through user scoring, or acquired through user behavior analysis, or acquired with the approaches of Web semantic Suppose user U_j has rated several items and the rating matrix set is $AS = \{A(U_j, P_1), A(U_j, P_2), ... A(U_j, P_t)\}$, where $A(U_j, P_i)(i = 1, 2, ... t)$ is user U_j's rating matrix for product i (i.e., P_i). This paper applies the rating matrix set to establishing the user interest model. The specific steps are as follows.

1. Calculating the feature weight vector of each rating matrix, and then acquire the feature weight vector set

$$VS = \{V_{U_j}^{P_1}(w_1, w_2, w_3, ... w_{size(A(U_j, P_1))}), V_{U_j}^{P_2}(w_1, w_2, w_3, ... w_{size(A(U_j, P_2))}) ... V_{U_j}^{P_t}(w_1, w_2, w_3, ... w_{size(A(U_j, P_t))})\}.$$

Where $V_{U_j}^{P_i}(w_1, w_2, w_3, ... w_{size(A(U_j, P_i))})$ denotes the feature weight vector of the user rating matrix $A(U_j, P_i)(i = 1, 2, ... t)$ and $size(A(U_j, P_i))$ denotes the length of the feature weight vector.

2. According to the category of each attribute, calculate the user interest weights of the relevant attribute in the related resource category. Referring to the methods, we propose the following formula for calculating the degree of the user interest.

$$Va(U_j, a_y, n) = \frac{\sum_{k=1}^{n} A(U_j, P_k) \times V_{U_j}^{P_k}(w_y)}{n} \tag{1}$$

Where $Va(U_j, a_y, n)$ denotes the degree to which user U_j is interested in attribute a_y. n is the number of the items which has attribute a_y and user U_j have rated. $A(U_j, P_k) \times V_{U_j}^{P_k}(w_y)$ (k=1, 2, 3,...n) denotes the degree of user U_j's interest in attribute a_y of product P_k, which indicates how user U_j's preference on item P_k is mostly determined by attribute a_y.

3   Collaborative Filtering Recommendation Algorithm Based on Multi-attribute Group Decision-Making

Firstly, we introduce the calculation of the value of user impact weight. This value is an important indicator to measure the degree of evaluation information consistency between a user and the others. The user matrix with higher group evaluation consistency will get higher weight. Vise versa. This paper adopts the concept of user rating similarity [6, 7]. We turn all the similar $n \times n$ user rating matrixes into $n^2 \times 1$ one dimensional vector. The user U_k judgment matrix A^k could be denoted as $V^k = \{a_{11}^k, a_{12}^k, a_{13}^k...a_{1n}^k, a_{21}^k, a_{22}^k, a_{23}^k...a_{2n}^k,...a_{n1}^k......a_{nn}^k\}$. Pearson similarity formula to calculate the rating matrix between the user U_k and the user U_l is show as follows:

$$Si(A^k, A^l) = \frac{\sum_{i=1}^{n^2}(V^k(i) - \overline{V^k}) \times (V^l(i) - \overline{V^l})}{\sqrt{\sum_{u=1}^{n^2}[V^k(i) - \overline{V^k}]^2} \times \sqrt{\sum_{u=1}^{n^2}[V^l(i) - \overline{V^l}]^2}} \quad (2)$$

$\overline{V^k}$ is the average value of all elements of user U_k rating matrix.

$$\overline{V^k} = \frac{a_{11}^k + a_{12}^k + ... + a_{nn}^k}{n^2}$$

The similarity between user k and other users could be calculated as follows:

$$Si_k = \sum_{l=1, l \neq k}^{p} Si(A^k, A^l)/(p-1).$$

where p denotes the number of users. We propose a formula $D_k = 1 - Si_k$ as the approximate measure of variance, which indicates the deviation degree of evaluation matrix. The approximate influence weight of user U_k is shown as follows:

$$\theta_k = \frac{(1 - \max\{Si_l, l = 1, 2,...p\})^2}{D_k^2} \quad (3)$$

After acquiring the similar user influence weight, we suppose the group integrated approximate evaluation matrix of p users is A^*, and the value of each element ω_{ij}^* in matrix A^* is as following:

$$\omega_{ij}^* = \sum_{k=1}^{p} \theta_k \times \omega_{ij}^k / \sum_{k=1}^{p} \theta_k \tag{4}$$

Matrix A^* is not a positive reciprocal matrix. Suppose X is a positive reciprocal matrix composed of x_{ij}. This paper uses the least square method to modify X and propose the following formula:

$$F(X) = \min \sum_{i=1}^{n} \sum_{j=1}^{n} (x_{ij} - \omega_{ij}^*)^2$$

$$s.t \begin{cases} x_{ij} \times x_{ji} = 1 \\ x_{ij} > 0 \quad (i, j = 1, 2, ...n) \end{cases} \tag{5}$$

There are two important indicators in this article: compatibility and comprehensive compatibility. Their definitions are as follows:

Definition 1: Suppose X is the group user comprehensive evaluation matrix obtained by using the method of the least squares. Then the judgment matrix compatibility between user k and the other users is as follows:

$$S(A^k, X) = \frac{\sum_{i=1}^{n} \sum_{j=1}^{n} \dfrac{\omega_{ij}^{(k)} \times x_{ij}}{\max((\omega_{ij}^{(k)})^2, (x_{ij})^2)}}{n^2 - \alpha} \tag{6}$$

Although paper [25] has defined expert judgment matrix compatibility in usual cases, it does not consider the incomplete value. Formula [6] is a modified approach to solve the problem. Firstly, the block that the user does not rate is processed and given the value 0. Then α is used to indicate the number of 0. The aim of this approach is to eliminate the influence of user judgment matrix on compatibility indicator.

Definition 2: Suppose A^1、A^2... A^p are the compatibility correction of matrixes of p users' judgment matrixes. Then we get the comprehensive consistency indicator $\bar{S}$, as follows:

$$\bar{S} = \frac{\sum_{k=1}^{p} S(A, A^{k'})}{p} \tag{7}$$

Readers can refer to the simulation result of article [19]. When S(A,B)>= 0.8, the two evaluation matrixes is considered nearly compatible. When $\bar{S} \geq 0.8$, evaluation matrixes of all p similar users is considered compatible.

4   Experimentation

In order to validate the effectiveness of this algorithm, we build an experiment environment to execute our algorithm at current conditions. The environment is described as follows:

Ontology and the relevant methods are adopted to design and develop the movie information database. Jena 2.6.2 is applied to store the movie information in RDF format and ARQ-2.2 is used to manage the movie information. We have imported 300 movies which involve 10 categories. A semantic analysis of each movie is conducted to get key words and form the initial attribute set. Then the synonyms and the similar words in the initial set are combined. Take some topical words as the characteristic attributes and use them to represent these movies. Finally, 15 attributive categories and 282 concrete attributes are extracted. Then an online multi-attribute rating system based on the movie database and a collaborative filtering recommendation system based on group-decision making are designed and developed.

The concrete process that tests the algorithm is as follows:

1. Select four evaluated movies in which $G(u, p)$ is comparatively big and use them as the testify set. They respectively include 6,7,8 and 9 attributes. Then, use the target user evaluation matrixes which are further used as the real weight vectors to calculate the user interest vectors for each movie.

2. Based on the user-evaluated movies set (excluding the 4 movies in the test set), apply the methods in sections 2.3 and 2.4 to searching the most similar user set for the target user (i.e., the similar interest distributions).

Take Movie 1 with 6 attributes as an example. The real interest vectors are S=[3.7288,   2.7053, 1.9627, 0.4657, 0.3293, 0.3293]. The total score of this movie is 4.5 which indicates that the target user has a high preference to this movie. Moreover, the preference is mainly determined by the first three attributes. Totally, 9 similar users have evaluated this movie. Firstly, the traditional collaborative filtering algorithm is applied to obtaining the weighted average of the total score of this movie and gets the result 3.94. We are not sure whether the target users have interests in this movie. Thus, we need use the similar user evaluation matrixes to make judgments. The evaluation matrixes of six similar users are listed as follows:

$$A=\begin{bmatrix} 1 & 2 & 2 & 5 & 7 & 9 \\ 1/2 & 1 & 1 & 6 & 5 & 6 \\ 1/2 & 1 & 1 & 7 & 7 & 6 \\ 1/5 & 1/6 & 1/7 & 1 & 1 & 2 \\ 1/7 & 1/5 & 1/7 & 1 & 1 & 3 \\ 1/9 & 1/6 & 1/6 & 1/2 & 1/3 & 1 \end{bmatrix}$$

$$B=\begin{bmatrix} 1 & 2 & 3 & 3 & 7 & 7 \\ 1/2 & 1 & 0 & 4 & 7 & 6 \\ 1/3 & 0 & 1 & 0 & 4 & 5 \\ 1/3 & 1/4 & 0 & 1 & 1 & 2 \\ 1/7 & 1/7 & 1/4 & 1 & 1 & 3 \\ 1/7 & 1/6 & 1/5 & 1/2 & 1/3 & 1 \end{bmatrix}$$

$$C=\begin{bmatrix} 1 & 2 & 2 & 4 & 0 & 0 \\ 1/2 & 1 & 1 & 3 & 0 & 0 \\ 1/2 & 1 & 1 & 2 & 0 & 0 \\ 1/4 & 1/3 & 1/2 & 1 & 0 & 0 \\ 0 & 0 & 0 & 0 & 1 & 0 \\ 0 & 0 & 0 & 0 & 0 & 1 \end{bmatrix}$$

$$D=\begin{bmatrix} 1 & 2 & 3 & 4 & 6 & 8 \\ 1/2 & 1 & 2 & 2 & 4 & 6 \\ 1/3 & 1/2 & 1 & 1/2 & 4 & 7 \\ 1/4 & 1/2 & 2 & 1 & 3 & 2 \\ 1/6 & 1/4 & 1/4 & 1/3 & 1 & 2 \\ 1/8 & 1/6 & 1/7 & 1/2 & 1/2 & 1 \end{bmatrix}$$

$$E=\begin{bmatrix} 1 & 2 & 0 & 7 & 8 & 0 \\ 1/2 & 1 & 2 & 8 & 7 & 7 \\ 0 & 1/2 & 1 & 0 & 7 & 8 \\ 1/7 & 1 & 0 & 1 & 1 & 2 \\ 1/8 & 1/7 & 1/7 & 1 & 1 & 1 \\ 0 & 1/7 & 1/8 & 1/2 & 1 & 1 \end{bmatrix}$$

$$F=\begin{bmatrix} 1 & 2 & 4 & 0 & 7 & 0 \\ 1/2 & 1 & 2 & 6 & 7 & 7 \\ 1/4 & 1/2 & 1 & 0 & 2 & 2 \\ 0 & 1/6 & 0 & 1 & 0 & 2 \\ 1/7 & 1/7 & 1/2 & 0 & 1 & 1 \\ 0 & 1/7 & 1/2 & 1/2 & 1 & 1 \end{bmatrix}$$

(3) Use the following four algorithms to calculate the score of the four movies and make comparisons on the deviations of the real weight vectors of the target users. The result is listed as follows:

Table 1. The comparison between algorithms

	Movie 1 (6 order)	Movie 2 (7 order)	Movie 3 (8 order)	Movie 4 (9 order)
Arithmetic weighted average method	0.1589	0.0564	0.1985	0.1132
Logarithmic least squares method	0.1054	0.0534	0.1398	0.0831
Compatibility correction algorithm	0.0877	0.0556	0.1042	0.0687
Our algorithm	0.0780	0.0543	0.0885	0.0683

As shown in Table 1, when the scores of a part of similar users have a large deviation from those of the other users, the algorithm proposed in this paper can solve the problem of early convergence better than the other algorithms and obtain an accurate result. The core of our algorithm is the revised values of the comprehensive evaluation matrix determined by the majority of users. On this basis, the highly deviated evaluation values are revised. The result of seven order matrix experiment shows that the deviations of the result of any algorithms are not notable when all the similar users have unanimous evaluation matrixes,. The result of nine order matrix experiment shows that the result of the proposed algorithm is similar to that of compatibility correction algorithm when all the similar users have unanimous evaluation matrixes, while still have some incomplete values, and is better than the other two algorithms obviously. When there are 5 similar users and six order evaluation matrix is executed/ implemented with our algorithm, the change tendencies of the main indicators are shown in Figure 1:

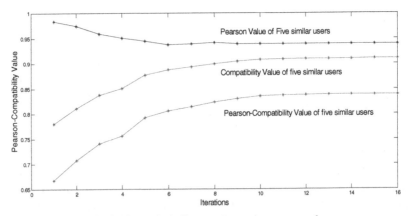

Fig. 1. The main indicators change in our example

(4) Take movie one with the six order evaluation matrix as an example. The influence of the user number on the accuracy of recommendation results is examined. Suppose the user number is 3,5,7 and 9. The accuracy and the number of iterations are calculated with different means of permutation and combination. Part of the result is shown in Table 2:

Table 2. The comparison of different similar user numbers

User number	3	5	7	9
initial Indicator of Comprehensive consistency degree	0.5872	0.6890	0.6872	0.7081
Deviation of result	0.1680	0.1093	0.0828	0.0780
Number of iterations	12	16	28	37

When the user number increase, more deviation items are generated. Thus, the iterations of this algorithm raise. This test indicates that the effectiveness of this algorithm is highly related to the initial consistency degrees of all users and the number of users. In general, when the initial consistency degree is low and the similar user set is limited (e.g. there are 3 users), it is hard for the algorithm to dig out the common information among the users. Therefore, the result deviation is huge. However, when the number of similar users increases to a certain degree (e.g. the number is equal or bigger than 7), this algorithm still remains a good accuracy, even if the initial compatibility is low.

In the aspect of providing personalized services to the target users, this paper calculates the comprehensive evaluation weight vectors of each movie with the group-decision making model. Take movie one with 6 attributes as example. The comprehensive evaluation score of nine similar users is $G(u, p)$ =3.94. The comprehensive evaluation vectors are V= [4.0653 2.9492 1.7630 0.3972 0.3044 0.3607]. Each value of the weight vector represents the potential interest degree of the target user on the corresponding product attributes. Thus, the total score calculation formula is

$$TScore = G(u, p) \times \sum_{i=1}^{n} V_i / n \qquad (10)$$

where *TScore* denotes the total score, n denotes the number of attributes, and V_i denotes the comprehensive evaluation value of the (i)th attribute of the product. The recommendation set can be fixed through the way of ranking or threshold setting. The total scores of the four movies is shown in Figure 2:

As shown in Figure 2, the movie one has the highest score with six attributes. The characters of this movie are analyzed as follows using the user interest model. Firstly, attribute V_i of weight vector V is normalized and generate vector $\overline{V} = [0.4131, 0.2997, 0.1792, 0.0404, 0.0309, 0.0367]$. The three attributes whose values are bigger than the average value 0.1666 are picked out. When the attribute value is bigger than 0.1666, the majority of users have evident preference on movie one. In the target user interest model, there are 124 attributes totally. The 3 attributes of movie one that are bigger than the average value are connotation, characteristic and special efficiency are still larger than the average value (1/124=0.0081) among 124 target user attribute preferences. This result indicates that target user has evident preference to these 3 attributes and the popularity of this movie is mainly determined by these attributes. Therefore, we could introduce movie one to target user and

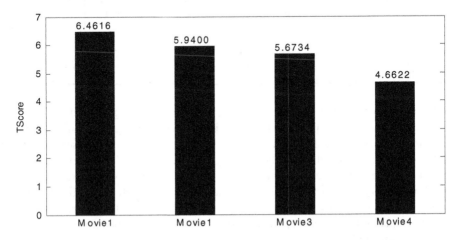

Fig. 2. The TScore of four movies

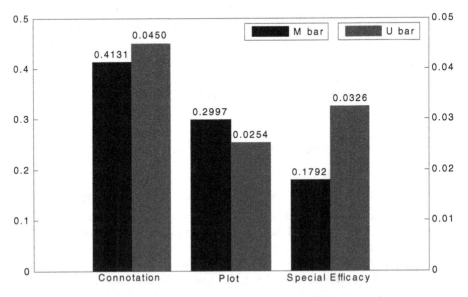

Fig. 3. Comparison analysis histogram of movie one with target user interest

provide the reasons why this movie is introduced. We also could use semantic analysis technique to describe each attribute in detail and provide more personal service to target user. The comparison analysis histogram is shown in Fig. 3.

5   Conclusion

Currently, the collaborative filtering personal recommended algorithm lesser consider the multi-attribute problem. We take the method which is based on the group-decision making, then build an improved Pearson-Compatibility algorithm and apply it into the collaborative filtering recommend field. And we also build a virtual recommend environment and testify the effectiveness and feasibility of this algorithm. The collaborative filtering personal recommended algorithm which is based on group-decision making have some advantages as following:

Firstly, we could find a more suited similar users set for the target user. Through field subdivision based on field attributes, we could get a more accurate target user model. Take the model as a foundation, we could find users who have similar interest distribution with target user and build the similar users set.

Secondly, our algorithm could provide more accurate and personal recommend service to our target user. The traditional collaborative filtering method merely could recommend a result set to target user, but could not provide analysis service. Our method overcome this weakness, making a information integration to know what are mainly factors determining the user preference, so that we could handle the user need more accurate.

Thirdly, we consider evaluation deviation between the similar users and revised the user evaluation. Compared with the traditional method of weighted mean, we use group-decision making method to calculate the comprehensive evaluation score. We believe deleting the deviation item and revising the evaluation matrix could make the result have a better fitting effect. We also applied the collaborative filtering method which is based on Pearson-Compatibility to the personal recommended field. The experiment result shown that this algorithm is stable when facing the deviation items and could find the common preference information between similar users.

If we want to apply this algorithm to real business environment, we need a new user evaluation model as a foundation. For there are little related research currently, the next step is to apply internet technique to build user online evaluation system. After collecting lots of user data, we could research this model further to testify its effective.

References

1. Adomavicius, G., Tuzhilin, A.: Toward the next generation of recommender systems: A survey of the state-of-the-art and possible extensions. IEEE Trans. on Knowl. and Data Eng. 17(6), 734–749 (2005)
2. Su, X., Khoshgoftaar, T.M.: A survey of collaborative filtering techniques. Advances in Artificial Intelligence (2009)

3. Goldberg, D., Nichols, D., Oki, B.M., Terry, D.: Using collaborative filtering to weave an information tapestry. Communications of ACM 35(12), 61–70 (1992)
4. Resnick, P., Varian, H.R.: Recommender systems. Communications of the ACM 40(3), 56–58 (1997)
5. Goldberg, K., Roeder, T., Gupta, D., Perkins, C.: Eigentaste: a constant time collaborative filtering algorithm. Information Retrieval 4(2), 133–151 (2001)
6. de Campos, L.M., Fernández-Luna, J.M., Huete, J.F., Miguel, A.: Rueda-MoralesCombining content-based and collaborative recommendations: A hybrid approach based on Bayesian networks. International Journal of Approximate Reasoning 51(7), 785–799 (2010)

Value Model of Knowledge Diffusion in High Technology Innovation Networks

Yu Xiao and Jingti Han

School of Information Management and Engineering,
Shanghai University of Finance of Economics, Shanghai, China, 200433
jxndtbxiaoyu@163.com

Abstract. To measure the influence of knowledge diffusion and information exchange between enterprises on high-tech innovation networks' production and operation, a production model and innovation model based on a network diffusion process are introduced. The knowledge diffusion process treated as an learning-by-observing process in a random network are influenced both by network's structure and non-structure properties. We analyze the influence of diffusion process theoretically and find that, if given the precondition that initial belief and belief elasticity follow a normal distribution, an increase in mean of initial belief would lead to increase in PV and IV; otherwise, mean of belief elasticity would have a opposite effect on PV and IV under some different conditions. Finally, we give the condition to compare knowledge diffusions in two high-tech networks with same mean degree but different variance.

Keywords: High-tech innovation networks, Social learning, Knowledge diffusion, Diffusion value, Degree distribution.

1 Introduction

For high-tech enterprises, continuous technological innovation is one of key factors to maintain their core competitiveness. Technological innovation depends largely on the partnerships they coordinate with other companies within the industry [1].

As a substrate of knowledge transferring between high-tech enterprises, high-tech innovation network has an important impact on the dissemination process of knowledge between enterprises[2]. For example, Uzzi (2005) found that large-scale structure of the network has a significant effect on musicians' creativity, art of music composed and profitability[3]. Schilling (2007) found that structure of inter-enterprise cooperation networks influence their knowledge creation and that enterprises cooperative networks in which have a higher clustering coefficient and less redundant links would have higher knowledge creation capability[4]. Phelps (2010) found that structure and composition of alliance networks have a significant impact on the ability of enterprises to explore innovation, corporate partners' technical diversity has a positive influence on its ability to explore new knowledge, while the density of network structure plays as regulatory role[5]. These empirical findings provide new reference for companies to acquire knowledge and set off a wave of knowledge diffusion research of high-tech innovative networks.

K. Liu et al. (Eds.): ICISO 2014, IFIP AICT 426, pp. 331–339, 2014.

With above empirical findings and the rise of complex network studies[6][7][8], a large number of scholars have focused on dynamic characteristics of large-scale network structure and knowledge emergence properties in these networks. Cowan (2004) examined the relationship between network structure and diffusion performance, and concluded that knowledge diffusion in small-world networks with different structure properties have great difference[9]. These studies have used simulation to explore knowledge diffusion process, but did not analyze the impact of such knowledge diffusion on the overall economy of high-tech innovation networks. In this paper, we define knowledge as a group of technical knowledge which would have a positive impact on production, operation and business activities (or reduce production costs and improve product quality). Although technical cooperation network can accumulate knowledge and innovate technologies, thus increase the whole profit, the implementation of these activities may bring risks and costs, so companies will evaluate the risk and decide whether to absorb new knowledge or not. Based on this consideration, this paper, which is different from previous studies, treat knowledge dissemination process as a learning process, companies will observe business-to-business alliances' adoption of new knowledge in return each period, and then evaluate the impact of new knowledge on their production and management, and finally decide whether to adopt new knowledge.

We build high-tech innovation network with mean-field approximation[10][11][12], with the aim to discuss the heterogeneity of degree distribution on knowledge diffusion. In addition, this article focuses on the overall impact of knowledge diffusion on the high-tech innovation network. Based on knowledge diffusion models, we also construct knowledge diffusion production value model and inter-enterprises impact value model. This article focuses on answering these questions: How is the impact of cost and actual knowledge value on adoption rate, production value (short for PV) and influence value (short for IV) in high-tech innovation network? How is the impact of initial belief of knowledge value and elasticity of evaluating of knowledge value on adoption rate, PV and IV? What about the heterogeneity of degree distribution's regulated role in these relationships?

2   Assumptions and Individual-Level Model

We regard knowledge dissemination process in the high-tech innovation network as a process of enterprises' evaluating benefit of adopting new knowledge. The transmission of knowledge isn't the same that of information or viral, but is an active behavior of knowledge acceptors. In this process, high-tech enterprises evaluate knowledge value repeatedly, combine together adoption cost and adoption risk of knowledge, and then decide whether to adopt new knowledge or not.

To simplify the process, we firstly make the following assumptions: 1) each period enterprise i can observe new knowledge adoption behavior of other k_i enterprises, a_i of which have adopted new knowledge; 2) For those enterprises who have adopted new knowledge, they produce a unit of information about the adoption of return every period which are independent from each other, the value return follows a normal distribution $I \sim N(\mu, \sigma^2)$; 3) Enterprise has a neutral risk preferences, information obtained in each period is independent with each other; 4) enterprises have the same cost c and value return of using knowledge; 5)the diffusion process follows a mean-field approximation process.

2.1   High-Tech Innovation Networks

The high-tech innovation network is represented as $DG = (V, E)$. The enterprises in the network are represented as node set $V = \{1, 2, ..., n\}$, and their relationship is represented as edge set $E = \{e_{ij}; i, j = 1, 2, ..., n\}$. If enterprise i observes the production return of enterprise j, and then there is a relationship between them, in other words $e_{ijt} = 1$; if not, then $e_{ijt} = 0$. This relationship between nodes is not fixed, but each node observes fixed number of other nodes across different period; the number k_i is featured as the degree of that node. Further, this relationship is unidirectional observation. In other words, $e_{ij} = 1$ doesn't mean $e_{ji} = 1$. To facilitate the analysis, we assume in_degree equals to out_degree. The proportion of node with degree k in the network is represented as $p(k)$, so the degree distribution could be represented as $P(k) = \{p(k); k = 1, 2, ..., k_{max}\}$.

2.2   Knowledge Adoption Rules Based on Learning from Observation

If enterprises have complete information of knowledge value, and $\mu > c$, then all would adopt the knowledge at the initial stage. In reality, Enterprises actually don't, however, know that kind of information. But they have a prior belief of the knowledge value, which is represented as v_{i0}. With the accumulation of information about knowledge value, they would also update their belief about knowledge value. When the posterior belief b_{it} at stage t is strong enough, enterprise i would decide to adopt the knowledge. Here we use a standard normal-normal belief updating rule[16][17].

At the initial stage, enterprise i's initial belief of knowledge value is v_{i0}. A low v_{i0} means that enterprise i has a negative attitude towards that knowledge. τ_i represents the elasticity of enterprise i's belief updating. As time goes, enterprises get information from its neighbors, and then update their belief. At t period, if there are a_i adopted neighbors, enterprise i would obtain a_i units of information. For that information is independent from each other, we can get the mean of knowledge value $\bar{I}_{it} \sim N(\mu, \frac{\sigma^2}{a_{it}})$. Followed as standard norm-norm updating rules, enterprise i's bayesian posterior belief can be expressed as the weighted average of prior valuation and the information obtained

$$v_{it} = \frac{\tau_i}{a_{it} + \tau_i} \cdot v_{i0} + \frac{a_{it}}{a_{it} + \tau_i} \cdot \bar{I}_{it}$$

When $v_{it} > c$, enterprise i will adopt the knowledge.

3   A Knowledge Diffusion Dynamic Model in Random Network

Each stage, suppose that enterprise i selects k_i enterprises randomly from the network to get information about knowledge usage. In the initial period, enterprises who meet the condition $v_{i0} > c$ would adopt knowledge and then create information for others next stages. Meanwhile, those adopted enterprises would, if their belief of knowledge value is larger than cost, give up using new knowledge.

We use $\rho_k(t)$ to represent knowledge adoption rate of sub-class featured with degree k in t period, and $\rho(t)$ to represent knowledge adoption rate of innovation network. Obviously, we have

$$\rho(t) = \sum_k \rho_k(t) p(k) \tag{1}$$

in which $0 \leq \rho_k(t), \rho(t) \leq 1$. Since enterprises may get several other enterprises' information, the probability of enterprise's observing an adopted counterpart is represented as

$$\theta(t) = \frac{\sum_k k p(k) \rho_k(t)}{\langle k \rangle} \tag{2}$$

in which $\langle k \rangle = \sum_k k p(k)$ is mean degree of the network. Thus, expected amount of information of enterprise i could be represented as

$$I_k(\theta(t)) = \sum_{a=0}^{k} C_k^a \theta(t)^a (1 - \theta(t))^{k-a} a \tag{3}$$
$$= k \cdot \theta(t)$$

For enterprise i, the bayesian posterior belief of knowledge value at stage t is

$$v_{it} = \frac{\tau_i}{k_i \theta(t) + \tau_i} \cdot v_{i0} + \frac{k_i \theta(t)}{k_i \theta(t) + \tau_i} \cdot \bar{I}_{it}, \tag{4}$$

in which $\bar{I}_{it} \sim N(\mu, \frac{\sigma^2}{k_i \theta(t)})$. When $v_{it} > c$, enterprise i would adopt knowledge, and

then we have $\frac{\tau_i v_{i0} + k_i \theta(t) \cdot \bar{I}_{it}}{k_i \theta(t) + \tau_i} > c$. Suppose $X \sim N(0,1)$, then

$$(\tau_i v_{i0} + k_i \theta(t)) \cdot \mu + \frac{(\tau_i v_{i0} + k_i \theta(t))\sigma}{\sqrt{k_i \theta(t)}} \cdot X > (k_i \theta(t) + \tau_i) \cdot c$$

which implies

$$\theta(t) > \frac{\tau_i(C - \mu v_{i0})}{k_i(\mu - C)} - \frac{(\tau_i v_{i0} + k_i \theta(t))\sigma}{(\mu - C) \cdot \sqrt{k_i \theta(t)}} \cdot X$$

Now we can define the expected information level for enterprise i adopting knowledge

$$\theta_i = \frac{\tau_i(c - \mu v_{i0})}{k_i(\mu - c)} \tag{5}$$

when $\theta(t) > \theta_i$, enterprise i would be inclined to adopt knowledge. Without lose of generality, suppose that when $\theta(t) > \theta_i$, enterprise i will adopt knowledge. For sub-class k, we have:

$$Z(\tau_i, v_{i0}; k) = \frac{\tau_i(c - \mu v_{i0})}{k(\mu - c)} \tag{6}$$

Suppose it's a continuous process, then the growth of adoption rate of sub-class k could be characterized as

$$\overset{\circ}{\rho_k}(t) = F(\theta(t); \tau_i, v_{i0}, k) - \rho_k(t) \tag{7}$$

$$\overset{\circ}{\theta}(t) = R(\theta(t)) - \theta(t) \tag{8}$$

$$\overset{\circ}{\rho}(t) = \sum_k p(k)F(\theta(t); \tau_i, v_{i0}, k) - \rho(t) \tag{9}$$

$$R(\theta(t)) = \frac{\sum_k kp(k)F(\theta(t); \tau_i, v_{i0}, k)}{\langle k \rangle} \tag{10}$$

When $R(\theta(t)) = \theta(t)$, equilibrium state is reached. Recall that the transitive from adopted to non-adopted is always possible. Hence, the equilibrium only refers to the value of $\rho(t)$ and $\theta(t)$.

4   Knowledge Diffusion Value for High-Tech Innovation Network

After modeling knowledge dynamics in high-tech innovation network, a following question would come as 'How is this diffusion's impact on the whole high-tech network?', and 'what's the role of the interaction between enterprises?'. Most literatures didn't, however, discuss these questions. For an analytical purpose, we construct a PV model and IV model, which is similar as customer value and influence value in Ho(2012). PV measures accumulated value from all enterprises' using new knowledge, and IV measures value raised from the interaction among enterprises, both of which are influenced by network structure.

Firstly we introduce discount coefficient r and valid period of knowledge. For a particular adopted enterprise, suppose that its PV each period is equal to μ. If enterprise i adopts knowledge at t, its PV could be represented as

$$PV_i = \sum_{s=t}^{T} \mu e^{-rs} \tag{11}$$

Except adopters in the initial stage, all new added adopters are influenced by earlier adopters whose influences are related to their degree. Thus, accumulated IV of adopted enterprise i with degree k_i could be represented as

$$IV_i = \int_t^T \omega \frac{k_i}{n \cdot \langle k \rangle \theta(s)} \cdot n \cdot \overset{\circ}{\rho}(s) \cdot \mu e^{-rs} ds$$
$$= \frac{k_i \omega \mu}{\langle k \rangle} \int_t^T \frac{\overset{\circ}{\rho}(s) \cdot e^{-rs}}{\theta(s)} ds \tag{12}$$

in which $0 < \omega < 1$ and $t \geq 1$. ω is coefficient of IV. Thus, PV and IV of knowledge in its life cycle could be represented as

$$PV = n\mu \int_0^T \int_t^T e^{-rs} \overset{\circ}{\rho}(s) ds dt \tag{13}$$

$$IV = \frac{n\mu\omega}{\langle k \rangle} \int_0^T e^{-rt} \overset{\circ}{\rho}(t) dt \tag{14}$$

PV characterizes the direct influence of knowledge on enterprises' production and operation, and is also influenced by the shape of knowledge adoption curve. Obviously, for two knowledge diffusion processes who have the same final adoption rate, the one having a higher initial adoption rate would also have a larger PV and a smaller IV. On the contrary, the rate of IV to PV mirrors the characteristics of diffusion curve. In this view, knowledge payoff, cost, enterprises' characteristics, and structure of high-tech innovation network all influence the shape of diffusion curve, would in turn influence PV and IV.

5   Theoretical Analysis

The diffusion process is influenced not only by knowledge payoff and cost, but also by distribution of initial belief b_0 and of elasticity τ and by degree distribution $P(k)$. If $\max\{v_{1,0}, v_{2,0}, ..., v_{i,0}, ..., v_{n,0}\} < c$, all enterprises would not adopt that knowledge at initial stage, which in turn lead to no information for next stage and finally to the failure of knowledge diffusion. This phenomenon could be found in practice— some technologies or knowledge are too expensive or revolutionary, giving enterprises a sense of risk, and thus all enterprises are waiting. As for this case, if $\mu > c$, the creator of knowledge could take some measures to handle with, such as giving discount to initial adopted enterprises or signing an agreement about sharing risky. Then, we have proposition 1.

Proposition 1: If all enterprises' initial belief of knowledge payoffs are lower than cost, or actual knowledge payoff is lower that cost, knowledge would fail to diffusion in the high-tech network.

For the sake of deeply understanding the model, we suppose that v_0 and τ follow a normal distribution. And also we will take the discrete version of this model.

Proposition 2: Suppose $v_0 \quad N(\mu_1, \sigma_1^2)$ and $\tau \sim N(\mu_2, \sigma_2^2)$, then

1) an increase in μ_1 would lead to increase in PV and IV,

2) when $c < b\mu$, an increase in μ_2 would lead to increase in PV and IV; when $c > b\mu$, an increase in μ_2 leads to decrease in PV and IV.

Proof. According with equation (6)

$$Z(\tau_i, v_{i0}; k) = \frac{c - \mu v_{i0}}{k(\mu - c)} \cdot \tau_i$$

suppose $\tau_i = \tau = 0$, then $Z \quad N(\frac{\tau(c - \mu \cdot \mu_1)}{k(\mu - c)}, \frac{\tau\mu}{k(\mu - c)} \cdot \sigma_1^2)$, combining with equation (7), we get

$$\theta(t+1) = \frac{\sum_k kp(k)\Phi\left(\frac{k(\mu - c)\theta(t) - c\tau + \tau\mu\mu_1)}{\sigma_1\sqrt{k\tau\mu(\mu - c)}}\right)}{\langle k \rangle}$$

in which $\Phi(\cdot)$ is CDF of normal distribution. Obviously, an increase in μ_1 leads to an increase in knowledge diffusion speed. If the diffusion achieve dynamic equilibrium at θ^*, then

$$\theta^* = \frac{\sum_k kp(k)\Phi\left(\frac{k(\mu - c)\theta^* - c\tau + \tau\mu\mu_1)}{\sigma_1\sqrt{k\tau\mu(\mu - c)}}\right)}{\langle k \rangle}$$

If there is θ^*, at this point, an increase in μ_1, the equilibrium state would be disrupted. Thus, would gain a growth. Combining equations (13) and (14), we can achieve proposition 1).

If b_{i0} equals to b and $b \neq \frac{c}{\mu}$, $Z \quad N(\frac{c - \mu v}{k(\mu - c)} \cdot \mu_2, \left|\frac{c - \mu v}{k(\mu - c)}\right| \cdot \sigma_2^2)$, combined with equation (7), we get

$$\theta(t+1) = \frac{\sum_k kp(k)\Phi\left(\frac{k(\mu - c)\theta(t) - (c - \mu b)\mu_2}{\sigma_2\sqrt{k(\mu - c)}|c - \mu b|}\right)}{\langle k \rangle}$$

Then we can achieve proposition 2) with the same method used for proposition 1). As in proposition 1, distributions of b_0 and τ have an impact on diffusion curve. b_0's influence is intuitive, τ's is, however, depend on different constrains.

Proposition 3: If there are two high-tech networks: network a with degree distribution $P_a(k)$ depicted by mean $\langle k_a \rangle$ and variance σ_a^2; network b with $P_b(k)$ depicted by $\langle k_b \rangle$ and σ_b^2. Then

1) If $P_a(k)$ FOSD $P_b(k)$ and $F(\theta,k)$ is, for any θ, a non-decreasing function of k, then there is more PV and IV in network a than that in network b.

2) If $P_a(k)$ SOSD $P_b(k)$ and $F(\theta,k)$ is, for any θ, a weak concave function of k, then there is more PV and IV in network a than that in network b.

Proof.
The proposition is easy to achieve with definition of First Order Statistical Dominance (short for FOSD) and Second Order Statistical Dominance (short for SOSD) given by Jackson (2006). $P_a(k)$ FOSD $P_b(k)$ means that $\langle k_a \rangle > \langle k_b \rangle$, then we can conclude that in two random network a and b, if average degree of a is larger than that of b, there would be also a larger PV and IV in high-tech network a. $P_a(k)$ SOSD $P_b(k)$ means that $\langle k_a \rangle \geq \langle k_b \rangle$ and $\sigma_a^2 > \sigma_b^2$, and we can draw the conclusion that in two networks with same average degree and different degree variance, the one with larger variance would also have larger PV and IV. For example, in a scale-free network and a regular network, PV and IV in the former one are larger that those in the later one.

The discount effect of knowledge also has an important influence on PV and IV. If $T \rightarrow \infty$, time axis would, for a knowledge diffusion process with a low discount coefficient, have little effect on PV and IV. In this situation, the equilibrium state of knowledge diffusion would have a decisive influence on PV and IV. If, however, a knowledge diffusion process is highly risky, which implies there is a large discount coefficient, then the initial stage of diffusion is vital to determine PV and IV.

6   Conclusion

Knowledge diffusion in high-tech networks is of importance in research area of knowledge management. We construct a knowledge dynamic diffusion model in high-tech networks with degree distribution based on observation learning and mean-field approximate method. In this high-tech network, every enterprise observes fixed amount of knowledge payoff from others, and then updates its belief of knowledge payoff. With mean-field approximation, we elicit a threshold of information level for each enterprise to decide whether to adopt new knowledge or not. Besides, we construct production value model of knowledge for high-tech networks and influence value model of the interaction between enterprises.

The result shows that new knowledge would, if all enterprises have too low belief of knowledge value, fail to diffusion in high-tech networks. If given precondition that initial belief and belief elasticity follow a normal distribution, an increase in mean of initial belief would lead to increase in PV and IV; otherwise, mean of belief elasticity would pose an opposite effect on PV and IV under different conditions. Finally, we give the condition to compare knowledge diffusions in two high-tech networks with same mean degree but different variance. The research in future would construct multiple-agents model to analyze different properties of high-tech on knowledge diffusion, and also on PV and IV.

Acknowledgments. This research is supported by projects: National Natural Science Foundation of China (71271126); research Fund for the Doctoral Program of Higher Education (20120078110002); the 6th graduate innovative fund of Shanghai University of Finance and Economics (CXJJ-2012-427); the 4th stage of 211 project of Shanghai University of Finance and Economics.

References

1. Phelps, C.C., Heidl, R., Wadhwa, A.: Wadhwa Knowledge, networks, and knowledge networks: a review and research agenda. Journal of Management 38(4), 1115–1166 (2012)
2. Uzzi, B., Spiro, J.: Collaboration and creativity: the small world problem. American Journal of Sociology 111(2), 447–504 (2005)
3. Melissa, A., Schilling, C.C.: Inter-firm Collaboration Networks: The Impact of Large-Scale Network Structure on Firm Innovation. Management Science 53(7), 1113–1126 (2007)
4. Phelps, C.C.: A longitudinal study of the influence of alliance network structure and composition on firm exploratory innovation. Academy of Management Journal 53(4), 890–913 (2010)
5. Newman, M.E.J.: The structure and function of complex networks. SIAM Review 45(2), 167–256 (2003)
6. Barabasi, A.L., Albert, R.: Emergence of scaling in random networks. Science 286(15), 509–512 (1999)
7. Watts, D.J., Strogatz, S.H.: Collective dynamics of small-world networks. Nature 393(10), 440–442 (1998)
8. Enyu, Z., Guanrong, C., Gang, F.: A network model of knowledge accumulation through diffusion and upgrade. Physica A 390, 2582–2592 (2011)
9. Cowan, R., Jonard, N.: Network structure and the diffusion of knowledge. Journal of Economic Dynamics and Control 28(8), 1557–1575 (2004)
10. Jackson, M.O., Yariv, L.: Diffusion of behavior and equilibrium properties in network games. American Economic Review 97(2), 92–98 (2007)
11. Pintado, D.L.: Diffusion in complex social networks. Games and Economics Behavior 62(2), 573–590 (2008)
12. Pintado, D.L.: Influence networks. Games and Economics Behavior 75, 776–787 (2012)
13. Teck-Hua, H., et al.: Customer Influence Value and Purchase Acceleration in New Product Diffusion. Marketing Science 31(2), 236–256

Developing a Knowledge Management System Using an Ontological Approach in Global Organization

Seung-Hwa Chung[1], Simon Robertson[1], Andre Minnaar[1],
Mark Cook[1], and Lily Sun[2]

[1] United Bible Societies, UK
schung@biblesocieties.org
[2] University of Reading, UK
lily.sun@reading.ac.uk

Abstract. This paper introduces an ontology-based knowledge model for knowledge management. This model can facilitate knowledge discovery that provides users with insight for decision making. The users requiring the insight normally play different roles with different requirements in an organization. To meet the requirements, insights are created by purposely aggregated transactional data. This involves a semantic data integration process. In this paper, we present a knowledge management system which is capable of representing knowledge requirements in a domain context and enabling the semantic data integration through ontology modeling. The knowledge domain context of United Bible Societies is used to illustrate the features of the knowledge management capabilities.

Keywords: Knowledge management system, Knowledge model, Ontology, Global organization.

1   Introduction

Knowledge management acquires information from multiple resources and uses the acquired information to generate value for an organization [1]. For a knowledge management system, there is a need to integrate an increasing set of diverse devices and information systems within an enterprise [2], e.g. inventory tracking systems, sales systems, finance systems, human resource systems, and so on, to effectively share the organizational knowledge [3]. Typically these devices and information systems are produced by a variety of developers with different data schemas. The information integration of such heterogeneous data using traditional data integration [4], which offers uniform access to a set of data sources through a mediated schema [5], is a specialist and brittle process, such that changing the structure of just one data source can force an integration redesign [6]. Data integration without involving semantics limits the data use to pre-defined functions, which are implemented by a rigorously agreed specification with the pre-defined meaning of terms for the exchange of data.

K. Liu et al. (Eds.): ICISO 2014, IFIP AICT 426, pp. 340–347, 2014.

This makes it difficult to manipulate the data according to the users' needs and to extract reasoned information from the data. Adding semantics to the data avoids these difficulties [7]. OWL (Web Ontology Language) is a well-known technology that enables semantics to be encoded with the data [8]. This technology formally represents the meaning involved in information (in other words, an ontology that specifies concepts and describes relationships between things and categories of things). The ontological approach to build a knowledge model offers significant advantages on sharing and generating value of the information for it enables the reasoning over data and handles the data exchange and integration for more flexibly.

There have been several investigations in this research field [9]. The data integration research trend is moving toward semantic data integration using ontology due to it having the capability of specifying relationships between concepts and facilitating reasoning [10]. In industrial practices, major information service enterprises such as Google, Yahoo and Microsoft have agreed on shared vocabularies with encoded semantics to publish the data on the Web [11]. This work surveyed existing industrial practices of knowledge management system developed using the ontological approach. We were, however, unable to find examples of best practice, which describe an empirical usage of knowledge management systems with a practical industrial dataset, to refer to for the development of the knowledge management system in our organization. However, it is understandable that industries treat their knowledge models and management systems as intellectual property [12] as they are important assets that help provide a competitive edge.

This paper introduces an ontology-based knowledge model and the core features of the proposed knowledge management system. The United Bible Societies want such a system to assist with information and service provision.

2   The Knowledge Domain Context

United Bible Societies (UBS) [13] is one of the world's largest Christian ministries. UBS is made up of 146 Bible Societies operating in more than 200 countries and territories. They translate, publish, and distribute the Bible, help people engage with content of the Bible, and are also active in areas such as literacy training, HIV/AIDS education and trauma healing. Bible Societies work in partnership and cooperation with all Christian churches and with some non-governmental organizations. Bible Societies' activity is expressed in over a thousand projects to facilitate the funding of these activities. A Global Mission Team (GMT) supports Bible Societies by helping them work together through consultation, coordination and the provision of shared services in areas such as international finance, project registration, capacity building, etc. The organizational structure of UBS is shown in Fig. 1. UBS is multi-cultural and multi-lingual, working in a geographically dispersed and collaborative way across the world - together these attributes make UBS a unique organization.

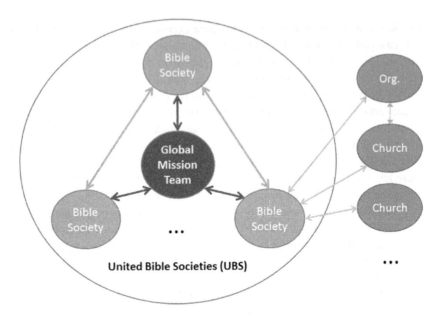

Fig. 1. The structure of the United Bible Societies

3   Information and Information Sources

This work analyzes the information systems in UBS. There include DBL (Digital Bible Library) system, UBS Community system, TMS (Translation Management System), Salesforce system, Project Registry system, and PSFinancials system. Fig. 2 shows the overview of the GMT core systems, and Table 1 shows a list of the existing information systems with the roles.

Each system is supporting Bible Societies in different domains. For example, DBL and TMS in the Bible domain, Project Registry in the Project domain, PSFinancials in the Financial domain, UBS Community in the Community domain, and HR.net and Salesforce in the Human resource domain. Currently, most of the data is searchable only vertically, which means that the information is only available within the domain [14]. Due to the independent design of the different systems, there is only limited syntactically integrated and shared data between the systems. As these systems evolve, it becomes increasingly difficult to extend and share the data. For example, Bible translation information in TMS system cannot be shared with the project information in the Project Registry system. Currently, the user needs to vertically search each domain manually to relate the search results from one domain to another. Integrating data syntactically, to enable a horizontal search to share the information between different domains, requires redesigning the system each time there is a need for new information sharing, and this does not allow for easy evolution.

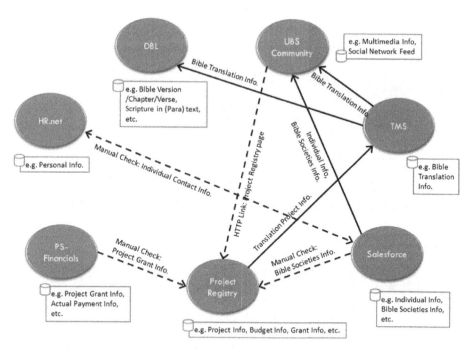

Fig. 2. Overview of GMT's core information systems

Table 1. List of GMT's core information systems and roles

System	Key Role
Project Registry	Keeping track of projects in UBS
PSFinancials	GFS (Global Financial Service) Project Ledger
HR.net	Keeping Personal Information in GMT for Human Resource Management
Salesforce	One central location for contact information of Individual and Bible Societies
DBL	A portal to allow people to access different Bible translations in one central location
TMS	Keeping track of Bible translation projects in detail
UBS Community	A portal for one contact point to access other systems in UBS

4 Design of the Knowledge Management System

Fig. 3 depicts the ontology-based knowledge management system (KMS) which enables creation of insights by processing the transactional data from the resources such as existing information systems. Each resource requires one plugin component, so when there is a need to import new resource, this can be handled by simply adding an additional plugin component. In this architecture, the system can easily evolve to incorporate the new imported information.

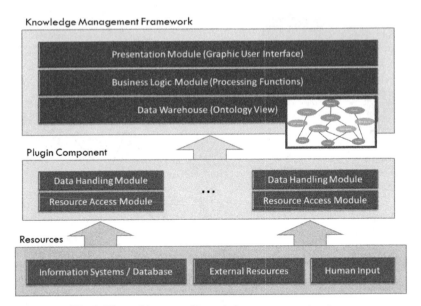

Fig. 3. The architecture of knowledge management system

The information from each domain will be aggregated and molded into the ontology model. This model dynamically generates the knowledge presentation to facilitate the discovery of new insight. Fig. 4 shows an example of the knowledge model developed to enable the sharing of information from different domains.

The requirements for the knowledge model for the UBS have been identified as followings.

1. The model needs to import data from different sources:
   The ontology-based knowledge model can aggregate the information from different domains (even from outside the UBS domain, such as the CIA World Factbook [15] and UN Human Development Reports [16]) in one ontology knowledge model.

2. The model needs to keep relationships between entities:
   The ontology-based knowledge model can formally describe the semantics of classes (general things in domains of interest), properties (attributes those things may have) and relationships that can exist among things [17].

3. The model needs to generate different knowledge presentations:
   The ontology-based knowledge model can generate dynamically the knowledge presentations according to each entity defined in the ontology without altering the knowledge model [18].

4. The model needs to be applied by certain rules to enable the semantic search:
   The ontology-based knowledge model can be semantically searched by query syntax such as SPARQL query [19] or SWRL rule [20]. For example, show Bible Societies making grants of more than $100,000 to literacy projects which are implemented in Swahili-speaking countries in Africa.

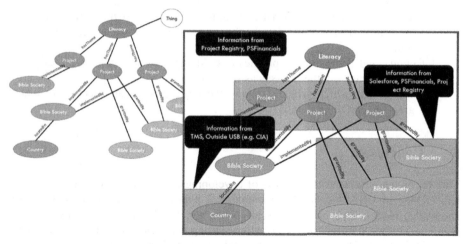

Fig. 4. The knowledge model using heterogeneous information resources

5   Application of the Knowledge Model

From the knowledge model we have proposed, the following interaction can be enabled, as an example. Fig. 5 shows the information details of each or group of entities in the model.

1. A Bible Society (BS) wants to make a funding grant to a literacy project. However, it does not know which projects or countries have the greatest needs.
2. The Knowledge Management System generates a literacy oriented knowledge presentation from the knowledge model. In the figure, Projects are the first information related to the literacy. The knowledge representation needs to be customized by user requirements. For example, Countries can be the first information to be related to the literacy if they are more appropriate for the user.

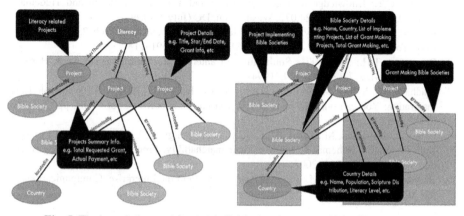

Fig. 5. The knowledge model using individual and group entities of information

3. BS receives summary information (e.g. total grant requests/payments) of existing literacy projects and details of each project as shown in the left side of figure.
4. Country and Bible Society profiles (e.g. literacy rate and population) are presented along with the projects as shown in the right side of figure.
5. BS discovers which projects require the most support, and decides to make grants to certain projects.

6   Conclusion

This paper has described the process of developing a Knowledge Management System (KMS) in UBS that takes the ontological approach, using an ontology-based knowledge model. This model aims to enable horizontal searches, not just vertical searches within a domain, and information sharing between different data sources in different domains. The KMS, using an ontology-based knowledge model, will shape the information into knowledge by aggregating, molding, linking and reasoning with the data. This will facilitate the discovery of new insights by revealing implicit information, which could be hidden without applying semantics to the data.

For the future work, we will further design the technical functions in the KMS and deploy the KMS in the day-to-day operations of UBS. Rigorous data collection and processing will be undertaken, followed by rigorous validation of the knowledge model. A successful implementation will also require the consideration of issues related to user motivation and change management.

Acknowledgement. The development of the knowledge management system is partially funded by Technology Strategy Board (TSB) (KTP009100-508802) and supported by University of Reading.

References

1. Havens, C.T.: Knowledge management system and method, U.S. Patent and Trademark Office, U.S. Patent No. 5,924,072, Washington, DC (July 13, 1999)
2. Rho, S., Park, J.: Ontology: The key of Internet Evolution, from Web 2.0 to Web 3.0, Gods'Toy Business, Korea, ch. 1 (2007) ISBN13-9788995919118
3. Davenport, T.H.: Saving IT's Soul: Human-Centered Information Management. Harvard Business Review 72(2), 119–131 (1994)
4. Madhavan, J., Jeffery, S., Cohen, S., Dong, X., Ko, D., Yu, C., Halevy, A.: Web-scale Data Integration: You can only afford to pay as you go. In: Proceedings of CIDR, pp. 342–350 (2007)
5. Chai, X., Sayyadian, M., Doan, A., Rosenthal, A., Seligman, L.: Analyzing and Revising Data Integration Schemas to improve their matchability. Proceedings of the VLDB Endowment 1(1), 773–784 (2008)
6. Bernstein, P.A., Haas, L.M.: Information Integration in the Enterprise. Communications of the ACM 51(9) (2008)

7. Waters, J., Powers, B.J., Ceruti, M.G.: Global Interoperability Using Semantics, Standards, Science and Technology (GIS3T). J. Computer Stands and Interfaces 31(6), 1158–1166 (2009)
8. Antoniou, G., Harmelen, F.V.: Web Ontology Language: OWL. In: Handbook on Ontologies, pp. 67–92. Springer, Heidelberg (2004)
9. Noy, N.F.: Semantic Integration: a survey of ontology-based approaches. ACM Sigmod Record 33(4), 65–70 (2004)
10. Gardner, S.P.: Ontologies and Semantic Data Integration. Drug Discovery Today 10(14), 1001–1007 (2005)
11. Schema RDFS Organization, Linked Data Community: Supporting Schema.org deployment and usage with a special focus on Linked Data (2011), http://schema.rdfs.org/
12. Castle, D., et al.: Knowledge Management and the Contextualisation of Intellectual Property Rights in Innovation Systems. Journal of Law, Technology and Society 7(1), 32–50 (2010)
13. The United Bible Societies, Swindon, UK (2014), http://www.unitedbiblesocieties.org/
14. Shettar, R., Bhuptani, R.: A Vertical Search Engine–Based On Domain Classifier. International Journal of Computer Science and Security 2(4), 18–27 (2007)
15. The World Factbook by Central Intelligence Agency, Washington DC, US (2013), https://www.cia.gov/library/publications/the-world-factbook/index.html
16. Human Development Reports by United Nations Development Programme (2012), http://hdr.undp.org/en/data
17. World Wide Web Consortium (W3C), OWL Web Ontology Language Use Cases and Requirements, W3C Recommendation (2004), http://www.w3.org/TR/webont-req/
18. Katifori, A., Halatsis, C., Lepouras, G., Vassilakis, C., Giannopoulou, E.: Ontology Visualization Methods - A Survey. ACM Computing Surveys (CSUR) 39(4), 10 (2007)
19. World Wide Web Consortium (W3C), SPARQL Query Language for RDF, W3C Recommendation (2008), http://www.w3.org/TR/rdf-sparql-query/
20. World Wide Web Consortium (W3C), SWRL: A Semantic Web Rule Language Combining OWL and RuleML, W3C Recommendation (2004), http://www.w3.org/Submission/SWRL/

Knowledge Sharing Idiosyncrasies of University Students in Ghana

Michael Dzigbordi Dzandu[1], Henry Boateng[2], and Yinshan Tang[1]

[1] Informatics Research Centre, Henley Business School, University of Reading,
RG6 6UD, Reading, UK
m.d.dzandu@pgr.reading.ac.uk, y.tang@henley.ac.uk
[2] Department of Marketing and Customer Management,
University of Ghana Business School, Legon, Ghana
hboateng@st.ug.edu.gh

Abstract. This study explored the factors affecting knowledge sharing behaviour of students in a higher institution of learning. Using a model derived from the Social Cognitive Theory and the Theory of Reason Action, six hypotheses were tested from a cross-sectional data collected from 371 undergraduate students on a 4-year degree programme in the University of Ghana. Five out of the six hypotheses were supported. The results showed that the knowledge sharing behaviour (KSB) of the students was significantly related to five of the human and environmental factors (F=639.9, df=5, 290, p<0.05) with a co-efficient of variation of R^2=0.917 (91.7%). The knowledge sharing behavior of the students was, however, not significantly dependent on their personal characteristics. The study makes a case for increased attention in understanding the human and environmental factors of knowledge sharing since knowledge sharing is largely a people activity shaped by culture.

Keywords: Knowledge sharing, Knowledge sharing behavior, Ghana·university, Students,·Human factors, Environmental factors.

1 Introduction

Knowledge sharing and learning from each other is part of human life and have been in existence since the beginning of social and community life [1]. Knowledge sharing behaviour is an important component of knowledge management activities, whether in individual or organizational learning [2]. Knowledge cannot be extricated from an individual's ego and occupational meanings; it is woven to people's egos and competitiveness in their occupations and therefore does not flow simply from the knowledge holder to others [3]. Knowledge sharing behaviours and barriers are not limited to organizations alone students also show such tendencies [4]. Over the years scholars have tried to ascertain knowledge sharing behaviour at the organisational level [5] and at the individual level [6]. In the academia, some studies exist. According to Modh et al. [7] found that students were motivated by the need to learn from others and caring for each other to share their knowledge. Again, Isika et al. [8]

K. Liu et al. (Eds.): ICISO 2014, IFIP AICT 426, pp. 348–357, 2014.

reported that the motivating factors for knowledge sharing among students differ from what is found in the corporate world, due to the difference in goals of students. In many instances, students "store" their knowledge and feel reluctant to share because they perceive it to be their personal possession and also as power [9]. More to these points, the lack of in-depth bond between the source and destination of knowledge [10], willingness to share [11], lack of motivation to share and lack of knowledge sharing culture in the learning environment [12] affect knowledge sharing among students.

Additionally, some studies have employed different theories to explain the knowledge sharing behaviour of individuals in organizations. For example, Endres et al. [13] used self-efficacy theory; [14] used Social exchange theory whilst [15] integrated social capital theory and social cognitive theory to understand knowledge sharing. Also, Chow and Chan [5] integrated social capital theory with Theory of Reason Action to whilst other scholars have proposed integration of social cognitive theory and social exchange theory to study knowledge sharing behaviour [16]. This study, however, tries to integrate the Social Cognitive theory and Theory of Reason Action to ascertain knowledge sharing behaviour of undergraduate students of the University of Ghana. This will help compliment the weakness of one model with the strength of the other and also help to adequately discuss from the human and environment factors perspectives.

A cursory look into the knowledge management literature shows a paucity of literature on knowledge sharing behaviour among students in higher education in Sub-Saharan Africa although globally a lot of studies exist ([4], [24], [27], [28]). This is particular so in Ghana, where knowledge sharing behaviour among students in universities is virtually non-existing ([17], [18], [19]). Although considerable studies have been done on knowledge management in Ghanaian context ([17]; [18], [19]), these studies do not consider knowledge sharing behaviour of students in higher institutions of learning. Again looking at the structural and cultural disparities between Ghanaian universities and those other countries and the universities in the aforementioned countries where similar studies have been conducted, this study is justified from a developing country context. The rest of the paper is divided into four parts. Part one focuses on reviewing relevant literature while part two discusses the methodology employed. Part three focuses on results and discussion of findings and the last part contains the conclusions.

2   Background

2.1   Cognition and Reason

The literature covers three themes, namely the Social Cognitive theory, Theory of Reason Action and knowledge sharing, knowledge sharing among students and factors affecting knowledge sharing.

The Social cognitive theory adopted for this study posits that individual behaviour is not static, but reciprocal or interactive network of personal factors, behaviour and context dependent [20]. The model of reciprocal causation, posits that behaviour, cognition and other personal factors, and environmental effects operate as interacting effects that affect each other bi-conditionally [21]. Social cognitive theory has been linked with the model of causation consisting of triadic reciprocal determinism. The theory of reasoned action, a principal factor in the theory of planned behaviour is the individual's intention to act in a given manner [22]. According to the theory, the proximal determinants of behaviour are intentions to engage in the behaviour and perceived behavioural control over the behaviour. The environment may denote the students, faculty members, policies and other objects within the institution. By inference it can be argued that students may share their knowledge when the academic environment encourages collaborative learning and social networking.

Several scholars have described the knowledge sharing process as the processes through which people be it individuals, group or organization mutually exchange knowledge and jointly create new knowledge ([23], [4]). Knowledge sharing is one of the most important aspects of knowledge management. The subject has become topical in recent times among people in organizations; teachers and students in universities as well as schools; and even among countries [7]. Knowledge sharing among students is the focus of this study, particularly as academic environments are considered knowledge intensive settings.

The extant literature provides broad evidence of knowledge sharing in academic environments ([24]; [25]). Some scholars have provided evidence of factors affecting knowledge sharing behaviour of students. Also, Schrader [26] found that the main reason why students share their knowledge is to solve their problems. In a related study, Zia-ur-Rehman et al. [27] noted that factors such as perceptions about knowledge sharing, trust and lack of knowledge to share [28], willingness to share and ability to share, instructor support and technology factors affect knowledge sharing among students [29].

According to Yuen and Majid [4], students share their knowledge because their colleagues would benefit from them. Nonetheless, some students equate knowledge to power, and source of competitive advantage and therefore are reluctant to share their knowledge [30]. Students are not willing to share knowledge for academic activities that were graded [4]. Furthermore, lack of mutual bond or relationship among students [10], lack of motivation or rewards to share [4]; lack of time [31] and non-existence of knowledge sharing culture in the learning environment [12] have been noted as the barriers to knowledge sharing among students.

Some scholars have also tried to investigate the mode of communication of knowledge among students. For example, Yuen and Majid [4] and Caipang [28] both found that face-to-face communication is the most preferred channel for most students to share knowledge, followed by online chat, email, and telephone, with the online message board or Short Message Service (SMS) being least preferred.

2.2   Factors Affecting Knowledge Sharing

It has been observed in the literature so far that for people who are willing to share their knowledge, the norm of reciprocity is important-they expect others to contribute as well [32]. Among the myriad of factors that facilitate or impede knowledge sharing, prior research has consistently identified culture as one of the most important [33]. The literature has also established lack of time, lack of social network, education, fear of loss of ownership, among others as barriers to effective [34]. Technology also plays a role in stimulating a positive knowledge sharing culture [35]. Perception affects knowledge sharing [36] and institutions that provide an environment that supports a positive perception are more likely to influence students or faculty members to share their knowledge [14].

Another factor that has been established in the literature as limiting knowledge sharing is the issue of kind of knowledge. Tacit knowledge essentially resides in the minds of the knower and it is therefore almost impossible for tacit knowledge to be shared without the active participation and cooperation of the knower ([37], [38]). Apart from the type of knowledge, various dimensions of the human factor also affect knowledge sharing. The active participation of the people involved in the knowledge sharing activities hinges on confidence, teamwork, interpersonal skills and ultimately self-esteem. Some people may have the feeling that the recipient of their knowledge will misuse it, and also the knowledge being shared might not be accurate and credible [39]. The attitude [29] and motivation [4] factors as well as personal characteristics of the person involved in the knowledge sharing are also noted.

Personal characteristics of individuals such as gender and age, education among others are likely to be factors that motivate knowledge sharing were viable predictors [36]. For example, Senge [9] in his study noted that factors such as age, race, faculties, and nationality have significant impact on knowledge sharing in a higher learning institution. Also, Ojha [40] found a relationship between group compatibility and knowledge sharing. The more compatible a person was with the group in terms of age, gender and other factors, the more likely he or she was to practice knowledge sharing; and conversely individuals who perceive themselves in a minority (e.g., gender, marital status, education, etc.) are less likely to participate in knowledge sharing.

A critical look at the theories and the literature reviewed for the study point to knowledge sharing as being a human activity within a defined environment or culture as shown in the proposed model in Fig. 1.

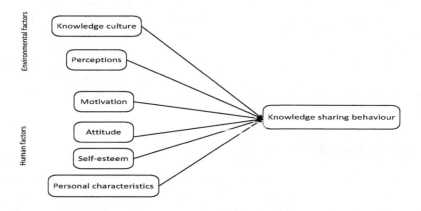

Fig. 1. Human-Environmental Model of Knowledge Sharing

The human factors were derived largely from the Social Cognitive Theory whilst the environmental factors were derived from the Theory of Reasoned Action together with extant literature. Based on this model, we have developed the following hypotheses which will be tested in this study:

H1: Knowledge sharing influences knowledge sharing behaviour
H2: Perceived limiting factors affect knowledge sharing
H3: Motivation influences knowledge sharing
H4: Self-esteem affects knowledge sharing behaviour
H5: Attitude influences knowledge sharing behaviour
H6: Personal characteristics influences knowledge sharing behaviour

3   Methodology

This study employed the exploratory approach where previous studies on knowledge sharing behaviour were reviewed to identify variables that formed the basis of the proposed model used for the study. Twenty variables were arrived at from the reviews, which were subsequently grouped into two main factors for environmental namely knowledge sharing culture and perception of knowledge sharing; and the human factors namely motivation, self-esteem and attitude. Five of the questions measured motivation, 3 questions each measured self-esteem, culture and perception, and 6 questions were for attitude. The number of questions used in measuring each variable was informed by the need for questions and counter questions on the same issues in order to ensure consistency in the responses and enhance the reliability of the measures. This was also informed by the decision to make for easy and simplistic aggregation of the scores which sums up to 100 (maximum score of 5 * 20questions). The twenty variables formed the basis of the questions that were designed on a Likert scale questionnaires for the study. The questionnaire was then administered to a randomly selected cluster of students at lecture sessions. In all 371 undergraduate students of the University of Ghana participated in the study. The students were required to indicate the extent to which the questions applied to them on a scale of 1-5, where 1-strongly disagree, 2-disagree, 3-neutral, 4-agree and 5- strongly agree. Data was also collected on the personal characteristics of the students. The summated scale was used to arrive at the average scores for both the independent and the dependent variables. The reliability test for the pilot study gave a high Cronbach Alpha of 0.71 for the 20-item Likert-scale used in measuring the knowledge sharing behaviour. Descriptive and inferential statistics were used and analytical tools namely regression, correlation, ANOVA and t-test were used to test the hypotheses for the study at the 95% significance level.

4   Results and Discussion

The researchers tested six hypotheses on the relationship between knowledge sharing behaviour and the independent variable namely knowledge sharing culture, motivation, self-esteem, attitude and perception and personal characteristics. A look at the background of the students showed that they were made of 51.5% males and

48.5% females in their 1st (3.5%), 2nd (50.6%), 3rd (25.6%) and 4th (20.3%) years on the 4-year undergraduate programmes at the University of Ghana. The students ranged in age between 18-36 years with a mode of 20 years, median of 21.0 years and mean of 21.8 years. Their programme composition was BA (58.3%), BSc (41.0%) and the BFA (0.6%). The majority (70.9%) were resident on campus whilst 29.1% were non-resident students. The proportion of Ghanaians to foreigners was 97% to 3% for the sample drawn for the study. The students were from four main faculties namely Arts (20.3%), Business (41.5%), Science (0.9%) and Social Sciences (37.3%). The study found no significant differences in the knowledge sharing behaviour of the students with respect to any of these personal characteristics ($p>0.05$). Therefore hypothesis H6 was not supported; that is the knowledge sharing behaviour of the students was not significantly dependent on their personal characteristics.

The data for the study revealed a significant relationship between knowledge sharing behaviour and the independent variables (F=639.9, df=5, 290; p<0.05) (Table 1). This shows that the regression model was robust in establishing the relationship between the dependent (knowledge sharing behaviour) and the independent variables.

Table 1. ANOVA Test of the Regression Model for the Factors of Knowledge Sharing Behaviour

Model[b]	Sum of Squares	df	Mean Square	F	Sig.
Regression	11892.560	5	2378.51	639.87	.000[a]
Residual	1077.977	290	3.72		
Total	12970.537	295			

a. Predictors: (Constant), P, MOT, ATT, KSC, SE;   b. Dependent Variable: KSB

The regression co-efficient obtained was R=0.958, $R^2 = 0.917$. Thus the strength of the relationship between the knowledge sharing behaviour and the independent variables was (95.8%) and as much as 91.7% of the knowledge sharing behaviour of the students can be explained by changes in the independent variables considered in this study.

All the five independent factors yielded positive co-efficients which were all significant in establishing a regression model for the knowledge sharing behaviour and the independent factors (p<0.05).

Table 2. Regression Coefficients for the Factors of Knowledge Sharing Behaviour

Model[a]	Coefficients		t	Sig.
	B	Std. Error		
(Constant)	14.160	1.067	13.28	.000
Attitude (ATT)	1.014	.077	13.18	.000
Motivation (MOT)	1.240	.061	20.21	.000
Self-esteem (SE)	.931	.055	16.90	.000
Knowledge Culture (KC)	1.031	.058	17.84	.000
Perception (P)	1.031	.055	18.76	.000

a. Dependent Variable: KSB

The regression model as per the results in Table 2 can thus be expressed as:

$$KSB = 14.16 + 1.01(ATT) + 1.24(MOT) + 0.93(SE) + 1.03 (KSC) + 1.03(P) . \quad (1)$$

The results in Table 3 show that the perceptions of the students about knowledge sharing correlated strongest and positively with their knowledge sharing behaviour (0.642), followed by self-esteem (0.626), knowledge sharing culture (0.572), motivation (0.495), and attitude (0.495) which correlated least with their knowledge sharing behaviour, albeit positively and significantly at the 0.05 level.

Table 3. Correlation Matrix for the Factors of Knowledge Sharing Behaviour

Knowledge sharing factors		ATT	MOT	SE	P	KC
KSB	R	.495**	.548**	.626**	.642**	.572**
	p-value	.000	.000	.000	.000	.000
	N	296	296	296	296	296
ATT	R		.186**	.180**	.156**	.120*
	p-value		.001	.001	.004	.027
	N		337	349	343	342
MOT	R			.200**	.141*	.050
	p-value			.000	.010	.364
	N			336	330	331
SE	R				.333**	.229**
	p-value				.000	.000
	N				345	341
P	R					.313**
	p-value					.000
	N					336

*. Correlation is significant at the 0.05 level (2-tailed);   **. Correlation is significant at the 0.01 level (2-tailed).

Thus hypotheses H1, H2, H3, H4 and H5 were supported by the data for the study (Tables 2 and 3) but hypothesis 6 was not supported since the knowledge sharing behaviour of the students was not significantly ($p>0.05$) dependent on the personal characteristics of the students (gender, age, and nationality).

The students tended to share more tacit (51.7%) than explicit (49.3%) knowledge. The direction of the knowledge sharing activities of the students was one of reciprocal tendencies (89.3%) with a focus on views of others they have learnt (46.7%) rather than on common views (37.5%) or an emphasis on their own views (15.8%). The students desire to share knowledge with their peers was most challenged by lack of time (49.9%) and least affected by perceived high cost of sharing knowledge (5.1%).

Technology has been described as an enabler of knowledge sharing, providing enhanced tools for general knowledge management activities and a platform, particularly for knowledge sharing. The study found that most of the students indicated face-to-face (59.0%), followed by WhatsApp (26.3%) and mobile phone (8.0%) as their most preferred medium for knowledge sharing whilst the least used medium was SMS (3.5%).

5   Conclusions

The study set out to explore the factors that affect the knowledge sharing behaviour of students in a higher institution of learning. The study revealed a significant relationship between the knowledge sharing behaviour of the students and both the environmental or cultural factors and the human factors of attitude, motivation and self-esteem with an explainable variation of 91.7%. Whilst acknowledging that knowledge sharing is an obvious activity in academic environment like the university, students' knowledge sharing behaviour especially among themselves is a very important aspect of university training in the area of teamwork, interpersonal skills and developing self-confidence for academic, social and future work life adjustments. The findings are evident of the Social Cognitive theory and Theory of Reason Action from which the proposed human-environmental factors of knowledge sharing model have been developed. The study makes significant contribution to the essence of informatics by trying to explore the interactions between human and information systems. The study is suggestive of the fact that the internal human dynamics of attitude, self-esteem and motivation within the constraints of perceived limiting factors and the context of pervasive environmental or cultural factors to a large extent influence the knowledge sharing behaviour of students.

The study recommends that university management should promote activities that help students to develop positive attitude, high self-esteem and motivation, coupled with positive perceptions whilst creating a knowledge sharing culture in the university environment. The study is, however, exploratory, therefore the proposed model need to be tested within different settings and with robust data in order to make generalizations. Also, it would be important to undertake series of test of reliability of the variables adopted for the study or at best adopt more standardised instruments for measuring the human factors from the domain of Psychology in order to enhance the validity and reliability of the data and results across different cultures. The authors also acknowledge the difficulty in defining what knowledge is; and knowledge as used in the context of this study was generic knowledge rather than specific knowledge. In effect the responses only represent what the students understood and perceived as knowledge. These do not in any way affect the findings of the study. The study makes a case for further research on understanding the human factors of knowledge sharing within defined cultures since knowledge sharing is primarily a human driven activity.

References

1. Malafsky, G.P.: Technology for Acquiring and Sharing Knowledge Assets. In: Holsapple, C.W. (ed.) Handbook on Knowledge Management 2: Knowledge Directions, pp. 85–107. Springer, Heidelberg (2003)
2. Nonaka, I.: A Dynamic Theory of Organizational Knowledge Creation. Organization Science 5(1), 14–37 (1994)
3. Davenport, T.H., De Long, D.W., Beers, M.C.: Successful knowledge management projects. Sloan Management Review 39(2), 43–57 (1998)

4. Yuen, T.J., Majid, M.S.: Knowledge-sharing patterns of undergraduate students in Singapore. Library Review 56(6), 485–494 (2007)
5. Chow, W.S., Chan, L.S.: Social network, social trust and shared goals in organizational knowledge sharing. Information & Management 45(7), 458–465 (2008)
6. Haas, M.R., Hansen, M.T.: When using knowledge can hurt performance: the value of organizational capabilities in a management consulting company. Strategic Management Journal 26(1), 1–24 (2005)
7. Mohd, S.N.H., Goh, G.G.G., Fathi, N.M.: Factors Affecting Motivations to Share Knowledge among University Students. In: Proceeding of the International Conference on Management, Economics and Finance (ICMEF 2012), pp. 693–703 (2012)
8. Isika, E., Ismail, M.A., Khan, A.F.: Knowledge sharing behaviour of postgraduate students in University of Malaya. The Electronic Library 31(6), 713–726 (2013)
9. Senge, P.: Sharing knowledge. Executive Excellence 14, 1–3 (1997)
10. Cross, R., Baird, L.: Technology is not enough: Improving performance by building organizational memory. Sloan Management Review 41(3), 69–79 (2000)
11. Liyanage, C., Elhag, T., Ballal, T., Li, Q.: Knowledge communication and translation: A knowledge transfer model. Journal of Knowledge Management 13(3), 118–131 (2009)
12. Syed-Ikhsan, S.O.S., Rowland, F.: Benchmarking knowledge management in a public organisation in Malaysia. Benchmarking: An International Journal 11(3), 238–266 (2004)
13. Endres, M., Endres, S., Chowdhury, S., Alam, I.: Tacit Knowledge Sharing, Self-Efficacy Theory and Application to the Open Source Community. Journal of Knowledge Management 11(3), 92–103 (2007)
14. Liang, P., Jansen, A., Avgeriou, P.: Selecting a high-quality central model for sharing architectural knowledge. In: Proceedings of the 8th International Conference on Quality Software (QSIC), pp. 357–365. IEEE Computer Society Press (2008)
15. Chiu, C.M., Hsu, M.H., Wang, E.T.G.: Understanding knowledge sharing in virtual communities: An integration of social capital and social cognitive theories. Decision Support Systems 42(3), 1872–1888 (2006)
16. Okyere-Kwakye, E., Nor, K.M.: Individual factors and knowledge sharing. Journal of Economic and Business Administration 3(5), 66–72 (2011),
http://thescipub.com/pdf/10.3844/ajebasp.2011.66.72
17. Narteh, B.: Knowledge transfer in developed-developing country inter-firm collaborations: a conceptual framework. Journal of Knowledge Management 12(1), 78–91 (2008)
18. Narteh, B.: Knowledge transfer and performance in Danish-Ghanaian strategic alliances. International Journal of Knowledge Management Studies 4(2), 198–215 (2010)
19. Boateng, H.: Knowledge transfer from academia to industry: A study of Ghanaian graduate students. Unpublished Masters Thesis University of Ghana, Legon (2012)
20. Bandura, A.: Social Cognitive Theory. In: Vasta, R. (ed.) Annals of child development, vol. 6, pp. 1–60 (1989)
21. Bandura, A., Adams, N.E.: Analysis of self-efficacy theory of behavioral change. Cognitive Therapy and Research 1, 287–310 (1977)
22. Ajzen, I., Fishein, M.: Understanding Attitudes and Predicting Social Behaviour. Prentice-Hall, Englewood Cliffs (1980)
23. Van den Hooff, B., Van Weenen, F.D.L.: Committed to share: commitment and CMC use as antecedents of knowledge sharing. Knowledge and Process Management 11(1), 13–24 (2004a)
24. Ho, S.P., Hsu, Y., Lin, E.: Model for Knowledge-Sharing Strategies: A Game Theory Analysis. The Engineering Project Organization Journal 1(1), 53–65 (2011)

25. Nazemi, J., Seyed-Hosseini, S., Fadaei, M.A.: Game-Theoretic Approach to Knowledge Sharing between Suppliers. A Case Study in the Iranian Automotive Industry (SAIPA). Australian Journal of Basic and Applied Sciences. 5(11), 1731–1741 (2011)
26. Schrader, S.: Informal technology transfer between firms: co-operation through information trading. Research Policy 20, 153–170 (1991)
27. Zia-ur-Rehman, K.A.J., Bin Dost, M.K., Wassan, A.A., Rasool, N.: Knowledge sharing behaviour of the students: comparative study of LUMS and COMSATS Kuwait Chapter of Arabian Journal of Business and Management Review. Journal of Business and Management Review 1(4), 138–149 (2011)
28. Caipang, C.L.A.: Perception on Knowledge-sharing Activities among Industrial Technology Students in a Public Higher Education Institution. Research Journal of Applied Sciences, Engineering and Technology 6(8), 1418–1423 (2012)
29. Wangpipatwong, S.: Factors influencing knowledge sharing among university students. Paper presented at the Proceedings of the 17th International Conference on Computers in Education, Asia-Pacific Society for Computers in Education, Hong Kong (2009)
30. Chaudhry, A.B.: Knowledge sharing practices in Asian institutions: A Multi-Cultural Perspective from Singapore. IFLA, Oslo (2005)
31. Hussein, A.R.H., Nassuora, A.B.: Jordanian student's attitudes and perceptions towards knowledge sharing in institutions of higher education. Int. J. Acad. Res. 3, 401–405 (2011)
32. Adler, P.S., Kwon, S.-W.: Social Capital: Prospects for a new concept. Academy of Management Review 27(1), 17–40 (2002)
33. Abzari, M., Teimouri, H.: The effective factors on knowledge sharing in organizations. The International Journal of Knowledge, Culture and Change Management 8(2), 105–113 (2008)
34. Riege, A.: Three-dozen knowledge sharing barriers managers must consider. Journal of Knowledge Management 9(3), 18–35 (2005)
35. Sveiby, K.E., Simons, R.: Collaborative climate and effectiveness of knowledge work. Journal of Knowledge Management 6(5), 420–433 (2002)
36. Connelly, C.E., Kelloway, K.: Predictors of employees' perceptions of knowledge sharing cultures. Leadership & Organizational Development Journal 24(5/6), 294–301 (2003)
37. Davenport, T.H., Prusak, L.: Working Knowledge. Harvard Business Press, Boston (1998)
38. Nonaka, I., Takeuchi, H.: The Knowledge Creating Company. Oxford Press, New York (1995)
39. Naftanaila, I.: Factors Affecting Knowledge Transfer in Project Environment. Review of International Comparative Management 11(5), 834–840 (2010)
40. Ojha, A.K.: Impact of team demography on knowledge sharing in software project teams. South Asian Journal of Management 12(3), 67–78 (2005)

A Logical Pattern for Integrating Business Intelligence into Information Systems Design

Stephen Opoku-Anokye and Yinshan Tang

Informatics Research Centre, Business Informatics, Systems and Accounting,
Henley Business School, University of Reading, Whiteknights, Reading, RG6 6UD, UK
s.opoku-anokye@pgr.reading.ac.uk, y.tang@henley.ac.uk

Abstract. In this paper, we review, literature concerning the relationship between the requirements for information systems design and business intelligence (BI). This is to provide a basis for discussion on the need for the integration of BI into information systems design. Literature on the current design patterns for information systems and BI were reviewed to identify design trends that are contributing to the use of BI that are based on only the data extracted from source information systems. We observe three main layers of logical design pattern for computer-supported information systems, namely, information presentation layer, domain model layer and information source layer. We classified according to the design purpose of each layer, which are, purposeful use of information presentation (Pragmatics design layer), meaning and understanding of information within particular business domains (Semantics design layer) and storage of signs for information captured and encoded into data (Syntactic design layer). We propose LOPIBIS as a logical pattern for integrating BI into information systems design, which is to support the use of a single version of business rules (SVOBR) to capture, process and recall same sets of data in source information systems. Subsequently enabling to the use of BI that are based on not just the data extracted from source information systems, but data with the contexts of business actions.

Keywords: Information Systems Design, Business Intelligence, Logical Design Pattern.

1 Introduction

Traditionally, the design efforts for a computer-supported information system (CSIS) focus on how to provide support for a more efficient and productive business operations [1] or appropriate and effective decision making [2]. The issues considered during the initial design of CSIS are largely the collection, processing, display and storage of information for purposeful use to support business actions or decision making. Information system design involves the gathering and analysis of business requirements to produce specifications for the information system. These specifications are used to produce abstract models for implementation to support information collection, processing, display and storage. Given the focus on either efficient and effective business actions or appropriate and effective business decision

K. Liu et al. (Eds.): ICISO 2014, IFIP AICT 426, pp. 358–367, 2014.

making; the initial specifications are, largely, for the design and implementation of CSIS that aims to provide support for business actions or decision making cycles. These include the need for the design of CSIS to process, store and/or retrieve transaction information, analytical information, collaborative information, etc. Business Intelligence (BI) is usually given almost negligible consideration during the design of CSIS to support business operations, collaboration or decision making. Due consideration is given, when end-users of CSIS begin to make demands for capabilities "to explore, make sense of, and gain actionable insight into rapidly changing business ecosystems." [3] Usually, by the time system designers begin to consider BI, a number of disparate and varied CSIS would have been in use for some time and are generating varieties of data at high volumes and velocity.

BI solutions are designed and implemented in organisations to provide support for the making of effective and appropriate business decisions or the taking of efficient and effective business actions or all. Its aim is to enable people within and across organisations to make sense of data that are being captured by the various information systems that support the process of business decision making and the taking of business actions. The objectives of implementing a BI solution in an organisation include the provision of support for "complex decision making and problem solving" [4]. This objective is achieved by enabling end-users of BI to answer fundamental business questions that the operations and decision-making cycle in every organisation depends on [5]. The primary aim of designing a BI solution can therefore be said to provide support for (1) effective and appropriate business decision making; (2) improving the efficiency with which decisions are made [6]; and (3) improving efficiency and effectiveness of business actions. In current industry practice, BI is either perceived to be a concept that is commonly used to describe "technologies, applications, and processes for gathering, storing, accessing, and analysing data." [7] or "architecture and collective use of integrated operational and decision-support applications and data-bases" [8]. BI design, therefore, involves the extraction of data from operations, collaborations or decision support systems. The extracted data is cleansed and then transformed into information and subsequently into knowledge. This information is then presented to BI end-users as reports, dashboards, scorecards, query results or analytical models. Often, the extracted-cleansed-transformed data are first loaded into a database or databases that are dedicated for BI use only. Examples of such databases include data-marts, operational data stores, analytical data stores, some data warehouse implementations, data cubes, etc.

Transformation of data as part of the BI process is achieved with the use of business rules to extract, cleanse, consolidate, aggregate, transform and make sense of data that were captured and stored within disparate CSIS. These business rules are often different from the business rules that exist in respective CSIS where the data are processed, captured and stored. The use of one set of business rules within an information system to capture and store information, and a different set of business rules to retrieve the same set of information through BI; thus presents a real risk, where, the data retrieved via BI may not have the same context as the data captured during the processing of such information. This creates gaps between the semantics of data captured and stored and information presented through BI. The existence of semantic gaps between any two or more information sources exacerbate the "levels of deceit in data and information manipulation [9]" that may go on within and across organizations. We argue these semantics gaps could be bridged when BI is integrated into information systems designs. We define two main criteria for such integration as follows:

1. The design of CSIS does not to consider just the display, processing with business rules and storage of data, but also the interaction of business rules that generated the data.
2. CSIS are designed to recall facts with context based on data with consideration to business rules interactions.

In this paper, we propose a logical pattern for the integration of BI into the design of information systems.

2   Design Pattern for Information Systems and Business Intelligence

The design of CSIS includes considerations for architecture and collective use of integrated operational systems, collaborative systems, decision-support systems, databases and business rules storage systems. The physical distribution of such architectures and integrated systems are different from the understanding of their logical designs and distributions [8]. Thus the physical distribution of any information system could be different from the understanding of its logical designs and distributions. A typical internal model for a CSIS follows n-tier client-server pattern with a clear division between data and application tiers. The pre-defined business rules that are used to control data flow and processing logic usually form part of the application tier or may be separated into several layers. Sometimes, the components that make up these two tiers could be separated into several layers. [10] describe three principal layers of logical CSIS design as presentation, domain and data source. We classify each of these three logical design layers according to the design purpose of each layer and map them to the three levels of abstractions for sign-systems as: (1) a model for the purposeful use of information that are presented (i.e. pragmatic model), (2) a model for the meaning and understanding of information within particular business domains (i.e. semantics model) and (3) a model for capturing, processing, forwarding and storage of signals (i.e. syntactic model). Fig. 1 is a diagram that describes our understanding of the current logical design pattern for CSIS and BI.

Current implementations of CSIS involve the design to encode facts with the contexts of business actions into data for processing and storage. Multiple version of business rules (MVOBR) are used to capture, forward, process, encode, store, recall and decode the same sets of data. Business data are often stored in a database or databases without the interactions of business rules that were used to process and encode the information into data. The use of these data without the associated interactions of business rule that created the data, excludes critical details about the facts that can be obtained from such data. These exclusions include information about what, how, when, where and why a particular piece of information was processed, encoded into data and stored during business operations or decisions making cycle. The contexts of business actions for the facts that are obtained from data that stored within the physical implementation of CSIS exist as part of the interactions of business rules that created such data. Thus, the facts represented by the data stored within database systems without the associated interactions of business rules may not have the same contexts of business actions as that of the data captured and encoded. In order to preserve the semantics of information presented to end-users through BI, design of CSIS need to encode facts with the contexts of business actions and store them as data with associated interactions of business rules. BI solutions can use these same business rules to decode the data stored within database systems into the facts with the contexts of business actions. Facts with the contexts of business actions enables end-users to 'process information into knowledge', which are then used to support business operations, collaborations and/or decision making. Design of CSIS needs to consider the capturing, encoding, recalling and decoding of data, whiles putting particular emphasis on maintaining the semantics of data captured. To achieve this would require an integrated approach to the design of domain models and data sources for CSIS and to enable BI across the organisation. This suggests the need for a unified approach to the collection, processing and encoding of information into data, the recalling decoding of data into the facts with the associated contexts of business actions, and the storage of data with associated interactions with business rules. Such a unified design approach must not only consider integration between knowledge and operations support as described by [11]; but also the integration of knowledge, business collaborations, decision making and BI requirements. Such integration will ensure consideration for the preservation of semantics (i.e. fact with the contexts of business actions) of data captured and encoded. This will thus ensure the design of CSIS give due consideration to the capture, processing, encoding and storage of data with associated interactions of business rules.

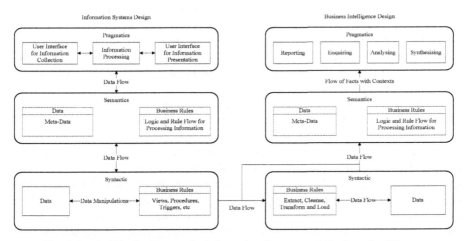

Fig. 1. Logical Design Pattern for Information Systems and Business Intelligence

3   Integration of BI into Information Systems Design

We propose LOPIBIS as a logical pattern for integrating BI into CSIS design. The proposed integration is to enable for the use of a single version of business rules (SVOBR) to capture, process and recall same sets of data. LOPIBIS follows the three principal layers of logical design that were described by [10] (i.e. presentation, domain model and data sources), except that LOPIBIS considers the interactions of business rules with data during the design of domain models and the storage of data with associated business rules interaction into respective information sources (see Fig. 2). The design pattern for the presentation layer of LOPIBIS remains the same as the current logical design pattern as described by [10]. That is, it is composed of two main information presentation design sets. One design set for the presentation of information to support business operations, collaboration and decision making (i.e. information collection, processing and display); and the other design set for the presentation of information to satisfy business intelligence requirements (i.e. reporting, inquiring, analysing and synthesising information). Information presentation design for BI considers the delivery of functionalities that enable capabilities for end-users to report, enquire, analyses and syntheses the facts with contexts of business action of data obtained from multiple and disparate business information sources. LOPIBIS integrates the domain model design of into consistent and unified facts with contexts of business actions (CUFCOBA). The CUFCOBA model contains two sets of meta-data and one set of meta-business-rules. One set of meta-data describes the business data capture, whiles the other describes business data recall. The meta-business-rules describe the business rules interactions that process, encode and decode business data. One set of meta-data are designed with associated meta-business-rules to capture facts with contexts of business actions and encode it into data for storage. The other set of meta-data are designed with associated meta-business-rules to recall and decode data into the facts with contexts of business actions for presentation. These two sets of meta-data and the meta-business-rules within the CUFCOBA model are used to provide support for the storage and sourcing of data with business rules, which include the extraction of data with business rules interactions either during processing of information or integration of information from disparate sources.

McFadden and Hoffer [12] quoted in [13] describe meta-data as "data about data". Meta-business-rules, however, represent business rules about the interactions of business rules. Meta-data and meta-business-rules together provide information about why, when, who, where, when, what and how a particular piece of data is captured, processed, stored and recalled. The CUFCOBA model ensures the design of meta-data and meta-business-rules use a locking and key mechanism with a business rules key and associated business rules executions key attached to each piece of raw data. Implementation and use of systems that are based on the CUFCOBA logical design pattern will help to eliminate the use of MVOBR within physical implementations of CSIS and BI. Therefore, CSIS that are designed based on the LOPIBIS, will bridge the semantic gaps between the facts with contexts of business action of data captured and stored within physical implementations of CSIS and the facts with contexts of business action that are obtained from the data recalled and presented through BI. Semantics contents (i.e. facts with business activity context) are encoded into data with business rules for computers to store using suitable database management systems and business rules management systems. LOPIBIS integrates information source design of CSIS and BI into a unified data with business rules (UDBR). UDBR contains a data store and a business rules store; it does focus design attention on the storage of data with business rules interactions, rather than the storage of just data. Data with business rules interactions stores are designed to be implemented using data with business rules interactions management systems (DBRIMS), whiles associated business rules stores are designed to be implemented using business rules management systems (BRMS). An Implementation of CSIS that is based on CUFCOBA and UDBR logical design patterns would enable CSIS to capture and recall data and BI to recall the same set of data with the same set of business rules. Facts with context of business actions are implemented using a set meta-data and meta-business-rules. These sets of meta-data and meta-business-rules are used to encode and store facts with contexts of business actions into data with business rules interactions; and also to source data with business rules interactions for decoding into the facts with contexts of business actions. This ensures the semantics contained business data that are captured and stored using the physical implementations of CSIS are maintained when such data are recalled into for decoding and presentation to satisfy BI requirements.

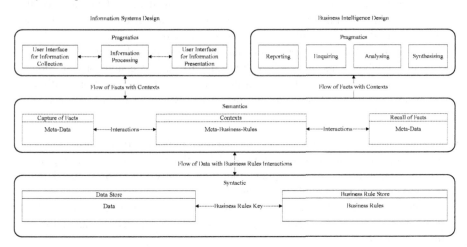

Fig. 2. A Logical Pattern for Integrating Business Intelligence into Information Systems Design

3.1   Integrating BI into Semantic Models

The integrated design of semantic layers with considerations for BI requirements would allow for the implementation and use of two sets of meta-data and a set of meta-business-rules, which are used to:

- Capture facts with the context of business actions and encode them into data for processing and storage along with the interactions of business rules.
- Recall and decode data with associated business rules interactions into facts with the context of business actions that are presented for purposeful use.

Meta-data with associated meta-business-rules for data capture describes how facts with the context of business actions are captured and encoded into data with the interactions of business rules, and how to store these into respective data or business rules stores. The meta-data with associated meta-business-rules that are used for data capture should be designed as a locking mechanism with an informative collection key (ICK). ICK will be used by application programs to encode captured facts and the context of business actions into data with the interactions of business rules, which can then be stored into their respective data and business rules stores as business rules key. Meta-data with associated meta-business-rules for data recall, describes how to recall and data with business rules interactions, and how to decode them into facts with the context of business actions. The meta-data with associated meta-business-rules that are used for data recall should be designed using an unlocking mechanism with a business intelligence key (BIK). BIK will be used by application programs to recall and decode data with the business rules keys that are associated with the original interactions of business rules into facts with the context of business actions. For each ICK within the unified semantic model, there must be a corresponding BIK. This ensures the semantics of data captured are maintained when the data is recalled, irrespective of the original purpose of the design of the application program that was used to capture the data. An integrated approach to the design of semantic models for implementation of application programs that are used to provide support for business operations, collaborations, decision making and BI; would enable organisations to implement and use consistent facts with the contexts of business actions within and across business domains. Such semantic model will have four main functions, which are to:

- Facilitate for the collection, processing and display information to provide support purposeful use of business operations, collaborations and decision making; and to provide capabilities for reporting, inquiring, analyzing and synthesizing of information as dictated by BI requirements.
- Encode facts with the contexts of business actions into the data with the interactions of business rules for storage into a unified organization-wide information store.
- Decode data with the interactions of business rules that are sourced from the unified organization-wide information store into the facts with the contexts of business actions.
- Facilitate for storage of data with the interactions of business rules that are used to capture, encode, process, recall and decode the data into the unified organisation-wide information store.

The integrated semantics model meets the following criteria, which we argued are needed to help resolve semantic gaps between CSIS that are designed to provide support for business operations, collaborations or decision making and BI:

- CSIS are designed to consider the display of information, processing with business rules and storage of data with the interaction of business rules that generated the data.
- CSIS are designed to recall data and decode them into facts with context based on data with consideration to business rules interactions.

3.2   Integrating BI into Syntactic Models

The CUFCOBA semantics, design pattern enables the design and implementation of domain models that are based on common sets of meta-data for data capture and recall and meta-business-rules for their interactions with business rules. These meta-data and meta-business-rules can be used to recall data with associated business rules interactions for decoding into the facts with the contexts of business actions without the need to for a separate data storage design layer for business intelligence specific data. Therefore the need for ETL process becomes unnecessary, particularly the cleansing and transformation of data. Extraction of data with associated business rules interactions from one information source to another may be necessary for the purposes of information backup and consolidation, as well as, other business, functional or technical reasons. In recent years, technologies such as in-memory database architectures, disk-based architectures and many more have been made available to offer fast read-write to and from data stores or business rule stores. Also, technologies that enable the use of meta-information on data and business rules are available to enable separation of applications from data and business rule stores. Availability of these technologies makes it possible for the implementation and use of UDBR models. Such implementation in an organization will enable storage and sourcing of data with business rules and will invalidate the need for ETL, particularly the cleansing and transformation of data. Extraction of data with business rules from one UDBR source into another may be necessary for the purposes of backup, consolidation and other business, functional or technical reasons. BI can thus be used to recall and decode data with associated business rules interactions into the facts with the contexts of business actions, without the need for separate data storage for BI or the associated ETL process. These enable the facts with the contexts of business actions that may be presented through BI to be based on data with the associated business rules interactions that generated the data, instead of being based on data with recreated versions of the interactions with business rules. Thus, it ensures the semantics of the data captured, processed and encoded during business operations, collaboration and decision making are preserved in the data recalled and decoded during BI.

4   Discussions and Conclusion

BI enables use of evidence from past business actions and decisions to support decisions and actions in the present. It also enables use of evidence past and present actions and decisions to anticipate or predict future business actions and decisions and their possible effect on the organization and its environments. The current design of domain models and information sources for an information system gives little consideration to the requirements to enable BI. The requirements for BI are considered when end-user communities start to request for information from the physical implementations of CSIS to satisfy complex business reporting and analytical requirements. Usually reports produced from these physical implementations of CSIS to satisfy these requests are satisfactory for BI purposes when the volume, velocity and variety of information are very low. Thus, as the volume, velocity and variety of data captured by BSS increases, so does the BI obtain from these systems becomes limited. The disparate nature of CSIS that are implemented across an organisation, presents particular challenges when attempting to obtain BI from these disparate CSIS without the original business rules used to capture, process and encode the data. New sets of business rules that may not be the same as the original business rules are used within BI to decode the data into the facts with contexts of business actions. Without the original business rules and associated interactions, the facts obtained from data stored lacks the contexts of business actions; and facts without the contexts of business actions encourages the interpretation of facts with made-up contexts of business actions or to put it simply, misinterpretations. The consequences of these include the:

- Problems associated with inconsistent versions of the same information that may exist in an organization. These are usually due to the use of MVOBR to capture, process and recall from multiple and often disparate data sources.
- Gaps in the semantics between data captured and stored within physical implementations of CSIS and data recalled and decoded into information through BI. The gap is worsened by lack of contextual details about the circumstance in which the data was captured or simply put, lack of data with its original contexts.

Various degrees of differences exist in the interactions of business rules through which information is collected, processed and encoded into data and the interactions of business rules that recall and decode data into the facts with contexts of business actions for presentation through BI. These differences in the interactions of business rules can partly be attributed to the lack of consideration for BI requirements during CSIS design. As a result, most implementations of CSIS would have business rules embedded into the very core (i.e. application code) of these systems. These make it very difficult to recall and decode data stored with the business rules interactions that generated the data; and therefore difficult to recall with the data, the context within which it was captured, processed and encoded. Especially when the data is being recalled from an information system that is not part of the original information system used to capture and encode it. It is, thus, often practical to extract only the data and then transform it into information using a new set of business rules. LOPIBIS is composed of separate pragmatics design layers for CSIS and BI, an integrated semantics design layer called CUFCOBA and an integrated syntactic design layer called UBDR. We argued the CUFCOBA design pattern is needed to help resolve semantic gaps between data that are captured, process and stored within the physical implementations of CSIS and data that are recalled and decoded within BI. The UDBR model advocates integration of BI into the syntactic design layers of CSIS. The UDBR design pattern enables implementation of information storage systems for data with business rules interactions by co-designing databases and business rule stores. This offers a unified approach to the capturing, processing, encoding, recalling and decoding of data both in the physical implementations of CSIS and BI; ensuring the facts obtained from data that are recalled through BI will have the same contexts of business actions as that of the data that were captured, processed, encoded and stored. Thereby helping to preserve the contexts of business actions of data regardless of the purpose and mechanism that is used to recall and decode the data.

References

1. Duan, L., Xu, L.: Business Intelligence for Enterprise Systems: A Survey. IEEE Transactions on Industrial Informatics PP, 1 (2012)
2. Remenyi, D., Sherwood-Smith, M.: Business benefits from information systems through an active benefits realisation programme. International Journal of Project Management 16, 81–98 (1998)
3. Basole, R.C., et al.: Visual Analytics for Converging-Business-Ecosystem Intelligence. IEEE Computer Graphics and Applications 32, 92–96 (2012)
4. Shim, J., et al.: Past, present, and future of decision support technology. Decision support systems 33, 111–126 (2002)
5. Mosimann, R.P., et al.: The Performance Manager: Proven Strategies for Turning Information into Higher Business Performance. Cognos Press, Ottawa (2007)
6. Ariav, G., Ginzberg, M.J.: DSS design: a systemic view of decision support. Commun. ACM 28, 1045–1052 (1985)
7. Wixom, B., Watson, H.: The BI-based organization. International Journal of Business Intelligence Research 1, 13–28 (2010)
8. Moss, L.T., Atre, S.: Business intelligence roadmap: the complete project lifecycle for decision-support applications. Addison-Wesley Professional (2003)
9. Fisher, C., Downes, B.: Performance measurement and metric manipulation in the public sector. Business Ethics: A European Review 17, 245–258 (2008)
10. Fowler, M.: Patterns of enterprise application architecture. Addison-Wesley Professional (2003), 2003
11. Cody, W.F., et al.: The integration of business intelligence and knowledge management. IBM Systems Journal 41, 697–713 (2002)
12. McFadden, F.R., Hoffer, J.A.: Data Base Management. Benjamin-Cummings Publishing Co. Inc., Menlo Park (1988)
13. Ricketts, J.A., et al.: Data reengineering for application systems. In: Proceedings of the Conference on Software Maintenance, pp. 174–179 (1989)

The Adoption of Mobile Games in China: An Empirical Study

Shang Gao[1,2], Zhe Zang[1], and John Krogstie[2]

[1] School of Business Administration,
Zhongnan University of Economics and Law, Wuhan, China
[2] Department of Computer and Information Science,
Norwegian University of Science and Technology
shangkth@gmail.com, zz-whalerider@163.com, krogstie@idi.ntnu.no

Abstract. Mobile games have become very popular in recent years in China. This research aims to investigate the potential factors that influence users' intention to play mobile games. Through the employment of structural equation modeling technology, a research model by extending technology acceptance model (TAM) with flow experience and social norms was proposed. This research model was empirically evaluated using survey data collected from 388 users about their perceptions of mobile games. Eleven research hypotheses were proposed in the study. Eight research hypotheses were positively significant supported, while three research hypotheses were rejected in this study. The result indicates that attitude and flow experience explain about 75% of uses' intention to playing mobile games. It was found that social norms do not have direct effect on the intention to play a mobile game. But it affects the attitude directly. In addition, flow experience, perceived ease of use and perceived usefulness all have direct effects on users' attitude toward playing a mobile game, and the effect from flow experience is quite strong. Flow experience plays an important role in the adoption of mobile games according to the analytical results of our study.

Keywords: Mobile game, TAM, Flow experience, Social norms.

1   Introduction

With the widespread application of the 3G network and handheld technologies in recent years, a number of new mobile innovations have been pushed into the market. Mobile games are one of the most promising and profitable services among them. It is growing rapidly worldwide. According to a report from iResearch in January 2014, the users of mobile game in China were more than 300 million in 2013, and the market revenue of mobile game had reached 11.24 billion, 246.9% higher than last year. Consequently, China is estimated to be one of the largest and fastest-growing mobile markets in the world.

It is found that mobile games are getting increasingly popularity and more and more important in mobile industry [8]. The object of this research is to study the

K. Liu et al. (Eds.): ICISO 2014, IFIP AICT 426, pp. 368–377, 2014.

adoption of mobile games in China. We attempt to investigate potential factors that impact users' intention to play mobile games in China in this research.

Technology Acceptance Model (TAM) [3] has received considerable attention of researchers in the information system field over the past years, and it has been applied to examine IT usage. Many previous studies (e.g., [1, 17]) have verified that user's perceived ease of use and usefulness are key determinants of individual technology adoption. However, perceived ease of use and perceived usefulness may not reflect the motivation of mobile game users exactly. Depending on the specific technology context, additional explanatory variables may be needed beyond the ease of use and usefulness constructs [5-6]. In this study, we proposed additional variables, such as flow experience and social norms to enhance our understanding of mobile game user behavior. Flow theory was used to study the influence of user concentration on task activity [2]. Flow has been studied in the context of information technologies and has been recommended as useful in understanding user behavior. Furthermore, several theories suggest that social influence is important in shaping user behavior. Innovation diffusion research [19] also suggests that user adoption decisions are influenced by a social system beyond an individual's decision style and the characteristics of the information technology. Both the additional variables are necessary to consider in understanding the user behavior of the mobile game context. We used the structure equation model to assess the relationships of variables in the extended TAM in this study.

The remainder of this paper is organized as follows: Section 2 discusses the theoretical background of this study. The research model and hypotheses are presented in Section 3. The research method and results are described in Section 4. This is followed by a discussion of the findings in Section 5. Section 6 concludes this research.

2   Literature Review

The literature related to this research is discussed in this section.

2.1   Technology Acceptance Model (TAM)

TAM is widely acknowledged as one of the most robust and influential models for explaining user acceptance behavior. It has been revised to incorporate additional variables in specific contexts, such as the Internet [20], WWW [18], and so on. Numerous extended variables with specific contexts have been added to TAM, such as perceived playfulness proposed for studying WWW acceptance, perceived enjoyment [10] in using the Internet, trust [7] in using mobile information services, compatibility in virtual stores, flow and environmental psychology in a web-based store, and perceived critical mass in groupware usage. These studies with extended beliefs were proposed to improve the understanding of user acceptance behavior for specific contexts, and better explanations were enabled as a result.

In the context of mobile games, social factors and flow experience are considered as additional variables. Flow experience has been studied as a possible measure of mobile user experience. As game playing may involve unique experiences for players, flow experience was proposed as a motive for playing games in our study. Additionally, technical barriers may have a negative impact on flow experience, consequently, we also considered technical barriers here. Besides, social interaction has critical impact on game players. Therefore, social norms have been assumed to influence user participation and added as the additional belief.

2.2   Flow Experience

The original concept of flow was first introduced by Csikszentmihalyi [2], and has been defined as the holistic experience that people feel when they act with total involvement. In previous studies, flow has been widely used in information system and electronic commerce contexts, such as web navigation, World Wide Web, online shopping, online game and so on. It suggests that online user behavior is significantly affected by the flow experience. Recently, with the development of the mobile devices, flow has also been studied in the mobile environment. For example, Tao Zhou et al. [24] examined the effect of flow experience on mobile social networking service (SNS) users' loyalty, and the results showed that both information quality and system quality significantly affected users' trust and flow experiences, which further determined their loyalty. Moreover, Chia-Liang Hung et al. [12] did a research which examined the influence of usability and flow on user satisfaction of mobile gaming. They built two structural equation models tested the influences resulted from usability and flow, and found the integrative model of usability and flow could explain user mobile satisfaction well.

In summary, most of the previous studies about flow focus on the online environments. The study of flow experience in the mobile environment is just at the beginning, especially for mobile games. In addition, approaches to measuring flow can be broadly characterized as unidimensional or multi-dimensional. In most cases, flow is treated as a multi-dimensional construct and it has characteristics of control, enjoyment, concentration, intrinsic interest, curiosity, etc. Flow is defined as an extremely enjoyable experience in this study. Accordingly, an individual will engage in a mobile game activity with total involvement, control, concentration, enjoyment and intrinsic interest in the flow experience.

2.3   Technical Barriers

In diffusion research theory, barriers are relevant in explaining the difference between innovators and early adopters and other ideal types of adoption behavior, such as the early and late majority and laggards [19]. According to research from Kim et al. [14]., he technicality, defined as the degree to which a mobile service is perceived as being technologically excellent in the process of providing services, was considered as a sacrifice component of the perceived value of an advanced mobile service, reducing the value and intended adoption of a service. Technological barriers may reduce the self-efficacy or perceived behavioral control of users. The technicality of smartphones and mobile services can be translated into the time and effort required to learn and use a system, which may have a negative impact on perceived behavioral control that is one of the characteristics of flow experience. Lack of technical support and training in using mobile systems, are argued to have a negative influence on the adoption of advanced mobile technologies and services [23].

2.4   Social Norms

Social norms represent a factor that is assumed to have a direct impact on perceived utility [15]. Some theories (e.g., [15]) suggest that social norms are crucial in shaping user behavior. Social norms consist of two distinct influences: informational influence and normative influence. Informational influence occurs when a user accepts information obtained from other users as evidence about reality, while normative influence refers that when a person conforms to the expectations of others to obtain a reward or avoid a punishment [4]. Informational influence is an internalization process that occurs when a user perceives information as enhancing his/her knowledge above that of reference groups [13]. Normative influence consists of two processes: identification, which occurs when a user adopts an opinion held by others because he/she is concerned with defining himself/herself as related to the group, and compliance, which occurs when a user conforms to the expectations of another to receive a reward or avoid rejection and hostility. In this study, we define social norms as the extent to which the user perceives the others' approval of his/her mobile game playing.

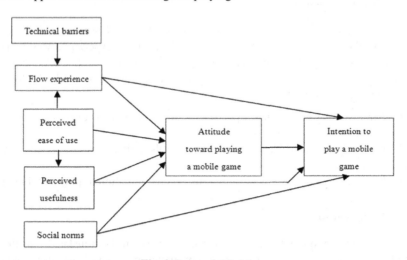

Fig. 1. Research Model

3   Research Model and Hypotheses

The proposed research model (See Figure 1) is an extension of TAM, with a consideration of flow experience, social norms, and technical barriers in addition to perceived ease of use and perceived usefulness, to study the user adoption of mobile games. The perceived usefulness is defined as the degree to which the user believes that playing mobile games will fulfill the purpose. The perceived ease of use to mobile game playing is defined as the degree to which users feel free from engaging in mental and physical efforts. The attitude toward playing a mobile game is defined as user preferences as to mobile game playing. Moreover, the intention to play a mobile game is the degree to which the user would like to reuse mobile games in future.

3.1   Perceived Ease of Use, Perceived Usefulness, Attitude from TAM

In this study, the research model is based on the TAM model. Therefore, our research model adopted the belief-attitude-intention-behavior relationship. According to the TAM, the following hypotheses were proposed in the context of mobile game playing:

H1: Perceived ease of use has a positive effect on the attitude toward playing a mobile game.

H2: Perceived ease of use has a positive effect on perceived usefulness.

H3: Perceived usefulness has a positive effect on the attitude toward playing a mobile game.

H4: Perceived usefulness has a positive effect on the intention to play a mobile game.

H5: Attitude has a positive effect on the on the intention to play a mobile game.

3.2   Flow Experience

A positive relationship between flow and perceived ease of use was identified from the past studies. Besides, Webster el al. found that flow experience was related to positive subjective experience and exploratory behavior [22]. Flow experience seemed to prolong Internet usage. On the basis of the former research, the following hypotheses were proposed:

H6: Perceived ease of use has a positively effect on the flow experience of playing a mobile game.

H7: Flow experience has a positively effect on the attitude toward playing a mobile game.

H8: Flow experience has a positively effect on the intention to play a mobile game.

3.3   Technical Barriers

The technicality of smartphones and mobile services can be translated into the time and effort required to learn and use a system, which may have a negative impact on perceived flow experience. Accordingly, we argue that technical barriers influence the acceptance of mobile games by reducing users' flow experience. Therefore, we proposed the following hypothesis:

H9: Technical barriers have a negative effect on flow experience of playing a mobile game.

3.4   Social Norms

Numerous empirical studies have found that social factors positively impact on user's IT usage. For instance, Venkatesh et al. noted that social norms represent a factor that is assumed to have a direct impact on perceived utility [21]. Accordingly, the following hypotheses were proposed:

H10: Social norms have a positive effect on the attitude toward playing a mobile game.

H11: Social norms have a positive effect on the intention to play a mobile game.

4   Data Analysis

Empirical data was collected by conducting an online survey. We choose college students as the major participants for the following reasons. According to iResearch, the users of mobile game are relatively young, and more than 60% concentrated in 18-30 years old in 2012. Meanwhile, almost 57.6% of the mobile game users have the college degree at least. Therefore, the college students are very representative as the participants for our study.

The survey yielded 412 responses both online and offline, 396 of them were usable. Among the participants, 98.0% had the experience of playing mobile game. Thus, we considered the 388 respondents as our analysis objects. 29.9% of the participants were male, and 70.1% were female. 88.9% of the respondents played mobile game on smartphones. Furthermore, 43.8% were most likely to play mobile game in the dormitory. Besides, about 80% had played mobile games for more than 1 year.

Developed from the literature, the measurement questionnaire consisted of 22 items. A seven point Likert scale, with 1 being the negative end of the scale (strongly disagree) and 7 being the positive end of the scale (strongly agree), was used to examine participants' responses to all items in the survey. In addition, data were analyzed using the structural equation modeling (SEM).

4.1   Measurement Model

The fitness measures are shown in Table 1. Except for the GFI and RMESA, the other fitness measures were all within acceptable range. In practice, GFI values above 0.8 are considered to indicate a good fit. Meanwhile, RMESA is also acceptable when it is less than 0.08 [9]. Consequently, all the fitness measures are within acceptable range. Therefore, we consider the measurement model is acceptable, and the measures indicate that the model fit the data.

The item reliabilities range from 0.51 to 0.93, which exceed the acceptable value of 0.5. Table 2 shows the composite reliability and average variance extracted. All the reliabilities exceed the threshold value of 0.7. Meanwhile, the average variances extracted for all constructs exceed the benchmark of 0.5. As the three values of reliability are above the recommended values, the scales for measuring these constructs are deemed to exhibit satisfactory convergence reliability.

Table 1. Fit indices for the measurement model

Measures	Recommended criteria	Measurement model
Chi-square/d.f.	<3.0	2.950
GFI	>0.9	0.880
AGFI	>0.8	0.844
CFI	>0.9	0.903
RMESA	<0.05	0.071

Table 2. Construct reliabilities

Construct	Composite reliability	Average variance extracted
Technical barriers	0.744	0.509
Social norms	0.957	0.917
Perceived ease of use	0.879	0.709
Perceived usefulness	0.910	0.772
Flow experience	0.873	0.579
Attitude	0.919	0.791
Intention to play	0.833	0.624

Furthermore, the variances extracted by the constructs are more than the squared correlations among variables. The fact reveals that constructs are empirically distinct. As the convergent and discriminant validity measures are quite well, the test of the measurement model is satisfactory.

4.2   Tests of the Structural Model

The structural model was tested using Amos 20. The results of the structural model are shown in Fig. 2.

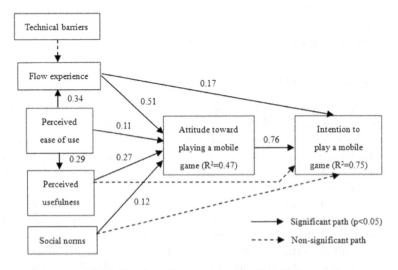

Fig. 2. Results of structural modeling analysis

The standardized path coefficients between constructs are presented, while the dotted lines stand for the non-significant paths. As a result, eight hypotheses were supported, while three hypotheses were rejected in the research model. The path coefficient from flow experience, perceived ease of use, perceived usefulness and social norms to attitude toward playing a mobile game are all statistically significantly. The positive effects of flow experience and perceived usefulness on attitude were relatively strong, as shown by the path coefficient of 0.51 and 0.27 ($P<0.001$). The other path coefficients of perceived ease of use and social norms were statistically positively significant at $P<0.05$. The path from flow experience, perceived ease of use, perceived usefulness and social norms explains 47% of the observed variance in attitude toward playing a mobile game. Thus, H1, H3, H7 and H10 were supported. The effect of attitude toward playing a mobile game on intention to play a mobile game is quite strong, as indicated by the path coefficient of 0.76 ($P<0.001$). The other path coefficient from flow experience to intention to play a mobile game is statistically significant at $P<0.05$. Besides, 75% of the observed variance in intention to play mobile games can be explained by the two paths. Therefore, H5 and H8 were supported. Furthermore, H2 and H6 are also supported with the perceived ease of use positively related to flow experience and perceived usefulness by the path coefficients of 0.34 and 0.29 at $P<0.001$.

5   Discussion

In our study, we find that three hypotheses are not supported. Firstly, technical barriers do not directly affect uses' flow experience. In previous study, it was found that the technicality have a negative impact on perceived behavioral control which is one of the characteristics of flow experience. But, according to our results, technical barriers did not appear to directly affect flow experience. The possible explanation might be that most users are young people and they have skills in playing games. Meanwhile, most mobile games are relatively easy to use. Thus, technical barriers may not be the obstacles in enjoying flow experience for the users. Secondly, the results show that perceived usefulness directly affect the attitude toward playing a mobile game, but it does not motivate users to play mobile games. Some previous studies found the similar results too (e.g.,[16] [11]). It seems reasonable that users would like to play mobile games if they find them useful, while mobile games can entertain the users and bring enjoyment to them. But the results indicate that perceived usefulness does not appear to drive users' participation. The users consider mobile games as an entertainment technology, and they usually want to kill time by playing mobile games. Thus, the significant effect of perceived usefulness to intention to play a mobile game might decrease. Thirdly, the hypothesis that social norms have positive effect on intention to play a mobile game is also not supported. The social norms directly affect the attitude towards playing a mobile game but it does not motivate users to play mobile games similar to the perceived usefulness. Users of mobile games may draw their attention to some mobile games when their friends or classmates recommend them. The systems on the mobile devices will recommend the new and popular games to the users. They can easily find most popular and newest games through the mobile systems. As most users regard the mobile game as an entertainment technology, they always choose the most convenient way to find a mobile game to play. Therefore, the users are more likely to play a mobile game recommended from the mobile systems than from the friends or classmates. In summary, social factors may have positive effect on the adoption of mobile games for the users to some extent, but the influence might not be strong.

Flow experience plays an important role in the adoption of mobile games. It has strong effect on the attitude to mobile game playing, and it also directly affects the intention to play a mobile game. We find that if the users have ever experienced being absorbed in playing a mobile game, they are more likely to adopt a mobile game.

We find that perceived ease of use has positive effect on both flow experience and perceived usefulness. The user-friendly interface of a mobile game is an important factor in forming flow experience of the users. If a user has difficulty in playing a mobile game, he/she may not have the flow experience and may not perceive the usefulness of the game, and then he/she may give up playing the mobile game.

6   Conclusion

With the development of mobile technology, mobile games are becoming more and more popular among the mobile users, but only few studies are concerned with identifying the factors that affect user behavior of mobile games. This study examined users' adoption of mobile games by extending TAM with two additional construct, flow experience and social norms. A research model with 11 research hypotheses was proposed in the study. Eight research hypotheses were positively significant supported, while three research hypotheses were rejected in this study. The results indicated that perceived ease of use directly affects the flow experience, and the flow experience has positive effect both on the attitude and intention to playing mobile games for the users. Meanwhile, social norms do not have positive effect on user's intention to play mobile games, but it affects uses' attitude toward playing mobile games directly. Thus, mobile game providers should be concerned with both flow experience and social factors to facilitate user adoption and usage of mobile games.

Acknowledgement. This research is supported by the Fundamental Research Funds for the Central Universities, China (Project No. ZNUFE. 2012065) and the experimental project funds from Zhongnan University of Economics and Law (Project No. 2012SY25).

References

1. Chen, L.-D., Gillenson, M.L., Sherrell, D.L.: Enticing online consumers: an extended technology acceptance perspective. Information & Management 39(8), 705–719 (2002)
2. Czikszentmihalyi, M.: Flow: The psychology of optimal experience. Lidové Noviny, Praha (1990) (cited on page)

3. Davis, F.D.: Perceived usefulness, perceived ease of use and user acceptance of information technology. MIS Quarterly 13, 319–340 (1989)
4. Deutsch, M., Gerard, H.B.: A study of normative and informational social influences upon individual judgment. The Journal of Abnormal and Social Psychology 51(3), 629 (1955)
5. Gao, S., Krogstie, J., Gransæther, P.A.: Mobile Services Acceptance Model Proceedings of ICHIT. IEEE Computer Society (2008)
6. Gao, S., Krogstie, J., Siau, K.: Developing an instrument to measure the adoption of mobile services. Mobile Information Systems 7(1), 45–67 (2011)
7. Gao, S., Moe, S.P., Krogstie, J.: An Empirical Test of the Mobile Services Acceptance Model. In: 2010 Ninth International Conference on Mobile Business and 2010 Ninth Global Mobility Roundtable (ICMB-GMR), pp. 168–175 (2010)
8. Gao, S., Zang, Z., Gopalakrishnan, S.: A study on distribution methods of mobile applications in China. In: 2012 Seventh International Conference on Digital Information Management (ICDIM), pp. 375–380 (2012)
9. Hayduk, L.A.: Structural equation modeling with LISREL: Essentials and advances. JHU Press (1988)
10. Heijden, H.V.D.: User Acceptance of Hedonic Information Systems. MIS Quarterly 28(4), 695–704 (2004)
11. Hsu, C.-L., Lu, H.-P.: Why do people play on-line games? An extended TAM with social influences and flow experience. Information & Management 41(7), 853–868 (2004)
12. Hung, C.-L., Chou, J.C.-L., Ding, C.-M.: Enhancing Mobile Satisfaction through Integration of Usability and Flow. Engineering Management Research 1(1) (2012)
13. Kelman, H.C.: Processes of opinion change. Public opinion quarterly 25(1), 57–78 (1961)
14. Kim, H.-W., Chan, H.C., Gupta, S.: Value-based adoption of mobile internet: an empirical investigation. Decision Support Systems 43(1), 111–126 (2007)
15. López-Nicolás, C., Molina-Castillo, F.J., Bouwman, H.: An assessment of advanced mobile services acceptance: Contributions from TAM and diffusion theory models. Information & Management 45(6), 359–364 (2008)
16. Liu, Y., Li, H.: Exploring the impact of use context on mobile hedonic services adoption: An empirical study on mobile gaming in China. Computers in Human Behavior 27(2), 890–898 (2011)
17. Lou, H., Luo, W., Strong, D.: Perceived critical mass effect on groupware acceptance. European Journal of Information Systems 9(2), 91–103 (2000)
18. Moon, J.-W., Kim, Y.-G.: Extending the TAM for a World-Wide-Web context. Inf. Manage. 38(4), 217–230 (2001)
19. Rogers, E.M.: The diffusion of innovations. Free Press, New York (1995)
20. Teo, T.S., Lim, V.K., Lai, R.Y.: Intrinsic and extrinsic motivation in Internet usage. Omega 27(1), 25–37 (1999)
21. Venkatesh, V., Bala, H.: Technology acceptance model 3 and a research agenda on interventions. Decision sciences 39(2), 273–315 (2008)
22. Webster, J., Trevino, L.K., Ryan, L.: The dimensionality and correlates of flow in human-computer interactions. Computers in Human Behavior 9(4), 411–426 (1994)
23. Wu, J.-H., Wang, S.-C., Lin, L.-M.: Mobile computing acceptance factors in the healthcare industry: A structural equation model. International Journal of Medical Informatics 76(1), 66–77 (2007)
24. Zhou, T., Li, H., Liu, Y.: The effect of flow experience on mobile SNS users' loyalty. Industrial Management & Data Systems 110(6), 930–946 (2010)

Nash Negotiation Method of Conflict Resolution for MSC Production Marketing Coordination Based on Multi-Agent

Tong Du and Guorui Jiang

The Economics and Management School, Beijing University of Technology,
100124 Beijing, China
jianggr@bjut.edu.cn

Abstract. In the face of increasingly market competition and diversified demand, manufacturers and dealers of Manufacturing Supply Chain (MSC) pay great effort to achieve production marketing coordination. However, it often generates conflicts in the process of production marketing coordination. For this kind of conflict problem, Multi-Agent technology is introduced. Enterprises of the supply chain are represented by Agents. The conflicts among Agents are resolved through Nash negotiation. A model of Nash Negotiation based on Agents is established. The conflict point of negotiation is determined by Stackelberg differential game. A Memetic Algorithm is proposed to solve the model. Finally, the validity of the algorithm and the model is verified by numerical experiment.

Keywords: Supply chain based on Multi-Agent, Production marketing coordination, Conflict, Nash negotiation, Memetic Algorithm, Differential game.

1 Introduction

Production marketing coordination includes core businesses of supply chain, and it is the most important activity of manufacturing [1]. Because each member of the supply chain is independent individual, the operation among members in supply chain often has the characteristics of autonomy, distribution and so on, which leads to that conflicts in the process of production marketing coordination are hard to avoid [2]. If conflicts are not resolved in a timely and effective way, it will affect the effect of coordination and reduce the competitiveness of supply chain [3]. Traditional supply chain management can't resolve the problem of conflict in production marketing coordination effectively. With the development of the distributed object technology and artificial intelligence technology, it has been an important method to research and implement supply chain management that uses Multi-Agent technology to simulate, optimize and control the operation of supply chain [4].

The conflicts in production marketing coordination for supply chain based on Multi-Agent have drawn the attention of some scholars. Zhang establishes a coordination model of supply chain based on Multi-Agent to solve order conflicts,

K. Liu et al. (Eds.): ICISO 2014, IFIP AICT 426, pp. 378–387, 2014.
© IFIP International Federation for Information Processing 2014

and puts forward a negotiation method based on fuzzy theory and Bayesian learning theory to solve the model [5]. For the problem of order fulfillment, Lin establishes a coordination model of Multi-Agent supply chain based on distributed constraint satisfaction, proposes a conflict resolution method based on the negotiation and analyzes the effect of constraint satisfaction algorithm under different form of demand [6]. Zheng analyzes the generating mechanism of conflict of supply chain from the aspect of information coordination, explores the application of multi-Agent system in supply chain management and establishes a supply chain model based on Multi-Agent which can solve the problem of asymmetric information [7]. Behzad considers the conflict between enterprises caused by the difference of goals and information asymmetry, and puts forward to a negotiation method based on Multi-Agent to resolve conflicts between enterprises for the problem of order acceptance in the case that demand is uncertain [8].

However, so far the existing research did not pay much attention on the combination between Game Theory and Multi-Agent. For the conflicts in production marketing coordination of supply chain, this paper introduces the method of Nash negotiation to resolve conflicts, establishes a model of Nash Negotiation based on Multi-Agent, and presents a method based on Memetic Algorithm to solve the model. The method is available to the case that objective function of Nash negotiation cannot be calculated by mathematical derivation.

2   Problem Description and Basic Mathematics Model

For convenience, we restrict that one manufacturer and one dealer in MSC is discussed in this paper. In order to meet the market demand $D(t)$, the dealer purchases a certain amount of products from manufacturer. The dealer decides the price of product $p(t)$, the manufacturer provides products for dealer at the wholesale price $w(t)$. The manufacturing cost of manufacturer is cm, the sales costs of dealer is cr. Let $A(t)$ is manufacturer's advertising investment, $C_a(t)$ is the manufacturer's advertising costs, h is the advertising costs factor of manufacturer, manufacturer advertised to the market to promote product sale, the relation between the manufacturer's advertising cost and the manufacturer's advertising investment is [9]: $C_a(t) = hA(t)^2$.

According to advertising theory, the differential equation of reputation that changes over time is: $\dfrac{dG(t)}{dt} = kA(t) - \varphi G(t)$ .where $G(t)$ represents the reputation, k represents the impact degree on the reputation exerted by the advertising investment of manufacturer, φ represents the attenuation degree of the manufacturer's reputation. The reason of the reputation attenuation is that the consumer turn to other company's products because of the impact of their advertising activities.

Supposed that the price demand function of dealer is [10]: $D(t) = \alpha - \beta P(t) + \eta G$. Where $D(t)$ is the product demand, α, β, η are all the constant number over zero. Among this, the α is the market capacity, the β is the price-sensitive factor. The higher the β value, the more sensitive the demand to price. If the price decreases, the demand increases. The η represents the advertisement-sensitive factor, the higher the η value, the more sensitive the demand to reputation.

Assumed that manufacturer and dealer have the same and positive discount rate μ, the goal of manufacturer is to find the wholesale price strategy and advertising strategy which can optimize itself profit in the infinite time. Then the manufacturer revenue function is as follow:

$$\prod_m = \int_0^\infty e^{\mu t}[(w(t) - c)(\alpha - \beta P(t) + \eta G) - hA(t)^2]dt \tag{1}$$

The dealer revenue function:

$$\prod_r = \int_0^\infty e^{\mu t}[(P(t) - w(t))(\alpha - \beta P(t) + \eta G)]dt \tag{2}$$

Both manufacturer and dealer make decision aiming to maximize their own benefits, which leads to inconsistencies in the decision variables, so conflicts occur. We resolve the conflicts by the method of Nash Negotiation.

3   Nash Negotiation Model Based on Multi-Agent

3.1   Model of Nash Negotiation

The Model of Nash negotiation based on Multi-Agent can be described by the following group with eight elements.

$$NM =< M, D, ME, x, u_m(x), u_r(x), d_m, d_r, S >$$

where M and D represent manufacturers and dealers respectively; ME negotiation coordination Agent; x the issue of negotiation, it is also the decision variable of production marketing coordination. $u_m(x)$ and $u_r(x)$ represent the utility function of manufacturers and dealers respectively. The utility function is represented by revenue function.

d_m and d_r is the conflict point of manufacturers and dealers respectively, which meet the condition $(u_m(x^*), u_r(x^*)) > (d_m, d_r)$, $(u_m(x^*), u_r(x^*)) = \arg\max$ $\prod_{m,d}(u_i(x) - d_i)$, and $(u_m(x^*), u_r(x^*)) \in S$, S is strategy space. It is bottom line of decision maker which means utility of participant i cannot be less than d_i. When the participants are not come to an agreement, conflicts are unable to be resolved. Then d_i is conflict utility of participant i.

Fig. 1. Process of Nash negotiation based on Agent

Model of Nash negotiation can be solved by mathematical derivation if the object function is simple. We can get the solution to set the first derivative is equal to zero and the second derivative is less than zero. But when $\prod_i (u_i(x) - d_i)$ is not differentiable

or the workload of derivation is huge with a very complex form, the mathematical derivation is not available. We can use computer algorithm to get optimal solution.

3.2   The Determination of Conflict Point

The Stackelberg game result is applied as the conflict point of Nash negotiation. he process of Stackelberg game is as follow.

It is a master-slave relationship between manufacturer and dealer when they play Stackelberg game. Manufacturer is master and dealer is slave. We first solve the problem of dealer's optimal control. The optimal function of dealer $V_r(G)$ has to satisfy the HJB equation:

$$\mu V_r(G) = \max_{P(t)} \{ (P(t) - w(t))(\alpha - \beta P(t) + \eta G) + \lambda_r(kA(t) - \varphi G) \} \quad (3)$$

where $\lambda_r = \dfrac{dV_r(G)}{dG}$. Let the first derivative about $P(t)$ at the right side is zero, we

get $P^*(t) = \dfrac{\beta w(t) + \eta G + \alpha}{2\beta}$.

HJB equation of manufacturer :

$$\mu V_m(G) = \max_{w(t),A(t)} \{ (w(t) - c)(\alpha - \beta P(t) + \eta G) - hA(t)^2 + \lambda_m(kA(t) - \varphi G) \} \quad (4)$$

Take $P^*(t)$ into (4) and solve the optimal problem about $A(t)$ and $w(t)$:

$w^*(t) = \dfrac{\eta G + \alpha + \beta c}{2\beta}$, $A^*(t) = \dfrac{k\lambda_m}{2h}$.

We assume that $V_m(G) = \dfrac{B_1}{2}G^2 + B_2 G + B_3$, so $\lambda_m = B_1 G + B_2$. Take λ_m , $P^*(t)$, $w^*(t)$, $A^*(t)$ into right side of (4), take $V_m(G)$ into the left side of (4). Then we compare the coefficient about G of the both side of (4), and get the equation set about B_1, B_2, B_3 .

$$\begin{cases} \dfrac{\mu B_1}{2} = \dfrac{3h\eta^2 - 2\beta(k^2 - 2k)B_1^2 - 8\beta h\varphi B_1}{8\beta h} \\ \mu B_2 = \dfrac{4h\eta(\alpha - \beta c) - 4\beta(k^2 - 2k)B_1 B_2 - 8\beta h\varphi B_2}{8\beta h} \\ \mu B_3 = \dfrac{h(\alpha - \beta c)^2 - 2\beta(k^2 - 2k)B_2^2}{8\beta h} \end{cases} \qquad (5)$$

We get B_1, B_2, B_3 by equation set (5). C_1, C_2, C_3 can be derived in a similar way under the assumption that $V_r(G) = \dfrac{C_1}{2}G^2 + C_2 G + C_3$. Then we solve differential equation of G about t.

$$\dfrac{dG}{dt} = k\dfrac{kB_1 G + kB_2}{2h} - \varphi G \Rightarrow \dfrac{dG}{dt} + \dfrac{2h\varphi - k^2 B_1}{2h}G = \dfrac{k^2 B_2}{2h} \quad,$$

$$\Rightarrow G = e^{-\int\frac{2h\varphi - k^2 B_1}{2h}dt}[C_0 + \int\dfrac{k^2 B_2}{2h}e^{\int\frac{2h\varphi - k^2 B_1}{2h}dt} dt] = C_0 e^{-\frac{2h\varphi - k^2 B_1}{2h}t} + \dfrac{k^2 B_2}{2h\varphi - k^2 B_1}$$

$$G(0) = 0 \qquad \Rightarrow C_0 = -\dfrac{k^2 B_2}{2h\varphi - k^2 B_1}$$

Lemma: the optimal decision under Stackelberg Game is as follow:

$$P^*(t) = \dfrac{3\eta G + 3\alpha + \beta c}{4\beta}, w^*(t) = \dfrac{\eta G + \alpha + \beta c}{2\beta}, A^*(t) = \dfrac{k(B_1 G + B_2)}{2h}$$

$$G = -\dfrac{k^2 B_2}{2h\varphi - k^2 B_1}e^{-\frac{2h\varphi - k^2 B_1}{2h}t} + \dfrac{k^2 B_2}{2h\varphi - k^2 B_1} \text{ and } B_1, B_2, B_3 \text{ satisfy the equation set of}$$

(4), $B_1, B_2, B_3 > 0$.

Proof: Take B_1, B_2, B_3 to G, we get above expression about G. Then take G into $P^*(t)$, $w^*(t)$, $A^*(t)$, we get relevant sales price, wholesale price and advertising.

Proposition: If $2h\varphi - k^2 B_1 > 0$, then the optimal decision under Stackelberg game tends to a stable state, by this time $G = \dfrac{k^2 B_2}{2h\varphi - k^2 B_1}$

Proof: $2h\varphi - k^2 B_1 > 0 \Rightarrow -\dfrac{2h\varphi - k^2 B_1}{2h} < 0$

$$\lim_{t \to \infty} G = \lim_{t \to \infty}(-\dfrac{k^2 B_2}{2h\varphi - k^2 B_1}e^{-\frac{2h\varphi - k^2 B_1}{2h}t} + \dfrac{k^2 B_2}{2h\varphi - k^2 B_1}) \Rightarrow \lim_{t \to \infty} G = \dfrac{k^2 B_2}{2h\varphi - k^2 B_1}$$

Reputation cannot increase unlimited in real life. Otherwise demand will not increase without limit with the increase of reputation.

3.3   The Method of Solving the Nash Negotiation Model

This paper set conflict point as the result of Stackelberg game. Profit of manufacturer and dealer is as follow:

$$\Pi_m = \int_0^\infty e^{\mu t}[(w^*(t)-c)(\alpha-\beta P^*(t)+\eta G)-hA^*(t)^2]dt \qquad \Pi_r^* = \int_0^\infty e^{\mu t}[(P^*(t)-w^*(t))(\alpha-\beta P^*(t)+\eta G)]dt$$

Model of Nash negotiation can be described as follow:

$$\max \ (\Pi_m - \Pi_m^*)(\Pi_r - \Pi_r^*) \tag{6}$$

$$s.t. \ (\Pi_m, \Pi_r) > (\Pi_m^*, \Pi_r^*)$$

As a result that we use differential game to study dynamic decision problems, the model is difficult to solve by the method of mathematical derivation. We can know that the function form of $P(t), w(t), A(t)$ is as $-K_1 e^{-K_3 t} + K_2$. So we assume that

$$P(t) = -X_1 e^{-X_3 t} + X_2, w(t) = -Y_1 e^{-Y_3 t} + Y_2, A(t) = -Z_1 e^{-Z_3 t} + Z_2, \text{ then}$$

we transfer the solving problem to search 9 d vector $(X_1, X_2, X_3, Y_1, Y_2, Y_3, Z_1, Z_2, Z_3)$ which satisfies the condition of $(\Pi_m, \Pi_r) > (\Pi_m^*, \Pi_r^*)$ and the vector can maximize $(\Pi_m, \Pi_r) > (\Pi_m^*, \Pi_r^*)$. So the key problem is the design and implementation of algorithm.

4   Memetic Algorithm

4.1   Local Search of MA

The local search process occurs after the evolutionary operation. Because the basic Powell algorithm is quadratic termination, so it uses an improved algorithm [11]. The specific process of algorithm is as follow.

Step 1 : Setting the initial point $x^{(1)}$, n linearly independent directions $d^{(1)}$, $d^{(2)}, \cdots, d^{(n)}$, Accuracy demand ε ,generation of search $k=1$, max generation K ;

Step 2 : Let f is fitness function, solving the one-dimensional problem : $\min \phi_i(\alpha) = f(x^{(i)} + \alpha d^{(i)})$ get α_i, define $x^{(i+1)} = x^{(i)} + \alpha d^{(i)}$, $(i=1,2,\cdots,n)$.

Step 3 : Defining $\mu = \max \{f(x^{(i)}) - f(x^{(i+1)}) \mid i=1,2,\cdots n\} = f(x^{(m)}) - f(x^{(m+1)})$

Step 4 : Setting $u = x^{(n+1)} - x^{(1)}$, solving the one-dimensional problem: $\min \phi(\alpha) = f(x^{(1)} + \alpha u)$, get $\bar{\alpha}$, setting $x^{(n+2)} = x^{(1)} + \bar{\alpha} u$.

Step 5 : Let $k = k+1$, if $k > K$ or $\| x^{(n+2)} - x^{(1)} \| \le \varepsilon$, stop calculating (set $x^{(n+2)}$ as the solution of problem)

Step 6 : If $|\bar{\alpha}| > \sqrt{\dfrac{f(x^{(1)}) - f(x^{n+2})}{\mu}}$, then calculating $d^{(i)} = d^{(i+1)}$,

$i = m, m+1, \cdots n-1$ and $d^{(n)} = u$.

Step 7 : Setting $x^{(1)} = x^{(n+2)}$, then transfer to step 2.

4.2   Global Search of MA

A global search algorithm is a kind of adaptive genetic algorithm. Algorithm is detailed as follows. *Coding* : Using binary encoding, $[lb_i, ub_i]$ is the range of issue i , lb_i' is the biggest integer that is not more than lb_i, ub_i' is the most small integer that is not less than ub_i. The value of issue i is represented by binary. The length of binary code is $NI_i + MI_i$. NI_i is the length of the binary code $ub_i' - lb_i'$. MI_i is accuracy which means correct to $1/2^{MI_i}$ in the process of Algorithm implementation. *Population initialization:* Generating initial population in a random way. *Fitness function:* in the interaction negotiation, fitness function is the objective function of Nash negotiation. *Selection rules:* adopting Roulette method to select individual which is the most commonly used in genetic algorithm. *Crossover:* Use the simplest way of single-point crossover. Cross point is selected randomly. Crossover probability changed automatically along with the parent fitness and has the feature of nonlinear variation. The adaptive crossover probability:

$$pc = \begin{cases} \dfrac{(pc_{max} - pc_{min})}{(1 + \lambda_c \sqrt{\dfrac{fit' - fit_{avg}}{fit_{max} - fit_{avg}}})} + pc_{min} & fit' > fit_{avg} \\ pc_{max} & fit' \le fit_{avg} \end{cases} \qquad (7)$$

Where fit_{max} is the fitness of the best individual in a population, fit_{avg} is the average fitness of the generation population. fit' is the fitness of the better individual in crossover. pc_{max} and pc_{min} are respectively upper limit and lower limit of crossover probability. λ_c is a fixed constant. **Mutation:** we introduce new gene can keep the population diversity and avoid precocity to some extent. Mutation point is selected randomly. Mutation probability has the feature of nonlinear variation

$$pm = \begin{cases} \dfrac{(pm_{max} - pm_{min})}{(1 + \lambda_m \sqrt{\dfrac{fit'' - fit_{avg}}{fit_{max} - fit_{avg}}})} + pm_{min} & fit'' > fit_{avg} \\ pm_{max} & fit'' \le fit_{avg} \end{cases} \qquad (8)$$

Where pm_{max} and pm_{min} are respectively upper limit and lower limit of mutation probability, λ_m is a fixed constant. fit'' is the fitness of mutation individual.

5 Example

5.1 The Conflict Point

The values of parameter listed below: advertising coefficient cost is 20, advertising sensitive coefficient is 2, the attenuation degree of reputation is 0.3, market capacity is 80, price sensitive coefficient is 5, the discount rate is 0.6, unit cost of production is 7. According to the above parameters, we can achieve function graph of reputation about time and advertising sensitive coefficient. The graph shows the conclusions as follow. When advertising sensitive coefficient is fixed, reputation increases over time. But when time increases to a certain value, the increase of reputation becomes very slow. Reputation tends to a constant when time tends to infinity. When time is fixed, reputation increases with the increasing of advertising sensitive coefficient at an accelerating speed.

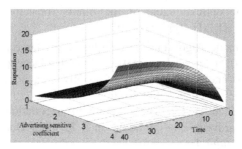

Fig. 2. Function graph of reputation about time and advertising sensitive coefficient

Make advertising sensitive coefficient is equal to 2. Put the parameter of table 1 into equation (12), and we can get: $B_1 = 0.5$, $B_2 = 10$, $B_3 = 225$ .According to B_1, B_2, B_3, we can get the expression of reputation(the initial reputation is zero):

$G = -4e^{-\frac{1}{4}t} + 4$. It can be seen from **Fig.1** that the change of reputation is very small when t is more than 20. Reputation is very close to the limit value. Decision will reach a relatively stable situation which is expressed in the proposition in section 2. $\prod_m^*$ and $\prod_r^*$ are the integral in the infinite time. It is easy to know that the value is infinity. So we choose a larger value to replace the original upper limit of integral which is positive infinity. We set $T = 100$. The approximation of conflict point can be expressed as:

$$\prod_m^* = \int_0^{100} [\frac{112e^{0.1t} + 5024e^{0.6t} - 1504*e^{0.35t}}{80}]dt \quad , \quad \prod_r^* = \int_0^{100} [\frac{64e^{0.1t} + 2809\,e^{0.6t} - 848\,e^{0.35t}}{80}]dt$$

5.2 The Process and Results of Nash Negotiation Based on Memetic Algorithm

$\prod_m$ and $\prod_r$ can be expressed by the expression which contain $P(t)$, $w(t)$, $A(t)$ .So we can get the expression of $(\prod_m - \prod_m^*)(\prod_r - \prod_r^*)$. We use MATLAB programming to implement the negotiation process. The key part of code for getting conflict point is as follow.

```
% the expression of conflict point
        my=exp(0.6*t)*((W-7)*(80-5*P+2*G)-20*A*A);
        ry=exp(0.6*t)*(P-W)*(80-5*P+2*G);
%To solve the definite integral, (Fun1, Fun2) is conflict point
        fun1=int(my,t,0,50);
        Fun1=double(vpa(fun1)/10^14);
        fun2=int(ry,t,0,50);
        Fun2=double(vpa(fun2)/10^14);
```

We use integral solving function int() of MATLAB to get the conflict point $(\Pi_m^*, \Pi_r^*) = (11.2, 6.3)$ (Numerical narrow 10^{14} times). Then we apply Memetic Algorithm to get the optimal value of the fitness (objective function of Nash negotiation). $fitness = (\Pi_m - \Pi_m^*)(\Pi_r - \Pi_r^*)/10^{28}$.

Parameters of Memetic Algorithm are as follows: the largest iterative algebra of Powell algorithm is 50, and accuracy is 0.01. 12 linearly independent initial directions are chosen randomly. The population size of adaptive genetic algorithm is 20. The largest evolution algebra is 50. Initialization, selection, crossover and mutation process are as described in 4.2. The program of negotiation implement on the computer with the hardware configuration: Intel Pentium Dual T3200, 2.00GHz, 2GB. Final result is as *table 1*.

Table 1. Result of Nash Negotiation

	A_i	B_i	C_i	Π_m	Π_r	fitness	runtime
1	1.25	1.64	2.42				
2	14.47	12.56	2.61	18.69	13.55	54.49	59.4s
3	0.12	0.57	1.16				

Table 1 shows that Memetic Algorithm can effectively solve the model of Nash negotiation in this paper. The result of Nash negotiation is superior to the conflict point. After negotiation, the manufacturer' profit increase by 66.9%, dealers' profit increased by 115%. From the aspect of distribution of profit, the manufacturers always occupy dominant position. In addition, the runtime is within tolerable range.

6   Conclusion

For the problem of coordinated decision of manufacturer and dealer in the downstream of supply chain, we take use of Nash negotiation to resolve conflicts and establish a model of Nash negotiation based on multi-Agent. We get conflict point by the master-slave differential game. Because the objective function of Nash Negotiation contains integral which makes that solution is difficult to get by the method of mathematical derivation, so we put forward a method based on Memetic Algorithm to solve the model. Finally we use a numerical experiment to validate the effectiveness of proposed model and algorithm.

Acknowledgments. The work in this paper is supported by the National Natural Science Foundation of China (71371018) and the Social Science Fund of Beijing-13JDJGB037.

References

1. Maxime, O., Dat, C.V., Julien, B., et al.: Decentralised planning coordination with quantity discount contract in a divergent supply chain. International Journal of Production Research 51(9), 2776–2789 (2013)
2. Shima, M., Li, X.: Designing intelligent agents to support long-term partnership in two echelon e-Supply Networks. Expert Systems with Applications 39(18), 13501–13508 (2012)
3. Jiang, G., Duan, X., Zhang Supply, H.: chain coordination planning based on conflict detection. Computer Engineering 36(3), 247–249 (2010)
4. Shima, M., Li, X.: Designing intelligent agents to support long-term partnership in two echelon e-Supply Networks. Expert Systems with Applications 39(18), 13501–13508 (2012)
5. Qingmin, Z., Shiliang, W., Shulei, S., et al.: A Negotiation model of supply chain inventory management in conflict. Journal of Industrial Technological Economics 207(1), 12–15 (2011)
6. Lin, F., Lin, Y.: Integrating multi-agent negotiation to resolve constraints in fulfilling supply chain orders. Electronic Commerce Research and Applications 190(5), 331–335 (2006)
7. Zheng, J.: Conflict mechanism and Multi-Agent systems in supply chain. Industrial Engineering Journal 9(4), 101–105 (2006)
8. Behdani, B., Adhitya, A., Lukszo, Z., et al.: Negotiation-based approach for order acceptance in a multiplant specialty chemical manufacturing enterprise. Industrial and Engineering Chemistry Research 50(50), 5508–5519 (2011)
9. Karray, S., Martı́n-Herrán, G.: A dynamic model for advertising and pricing competition between national and store brands. European Journal of Operational Research 193(2), 451–467 (2009)
10. Erickson, G.M.: A differential game model of the marketing-operations interface. European Journal of Operational Research 211(2), 394–402 (2011)
11. Yi, X.: Optimization theory and method. Beijing industrial university press, Beijing (2004)

The Construction of a Clinical Decision Support System Based on Knowledge Base[*]

Jianwu Xu[1,2], Xiumei Zhang[1,2], Yuhua Cheng[2], Gongliang Yang[2], and Junli Liu[2]

[1] Institute of Scientific and Technical Information of China
[2] Beijing Wanfang Data Co., Ltd.
{xiumei,xujianwu,chengyh,yanggl}@wanfangdata.com.cn

Abstract. Based on a review of domestic and foreign research, application status, classification, composition, and the main problem of a clinical decision support system, this paper proposed a CDSS mode based on a knowledge base. On KB-CDSS mode, this paper discussed the architecture, principle, process, construction of the knowledge base, system design, and application value, then introduced the application WanFang Data Clinical Diagnosis and Treatment Knowledge Base.

Keywords: Clinical Decision Support System, CDSS, Knowledge Base.

1 Background

Errors made by medical staff in the health care activities have become a social problem of common concern at home and abroad. In 1999, the research report "To err is Human," published by the Institute of Medicine (IOM), noted that the number of medical errors was alarming. Death caused by medical errors has been ranked No. 5 among the top ten causes of human death. Medical errors caused by human factors account for a large proportion of errors, but most of such medical errors can be avoided by the operation of a computer system. Therefore, how to improve medical quality, control medical errors, and enhance patient safety have become urgent tasks for the current health care sector. Accordingly, clinical decision-making research has gradually become an important field in clinical medicine [1].

Doctors need to have a relevant knowledge of disciplinary expertise, drug, examination, diagnosis and treatment, etc., to make scientific clinical decisions. General practitioners and interdisciplinary doctors are required to have more knowledge.

A high quality design of Clinical Decision Support System (CDSS) can provides guarantees to compensate the limitations of doctors' clinical knowledge, reducing human negligence regarding diagnosis, treatment, examination, and drug use and avoiding repeated treatment and unnecessary medication; however, there are few CDSSs that can be widely applied to clinical treatment at home and abroad. The main

[*] Found project: National Natural Science Foundation of China, "research on China's information resource industry development policy and management" (ID: 71133006).

K. Liu et al. (Eds.): ICISO 2014, IFIP AICT 426, pp. 388–397, 2014.

reasons include great difficulty in the combination of computer science and clinical work mode, difficulties in the construction of an authoritative knowledge base, rapid updating of medical knowledge, more clinical diagnosis uncertainties, and complex inference mechanisms. Based on this, our team integrated a variety of limitations in the study and practice, proposed the idea of building a CDSS from the perspective of the medical knowledge base, and made attempts to do so [2], [3], [4], [5], [6], [7], [8].

2   The Status of CDSS

2.1   Definition and Development Status of CDSS

Currently, there are many definitions of clinical diagnosis and treatment knowledge systems. Combining them, a CDSS is an expert system that provides decision support and serves as a diagnosis and treatment reference for clinicians or patients, with any patient-related clinical data as input information and in combination with clinicians' work as well as a knowledge base and reasoning analysis.

The world's first fully functional CDSS was MYCIN, developed by Stanford University in the 1970s. MYCIN is mainly used for diagnosis and treatment of bacterial infections. CDSSs with different functional characteristics emerged later, such as QMR of the University of Pittsburgh, HELP of the University of Utah in Salt Lake City[12], Uptodate of Wolters Kluwer[13], [14], [16], Elsevier's MD Consult[15], [17]and so on.

China's CDSS was developed late and is mostly still in the theoretical research stage. There is a large gap compared with foreign countries. The existing CDSS mainly gives priority to single-disease or single-discipline diagnosis and mostly remains in the stage of theoretical studies and laboratory studies, such as the OCDSS of Shanghai University[18], the bone tumor aided diagnosis system of the Fourth Military Medical University[19], the urology clinical decision support system of Chongqing University[20], the intelligent decision support system of acute myocardial infarction diagnosis of Harbin Institute of Technology[21], and the neurosurgery clinical decision support system of Fudan University[22].

2.2   Classification and Main Components of CDSS

In Lei Jianbo's "Core Value and Clinical Decision Support of Electronic Medical Records",CDSSs can be classified according to their internal decision-making mechanisms, system functions, method of recommended, man-machine interaction, communication, and extent of decision support.(table. 1) [12]

The application of CDSS and electronic medical record (Electronic Medical Record, EMR) is closely related.In the EMR Adoption Model (EMRAM) developed by HIMISS Analytics and the Application Level Grading Evaluation Methods and Standards of Electronic Medical Record System Function (Trial) launched by China's Ministry of Health, the requirements of CDSS in different levels of EMRs are also different. [24], [25].

CDSSs are generally composed of a database(scientific data such as clinical pathways and clinical guidelines, and empirical data such as evidence-based literature and case reports), human-computer interaction and logical reasoning, a user interface, and users(doctors, nurses, and inspectors) (Fig. 1).

Table 1. Classification of CDSS Dimension

Classification of dimension	Content
Internal decision-making mechanism	Based on Bayesian algorithm, decision tree analysis, predetermined rule process approach, neural networks, similarity algorithm
System function	Determination of the current diagnosis, follow-up strategy for current diagnosis
The recommended way	Automated alerting (active), active queries (passive)
Man-machine interaction	Standalone system (can independently exist), integration system (integrate with other systems)
Communication way	Consultant way, criticism way
The degree of decision support	Directly (give decision conclusion), indirectly (provide decision-making reference)

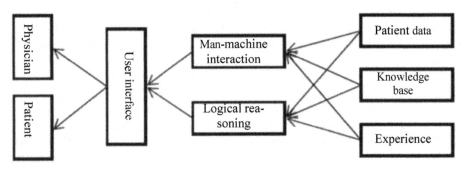

Fig. 1. Main components of CDSSs

2.3   Problems of CDSSs

Although there are many theoretical and system development studies on CDSSs at home and abroad, CDSSs have not yet been widely used on a large scale, the main reasons for which are as follows:

1. CDSSs involve difficult interdisciplinary problems of computers, clinical medicine, psychology, etc. Any CDSS developer who does not have profound clinical knowledge will not be able to meet doctors' demand.

2. CDSSs require a strong and authoritative clinically relevant knowledge base. It is not difficult to build a single-disease or single-discipline knowledge base, but it is very hard to build a knowledge base that can meet all disciplines.

3. Clinical medicine is a rapidly growing discipline. Rapidly updating medical knowledge and conflict among medical views are also factors limiting the usefulness of CDSSs.

4. CDSSs can only achieve their maximum value by closely combining with HIS/EMR systems. Currently, except in large general hospitals, most medium and small hospitals have not established a perfect HIS/EMR system, which also limits CDSSs' ability in the actual docking.

Although CDSSs face many problems, more and more clinicians need the support of a CDSS for making clinical decisions on information acquired in the hospital. Currently, theoretical research on CDSSs, computer technology, and Internet technology has developed greatly, which also provides a good environment for the application of CDSSs. A growing number of HIS manufacturers and medical publishers are entering this market.

3   Construction of a CDSS Based on a Clinical Knowledge Base

3.1   KB-CDSS Construction Ideas and Structure

Based on the current development status of and demand for a CDSS and combined with our rich experience in the construction of large-scale databases, our team proposed Knowledge Base-Clinical Decision Support System (KB-CDSS), which creates different types of clinical databases on the basis of clinical knowledge and vast literature; provides a variety of services for different platforms including organization, search, navigation, interface, and security technology; and offers targeted, timely content according to the user's needs through the interface technology embedded in the electronic medical record system, with the architecture shown in Fig. 2.

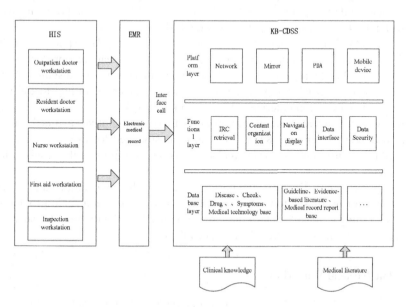

Fig. 2. KB-CDSS Architecture

3.2   Construction Principles

The KB-CDSS-based system architecture mainly sticks to the following principles in the construction process:

1. Authoritative content: The knowledge bases supporting KB-CDSS are all written and audited by physicians with extensive clinical experience. Writers and auditors are all served by physicians with vice-senior titles or above and certain academic achievements in their disciplines.
2. Content objectivity: The knowledge sources of the knowledge bases supporting KB-CDSS all refer to openly published information required not to contain personal subjective points of view and that underwent a process of text editing review and expert content review.
3. Modularity: Based on the different types of resources, KB-CDSS is divided into a clinical knowledge base and a clinical document base. The basic clinical knowledge base includes a disease base, a symptoms base, a check base, and a drug base. The clinical document base includes clinical-related academic literature, such as guide specifications, case reports, system evaluations, and meta-analyses. Knowledge bases are maintained and regularly updated by experts in various fields to make it easy for clinicians to gain the latest knowledge. In terms of service, they are divided into literature services, knowledge content services, client services, and interface services.
4. Low coupling: KB-CDSS docks with the EMR system through the system interface. The benefits of using this method are that on the one hand it reduces the cost of the EMR developer so that KB-CDSS data can be called through the interface, while on the other hand it reduces KB-CDSS operation problems, which will not affect the normal operation of the EMR.
5. Immediacy: The clinician in the diagnosis process usually requires immediate decision feedback to facilitate the development of treatment programs. KB-CDSS is able to automatically provide relevant content for instant reference through the internal mapping and retrieval mechanism according to the information in CPOE(computerized physician order entry).
6. Relevance: Clinical treatment involves a variety of disciplines and tasks as well as different use groups. KB-CDSS can be customized for different clients according to different user roles and tasks to provide users with closely related content.
7. Low interference: Doctors' diagnostic process is a highly centralized procedure. The doctor needs support only when encountering insurmountable problems or when failing to make a determination, so the KB-CDSS only provides support in the form of reminders when doctors need them.

3.3   The Clinical Workflow

Clinical diagnostic work involves many roles, such as doctors, patients, nurses, and inspectors. Each role at different stages requires different degrees of clinical knowledge support.

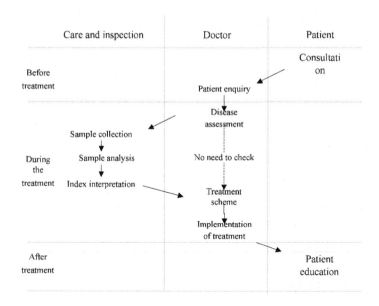

Fig. 3. Clinical workflow

Before treatment, patients need to have an understanding of their own symptoms and disease to provide a reference for effective treatment. Doctors conduct inferential analysis according to the patient's description. The main input information at this stage includes patient history data and descriptions of symptoms. Based on this information, the doctor determines the initial disease. KB-CDSS provides relevant descriptive reference information for support.

In the treatment process, the doctors make a determination according to the patient information. If necessary, they arrange for the patient to be tested to provide more patient information to develop and implement disease treatment programs. At this stage, KB-CDSS is divided into active and passive methods of support. The active method is aimed to prevent the serious consequences of improper treatment emerging in the treatment program, such as disease drug contraindications and drug incompatibility. The passive method means that physicians acquire relevant evidence regarding their decisions according to their experience, including basic knowledge and guidelines on diseases, medicines, examinations, system evaluations/meta-analyses, and case reports.

After treatment, Most of the time patient treatment time is short, and there is a lack of relevant health information literacy. KB-CDSS can provide some support for patient education, as shown in Fig. 3.

3.4   Construction of the Clinical Knowledge Base

The clinical knowledge base is the basis of KB-CDSS. The richness and authority of the knowledge base has a direct impact on the application effect of the system. According to the characteristics, the knowledge base is divided into three categories, as shown in Table 2.

Table 2. Clinical Knowledge Base

Data type	Examples	Source	Requirement	Organization method
Patient data	Electronic medical records	HIS/EMR	Authentity and interity	HL7
Scientific knowledge	Disease,symptoms, examination, harmaceuticals, medical technology	Textbooks, authoritative treatment manuals, etc.	Objectivity and authority	ICD-10, pharmacopeia, examination means
Experience knowledge	Guideline, meta-analysis, system evaluation, case reports	Openly published literature	Open publishing and source quality	Literature types, content topics

3.5 KB-CDSS Design

KB-CDSS design includes four parts: database construction, functional design, interface design, and platform applications.

1. Database construction: KB-CDSS is based on Wanfang Data IRC technology, which can support the retrieval needs of massive data, multiple fields and multiple languages. KB-CDSS database is divided into the disease base, check base, drug base, guideline base, case report base, evidence-based medicine base, literature citations database, and full-text database, which can be used for different types of applications.

2. Functional design: KB-CDSS functions include knowledge content retrieval, resource navigation, sorting methods, and related recommendations to provide support for different application environments. Knowledge content retrieval provides knowledge content points of different particle sizes and supports precise and fuzzy searches; resource navigation is organized according to the characteristics of content to be easy to read; and sorting is performed according to time, relevance, quality, and content. Related recommendations can recommend the most relevant content according to the current browsing information.

3. Interface technology: KB-CDSS interface technology can support major system types, such as B/S and C/S, and provide return value according to different input parameters, including information on knowledge content, knowledge entry, literature, and clustering results. Data are saved in JSON format.

4. Platform application: KB-CDSS provides different versions depending on the different application environment. (1) Network version: Doctors generally have the most contact with the Internet. As long as they have access rights, users have access to the necessary knowledge through the network version anytime and anywhere. (2) Mirror version: Most doctors cannot access the Internet at work. The mirror version enables doctors to access knowledge when they cannot access the external network. (3) Client: In order to better support physician workflow and

HIS data calls, it can provide more functions that cannot be achieved through the network version. (4) Mobile version: currently, many large hospitals have adopted PDAs or mobile phones as part of their hospital information technology system. The mobile version is quick and easy to use.

4   Discussion and Cases of the Application's Value

The electronic medical record system is an important part of hospital information. A high-quality electronic medical record system must have CDSS functions, so the CDSS plays an important role in hospital information and should be a necessary part of the hospital information system.

A CDSS can significantly improve the quality of medical work, such as by shortening diagnosis time and improving screening accuracy rates.

Currently, the most widely used CDSS is the rational drug use system. The CDSS has a positive effect on reducing the incidence of misdiagnosis, preventing drug incompatibility, and handling medication for special populations.

From the perspective of the medical economy, the CDSS improves doctors' work efficiency, thereby decreasing the number of clinics. Accidents caused by medical errors are reduced, thereby reducing damages to the hospital.

The CDSS also has a significant impact on treatment methods. More and more patients pay close attention to the relevant medical knowledge after treatment and before treatment, and know about them due to the Internet and other means before treatment.

Currently, the Wanfang Data Clinical Diagnosis and Treatment Knowledge Base developed by Wanfang Data has been formally launched and has dozens of official users and dozens of trial users. Feedback from some hospitals is shown in Table 3.

Table 3. KB-CDSS Use Situation of Some Users

User	Version	Advantages	Suggestions
Beijing Grade-III General Hospital	Network version	Simple interface, easy retrieval, rich data types. Associated with literature	Extensive knowledge, patient-oriented education. Recent progress in improving treatment
Shandong Grade-III Hospital	Client	Easy installation, rich data types, provide expertise and literature	Extensive knowledge, subdivided according to the type of user, sound reasoning mechanism

5   Conclusions and Limitations

Through a study of the theory and application of CDSSs at home and abroad, this paper analyzed the main composition and classification of CDSs and the main problems facing CDSSs, proposed KB-CDSS construction ideas, and described perspectives on KB-CDSS construction ideas, construction principles, clinical work-flow analysis, clinical knowledge base construction, and KB-CDSS design. The Wanfang Data Clinical Diagnosis and Treatment Knowledge Base guided by KB-CDSS has been running successfully in some hospitals.

KB-CDSS involves a wide range of theoretical research and design development. This study only describes the basic ideas of KB-CDSS and cannot deeply discuss the clinical workflow, knowledge base construction, and system design. In practice, the content and functionality of the Wanfang Data Clinical Diagnosis and Treatment Knowledge Base need to be improved.

With the development of computer science, evidence-based medicine and hospital information technology, more CDSSs will be applied to electronic medical record systems in hospitals. Doctors' diagnoses are no longer based on personal experience, but they make clinical decisions with the help of CDSSs. KB-CDSS-based Wanfang Data Clinical Diagnosis and Treatment Knowledge Base aims to achieve the purpose of assisting clinical decision-making through continuous improvement and upgrades.

References

1. Kohn, L.T., Corrigan, J.M., Donaldson, M.S.: To err is human: building a safer health sys-tem. National Academy Press, Washirlgton, D.C (2000)
2. Zhao, C.W., Yan, Z.Z., Sun, Y.G., et al.: design concept of OCDSS. Beijing Biomedical Engineering 1, 85–88 (2006)
3. Lin, H.C., Wu, H.C., Chang, C.H., et al.: Development of a real-time clinical decision sup-port system upon the web mvc-based architecture for prostate cancer treatment. BMC Medical Informatics and Decision Making 1, 16 (2011)
4. Garg, A.X., Adhikari, N.K.J., McDonald, H., et al.: Effects of computerized clinical deci-sion support systems on practitioner performance and patient outcomes. JAMA: The Jour-nal of the American Medical Association 10, 1223–1238 (2005)
5. Fang, L.X., Deng, Q.D., Wang, S.P., et al.: Study of Electronic Medical Record Clinical Decision Support System. Modern hospital 2, 9–11 (2011)
6. Yang, Y.: Design and implementation of CDSS based on clinical guidelines. Zhejiang University of Technology (2008)
7. Yang, Y.: Study on urology clinical decision support system based on data mining. Chongqing University (2011)
8. Sun, B.Q., Feng, Y.J.P., Qi, S., et al.: Intelligent Decision Support System of acute myo-cardial infarction diagnosis. System engineering theory and practice 10, 141–144 (2006)
9. Van, B., Musen, M.A., Bao, H.F., Zheng, X.P.: Medical informatics. Shanghai scientific & Technical Publishers (2002)
10. Su, S.S., Du, Y.: Discussion on CDSS based on HIS. Medical information 12, 1610–1611 (2005)
11. Sim, I., Gorman, P., Greenes, R.A., et al.: Clinical decision support systems for the prac-tice of evidence-based medicine. Journal of the American Medical Informatics Associa-tion, 6, 527–534 (2001)
12. Lei, J.B.: Core Value and Clinical Decision Support of Electronic Medical Records. China Digital Medicine 3, 26–30 (2008)
13. Isaac, T., Zheng, J., Jha, A.: Use of UpToDate and outcomes in US hospitals. Journal of Hospital Medicine 2, 85–90 (2012)

14. Ahmadi, S.F., Faghankhani, M., Javanbakht, A., et al.: A comparison of answer retrieval through four evidence-based textbooks (ACP PIER, Essential Evidence Plus, First Consult, and UpToDate): A randomized controlled trial. Medical Teacher 9, 724–730 (2011)
15. Wang, J.F., Li, Y.Q., Xiong, M.L., et al.: MD Consult Introduction to Clinical Medicine Knowledge Base. Journal of Medical Informatics 5, 341–342 (2006)
16. Uptodate Homepage, http://www.uptodate.com/home
17. Mdconsult Homepage,
    http://www.mdconsult.com/php/432354867-666/home.html
18. Zhao, C.W., Yan, Z.Z., Sun, Y.G., et al.: Design concept of OCDSS. Beijing Biomedical Engineering 1, 85–88 (2006)
19. Liu, J.H., Qian, Z.C., Qu, J.H., et al.: Establishment of Clinical Knowledge Base in Computer-Aided Diagnostic Expert System for Osteoma. Journal of the Fourth Military Medical University 2, 179–181 (2003)
20. Yang, Y.: Study on urology clinical decision support system based on data mining. Chongqing University (2011)
21. Sun, B.Q., Feng, Y.J.P., Qi, S., et al.: Intelligent Decision Support System of Acute Myocardial Infarction Diagnosis. System Engineering Theory and Practice 10, 141–144 (2006)
22. Deng, H.H., Xin, J.B., Mo, M.Q., et al.: Neurosurgical Clinical Decision Support System Design Research. Shanghai Biomedical Engineering 4, 208–212 (2007)
23. Himss Homepage, http://www.himssanalytics.org/emram/emram.aspx
24. Electronic medical records,
    http://www.moh.gov.cn/mohyzs/s3585/201012/50229.shtml

Assisting an Elderly with Early Dementia Using Wireless Sensors Data in Smarter Safer Home

Qing Zhang[1], Ying Su[2], and Ping Yu[3]

[1] Australian e-Health Research Centre/CSIRO Computational Informatics, Australia
[2] Institute of Scientific and Technical Information of China, China, 100038, Beijing, China
[3] Health Informatics Research Laboratory, University of Wollongong, Australia
qing.zhang@csiro.au, suy.rspc@istic.ac.cn, ping@uow.edu.au

Abstract. The primary aim of this study is to develop a Smart Assistive Living (SAL) platform to enable old people suffering from dementia to stay at home as long as possible. The technology used includes wireless sensor network and broadband network connectivity. The assistive technology aggregates sensor information about environmental, cognitive, physical and physiological factors and integrate them to support the delivery of telehealth and telecare services to older people with mild dementia. The plan for the testing and implementation of the technology and commercial roll out is also briefly outlined.

Keywords: Wireless Sensor Network, Smart home, Activity recognition, Activity of daily living, ADL, Aged carer, Community care, Time series analysis, Information quality.

1 Introduction

The looming dementia epidemic has plagued all nations around the world, with its social and economic impact widely acknowledged by World Health Organisation, health organizations and governments. For example, about 14 million people in the Asia Pacific Region, the largest continent with more than half of the world population, are plagued by dementia. Alzheimer's Disease International (ADL) estimated that by 2050 the amount of people with dementia will be tripled to 65 millions.

The cost of dementia in 2003 was $60.4 billion for an estimated 12.6 million people with dementia in Asia Pacific region. With an estimated cost of around 1% of GDP, dementia will become the third largest source of health and residential aged care spending in Australia within two decades. The devastating impact of dementia on the social and public health systems is not only due to it being the most disabling of all chronic diseases, but also its enormous economic impact on health system, care services, and productivity losses. Therefore, dementia presents significant challenges to policymakers and public healthcare system.

While there is no cure to dementia, efforts can be made to delay or reduce the number of people suffering from it. The possible preventive and interventive

K. Liu et al. (Eds.): ICISO 2014, IFIP AICT 426, pp. 398–404, 2014.

mechanisms include improving social and physical living environment to prevent or slow down the progression of the disease, early interventions (lowering incidence), and improvements in treatment and care to increase survival.

Wellness is about well-being of people. It is indicated by the capability of people in performing their daily activities of living and work. A wellness determination process helps Data related to the wellness indices and behavior recognition can guide the healthcare professionals to identify the variations of people's performance on maintaining or improving health and wellness.

To address the challenge taking the advantage of information and communication technology, we propose a solution called "Smarter and Safer Home" that we hope to enable old people with early dementia (PWED) to remain independently in their homes as long as possible. The second aim of our solution is to enhance quality of life (QoL) for these people, as well as QoL for their family carers. Our strategy is to deploy environmental sensors in their homes, acting as non-intrusive monitoring devices for human behaviour. These sensors are expected to continuously stream data to our central server, where we can then extract and analyse these data to identify the pattern of a person's daily activities. Through the mechanism of machine learning, new activities will be benchmarked against the established patterns to identify those 'abnormal' situations. Once an abnormal signal was detected, an alert will be provided to family carers, such as unattended stove or bathroom flooding. We hope that the 'signal' from the sensors will notify, motivate, and encourage older people and their family carers to take appropriate precaution or intervention. Our proposed technology will lead to new method in assessing the severity of dementia, early detection of abnormal health conditions and development of targeted prevention or early intervention. This will again lead to the reduction of occurrence of behavioural or psychological symptoms and relief burden for family carers to look after their beloved ones. The ultimate goal is to maintain the ADL of people with dementia, improve their QoL and QoL for their family members. This paper will outline the design of our smart home and the plan to implement it.

2   The Architecture of the System

We employ the Smarter Safer Home system developed at CSIRO [4] to collect and analyse sensor data from homes of dementia patients. The system consists of two components: (i) Wireless Sensor Network (WSN) for data transmission and (ii) intelligent home monitoring system to collect sensor data, perform data analysis and present results to end user.

2.1   Wireless Sensor Network

Although there are many previous work on monitoring ADL of people with dementia through wearable sensors such as RFID markers and wearable accelerometers detecting falls ([1,2,3]), the innovative aspect of our proposed solution is to place the sensors in the person's living environment, instead attached to their body for non-intrusive monitoring of human behavior. The two advantages of this solution are: First, wearable sensors are not always convenient for users to carry around. This is particularly relevant for people with mild dementia as they easily forget things; second, sensors placed in environment is out of the sight of the users, thus has less interference with their daily lives. Third, the data recorded by sensors are anonymous, containing very little information about personal privacy. Table 1 describes all types of in-house sensors that will be used in our smart home system.

Table 1. List of environmentally placed sensors

Sensor type	Data collected
Motion sensor	Incidents of movements
Accelerometer	Mattress movements
Power sensor	Electrical power draw by appliances
Acoustic sensor	Water flows in pipes
Temperature sensor	Temperature readings
Humidity sensor	Humidity readings
Read switch	Doors open/closed
Pressure sensor	Sofa/couch being attended

2.2   Intelligent Home Monitoring System

Figure 1 illustrates the function of the smart home: data collection, analyses and presentation.

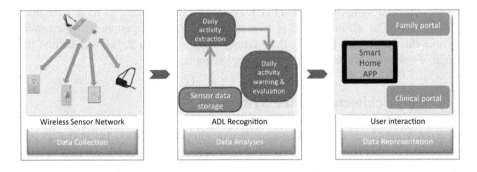

Fig. 1. Smart Home platform architecture

Data Collection
This module gathers continuously recorded, daily activity data of a person from the non-intrusive sensors deployed at invisible locations at home. Figure 2 presents the places where these sensors are likely to be located.

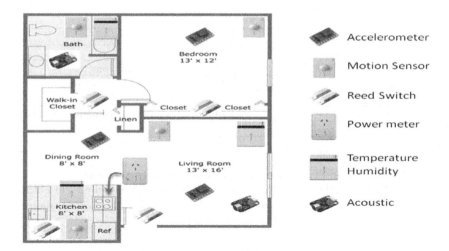

Fig. 2. Typical places where the sensors will be installed

Data Analyses

This module analyses raw sensor data captured to extract information about a person's routine behaviour and ADL. It will extract activity patterns and measure the person's physical, health and mental functions. Based on statistical data analysis and machine learning, it will provide warning/alert of abnormal situations in real time when such situation happens. By triangulating data from other sources, it is anticipated that the level and type of assistance that a person with early onset of dementia requires can be estimated and be provided to enable him or her to live independently as long as possible.

Raw sensor data is initially processed at the in-house local server. The output is converted to semantically meaningful representation of observed actions. The design and implementation of information presentation and service provision will benefit from semiotics, a well-established discipline of signs and human communication in social context. The semiotic framework will guide us in taking account of syntactic, semantic and pragmatic levels of system functions and service provision to the different stakeholders. In our system, sensors collect simple actions such as turn on/off the microwave, move in/out of the bathroom. These actions, along with their temporal features, are then transmitted to the database server for more complex activity extractions. An activity is a more complex motion pattern, typically composed of many actions and with longer durations. For example, turning on a microwave is considered an action, while preparing a meal is an activity. Typical activities of daily living, as a concept that is first established by Katz, include bathing, dressing, toileting, transferring, continence and feeding [5]. It is well known that maintaining ADL becomes a major focus for care of people with dementia. Table 2 shows a non-exhaustive list of ADLs that could be automatically extracted from the related sensors in our system.

Table 2. Extracting ADLs from sensors

Daily activities	Sensor types
Indoor walking/wandering	Motion sensors
Sleep	Motion sensors, accelerometer
Preparing meals	Motion, Power, Acoustic sensors
Washing cloth	Power, Motion sensors, Reed switch
Visiting bathroom	Motion, Temperature, Humidity sensors
House cleaning	Motion, Power, Acoustic sensors
Postural transfer	Pressure, Motion sensor

Wellness Determination Process through Monitoring Daily Activities

Fig. 2 shows the schematic representation of the determination of wellness of elderly in the proposed Smart Home. The recognition of basic ADLs and determination of wellness of the elderly are described in the following Equations.

$$P(t|c) = \frac{N_{ct}+1}{\sum_{t' \in V}(N_{ct'}+1)} = \frac{N_{ct}+1}{\sum_{t' \in V}N_{ct'}+K'} \tag{1}$$

where N_{ct} is the number of times a particular sensor ID occurs in activity 'c'. V is the set of sensor IDs. $K'=|V|$ is the number of unique sensor IDs. The first function(β_1) indicates about the non-usage or inactive duration of the appliances, and the second function (β_2) is about the over-usage of specific household appliances. The following are the details:

$$\beta_1 = 1 - \frac{t}{T}; \beta_2 = 1 + (1 - \frac{T_\alpha}{T_n}) \tag{2}$$

Data Presentation

In order to improve awareness and facilitate self monitoring, data will be presented in tablet PC or mobile phone. This will enable family members to gain an insight into the capacity and condition of living of their beloved ones; assist health care providers to get a whole picture of the person's daily lives, routines and health status. The awareness and information will facilitate the timely provision of intervention through telehealth and telecare.

The data will be presented to the person for whom home monitoring service is provided, to family care givers and to clinical professionals providing health services to the person. It can be used by the person for the purpose of self-monitoring, by care givers as a means for remote monitoring and care assistance, and by clinicians to support their diagnostic and treatment decision through examining the changes/trends in ambient and activities of daily living, psychological, behavioral and vital signs, respectively, for older people with early dementia, which is particularly useful for those living at home alone. For the later, we will provide a tablet-based application for them to self-monitor their daily activities and conduct physiological assessments regularly.

Implementation Studies
The Smart Home system will be developed and implemented in the relevant population to develop and test the system implementation methods. The purpose of the trial is to (1) develop and fine-tune the technology; (2) understand the facilitators and barriers for acceptance and usage of the system; (3) test acceptance, usage and impact of the system on people with mild dementia and their family carers; (4) develop the relevant training and support services to foster adoption and usage; and (5) develop the business model for the commercial roll out of the solution to large population. These will be achieved in three stages.

Stage 1. Develop and Fine-Tune the Technology, and Develop Understanding about Facilitators and Barriers for System Adoption
This trial will be conducted in small population with five to ten people who suffer from mild dementia. The selection of sample will take into account a balance of genda, living environment and life style. Both engineers and system analysts will be involved in the trial. In addition to the data collected by the sensors, human factors for system implementation will also be collected through interview and observation. These data are important in guiding the development of user-friendly interface that will be accepted by the people with dementia and their family carers. The indicators for human factors include the interface design that is acceptable by the end users, the older people's preference for navigating the system and the type of devices with optimal opportunity to be accepted and used. The functions and messages that are useful for the intended population will also be identified.

Stage 2. Pilot Trial of the System in Small Population Group
After the initial validation, the system will be further implemented in a small population group of 30 to 50 people with dementia to further test the functionality, user acceptance, usage and effectiveness of the system. Any issues identified will be timely fixed, with system improved. This test and improvement process will be continuously conducted and evolved until enough evidence has been gathered to prove that the system has achieved its objectives.

Stage 3. Large Scope Implementation to Develop the Business Model for Rolling Out the System
After the efficacy of the system is validated, the solution will be rolled out in the scope of a city or province to further test its efficacy for large population. The relevant business model for technology roll out will be developed. This include costing model for the solution, implementation strategies, end user support and roles and responsibilities of the relevant stakeholder groups, etc.

3   Conclusions

This paper briefly outlines a comprehensive Smart Home solution to assist people with mild dementia to live at home. It first presents the technical solution, then the empirical technology development, pilot testing and implementation strategies for rolling out the system to the population. Different from the solutions with wearable devices, the sensors of our Smart Home are placed at various locations in the residency of a person, which will bring in the advantage of no intrusion thus comfort of use. We plan to develop and introduce the system through a rigorous technology development and implementation strategy and practice. The human factors that either facilitate or hinder the adoption of the Smart Home solution will be fully noticed with solution developed. The conduct of the project will contribute to Smart Home technology development and knowledge about effective ICT solutions to assist people with memory loss. It will also contribute to addressing the biggest challenge of population ageing in the current world – dementia, taking advantage of current advancement of ICT [7,8,9].

Acknowledgements. This work was financially supported by the National Soft Science Planning (2011GXQ4K029), and all sensor data will be collected via National Population and Reproductive Health Science Data Center of National Scientific Data Sharing Platform for Population and Health.

References

1. Zouba, N., Boulay, B., Bremond, F., Thonnat, M.: Monitoring Activities of Daily Living (ADLs) of Elderly Based on 3D Key Human Postures. Cognitive Vision (2008)
2. Sangwan, R.S., Qiu, R.G., Jessen, D.: Using RFID tags for tracking patients, charts and medical equipment within an integrated health delivery network. In: IEEE Networking, Sensing and Control (2005)
3. Cañas, J.M., Marugan, S., Marrón-Romera, M., Garcia, J.C.: Visual Fall Detection for Intelligent Spaces. In: 6th IEEE International Symposium on Intelligent Signal Processing (2009)
4. Zhang, Q., Karunanithi, M., Rana, R., Liu, J.: Determination of Activities of Daily Living of independent living older people using environmentally placed sensors. In: 2013 35th Annual International Conference of the IEEE Engineering in Medicine and Biology Society (EMBC), pp. 7044–7047 (2013), doi:10.1109/EMBC.2013.6611180
5. Plan, T.H.: Katz Activities of Daily Living (ADL), pp. 1–8 (2008)
6. National Population and Reproductive Health Science Data Center on, http://www.poprk.org/
7. Yu, P.: Aged care IT in Australia – the past, present and future. eJournal of Health Informatics 7(2), e2 (2012)
8. Yu, P.: A multi-method approach to evaluate health information systems. Studies in Health Technology and Informatics 160(2), 1231–1235 (2010)
9. Su, Y., et al.: Consumer-centered eHealth: challenges and opportunities for China. Advanced Science Letters 7, 257–260 (2012)

Health Outcomes and Cost Benefit of Home e-Health in Helping to Manage Heart Failure

Yuan Yao[1] and Ying Su[2]

[1] Military Medical Sciences and PLA General Hospital, China
[2] Institute of Scientific and Technical Information of China, China,
100038, Beijing, China
yaoyuan301@sina.cn, suy.rspc@istic.ac.cn

Abstract. This study presents a systematic review of the nature and magnitude of outcomes associated with e-Health of cardiac diseases. Methods: A comprehensive literature search was conducted on Medline and the Cochrane Library to identify relevant articles published between 2000 and 2014 in which the outcome measure used was one or more of health outcome, proxy health outcome, patient compliance or cost. Studies identified were subjected to narrative review. The magnitude and significance of the Home e-Health effects on patients' conditions (e.g., early detection of symptoms, decrease in blood pressure, adequate medication, reduced mortality) still remain inconclusive for cardiac diseases. However, the results of this study suggest that regardless of their nationality, socioeconomic status, or age, patients comply with Home e-Health programs and the use of technologies. Importantly, the Home e-Health effects on clinical effectiveness outcomes (e.g., decrease in the emergency visits, hospital admissions, average hospital length of stay) are more consistent in Heart Failure. Home e-Health of cardiac diseases seems to be a promising patient management approach that produces accurate and reliable data, empowers patients, influences their attitudes and behaviors, and potentially improves their medical conditions. Future studies need to build evidence related to its clinical effects, cost effectiveness, impacts on services utilization, and acceptance by health care providers.

Keywords: Chronic heart failure, Blood pressure control, Lung transplantation, Monitoring system, Pulmonary function, Diabetes control, Self-measurement, Controlled trial, Hypertensive patients, African Americans.

1   Introduction

It is over a decade since e-Health started to be explored as a tool in the reduction of exposure to risk factors for disease, and in the management of illness. It has taken various forms as technology has evolved, but with the exception of the remote interpretation of images, has failed to become part of mainstream medicine in, for instance, the UK. In previous research, most of intelligent works were centralized at healthcare center and the function of telemedicine terminal device was mainly

K. Liu et al. (Eds.): ICISO 2014, IFIP AICT 426, pp. 405–411, 2014.
© IFIP International Federation for Information Processing 2014

focused on the acquisition and transmission of physiological data. Heart Failure has features which appear to make it particularly suitable for management involving e-Health: measurement in healthcare settings may be spuriously high ("white coat cardiac diseases"); people with mild to moderate cardiac diseases feel well when off medication but may feel unwell on treatment so may not use it conscientiously; the information to be conveyed between the individual and the healthcare professional is simple; the individual's use of the equipment is unlikely to be comprised by their being acutely anxious or fearful because of the condition. We created a generic workflow model based on interviews and observations at three CR clinics.

2   Methods

A comprehensive literature search was conducted on Medline and the Cochrane Library to identify relevant articles published between 2003 and 2013. The keywords that were used include telemonitoring, telecare, telemedicine, telematics, telehealth, and telehomecare.. All abstracts were read to identify how many studies were reported in the literature. The inclusion criteria required that the studies: (1) have an experimental design involving direct data collection from patients with any of the four considered chronic diseases, (2) be published in the English language and appear in peer-reviewed journals, and (3) document telemonitoring effects. The abstracts and papers were reviewed by two independent readers.

Table 1. Overview of Research Designs

Sensor type	Cardiac Diseases
Total number of studies	16
Type of design	7
Adults with congestive heart failure	15
Size of experimental group	Minimum:10; Maximum 230
Study duration	Minimum:1 month; Maximum 36 months
Main types of data being transferred	Basic vital signs; Symptoms
Frequency of data transmission	More than once a day 4, Once a day 8

3   Results

3.1   Literature Search

Forty three abstracts were found, and led to the identification of 14 relevant RCTs. The 29 abstracts were rejected because they did not report information on health outcome, proxy health outcomes, treatment process, patient compliance and/or cost with particular respect to management of cardiac diseases. Some were excluded as they were trialing mobile phone-based interventions with no e-Health element.

3.2   Health Outcome

With the exception of pulmonary diseases that represent a variety of medical conditions, telemonitoring of cardiac diseases was specific to each of these illnesses, and involved adult patients suffering from these medical conditions. Only in few cases, subgroups of the general population (e.g., children, veterans, pregnant women) were considered.

3.3   Proxy Health Outcome

Four RCTs evaluated the efficacy of e-Health in controlling cardiac diseases, with somewhat conflicting results.

Kirtava, Z., et al 2013[1] randomised 54 patients with main medical results, Quality of Service (QoS), Quality of Experience (QoE), cost-efficiency and remaining challenges - is presented, as well as the outline of its continuation - MTM-2 project, which aims improvement of decision making for emergency cardiac patients and usage of mHealth applications for integrated care provision in remote regions of Georgia. This result was confirmed by two other RCTs. Goroso, D. G et al 2013 [2] provide a mobile tool to prevent early cardiac arrhythmia by means of monitoring on-line and assessing heart rate variability. Preliminary results proved effective in Sao Paulo for study of heart rate variability. This new service uses mobile phone to record, evaluate and transmit information, which currently is in clinical validation. Foche-Perez et al 2012 [3] twelve patients have been auscultated by all the physicians using the tele-stethoscopy system, versus a local auscultation using traditional stethoscope. The system must allow listen the cardiacpatientspatients (systolic and diastolic murmurs, gallop sound, arrhythmias) and respiratory (rhonchi, rales and crepitations, wheeze, diminished and bronchial breath sounds, pleural friction rub) sounds[3].

An architectural framework of a system utilising mobile technologies to enable continuous, wireless, electrocardiogram (ECG) monitoring of cardiac patients. The proposed system has the potential to improve patients' quality of life by allowing them to move around freely while undergoing continuous heart monitoring and to reduce healthcare costs associated with prolonged hospitalisation, treatment and monitoring[4]. At follow up, 36% of those allocated to 'e-Health' had pressures below 140/90 as did 31% of those receiving usual care. Only those in the third arm -'e-Health' as above plus web delivered pharmacist support - did significantly better than those receiving usual care (56% controlled)[5].

3.4   Process of Care

Telemonitoring projects of cardiac diseases had the largest samples of patients, which exceeded by far the size of the experimental and the largest average study durations (Table 1).

Fanucci et al 2013 [6] evaluated a complete and integrated Information and Communication Technology system (CHF patients to daily collect vital signs at home and automatically send them to the Hospital Information System, allowing the physicians to monitor their patients at distance and take timely actions in case of necessity.) against usual care in confirming suspected cardiac diseases in 74 adults. All 74 underwent 24 hour ambulatory monitoring; e-Health appeared superior in detecting true cases (64%) to usual care (26%). E-Health was also more rapid in confirming or refuting the suspicion of cardiac diseases.

Nowadays, chronic heart failure (CHF) affects an ever-growing segment of population, and it is among the major causes of hospitalization for elderly citizens[6]. Dennis et al 2013 [7] addressed Telephone coaching for people with chronic conditions can improve health behaviour, self-efficacy and health status: telemedical home blood pressure measurement (5 days, duplicate measurement, four times daily), clinic blood pressure or ambulatory blood pressure monitoring. They confirmed the existence of "white coat cardiac diseases", but showed an increasingly good correlation between telemedical and ambulatory monitoring over the five day periods, with the afternoon readings having the best correlation with the ambulatory value. Cowie et al 2013 [8] performed an equivalence study to e-Health innovation in detecting uncontrolled cardiac diseases over one year in 62 out-patients of a cardiac diseases clinic. Each patient had e-Health and face-to-face consultations on the same days, the order of the two encounters being randomised. The e-Health system was found to be equivalent to in-person consultation in detecting uncontrolled cardiac diseases, in the physicians' use of additional tests, and in the associated therapeutic decisions. ESC has invested in innovation in education and learning by delivering rich content from its meetings online, by delivering a variety of specialty courses on webinars, and last but not least by delivering clinical guidelines to the personal digital assistants of specialists.. Munoz et al 2011 [9] explored a case series of pediatric patients teleassisted from the Cardiac Intensive Care Unit (CICU) at Children's Hospital of Pittsburgh of University of Pittsburgh Medical Center, Pittsburgh, PA, to the CICU at Hospital Valle del Lili, Cali, Valle, Colombia, between March and December 2010. Seventy-one recommendations were given regarding 53 patients. Median age and weight were 10 months and 7.1 kg, respectively. Ventricular septal defect, transposition of the great vessels, and single ventricle accounted for most cases. The most frequent recommendations were related to surgical conduct, management of arrhythmias, and performance of cardiac catheterization studies. No technical difficulties were experienced during the monitoring of the patients. Satisfaction rates were equally high for technical and medical aspects of telemedicine service.

Duck Hee et al 2012 [10] showed that the fall in blood pressure in their e-Health group was (ECG) signal preprocessing including filtering, power noise canceling, and level shifting adherence of 17.7%.

3.5   Cost of Care

Kifle, M., et al. [11] examines the role of Tele-Medicine in the healthcare system and analyzes the costs and benefits of introducing Tele-Cardiology services in Ethiopia (a Sub- Saharan African country). This is a cost comparison study for the treatment of cardiac patients traveling abroad versus patients treated via Tele-Cardiology. Our findings show that Tele-Cardiology is clinically more feasible and more cost effective compared to patients traveling abroad for treatment. Those monitoring themselves made on average 1.2 fewer cardiac diseases related consultations in the year which represented a cost saving despite the expense of the equipment. Martin et al 2013 [8] need to be involved, and to collaborate with engineers and other key stakeholders at each stage of the process: the technology design and integration, the assessment of the value of e-health innovation (in terms of the impact on patients, the healthcare system, and the costs), the education and support of healthcare professionals and patients, the development of guidelines, and the standardization of systems and models.

4   Discussions

The introduction of e-Health is a change to the structure of healthcare, so it is appropriate to consider its effect on the processes and outcomes of care. This survey of papers reporting RCTs shows that it is feasible, at least experimentally, to introduce e-Health into the process of identifying and working with individuals with cardiac diseases to reduce their subsequent risk of stroke, ischaemic heart disease and sudden death. It also confirms that this has not been introduced into everyday clinical practice in countries which take an 'evidence based' approach to healthcare, though the literature has developed [12-14]from that available to the guideline development groups producing the CSIRO (Commonwealth Scientific and Industrial Research Organisation) and the Queensland Government have jointly established the Australian e-Health Research Centre (AEHRC) Guideline 97 (Risk estimation and prevention of cardiovascular disease February 2011). The former guideline says "Routine use of automated ambulatory blood pressure monitoring or home monitoring devices in primary care is not currently recommended because their value has not be adequately established; appropriate use in primary care remains an issue for further research" and the latter does not mention it at all.

There is no definitive evidence that e-Health improves the ultimate health outcomes of the management of cardiac diseases. Our synthesis of the literature indicates that e-Health is likely to be beneficial in controlling cardiac diseases, and thus has the potential to improve health outcomes. Little is known about how this effect is mediated - there is one suggestion that it is through improved compliance. E-Health can also reduce the requirement of hospital care and the number of mortalities. Modern e-health systems can control successfully such diseases as cardiac, diabetic or pulmonary diseases.

The major weakness of this paper is that it is narrative review not a systematic review or a meta-analysis. This is compounded by the fact that the RCTs available are generally small and/or have short follow-up times, so should not be over-interpreted. A more quantitative approach would add value, but, given that there are some relevant trials that have finished recruiting participants but not yet reported (The European Commission has undertaken to support member states in deploying e-health solutions for chronic disease management and in setting quantitative targets such as reduction in hospitalization for heart failure, reduction in healthcare resources by patients with diabetes, and improvement in quality and length of life.), there will be a more optimal opportunity for formal meta-analysis in the near future. We also note that Fayn et al are about to start another trial building an operational e-health infrastructure including pervasive services and remote distributed applications servers in the cardiology domain[15].

5   Conclusions

So far, despite the recent history of home e-Health, a significant body of knowledge has been developed and made available to policymakers and clinicians. Based on the results of this review, home e-Health of cardiac diseases seems to be a promising patient management approach that produces accurate and reliable data, empowers patients, influences their attitudes and behaviors, and potentially improves their medical conditions. Nevertheless, some studies have shown that there is an overall reduction in both systolic and diastolic values, and the presumed mechanism is better patient engagement in disease control and compliance. For insurance companies and governments to consider future endorsement of this patient management approach, and subsequent reimbursement for the services provided, it is important to demonstrate its feasibility at the population level. More rigorous research on home e-Health would build stronger evidence that lead to changes in the practice and management of these cardiac illnesses, to acceptance of this patient management approach by payers and providers, and to its future integration in the overall process of care.

Acknowledgements. The researchers acknowledge the support of the National Soft Science Planning (2011GXQ4K029), and National Population and Reproductive Health Science Data Center of National Scientific Data Sharing Platform for Population and Health funded by Ministry of Science and Technology, China; the research volunteers and the respondees.

References

1. Kirtava, Z., Gegenava, T., Gegenava, M.: mHealth for cardiac patients telemonitoring and integrated care. In: 2013 IEEE 15th International Conference on E-Health Networking, Applications and Services (Healthcom 2013), pp. 5–21 (2013)
2. Goroso, D.G., da Silva, R.R., Battistella, L.R., Odstrcil, M., Paolini, M.: Monitoring heart rate variability on-line used mobile telephone 3G e-health service oriented. Journal of Physics: Conference Series 477, 12036(8 pp.) (2013)
3. Foche-Perez, I., Ramirez-Payba, R., Hirigoyen-Emparanza, G., Balducci-Gonzalez, F., Simo-Reigadas, F.-J., Seoane-Pascual, J., et al.: An open real-time tele-stethoscopy system. Biomedical Engineering Online 11 (August 23, 2012)
4. Sneha, S., Varshney, U.: A wireless ECG monitoring system for pervasive healthcare. International Journal of Electronic Healthcare 3, 32–50 (2007)

5. Pare, G., Jaana, M., Sicotte, C.: Systematic review of home telemonitoring for chronic diseases: The evidence base. Journal of the American Medical Informatics Association 14, 269–277 (2007)
6. Fanucci, L., Saponara, S., Bacchillone, T., Donati, M., Barba, P., Sanchez-Tato, I., et al.: Sensing Devices and Sensor Signal Processing for Remote Monitoring of Vital Signs in CHF Patients. IEEE Transactions on Instrumentation and Measurement 62, 553–569 (2013)
7. Dennis, S.M., Harris, M., Lloyd, J., Powell, G., Faruqi, N., Zwar, N.: Do people with existing chronic conditions benefit from telephone coaching? A rapid review. Australian Health Review 37, 381–388 (2013)
8. Cowie, M.R., Chronaki, C.E., Vardas, P.: E-Health innovation: time for engagement with the cardiology community. European Heart Journal 34, 1864–1868 (2013)
9. Munoz, R.A., Burbano, N.H., Motoa, M.V., Santiago, G., Klevemann, M., Casilli, J.: Telemedicine in Pediatric Cardiac Critical Care. Telemedicine and E-Health 18, 132–136 (2012)
10. Duck Hee, L., Rabbi, A.F., Root, N., Fazel-Rezai, R., Jaesoon, C., de Leon, P., et al.: A heart monitoring system for a mobile device. International Journal of Handheld Computing Research 3, 22–39 (2012)
11. Kifle, M., Mbarika, V.W.A., Datta, P.: Interplay of cost and adoption of tele-medicine in Sub-Saharan Africa: The case of tele-cardiology in Ethiopia. Information Systems Frontiers 8, 211–223 (2006)
12. Hickey, K.T., Johnson, M.P., Biviano, A., Aboelela, S., Thomas, T., Bakken, S., et al.: Cardiac e-Learning: Development of a Web-Based Implantable Cardioverter Defibrillator Educational System. Telemedicine and E-Health 17, 196–200 (2011)
13. Hansen, D.P., Gurney, P., Morgan, G., Barraclough, B.: The Australian e-Health Research Centre: enabling the health care information and communication technology revolution. Medical Journal of Australia 194, S5–S7 (2011)
14. Karunanithi, M., Varnfield, M., Ding, H., Garcia, E., Whittaker, F., Sarela, A., et al.: Care Assessment Platform: An ICT-Enabled Home Care Model for Secondary Prevention of Cardiovascular Diseases. In: 2010 Annual International Conference of the IEEE Engineering in Medicine and Biology Society, pp. 5266–5266 (2010)
15. Fayn, J., Ghedira, C., Telisson, D., Atoui, H., Placide, J., Simon-Chautemps, L., et al.: Towards new integrated information and communication infrastructures in e-health. Examples from cardiology, Computers in Cardiology 2003 (IEEE Cat. No.03CH37504), 113–116 (2003)

Concerns of Ageing and Interest in Assistive Technologies – Convenience Sampling of Attendees at an Aged Care Technology Exhibition in China

Jeffrey Soar[1] and Ying Su[2]

[1] School of Management & Enterprise, Faculty of Business, Education, Law & Arts,
University of Southern Queensland, Australia 4350
soar@usq.edu.au
[2] Institute of Scientific and Technical Information of China,
No.15 Fuxing Road, Beijing, 100038 China
suy.istic@gmail.com

Abstract. As in many countries, ageing and aged care in China is an important issue. There is a need for more research on the potential for technology to assist older people and their families, particularly given the disappointing levels of adoption in developed countries. Accordingly this paper aims to gain insight into the perceptions of older people and stakeholders in relation to issues of ageing and their interest in adoption of technology. Using convenience sampling, the authors surveyed 277 participants to understand peoples concerns concerning ageing and use of technologies. Results from this study provide a basis for discussion with stakeholders, particularly concerning ageing in China.

Keywords: China, Ageing, Technology.

1 Background

This research was conceived as an initial step in a long-term program to gain greater insight into the perceptions of older people and stakeholders in relation to issues of ageing and their interest in adoption of technology. The adoption of home telehealth and intelligent assistive technology has to date been disappointing [1] and there is a lack of convincing research evidence of its benefits. The needs and concerns of older adults as computer users may be different from those of younger users as a result of the changes associated with the ageing process [2]. There is a need for a greater appreciation of ageing and adoption of assistive technologies from the perspective of older people and their families.

The increased use of healthcare associated with ageing is well documented [3] including the increasing use of medications needed to manage chronic conditions [4]. Other challenges of ageing include elder abuse particularly financial abuse [5]. Associated with increasing use of health and support services is the need to manage documentation and processes for making claims on government or health insurance. It can be a challenge for carers of the frail elderly, likely to be elderly themselves [6], to navigate the complexity. ICTs offer potential benefits for older people including

K. Liu et al. (Eds.): ICISO 2014, IFIP AICT 426, pp. 412–419, 2014.
© IFIP International Federation for Information Processing 2014

management of records, personal safety, comfort for families, reminders for medications and other needs, remote access to clinical and other care services, social connections, quality information for self-care, GPS (Global Positioning Systems) tracking and assistance in way-finding, support for people with specific disabilities amongst many others [7].

The stoicism of the War Generation may result in a reluctance to seek help or to report instances of breaches of privacy. Anecdotally a commonly-reported comment from older people is they don't want to be a "bother" to people. Entry into the aged care system can occur through a catastrophic event such as a serious fall or from a visit from a relative who observes the older person is no longer able to care for themselves. Better use of ICTs (Information and Communication Technologies) such as Personal Alarms or other sensors and monitors may allow difficulties to be known earlier and for help to be obtained to assist someone to live at home. Trials of Telecare and telehealth have shown these to be well-accepted by consumers and their families.

ICTs are usually designed by young people with good eye-sight, dexterity and familiarity with technologies. Older people often have poorer vision; there are slower connections in the brain. The choice of fonts is rarely undertaken with cognisance of the needs of older users. The ICT hardware and software that older people have may not be updated as frequently as that of other ICT users. They may not understand how to use the automatic updates that software vendors provide leaving them vulnerable to the security gaps these fixes may have addressed.

The cohort of older adults today is very different from previous cohorts of older people, and the next cohort of the elderly, the "baby boomers," is also likely to be different from today's elderly [8]. Baby boomers can be expected to continue their high use of ICTs into their older years. They will have high expectations of services that can be delivered, of ways they can manage their own care. An issue for them will be maintaining their competencies in the face of the relentless change of technologies; already there is a large gap between teenagers and older people in the social networks and other applications used. The nature of cyber-attacks has changed considerably and baby-boomers may find it a challenge to keep up to date with technology change.

2   Chinese Government Policy on Ageing, Aged-Care and Technology

Ageing is an area of high priority for governments in China as evidenced by the 12th Five-Year Plan [9] and the conclusions of the third plenum session of 18th Party Congress [10]. Included in the "CCP (Chinese Communist Party) decision on deepening the reform of some major issues" latter amongst other recommendations for health and aged care services is "Make full use of information technology tools to promote high-quality medical resources longitudinal flow".

3   Methods

The researchers are involved in organising an annual Aged Care Exhibition in Nanjing, China. This is hosted by the Department of Civil Affairs of Jiangsu, Office of Jiangsu Provincial Committee on Aging, and the China Council for the Promotion of International Trade, Jiangsu Sub-Council. Exhibits include products for mobility, nutrition and dietetics, dietary supplements, mobility devices, training, TCM (Traditional Chinese Medicine) and complementary therapeutics, age-specific real estate, assistive devices, diagnostic devices, "age-friendly" household articles and construction materials, accident prevention products, bathroom products, communication devices, positioning systems and many others. Attendees include government officials, providers of services for the aged, and suppliers; the attendees are largely consumers and the event attracts large numbers of older people. Lectures and presentations are provided by suppliers, researchers, government officials and others covering topics such as analysis of the "silver" market, government policies, the plans of care service organisations and workshops on specific topics such as on ophthalmology and prevention and treatment of cardiovascular diseases. Nanjing was selected as the venue for the annual event; it has an older demographic than most of China, it is easily accessible and it is seen as a desirable city that is a popular venue for conferences.

In 2013 the opportunity was taken to try to survey attendees about concerns of ageing and opinions of assistive technologies. Convenience sampling was undertaken of attendees of the annual Aged Care Technology Expo at Nanjing over three days in November 2013. Approval for a survey of attendees was granted by ISTIC through their processes for research and a survey form developed and tested. This asked for ranking of concerns of ageing and indications of technologies that attendees might be interested in. The options were decided upon following a focus group of aged care policy officials and researchers.

A volunteer assisting at the conference agreed to invite attendees to complete the survey form and a reward was offered in the form of a plastic finger massage device. The volunteer was located at a booth near the main entrance to the Exhibition. Consequently approaches were made only to people who passed near the booth, as the entrance to the exhibition was across several large doors to the Exhibition only a minority of attendees was invited to complete it.

4   Results

277 attendees completed the survey form which is a very small level of participation given that attendance at the event is around 50,000 people. The numbers of attendees might itself have been a barrier to participation as only a small number of people would have been able to see the volunteer due to the large numbers of people and that entry to the event was through a large open doorway. The volunteer only asked people who passed near her particular booth; there were 190 exhibitors at the event using booths or other displays for their projects and services.

Of the ten options provided on the form for concerns of ageing the responses, in priority order were: health (190), maintaining social activities (140), physical decline (134), accessing public transport (130) Family not taking care of you (113), not having enough money (111), mental decline (99), house not suitable for an older person (76), and family taking your money and assets (63). No respondees selected "other". The responses to the question "Which of the devices people would be happy to purchase" the responses to the options given were: Home telehealth device for on-line medical consultations (117), Reminder service (appointments, medications etc) (102), Home sensors (87), GPS tracking device in case I get lost (71), Home cameras so my family can see I am OK (69), other products/services (0). No respondees selected "other".

5   Discussion

Concerns of people about their own ageing are many and varied. There are concerns about a decline in health, increasing chronic disease and disability. Of concern to consumers, funders and care providers is the correlation between the rising number of chronic conditions accumulated with ageing and rising healthcare costs [11]. There are expectations and some evidence that a greater use of technology might assist consumers and their carers to better manage health including remote access to care services. In this sample health and physical were the major concerns of ageing ranked first for health and third for physical decline. There is some evidence of the benefits of maintaining social activities for health and well-being and that was the second major concern of the respondees. Despite China, and especially Nanjing, having a reasonable public transport system in terms of a metro, bus and train networks, accessing public transport was the next concern of respondees. There are indications that transfers are the greatest risk for frail elderly in accessing transport although most Metro and train stations have elevators as well as escalators.

China is a nation influenced by the Confucian tradition which values age and places expectations that your family will be taking care of you in older age. The option of "family not taking care of you scored 113 responses suggesting it is a concern of some older people. Nanjing is in the developed east coast strip where greater wealth is evident compared to inner or western Chin yet "not having enough money" scored 111 responses. Lower scores were received for "mental decline" (99) and "house not suitable for an older person" (76). Most Chinese live in apartments and depending on whether they were serviced by elevators might indicate their suitability for frail aged.

Elder abuse is a sad feature of societies and ICTs could offer an additional channel for this to occur, particularly financial abuse [12]. Older people often use ICTs to manage their retirement savings and investments. They may be less alert to instances of fraud or errors by financial institutions and may be more trusting of institutions such as banks; they may need help to access accounts and manage security including password changes. It may be tempting for people assisting to take advantage of that trust. In this research the concern of "family taking your money and assets scored low (63) but enough to indicate this was a concern of some older people.

6   Technology and New Service Models

The need for streamlined service models for aged care has been identified [13] and technology has potential to help transform the experience of ageing and the delivery of care and support services. While a great deal of work has been done on pilot studies, time-limited trials and telehealth frameworks for health delivery [14] very little research has been done on analysing the critical successes and failures of the delivery models. There is disappointment in governments, providers and remote clients that telehealth has not been adopted at an expeditious rate and the reasons for this warrant investigation [15].

This research invited responses to the question "Which of the devices you would be happy to purchase". The highest response was for the option "Home telehealth device for on-line medical consultations" (117 responses). Telehealth has the potential to automatically provide a consultation including taking of vital signs through peripheral devices. A Reminder service (appointments, medications etc) (102) was the second most popular item followed by Home sensors (87), GPS tracking device in case I get lost (71) and Home cameras so my family can see I am OK (69). The form provided space for respondees to indicate other devices but no reponses were received for "other".

Technology along with innovations such as universal housing design [16] has the potential to meet people's needs at various stages of their lives. These can make our homes safer and reduce the need to move home in the event of illness, frailty or disability. The aged and community care sector is yet to fully embrace the wide range of technology innovations that are increasingly available.

Smart home technologies include Telecare, Telehealth, robotics, wearable devices, and ubiquitous sensors on appliances such as microwave ovens and light switches. The needs of people with dementia that technologies could assist with are great and varied. This includes reminders for ADLs (Activities of Daily Living) and medications. Consumers, families and carers could access care through Telehealth technologies; that is technologies that can provide an automated consultation, a link to a remote clinician when required and information for guided self-care. Similarly these and other devices can facilitate social connections and some residential care facilities already make Skype available for residents. Telecare can help keep people safe through movement detectors, out-of-bed sensors, automated lighting to guide someone to the toilet when they get out of bed in the night, sensor for extreme heat in the kitchen and flooding in the bathroom. Signals can be selectively routed such that an alert about a fall might have a different recipient than an alert about a fire.

As many people are aware the responsibility of caring for a person with dementia can be consuming and allow little time for other responsibilities. Through the technology families can have reassurance that their family member is safe. Sensors can detect if a person opens a door, uses the microwave or other appliances, has a fall, and is taking medications and otherwise following ADLs. The technology can give respite to families so they can live more of their own lives or even to be able to go shopping knowing they will receive an alert in the event of an adverse event such as a fall or in the case of wandering. Technology has the potential to relieve clinicians of much of the non-clinical tasks that clinicians need to deal with, allowing them to focus more on the functions they were trained for.

Sensor networks can be connected to Big Data tools that can analyse massive amounts of data that various sensors can capture. The analytical tools can detect subtle changes in behaviour that might otherwise be missed by busy clinicians. Home visiting care staff members typically spend significant hours driving from client to client. The technology can assist to triage and prioritise visits it can also indicate when the client may not need a personal visit. Clinical staff can reduce unnecessary visits and instead focus on more critical needs for their skills. Overseas these technologies have been demonstrated to reduce admissions, readmissions, and length of stay when a client is admitted. There is also an environmental benefit in reducing client and carer travel to access services.

Despite the long-anticipated benefits the adoption of Smart Home technologies for care has been slow but there are signs that the pace of adoption is starting to accelerate. There have been a small but increasing number of larger-scale roll-outs. There is more available evidence to support the expectations of benefits from Smart Home technologies. The better known studies include the Whole System Demonstrator in the UK [17] which involved over 6000 patients in a randomised controlled trial. It found show that Telehealth can deliver a 15% reduction in A&E/ED (Accident & Emergency or Emergency Department) visits, a 20% reduction in emergency admissions, a 14% reduction in elective admissions, a 14% reduction in bed days and an 8% reduction in tariff costs and a 45% reduction in mortality rates. This was not dissimilar from the evaluation of a similar project in the Veterans Administration system in the USA which found 25% reduction in bed days, 19% reduction in hospital admissions and high consumer satisfaction at a relatively modest cost [18].

There is an expectation that the move of Baby-boomers into the age when they will require aged care services will have significant impacts. This is in terms of their political pressure for improvements including greater access to technology as well as provide markets for "killer aps", that is innovations that perhaps have not yet been invented but which by themselves will drive massive-scale adoption. Another driver may be the ageing cohorts in Asia which already has the countries with the largest numbers of older people (India and China), the regions with the most aged demographics (Hong Kong, Macau, Japan) and the most rapidly ageing countries (Korea and Taiwan).

Smart home technology has matured significantly over the past decade and there is much to learn from the way different technologies are being used successfully in different services and different countries. There is no lack of technology innovations but there is much to be done in learning how to adopt and realise the benefits. It appears many of the Smart Home projects in Australia and overseas are not independently evaluated which can mean that valuable lessons are lost. Care providers are encouraged to partner with some of the many researchers in this field who can assist in finding research grant funds and in distilling the learning to the benefit of all.

7   Limitations of the Study

The study had many limitations. It was a convenience study of people attending an aged care event so only people with the capacity and means to attend the event could be included in sampling. The volunteers invited people who came near their booth but had no way of knowing their age, whether they were visitors to the event or participating in another capacity such as an exhibitor, presenter or accompanying family member. The volunteer's booth was near the main entrance so many of the respondees would not have seen the many technologies on display which may account for no-one selecting "other" as technologies they would like to adopt.

Acknowledgements. The researchers acknowledge the support of the National Soft Science Planning (2011GXQ4K029), and National Population and Reproductive Health Science Data Center of National Scientific Data Sharing Platform for Population and Health funded by Ministry of Science and Technology, China; the research volunteers and the participants.

References

1. Soar, J., Wang, H., Su, Y.: A model for regional innovation and information sharing to reduce falls amongst the elderly through intelligent technologies. In: Proceedings COINFO 2011: 6th International Conference on Cooperation and Promotion of Information Resources in Science and Technology: Coordinative Innovation and Open Sharing, Hangzhou, China, November 12-14 (2011)
2. Wagner, N., Hassanein, K., Head, M.: Computer use by older adults: A multi-disciplinary review. Computers in Human Behavior 26(5), 870–882 (2010)
3. Oliver, D.: Managing risk in older hospital inpatients. Clinical Risk 18(5), 161–162 (2012)
4. Marek, K.D., Antle, L.: Medication Management of the Community-Dwelling Older Adult. In: Hughes, R.G. (ed.) Patient Safety and Quality: An Evidence-Based Handbook for Nurses. Rockville (MD): Agency for Healthcare Research and Quality (US), ch. 18 (April 2008), http://www.ncbi.nlm.nih.gov/books/NBK2670/ (accessed December 28, 2013)
5. Clare, M., Blundell, B., Clare, J.: Examination of the Extent of Elder Abuse in Western Australia: A Qualitative and Quantitative Investigation of Existing Agency Policy. In: Service Responses and Recorded Data. Crime Research Centre, The University of Western Australia (April 2011)
6. ABS. Older Carers. 4102.0 - Australian Social Trends. Australian Bureau of Statistics. (December 2012)
7. Ying, S., Soar, J., Talburt, J., Jadad, A.R.: Consumer-Centered Ehealth: Challenges and Opportunities for China. Advanced Science Letters 7, 60–257 (2012)
8. Czaja, S.J., Sharit, J.: The Aging of the Population: Opportunities and Challenges for Human Factors Engineering. The Bridge on Technologies for an Aging Population. NAE. Spring 39(1) (2009)
9. State Council of the people's Republic of China, The planning and construction of social endowment service system (2011-2015), http://www.gov.cn/xxgk/pub/govpublic/mrlm/201112/t20111227_64699.html
10. Xinhua Daily telegraph, CCP decision on deepening the reform of some major issues (November 21, 2013), http://news.xinhuanet.com/mrdx/2013-11/16/c_132892941.htm

11. Thomas Lehnert, T., Heider, D., Leicht, H., Heinrich, S., Corrieri, S., Luppa, M., Riedel-Heller, S., König, H.: Review: Health Care Utilization and Costs of Elderly Persons With Multiple Chronic Conditions. Med Care Res Rev 68, 387–420 (2011)
12. Clare, M., Blundell, B., Clare, J.: Examination of the Extent of Elder Abuse in Western Australia: A Qualitative and Quantitative Investigation of Existing Agency Policy, Service Responses and Recorded Data. Crime Research Centre. The University of Western Australia (April 2011)
13. O'Reilly, M.T., Courtney, M.D., Edwards, H.E., Hassall, S.: Clinical outcomes in residential care: setting benchmarks for quality. Australasian Journal on Ageing 30(2), 63–69 (2011)
14. Barrientos, J., Soar, J., Su, Y.: Impact analysis of assessment, consultation and education services to support the adoption of smart home technologies, innovations for chronic disease prevention and solutions for independent living. In: 10th International Conference on Smart Homes and Health Telematics: Impact Analysis of Solutions for Chronic Disease Prevention and Management (ICOST 2012), Artimino, Italy, June 12-15 (2012)
15. Goodwin, N.: The State of Telehealth and Telecare in the UK: Prospects for Integrated Care. Journal of Integrated Care 18(6), 3–10 (2010)
16. Demirbileka, O., Demirkan, D.: Universal product design involving elderly users: a participatory design model. Applied Ergonomics 35(4), 361–370 (2004)
17. Department of Health 2011, Whole system demonstrator programme: Headline findings – (December 2011)
18. Darkins, A., Ryan, P., Kobb, R., Foster, L., Edmonson, E., Wakefield, B., Lancaster, A.E.: Care Coordination/Home Telehealth: The Systematic Implementation of Health Informatics. Home Telehealth, and Disease Management to Support the Care of Veteran Patients with Chronic Conditions Telemedicine and e-Health 14(10), 1118–1126 (2008)

A Fast Method for Abrupt Change Detection from Large-Scale Electrocardiogram (ECG) Time Series

Jin-Peng Qi[1], Qing Zhang[3], Jie Qi[1], and Ying Zhu[2]

[1] College of Information Science & Technology, Donghua University,
Shanghai 201620, P.R. China
{qipengkai,jieqi}@dhu.edu.cn
[2] Hunter New England Health, Royal North Shore Hospital, New South Wales, Australia
ying.zhu@hnehealth.nsw.gov.au
[3] Australian e-Health Research Centre, CSIRO, UQ HSB 901/16, RBWH, Brisbane,
QLD 4060, Australia
qing.zhang@csiro.au

Abstract. In previous work, we proposed a promising method, named HWBST, for Change-Point (CP) detection from time series. However, the performance of HWBST is affected partly by the search criteria in terms of Binary Search Tree (BST). In this paper, we propose an improved method for fast CP detection from large-scale ECG time series, based on multi-level Haar Wavelet and Ternary Search Tree (HWTST, for short). In this method, we construct a ternary search tree termed TSTcD from a diagnosed time series by using multi-level HW. Then, we implement fast detection abrupt change from root to leaf nodes in TSTcD, by introducing two search criteria in terms of the data fluctuation in the left, right, and virtual middle branches of TSTcD. Based on the assembled and abnormal ECG samples, we evaluate the proposed HWTST by comparing with HWBST, KS, and T methods. The results show that the proposed HWTST is a faster and more efficient than HWBST, KS and T in terms of the computation time, error, accuracy, and distance of e.c.d.f.

Keywords: CP detection, ECG Time series, Large-Scale, Haar Wavelet (HW), Ternary Search Tree (TST).

1   Introduction

Currently, Change-Point (CP) detection has attracted considerable attention in the fields of data mining and statistics. CP detection has been widely studied in many real-world problems, such as atmospheric and financial analysis [1], intrusion detection in computer network [2], signal segmentation in data stream [3], as well as fault detection in engineering system [2, 4]. In the past decade, Wavelet Transform (WT), and its revised approaches have emerged as an important mathematical tool for analyzing time series [5-10]. WT is a promising approach for CP detection. It has found applications in anomaly detection, time series prediction, image processing, and noise reduction [6, 10-12]. WT can represent general functions at different scales and positions in a versatile and sophisticated manner, so the data distribution features can

K. Liu et al. (Eds.): ICISO 2014, IFIP AICT 426, pp. 420–429, 2014.

be easily extracted from different time or space scales [12, 13]. As a simple WT, Haar Wavelet (HW), owns some attracting features including fast for implementation and able to analyze the local feature. HW is very useful to find discontinuity and high frequency change in time series, so it is a potential candidate in modern electrical and computer engineering applications, such as signal and image compression, as well as abnormality detection from time series [14, 15].

Previously, we proposed a HWBST method for fast CP detection [16]. HWBST is a promising method for detecting abrupt change from large-scale time series. However, the performance of HWBST is affected partly by binary search criteria, especially when abrupt change occurs near the middle boundary of BST. To resolve this problem, in this paper, we propose an improved method for fast CP detection from large-scale time series, named HWTST, based on multi-level HW and ternary search tree. In the proposed method, a ternary search tree (TST), named TSTcD is built based on a binary search tree, TcD derived from a diagnosed time series, by adding a virtual middle sub-tree; and then abrupt change is detected from TSTcD in terms of two search criteria. To evaluate the proposed method, we apply the HWTST, HWBST, KS, and T to detect abrupt change from both the assembled and the abnormal ECG samples. The detailed HWTST method is implemented as follows.

2   Method

2.1   Definition and Assumption [16]

Suppose $Z = \{z_1,...,z_N\}$ is a diagnosed time series, we observe

$$Z = f(i/n) + X, i = 1,...,N, \tag{1}$$

where $X = \{x_i\}_{i=1,...,N}$ are discrete and centred i.i.d. random variables, and f is a noisy mean signal with unknown distribution.

Definition 1: We define the data fluctuation between two adjacent segments in Z as,

$$D_{mn}(c) = \sup_{1 \le L, R \le N} | \frac{1}{m} \sum_{L=a}^{c} z_L - \frac{1}{n} \sum_{R=c+1}^{b} z_R |, \tag{2}$$

where $Z = \{Z_L, Z_R\}$, $Z_L = \{z_a,...,z_c\}$, $Z_R = \{z_{c+1},...,z_b\}$, and $m = c - a$, $n = b - c - 1$, and $m + n \le N$. If a change point c occurs in Z, there exists a value c satisfies $D_{mn}(c) > \delta$, $z_c \in [z_1, z_N]$, and $\delta \in R$.

Hypotheses:
  (1) H_0: if $D_{mn}(c) \le \delta$, no abrupt change occurs in Z.
  (2) H_1: if $D_{mn}(c) > \delta$, abrupt change occurs in Z.
where $\delta \in R$ is a threshold of data fluctuation in a time series Z within an identical distribution. We wish to test H_0 against H_1 from observations. Thereafter, we assume that the number, the location, and the size of the function f are unknown. However, the upper bound of data fluctuation δ is supposed to be known.

2.2   Multi-level HW

Generally, as shown in Fig.1, by using multi-level HW, a discrete time-series signal $Z=\{z_1, z_2,..., z_N\}$, can be decomposed into the kth-level trend cA^k, and k level fluctuations, $i.e.$, $\mathbf{cD}^1$, cD^2,..., cD^k, $k=1, 2, ..,\log_2 N$. The k-level HW is the mapping H_k defined by [8],

$$Z \xrightarrow{H_1} (cA^k|cD^k|cD^{k-1}|..|cD^2|cD^1), \tag{3}$$

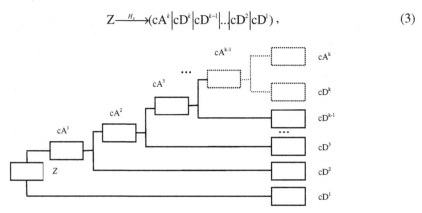

Fig. 1. The diagram of multi-level HW for a time-series signal Z, it is composed of k-level cA and cD vectors, $i.e.$, the average and difference coefficients vectors

Suppose a diagnosed sample $Z=\{z_1, z_2,..., z_N\}$ is decomposed by means of multi-level HW, we can represent the approximation and detail coefficient vectors by the following matrices, namely McA and McD:

$$McA=\begin{bmatrix} cA^0 \\ cA^1 \\ ... \\ cA^k \\ ... \\ cA^M \end{bmatrix}=\begin{bmatrix} cA_{0,1} & ... & ... & ... & ... & cA_{0,N} \\ cA_{1,1.} & ... & ... & ... & cA_{1,N/2} \\ ... & ... & ... & ... \\ cA_{k,1} & ... & cA_{k,j} \\ ... & ... \\ cA_{M,1} \end{bmatrix} \quad McD=\begin{bmatrix} cD^0 \\ cD^1 \\ ... \\ cD^k \\ ... \\ cD^M \end{bmatrix}=\begin{bmatrix} cD_{0,1} & ... & ... & ... & ... & cD_{0,N} \\ cD_{1,1.} & ... & ... & ... & cD_{1,N/2} \\ ... & ... & ... & ... \\ cD_{k,1} & ... & cD_{k,j} \\ ... & ... \\ cD_{M,1} \end{bmatrix}, \tag{4}$$

where $cA^0 = cD^0 = Z = \{z_1, z_2,..., z_N\}, 0 \le k \le M = log_2 N$, and $1 \le j \le N/2^k$.

2.3   Overview of HWTST Method

The scheme of integrated HWTST method (Fig.2) is composed of three parts. First, a ternary search tree, TSTcD, is constructed from a diagnosed time-series Z by multi-level HW method. Second, abrupt CP is detected from root to leaf nodes in TSTcD, in terms of two search criteria. Last, the proposed method is evaluated by comparing with HWBST, KS, and T methods.

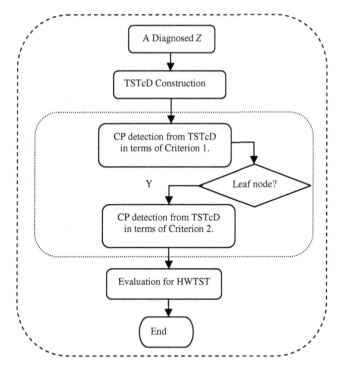

Fig. 2. The scheme of the integrated HWTST framework, it includes three parts: TSTcD construction, CP detection from TSTcD in terms of two ternary search criteria, and evaluation for HWTST method

2.4   Construction of TSTcD

First, we build a binary tree TcD, in terms of McD. As shown in Fig.3, we deal the element $cD_{k,j}$ in McD as the root, the other elements as non-leaf left and right child nodes, and the original $Z= \{z_1, z_2,\ldots, z_N\}$ as N leaf nodes, respectively. Then, a virtual middle-child node termed $cD_{k,j;M}$ is added into non-leaf parent node $cD_{k,j}$ in TSTcA.

2.5   CP Detection from TSTcD

Definition 2: Suppose the current non-leaf node $cD_{k,j}$ is selected in TSTcD, with its left, virtual middle, and right child non-leaf node, namely $cD_{k,j;L}$, $cD_{k,j;M}$, and $cD_{k,j;R}$, respectively. To measure the data fluctuation in different segments of Z, three statistic variables, $D_{k,j;L}$, $D_{k,j;M}$, and $D_{k,j;R}$ are defined as:

$$D_{k,j;L} = \left|cD_{k,j;L}\right| = \left|\frac{1}{(\sqrt{2})^{\wedge}(k-1)}(\sum_{L=a}^{aM-1} z_L - \sum_{R=aM}^{c} z_R)\right| , \qquad (16)$$

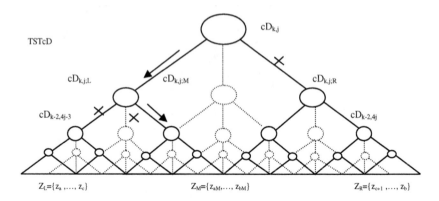

Fig. 3. The scheme of TSTcD construction, the virtual non-leaf middle-child node is added

$$D_{k,j;R} = |cD_{k,j;R}| = \left| \frac{1}{(\sqrt{2})^\wedge (k-1)} (\sum_{L=c+1}^{bM} z_L - \sum_{R=bM+1}^{b} z_R) \right| , \tag{17}$$

$$D_{k,j;M} = |cD_{k,j;M}| = \left| \frac{1}{(\sqrt{2})^\wedge (k-1)} (\sum_{L=aM}^{c} z_L - \sum_{R=c+1}^{bM} z_R) \right| , \tag{18}$$

where $a = 2^k(j-1)+1, b = 2^k * j$, and $c = 2^k(j-1)+2^{(k-1)}$; $aM = 2^{k-1}(2j-2)+2^{k-2}+1$, and $bM = 2^{k-1}(2j-1)+2^{k-2}$; $1 \le j \le N/2^k$, and $2 \le k \le \log_2 N$. Thereafter, we can introduce the first search criterion in terms of the data fluctuation defined above.

Criterion 1: Suppose the current non-leaf node $cD_{k,j}$ is selected in TSTcD, $2 \le k \le \log_2 N$,

(a) If $(\max(D_{k,j;L}, D_{k,j;R}, D_{k,j;M}) = D_{k,j;L})$ holds true, then the left-child node $cD_{k,jL}$ in TSTcD, is selected to be involved into the current search path;

(b) If $(\max(D_{k,j;L}, D_{k,j;R}, D_{k,j;M}) = D_{k,j;R})$ holds true, then the right-child node $cD_{k,jR}$ in TSTcD, is selected to be involved into the current search path;

(c) If $(\max(D_{k,j;L}, D_{k,j;R}, D_{k,j;M}) = D_{k,j;M})$ holds true, then the virtual middle-child node $cD_{k,jM}$ in TSTcD, is selected to be involved into the current search path.

In addition, we introduce another criterion to deal with the last leaf node in TSTcD, and then decide whether the selected leaf node is the potential CP or not. We define the second search criterion in terms of the data fluctuation in the last leaf node level as follows.

Criterion 2: Suppose the current selected non-leaf node is $cD_{k,j}$, $k = 1$, with left, and right-child leaf node, $cD_{0,2j-1}$, and $cD_{0,2j}$, namely, z_{2j-1}, and z_{2j},

(a) If $(|cD_{k,j}| > \sqrt{2}\alpha)$ is satisfied, then the right-child leaf node $cD_{0,2j}$, i.e., z_{2j} is selected, and dealt as the estimated CP in Z;

(b) If $(|cD_{k,j}| > \sqrt{2}\alpha)$ is satisfied, then there is no abrupt change detected from Z.

Based on two search criteria above, a fast CP detection is implemented, and then an estimated CP can be detected from root to leaf-nodes in TSTcD.

3   Results

To verify the performance of the proposed method further, we apply HWKS, and KS, HW, and T methods, to detect abrupt change from ECG time series provided by PhysioBank. In ECG experiments, we design the diagnosed ECG samples from different ECG datasets, including the MIT-BIH Normal Sinus Rhythm Database (NSRDB) [17], MIT-BIH Noise Stress Test Database (NSTDB) [18], and MIT-BIH Malignant Ventricular Arrhythmia Database (MVADB) [19].

3.1   CP Detection from Assembled ECG Samples

First, we select a normal ECG dataset, 16265m from NSRDB, and an abnormal ECG dataset, 118e00m from NSTDB. Specifically, we take the normal ECG segment of size m as X_m, and the abnormal segment of size n as Y_n, respectively, and then assemble the diagnosed ECG sample $Z=\{X_m, Y_n\}=\{x_1,\ldots, x_m, y_1,\ldots, y_n\}$. Then, a single CP test

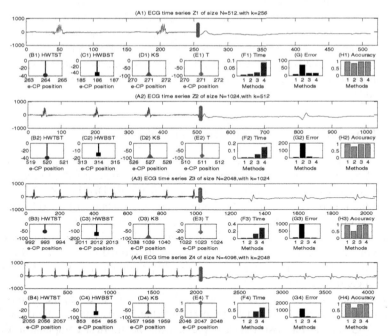

Fig. 4. The results of CP detection from the assembled ECG time series Z1-Z4. (A1)-(A4) the assembled Z1-Z4; (B1)-(B4),(C1)-(C4) ,(D1)-(D4), and (E1)-(E4) the e-CP detected from Z1-Z4, by HWTST, HWBST, KS, and T, respectively; (F1)-(F4) the diagram analysis for the computation time, (G1)-(G4) the error of e-CP, and (H1)-(H4) the accuracy for HWTST, HWBST, KS, and T, respectively. In histograms (F)-(H), '1', '2', '3', and '4' stands for HWTST, HWBST, KS, and T, respectively.

Table 1. The results of CP detection from the assembled ECG samples

Z \ M	Size, N / CP, k	2^7 / 2^6	2^8 / 2^7	2^9 / 2^8	2^10 / 2^9	2^11 / 2^10	2^12 / 2^11	2^13 / 2^12	2^14 / 2^13	Mean
Time	*HWTST*	*.0050*	*.0060*	*.0060*	*.0060*	*.0060*	*.0060*	*.0070*	*.0090*	*.0063*
	HWBST	.0060	.0060	.0070	.0080	.0080	.0100	.0140	.0240	.0103
	KS	.0100	.0130	.0200	.0440	.0119	.3910	1.420	5.431	.9176
	T	.0300	.0450	.0740	.1390	.2870	.6750	1.653	4.461	.9205
Error	*HWTST*	*9*	*8*	*8*	*8*	*31*	*8*	*8*	*8*	*11*
	T	63	63	15	1	1	1	1	1	18
	KS	15	15	15	15	15	90	52	70	36
	HWBST	62	4	70	198	988	1194	388	8074	1372
Accuracy	*HWTST*	*.9297*	*.9688*	*.9844*	*.9922*	*.9849*	*.9980*	*.9990*	*.9995*	*.9821*
	KS	.8828	.9414	.9707	.9854	.9927	.9780	.9937	.9957	.9675
	T	.5078	.7539	.9707	.9990	.9995	.9998	.9999	.9999	.9038
	HWBST	.5156	.9844	.8633	.8066	.5176	.7085	.9526	.5072	.7320

position is arranged at the middle part in each diagnosed ECG sample. The selected results are shown in Fig 4, and the results of the computation time, error and accuracy for all ECG samples of size from 2^7 to 2^{14} are summarized in Table 1.

In this assembled ECG experiments, the results of CP detection illustrated in Fig.2, and Table 1 show that, the proposed HWTST can estimate CP position efficiently, and then distinguish the normal and abnormal segments from the assembled ECG samples with faster, smaller error and higher accuracy than HWBST, KS, and T. For HWBST, although faster than KS, and T, it has the biggest error and the lowest accuracy in all four methods. For KS, although slightly bigger error than T, it is faster than T, and has smaller error and higher accuracy than HWBST. For T, it has smaller error and higher accuracy than HWBST, whereas, it needs the longest computation time in all methods. These results indicate the proposed HWTST is more sensitive and efficient than HWBST, for CP detection at the middle boundary. Especially, it has the shortest computation time, the smallest error, and the highest accuracy in all four methods.

3.2   CP Detection from Abnormal ECG Time Series

To verify the performance of the proposed method further, we apply HWTST, HWBST, KS, and T to analyze the abnormal ECG time series directly. In this part, we select the abnormal ECG segment from 615m in the MVADB, i.e., $Z=\{Y_n\}=\{y_1,..., y_n\}$, as a diagnosed ECG sample. To some extent, the distance of e.c.d.f can partly reflect the statistic fluctuation. Therefore, we take this variable as an indicator of the data fluctuation between two adjacent ECG segments divided by the estimated CP (e-CP) position. The selected results of CP detection are plotted in Fig.5, and the results for all abnormal ECG samples, including the e-CP position, computation time, and the variance of e.c.d.f are summarized in Table 2.

For abnormal ECG samples Z1-Z6 of size N from 2^{10} to 2^{15}, the results show that the proposed HWTST can detect the abrupt change position, and then divide the original ECG sample into two adjacent parts, with the shortest computation time in four methods; and it has bigger distance of e.c.d.f than HWBST, and T methods. For HWBST, although faster than KS, and T, it has the smallest variance of e.c.d.f in all four methods. For KS, it can detect CP with the maximal distance of e.c.d.f, whereas, it needs longer computation time than HWTST, HWBST, especially when ECG sample size is bigger. For T, it needs the longest averaged computation time in all four methods, although it has bigger variance of e.c.d.f than HWBST. These results show that HWTST can capture abrupt change position from the diagnosed ECG samples more quickly and efficiently than HWBST, KS, and T. On the other hand, the detected CP is very useful to find a critical time from the diagnosed ECG time series, where a patient might encounter an important conversion between two different states

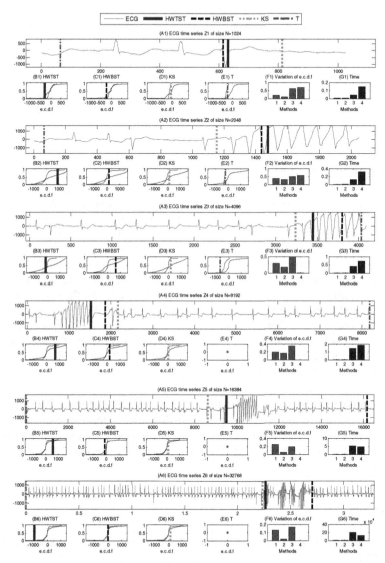

Fig. 5. The results of CP detection from abnormal ECG time series of size for 2^10 to 2^15. (A1)-(A6) the abnormal ECG sample Z1-Z6; (B1)-(B6), (C1)-(C6), (D1)-(D6), (E1)-(E6) the e.c.d.f derived from two adjacent ECG segments in Z1-Z6, by HWTST, HWBST, KS, and T, respectively; (F1)-(F6) the diagram analysis of the distance of e.c.d.f, and (G1)-(G6) the computation time of HWKS, KS, HW, and T in Z1-Z6, respectively. In histograms (F)-(H), '1', '2', '3', and '4' stands for HWTST, HWBST, KS, and T, respectively.

Table 2. The results of CP detection from the abnormal ECG samples

Z\M		Size, N	2^{10}	2^{11}	2^{12}	2^{13}	2^{14}	2^{15}	Mean
e-CP	HWTST	630	1478	3448	1520	9503	22640	NA
	HWBST	614	1437	3804	1863	16167	27054	NA
	KS	813	1153	3237	2164	8610	22361	NA
	T	66	65	4036	8190	1	1	NA
Time	HWTST	.0060	.0060	.0070	.0060	.0090	.0140	.0080
	HWBST	.0080	.0090	.0100	.0140	.0200	.0350	.0160
	KS	.0430	.1320	.4100	1.409	5.294	20.46	4.625
	T	.1450	.3170	.7440	1.855	4.685	13.02	3.461
Variance of e.c.d.f	KS	.6260	.4919	.4991	.3456	.1909	.1632	.3861
	HWTST	.1944	.3750	.2916	.1941	.2475	.1297	.2387
	T	.6770	.5811	.0079	0	0	0	.2110
	HWBST	.0983	.3249	.1786	.1616	.0496	.0162	.1382

of health. Therefore, HWTST is very meaningful for inspecting and diagnosing different states of health from diagnosed ECG time series more quickly and efficiently.

4   Conclusion

In this paper, based on multi-level HW and ternary search tree, an improved method, named HWTST, is proposed for fast CP detection from large-scale ECG time series. In the proposed HWTST method, a ternary search tree, TSTcD, is built by adding a virtual middle-child sub-tree into TcD, which is derived from a diagnosed time series Z; and two search criteria are defined in terms of the data fluctuation in TSTcD. Then, an abrupt change is detected from root to leaf nodes of TSTcD in terms of two search criteria. Comparing with previous HWBST, KS, and T methods, the results show that the proposed HWTST is more efficient for fast detection CP from large-scale ECG time series, due to the shortest computation time, the smallest error, the highest accuracy in all four methods, and bigger variance of e.c.d.f than HWBST and T. In addition, HWTST has better performance than HWBST, especially when abrupt change occurs near the middle boundary.

Acknowledgment. I would like to thank my supervisor Prof. Qing. Zhang and Prof. Mohan Karunanithi in the Australia E-Health Research Centre for their assistances, supports and advices for this paper. This paper is supported by National Natural Science Foundation of China (No.61104154), and the Fundamental Research Funds for the Central Universities.

References

1. Bolton, R.J., Hand, D.J.: Statistical fraud detection: A review. Statistical Science, 235–249 (2002)
2. Yamanishi, K., et al.: On-line unsupervised outlier detection using finite mixtures with discounting learning algorithms. Data Mining and Knowledge Discovery 8, 275–300 (2004)
3. Basseville, M.E., Nikiforov, I.V.: Detection of abrupt changes: theory and application (1993)

4. Murad, U., Pinkas, G.: Unsupervised profiling for identifying superimposed fraud. In: Żytkow, J.M., Rauch, J. (eds.) PKDD 1999. LNCS (LNAI), vol. 1704, pp. 251–261. Springer, Heidelberg (1999)
5. Gustafsson, F.: Adaptive filtering and change detection, vol. 1. Wiley, New York (2000)
6. Alarcon-Aquino, V., Barria, J.A.: Anomaly detection in communication networks using wavelets. IEE Proceedings-Communications 148, 355–362 (2001)
7. Khalil, M., Duchêne, J.: Detection and classification of multiple events in piecewise stationary signals: comparison between autoregressive and multiscale approaches. Signal processing 75, 239–251 (1999)
8. Kobayashi, M.: Wavelets and their applications in industry. Nonlinear Analysis: Theory, Methods & Applications 47, 1749–1760 (2001)
9. Percival, D.B., Walden, A.T.: Wavelet methods for time series analysis, vol. 4. Cambridge University Press (2006)
10. Salam, M., Mohamad, D.: Segmentation of Malay Syllables in connected digit speech using statistical approach. International Journal of Computer Science and Security 2, 23–33 (2008)
11. Qi, J., et al.: Kinetic theory approach to modeling of cellular repair mechanisms under genome stress. PloS One 6, e22228 (2011)
12. Tseng, V.S., et al.: Segmentation of time series by the clustering and genetic algorithms. In: Sixth IEEE International Conference on Data Mining Workshops, ICDM Workshops 2006, pp. 443–447 (2006)
13. Alarcon-Aquino, V., Barria, J.: Change detection in time series using the maximal overlap discrete wavelet transform. Latin American Applied Research 39, 145–152 (2009)
14. Darkhovski, B.S.: Nonparametric methods in change-point problems: A general approach and some concrete algorithms. Lecture Notes-Monograph Series, 99–107 (1994)
15. Walker, J.S.: A primer on wavelets and their scientific applications. CRC press (2002)
16. Qi, J.P., Zhang, Q., Qi, J.: A Fast Method for Change Point Detection from time series Based on Haar Wavelet and Binary Search Tree (HWBST). In: presented at the The 19th World Congress of the International Federation of Automatic Control Cape Town, South Africa (to be published)
17. Goldberger, A.L., et al.: Physiobank, physiotoolkit, and physionet components of a new research resource for complex physiologic signals. Circulation 101, e215–e220 (2000)
18. Moody, G.B., et al.: A noise stress test for arrhythmia detectors. Computers in Cardiology 11, 381–384 (1984)
19. SD, G.: Development and analysis of a ventricular fibrillation detector, M.S. thesis, MIT Dept. of Electrical Engineering and Computer Science (1986)

Research into Inventory Optimization of a Two-Echelon Distribution System Based on Particle Swarm Optimization (PSO)

Jingti Han[1], Mingliang Yu[1,2], and Lin Liu[1]

[1] School of Information Management and Engineering, Shanghai University of Finance and Economics, Shanghai 200433, China
[2] Labs of Economics and Management, University of Shanghai for Science and Technology, Shanghai 200093, China
{YU Mingliang,ymllw}@163.com

Abstract. Based on the assumption that distributor and retailers adopt different replenishment policies, this article gives consideration to the relationship between the inventory strategies of the two echelon. The authors construct an inventory model of a two-echelon distribution system under stochastic demand, and solve the problem based on algorithm of Particle Swarm Optimization (PSO) to quantitatively get the optimal ordering strategies of distribution center and retailers.

Keywords: Different replenishment policies, Two-echelon distribution system, Particle Swarm Optimization (PSO), Inventory model.

1 Introduction

Inventory optimization of two-echelon distribution system is exactly the typical problem in multi-echelon inventory control of supply chain, as for the demand uncertainty of actual management, many experts make research on two-echelon inventory system based on random demand. [1] established a two-echelon inventory system jointly operation model including a single supplier (or distributor) and many retailers. [2] proposed an inventory control model of a two-echelon distribution system based on decentralized control strategy. [3] put forward that queuing theory can be used to simulate the process retailers waiting for the delivery under the assumption of Poisson distribution, thus a two-echelon inventory model based on (R,Q) inventory replenishment policy under stochastic demand was established. [4] put great emphasis on quantitative impact of retailers inventory strategy on demands faced by suppliers.

In this paper, we study a typical two-echelon distribution system, the distribution system consists a distributor and many retailers. Based on the assumption that distributor and retailers adopt different replenishment policies, we assume retailers with (R,Q) policy and distributor with (s,S) policy, the order quantity Q remains unchanged for each order. This article gives consideration to the relationship between the inventory strategies of the two echelon, aim to minimum the average total cost,

K. Liu et al. (Eds.): ICISO 2014, IFIP AICT 426, pp. 430–438, 2014.

establish an inventory model of a two-echelon distribution system and solve the problem based on algorithm of Particle Swarm Optimization (PSO) with a numerical example.

2   Assumptions and Symbols

2.1   Assumptions

a. In the two-echelon distribution system, distributor sends ordering information to suppliers and provides single species products. **b.** The final demands of customers faced by various retailers are mutually independent random variables, and demands per unit time follow a Poisson distribution with the same parameters. **c.** The retailers adopt a continuous review (R,Q) strategy. Assuming $Q \geq R+1$, so that order crossover phenomenon will not occur within two successive cycles. **d.** Distributor adopt a continuous stock-taking (s,S) strategy and s <S, Where s and S are integer multiple of order quantity Q. **e.** Backorders are allowed in each echelon of the two-echelon system and are delay in delivery, backorders are sale without loss, namely Backorder mode, delay in delivery has a corresponding cost .**f.** Lead time a random variable, the lead time is independent from unit time demand of retailers and it is composed of transport time and random delay of distributor. **g.** Assuming transportation time and cost are the same from distributor to different retailers.

2.2   Symbols

N - The total number of retailers,

L_0 -Fixed lead time of distributor's purchases from suppliers,

A_0 - Fixed ordering cost per distributor order

h_0 - Holding cost of per unit goods within per unit time of distributor,

b_0 - Backorder cost of per unit goods within per unit time of distributor,

L_t - Fixed shipping time from distributor to different suppliers,

x_r - Retailers' demand per unit time, $x_r \sim P(\lambda_r)$,

h_r - Holding cost of per unit goods within per unit time of retailers,

A_r - Fixed ordering cost per retailor order,

b - Backorder cost of per unit goods within per unit time of retailers,

λ_0 -The average arrival rate of distributor's demand,

x_0 - The number of orders reaches distributor per unit time,

$D(t,t+\tau) = D(\tau)$ - Random demand of distributor from time period t to $t+\tau$,

$\delta_j(t)$ - The probability of the demand arrived at distribution center at moment t,

$\omega_j(\tau)$ The probability that the number of orders arriving at distributor is j in time period τ,

L_d - Random delay of retailers' orders at distribution center,

L_r -The lead time of retailers' orders.

3   An Inventory Model of a Two-Echelon Distribution System

3.1   An Inventory Model of Distribution Center

A.   Demand Analysis on Distribution Center

The average arrival rate of distributor's demand is

$$\lambda_0 = \sum_{i=1}^{N} \frac{\lambda_i}{Q} = \frac{N\lambda_r}{Q_r} \tag{3.1}$$

The orders received by distribution center x_0 obey Poisson distribution with parameter λ_0, that is $x_0 \sim P(\lambda_0)$, As the batch of each order is Q_r, the probability of the demand arrived at distribution center at moment t is

$$\delta_j = \frac{\lambda_0^{j/Q_r}}{(j/Q_r)!} e^{-\lambda_0}, \quad j/Q_r \in N^+ \tag{3.2}$$

The orders arrive as Poisson flow, thus the probability that the number of orders arriving at distributor equal to j within a time interval t τ is

$$\omega_j(\tau) = \frac{(\lambda_0\tau)^j}{j!} e^{-\lambda_0\tau}, \quad j = 0,1,2,\cdots \tag{3.3}$$

As the batch of each order is Q_r, the probability of the demand equal to d within a time interval t τ is

$$P\{D(\tau) = d\} = \omega_{d/Q_r}(\tau) = \frac{(\lambda_0\tau)^{d/Q_r}}{(d/Q_r)!} e^{-\lambda_0\tau} \tag{3.4}$$

μ presents for average demand per unit time of distribution center, then

$$\mu = \lambda_0 Q_r = N\lambda_r \tag{3.5}$$

B.   Analysis of Inventory Level

Suppose the holding inventory at moment t is $\{IP(t), t \geq 0\}$ and inventory level is $\{IL(t), t \geq 0\}$, So we can get the following properties,

$$IL(t + L_0) = IP(t) - D(t, t + L_0) = IP(t) - D(L_0) \tag{3.6}$$

$\{IP(t), t \geq 0\}$ is a random process with continuous parameters and discrete values, and the scope of $IP(t)$'s value is $\{s_0 + Q_r, s_0 + 2Q_r, \cdots, S_0\}$. We can see from the assumption (5) that, s_0 and S_0 are integral multiples of Q_r, assume $s_0 = k_0 Q_r$,, $S_0 = K_0 Q_r$, and $k_0, K_0 \in N^+$ here.

Suppose ρ_j to be the probability that the holding inventory $IP(t)$ reach j, $j = mQ_r$, $k_0 + 1 \leq m \leq K_0$. At the beginning of each order cycle, the orders of distribution centers ensure the holding inventory reach S_0, so $\rho_{S_0} = 1$. In an order cycle, each time t the arrival of the demand will cause transitions of holding inventory, and each holding inventory point can be reached at most once. Obviously, when $IP(t) = f > j$, if the next demand arriving at distribution center is $f - j$, then the holding inventory $IP(t) = j$, so, there is

$$\rho_j = \sum_{f>j} \rho_f \delta_{f-j} = \sum_{i=m+1}^{K_0} \rho_{iQ_r} \delta_{(i-m)Q_r} \text{, that is } \rho_j = \sum_{i=\frac{j}{Q_r}+1}^{K_0} \rho_{iQ_r} \delta_{iQ_r - j} \quad (3.7)$$

Here, $j = s_0 + Q_r, s_0 + 2Q_r, \cdots, S_0$. Only one solution can be get by solving equation (3.7), denoted by $\rho_j^*(j = s_0 + Q_r, s_0 + 2Q_r, \cdots, S_0)$. In fact, ρ_j^* also can be seen as the expected frequencies that holding inventory reaches j in one order cycle. Therefore, the frequency of average total demand in one order cycle is

$$\sum \rho_j^* = \rho_{s_0+Q_r}^* + \rho_{s_0+2Q_r}^* + \cdots + \rho_{S_0}^* = \sum_{i=k_0+1}^{K_0} \rho_{iQ_r}^* \text{ . As orders to distribution center obey}$$

compound Poisson process, and the average time intervals of demands to systems are always the same, therefore, under the stable state, the probability distribution of inventory location can be written as follow,

$$P\{IP = y\} = \frac{\rho_y^*}{\sum \rho_j^*} = \frac{\rho_y^*}{\sum_{i=k_0+1}^{K_0} \rho_{iQ_r}^*}, \quad y = s_{0+}Q_r, s_0 + 2Q_r, \cdots, S_0 \quad (3.8)$$

C. Holding Cost and Backorder Cost of Anticipation Inventory

For the given inventory level IL, inventory holding cost can be expressed as $h_0 \cdot E(\max(IL,0))$, and $\max(IL,0)$ as $(IL)^+$, then inventory cost can be expressed as $h_0 E(IL)^+$. In addition, the delayed delivery cost can be expressed as $b_0 \cdot E(\max(-IL,0))$, and $\max(-IL,0)$ as $(IL)^-$, then delayed delivery cost can be expressed as $b_0 E(IL)^-$. Assume inventory position of the distribution center is always $IP = y$, the following can be get from property(3.6).

$$P\{IL = x\} = P\{D(L_0) = y - x\}, \quad x \le y \quad (3.9)$$

When $IP = y$, $G(y)$ represents the sum of anticipation inventory cost and anticipation delayed delivery cost, so

$$G(y) = b_0 E(IL)^- + h_0 E(IL)^+ \quad (3.10)$$

Because $(IL)^- = (IL)^+ - IL$,

$$E(IL)^- = E((IL)^+ - IL) = E(IL)^+ - E(IL) \quad (3.11)$$

So, $G(y) = = -b_0(y - \mu L_0) + (h_0 + b_0) \sum_{i=1}^{y/Q_r} iQ_r \cdot P\{D(L_0) = y - iQ_r\} \quad (3.12)$

D. Anticipation Total Cost Per Unit Time of the Distribution Center

We can know from the analysis of (B) that the average number of holding inventories' changes in one order cycle is $\sum \rho_j^* = \sum_{i=k_0+1}^{K_0} \rho_{iQ_r}^*$, and every demand arrival can lead to changes of inventory levels, thus the average length of one order cycle is

$$T_0 = \sum_{i=k_0+1}^{K_0} \rho_{iQ_r}^* = \sum_{i=S_0/Q_r+1}^{S_0/Q_r} \rho_{iQ_r}^* \tag{3.13}$$

From the above analysis, we can know that anticipation total cost per unit time of the distribution center is

$$ATC_0(s_0,S_0) = \frac{A_0}{T_0} + \sum_{k=S_0/Q_r+1}^{S_0/Q_r} P\{IP = kQ_r\}G(kQ_r), in\frac{s_0}{Q_r}, \frac{S_0}{Q_r} \in N^+ \tag{3.14}$$

3.2   An Inventory Model of Retailers

A.   The Analysis on Lead Time of Retailers' Order

We can know from assumption(6) that the lead time of retailers' order consists of two parts, of which the fixed shipping time from distributor to different suppliers L_t is constant while random delay of retailers' orders at distribution center L_d is a random variable. Namely,

$$L_r = L_t + L_d \tag{3.15}$$

Just because the uncertainty distribution of L_d , its mean value is often used to represent the random variable in practice, we can get equation (3.16) from Little's formula in Queuing Theory,

$$\bar{L}_d = E(IL_0)^-/\mu_0 \tag{3.16}$$

Here, the numerator represents the average backorder level of distribution center, the denominator represents the average demand per unit time of distribution center. Substitute equation (3.5) and equation (3.11) into equation (3.16),

$$\bar{L}_d = \frac{1}{N\lambda_r}\{ \sum_{k=s_0/Q_r+1}^{S_0/Q_r} P\{IP=kQ_r\} \cdot [\sum_{i=1}^{k} iQ_r \cdot P\{D(L_0)=(k-i)Q_r\}-(kQ_r-N\lambda_r L_0)]\} \tag{3.17}$$

And $\bar{L}_r$ satisfies the following conditions, $\bar{L}_r = L_t + \bar{L}_d$ \tag{3.18}

B. Holding Cost of Inventory

From assumption (3), the demand during lead time x_r is a discrete random variable taking positive integers, provided the cumulative distribution function is $\phi(x)$, the probability distribution is $P(X_r = x) = \varphi(x)$, the expected value (average) is l. The average inventory in one cycle is $\overline{I_r} = \frac{1}{2}[R_r - l + Q_r + R_r - l] = \frac{Q_r}{2} + R_r - l$.

As $x_r \sim P(\lambda_r)$, according to the characteristics of Poisson distribution, the average demand per unit time is, λ_r and the order quantity is Q_r, then the average order times per unit time is $\frac{\lambda_r}{Q_r}$, thus the average length of one order cycle is $\frac{Q_r}{\lambda_r}$. Therefore, the average inventory holding cost of the retailers in one cycle is,

$$C_r^I = h_r \frac{Q_r}{\lambda_r}(\frac{Q_r}{2} + R_r - l) \tag{3.19}$$

C. Backorder Cost
Backorders occur when demands in the lead time exceed a reorder point, so the average value of backorders in one cycle is,

$$\sum_{x=R_r}^{+\infty}(x - R_r)\varphi(x) = \sum_{x=R_r}^{+\infty} x\varphi(x) - R_r[1 - \phi(R_r)]$$

Here, $\varphi(x)$ is the probability density function of demand X_r in the lead time, and $\varphi(x)$ is a cumulative distribution function of X_r.

Thus the average total backorder cost in a cycle is

$$C_r^S = b_r\{\sum_{x=R_r}^{+\infty} x\varphi(x) - R_r(1 - \phi(R_r))\} \tag{3.20}$$

D. The Average Total Cost Per Unit Time
From equation (3.19) and (3.20), the average total cost of the retailers and since the average time of one ordering cycle is $\frac{Q_r}{\lambda_r}$, the e average total cost of retailers per unit time is

$$ATC_r(R_r, Q_r) = \frac{\lambda_r}{Q_r} A_r + h_r(\frac{Q_r}{2} + R_r - l) + b_r \frac{\lambda_r}{Q_r}\{\sum_{x=R_r}^{+\infty} x\varphi(x) - R_r[1 - \phi(R_r)]\} \tag{3.21}$$

Retailers' demand per unit of time $x_r \sim P(\lambda_r)$, as convolution formula of Poisson distribution, demands during lead time meet $X_r \sim P(\overline{L}_r\lambda_r)$, so we have the followings in equation (3.21),

$$\varphi(x) = \frac{(\overline{L}_r\lambda_r)^x}{x!}e^{-\overline{L}_r\lambda_r} \tag{3.22}$$

$$\phi(R_r) = \sum_{x=0}^{R_r} \varphi(x) \tag{3.23}$$

$$l = \overline{L}_r\lambda_r \tag{3.24}$$

$\overline{L}_r$ can be get from (3.17) and (3.18).

Refer to equation (3.14) and (3.21), the function of anticipation total cost of the overall two-echelon distribution system per unit time can be expressed as follow,

$$ATC(s_0, S_0, R_r, Q_r) = ATC_0(s_0, S_0, Q_r) + N \cdot ATC_r(R_r, Q_r, \overline{L}_d(s_0, S_0)) \tag{3.25}$$

The goal of the model is to find the optimal $s_0^*, S_0^*, R_r^*, Q_r^*$, so that the anticipation total cost of the overall system per unit time to be minimum. So the problems to be solved by the model can be described as

$$\min\ ATC = ATC(s_0, S_0, R_r, Q_r) \tag{3.26}$$

$$s.t.\begin{cases} R_r, Q_r \in N \\ 0 < R_r + 1 \leq Q_r \\ {s_0}\!/\!{Q_r}, {S_0}\!/\!{Q_r} \in N^+ \\ s_0 < S_0 \\ Equation\ (3.1) \sim (3.25) \end{cases}$$

4   Solution Method for Model Based on Particle Swarm Optimization (PSO)

4.1   Coding and Fitness Function

Set particle size M=20, the maximum iteration K_{max}=30, adopt real number coding on the respective components of each vector's position X_i, the position vector X_i contains four dimensions, corresponding s_0, S_0, R_r, Q_r respectively, so the current position of each particle forms a solution vector, that is $X_i = (s_i, S_i, R_i, Q_i), i = 1, 2, \cdots 20$.

The goal of the two-echelon system joint inventory optimization is to optimize the total cost of distribution centers and the retailers, therefore, fitness function of algorithm can be defined as the sum of the cost of both, that is

$$fitness = ATC_0(s_i, S_i, Q_i) + N \cdot ATC_r(s_i, S_i, R_i, Q_i)$$

4.2   The Solving Process of Particle Swarm Optimization (PSO)

Step1: Its scale $M = 20$, Maximum iteration $k_{max} = 30$.

Step2: Determine the initial position of each particle $X_i^{(0)} = (s_i, S_i, R_i, Q_i), i = 1, 2, \cdots, M$, the initial velocity of each particle $v_i^{(0)} = (v_i^s, v_i^S, v_i^R, v_i^Q)$.

Step3: Measure the fitness of each particle based on (4.1) $f_i^{(0)}$, the optimal position of the each particle $p_i^{(0)} = f_i^{(0)}$.

Step4: Find out the global optimum $p_g^{(0)}$ from $p_g^{(0)} = \min\{p_1^{(0)}, p_2^{(0)}, \cdots p_M^{(0)}\}$.

Step5: Let iterations k=0 and k<—k+1, update particle velocity $v_i^{(k)}$ and particle position $X_i^{(k)}$ according to the following three equations. $X_i^k = X_i^{k-1} + v_i^{(k)}$

$$v_i^{(k)} = w^k v_i^{(k-1)} + c_1 r_1 (p_i - X_i^{(k-1)}) + c_2 r_2 (p_g - X_i^{(k-1)}), \quad w^k = w_{max} - \frac{w_{max} - w_{min}}{k_{max}} \cdot k$$

Here, r_1, r_2 are random numbers among [0,1], accelerated factor $c_1, c_2 = 0.7$, the maximum value of inertia factor w_{max} =0.9, minimum value w_{min} =0.7.

Step6: Measure the fitness of each particle fitness $f_i^{(k)}$ according to fitness function (4.1).

Step7: For each particle, compare its fitness $f_i^{(k)}$ with its historical optimal position $p_i^{(k-1)}$, place it as the current optimal position $p_i^{(k)}$ if it's better than p_i.

Step8: For each particle, compare its optimal position $p_i^{(k)}$ with the global optimal location of the whole group $p_g^{(k-1)}$, place it as the optimal location of the whole group $p_g^{(k)}$ $p_i^{(k)}$ if it's better than $p_g^{(k)}$, then $p_g^{(k)} = \min\{p_1^{(k)}, p_2^{(k)}, \cdots p_M^{(k)}\}$.

Step 9: Check the termination conditions, jump to step 6 if $k < k_{max}$; Otherwise, the maximum iteration, termination.

5   Examples

The distribution center face 40 retailers, that is $N = 40$, retailer's daily demand obey Poisson distribution, average demand $\lambda_r = 9$ units. Daily per holding cost of the distribution centers and retailers is $h_0 = h_r = 2$ yuan, unit backorder cost of the distribution centers is $b_0 = 4$ yuan, unit backorder cost of the retailers is $b_r = 8$ yuan, ordering fee of retailers each time is $A_r = 96$ yuan, ordering fee of the distribution centers each time $A_0 = 1200$ yuan, the lead time of distribution center is $L_0 = 2$ days, transportation time from the distribution center to the retailers is $L_t = 1$ day.

Take various parameters in the above application examples into the two-echelon distribution system and solve the problem based on algorithm of Particle Swarm Optimization (PSO) with the software MATLAB (R2008a).We will record once the current optimal solution every three times of iterations, the results refer to Table 1.

Table 1. Example 5.1 Iterative process records algorithm of PSO

Number	s_0	S_0	R_r	Q_r	Optimal fitness	Average fitness
0	663	1938	9	51	2755.69	7947.14
3	480	1440	11	40	2672.36	6148.03
6	480	1440	11	40	2672.36	4200.38
9	396	1672	11	44	2671.7	3345.47
12	540	1575	8	45	2651.01	2957.4
15	540	1575	8	45	2651.01	2870.4
18	484	1672	8	44	2648.03	2869.76
21	495	1620	9	45	2645.65	2711.55
24	484	1628	9	44	2644.08	2762.3
27	484	1584	9	44	2643.91	2884.25
30	473	1591	9	43	2643.52	2674.47

From the table1 we can clearly see the convergence process of particle swarm, the difference of the optimal fitness between adjacent two iterations is gradually reduced, and the gap between the average fitness of each particle and the optimal value is gradually narrowing, indicating that each particle convergences to the optimal position, its visible that the algorithm has preferable convergence.

6   Summary

This paper selects an important part of the multi-echelon inventory system- distribution system as the research object, the optimization of the two-echelon inventory system is studied under centralized control strategy. Distribution centers adopt (s,S) ordering strategy while retailers adopt (R,Q) ordering strategy, the lead time of distribution centers to retailers is a random variable while each retailer's demand is independent Poisson process, the authors construct an inventory model of a two-echelon distribution system under this assumption, and solve the problem based on algorithm of Particle Swarm Optimization (PSO) with inertia weights to achieve effective exploration on swarm intelligence technology on inventory optimization problems.

References

1. Federgruen, A., Zipkin, P.H.: Approximations of dynamic multi-location production and inventory problems. Management Science 30, 69–84 (1984)
2. Axsäter, S.: A simple decision rule for decentralized two-echelon inventory control. International Journal of Production Economics 93-94, 53–59 (2005)
3. Olsson, R.J., Hill, R.M.: A two-echelon base stock inventory model with Poisson demand and the sequential processing of orders at the upper echelon. European Journal of Operational Research 177, 310–324 (2007)
4. Thangam, A., Uthayakumar, R.: A two-level distribution inventory system with stochastic lead time at the lower echelon. The International Journal of Advanced Manufacturing Technology 41, 1208–1220 (2009)

Measuring Change Risk for Organisational Decision Making through a Hierarchical Model Process Approach

Charalampos Apostolopoulos[1], George Halikias[1],
Krikor Maroukian[2], and Georgios Tsaramirsis[3]

[1] School of Engineering & Mathematical Sciences,
City University London, Northampton Square, London, EC1V 0HB, UK
[2] School of Natural & Mathematical Science,
Department of Informatics, King's College London, Strand, London,WC2R 2LS, UK
[3] Department of Information Technology,
King Abdulaziz University, Jeddah, 21589, Saudi Arabia
{charalampos.apostolopoulos.1,g.halikias}@city.ac.uk,
krikor.maroukian@kcl.ac.uk, gtsaramirsis@kau.edu.sa

Abstract. Project Management has long established the need for risk management techniques to be utilised in the succinct identification and mitigation of associated risks in projects. Such techniques aim at the reconciliation of countervailing project activities to reduce scope creep, increase the probability of on-time and within-budget delivery. Uncontrolled changes, regardless of size and complexity, can develop risks to projects and affect project success or even an organisation's project delivery coherence. Ideally, a change or consequence based upon a decision should have a fairly high level of predictability and thus a low level of a potential risk materializing, which would significantly undo the decision taken. This paper proposes a novel modeling process approach; CRAM (Change Risk Assessment Model), which could significantly contribute to the missing formality of business models especially in the change risk assessment area.

Keywords: CRAM, Change Risk Assessment Model, Project Management, Change Management, Risk Management, Decision Analysis.

1 Introduction

Nowadays, a mission critical necessity for an organisation seems to be the adaptation to specific customer requirements and concepts such as: strategic business planning, customer satisfaction, market adaptation and subsequently efficient and effective business change management. However, the transitional period of change is not only time consuming but also a risky process. In this context, risk can be regarded as an integral part for both, businesses and management.

Nonetheless, the processes of change management and risk assessment are usually regarded as separate business domains and ones which should be generally implemented during the whole life cycle of a project. Besides the generic need for

K. Liu et al. (Eds.): ICISO 2014, IFIP AICT 426, pp. 439–448, 2014.
© IFIP International Federation for Information Processing 2014

change, implementing change is often perceived as an unsurpassable challenge due to several organisational barriers and behavioural aspects relating to human resources, who express considerable resistance to change which often hinders the overall process success.

Project management can have added strategic value, when the level of effectiveness and the efficiency with which a project is accomplished are interlinked and when project outcomes can provide overall business value. Furthermore, change management, also poses as a strategic and structured approach to transitioning individuals, teams and organisations from a current state to a desired future state.

The implementation of project management also requires changes, e.g. in the processes, tools, and methods used to fulfil organisational goals [1]. In effect, 'change' for project management can be seen as an integrated process which is related to controlling the project's requirements in an effort to change them so as to eventually place activities in order and conform to customers requirements.

This research paper, attempts to facilitate various organisational change risk factors which can influence project success by introducing a novel modelling approach named Change Risk Assessment Model (CRAM). The introduction of CRAM will allow the identification and definition of speculative relationships, between change risk events in the form of hierarchical risk model analysis.

Further to the introduction, this paper is organised as follows: section (2) presents existing literature findings. Section (3) discusses the methodology used to develop the model, section (4) provides an overview of the CRAM's processes. Research conclusions are presented in section (5) and finally, section (6) defines the next steps to future work.

2   Literature Review

There exist many different models and views for managing change, such as the three stage model (Unfreezing, Confusion, Refreezing), [2]; planned change phases (Exploration, Planning, Action, Integration), [3]; managing the transitional phases (Ending, Neutral and New Beginning), [4]. Even though, this work is significant, it corresponds mainly to a narrative and multi-stage process description which excludes any change risk-assessment process.

Change management, is often based on informal models with risk inconsistencies and generalisations that may lead to loss of meaning and semantic gaps. However, models depicting a simplification of reality withhold a significant advantage [5] and in most of the cases models can be used to deduce simplified conclusions about the real world [6].

Taking as example the two most established project management frameworks PRINCE2® (developed by UK Government) and PMBOK® (developed by Project Management Institute); project success takes into account several significant environmental exogenous and endogenous project factors ([7], [8]). It is clear that any changes in the project constraints as seen in Table 1, can influence the success or failure of the end result of a project or its deliverables. However, it is within the

Table 1. Project constraints comparison

PRINCE2® variables	PMBOK® competing constraints
Cost	Scope
Timescale	Quality
Quality	Schedule
Scope	Budget
Risk	Resources
Benefits	Risks

scope of this paper to examine different attributes far beyond the constraints which are extensively referenced in PMBOK® and PRINCE2®, showing that the four major ones: time, cost, scope and quality are just the peak of the iceberg.

If any one factor changes, at least one other factor is likely to be affected; effectively changing the project requirements or objectives may create in turn additional risks. Taking into account that project management and change management are integrated processes, an analogy can be found between the project and change influence factors. Critical success factors (CSFs) are requirements or deliverables that must have a satisfactory completion rate for the successful outcome of the project [9].

In a relative research [10] with sixty subjects it was indicated that 43.33% of the sample's respondents agreed that among other factors 'responsiveness to change' is a project success criterion. In a more practical approach [11], a change management toolkit was developed, which actually provides a numerical computation of change risk, irrespective of project management frameworks. The more identified risks before the initiation phase of the project, subject to project complexity, the better the expected outcome can be. Table 2, shows some indicative project risk categories:

Table 2. Project Risk Categories

Project Risk Categories	
Technical	Project
Quality	Legal
Performance	Environmental
Change	Scope
Organisational	Quality
External / Internal	Schedule
Business	Process
Cultural	Requirements

Changes and associated risks can occur during the whole life cycle of a project; however, it is vital to assess the possibility of success materialisation before the decision is made to proceed with the change or not. CRAM has the capacity to define the internal dynamics of change management within project management eliciting also risk cause-and-effect relationships. Effectively, stakeholders are allowed to describe a problem as they see it, refine the complexity and structure a hierarchy of attributes.

3   Methodology

The methodology in terms of scientific research used so as to develop the nodes and attributes of the prototype model, combined in depth literature review analysis and personal interviews in correlation with group meetings (Delphi technique). Interviews (high level executives from diversified industries) were proven more than assistive in coupling together not only professional experience, but also the personal reflection of the participants.

Taking into account that focused group discussions (Delphi Technique) was engaged as a further verification tool of the interviews results, it was more than obvious, that a group environment is beneficial for the respondent in gaining a deeper understating of the research questions. Professionals were able to discuss further their common opinions or disagreements; contribute more effectively either by listening to new ideas or even discussing in more depth with fellow participants.

The change risk categories that were identified are summarised in table 3.

Table 3. Identified Change Categories

Change Categories	
Individual	Rules / Regulations
Organisational	Evolutionary
Cost cutting	Revolutionary
Process	Strategic
Cultural	Transformational
Technical	Proactive /Reactive
Planned / Unplanned	Technological

In turn, the attributes were categorised based on rationalism, testing theory and practice. The key idea of categorisation was to construct the prototype model in a sense that can be used repeatedly in various industries, minimising any bias as possible.

4   Change Risk Assessment Model Overview

Even if project managers, change managers or other stakeholders discuss about change and associated risks; still, there is a lot of room for research improvement in this area.

Within the research scope, models are defined as the representation of a view of an interpreter about an entity or concept from the real world [12]. However, it is not uncommon to do business or perform business related activities without the use of models. Often, the modellers themselves have disappeared, and any knowledge that was not captured in the specialised models is inaccessible, forgotten, or written off [13]. This leads to the inability to address key business environment factors. Nevertheless, business models which can be combined and configured with project business seem to be an exploited research area [14].

The significance of CRAM is that, it can be considered as a prototype change risk assessment modelling method that can be applied in various project types' or organisations irrespective of size or complexity as seen below. The method can be tailored to specific customer or project needs, taking into account significant environmental change risk factors (add or delete risk attributes on a per case basis).

Because project's scope and objectives differ, in the same sense it is difficult to identify all potential risks.

- Product and Strategy Management   - Insurance
- Software / Technology Solutions   - Government
- IT / Telecoms   - Retail
- Service Provisioning   - Utilities
- Consulting   - Defence
- Engineering   - Banking

In addition, CRAM can be integrated with contemporary project management frameworks like for example PMBOK® and PRINCE2®. The proposed model attempts to enforce and integrate currently prevailing descriptive risk analysis methodologies, by engaging a semi-quantitative and qualitative change management risk modelling approach.

4.1   CRAM Processes

CRAM is composed of three interrelated processes which are continually recorded and monitored. CRAM processes accomplish specific risk objectives, which are applied to projects or at a greater extent to business environments with a view to facilitate and control change risks. A schematic interpretation of CRAM processes can be seen in Fig. 1.

Fig. 1. Change Risk Assessment Model Processes

Risk Identification

Risks can be found everywhere and in fact, the difficult part is not to identify but control them. The primary goal of *Risk Identification* is to recognise the threats and opportunities which may affect the project's objectives and consequently deliverables. Indicatively, risk(s) can be categorised as follows:

Known Risk: this kind of risk refers to an in-depth project analysis which has a considerably high probability of occurrence.

Predictable Risks: are those risks that past experience dictates one may face with high probability.

Unpredictable Risk: is the risk that could happen, but the probability of occurrence in terms, for example, of timing cannot be estimated accurately. The success of many projects is related to the level that this risk will be estimated [15].

Irrespective of risk categorisation, CRAM proposes the following tools and techniques so as to identify change risks:

-   SWOT analysis
-   Change/Risk surveys
-   Delphi technique
-   RACI diagrams
-   PERT diagrams
-   PESTEL analysis
-   Risk Breakdown Structure (RBS)
-   Interviews
-   Brainstorming sessions

Of course, potential risks and required changes can be identified and decided during the entire lifecycle of the project. Nevertheless, they have to be assessed and monitored the sooner the possible.

Risk Assessment

The basic aim of the proposed model among other objectives is *Risk Assessment* (Estimation and Evaluation). Change, if uncontrolled can be associated with activities of uncertain outcome(s) which would be deemed unwanted deliverables from project stakeholders. However, when change management and risk management are coupled together, risk aftermath can be reduced; risk is estimated at the planning stage of a project and consequently, there is time to develop a risk mitigation plan and take all necessary preventive actions, acting proactively.

A simple definition of risk in terms of probability of occurrence and its related impact is given by the formula ([9], [16], [17]):

$$Risk = Probability \times Impact. \tag{1}$$

The majority of quantitative methodologies use extensively probabilities being rather less ambiguous and imprecise; meaning that they are more objective as far as the assessment of the information and data on identified risks is concerned. The narrative approach of risk estimation has an advantage of providing contextual information but on the other hand does not allow the level i.e. magnitude of risk, to be measured. Qualitative and quantitative scales do indicate levels or rating but lack the information content.

Estimation can facilitate project risks in terms of the probability of occurrence and impact. On the other hand, *Evaluation* assesses the overall effect of all identified risks aggregated together. Some kinds of risks, like for example financial risks, can be evaluated in numerical terms.

Risk Assessment can be accomplished with the aid of a variety of methods and techniques, such as for example: Simulations, Monte Carlo analysis, CPM (Critical Path Method), AHP (Analytic Hierarchy Process), risk maps, Bayesian probability and statistics, probability trees or even fault tree analysis.

Concerning evaluation, this can be indicatively accomplished for example by a means of benchmark questions, like for example:

- Were all implemented non-standard changes assessed?
- Did the approved changes meet the intended goal?
- Concerning result, does it satisfy stakeholders and more specifically conform to customer requirements?
- Were there found any unplanned changes; which are the associated risks?
- Concerning the implementation phase, did it exceed the project's constraints?
- Are the results documented, for example, in the change risk log?

Risk Monitor and Control

The *Risk Monitor and Control* process mainly intends to: identify, analyse, control and track new risks. Risk monitor and control can be accomplished with the aid of a variety of methods and techniques, such as for example:

- Risk Reassessment
- Meetings (consultation, status update)
- Variance Analysis
- Trend Analysis
- Risk Auditing

Alongside the aforementioned CRAM processes an 'Experts' Judgment' may be proven overall constructive. An expert might be, for instance, an individual (project manager, change manager) of a group of executives (Project Steering Committee, Change Advisory Board) which can influence and advice on CRAM results. The hierarchy of CRAM per levels is shown in table 4:

Table 4. CRAM Nodes Hierarchy

Level 1 (Root Node)	Level 2 (Parent Nodes)	Level 3 (Child Nodes)
Change Risk	Leadership	Performance
	Communication	Motivation
	Culture	Appraisal
	Resistance	Rewards
	Requirements	Training
	Monitoring	
	Flexibility	
	Project Management Team	

An overall, schematic representation of the prototype risk tree is indicated in Fig. 2, which consists of one (1) core (root) node, eight (8) parent nodes, five (5) child nodes and its respective sixty-one (61) attributes.

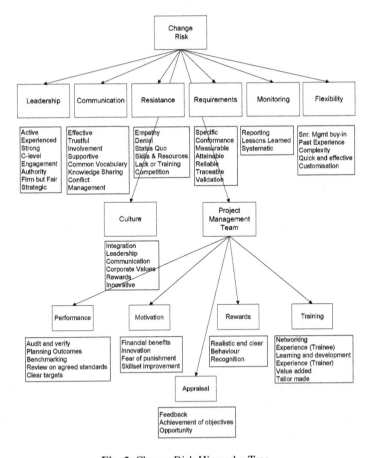

Fig. 2. Change Risk Hierarchy Tree

Definitions of CRAM's *Risk Attributes* can be seen at: www.changemodel.net [18].

The 'project management team' is the only parent node possessing child attributes indicating a third level of analysis due to the overall significance in the process of structured project management frameworks. In case a project lacks project management team, then it would be expected to lack coordination and clarity on deliverables.

Depending on the scope and deliverables of a project, CRAM nodes and related risk attribute's hierarchy per level, can change so as to accommodate more of fewer criteria. The only restriction on the hierarchic arrangement of elements is that any element in one level must be capable of being related to some elements in the next higher level, which serves as a criterion for assessing the relative impact of elements in the level below.

5   Conclusions

Changes and the process of managing related risks differ among organisations and business cultures. As far as change risk assessment modelling is concerned, there is no one-size-fits-all or all-you-can-eat model. Each customer is different, but what stays the same is the expectation and demand for project success, delivery of services and overall customer's expectations conformance. Each project may require different changes and handling which may be reflected in culture, leadership, decision making, norms and directives and consequently in the general way of implementing and managing projects.

CRAM attempts to take into account various environmental risk factors which influence project success. These risk factors are modeled, and can be assessed numerically in a top-down hierarchical model. Nevertheless, not all risks are the same or have the same priorities. Most of the objectives have to be measured to a certain degree.

On the other hand, there is no unique way to conform to project changes and estimate the relative risks, or to predefine the results of a project. This is because what may seem to be applicable on an individual basis or at a business level, might be inappropriate or insufficient for specific project environments where a number of vendors and clients coexist. Even though, CRAM may carry a degree of complexity on a per case basis, an aim of its scope is to collect data on a global basis, irrespective of specific structured project management framework approaches. In other words, an overall aim of CRAM would be its adoption in project business scenarios on a consistent and repetitive basis so as to identify patterns related to all parent nodes described previously.

Finally, CRAM does not actually dictate any direct or indirect walkthrough; rather it is regarded as a structured approach for facilitating change risk effectively. Even if for example, no project management framework is adopted, CRAM has exactly the same capabilities concerning change risk identification, assessment and monitor and control processes.

6   Future Work

Further to the key integration of Change Management, Project Management and Risk Management in terms of CRAM, future research efforts, will focus on the integration (numerical assessment) with quantitative analysis techniques. In addition, CRAM outcomes are characterised by environmental factors and attributes which can form the basis of an Environment-feature-driven model composition.

A framework capable of transforming such a model layer to subsequent models of lower level abstraction would require a pioneer approach to model-driven initiatives.

Such a framework, resides in the logic behind which the Model Driven Business Engineering (MDBE) framework was developed. In fact, it aims at the unification of model-driven aspects of software engineering and business process modeling, thus, attempting to reconcile the benefits of these two model-driven domains. The outcome could be a more attractive solution to model-driven initiatives for corporate entities whereas academia would have the opportunity to rethink an approach to the study of model based engineering and particularly, model-driven development.

References

1. Martinuso, M., Hensmen, N., Artoo, K., Kujala, J., Jaafari, A.: Project based management as an organizational innovation: Drivers, changes and benefits of adopting project-based management. Project Management Journal 37(3), 85–97 (2006)
2. Lewin, K.: Field Theory in Social Science. New York Harper and Row (1951)
3. Bullock, R.J., Batten, D.: It's just a phase we're going through: A review and synthesis of OD phase analysis. Group and Organization Studies 10(4), 383–412 (1985)
4. Bridges, W.: Managing Transitions. Addison-Wesley, Reading (1991)
5. Pidd, M.: Five simple principles of modelling. In: Proceedings of Simulation Conference, pp. 721–728 (1996)
6. Williams, T.: Modelling complex project. John Wiley & Sons (2002)
7. Office of Government Commerce. Managing Successful Projects with PRINCE2 Reference Manual, TSO, The Stationery Office (2009)
8. Project Management Institute. A guide to the project management body of knowledge (PMBOK® guide), 5th edn. (2013)
9. Heldman, K.: Project Manager's Spotlight on Risk Management, Jossey-Bass, A Wiley Imprint, San Francisco (2005)
10. Bryde, D.: Project management concepts, methods and application. International Journal of Operations and Production Management 23(7), 775–793 (2003)
11. Carnall, C.: Managing change in organizations. Prentice Hall, New York (2003)
12. Seidewitz, E.: What models mean. IEEE Softw. 20(5), 26–32 (2003)
13. Denno, P., Steves, M.P., Libes, D., Barkmeyer, E.J.: Model-Driven Integration Using Existing Models. IEEE Software, 59–63 (2003)
14. Wikström, K., Artto, K., Kujala, J., Söderlund, J.: Business models in project business. International Journal of Project Management 28, 832–841 (2010)
15. Rescher, N.: Risk. University Press of America, Lanham (1983)
16. Kendrick, T.: Identifying and Managing Project Risk, 2nd edn. Amacon, NY (2009)
17. Kerzner, H.: Applied project management. Wiley Publications, New York (2000)
18. Change Risk Assessment (CRAM) Glossary (February 2014),
    http://www.changemodel.net (retrieved)

A Novel Multimodal Data Analytic Scheme for Human Activity Recognition

Girija Chetty[1] and Mohammad Yamin[2]

[1] University of Canberra, Australia
[2] Department of MIS, King Abdulaziz University, Saudi Arabia
Girija.Chetty@canberra.edu.au, myamin@kau.edu.sa

Abstract. In this article, we propose a novel multimodal data analytics scheme for human activity recognition. Traditional data analysis schemes for activity recognition using heterogeneous sensor network setups for eHealth application scenarios are usually a heuristic process, involving underlying domain knowledge. Relying on such explicit knowledge is problematic when aiming to create automatic, unsupervised or semi-supervised monitoring and tracking of different activities, and detection of abnormal events. Experiments on a publicly available OPPORTUNITY activity recognition database from UCI machine learning repository demonstrates the potential of our approach to address next generation unsupervised automatic classification and detection approaches for remote activity recognition for novel, eHealth application scenarios, such as monitoring and tracking of elderly, disabled and those with special needs.

Keywords: Multimodal, PCA, LDA, RBM, Activity recognition, Feature learning.

1 Introduction

Automatic human activity recognition for complex eHealth application scenarios requiring unsupervised monitoring and tracking of elderly, disabled and those with special needs, is a very challenging problem, especially when data is captured remotely using heterogeneous sensor networks, with sensors capturing the data related to activities being performed by humans and objects in the environment. We investigate the potential of multimodal machine learning and data mining methods for discovering learning features for human activity recognition using heterogeneous sensor networks with humans and object in the environment.

Over the last few years, recognizing activity from motion sensors and accelerometer sensor data patterns has become a popular area of research in ubiquitous computing and computer vision area, and one of the most successful applications of image analysis and understanding. There is an urgent need for development of automatic activity recognition systems from such heterogeneous sensor data, for visualising the goal of a next-generation automatic surveillance technology for health care of elderly and disabled, with applicability to development

K. Liu et al. (Eds.): ICISO 2014, IFIP AICT 426, pp. 449–458, 2014.

of remotely instrumented home care environments. Several physiological and bio-mechanical studies have shown that most of the human activity in performing day-to-day activities is inherently multimodal, and is based on kinematic interaction between several motion articulators, involving lower and upper body parts and other bio-mechanics of joints. It is person specific based on body weight, height, joint mobility in the lower and upper body, and type of activity being performed and the objects in the environment. For an automatic recognition of an activity the human is performing, there is a need to take into consideration multimodal cues available from the human body parts, from the surrounding environment and from other objects present in the environment.

If automatic activity recognition systems can be built based on this concept, it will be a great contribution to eHealth area, particularly for remote activity monitoring and recognition using heterogeneous sensor networks in aged care and disability care sector. However, each of these cues or traits captured from heterogeneous wireless sensors on their own are not powerful enough for ascertaining activity: a combination or fusion of each of them, along with an automatic processing technique can result in robust activity recognition. In this article, we propose usage of a publicly available activity recognition dataset, and use of novel multimodal techniques based on semi-supervised machine learning for automatic activity recognition. It is to be noted, that since user cooperation is not mandatory upon data collection, this novel strategy is suitable for monitoring the elderly and disabled for remote home care monitoring scenarios.

In this article, we propose the use of a principled approach involving feature extraction techniques based on automatic semi-supervised discovery, such as principle component analysis (PCA) and linear discriminant analysis (LDA), and novel deep learning approach. Further, we propose that the score level fusion of these features can enhance the performance of activity recognition scheme as compared to single mode image features. Fusing features captured from heterogeneous sensors from the sensor network at the score level is more effective than fusion at feature level, as the incompatible, asynchronous sensors in the sensor network can be combined using different fusion rules in a synergistic manner[2]. The experimental evaluation of the proposed approach with a publicly available activity recognition database [1] shows a significant improvement in recognition performance as compared to other methods proposed in the literature. Rest of the article is organised as follows. Next Section describes the background and motivation for proposed work, followed by the proposed multimodal activity recognition scheme in Section 3. The details of the experiments performed are described in Section 4, and conclusions and plans for further work are described in Section 5.

2   Background

Activity recognition is an essential requirement for automatic monitoring of elderly disabled, and those with special needs, for next generation automated home care environments. In general, sensors, which are either worn on the body and/or embedded into objects and the environment, are utilized to capture aspects of movement or a human's behavior. Ideally, by applying data analysis, image and signal processing and pattern classification techniques, this sensor data can be automatically analyzed yielding a real-time classification of the activities that users (patients, humans who are aged or those who have special needs) are engaged in. Activity recognition can be considered a classical (multi-variate) time series or sequence analysis problem, for which the task is to detect and classify those contiguous portions of sensor data streams that cover activities of interest for the target application. The predominant approach to activity recognition is based on a sliding window procedure, where a fixed length analysis window is shifted along the signal sequence for frame extraction. Subsequent frames overlap to some degree in this sliding window approach, but are usually processed separately. Preprocessing then transforms raw signal data into feature vectors, which are subjected to statistical classifiers that eventually provide activity hypotheses. As for any pattern recognition task, the keys to successful activity recognition are: (i) choice of appropriate features to be extracted from raw sensor data; and (ii) the design of suitable learning classifiers. The machine learning and data mining literature describes a wide variety of supervised machine learning approaches involving the stages of feature extraction, feature selection and learning classifiers. By contrast, comparatively little systematic research has addressed the problem of feature design, with almost all previous work using heuristically selected general measures. These features are either calculated in the time domain, calculated on symbolic representations of the sensor data, or spectra based. The lack of systematic research on appropriate features for automatic unsupervised classification or even semi-supervised classification is one of the major shortcomings of current activity recognition systems. For example, it is questionable whether the next generation of eHealth applications for remote home-care scenarios for activity monitoring of elderly and disabled, for behavioral analysis, fall or injury detection, or monitoring of vital health parameters can be realized based on the use of such heuristically selected features alone, requiring constant human/expert intervention. Such problems require intelligent unsupervised or at least semi-supervised quantitative analysis of the underlying sensor data captured, which are beyond the capabilities of current procedures.

However, recent developments in the data mining and machine learning field have the potential to overcome this shortcoming by automatically discovering novel feature representations for such activity recognition from heterogeneous sensor networks. In this article, we present a novel approach to feature extraction and investigate the suitability of feature learning for activity recognition tasks. We utilize a learning framework, which automatically discovers suitable feature representations that do not rely on application-specific feature design and engineering by human experts. We use semi-supervised feature learning techniques, namely well-known principal component analysis and linear discriminant analysis, and recently proposed deep learning technique, and show how the automatic discovery of features outperform traditional statistical and supervised learning features for an activity recognition application. Such a novel feature extraction procedure has important implications for the development of future eHealth applications such as remote monitoring of home-care environments for elderly, disabled and those with special needs, since no manual optimization is required. The deep learning approach allows for in-depth analysis of the underlying multimodal data from different sensors, as the new representation based on semi-supervised machine learning implicitly highlights the most informative portions of the analyzed data [2, 3,4]. This is likely to be important for new classes of activity analysis such as new or anomalous activity recognition where there is no previous information available in the databases, which is normally the case with unstructured home care health environment.

Each of the sensor node, whether it is for tracking the person data or that of the other objects in the environment of the person, can contribute significantly to detecting the higher level activity being performed. While the sensor data captured from human body can be termed as primary sensor data, the sensor data captured from surrounding objects in the environment can be termed as a soft sensor data or secondary data. Soft or secondary data often captures the high level information of the environment where the human performs the activity, and though acts as weak information for recognising the human activity, does help in enhancing the robustness of activity recognition if multiple heterogeneous secondary sensor data from the environment is used in appropriate combination. [5, 6]. In other words, if we combine complementary information from another source, this multimodal combination is expected to be powerful for activity recognition. Further, use of an appropriate automatic processing scheme for processing this multimodal sensor network, can enhance the performance and robustness of the system. For example, researchers in [7, 8] have found that multi-modal scheme involving simple PCA features on combined heterogeneous sensor input results in significant improvement over single mode sensor data. In addition, other recent attempts to improve the recognition accuracy include multiple heterogeneous set of sensors has been reported in [9], [10]. The fusion of complementary sensor node information from disparate sources for activity recognition, however, did not attract much attention from the research community. This could be due to difficulty in acquiring the data, and processing and making sense out of them.

3   Dataset for Multimodal Activity Recognition

For experimental evaluation of our proposed multimodal activity recognition scheme, we used publicly available UCI OPPORTUNITY Activity Recognition Dataset [1]. The OPPORTUNITY Dataset for Human Activity Recognition from Wearable, Object, and Ambient Sensors is a dataset devised to benchmark human activity recognition algorithms. A subset of this dataset comprises the readings of motion sensors recorded while users executed typical daily activities:

- Body-worn sensors: 7 inertial measurement units, 12 3D acceleration sensors, 4 3D localization information.
- Object sensors: 12 objects with 3D acceleration and 2D rate of turn
- Ambient sensors: 13 switches and 8 3D acceleration sensors

- Recordings: 4 users, 6 runs per users. Of these, 5 are Activity of Daily Living runs characterized by a natural execution of daily activities. The 6th run is a "drill" run, where users execute a scripted sequence of activities.
- Annotations/classes: the activities of the user in the scenario are annotated on different levels: "modes of locomotion" classes; low-level actions relating 13 actions to 23 objects; 17 mid-level gesture classes; and 5 high-level activity classes.

The activity recognition environment and scenario has been designed to generate many activity primitives, yet in a realistic manner. Subjects operated in a room simulating a studio flat with a deckchair, a kitchen, doors giving access to the outside, a coffee machine, a table and a chair. Each subject was recorded in 6 different runs. Five of them, termed as activity of daily living (ADL), followed a given scenario. The remaining one, a drill run, was designed to generate a large number of activity instances. The ADL run consists of temporally unfolding situations:

- Start: lying on the deckchair, get up
- Groom: move in the room, check that all the objects are in the right places in the drawers and on shelves
- Relax: go outside and have a walk around the building
- Prepare coffee: prepare a coffee with milk and sugar using the coffee machine
- Drink coffee: take coffee sips, move around in the environment
- Prepare sandwich: include bread, cheese and salami, using the bread cutter and various knifes and plates
- Eat sandwich
- Cleanup: put objects used to original place or dish washer, cleanup the table
- Break: lie on the deckchair

The drill run consists of 20 repetitions of the following sequence of activities:

- Open then close the fridge.
- Open then close the dishwasher
- Open then close 3 drawers (at different heights)
- Open then close door 1
- Open then close door 2
- Toggle the lights on then off
- Clean the table
- Drink while standing
- Drink while seated

The annotations are done on five 'tracks'. One track contains modes of locomotion (e.g. sitting, standing, walking). Two other tracks indicate the actions of the left and right hand (e.g. reach, grasp, release), and to which object they apply (e.g. milk, switch, door). The fourth track indicates the high level activities (e.g. prepare sandwich). As can be seen, this dataset does provide an opportunity to benchmark many automatic activity recognition algorithms, consisting of classification, (semi-) supervised machine learning, automatic segmentation, unsupervised structure discovery, data imputation, multi-modal sensor fusion, sensor network research transfer learning, multitask learning, sensor selection, feature extraction and classifier calibration and adaptation. Our experiments involved the subset of data acquired from this large database consisting of sensor data recorded by the accelerometer attached to the right arm of the subject. We considered 10 low level activities of interest plus an unknown activity category. The acceleration data were sampled with 64Hz yielding approximately 4,200 frames. Fig. 1 shows the screen shot for the dataset we used in our experiments.

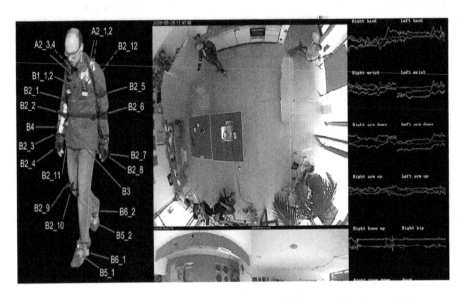

Fig. 1. Sample data from OPPORTUNITY activity recognition dataset [1]

4   Features for Multimodal Activity Recognition

To analyze the performance of different low level features and their fusion for proposed multimodal activity recognition, we performed experiments that compared the capabilities of different combinations of features extracted from sensor data streams. Further, we examined score level fusion, which means there is no requirement of having identical dimensionalities of features for objective comparisons. This stands in contrast to feature level fusion where small differences in the dimensionality of the underlying data and loss of synchronism in fusion can lead to catastrophic fusion, and can have a significant impact on the estimation procedure and hence on the capabilities of the models.

To extract the low level features from raw sensor data streams for activity recognition, we used a set of statistical measures to represent frames of contiguous multidimensional sensor data. Given the 192-dimensional analysis, frames (64 × 3) provided by our sliding window procedure, we first calculated pitch and roll values. Subsequently, for each source channel (i.e. x, y, z, pitch, and roll) we then calculated mean, standard deviation, energy, and entropy. Together with three correlation coefficients (estimated for all combinations of the x, y, z axes) this yielded a 23-D representation of the raw signal data covered by an analysis frame.

4.1   PCA-LDA Features

Principle component analysis is a way of identifying patterns in data, and expressing the data in such a way as to highlight their similarities and differences. On the other hand, the LDA attempts to model the difference between the classes of data [9,10]. PCA does not take into account any difference in class, and factor analysis builds the feature combinations based on differences rather than similarities. Discriminant analysis is also different from factor analysis in that it is not an interdependence technique: a distinction between independent variables and dependent variables (also called criterion variables) must be made. LDA works when the measurements made on independent variables for each observation are continuous quantities. When dealing with categorical independent variables, the equivalent technique is discriminant correspondence analysis. And in our experiment, LDA shows more promising results than PCA does. We performed experiments utilizing PCA and LDA based features where the projection sub-space is spanned by those eigenvectors that correspond to the $c = 18, 23, 30$, and 39 largest eigenvectors. These selections of c are justified by significant drops in the eigenvalue spectrum of the data and correspond to the selected target dimensionalities of the other approaches investigated. No significant changes in classification accuracy were observed for the four choices of c, hence we present the results for $c = 30$.

4.2   Deep Learning Features

Auto encoder networks have proved to be a powerful tool for the generic semi-supervised or unsupervised discovery of features [11, 12]. These aim to learn a lower-dimensional representation of input data, which produces a minimal error when used for reconstructing the original data. As an alternative to PCA or LDA based feature extraction for continuous sensor streams we employed deep learning methods for auto encoder based feature learning on sequential data. The desired representation is discovered by means of a feed-forward neural network that consists of one input layer, one output layer and an odd number of hidden layers. Every layer is fully connected to the adjacent layers and a non-linear activation function is used. The objective function during training is the reconstruction of the input data at the output layer. The auto encoder transmits a description of the input-data across each layer of the network. Since the innermost layer of the network has a lower dimensionality, the transmission of a description through this bottleneck can only be achieved as result of a meaningful encoding of the input.

This non-linear low-dimensional encoding is hence an automatically learned feature representation in an semi-supervised manner. For robust model training, we learn the layers of the auto encoder network greedily in a bottom-up procedure, by treating each pair of subsequent layers in the encoder as a Restricted Boltzmann

Machine (RBM). An RBM is a fully connected, bipartite, two-layer graphical model, which is able to generatively model data. It trains a set of stochastic binary hidden units which effectively act as low-level feature detectors. One RBM is trained for each pair of subsequent layers by treating the activation probabilities of the feature detectors of one RBM as input-data for the next. Once the stack of RBMs is trained, the generative model is unrolled to obtain the final fully initialized auto encoder network for feature learning. Different methods exist to model real-valued input units in RBMs. We employ Gaussian visible units for the first level RBM that activate binary, stochastic feature detectors (Gaussian-binary). The subsequent layers can then rely on the common binary-binary RBM. The final layer is a binary linear RBM, which effectively performs a linear projection.

During training the sensor data is processed batch-wise, where each batch ideally comprises samples from all classes in the training-set. Note that the availability of the class information is not mandatory, since we expect an unsupervised learning. RBMs can also be trained in a completely unsupervised manner. However, balancing the batches with respect to the distribution of the classes, (sort of semi-supervised training), improves the model quality since it removes the potential for artificial biases.

Auto encoder networks contain a number of free parameters, including the network topology, i.e., the number of internal layers and its dimensionalities. The optimized network layout consists of a 4-layer model with 1024 units in each hidden layer and 30 units in the top one (192-1024-1024-30). In all experiments, the first layer was trained for 100 epochs while the subsequent layers were trained for 50 epochs. To reduce biasing due to class imbalance, each batch was split equally among all classes, holding 10 samples for each.

5   Experimental Results

To evaluate the performance of the proposed multimodal scheme for activity recognition, we conducted a number of experiments to examine the performance of different features and their multimodal fusion. Sensor data was analysed by means of a sliding window procedure, extracting frames of n = 64 contiguous samples, which overlap by p = 50 percent. Feature extraction was then performed on a frame-by-frame basis. The focus of our experimental evaluation was on the capabilities of the proposed feature representations. Accordingly, we did not focus on classifier optimisation but on the features themselves. So, we selected a standard, instance-based Nearest Neighbour (NN) classifier, and applied it "as is" to all tasks. Given ground truth annotations we report the classification accuracy as percentages of correct predictions provided by the NN classifier. The experiments were performed as N =7-fold cross validations. Folds were created by randomly choosing samples from the original dataset thereby respecting fold-wise balanced distributions of all classes (i.e. activities to be recognized).

The experiments involved examining the classification accuracy for different single mode features and multimodal features (score level fusion of features) proposed. As can be seen in Figure 2, it was possible to achieve classification accuracy between 65% to 75% for different feature and their combinations. The classification accuracy obtained was 65.2% for PCA features, 67.6% for LDA features, 70.5% for RBM features, 72.4% for score level fusion of PCA and RBM features, and 74.7% for score level fusion of LDA and RBM features. We used a weighted fusion method, where the weight for each feature is assigned based on the classification score achieved in single mode classification. This strategy allows us to achieve an adaptive fusion that can be automated in future without manual intervention.

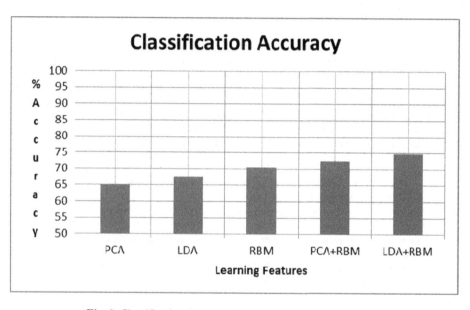

Fig. 2. Classification Accuracy for Different Learning Features

6   Conclusions and Further Plan

In this article, we proposed a novel activity recognition scheme based on multimodal fusion of semi-supervised low level features obtained from raw accelerometer sensor data. We investigated the role of simple semi-supervised subspace features which can result in development of better automatic activity recognition systems for eHealth application scenarios for monitoring the activities of elderly, disabled or those with special needs. We also examined the benefits achieved with multimodal fusion of efficient subspace features in enhancing the classification accuracy. Experimental evaluation of the proposed multimodal activity recognition scheme for a data subset from a publicly available OPPORTUNITY activity recognition UCI dataset [1], showed a significant improvement in recognition accuracy for score level fusion of features as compared to single mode features. Further research will involve investigating novel unsupervised learning approaches and combining the data from several other sensors available for activity recognition in this dataset.

References

1. Sagha, H., Digumarti, S.T., José del, R.M., Chavarriaga, R., Calatroni, A., Roggen, D., Tröster, G.: Benchmarking classification techniques using the Opportunity human activity dataset. In: IEEE International Conference on Systems, Man, and Cybernetics, Anchorage, AK, USA, October 9-12 (2011)
2. Huang, L.: Person Recognition By Feature Fusion. Dept. of Engineering Technology Metropolitan State College of Denver, IEEE, Denver, USA (2011)
3. Jain, A.K.: Next Generation Biometrics, Department of Computer Science & Engineering. Michigan State University, Department of Brain & Cognitive Engineering, Korea University (2009)
4. Yampolskiy, R.V., Govindaraja, V.: Taxonomy of Behavioral Biometrics. Behavioral Biometrics for Human Identification, 1–43 (2010)
5. Meraoumia, A., Chitroub, S., Bouridane, A.: Fusion of Finger-Knuckle-Print and Palmprint for an Efficient Multi-biometric System of Person Recognition. In: IEEE Communications Society subject matter experts for publication in the IEEE ICC (2011)
6. Ross, A., Jain, A.K.: Information fusion in biometrics. Pattern Recognition Letters 24, 2115–2125 (2003)
7. Chang, K., et al.: Comparison and Combination of Ear and Face Images in Appearance-Based Biometrics. IEEE Trans. PAMI 25, 1160–1165 (2003)
8. Kittler, J., et al.: On combining classifiers. IEEE Trans. Pattern Anal. Mach. Intell. 20, 226–239 (1998)
9. Hossain, E., Chetty, G.: Multimodal Identity Verification Based on Learning Face and Gait Cues. In: Lu, B.-L., Zhang, L., Kwok, J. (eds.) ICONIP 2011, Part III. LNCS, vol. 7064, pp. 1–8. Springer, Heidelberg (2011)
10. Multilayer Perceptron Neural Networks, The Multilayer Perceptron Neural Network Model, http://www.dtreg.com
11. Hinton, G.E.: To recognize shapes, first learn to generate images. Progress in Brain Research 165, 535–547 (2007)
12. Hinton, G.E., Osindero, S., Teh, Y.W.: A fast learning algorithm for deep belief nets. Neural computation 18(7), 1527–1554 (2006)

Usability Challenges in Smartphone Web Access: A Systematic Literature Review

Mazen Al-Ismail and A.S.M. Sajeev

School of Science & Technology, University of New England, Australia
`malismai@myune.edu.au, sajeev@une.edu.au`

Abstract. Systematic literature reviews facilitate methodical understanding of current advances in a field. With the increasing popularity of smartphones, they have become an important means to access the web. Although the literature on this topic is growing in recent times, there has been no effort yet to systematically review it. This paper reports on a systematic literature review of primary studies from 2007 to 2012 that concern mobile web usability. We identify the usability dimensions tested and the testing procedures adopted in the literature. We anticipate that our work will not only help researchers understand the current state of usability testing of mobile web but also identify the areas where further research is needed in addressing the challenges identified.

Keywords: Mobile web, Systematic literature review, Web usability, User experience.

1   Introduction

Web access through wireless devices has exploded in recent times with the increased popularity of smartphones and tablets that run on mobile operating systems such as Android [1] and IOS [2]. According to International Telecommunication Union (ITU), mobile phone subscribers have grown from around two billion in 2005 to close to seven billion by 2013. Mobile broadband access has grown from 268 million in 2007 to 2.1 billion in 2013 [3]. While these developments put unprecedented pressure on designers to make web sites easy to access from mobile devices, growth in mobile-friendly websites has been slow. Google, in a survey of its largest advertisers in 2011, found that only 21% of them have mobile friendly websites [4].

In the mean time, the capabilities of mobile phones have increased from just being able to make phone calls and text messages, to become a sophisticated computing and communication device which can handle internet surfing, send and receive emails, play multimedia and run advanced apps in varying fields from social networking to health to commerce and education. As the number of users of these devices increase and the capabilities of the devices improve, there is a need to understand the challenges that both web developers and web users face in achieving high quality browsing experience on a mobile device. This paper provides a systematic review of the literature on mobile web usability.

K. Liu et al. (Eds.): ICISO 2014, IFIP AICT 426, pp. 459–470, 2014.
© IFIP International Federation for Information Processing 2014

Systematic literature reviews (SLR) facilitate methodical understanding of current advances in a field. They help both in recording the achievements in well established fields such as medicine, and at the same time, offering in-depth understanding of developments in emerging fields such as in Information Technology. An example of the former is the SLR of effective methods of giving information to cancer patients by McPherson, et al. [5], and an example of the latter is the SLR of empirical work in global software engineering by Šmite, et al. [6].

Holzinger [7] identifies five characteristics of usability, namely, learnability, efficiency, memorability, low error rate and satisfaction. The International Standards Organisation, on the other hand, gives a more general definition of usability as "the extent to which a product can be used by specified users to achieve specified goals with effectiveness, efficiency and satisfaction in a specified context of use" [8].

Therefore, it is safe to say that usability determines the relationship between a product and its user [9]. From an engineering point of view, usability is reducing the complexity of the interface as much as possible so users can focus on their tasks rather than concentrating on the product. We explore how these dimensions are tested. Our research questions are:

RQ1: What dimensions of usability are examined in mobile web testing?
RQ2: What are the different purposes for which mobile web usability testing is conducted?

The main contributions of the paper are:

- It explores the dimensions of usability that are identified in the literature and explain how these dimensions have been assessed with respect to mobile web usability.
- It explains the current usability testing practices in mobile web and their limitations.
- It applies the systematic review approach illustrated by Kitchenham, et al. [10], thus ensuring that papers reviewed are those meeting pre-specified search and quality criteria within the search period.

The rest of the paper is organised as follows. In the next section, we explain the research method. In Section 3, we explore the different dimensions of usability testing and review how researchers conduct usability tests. In Section 4 we identify some of the limitations of this research, and finally, in Section 5 we give the conclusions.

2   Research Method

In order to conduct a systematic literature review, we used the research method explained by Kitchenham and Chatters [11]. Accordingly, a protocol for literature search was formulated around our research questions. The protocol decided our search terms, choice of search engines, and inclusion and exclusion criteria for the selection of papers. This selection process is explained further in Section 2.1. The papers selected were then assessed based on a set of quality criteria as explained in Section 2.1.1; a score was given to each paper with a view of excluding those that scored less than a threshold value. Finally, the contents of the short-listed papers were compiled and analysed to formulate the answers to our research questions.

2.1   Search Process

The search engines we used were:

- Google Scholar: http://scholar.google.com.au
- ACM Digital Library: http://dl.acm.org
- IEEE Digital Library: http://ieeexplore.ieee.org

All search processes were conducted online using the above mentioned libraries. We used the search terms: ((Mobile AND Usability) AND (Web OR Website OR Site) in the title of the article, and year of publication between 2007 and 2012. Even though, we tried to search for literature using the keyword "smartphone", the term has not been widely used in the literature with respect to usability for our period of interest; hence our use of the word "mobile" instead.

We chose to include papers published from 2007 in our review for the following reason. The era of smartphones started largely with the release of iPhones in June 2007. Even though, there were mobile devices such as personal digital assistants (PDA) and WAP (Wireless Access Protocol) capable phones before then, they were not suitable for widespread mobile web access. Thus web usability has become a serious research issue with the advent of smartphones in 2007. The search resulted in 35 papers as shown in Table 1.

Table 1. Number of papers from initial search

Digital Library Name	Number of Papers identified
Google Scholar	27
ACM Digital Library	4
IEEE Digital Library	4

The results were pruned to remove duplicate entries from different search engines. The following inclusion criteria for the SLR were then applied:

- The paper is on the topic of mobile web usability
- The paper reports a primary study
- The paper is peer-reviewed and is written in English
- The paper was not published before 2007
- If the paper is a book chapter, then the book includes at least one other paper on mobile web usability

In the search results, there were eight duplicate entries, three non-English papers, two papers that were not peer-reviewed, and three papers unrelated to the topic; these were discarded. After this step, we ended up with 19 papers which are listed in Table 2.

2.2   Quality Assessment

Each paper's quality for inclusion was evaluated using the following criteria:

- [Q1] Does the paper provide a clear method on usability testing or suggest an approach for designing a mobile web page to enhance the usability?
- [Q2] Does the paper test any usability dimensions?

Each paper was given a score based on a subjective assessment of how well it answered each of the questions (1 means very well, 0.5 means partly and 0 means not at all) and the net quality rating was the sum of the three scores. The minimum required quality rating was set at 1; all the 19 papers met this rating as shown in Table 2.

Table 2. Papers selected for the study and their quality rating

Authors, year and citation	Title	Q1	Q2	Total
Rosario et al (2012) [12]	A Study in Usability: Redesigning a Health Sciences Library's Mobile Site	3	2	5
Yeh & Fontenelle (2012) [13]	Usability Study of a Mobile Website: the Health Sciences Library, University of Colorado Anschutz Medical Campus, Experience	3	2	5
Hong and Kim (2011) [14]	Mobile Web Usability: Developing Guidelines for Mobile Web via Smart Phones	3	2	5
Tsiaousis & Giaglis (2010) [15]	An Empirical Assessment of Environmental Factors that Influence the Usability of a Mobile Website	0	2	2
Shrestha (2007) [16]	Mobile Web Browsing: Usability Study	3	2	5
Schmiedl et al (2009) [17]	Mobile Phone Web Browsing: A Study on Usage and Usability of the Mobile Web	0	2	2
Jeong & Han (2011) [18]	Usability Study on Mobile Web Newspaper Sites	3	0	3
Wessels et al (2011) [19]	Usability of Web Interfaces on Mobile Devices	3	0	3
Carta et al (2011) [20]	Support for Remote Usability Evaluation of Web Mobile Applications.	3	0	3
Diaz et al (2008) [21]	Evaluating the Usability of the Mobile Interface of an Educational Website	3	2	5
Frederick & Lal (2009) [22]	Mobile Web Usability	3	0	3
Brown et al (2010) [23]	Blind Leading the Blind: Web Accessibility Research Leading Mobile Web Usability	3	0	3
Pendell & Bowman (2012) [24]	Usability Study of a Library's Mobile Website: An Example from Portland State University	3	2	5
Kristjansdottir et al (2011) [25]	Written Online Situational Feedback via Mobile Phone to Support	1.5	2	3.5
Amelung et al (2009) [9]	Mobile Usability	3	2	5
Kaasalainen (2009) [26]	Designing for Mobility	1.5	0	1.5
Vartiainen (2009) [27]	Designing Mobile User Interfaces for Internet Services	3	2	5
Tsiaousis & Giaglis (2008) [28]	Evaluating the Effects of the Environmental Context-of-Use on Mobile Website Usability	3	1	4
Ivanc et al (2012) [29]	Usability Evaluation of a LMS Mobile Web Interface	3	0	3

3   Usability Design and Testing Practices

3.1   Summative versus Formative Evaluation

Usability tests can be formative or summative [9]. Formative evaluation occurs during the development process, whereas summative evaluation occurs after the mobile site is designed and constructed. For formative evaluation, since the system development is not complete, testing is conducted using a software emulator. Another common method of formative evaluation is to use *website wireframes* which are skeletal page-layouts drawn on paper. When a participant "clicks" on a button, the sheet showing the page resulting from the click replaces the current sheet.

While summative tests can use field tests or laboratory tests, formative testing needs a laboratory setup because prototype testing is difficult to perform in the field.

3.2   Testing Different Dimension of Usability

From the ISO definition [8] given in Section 1, we can deduce three dimensions of usability, namely, effectiveness, efficiency and user satisfaction. These three are the most common dimensions for which usability testing is conducted. Generally, as part of the test, participants are asked to use their mobile phones to perform a number of tasks (e.g., a task in [20] is to check the United Airlines departure flights to Chicago). Effectiveness of a mobile web page was measured by the successful number of completed tasks and efficiency as the time taken for task completion. A high completion rate and a short period of time required to complete the tasks indicate that the examined system is effective and efficient, respectively. Satisfaction is the degree of accessibility and comfort perceived by the user of the measured system. It is measured by interviewing or surveying the participants to explore their user experience with the system. The normal practice is to use a post-test questionnaire of various satisfaction items with responses measured on a Likert-type scale. As exceptions, Kristjánsdóttir, et al. [25] used semi-structured interviews in addition to a questionnaire, and Yeh and Fontenelle [13] used product reaction cards [32] which are explained later in this section.

In exploring the above three dimensions of usability, authors have used various usability terms which include error rates [14, 15, 20, 24, 28], ease of use [24], user experience [16, 17, 24, 25], usefulness [13, 24, 25], appearance [24], feasibility [25], accessibility [16, 24], effort [16], understandability [13, 25], clarity [16, 24] and relevance [13]. These terms are not all independent (for example, a low error rate is discussed in the context of effectiveness, and ease of use in the context of satisfaction), which leads to a classification of usability dimensions as shown in Fig. 1. Next, we provide the dimensions and the contexts of usability tests in the literature. The tests include investigating usability of websites on mobile phones vis-à-vis desktops, and mobile optimized sites vis-à-vis non-optimised sites; they also include studying the effect of environmental factors such as background noise on mobile web usability, and studying specific web applications related to library access and health intervention.

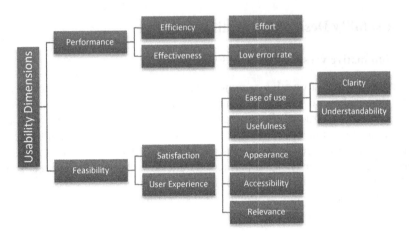

Fig. 1. Classifying usability dimensions

Rosario et al. [12] tested the effectiveness of redesigning a health science library's mobile site. Firstly they implemented open-ended questions where participants (library users) identified the most needed services, namely the need to search journal databases, access full-text articles, access databases, access e-books, search library catalogue, and find the library hours. After that, participants were invited to perform tasks using a prototype design on paper, simulating the intended mobile library web. While all participants could complete tasks such as finding the library hours, only 10% could complete the task of viewing full-text of an article on line; they found the search interface confusing and the screen size inadequate. Finally, the mobile library web was designed with basic HTML incorporating the results of the usability testing of the prototype.

A similar study done by Yeh and Fontenelle [13] measured the effectiveness, efficiency and satisfaction of a health sciences library by comparing optimized and non-optimized mobile websites. Effectiveness and efficiency were measured by asking participants to perform 10 information retrieval tasks. Yeh and Fontenelle used Microsoft's desirability toolkit with product reaction cards [32] to measure satisfaction; each card has a word that could describe a usability facet (examples are words like accessible, confusing, efficient, frustrating etc.) and participants are asked to select cards that reflect their user experience. As a further measure of satisfaction, participants are later interviewed to find reasons for their choice of reaction cards. Unlike a Likert-type questionnaire that tends to have mostly positive statements, which might result in participants unintentionally selecting positive answers, the product reaction cards are designed with 40% negative words and the remaining positive words. The authors found that optimized websites significantly improved the effectiveness (19% improvement) and efficiency (9% improvement) of information retrieval on smartphones. With respect to user satisfaction, there were less number of negative words (slow and unrefined) chosen by the participants in the case of the optimised site than in the case of non-optimised site (confusing, difficult, hard to use, ineffective, not valuable, slow, time consuming, and unrefined).

In another usability experiment, Pendell and Bowman [24] tested an existing mobile-optimized library website by asking participants to perform five tasks to measure effectiveness, efficiency and satisfaction. Effectiveness was measured in terms of errors which they classified into three categories: fatal (for example, not being able to complete a task), major (for example, being able to complete a task but with delays) and minor (completing a task with errors easily corrected by the participant). Satisfaction was measured by asking participants to take notes of their experience and further through a post-test survey on the site's appearance and ease of use. As in the case of [12], all participants completed the task of finding the library hours successfully. However, many users took a long time to search for a book; one of the reasons was that the developers included in the mobile site pull down menus and options to search different types of collections simply because they were available in the full site; this is an example of a challenge in mobile optimization where judicious decisions need to be made on what to exclude from the full site in order to improve usability.

Tsiaousis & Giaglis [15] reported a very different kind of study where they tested the impact of environmental contexts on effectiveness, efficiency, and satisfaction of general mobile web access. The study was conducted in a laboratory to control and simulate environmental contexts. For example, they studied the impact of meaningful sound (e.g. someone talking) versus background noise (e.g printer or fax sound) on participants who were browsing a mobile website; they found that sounds with 'semantics' significantly decreased effectiveness and efficiency compared to meaningless noise. This test was conducted in a laboratory since it is hard to control background sound in a field test; field factors can be easily controlled in a laboratory, for example, by turning on printers to create noise and asking volunteers to start dialogues with participants to create sound with semantics.

In another study, Schmiedl et al. [17] measured efficiency by comparing the access on a mobile phone of a full website versus the corresponding mobile optimized site. They used five mobile optimised sites such as ebay and amazon and asked the participants to perform three to four tasks first on the full website and then on the mobile optimised site, and the time of accomplishing tasks were measured. They found 30 to 40% increase in efficiency in accessing mobile-optimized sites compared to the non-optimized versions. User satisfaction was also measured by seeking post-test comments from the participants, and interestingly, feature limitations were reported as annoying by the participants. This illustrates the dilemma between increasing efficiency by reducing features to make access faster, and achieving user satisfaction by providing a feature rich site. Schmiedl et al. also found that touch screen phones were preferred for surfing, with an additional keyboard found as an advantage whereas use of a pen for navigation was disliked.

Although many studies measured effectiveness by the number of successful tasks completed, Hong and Kim [14] measured it by the number of errors that were made by participants. They conducted three studies. In the first study, participants were observed to find out when and where they made errors during web browsing on mobile. They used the think-aloud technique were participants are asked to speak their mind while performing the tasks and the session was video recorded. The common errors were related to (a) interaction where novice users had trouble with finding the right icons and hyperlinks on the screen and (b) navigation from one page to another. In the second study the participants were interviewed to collect qualitative data on their browsing experience. The most frequent complaint was the complexity of the websites accessed. Finally, 33 mobile sites were analysed for their efficiency of design layout which resulted in recommendations on good layout.

Shrestha [16] measured effectiveness, efficiency, and satisfaction by asking participants to complete four tasks on a desktop browser and then on a mobile browser. The tasks on both the desktop and mobile browsers were similar in scope, and the websites were not optimized for mobile devices. The number of completed tasks on the mobile phone was compared with the number of completed tasks on the desktop, which reflected effectiveness. In order to measure efficiency, the tasks were timed to compare the completion time on mobile versus desktop. Finally, participants were asked to rate their level of satisfaction with each task performed. This is one of the earliest papers in our study literature when there was hardly any mobile optimized sites. Understandably, too much scrolling and getting visibly lost in the website were the highest reported usability problems. Of the total time spend on tasks 80% was on mobile device and only 20% on desktop thus indicating the difficulty of web tasks on mobile phones when the experiment was conducted.

Whereas all of the studies above measured effectiveness and/or efficiency, one study that did not use these "standard" dimensions of usability testing is by Kristjánsdóttir, et al. [25]. They tested a mobile-web solution for cognitive behavioural intervention for people with chronic pain; essentially, patients kept an online diary of their feelings and behaviour on the web using a mobile phone and received feedback from a therapist in the same way. The usability test involved testing feasibility and usefulness of the mobile web-based intervention. Feasibility was measured in terms of user experience and satisfaction which were assessed through questionnaires and semi-structured interviews. Usefulness of the feedback received was also measured through a daily two-item questionnaire. Most participants found the mobile web-based solution "supportive, inspiring and meaningful". Two-thirds of the participants reported that the solution has increased their insights into their symptoms and taught them new methods to cope with their symptoms. However, negative issues included frustrations with filling out the diary and receiving a validation error because of poor internet connection, frustration with a patient feeling misunderstood and not being able to explain herself and the therapist sending feedback to the wrong patient by clicking the wrong button; problems that probably would not occur in a face-to-face situation.

4   Limitations

As in any research, this review has several limitations. We have chosen the research period from 2007 to 2012 which means that papers published outside this period are not included. Web access on mobile devices has been of interest in the days of PDAs and feature phones, and therefore, there will be usability studies on them which we have not covered. We did not include them in our research primarily because the issues identified in those days are probably of less interest with the paradigm shift that smartphones have achieved. We note that some of the early tests within our period of study also used feature phones and therefore their results may not be as relevant as later studies.

Even though, we believe that google-scholar is very comprehensive in its literature search capability, our choice of search engines and keywords may have caused some relevant papers not to be discovered.

Our search term used the word "mobile", however, all the papers resulted from the search used mobile phones for their usability testing; in future, other popular devices such as android tablets and iPads will also become part of usability test literature.

5   Discussion and Conclusion

As the capabilities of mobile devices increase, they are rapidly becoming popular for browsing the web. However, recent surveys have shown that even commercial companies, for which web as a medium for marketing and advertising is critical, are lacking in optimizing their web sites for mobile access [4, 30]. This adds to the usability challenges of browsing the web from a mobile device. A systematic literature review is often used to methodically identify the issues reported in the literature. We employed the same method to answer the research question:
What dimensions of usability are examined in mobile web testing?

We identified the usability factors that are tested by different researchers. The three dimensions most studies used are effectiveness, efficiency and satisfaction. Effectiveness and efficiency are measured quantitatively whereas satisfaction is measured often through post-test surveys or interviews with the users; use of product reaction cards [32] was also found in one study. These dimensions were found to be subsuming a larger number of usability factors, the relationships between which we captured in Fig. 1.

Our final research question was:

What are the purposes for which mobile web usability testing is conducted?

We found that researchers conducted usability tests to:

- Compare user experience between mobile optimized sites and non-optimized sites
- Compare user experience between websites accessed on desktops and accessed on mobile phones
- Study the effect of environmental factors such as background noise on mobile web usability
- Study the effectiveness of mobile web-based applications such as in health
- Test the usability of web sites such as University library sites after optimizing them for mobile devices.

Both formative and summative evaluations are presented in the literature. We observed the following major limitations in the current usability testing practices:

- Most studies use small samples which makes statistical analysis difficult. The absence of discussions on generalizability of the results in most of the studies is a consequence of this limitation.
- The use of software tools to streamline the collection and analysis of data is also found to be lacking. A few researchers have used tools to draw paper prototypes for formative studies but not for the collection and analysis of data. One of the papers in the period of study described a software tool for collection of usability data [20] which is promising; however, this or other tools are not used in the empirical papers reviewed. Tool support will assist in measuring, particularly, effectiveness and efficiency in web usability.
- Some tests were not controlled for variability in the mobile devices used; this could particularly be a problem since device heterogeneity is one of the challenges in mobile web usage.

In summary, the systematic literature review has identified and categorised the usability dimensions that are tested by mobile web researchers, and the purposes for which usability testing is currently employed. We believe, this study will assist researchers and practitioners in understanding the current challenges and limitations of mobile web usability, and encourage them to work on addressing them.

Acknowledgments. An earlier draft by the first author was edited with the help of Scribendi website.

References

1. Burnette, E.: Hello, Android: introducing Google's mobile development platform. Pragmatic Bookshelf (2009)
2. Grossman, L.: Invention of the year: The iPhone. Time Magazine Online 1 (2007)
3. International Telecommunication Union, Key Global Telecom Indicators for the World Telecommunication Service Sector (2012), http://www.itu.int/ITU-D/ict/statistics/at_glance/keytelecom.html
4. Ha, A.: Google Pushing Advertisers to Build for Mobile Search. Adweek (2011)
5. McPherson, C.J., Higginson, I.J., Hearn, J.: Effective methods of giving information in cancer: a systematic literature review of randomized controlled trials. Journal of Public Health 23, 227–234 (2001)
6. Šmite, D., Wohlin, C., Gorschek, T., Feldt, R.: Empirical evidence in global software engineering: a systematic review. Empirical Software Engineering 15, 91–118 (2010)
7. Holzinger, A.: Usability engineering methods for software developers. Communications of the ACM 48, 71–74 (2005)
8. International Standards Organization, Ergonomic Requirements for Office Work with Visual Display Terminals - Part 11: Guidance on Usability, in ISO 94241-11, ed: ISO (1998)
9. Amelung, H., Ohl, C., Schade, G., Wagner, S.: Mobile Usability. In: Mobile Web 2.0: Developing and Delivering Services to Mobile Phones, pp. 57–69. Auerbach, Hoboken (2009)

10. Kitchenham, B., Pearl Brereton, O., Budgen, D., Turner, M., Bailey, J., Linkman, S.: Systematic literature reviews in software engineering–a systematic literature review. Information and software technology 51, 7–15 (2009)
11. Kitchenham, B., Charters, S.: Guidelines for Performing Systematic Literature Reviews in Software Engineering. Keele University, EBSE-2007-12007(2007)
12. Rosario, J.A., Ascher, M.T., Cunningham, D.J.: A Study in Usability: Redesigning a Health Sciences Library's Mobile Site. Medical Reference Services Quarterly 31, 1–13 (2012)
13. Yeh, S.T., Fontenelle, C.: Usability study of a mobile website: the Health Sciences Library, University of Colorado Anschutz Medical Campus, experience. Journal of the Medical Library Association: JMLA 100, 64 (2012)
14. Hong, S., Kim, S.C.: Mobile web usability: Developing guidelines for mobile web via smart phones. In: Marcus, A. (ed.) HCII 2011 and DUXU 2011, Part I. LNCS, vol. 6769, pp. 564–572. Springer, Heidelberg (2011)
15. Tsiaousis, A.S., Giaglis, G.M.: An Empirical Assessment of Environmental Factors that Influence the Usability of a Mobile Website. In: 2010 Ninth International Conference on Mobile Business and 2010 Ninth Global Mobility Roundtable (ICMB-GMR), pp. 161–167 (2010)
16. Shrestha, S.: Mobile web browsing: usability study. In: Proceedings of the 4th International Conference on Mobile Technology, Applications, and Systems and the 1st International Symposium on Computer Human Interaction in Mobile Technology, Singapore, pp. 187–194 (2007)
17. Schmiedl, G., Seidl, M., Temper, K.: Mobile phone web browsing: a study on usage and usability of the mobile web. In: Proceedings of the 11th International Conference on Human-Computer Interaction with Mobile Devices and Services, Bonn, Germany, pp. 1–2 (2009)
18. Jeong, W., Han, H.: Usability study on mobile Web newspaper sites. In: Proceedings of the American Society for Information Science and Technology, vol. 48, pp. 1–4 (2011)
19. Wessels, A., Purvis, M., Rahman, S.S.: Usability of Web Interfaces on Mobile Devices. In: Eighth International Conference on Information Technology: New Generations (ITNG), pp. 1066–1067 (2011)
20. Carta, T., Paternò, F., Santana, V.: Support for remote usability evaluation of web mobile applications. In: Proceedings of the 29th ACM International Conference on Design of Communication, pp. 129–136 (2011)
21. Diaz, F.J., Harari, B.S.I., Paola, B.: Evaluating the Usability of the Mobile Interface of an Educational Website. In: Innovative Techniques in Instruction Technology, E-learning, E-assessment, and Education, pp. 47–52 (2008)
22. Frederick, G.R., Lal, R.: Mobile Web Usability. Beginning Smartphone Web Development, 163–186 (2009)
23. Brown, A., Yesilada, Y., Jay, C., Harper, S., Chen, A.Q.: The blind leading the blind: Web accessibility research leading mobile Web usability. In: Ahson, S.A., Ilyas, M. (eds.) Mobile Web 2.0: Developing and Delivering Services to Mobile Devices, pp. 71–94. Taylor and Francis, Boca Raton (2011)
24. Pendell, K.D., Bowman, M.S.: Usability Study of a Library's Mobile Website: An Example from Portland State University. Information Technology and Libraries 31, 45–62 (2012)

25. Kristjánsdóttir, Ó., Fors, E., Eide, E., Finset, A., van Dulmen, S., Wigers, S., Eide, H.: Written online situational feedback via mobile phone to support self-management of chronic widespread pain: a usability study of a Web-based intervention. BMC Musculoskeletal Disorders 12, 51 (2011)
26. Kaasalainen, J.P.: Designing for Mobility. In: Ahson, S.A., Ilyas, M. (eds.) Mobile Web 2.0: Developing and Delivering Services to Mobile Phones, pp. 1–32. Taylor and Francis, Boca Raton (2011)
27. Vartiainen, E.: Designing Mobile User Interfaces for Internet Services. In: Ahson, S.A., Ilyas, M. (eds.) Mobile Web 2.0: Developing and Delivering Services to Mobile Phones, pp. 33–56. Taylor and Francis, Boca Raton (2011)
28. Tsiaousis, A.S., Giaglis, G.M.: Evaluating the Effects of the Environmental Context-of-Use on Mobile Website Usability. In: 7th International Conference on Mobile Business, ICMB 2008, pp. 314–322 (2008)
29. Ivanc, D., Vasiu, R., Onita, M.: Usability Evaluation of a LMS Mobile Web Interface. In: Skersys, T., Butleris, R., Butkiene, R. (eds.) ICIST 2012. Communications in Computer and Information Science, vol. 319, pp. 348–361. Springer, Heidelberg (2012)
30. Cookson, R.: UK companies not ready for mobile internet. Financial Times (January 2, 2013),
http://www.ft.com/cms/s/0/bd059e26-4cf2-11e2-a99b-00144
feab49a.html-axzz2QrGnu9Db
31. Jones, M., Marsden, G.: Mobile interaction design. Wiley (2006)
32. Benedek, J., Miner, T.: Measuring Desirability: New methods for evaluating desirability in a usability lab setting. In: Proceedings of Usability Professionals Association Conference, Orlando, pp. 8–12 (2002)
33. Rabin, J., McCathieNevile, C.: Mobile Web Best Practices 1.0 (2008),
http://www.w3.org/TR/mobile-bp/

Face to Face or Facebook: 21st Century University Education: A Survey

Tom Gedeon[1] and Mohammad Yamin[1,2]

[1] Research School of Computer Science, Australian National University,
Acton ACT 0200, Australia
tom.gedeon@anu.edu.au
[2] Department of Business Administration, King Abdulaziz University,
Jeddah 21589, Saudi Arabia
doctoryamin@gmail.com

Abstract. University education has for centuries depended on face to face interactions between academic teachers and their students. In the 21st century, social media tools such as Facebook™ consume an increasing part of the time and attention of our students, who are also more and more stressed. Meanwhile, lecture attendance is down, student part-time work is up, and what has happened to the learning? Is there an ideal amount of Facebook engagement which will maximize outcomes (learning), and engagement (enthusiasm)? We survey the relevant literature to come to some initial conclusions and propose an experimental test of our conclusion.

Keywords: University education, Facebook, Social media, Student achievement, Student engagement, Predict marks.

1 Introduction

There are many possible goals in education, but for us the two primary ones are outcomes (learning), and engagement (enthusiasm) – which will lead to later learning as well as support current learning. In the area of this paper, there are a number of attributes that we could measure and a number of ways we could measure them, or measure proxies or somehow otherwise approximate these attributes if we cannot measure it directly. For outcomes, we will generally assume that we will use the student'a preferred proxy for learning, that of the grade or marks achieved in that course.

A non-exhaustive list of behaviours or actions we could measure include amount of time spent on social media, or in the classroom, the number of times certain kinds of actions such as reading or posting comments take place, or the time or proportion of time spent on those activities. In the subsequent discussion we will generally refer to social media by referring to Facebook, as it is the most commonly used such tool. We will refer to social media when discussing the work of others and want to be clear that that work did not take place with regards Facebook, or when we want to make a point that the issue being discussed has wider relevance.

K. Liu et al. (Eds.): ICISO 2014, IFIP AICT 426, pp. 471–477, 2014.
© IFIP International Federation for Information Processing 2014

The two main ways we can measure behaviours or actions is to survey the actors or observers, before and / or after the behaviour, or by actually observing and recording the behaviour.

Fig. 1. Model linking behaviours to social and tangible outcomes

The analysis model we use is illustrated in Fig. 1. The lower path provides objective measurable effects, and tangible outcomes, while the upper path is clearly more related to the social aspects of the behaviours as well as its data collection. The two paths are not independent and have effects on each other. As we will see subsequently, data collection along the top path is easier, but the data collected is less useful for tangible outcome prediction.

In subsequent sections we ask questions such as can we predict student outcomes, can we predict student engagement, what are the properties of reported or actual behaviour factors which we can use to build prediction models, and can we identify the causative links between factors and engagement or outcomes?

2   Predicting Student Outcomes

We discuss prediction of student outcomes (marks) in this section in terms of measure data (the lower path in Figure 1), and estimate data (the upper path in the figure), respectively.

2.1   Objective Data

We have done some previous work in predicting student marks in a first year Computing course [1]. The data consisted of the results from a number of laboratory exercises, assignments and a mid-term quiz all of which compose 40% of a student's mark for the subject. The marks were used in a neural network model to predict the final aggregate mark. The neural network was able to correctly classify the grade the student received based on the part-marks with a reliability of 86%.

More recent work used the Moodle [2] web-based on-line learning platform, to use students' web behaviour on Moodle to predict their final marks [3]. Table 1 shows the attributes used. The success rate in predicting final grades was 65%. The reduced prediction accuracy may be due to a less direct relationship between the measured attributes (web behaviour versus prior marks) and the predicted output (final mark).

Table 1. Attributes Used by Each Student in Summary File (from [3])

Name	Type	Description
Course	Input attribute	Identification number of the course
n_assigment	Input attribute	Number of assignments done
n_quiz_a	Input attribute	Number of quizzes passed
n_quiz_s	Input attribute	Number of quizzes failed
n_posts	Input attribute	Number of messages sent to the forum
n_read	Input attribute	Number or messages read on the forum
total_time_assignment	Input attribute	Total time used on assignments
total_time_quiz	Input attribute	Total time used on quizzes
total_time_forum	Input attribute	Total time used on forum
Mark	Class	Final mark the student obtained

2.2 Subjective Data

It has been shown that previous programming experience is beneficial in terms of student achievement in a first year computing course [4]. This was estimated for 75 students via questionnaire, with summary data shown in Table 2. Note that HTML experience was controversially included as a programming language. This fits with the language we use as instructors (such as "code up some HTML") and the students' perception, yet is in fact 'just' a markup language.

Table 2. Number of students with previous language experience (from [4], modified)

	Experience	Study
None	17	29
Pascal/Delphi	29	28
Basic/Visual Basic	22	21
C/C++	34	39
Java	4	4
HTML	43	16
CGI/Perl	4	2
Other	17	15
Total	97	97

	Experience	Study
None	18	18
1 language group	10	2
2 language groups	3	1
>= 3 language groups	3	0
Total	34	21

A significant effect was found for achievement by experienced students, and this difference was related to the number of languages previously studied or used. The effect was stronger for those students who formally studied programming previously as opposed to 'mere' use of the same number of programming languages. While this work [4] did not predict final marks, the data reported would support such an activity, and given the reported results it is highly likely that including the surveyed prior language experience would enhance the prediction. So we can posit that the use of subjective survey data at least enhances prediction of student final marks.

The connection between Facebook usage and final marks has been examined [5], in a large survey of reported detailed Facebook usage and reported GPA.

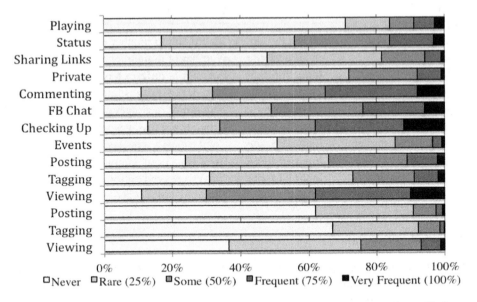

Fig. 2. Self-reported frequency of participation in Facebook activities (from [5], modifed)

The results were that Facebook use for collecting and sharing information (checking to see what friends are up to and sharing links, respectively) is positively predictive of outcomes while using Facebook for socializing (status updates and chatting) is negatively correlated. Overall time spent on Facebook is negatively related to overall GPA.

An analysis of the factors affecting the success of non-majors in learning to program [6] found that both self-efficacy and knowledge organization had a positive affect on student grade. Prior experience affected self-efficacy but not knowledge organization. In this context, we can understand the relatively low accuracy of results in [3] better, where here knowledge organization relates to prior study. Students' self-efficacy beliefs come from four sources of information [7]: personal experiences of mastery; second-hand experiences (observation); verbal persuasion, encouragement by others etc; and emotional arousal. Of the sources of self-efficacy beliefs, personal experience of successfully mastering a task is the most direct and most powerful. Social media benefits could only arise via persuasion and this is at most of minor positive benefit.

Another study on on-line achievement [8] found that, as we would now expect, prior GPA is the best predictor of results, and that while factors related to self-efficacy had either no effect or were positively correlated, desire for interaction was negatively correlated with results. This accords with the negative effect of the quantity of on-line social interaction negatively correlating with student achievement, and suggests that the social interaction and course achievement goals are not the same or even similar, and that time spent on one is at the cost of the other.

3   Predicting Student Engagement

We could not find any studies linking measure data to student engagement. This is a possible hole in the literature, which could do with investigation. There is an abundant literature on estimate / survey data relating numerous factors to student engagement. We focus on three indicative studies particularly relevant to the focus of our work.

3.1   Estimate Data

A study using job design and work stress theories examined the relation between psychosocial work characteristics, well-being and satisfaction, and performance [9].

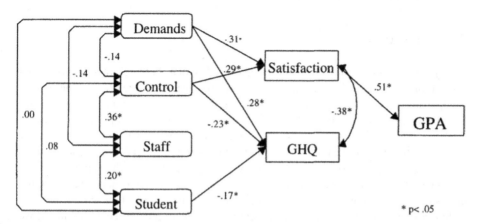

Fig. 3. Relating job characteristics, psychological outcomes, and performance in university students (additive structural model from [9], GHQ = General Heath Questionnaire [10])

Social interaction is an important motivational factor for 'job design', which relates to satisfaction here, which has a statistically significant impact on GPA. A difference was found with regards to quantity of interaction versus quality of interaction, with as expected the latter being the most effective. This is consistent with studies on student achievement in that quantity of hours was generally found to be negative and that the higher quality of interactions are most significant. The study also concluded that both prior to examinations (expected) and at the commencement of the subsequent semester, high levels of distress and demotivating effect of low satisfaction were found, which may lead to underachievement. This is relevant to our goals as it known that high levels of stress negatively affect students' cognitive processes such as concentration and memory [11] which must clearly impact on their ability to learn and hence on student achievement overall.

On the other hand, it was found that overall time spent online including Facebook was positively correlated with student engagement [12]. It is possible this difference in the more recent survey is due to better on-line targeting of time in general, though we consider it more likely to be the difference between prediction of achievement as opposed to prediction of engagement.

4   Reliability of Measures for Student Outcomes and Engagement

The major limitation in the reliability of most of the work in the literature is the reliance on self-report data. Media use is thought to be particularly difficult to measure accurately using self-report data [13]. Self-reporting of GPA is also fraught and is readily affected by priming [14], such that participants primed with attachment security were statistically significantly less willing to lie about their GPA in an achievement context, than those primed with attachment anxiety. Yet as we have seen that high levels of distress are often concomitants of student study life, we must be skeptical of correlations and results from surveys without other forms of validation.

5   Causation

A major limitation of all of the studies discussed is that they are cross-sectional and correlational in nature, and therefore it is impossible to determine the causal mechanisms between social factors / social media / Facebook use and engagement or achievement [8, 12, 5]. Of course, while these designs are inappropriate for drawing causal inferences from the data because of the lack of a comparison condition, they are perfectly appropriate for investigating relationships [8]. The key point for us is that both large numbers of hours of Facebook use and low achievement may be correlated, they may be the causal outcome of some other factor, hence reducing the number of Facebook hours may have no or even detrimental effect on achievement.

In our own prior work [1], using student part-marks to predict their final mark, we used causal indices to identify the rules being used by the neural network in making the high quality conclusions we achieved. It must be noted that this causation is in terms of the neural network model making the prediction and says nothing about the real world setting being modeled by the neural network. Thus, we had available some parts (the part-marks worth 40%) of the final mark, and clearly the addition of part-marks and exam marks produces the final mark. We could perhaps consider these part-marks to be 40% causal to the final mark? Anecdotally, a predicted high mark could cause a lower than predicted final mark due to complacence, whereas a lower predicted mark than desired could lead to a greater effort and a final mark higher than that predicted. By these arguments we conclude that the objective measures (lower path in Fig. 1) have no intrinsic greater claim to having identified causation of student levels of achievement.

6   Conclusion and Proposal for Further Work

We can conclude that there appears to be some approximately ideal amount of Facebook time, which is correlated with student engagement, though this number of hours has not as yet been identified. We can also conclude that measures of actual behaviour are needed (as opposed to self-reporting) to be able to produce reliable predictions of student performance. We have seen that self-reporting is fraught is the areas of interest to us.

For progress to be made which can be relied on pro-actively to improve student achievement and/or engagement, we believe it is necessary to: i) measure actual Facebook behaviour including patterns of behaviour; ii) measure student achievement (marks) as well as engagement (necessarily will need to be done primarily by questionnaire, but should be enhanced by measures of participation in voluntary study activities); iii) plausible causative models developed; and iv) testing of causative models by interventions. So far, none of these steps have been taken, to our knowledge, and reported in the literature. Our future work is in this direction, we have already begun work on steps *i* and *ii*.

References

1. Gedeon, T.D., Turner, S.: Explaining student grades predicted by a neural network. In: Proceedings of 1993 International Joint Conference on Neural Networks, IJCNN 1993-Nagoya, vol. 1, pp. 609–612. IEEE (October 1993)
2. Moodle.org (accessed January 31, 2014)
3. Romero, C., Espejo, P.G., Zafra, A., Romero, J.R., Ventura, S.: Web usage mining for predicting final marks of students that use Moodle courses. Computer Applications in Engineering Education 21(1), 135–146 (2013)
4. Hagan, D., Markham, S.: Does it help to have some programming experience before beginning a computing degree program? ACM SIGCSE Bulletin 32(3), 25–28 (2000)
5. Junco, R.: Too much face and not enough books: The relationship between multiple indices of Facebook use and academic performance. Computers in Human Behavior 28(1), 187–198 (2012)
6. Wiedenbeck, S.: Factors affecting the success of non-majors in learning to program. In: Proceedings 1st International workshop on Computing Education Research, pp. 13–24. ACM (2005)
7. Gist, M.E., Mitchell, T.R.: Self-efficacy: a theoretical analysis of its determinants and malleability. Academy of Management Review 17, 183–211 (1992)
8. Bernard, R.M., Brauer, A., Abrami, P.C., Surkes, M.: The development of a questionnaire for predicting online learning achievement. Distance Education 25(1), 31–47 (2004)
9. Cotton, S.J., Dollard, M.F., de Jonge, J.: Stress and student job design: Satisfaction, well-being, and performance in university students. International Journal of Stress Management 9(3), 147–162 (2002)
10. Goldberg, D.P.: Manual of the General Health Questionnaire. Nfer-Nelson, Windsor (1978)
11. Fisher, S.: Stress in academic life. The Society for Research into Higher Education and Open University Press, Buckingham (1994)
12. Junco, R.: The relationship between frequency of Facebook use, participation in Facebook activities, and student engagement. Computers & Education 58(1), 162–171 (2012)
13. Turner, J.S., Croucher, S.M.: An examination of the relationships among United States college students' media use habits, need for cognition, and grade point average. Learning, Media and Technology (ahead-of-print), 1–16 (2013)
14. Chugh, D., Kern, M.C., Zhu, Z., Lee, S.: Withstanding moral disengagement: Attachment security as an ethical intervention. Journal of Experimental Social Psychology 51, 88–93 (2014)

Author Index

Printed in the United States
By Bookmasters